LaunchPad for *Media Essentials* goes beyond the printed textbook.

Media Essentials emphasizes convergence and practices it, too. LaunchPad for *Media Essentials*, Macmillan Learning's online course space, includes a number of key features that engage readers in media concepts and support learning.

Video Clips

Callouts in the boxes and margins throughout the book point you to a wealth of video clips, which are divided into two distinct types:

- **Web Clips**, which suggest an easily accessible third-party video clip and provide a related discussion question; links are included in LaunchPad.
- **LaunchPad video quizzes**, where you can view a video directly on LaunchPad, respond to accompanying critical thinking questions, and have your answers recorded in the gradebook.

We've included clips from movies, TV shows, online sources, and other media texts, in addition to insightful interviews with media experts and newsmakers. For a complete list of available clips, see the last book page.

LearningCurve

LearningCurve is a gamelike adaptive quizzing system designed to help you review. Each chapter's LearningCurve uses a wealth of review questions and adaptive technology that analyzes your answers, helping you figure out what you already know and master the concepts you still need to learn.

Digital Timeline

A digital timeline feature will help you dive into the history of mass communication and see how one event or advancement led to the next.

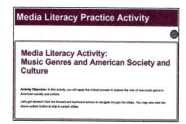

Media Literacy Practice Activities

Included in each chapter of LaunchPad, these activities help you apply and practice your media literacy skills.

LaunchPad for *Media Essentials* can be packaged with the book or purchased on its own. To learn more, see the inside back cover or visit **launchpadworks.com**.

For more information about *Media Essentials*, please visit **macmillanlearning.com/communication**.

MEDIA ESSENTIALS

MEDIA ESSENTIALS

A Brief Introduction

Fifth Edition

Richard Campbell
MIAMI UNIVERSITY

Christopher R. Martin
UNIVERSITY OF NORTHERN IOWA

Bettina Fabos
UNIVERSITY OF NORTHERN IOWA

Shawn Harmsen
COE COLLEGE

For Bedford/St. Martin's

Vice President, Editorial, Macmillan Learning Humanities: Leasa Burton
Senior Program Director for Communication and College Success: Erika Gutierrez
Marketing Manager: Amy Haines
Director of Development: Jane Knetzger
Senior Developmental Editor: Christina Lembo
Senior Content Project Manager: Harold Chester
Senior Media Editor: Tom Kane
Media Project Manager: Sarah O'Connor Kepes
Senior Workflow Project Supervisor: Susan Wein
Associate Editor: Kathy McInerney
Copy Editor: Jamie Thaman
Indexer: Julie Grady
Photo Researcher: Brittani Morgan Grimes
Director of Rights and Permissions: Hilary Newman
Director of Design: Diana Blume
Text Design: Rick Korab
Cover Design: William Boardman
Cover Photo: Ezra Bailey/Getty Images
Composition: Lumina Datamatics, Inc.
Printing and Binding: LSC Communications, Crawfordsville

Copyright © 2020, 2018, 2016, 2013 by Bedford/St. Martin's. All rights reserved. No part of this book may be reproduced, stored in a retrieval system, or transmitted in any form or by any means, electronic, mechanical, photocopying, recording, or otherwise, except as may be expressly permitted by the applicable copyright statutes or in writing by the Publisher.

Manufactured in the United States of America

1 2 3 4 5 6   24 23 22 21 20 19

For information, write: Bedford/St. Martin's, 75 Arlington Street, Boston, MA 02116 (617-399-4000)

ISBN 978-1-319-20817-2 (Paperback)
ISBN 978-1-319-26606-6 (Loose-leaf Edition)

Acknowledgments

Acknowledgments and copyrights appear on the same page as the text and art selections they cover; these acknowledgments and copyrights constitute an extension of the copyright page. It is a violation of the law to reproduce these selections by any means whatsoever without the written permission of the copyright holder.

About the Authors

Richard Campbell is the former and founding chair of the Department of Media, Journalism, and Film at Miami University, as well as the 2019 recipient of the university's Benjamin Harrison Medallion for his "Outstanding Contribution to the Education of the Nation." Campbell is the author of *"60 Minutes" and the News: A Mythology for Middle America* (1991) and coauthor of *Cracked Coverage: Television News, the Anti-Cocaine Crusade, and the Reagan Legacy* (1994). He has written for numerous publications, including *Columbia Journalism Review*, *Critical Studies in Mass Communication*, and *TV Quarterly*. Campbell is cocreator of *Stats+Stories*, listed on NPR's podcast directory, and founder of Report for Ohio, an initiative aimed at getting young journalists hired in rural and urban communities. He is executive producer of a 2019 documentary on the role that Oxford, Ohio, played in 1964's Freedom Summer, titled *Training for Freedom: How Ordinary People in an Unusual Time and Unlikely Place Made Extraordinary History*. He served for ten years on the board of directors for Cincinnati Public Radio and holds a PhD from Northwestern University.

Courtesy of Dianna Campbell

Christopher R. Martin is a professor of digital journalism at the University of Northern Iowa and author of *No Longer Newsworthy: How the Mainstream Media Abandoned the Working Class* (2019) and *Framed! Labor and the Corporate Media* (2003). He has written articles and reviews on journalism, televised sports, the Internet, and labor for several publications, including *Communication Research*, *Journal of Communication*, *Journal of Communication Inquiry*, *Labor Studies Journal*, and *Culture, Sport, and Society*. He is also on the editorial board of the *Journal of Communication Inquiry*. Martin holds a PhD from the University of Michigan and has also taught at Miami University.

Courtesy of Bettina Fabos

Bettina Fabos, an award-winning video maker and former print reporter, is a professor of visual communication and interactive media studies at the University of Northern Iowa. She is writer, producer, and creator of the award-winning multimedia project *Proud and Torn: A Visual Memoir of Hungarian History* (2018) at proudandtorn.org, and author of *Wrong Turn on the Information Superhighway: Education and the Commercialized Internet* (2003). Her areas of expertise include critical media literacy, Internet commercialization and education, and media representations of popular culture. Her work has been published in *Library Trends*, *Review of Educational Research*, and *Harvard Educational Review*. Fabos has a PhD from the University of Iowa.

Courtesy of Christopher Martin

Shawn Harmsen teaches courses in journalism, digital and broadcast media production, and critical media studies at Coe College. Harmsen worked in radio and television news for over a decade, at various times working as reporter, photojournalist, anchor, producer, and news director. Harmsen has an MA from the University of Northern Iowa and a PhD from the University of Iowa. A former editor of the *Journal of Communication Inquiry* and coauthor of work published in *Journalism Practice* and *Journalism and Mass Communication Quarterly*, his research focuses on sociology of news, cultural studies, news framing, and political and social movements. His local activism accomplishments include managing the successful city council campaign of the first Sudanese American immigrant to win elected office in the United States.

Courtesy of Paul W. Jensen

Brief Contents

MASS MEDIA INDUSTRIES

1. Mass Communication: A Critical Approach 3
2. Books and the Power of Print 31
3. Newspapers to Digital Frontiers: Journalism's Journey 57
4. Magazines in the Age of Specialization 99
5. Sound Recording and Popular Music 125
6. Popular Radio and the Origins of Broadcasting 157
7. Movies and the Impact of Images 187
8. Television, Cable, and Specialization in Visual Culture 219
9. The Internet and New Technologies: The Media Converge 253
10. Digital Gaming and the Media Playground 283

MEDIA FRAMING INDUSTRIES

11. Advertising and Commercial Culture 313
12. Public Relations and Framing the Message 347

MEDIA EXPRESSIONS

13. Legal Controls and Freedom of Expression 373
14. Media Economics and the Global Marketplace 403
15. Media Effects and Cultural Approaches to Media Research 431

Preface

THE DIGITAL FUTURE OF MASS MEDIA HAS ARRIVED, and we're experiencing it firsthand. Not only has there been a fundamental change in the ways we use and consume media, but we are seeing a change in the many ways that media messages saturate our lives. As media industries continue to evolve and converge, we want students to have the critical tools they need to understand the media-saturated world around them. These tools, and an understanding of the fundamentals of media studies, are exactly what we had in mind when we wrote *Media Essentials*.

Media Essentials distills media industries and major concepts like digital convergence and legal controls down to their essence. Each chapter offers incisive historical context, frames key concepts up front, and uses pivotal examples to tell the broader story of how different forms of media have developed, how they work, and how they connect to us today. For example, Chapter 5, "Sound Recording and Popular Music," explores the roots of sound recording, tracing its evolution from cylinders and flat disks to classic vinyl, tape, and eventually a number of digital formats. The chapter goes on to describe how popular music shook up American (and global) culture, most dramatically starting in the 1950s with rock and roll and continuing with the emergence of folk, country, soul, punk, and hip-hop. It then follows the money through an in-depth section on the economics of sound recording, explaining how digital formats of recorded music have completely upended the music industry, leaving music fans more likely to stream music on their smartphones than assemble a collection of music, like previous generations of fans might have done. The chapter concludes with a discussion of music's role in a democratic society.

In addition to the wealth of content offered in every chapter, *Media Essentials* continues to be substantially briefer than competing books. Throughout the book, our coverage is succinct, accessible, and peppered with memorable examples, and the book's unique approach—distilling media information to its core—gives instructors the space to add in personal research or social perspectives.

In this fifth edition, Chapter 1 has been revised and restructured to provide **greater emphasis on two of the text's hallmark topics: the cultural approach and the critical process**. An expanded section on the cultural approach covers this foundational topic in more detail up front, and in response to reviewer requests, more coverage has been added about the critical approach to media literacy and the five stages of the critical process: description, analysis, interpretation, evaluation, and engagement. The chapter also includes expanded coverage of the development of mass media industries over time, particularly during the electronic and digital eras.

In addition, the fifth edition continues to emphasize the importance of the digital turn and the value of media literacy by including case studies on these topics in every chapter. **Digital Turn Case Studies** explore the shift in media use and consumption resulting from the emergence of the Internet as a mass medium, and new topics in this edition include how poetry's popularity on Instagram has translated to offline book sales; the continuing harassment and intimidation of journalists around the world; competition for ad dollars between streaming's free tier of service and "traditional" terrestrial radio; and the impact of social media fraud on our elections and the democratic process. **Media Literacy Case Studies** in this fifth edition—each with an accompanying Applying the Critical Process activity—explore new topics, such as the Music Modernization Act, the polarization of talk radio, the invisible hand of PR, Netflix and the business of content creation, and the implications of depicting suicide on TV.

Because currency is so crucial in mass communication, we have also included **updated coverage of all the latest developments in the world of mass media**. New chapter openers examine Netflix as a disruptor, the ubiquity of smart devices and resulting privacy concerns, the success of eSports, the increasing popularity of podcasts, Chance the Rapper's unique approach to the music industry, and public relations problems at the NFL. New and expanded coverage of timely topics throughout the text includes a look at our changing understanding of fake news, including how the term itself has taken on new and more diverse meanings; the #MeToo and #TimesUp movements in the media industries; net neutrality; media mergers between Disney and 21st Century Fox and between AT&T and Time Warner; the growth of Internet and mobile advertising; and the impact of streaming across the movie, TV, and film industries.

Because the book also practices convergence, *Media Essentials* has an online video program accessible in LaunchPad, with clips that offer students firsthand experience with important (and attention-grabbing) media texts, covering everything from groundbreaking blockbusters like *Black Panther* to controversial streaming hits like *13 Reasons Why*. **Half of the suggested video clips** accompanying the text's case studies are new to the fifth edition, and **additional new video clips**—on topics as diverse as special effects in *Star Wars: The Last Jedi*, *Essence* magazine's brand identity, Amazon's retail strategy, how streaming is saving the music industry, and Edison sound recordings from a century ago—are spotlighted throughout the text and available with accompanying questions on LaunchPad. LaunchPad also includes access to LearningCurve, an adaptive quizzing system that helps students figure out what they know—and what material they need to review. LaunchPad for *Media Essentials* contains the e-book and is a complete learning solution that can be integrated with most campus LMS systems. LaunchPad can also be packaged with the book.

Hallmark Features of *Media Essentials*

Clear, streamlined, and accessible. Significantly briefer than competing texts, *Media Essentials* addresses all the topics typically covered in introductory mass communication books. From media industries to legal controls, it offers just the right amount of detail, ensuring that students have enough information to make connections and develop media literacy.

An organization that supports learning. *Media Essentials* offers a chronological table of contents and consistent organization. Each chapter includes a brief history of the topic; a discussion of the evolution of the medium; a look at media economics; and coverage of the medium's relationship to democracy, media literacy, and convergence enabled by the digital turn. This consistent organization and focus help students make their way through the material while they grasp themes both large and small. Under each major heading, a preview paragraph highlights key ideas and contextualizes them, guiding students through the material.

Learning tools help students master the material. Each chapter opens with an outline highlighting what topics will be covered, while The Digital Turn and Media Literacy Case Study boxes address relevant topics in greater detail and help students think critically about them. Finally, each chapter concludes with Chapter Essentials, a useful study guide that helps students review material and prepares them for quizzes and exams.

New to This Fifth Edition

Print and media that converge with LaunchPad. LaunchPad for *Media Essentials*, Fifth Edition, Macmillan Learning's online course space, meets students where they love to be—online. Available to be purchased on its own or packaged with the text at a significant discount, LaunchPad for the fifth edition includes the following updated features:

- **Half of the video clips** accompanying the text's case studies are new to the fifth edition, and the clips throughout the text are divided into two distinct types:
  - **Web clips**, which suggest an easily accessible third-party video clip and provide a related discussion question; links are included in LaunchPad.
  - **LaunchPad video quizzes**, where students can view a video directly on LaunchPad, respond to accompanying critical-thinking questions, and have their answers recorded in the gradebook.

We've included thought-provoking clips from movies, TV shows, online sources, and other media texts, such as *Black Panther*, *Star Wars: The Last Jedi*, and *13 Reasons Why*; videos offering analysis from Bloomberg; and insightful interviews with media experts and newsmakers. For a complete list of available clips, see the inside back cover.

- **Updated LearningCurve and iClicker questions**, along with a fully revised set of instructor resources, are available directly on LaunchPad.

Increased emphasis on foundational topics in Chapter 1. Chapter 1 has been thoroughly revised and restructured to better emphasize the cultural approach to media studies and the critical process behind media literacy, including the five stages of the critical process: description, analysis, interpretation, evaluation, and engagement. In addition, the chapter includes expanded coverage of the development of mass media industries over time—particularly during the electronic and digital eras—to illustrate how past innovation and change have contributed to the development of our current media world.

A spotlight on the digital turn and media literacy. The fifth edition continues to emphasize the importance of the digital turn and the value of media literacy by including case studies on each of these topics in every chapter.

- **New Digital Turn Case Studies**, which address the shift in media use and consumption resulting from the emergence of the Internet as a mass medium, include the rise of Instapoets and how Instagram popularity has translated to real-world book sales; the harassment and intimidation of journalists in the United States and around the world; competition between streaming sites' free tier and terrestrial radio; and social media fraud and its impact on our elections.
- **New Media Literacy Case Studies**—each accompanied by an Applying the Critical Process activity—examine such issues as streaming, royalties, and the Music Modernization Act; the polarization of talk radio; the invisible hand of PR; Netflix and the business of content creation; and the implications of depicting suicide on TV.

Cutting-edge coverage of what's new in the world of mass media.

- New chapter openers bring students into the stories of the media with current and attention-grabbing coverage of recent events, including Netflix as a disruptor, the ubiquity of smart devices and resulting privacy concerns, the success of eSports, the increasing popularity of podcasts, Chance the Rapper's unique approach to the music industry, and public relations problems at the NFL.
- New and expanded coverage of current media issues includes social media fraud in the 2016 election; our changing understanding of fake news, including how the term itself has taken on new and more diverse meanings; the #MeToo and #TimesUp movements in the media industries; literal and figurative attacks on journalism, both domestically and globally; net neutrality; media mergers between Disney and 21st Century Fox and between AT&T and Time Warner; the

growth of Internet and mobile advertising; and the impact of streaming across the movie, TV, and film industries.
- Updated examples in the text discuss Instapoet Rupi Kaur, Pulitzer Prize–winning rapper Kendrick Lamar, *Overwatch* and the rise of MMPORGs and MOBAs, *Black Panther*, *13 Reasons Why*, and *Deadpool 2*, among others.
- Fully updated figures, tables, and graphs incorporate the latest in industry data.

Digital and Print Formats

Whether it's print, digital, or a value option, choose the best format for you. For more information on these resources, please visit the online catalog at **macmillanlearning.com**.

- **LaunchPad for *Media Essentials* dramatically enhances teaching and learning.** LaunchPad combines the full e-book with video activities, LearningCurve adaptive quizzing, Media Literacy Practice activities, an interactive timeline, instructor's resources, and chapter quizzes. For access to all multimedia resources, package LaunchPad with the print version of *Media Essentials* (**ISBN: 978-1-319-31378-4**) or order LaunchPad on its own (**ISBN: 978-1-319-28029-1**).
- **The Loose-Leaf Edition of *Media Essentials*** features the print text in a convenient, budget-priced format, designed to fit into any three-ring binder. The loose-leaf version can also be added to LaunchPad for a small additional cost (**ISBN: 978-1-319-31384-5**).
- ***Media Essentials* is available as a print text.** To get the most out of the book, package LaunchPad with the text (**ISBN: 978-1-319-31378-4**).
- **E-book.** *Media Essentials* is available as an e-book for use on computers, tablets, and e-readers. See **macmillanlearning.com/college/us/digital/ebooks** to learn more.
- **You want to give your students affordable rental, packaging, and e-book options.** So do we. Learn more at **store.macmillanlearning.com**.
- **Customize *Media Essentials* using Bedford Select for Communication.** Create the ideal textbook for your course with only the chapters you need. You can rearrange chapters, delete unnecessary chapters, and add your own original content to create just the book you're looking for. With Bedford Select, students pay only for material that will be assigned in the course, nothing more. For more information, visit **macmillanlearning.com/selectcomm**.

Student Resources

For more information on student resources or to learn about package options, please visit the online catalog at **macmillanlearning.com**.

LaunchPad: Where Students Learn

Digital tools for *Media Essentials*, Fifth Edition, are available on LaunchPad, a dynamic online platform that combines a curated collection of videos, homework assignments, e-book content, and the LearningCurve adaptive quizzing program, organized for easy assignability, in a simple user interface. LaunchPad for *Media Essentials* features:

- **A fully interactive e-book.** Every LaunchPad e-book comes with powerful study tools, multimedia content, and easy customization tools for instructors. Students can search, highlight, and bookmark, making studying easier and more efficient.
- **LearningCurve adaptive quizzing.** In every chapter, call-outs prompt students to tackle the gamelike LearningCurve quizzes to test their knowledge and reinforce learning of the material.
- **Integrated video clips that extend and complement the book.** A rich library of LaunchPad videos and suggested web clips offers easy access to clips from movies, TV shows, interviews, and more.
- **An interactive timeline.** This timeline helps students explore and understand the development of mass communication through the years.
- **Media Literacy Practice activities.** Included in each chapter of LaunchPad, these activities encourage students to apply and practice their media literacy skills.
- **The newest edition of our *Media Career Guide*.** LaunchPad includes a digital version of this practical, student-friendly guide to media jobs, featuring tips and career guidance for students considering a major in the media industries.

To learn more about LaunchPad for *Media Essentials* or to purchase access, go to **launchpadworks.com**.

Media Career Guide: Preparing for Jobs in the 21st Century, Twelfth Edition

Practical, student-friendly, and revised to address recent trends in the job market, this guide includes a comprehensive directory of media jobs, practical tips, and career guidance for students who are considering a major in the media industries. *Media Career Guide* can be packaged at a significant discount with the print book. An electronic version comes integrated in LaunchPad for *Media Essentials*.

New! *The Essential Guide to Visual Communication*

A concise introduction to the evolution, theory, and principles of visual communication in contemporary society, this guide helps students develop the skills they need to become critical consumers of visual media by examining images through the lens of visual rhetoric. Students see how images influence and persuade audiences, and how iconic images can be repurposed to communicate particular messages. *The Essential Guide to Visual Communication* can be packaged at a significant discount with the print book.

Instructor Resources

For more information or to order or download the instructor resources, please visit the online catalog at **macmillanlearning.com**.

LaunchPad for *Media Essentials*, Fifth Edition

At Bedford/St. Martin's, we are committed to providing online resources that meet the needs of instructors and students in powerful yet simple ways. We've taken what we've learned from both instructors and students to create a new generation of technology featuring LaunchPad. With its student-friendly approach, LaunchPad offers our trusted content—organized for easy assignability in a simple user interface. Access to LaunchPad can be packaged with *Media Essentials* at a significant discount or purchased separately.

- **An easy-to-use interface.** Ready-made interactive LaunchPad units give you the building blocks to assign instantly as is or to customize to fit your course. A unit's worth of work can be assigned in seconds, significantly decreasing the amount of time it takes for you to get your course up and running.
- **Intuitive and useful analytics.** The gradebook quickly and easily allows you to gauge performance for your whole class, for individual students, and for individual assignments, making class prep time as well as time spent with students more productive.
- **A fully interactive e-book.** Every LaunchPad e-book comes with powerful study tools, multimedia content, and easy customization tools for instructors. Students can search, highlight, and bookmark, making studying easier and more efficient.
- **LearningCurve adaptive quizzing.** In every chapter, call-outs prompt students to tackle the gamelike LearningCurve quizzes to test their knowledge and reinforce learning of the material. Based on research as to how students learn, LearningCurve motivates students to engage with course materials, while the reporting tools let you see what content students have mastered, allowing you to adapt your teaching plan to their needs.
- **Integrated video clips that extend and complement the book.** A rich library of LaunchPad videos and suggested web clips offers easy access to clips from movies, TV shows, interviews, and more.
- **An interactive timeline.** This timeline helps students explore and understand the development of mass communication through the years.
- **Media Literacy Practice activities.** Included in each chapter of LaunchPad, these activities encourage students to apply and practice their media literacy skills.
- **Instructor resources.** The Instructor's Resource Manual, Test Bank, lecture slides, and iClicker questions, as well as a twenty-question review quiz for each chapter, are all available in LaunchPad for *Media Essentials*, Fifth Edition.

Find out more at **www.launchpadworks.com**, or contact your Bedford/St. Martin's sales representative for more details.

Instructor's Resource Manual

This downloadable manual provides instructors with a comprehensive teaching tool for the Introduction to Mass Communication course. Every chapter offers teaching tips and activities culled from dozens of instructors who teach thousands of students. In addition, this extensive resource provides a range of teaching approaches, tips for facilitating in-class discussions, writing assignments, outlines, lecture topics, lecture spin-offs, critical-process exercises, classroom media resources, and an annotated list of more than two hundred video resources.

Test Bank

The Test Bank includes multiple-choice, fill-in-the-blank, and essay questions for every chapter in *Media Essentials*. Feedback is provided.

Lecture Slides

Slide presentations to help guide each chapter's lecture are available for download.

iClicker Questions

Downloadable iClicker question slides help keep your students engaged and help you make your class even more interactive.

Acknowledgments

We wish every textbook author could have the kind of experience we've had while working on *Media Essentials* and would like to thank everyone at Bedford/St. Martin's who supported this project through its editions and stages, including Vice President Leasa Burton, Senior Program Director Erika Gutierrez, Marketing Manager Amy Haines, and Senior Editor Christina Lembo, who helped us develop this edition. We also appreciate the tireless work of Senior Content Project Manager Harold Chester, who kept the book on schedule while making sure all details were in place; Senior Workflow Project Supervisor Susan Wein; Senior Media Editor Tom Kane; and Associate Editor Kathy McInerney. We are also grateful to our research assistant, Susan Coffin. We extend particular and heartfelt thanks to past contributor Jimmie Reeves, particularly for his knowledge of the world of digital gaming.

We also want to thank the many fine and thoughtful reviewers who contributed ideas to earlier editions of *Media Essentials*: Aje-Ori Agbese, *University of Texas Pan American*; Julie Andsager, *University of Iowa*; Barbara Barnett, *University of Kansas*; Vince Benigni, *College of Charleston*; Michael Bowman, *Arkansas State University*; Scott Brown, *California State University–Northridge*; Ted Carlin, *Shippensburg University of Pennsylvania*; Cheryl Casey, *Champlain College*; Jerome D. DeNuccio, *Graceland University*; Don Diefenbach, *University of North Carolina–Asheville*; Scott Dunn, *Radford University*; Barbara Eisenstock, *California State University–Northridge*; Doug Ferguson, *College of Charleston*; Jennifer Fleming, *California State University–Long Beach*; David Flex, *College of DuPage*; Katie Foss, *Middle Tennessee State University*; Nathaniel Frederick, *Winthrop University*; Peter Galarneau Jr., *West Virginia Wesleyan College*; Mary-Lou Galician, *Arizona State University*; Neil Goldstein, *Montgomery Country Community College*; August Grant, *University of South Carolina*; Jennifer Greer, *University of Alabama*; Allison Hartcock, *Butler University*; Kirk Hazlett, *Curry College*; Amani E. Ismail, *California State University–Northridge*; Harvey Jassem, *University of Hartford*; Kate Joeckel, *Bellevue University*; Steven Keeler, *Cayuga Community College*; Sharon Mazzarella, *James Madison University*; Daniel G. McDonald, *Ohio State University*; Gary Metzker, *California State University–Long Beach*; James E. Mueller, *University of North Texas*; Robert M. Ogles, *Purdue University*; Ileana Oroza, *University of Miami*; Lawrence Overlan, *Wentworth Institute of Technology*; Daniel A. Panici, *University of Southern Maine*; Kenneth Payne, *Western Kentucky University*; Zengjun Peng, *St. Cloud State University*; Samantha Phillips, *University of Miami*; Selene Phillips, *University of Louisville*; David Pierson, *University of Southern Maine*; Jennifer Proffitt, *Florida State University*; Mark Raduziner, *Johnson County Community College*; D. Matthew Ramsey, *Salve Regina University*; Arthur A. Raney, *Florida State University*; Chadwick Lee Roberts, *University of North Carolina–Wilmington*; Steve H. Sohn, *University of Louisville*; Martin David Sommerness, *Northern Arizona University*; Jeff South, *Virginia Commonwealth University*; Mark Steensland, *Penn State Behrend*; Carl Sessions Stepp, *University of Maryland*; Andris Straumanis, *University of Wisconsin–River Falls*; Melvin Sunin, *Penn State Behrend*; Erin Szabo, *College of St. Benedict/St. John's University*; Mike Trice, *Florida Southern College*; Matthew Turner, *Radford University*; Richard West, *University of Texas–San Antonio*; Mark J. P. Wolf, *Concordia University Wisconsin*; and Yanjun Zhao, *Morrisville State College*.

We'd also like to thank the excellent reviewers who gave us feedback as we prepared the fifth edition: William Adams, *Clarion University*; James L. Aucoin, *University of South Alabama*; Elizabeth Blakey, *California State University–Northridge*; Douglas Carr, *El Paso Community College*; Phillip

Cunningham, *Quinnipiac University*; Jennifer Ehrhardt, *Pensacola State College*; Lisa Elliott, *El Paso Community College*; Jodi Hallsten Lyczak, *Illinois State University*; Larry D. Hansen, *Madison Area Technical College*; David Humphreys, *Southern New Hampshire University*; Ashley Marietta-Brown, *Ohio State University–Newark*; Carole McNall, *St. Bonaventure University*; Laurie T. O'Connor, *Georgia State University's Perimeter College*; Ginger Thomson, *South Dakota State University*; and Denitsa Yotova, *University of Maryland–College Park*.

Special thanks from Richard Campbell: I am grateful to all my former students at the University of Wisconsin–Milwaukee, Mount Mary College, the University of Michigan, and Middle Tennessee State University, as well as to my current students at Miami University. Some of my students have contributed directly to this text, and thousands have endured my courses over the years—and made them better. My all-time favorite former students, Chris Martin and Bettina Fabos, are coauthors, as well as the creators of our book's Instructor's Manual and Test Bank. I am grateful for all their work, ideas, and energy.

Special thanks from Christopher Martin and Bettina Fabos: We would like to thank Richard Campbell and Shawn Harmsen, who are both a delight to work with on this project. We also appreciate the great devotion, creativity, and talent that everyone at Bedford/St. Martin's brings to the book. We would like to thank reviewers and our own journalism and media students for their input and for creating a community of sorts around the theme of critical perspectives on the media. Most of all, we'd like to thank our daughters, Olivia and Sabine, who bring us joy and laughter every day, and a sense of mission to better understand the world of media in which they live.

Special thanks from Shawn Harmsen: I would like to thank Richard Campbell, Bettina Fabos, and Christopher Martin for years of generously given trust, support, and friendship, going back to the early 2000s, when I took my first class with Bettina as a student pursuing an MA. I am excited, humbled, and grateful to fully join the author team on this edition of *Media Essentials*. Thank you to Christina Lembo, who, in addition to being a supremely competent editor, was also an amazing colleague and collaborator through every stage of the research and writing process. I could not ask for better. For that matter, many thanks to the entire Bedford/St. Martin's team for all the work they do to make this book a reality. Thank you also to my students. You motivate me to provide the best information and insights possible throughout this text so that it will be truly valuable to you now and for years to come. And finally a very special thank you and my undying gratitude to my wife, Jody; my kids, Katy and Jack; and my Mom, Candi, for all the help, support, love, and encouragement.

NCA Learning Outcomes

Media Essentials, **Fifth Edition, connects to the learning outcomes of the National Communication Association (NCA).**

The National Communication Association has published learning outcomes for courses within the discipline. The following table shows how these learning outcomes are reflected in *Media Essentials,* Fifth Edition.

Learning Outcome	Campbell, *Media Essentials,* Fifth Edition
Employ communication theories, perspectives, principles, and concepts	**Chapter 1: Mass Communication: A Critical Approach** gives students a solid overview of mass communication. • "The Evolution of Mass Communication" section provides a knowledge base of all the types of mass communication, from the oral and written eras to the print revolution, through the electronic era, and into the digital era. • "The Development of Media and Their Role in Society" section invites students to begin thinking about the relevance of mass communication in their own lives, as well as the relationship between the media and society. • The "Cultural Approach to Media Studies" section defines the concept of culture and introduces the cultural model of media literacy. **Chapter 15: Media Effects and Cultural Approaches to Media Research** is directly focused on these learning outcomes and examines specific mass communication theories and both social scientific and cultural studies research perspectives. **Industry-specific chapters** throughout the book provide in-depth study and exploration of the types of mass communication: • Chapter 2: Books and the Power of Print • Chapter 3: Newspapers to Digital Frontiers: Journalism's Journey • Chapter 4: Magazines in the Age of Specialization • Chapter 5: Sound Recording and Popular Music • Chapter 6: Popular Radio and the Origins of Broadcasting • Chapter 7: Movies and the Impact of Images • Chapter 8: Television, Cable, and Specialization in Visual Culture • Chapter 9: The Internet and New Technologies: The Media Converge • Chapter 10: Digital Gaming and the Media Playground The **history of mass media** is threaded throughout the book. Book sections that specifically explore history include the following: • "The Evolution of Mass Communication" and "The Development of Media and Their Role in Society" in Chapter 1 • "The Early History of Books: From Papyrus to Paperbacks" and "The Evolution of Modern Publishing" in Chapter 2 • "The Early History of American Journalism" and "The Evolution of Newspaper Journalism: Competing Models and the Rise of Professionalism" in Chapter 3 • "The Early History of Magazines" and "The Evolution of Modern American Magazines" in Chapter 4 • "The Early History and Evolution of Sound Recording," "U.S. Popular Music and the Rise of Rock," and "The Evolution of Pop Music" in Chapter 5 • "The Early History of Radio" and "The Evolution of Radio" in Chapter 6

	- "The Early History of Movies," "The Evolution of the Hollywood Studio System," "Hollywood's Golden Age: The Development of Style," and "The Transformation of the Hollywood Studio System" in Chapter 7
- "The Early History of Television," "The Evolution of Network Programming," and "The Evolution of Cable Programming" in Chapter 8
- "The Early History of the Internet" and "The Evolution of the Internet: Going Commercial, Getting Social, Making Meaning" in Chapter 9
- "The Early History of Digital Gaming" and "The Evolution of Digital Gaming" in Chapter 10
- "The Early History of American Advertising: 1850s to 1950s" and "The Evolution of U.S. Advertising: 1950s to Today" in Chapter 11
- "Early History of Public Relations" in Chapter 12
- "The Origins of Free Expression and a Free Press" in Chapter 13
- "The Transition to an Information Economy" in Chapter 14
- "Early Media Research Methods" in Chapter 15

The **Interactive Digital Timeline**, available in LaunchPad, allows students to explore the histories of mass media industries and examine how these histories interact with one another and with the history of our society in general.

LaunchPad video activities in each chapter give students the opportunity to hear from industry professionals, analyze and make connections with film and TV clips, and explore current issues in media.

Digital Turn Case Studies in each chapter explore the concept of convergence and the shift in media use and consumption resulting from the emergence of the Internet as a mass medium. Topics include poetry's popularity on Instagram, FOMO in a digital world, competition for ad dollars between streaming services and terrestrial radio, and the impact of social media fraud on our elections and the democratic process. |
| Engage in communication inquiry | **Media Literacy Case Study boxes** in each chapter provide real-life examples of how we interact with the media, and an accompanying Applying the Critical Process activity in each case study helps students practice the art of critical thinking.

The **LaunchPad** for each chapter provides an interactive and assignable Media Literacy Practice activity, which allows students to practice their skills as critical consumers of the media. Even more Media Literacy Practice activities in the **Instructor's Resource Manual** provide instructors with ideas for additional practice that they can use as classroom activities or as inspiration for assignments. |
| Critically analyze messages | Richard Campbell's critical and cultural approach to the media, particularly his **Media Literacy Case Studies** and their accompanying **Applying the Critical Process activities**, gets students describing, analyzing, interpreting, evaluating, and engaging in topics in the media to actively build media literacy. Topics include the Music Modernization Act, the polarization of talk radio, the invisible hand of PR, Netflix and the business of content creation, and the implications of depicting suicide on TV.

Chapter 1: Mass Communication: A Critical Approach includes a discrete section, "**Critiquing Media and Developing Media Literacy**," that introduces the steps of the critical process and explains the benefits of examining media with a critical perspective.

Additional interactive and assignable **Media Literacy Practice activities** on LaunchPad allow students to practice their skills as critical consumers of the media. Even more Media Literacy Practice activities in the **Instructor's Resource Manual** provide instructors with ideas for additional practice that they can use as classroom activities or as inspiration for assignments. |
| Demonstrate the ability to accomplish communicative goals (self-efficacy) | The **Media Career Guide** that accompanies the book (available on LaunchPad) helps students define and achieve their career goals in the communication fields of their choice.

Additionally, the **Media Literacy Case Studies** and their accompanying Applying the Critical Process activities allow students the space to practice and develop their skills as critical consumers of the media. |

Apply ethical communication principles and practices	*Media Essentials* strives to help students understand contemporary issues and controversies. Content throughout the text discusses ethics issues across the media industries: • "Media Literacy Case Study: Masculinity and the Media" in Chapter 1 • "Media Literacy Case Study: Banned Books and 'Family Values'" in Chapter 2 • "Media Literacy Case Study: The Evolution of Photojournalism" in Chapter 4 • "The Digital Turn Case Study: 360 Degrees of Music" in Chapter 5 • "Media Literacy Case Study: How Did Talk Radio Become So One-Sided?" and "Manipulating Playlists with Payola" in Chapter 6 • "The Movies in a Democratic Society" (including the Hollywood Ten) in Chapter 7 • "The Digital Turn Case Study: Social Media Fraud and Elections," "Social Media and Democracy," "Targeted Advertising and Data Mining," and "Information Security: What's Private?" in Chapter 9 • "Trends and Issues in Digital Gaming: Immersion and Addiction" and "Trends and Issues in Digital Gaming: Violence and Misogyny" in Chapter 10 • "Online and Mobile Advertising Alter the Ad Landscape," "Persuasive Techniques in Contemporary Advertising," and "Commercial Speech and Regulating Advertising" in Chapter 11 • "Media Literacy Case Study: The Invisible Hand of PR," "The Digital Turn Case Study: Military PR in the Digital Age," "Cultivating Government Relations," "Tensions between Public Relations and the Press," and the chapter opener on the NFL's public relations problems in Chapter 12 • "The Digital Turn Case Study: Is 'Sexting' Pornography?" and "Media Literacy Case Study: Fake News, the First Amendment, and Fighting Propaganda" in Chapter 13 • "The Digital Turn Case Study: Are the Big Digital Companies Too Big?" in Chapter 14 **Chapter 3: Newspapers to Digital Frontiers: Journalism's Journey** digs into the ethics issues and judgment calls that journalists face every day. The chapter also explores the values that journalists promise to uphold, and it discusses the harassment and intimidation of journalists around the world. **Chapter 15: Media Effects and Cultural Approaches to Research** provides an in-depth study of media effects on society, taking students through early media research methods, research on media effects, cultural approaches to media research, and media research and democracy. Features include "The Digital Turn Case Study: Artificial Intelligence Gets Personal" and "Media Literacy Case Study: Does Art Imitate Life or Life Imitate Art? TV Depictions of Suicide and Copycat Fears." **Media Literacy Case Studies** (many of which have been noted here) and interactive Media Literacy Practice activities on LaunchPad help students hone their critical media skills.
Utilize communication to embrace difference	Content throughout the book explores the connection between communication and culture and incorporates a range of diverse perspectives and discussions. Examples include the following: • "The Cultural Approach to Media Studies" and the chapter opener on #BlackLivesMatter and the impact of hashtag activism in Chapter 1 • "Types of Magazines: Domination of Specialization" in Chapter 4 • "Rock and Roll Arrives" and "Rock Blurs Additional Boundaries" in Chapter 5 • "Global Cinema" and "Media Literacy Case Study: Breaking through Hollywood's Race Barrier" in Chapter 7 • "Media Literacy Case Study: Race, Gender, and Sexual Orientation in TV Programming" in Chapter 8 • "Media Literacy Case Study: Fighting the Dark Side of Gaming Culture: Anita Sarkeesian and Feminist Frequency" and "Alternate Voices" in Chapter 10 • "Media Literacy Case Study: Idiots and Objects: Stereotyping in Advertising" in Chapter 11 • "The Growth of Global Audiences" and "Cultural Imperialism" in Chapter 14 • "Cultural Approaches to Media Research" in Chapter 15

Influence public discourse	The relationship among politics, democracy, and the media is a recurring theme in *Media Essentials*. Examples can be found throughout: • "Books in a Democratic Society" in Chapter 2 • "Journalism in a Democracy Society" in Chapter 3 • "Magazines in a Democratic Society" in Chapter 4 • "Sound Recording in a Democratic Society" in Chapter 5 • "Radio in a Democratic Society" in Chapter 6 • "The Movies in a Democratic Society" in Chapter 7 • "Television in a Democratic Society" in Chapter 8 • "The Internet in a Democratic Society" in Chapter 9 • "Digital Gaming in a Democratic Society" in Chapter 10 • "Advertising in a Democratic Society" in Chapter 11 • "Public Relations in a Democratic Society" in Chapter 12 • "The First Amendment in a Democratic Society" in Chapter 13 • "The Media Marketplace in a Democratic Society" in Chapter 14 • "Media Research in a Democratic Society" in Chapter 15 **Chapter 13: Legal Controls and Freedom of Expression** takes a close look at the First Amendment and how it relates to mass media. Finally, the last step of the critical process discussed throughout the text is **engagement**, which urges students to become involved in the public discourse of media questions of our day.

Contents

ABOUT THE AUTHORS   vii
BRIEF CONTENTS   viii
PREFACE   ix

MASS MEDIA INDUSTRIES

1 Mass Communication: A Critical Approach   3

The Evolution of Mass Communication   6
    The Oral and Written Eras   6
    The Print Era   7
    The Electronic Era   9
    The Digital Era   10

The Development of Media and Their Role in Society   12
    The Evolution of Media: From Emergence to Convergence   12

THE DIGITAL TURN CASE STUDY   FOMO in a Digital World   13
    ▶ **Web Clip**   Social Media and FOMO   13
    Debating Media's Role in Everyday Life   14
    LaunchPad   Agenda-Setting and Gatekeeping   14

The Cultural Approach to Media Studies   16
    Moving from a Linear Model to a Cultural Model   17
    Surveying the Cultural Landscape   18
    Tracing Changes in Values   19

Critiquing Media and Developing Media Literacy   21
    Media Literacy and the Critical Process   22

THE CRITICAL PROCESS BEHIND MEDIA LITERACY   23

MEDIA LITERACY CASE STUDY   Masculinity and the Media   24
    LaunchPad   Masculinity on Screen: *Tough Guise 2*   24
    Benefits of a Critical Perspective   26

CHAPTER ESSENTIALS   28

Daniel Leal Olivas/AFP/Getty Images

LaunchPad   For videos, review quizzing, and more, visit **launchpadworks.com**.

Mandel Ngan/AFP/Getty Images

2 Books and the Power of Print 31

The Early History of Books: From Papyrus to Paperbacks 34
Papyrus, Parchment, and Codex: The Development Stage of Books 34
Writing and Printing Innovations: Books Enter the Entrepreneurial Stage 35
The Printing Press and the Publishing Industry: Books Become a Mass Medium 36

The Evolution of Modern Publishing 38
The Formation of Publishing Houses 38
Types of Books 39

Trends in Contemporary Book Publishing 41
Convergence: Books in the Digital Age 41
Self-Publishing 42
Audio Books 43
Influences of Television and Film in the Digital Age 43
▶ **LaunchPad** Based On: Making Books into Movies 43

The Organization and Economics of the Book Industry 44
The Conglomerates 44
The Structure of Book Publishing 46

THE DIGITAL TURN CASE STUDY The Epic Rise of Instapoets 47
▶ **Web Clip** Rupi Kaur: Instapoet 47
Selling Books 48
▶ **LaunchPad** Amazon's Brick-and-Mortar Bookstores 50

Books in a Democratic Society 50
Physical Deterioration 50
Censorship 51
Resiliency of Reading 51

MEDIA LITERACY CASE STUDY Banned Books and "Family Values" 52
▶ **LaunchPad** Banned Books on Screen: *Huck Finn* 52

CHAPTER ESSENTIALS 54

3 Newspapers to Digital Frontiers: Journalism's Journey 57

Granger—All rights reserved.

The Early History of American Journalism 59
    Colonial Newspapers and the Partisan Press 59
    The Penny Press: Becoming a Mass Medium 60
    Yellow Journalism 63

The Evolution of Newspaper Journalism: Competing Models and the Rise of Professionalism 65
    "Objectivity" and Professionalization in Modern Journalism 65
    Interpretive Journalism 67

MEDIA LITERACY CASE STUDY Investigative Journalism: In the "Spotlight" 68
    LaunchPad Investigative Journalism on Screen: *Spotlight* 68

Journalism Evolves across Media 70
    Journalism on the Airwaves 70
    Internet Convergence Accelerates Changes to Journalism 72

The Culture of News and Rituals of Reporting 73
    What Is News? 74
    Values in American Journalism 75
    When Values Collide: Ethics and the News Media 79

The Economics of Journalism in the Twenty-First Century 82
    A Business Model in Transition 82
    Newspaper Operations 84
    Consolidation and a Crash 85
    LaunchPad Newspapers and the Internet: Convergence 86

Changes, Challenges, and Threats to Journalism Today 87
    Social Media 87
    Citizen Journalism 89
    Satiric Journalism 89
    Fake News 90

THE DIGITAL TURN CASE STUDY Attacking Journalism: Trolls and State-Sponsored Troll Armies 92
    ▶ **Web Clip** Global Attacks on Journalism 92

Santi Visalli/Archive Photos/
Getty Images

Journalism in a Democratic Society 93
    Social Responsibility 93
    The Troubled Future of Journalism 94

CHAPTER ESSENTIALS 96

4 Magazines in the Age of Specialization 99

The Early History of Magazines 101
    The First Magazines: European Origins 102
    Magazines in Eighteenth-Century America: The Voices of Revolution 102
    Magazines in Nineteenth-Century America: Specialization and General Interest 102
    Going National as the Twentieth Century Approaches 103

The Evolution of Modern American Magazines 103
    Distribution and Production Costs Plummet 104
    Muckrakers Expose Social Ills 104
    General-Interest Magazines Hit Their Stride 105

MEDIA LITERACY CASE STUDY The Evolution of Photojournalism 106
    ▶ **Web Clip** The Power of Photojournalism 106
    General-Interest Magazines Decline 109

Types of Magazines: Domination of Specialization 110
    LaunchPad Magazine Specialization Today 110
    Men's and Women's Magazines 111
    Entertainment, Leisure, and Sports Magazines 111
    Age-Specific Magazines 112
    Elite Magazines 112
    Minority-Targeted Magazines 113
    Trade Magazines 113
    Alternative Magazines 114
    Supermarket Tabloids 114
    Online Magazines 114
    LaunchPad Narrowcasting in Magazines 115

The Organization and Economics of Magazines 115
    Magazine Departments and Duties 115
    Major Magazine Chains 118

THE DIGITAL TURN CASE STUDY Snapchats and Podcasts: Magazine Publishing Turns New Pages 119
    LaunchPad Magazines on Screen: *13 Going on 30* 119

Contents xxvii

Magazines in a Democratic Society 120

CHAPTER ESSENTIALS 122

5 Sound Recording and Popular Music 125

The Early History and Evolution of Sound Recording 127

    From Cylinders to Disks: Sound Recording Becomes a Mass Medium 128

    LaunchPad Sound Recordings from a Century Ago 129

    From Records to Tapes to CDs: Analog Goes Digital 129

    LaunchPad Recording Music Today 130

    From Downloads to Streaming: Sound Recording Goes through the Digital Turn 130

MEDIA LITERACY CASE STUDY The New Masters of Music Modernization: Daniel Ek, Spotify, and Streaming Services 132

    ▶ **Web Clip** Spotify and Streaming 132

    The Music Industry and Radio: A Rocky Relationship 134

U.S. Popular Music and the Rise of Rock 134

    The Rise of Pop Music 135

    Rock and Roll Arrives 136

    Rock Blurs Additional Boundaries 138

The Evolution of Pop Music 140

    The British Are Coming! 140

    Motown: The Home of Soul 141

    Folk and Psychedelic: Protest and Drugs 142

    Punk and Indie Respond to Mainstream Rock 143

    Hip-Hop Redraws Musical Lines 144

    The Country Road 146

The Economics of Sound Recording 146

    A Shifting Power Structure 147

    The Indies Grow with Digital Music 148

    Making, Selling, and Profiting from Music 148

THE DIGITAL TURN CASE STUDY 360 Degrees of Music 151

    LaunchPad Touring on Screen: Katy Perry 151

Sound Recording in a Democratic Society 152

CHAPTER ESSENTIALS 154

Mark Ralston/Getty Images

Heather Kennedy/Getty Images

6 Popular Radio and the Origins of Broadcasting 157

The Early History of Radio 159
Inventors Paving the Way: Morse, Maxwell, and Hertz 159
Innovators in Wireless: Marconi, Fessenden, and De Forest 160
Early Regulation of Radio 162
The Networks 164
The Radio Act of 1927 166
The Golden Age of Radio 167

The Evolution of Radio 169
Transistors: Making Radio Portable 169
The FM Revolution 170
The Rise of Format Radio 170

The Characteristics of Contemporary Radio 171
Format Specialization 172
Nonprofit Radio and NPR 173

MEDIA LITERACY CASE STUDY How Did Talk Radio Become So One-Sided? 174
  ▶ **Web Clip** News/Talk Radio on YouTube 174
Radio and Convergence 176
  LaunchPad Going Visual: Video, Radio, and the Web 177

THE DIGITAL TURN CASE STUDY Streaming Services Set Their Sights on Broadcast Radio 178
  ▶ **Web Clip** Streaming Music Videos 178

The Economics of Commercial Radio 179
Selling Ads and Paying for Programming 179
  LaunchPad Radio: Yesterday, Today, and Tomorrow 180
Manipulating Playlists with Payola 180
Radio Ownership: From Diversity to Consolidation 181

Radio in a Democratic Society 182

CHAPTER ESSENTIALS 184

7 Movies and the Impact of Images 187

LaunchPad Storytelling in *Star Wars* 188

The Early History of Movies 189
- Advances in Film Technology 189
- Telling Stories: The Introduction of Narrative 191
- The Arrival of Nickelodeons 192

The Evolution of the Hollywood Studio System 193
- Edison's Attempt to Control the Industry 193
- A Closer Look at the Three Pillars 194

Hollywood's Golden Age: The Development of Style 196
- Narrative Techniques in the Silent Era 196
- Augmenting Images with Sound 197
- Inside the Hollywood System: Setting the Standard for Narrative Style 198
- Outside the Hollywood System: Providing Alternatives 200

LaunchPad Breaking Barriers with *12 Years a Slave* 200

MEDIA LITERACY CASE STUDY Breaking through Hollywood's Race Barrier 202

LaunchPad A Hollywood Blockbuster: *Black Panther* 202

The Transformation of the Hollywood Studio System 204
- The Paramount Decision 204
- Flight to the Suburbs 205
- Television Changes Hollywood 205
- Hollywood Adapts to Home Entertainment 206

The Economics of the Movie Business 207
- Making Money on Movies Today 207
- Conglomerations and Synergy in the Movie Industry 208
- Theater Chains Consolidate Exhibition 209
- Convergence: Movies Adjust to the Digital Turn 210

THE DIGITAL TURN CASE STUDY Attracting an Audience in a Digital Age 212

▶ **Web Clip** Digital Marketing for Popular Movies 212

The Movies in a Democratic Society 214

LaunchPad More Than a Movie: Social Issues and Film 215

CHAPTER ESSENTIALS 216

© Walt Disney Studios Motion Pictures/Lucasfilm Ltd./Courtesy Everett Collection Inc

Netflix/Photofest

8 Television, Cable, and Specialization in Visual Culture 219

The Early History of Television 222
    Becoming a Mass Medium 222
    Controlling TV Content 224
    Staining Television's Reputation 224
    Introducing Cable 225
    LaunchPad Television Networks Evolve 225

The Evolution of Network Programming 226
    Information: Network News 227
    Entertainment: Comedy 227
    Entertainment: Drama 228
    LaunchPad Television Drama: Then and Now 229
    Talk Shows and TV Newsmagazines 230
    Reality Television 230
    Public Television 231

MEDIA LITERACY CASE STUDY Race, Gender, and Sexual Orientation in TV Programming 232
    LaunchPad Race in TV Programming: *Black-ish* 232

The Evolution of Cable Programming 234
    Basic Cable 234
    Premium Cable 235

Regulatory Challenges Facing Television and Cable 236
    Restricting Broadcast Networks' Control 236
    Reining in Cable's Growth—for a While 237

Technology and Convergence Change Viewing Habits 239
    Home Video and Recording 239
    The Internet, Smartphones, and Mobile Video 240

THE DIGITAL TURN CASE STUDY Bingeing Purges
    Traditional Viewing Habits 241
    LaunchPad Bingeable Series: *Stranger Things* 241
    DBS 242

The Economics of Television, Cable, and Streaming Video 242
    Production 242
    Distribution 243

Contents **xxxi**

Syndication Keeps Shows Going and Going . . . 244

Measuring Television Viewing 244

The Major Programming Corporations 246

Television in a Democratic Society 248

CHAPTER ESSENTIALS 250

9 The Internet and New Technologies: The Media Converge 253

The Early History of the Internet 256

Military Functions, Civic Roots 256

The Net Widens 258

The Evolution of the Internet: Going Commercial, Getting Social, Making Meaning 259

The Commercialization of the Internet 259

The Web Gets Social 262

LaunchPad The Rise of Social Media 262

The Next Era: The Semantic Web 265

LaunchPad The Internet in 1995: *The Net* 265

THE DIGITAL TURN CASE STUDY Social Media Fraud and Elections 266

▶ **Web Clip** Understanding Social Media Fraud 266

The Economics of the Internet 268

Ownership: Controlling the Internet 268

Targeted Advertising and Data Mining 270

MEDIA LITERACY CASE STUDY Net Neutrality 272

LaunchPad Reddit CEO on Net Neutrality 272

The Noncommercial Web 274

Security and Appropriateness on the Internet 274

Information Security: What's Private? 275

Personal Safety: Online Predators, Spreading Hate, and Deciding What's Appropriate 276

The Internet in a Democratic Society 277

Access: Closing the Digital Divide 277

Ownership and Customization 278

CHAPTER ESSENTIALS 280

Jinxy Productions/Getty Images

AFP Contributor/Getty Images

10 Digital Gaming and the Media Playground 283

The Early History of Digital Gaming 285
    Mechanical Gaming 286
    The First Video Games 287

The Evolution of Digital Gaming 288
    Arcades and Classic Games 288
    Consoles Power Up 289
    Computer Gaming 293
    The Internet and Social Gaming 293

Trends and Issues in Digital Gaming 295
    Communities of Play: Inside the Game 295
    Communities of Play: Outside the Game 296
    Immersion and Addiction 297

THE DIGITAL TURN CASE STUDY   Games in the Great Wide Open: *Pokémon Go* and the Future of Mobile Gaming 299
    ▶ **Web Clip**   *Pokémon Go* and Mobile Gaming 299
    Violence and Misogyny 300

MEDIA LITERACY CASE STUDY   Fighting the Dark Side of Gaming Culture: Anita Sarkeesian and Feminist Frequency 302
    LaunchPad   Anita Sarkeesian and #GamerGate 302

The Economics of Digital Gaming 304
    Selling Digital Games 304
    LaunchPad   Video Games at the Movies: *Resident Evil* 306
    Making Digital Games 306

Digital Gaming in a Democratic Society 307
    Self-Regulation 307
    Free Speech and Video Games 307
    Alternate Voices 308

CHAPTER ESSENTIALS 310

MEDIA FRAMING INDUSTRIES

11 Advertising and Commercial Culture 313

Gabe Ginsberg/Getty Images

The Early History of American Advertising: 1850s to 1950s 315
   The First Advertising Agencies 316
   Retail Stores: Giving Birth to Branding 316
   Patent Medicines: Making Outrageous Claims 317
   Department Stores: Fueling a Consumer Culture 317
   Transforming American Society 318
   Early Regulation of Advertising 318

The Evolution of U.S. Advertising: 1950s to Today 319
   Visual Design Comes to the Fore 320
   New Breeds of Advertising Agencies Are Born 320
   Ad Agencies Develop a Distinctive Structure 322
   Online and Mobile Advertising Alter the Ad Landscape 325
   LaunchPad Advertising in the Digital Age 325

THE DIGITAL TURN CASE STUDY Does the Digital Turn Spell Doom for Network TV? 328
   LaunchPad Internet vs. TV Ad Spending 328

Persuasive Techniques in Contemporary Advertising 329
   Using Conventional Persuasive Strategies 330
   Associating Products with Values 330

MEDIA LITERACY CASE STUDY Idiots and Objects: Stereotyping in Advertising 332
   ▶ **Web Clip** Parodying Ad Stereotypes 332
   Telling Stories 334
   Placing Products in Media 334

Commercial Speech and Regulating Advertising 335
   Targeting Children and Teens 335
   LaunchPad Advertising and Effects on Children 335
   Triggering Anorexia and Overeating 336
   Promoting Smoking 337
   Promoting Drinking 337
   Hawking Drugs Directly to Consumers 338
   Monitoring the Advertising Industry 338

Advertising in a Democratic Society 340

CHAPTER ESSENTIALS 344

Kirby Lee-USA Today Sports/Newscom

12 Public Relations and Framing the Message 347

Early History of Public Relations 350
- Age of the Press Agent: P. T. Barnum and Buffalo Bill 350
- Business Adopts Press Agent Methods 351
- Professional Public Relations Emerges 351

The Evolution of Public Relations 353

MEDIA LITERACY CASE STUDY The Invisible Hand of PR 354
- ▶ **Web Clip** The Influence of Edward Bernays 354
- PR Agencies and In-House PR Staffs 356
- A Closer Look at Public Relations Functions 356

THE DIGITAL TURN CASE STUDY Military PR in the Digital Age 358
- ▶ **Web Clip** Military PR and Lady Gaga 358
- Public Relations in the Internet Age 363

Tensions between Public Relations and the Press 364
- Elements of Interdependence 364
- Journalists' Skepticism about PR Practices 365
- **LaunchPad** Give and Take: Public Relations and Journalism 366
- Shaping PR's Image 366

Public Relations in a Democratic Society 367

CHAPTER ESSENTIALS 370

MEDIA EXPRESSIONS

Alex Wong/Getty Images

13 Legal Controls and Freedom of Expression 373

The Origins of Free Expression and a Free Press 376
- A Closer Look at the First Amendment 376
- Interpretations of Free Expression 377
- The Evolution of Censorship 377
- Unprotected Forms of Expression 379

THE DIGITAL TURN CASE STUDY Is "Sexting" Pornography? 385
- **LaunchPad** MTV Explores Sexting and the Law 385
- First Amendment versus Sixth Amendment 387
- **LaunchPad** Bloggers and Legal Rights 387

Film and the First Amendment 388

Citizens and Lawmakers Control the Movies 389

The Movie Industry Regulates Itself 389

The First Amendment, Broadcasting, and the Internet 391

The FCC Regulates Broadcasting 392

Dirty Words, Indecent Speech, and Hefty Fines 393

Political Broadcasts and Equal Opportunity 394

The Demise of the Fairness Doctrine 394

Communication Policy and the Internet 395

The First Amendment in a Democratic Society 396

MEDIA LITERACY CASE STUDY Fake News, the First Amendment, and Fighting Propaganda 398

▶ **Web Clip** Stopping the Spread of Fake News 398

CHAPTER ESSENTIALS 400

14 Media Economics and the Global Marketplace 403

CB2/ZOB/Supplied by WENN.com/Newscom

The Transition to an Information Economy 406

How Media Industries Are Structured 406

From Regulation to Deregulation 408

The Rise of Media Powerhouses 409

THE DIGITAL TURN CASE STUDY Are the Big Digital Companies Too Big? 411

LaunchPad The Impact of Media Ownership 411

Analyzing the Media Economy 412

How Media Companies Operate 412

How the Internet Is Changing the Game 413

Business Trends in Media Industries 414

The Age of Hegemony 415

Specialization and Global Markets 418

The Rise of Specialization and Synergy 418

Disney: A Postmodern Media Conglomerate 418

LaunchPad Disney's Global Brand: *Frozen* 421

The Growth of Global Audiences 421

MEDIA LITERACY CASE STUDY Netflix and Change: The Streaming Revolution and the Business of Content Creation 422

▶ **Web Clip** Netflix on YouTube 422

Social Issues in Media Economics 424

xxxvi Contents

      The Limits of Antitrust Laws 424

      The Fallout from a Free Market 425

      Cultural Imperialism 426

The Media Marketplace in a Democratic Society 426

CHAPTER ESSENTIALS 428

15 Media Effects and Cultural Approaches to Media Research 431

Brendan Smialowski/Getty Images

Early Media Research Methods 433

    Propaganda Analysis 434

    Public Opinion Research 434

    Social Psychology Studies 435

    Marketing Research 435

THE DIGITAL TURN CASE STUDY Artificial Intelligence Gets Personal 437

    ▶ **Web Clip** Amazon's Powerful Algorithm 437

Research on Media Effects 438

    Early Models of Media Effects 438

    LaunchPad Media Effects Research 439

    Conducting Media Effects Research 440

    Contemporary Theories of Media Effects 443

    Evaluating Research on Media Effects 446

Cultural Approaches to Media Research 446

    Early Developments in Cultural Studies Media Research 447

    Contemporary Cultural Studies Approaches 447

MEDIA LITERACY CASE STUDY Does Art Imitate Life or Life Imitate Art? TV Depictions of Suicide and Copycat Fears 450

    LaunchPad Suicide on TV: *13 Reasons Why* 450

    Evaluating Cultural Studies Research 452

Media Research in a Democratic Society 452

CHAPTER ESSENTIALS 454

    Notes N-1

    Glossary G-1

    Index I-1

MEDIA ESSENTIALS

Mass Media Industries

Mass Communication: A Critical Approach

6
The Evolution of Mass Communication

12
The Development of Media and Their Role in Society

16
The Cultural Approach to Media Studies

21
Critiquing Media and Developing Media Literacy

"Black people, I love you. I love us. Our lives matter." After a jury acquitted George Zimmerman in the shooting death of unarmed black teen Trayvon Martin on July 13, 2013, Alicia Garza used these words in a Facebook post describing her anger and heartbreak. When Garza's friend Patrisse Cullors saw the post and shared it along with the hashtag #BlackLivesMatter, these same words inspired a new chapter in civil rights activism: Garza and Cullors brought in friend Opal Tometi and together the three women cofounded the Black Lives Matter movement.[1]

The organization built an online presence using the hashtag #BlackLivesMatter on social media sites as a way to connect people and share information (including videos) about violence against black men and women—especially by police. Following the shooting death of Michael Brown in Ferguson, Missouri, in 2014, the "hashtag activism" of the Black Lives Matter movement moved offline as more than five hundred people descended on Ferguson to protest the shooting. Now more than six years old, the Black Lives Matter movement has nearly two dozen chapters, and the hashtag is used on Twitter an average of 17,002 times a day.[2]

◀ #BlackLivesMatter grew from a social media hashtag into an international movement that emphasizes both online and in-person **activism.** Daniel Leal Olivas/AFP/Getty Images

Hashtag activism—so called because of the use of the symbol # before a word or phrase on Twitter that communicates a larger idea or event—offers a compelling illustration of just how powerful social media can be when it is channeled toward a cause. In addition to #BlackLivesMatter, #MeToo spurred a flood of posts about the sexism, harassment, and violence experienced by women at the hands of men. This online participation can also translate to real-world engagement and real-life consequences: #MeToo helped bring down powerful Hollywood producer Harvey Weinstein, as multiple women—including many famous actresses—came forward with tales of sexual abuse by Weinstein.

But hashtag activism also captures another aspect of our relationship with social media: that it's complicated. According to a 2018 Pew Research Center survey, over half of U.S. adults have used social media to be "civically active"—for example, to engage with a cause, to look up information on local protests and rallies, or to talk others into taking action on issues. In addition, 80 percent of black respondents believe that sites like Twitter help get issues into the public discussion that wouldn't otherwise be covered. At the same time, 77 percent of all respondents feel that social media distracts from truly important issues, and 71 percent believe that hashtag activism can give people the false sense that they have accomplished something worthwhile—a phenomenon sometimes called "slacktivism."[3]

In this way, hashtag activism and other forms of online engagement defy simple evaluations of being either "good" or "bad"; rather, they can be both. As Alicia Garza explains, social media has benefits, but social media alone does not effect change: "Twitter is not going to save us. Twitter can be a vehicle that connects us and helps bring us together to strategize around how . . . to transform the world we live in."[4]

Nuanced though it may be, social media's impact on our lives is powerful, and it is here to stay. In this age of smartphones and lightning-fast Internet speeds, it's hard to imagine any successful effort to capture the public's attention that wouldn't make savvy use of social media—including a social movement. Hashtag activism illustrates just one of the many ways that mass media are integrated into our lives—now, more than ever before.

THE NEED TO COMMUNICATE WITH OTHERS—to tell stories, to persuade, to entertain and be entertained, to share values and ideas—is a defining feature of what it means to be human. Understanding how we use media to facilitate this communication, how our use of media has changed over time, and what these changes might mean for the present and future are all ideas that we consider in mass communication research.

Thinking about these ideas can generate many compelling questions. For example, how do media both reflect and shape society? Who owns and controls the different parts of the mass media? What responsibilities do the owners of mass media corporations have to the public? What responsibilities do we, as members of the public, have in the way we use mass media? Do digital developments like social media and online content streaming represent uncharted media territory, an extension of existing media forms, or both? In this book, we take up these questions and many more by examining the history and business of mass media and discussing the media as a central force in shaping our culture and our democracy.

At their best, mass media try to help us understand the events and trends affecting us. At their worst, they can erode the quality of our lives. For one thing, media outlets' appetite for telling and selling stories can lead them to misrepresent those events or exploit them (and the people they most affect) for profit. Many critics disapprove of how media—particularly TV and the Internet—hurtle from one event to another, often dwelling on trivial, celebrity-driven content. Critics also fault media for failing to fulfill their responsibility as watchdogs for democracy, which sometimes requires challenging our leaders and questioning their actions. Finally, the formation and growth of media industries, commercial culture, and new technologies have some critics worrying that we now spend more time consuming media than interacting with one another.

Like anything else, mass media have their good sides and bad sides, their useful effects and destructive ones. And that's why it is so important for us to acquire **media literacy**—an understanding of the media that are powerfully shaping our world (and being shaped by it). Only by being media literate can we become critical consumers and engaged participants who accept part of the responsibility for the shape and direction of our media culture.

In this chapter, we will take steps to strengthen media literacy by:

- **tracing the evolution of mass communication from oral and written forms to print, electronic, and digital incarnations**

- **examining mass media and the process of communication, including the steps a new medium travels on its journey to mass medium status, and the role that mass media play in our everyday lives**

- **exploring the complicated ways in which culture and mass media simultaneously reflect and shape each other**

- **exploring ways of critiquing the mass media and reflecting on the importance of doing so**

> **LaunchPad**
> launchpadworks.com
> Use **LearningCurve** to review concepts from this chapter.

The Evolution of Mass Communication

The mass media surrounding us have their roots in mass communication. **Mass media** are the industries that create and distribute songs, novels, newspapers, movies, Internet services, TV shows, magazines, and other products to large numbers of people. The word *media* is a Latin plural form of the singular noun *medium*, meaning an intervening material or substance through which something else is conveyed or distributed.

We can trace the historical development of media through several eras, all of which still operate to varying degrees. In the first two eras (oral and written), media existed only in tribal or feudal communities and in agricultural economies. In the last three eras (print, electronic, and digital), media became vehicles for **mass communication**: the creation and use of symbols (e.g., languages, Morse code, motion pictures, and binary computer codes) that convey information and meaning to large and diverse audiences through all manner of channels.

Although the telegraph meant that by the middle of the 1800s reporters could almost instantly send a report to their newspaper across the country, getting that news out to a mass audience still required the printing and delivery of a physical object. But with the start of the electronic age in the early twentieth century, radio and then television made mass communication even more widely—and instantly—accessible. If a person was in range of a transmitter, news and entertainment now came at the flick of a switch. By the end of the twentieth century, the Internet revolutionized the entire field of mass communication. We call this profound change in mass media the *digital turn*, and this change is still happening today. Interestingly, as shown throughout this book, older forms of communication don't go away but are adapted and *converged*, or joined together, with newer forms and technologies.

The Oral and Written Eras

In most early societies, information and knowledge first circulated slowly through oral (spoken) traditions passed on by poets, teachers, and tribal storytellers. However, as alphabets and the written word emerged, a manuscript (written) culture developed and eventually overshadowed oral communication. Painstakingly documented and transcribed by philosophers, monks, and stenographers, manuscripts were commissioned by members of the ruling classes, who used them to record religious works and prayers, literature, and personal chronicles. Working people, most of whom were illiterate, rarely saw manuscripts. The shift from oral to written communication created a wide gap between rulers and the ruled in terms of the two groups' education levels and economic welfare.

These trends in oral and written communication unfolded slowly over many centuries. Although exact time frames are disputed, historians generally date the oral and written eras as ranging from 1000 BCE to the mid-fifteenth century. Moreover, the transition from oral to written communication wasn't necessarily smooth. For example, some philosophers saw oral traditions (including exploration of questions and answers through dialogue between teachers and students) as superior, and feared that the written word would hamper conversation between people.

The Print Era

What we recognize as modern printing—the wide dissemination of many copies of particular manuscripts—became practical in Europe around the middle of the fifteenth century. At this time, Johannes Gutenberg's invention of movable metallic type and the printing press in Germany ushered in the modern print era. Printing presses—and the publications they produced—spread rapidly across Europe in the late 1400s and early 1500s. But early on, many books were large, elaborate, and expensive. It took months to illustrate and publish these volumes, which were typically purchased by wealthy aristocrats, royal families, church leaders, prominent merchants, and powerful politicians.

In the following centuries, printers reduced the size and cost of books, making them available and affordable to more people. Books were then being mass-produced, making them the first mass-marketed products in history. This development spurred four significant changes: an increasing resistance to authority, the rise of new socioeconomic classes, the spread of literacy, and a focus on individualism.

▶ Before the invention of the printing press, books were copied by hand in a labor-intensive process. This beautifully illuminated page is from an Italian Bible from the early 1300s. Scala/Art Resource, NY

Resistance to Authority

Since mass-produced printed materials could spread information and ideas faster and farther than ever before, writers could use print to disseminate views that challenged traditional civic doctrine and religious authority. This paved the way for major social and cultural changes, such as the Protestant Reformation and the rise of modern nationalism. People who read contradictory views began resisting traditional clerical authority. With easier access to information about events in nearby places, people also began seeing themselves not merely as members of families, isolated communities, or tribes but as participants in larger social units—nation-states—whose interests surpassed local or regional concerns.

New Socioeconomic Classes

Eventually, mass production of books inspired mass production of other goods. This development led to the Industrial Revolution and modern capitalism in the mid-nineteenth century. The nineteenth and twentieth centuries saw the rise of a consumer culture, which encouraged mass consumption to match the output of mass production. The revolution in industry also sparked the emergence of a middle class. This class was composed of people who were neither poor laborers nor wealthy political or religious leaders but who made modest livings as merchants, artisans, and service professionals such as lawyers and doctors.

In addition to a middle class, the Industrial Revolution gave rise to an elite class of business owners and managers who acquired the kind of influence once held by only the nobility or the clergy. These groups soon discovered that they could use print media to distribute information and maintain social order.

Spread of Literacy

Although print media secured authority figures' power, the mass publication of pamphlets, magazines, and books also began democratizing knowledge—making it available to more and more people. As literacy rates rose among the working and middle classes, some rulers fought back. In England, for instance, the monarchy controlled printing press licenses until the early nineteenth century to constrain literacy and therefore sustain the Crown's power over the populace. Even today, governments in many countries control presses, access to paper, and advertising and distribution channels for the same reason. In most industrialized countries, such efforts at control have met with only limited success. After all, building an industrialized economy requires a more educated workforce, and printed literature and textbooks support that education.

Focus on Individualism

The print revolution also nourished the idea of individualism. People came to rely less on their local community and their commercial, religious, and political leaders for guidance on how to live their lives. Instead, they read various ideas and arguments and came up with their own answers to life's great questions. By the mid-nineteenth century, individualism had spread into the realm of commerce. There, it took the form of increased resistance to government interference in the affairs of self-reliant entrepreneurs. Over the next century, individualism became a fundamental value in American society.

The Electronic Era

In Europe and America, the rise of industry completely transformed everyday life, with factories replacing farms as the main centers of work and production. During the 1880s, roughly 80 percent of Americans lived on farms and in small towns; by the 1920s and 1930s, most had moved to urban areas, where new industries and economic opportunities beckoned. This shift set the stage for the next era in mass communication: the electronic era, which saw the rise of the telegraph, radio, and television.

The Telegraph and Instant Communication

In America, the gradual transformation from an industrial, print-based society to one fueled by electronic innovation began with the development of the telegraph in the 1840s. Featuring dot-dash electronic signals, the telegraph made media messages instantaneous, no longer reliant on stagecoaches, ships, or the Pony Express. It also enabled military, business, and political leaders to coordinate commercial and military operations more easily than ever. And it laid the groundwork for future technological developments, such as wireless telegraphy, the fax machine, and the cell phone (all of which ultimately led to the telegraph's demise).

Radio, Television, and a Common Mediated Culture

The development of film at the start of the twentieth century and radio in the 1920s were important milestones, but the electronic era really took off in the 1950s and 1960s with the arrival of television—a medium that powerfully reshaped American life.

Through much of human history, people shared their strongest cultural ties with those who lived in the same village, city, or region. Shared language, experience, and customs moved relatively slowly in most cases, limited by the challenges of transportation and distance. This started to change with the print era, but the ability of formerly isolated groups to see themselves as part of a larger whole accelerated rapidly with the electronic age.

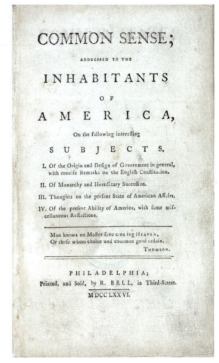

▲ Published in January 1776, Thomas Paine's pamphlet *Common Sense* not only made a case for American independence but made it in plain and simple language considered accessible to the broader colonial audience. The popular publication is often credited with helping build support for the break with Great Britain. Library of Congress, Prints & Photographs Division, Reproduction number LC-USZ62-10658 (b&w film copy neg.)

▲ Beginning in the 1920s, radios and then television sets—encased in decorative wood and sold as stylish furniture—occupied a central place in many American homes.
Camerique/ClassicStock/Getty Images

In America, the invention of both radio and television is credited with helping the country forge a shared national identity. News, sports, and entertainment could be shared instantly with vast audiences from coast to coast. President Franklin's fireside chats, the first steps of a man on the moon, coverage of the Civil Rights movement, and the bombing and collapse of the World Trade Center towers: These are just a few of the touchstones media historians point to when describing moments Americans experienced together as a nation via electronic mass media.

The Digital Era

With the arrival of cutting-edge communication gadgetry—ever-smaller personal computers, cable TV, e-mail, DVDs, DVRs, direct broadcast satellites, smartphones—the electronic era gave way to the digital era. In **digital communication**, images, texts, and sounds are converted (encoded) into electronic signals represented as combinations of ones and zeros, which are then reassembled (decoded) as a precise reproduction of, say, a TV picture, a magazine article, a song, or a voice at the other end of a phone.

New technologies developed so quickly during the digital era that traditional communication leaders lost some of their control over information. For example, beginning with the 1992 presidential campaign, ABC, CBS, and NBC News began to lose their audiences to cable channels and radio talk shows, and by the 2012 national elections, *social media* sites had become key players in news and politics. Social media sites have also reinvented oral culture, enabling people from all over the world to have online conversations, share stories, and generate their own media content.

This turn to digital media forms has fundamentally disrupted traditional media business models, the ways we engage with and consume media products, and the ways we organize our daily lives around various media choices. It has also led to two important hallmarks of the digital era: the digital turn and media convergence.

The Digital Turn

Each new form of mass media, from books to television, has led to powerful changes in how people consume information and entertainment. But more recently, we have experienced a **digital turn**: a shift in media use and consumption resulting from the emergence of the Internet as a mass medium, which enabled an array of media to come together in one space and be easily shared. The digital turn is characterized by its speed and by the way it dismantled the once-clear boundaries between different forms of media. An early medium like radio could take decades to fully emerge, while today a website or an app can reach similar audience thresholds in a matter of months or even days. Thus, while the foundations for this digital turn were laid in the 1990s, it is the ever-quicker download speeds and more portable and powerful devices of the last decade that have fundamentally changed the ways in which we access and consume media.

The digital turn has made us more fragmented even as it has made us more connected (see also "The Digital Turn Case Study: FOMO in a Digital World" on page 13). We might not be able to count on our friends all watching the same television show, but Facebook, Twitter, and even interactive games like *Fortnite* have made it easier for us to connect with friends—and strangers—and tell them what we watched, listened to, and read.

Media Convergence

Although it has its roots in the electronic era, the phenomenon of **media convergence** is one of the defining characteristics of the digital turn. This term has two very different meanings. According to one meaning, media convergence is the technological merging of content across different media channels. For example, magazine articles and radio programs are also accessible on the Internet; and songs, TV shows, and movies are now available on computers, tablets, and cell phones.

The term *media convergence* can also be used to describe a particular business model in which a company consolidates various media holdings—such as Internet connections, television and cable stations, radio stations, websites, movie studies, and theme parks—under one corporate umbrella. The goal of such consolidation is not necessarily to offer consumers more choices but to better manage resources, lower costs, and maximize profits. For example, a company that owns TV stations, radio outlets, and newspapers in multiple markets—as well as in the same cities—can deploy one reporter or producer to create three or four versions of the same story for various

▲ Comcast is one example of a converged media company, with diverse holdings that include Xfinity cable, TV networks like the E! channel, movie studios like Universal Pictures, and Universal Studios theme parks. In this tweet, the company promotes a show on a network it owns (*This Is Us* on NBC), which is broadcast on its Xfinity cable system.

media outlets. Thus, the company can employ fewer people than if it owned only one media outlet.

Although it's easy to see how a converged business model benefits media owners—more profits to those companies that downsize their workforce while increasing their media holdings in a variety of markets—this model presents some disadvantages for society. For one thing, it limits the range of perspectives from which messages are delivered, as media content becomes concentrated in fewer hands.

In every chapter in this book, we will discuss how both kinds of convergence have changed the way mass media work and how we use each medium. For example, in later chapters we will see how the music industry is coming to grips with streaming music, how convergence played a key role in damaging the business model of traditional news media, and how online piracy and copyright infringement remain major challenges for music and movie companies.

The Development of Media and Their Role in Society

To understand how mass media shape the communication process, let's look at how they develop—including the stages a medium goes through on its journey to becoming a mass medium. Then let's examine the ways in which the media have affected everyday life.

The Evolution of Media: From Emergence to Convergence

The development of most mass media is initiated not only by the diligence of inventors, such as Thomas Edison (see Chapters 5 and 7), but also by social, cultural, political, and economic circumstances. For instance, the Internet arose to meet people's desire to transport messages and share information more rapidly in an increasingly mobile and interconnected global population. Media innovations typically evolve through four stages:

1. First is the *development stage* (also called the *emergence* or *novelty stage*), in which inventors and technicians try to solve a particular problem, such as making pictures move, transmitting messages from ship to shore, or sending mail electronically.
2. Second is the *entrepreneurial stage*, in which inventors and investors determine a practical and marketable use for the new device. For example, the Internet had its roots in scientists' desire for a communication system that could enable their colleagues across the country to share time on a few rare supercomputers.

The Digital Turn

CASE STUDY

FOMO in a Digital World

For at least some of us, the social mediated version of ourselves becomes the predominant way we experience the world. As *Time* magazine noted, "Experiences don't feel fully real" until we have "tweeted them or tumbled them or YouTubed them—and the world has congratulated [us] for doing so."[1] But the flip side of promoting our own experiences on social media as *the most awesome happenings ever (and too bad you aren't here)* is the social anxiety associated with reading about other people's experiences and realizing that you're not part of them.

The problem is called Fear of Missing Out (FOMO), and one report defines it as "the uneasy and sometimes all-consuming feeling that you're missing out—that your peers are doing, in the know about or in possession of more or something better than you."[2] There are plenty of platforms for posting about ourselves and anxiously creeping on others; Facebook, Twitter, Snapchat, and Instagram are just a few of the sites that can feed our FOMO problem.

FOMO existed long before social media was invented. Photos, postcards, and those holiday letters usually put the most positive spin on people's lives. But social media, mobile technology, and other conveniences of the digital turn make being exposed to the interactions we missed a 24/7 phenomenon. There is potentially *always* something better we could have/should have been doing.

People with FOMO tend to tether themselves to social media, tracking "friends" and sacrificing time that might be spent having in-person, unmediated experiences.[3] Yet all this time on social media may not equal happiness. According to one study, the more a group of college students used Facebook, the more two components of well-being declined: how people feel moment to moment and how satisfied they are with their lives.[4] Even more seriously, an Australian study found that FOMO causes drivers, especially younger ones, to text or check their smartphones while behind the wheel—a practice found to increase the risk of accidents by more than six times.[5]

Studies about happiness routinely conclude that the best path to subjective well-being is having a community of close personal relationships. Social psychologists Ed Diener and Robert Biswas-Diener acknowledge that the high use of mobile phones, text messaging, and social media is evidence that people want to connect. But they also explain that "we don't just need relationships: we need close ones." They conclude, "The close relationships that produce the most happiness are those characterized by mutual understanding, caring, and validation of the other person as worthwhile."[6] Thus, frequent contact isn't enough to produce the relationships that lead to the most happiness.

Ironically, there has never been a medium better than the Internet and its social media platforms to bring people together. Still, according to Diener and Biswas-Diener, maintaining close relationships may require a "vacation" from social media from time to time, experiencing something together with friends. Of course (we hate to say it), you will still need to text, e-mail, or call to arrange that date.

▶ Web Clip

YouTube.com has many videos about FOMO. One good option to search for: "Do You Have FOMO?" by Soapboxing and Refinery29. Do you think an audience watching this video in five years will still relate to feelings of FOMO? In ten years? Why or why not?

3. Third is the *mass medium stage*. At this point, businesses figure out how to market the new device as a consumer product. To illustrate, Pentagon and government researchers helped develop early prototypes for the Internet, but commercial interests extended the Internet's global reach and business potential.
4. Finally, the fourth and newest stage in a medium's evolution is the *convergence stage*, in which older media are reconfigured in various forms into newer digital media (see the "Media Convergence" section earlier in the chapter). However, this does not necessarily mean that the older forms cease to exist. For example, you can still get the *New York Times* in print, but it's also now accessible—with additional content—on laptops and smartphones. During this stage, we see the merging of many different media forms onto online platforms, but we also see the fragmenting of large audiences into smaller niche markets. With new technologies allowing access to more media options than ever before, mass audiences are morphing into audience subsets that consume and chase particular products, lifestyles, politics, hobbies, and forms of entertainment.

launchpadworks.com

Agenda-Setting and Gatekeeping

Experts discuss how the media exert influence over public discourse.

Discussion: How might the rise of the Internet cancel out or reduce the agenda-setting effect in media?

Debating Media's Role in Everyday Life

For centuries, human beings have discussed and debated the media's merits and dangers. The longest-enduring arguments have revolved around the amount of influence media has over audiences, and what this means for the values and morals of a society. More recently, the debates over the role of media in our everyday lives have expanded to include questions about who owns and controls the various forms of media, and the impact of fewer and fewer people having more control.

The Social Impact of Mass Media

The earliest recorded media-related debates in Western society date back to the ancient Greeks—in particular, to Socrates, Euripides, and Plato, who questioned the impact of the written word on daily life. These men argued over whether theatrical plays would corrupt young people by exposing them to messages that conflicted with those promulgated by their teachers.

We still debate these sorts of questions. At the turn of the twentieth century, for example, newly arrived immigrants to the United States who spoke little English gravitated toward vaudeville shows and silent films, which they could enjoy without having to understand English. These popular events occasionally became a flash point for some groups. For example, the Daughters of the American Revolution, local politicians, religious leaders, and police vice squads feared that these "low" cultural forms would undermine what they saw as traditional American values. Today, with the reach of different types of media and the amount of time people spend consuming them (see Figure 1.1),

FIGURE 1.1 // DAILY ELECTRONIC MEDIA USE BY PLATFORM, 2018

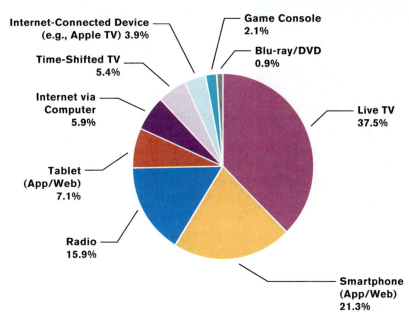

Data from: "Time Flies: U.S. Adults Now Spend Nearly Half a Day Interacting with Media," Nielsen, July 31, 2018, www.nielsen.com/us/en/insights/news/2018/time-flies-us-adults-now-spend-nearly-half-a-day-interacting-with-media.html. Note: These numbers do not include time spent with print media.

mass media now play an even more controversial role in society. For instance, some people are frustrated by the overwhelming amount of information available. Others decry what they view as mass media's overly commercial and sensationalistic quality.

People also keep grappling with the dual question: How much does mass media shape society, and how much does mass media simply respond to existing values and behaviors? For example, some researchers have designed studies to determine whether watching violent TV shows makes viewers more likely to commit violent acts, while others argue that people who have violent tendencies are drawn to violent TV shows, or that certain variables—such as age, upbringing, or genetics—might be the root cause of violence. Research into such questions hasn't yielded conclusive answers, but it does encourage us to keep analyzing and thinking critically about the media's role in our lives.

Concentration of Power
With American mass media industries earning more than $700 billion in 2017 (according to the U.S. Department of Commerce), the economic and societal stakes of media influence are high. Large portions of media resources go

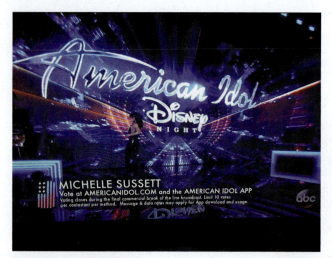

▲ In 2018, Disney night on *American Idol* featured a guest appearance by Mickey Mouse, contestants singing Disney songs, and judge Katy Perry dressed as Snow White. It isn't a coincidence that the singing competition airs on ABC, which is a Disney-owned TV network. Cross-promotions like this illustrate the powerful corporate reach of global media companies like Disney. Christopher Martin

toward studying audiences, capturing their attention through stories, and taking in their consumer dollars. To increase their revenues, media outlets try to influence everything from how people shop to how they vote.

Along with understanding the vast financial power of the mass media, it is important to understand the increasing concentration of that power. Especially over the past thirty years, as media influence has grown, the number of owners who control media businesses has shrunk. What does it mean, for example, that Disney owns both the *Star Wars* and Marvel franchises? Just two parts of a much bigger media empire, this nevertheless demonstrates the vast economic and cultural power under the control of one corporation's CEO and board of directors.

Like the air we breathe, the commercially based culture that mass media help create surrounds us. Its impact, like the air, is often taken for granted. But to monitor that culture's "air quality," we must first become media literate and attend more thoughtfully to a vast array of media stories that are too often taken for granted.

The Cultural Approach to Media Studies

One way to understand the impact of media on our lives is to explore the cultural context in which media operate. In its broadest sense, culture can be viewed as the ways in which people live and represent themselves at particular historical times, as manifested in things like fashion, sports, architecture, education, religion, science, and mass media.

Culture is made up of both the products that a society fashions and, perhaps more importantly, the processes that forge those products and reflect a culture's diverse values. Thus, **culture** may be defined as the symbols of expression that individuals, groups, and societies use to make sense of daily life and to articulate their values. When we listen to music, read a book, watch television, or scan the Internet, we assign meaning to that song, book, TV program, or website—and different people often assign different meanings to the same media content.

In this section, we will take a more detailed look at the relationship between media and culture. We'll introduce the cultural model of media literacy, which is one of the models that researchers use to explain how media messages are communicated. (For a more detailed examination of different models researchers use to study the media, including the cultural and media effects models, please see Chapter 15.) We'll also discuss two metaphors researchers use to describe the way people judge media content, and present ways to trace changes in our cultural values as media adapt and change.

Moving from a Linear Model to a Cultural Model

Among the many changes that came with the digital era was a shift in the models that media researchers use to explain how media messages and meanings are constructed and communicated in everyday life. One older and outdated explanation of how media operate viewed mass communication as a linear process of producing and delivering messages to large audiences. According to this *linear model*:

- Senders (authors, producers, and organizations) transmitted messages (programs, texts, images, sounds, and ads) through a mass media channel (newspapers, books, magazines, radio, television, or the Internet) to large groups of receivers (readers, viewers, and consumers).
- Gatekeepers (news editors, executive producers, and other media managers) filtered those messages by making decisions about what messages got produced for which audiences.
- The process allowed for feedback, in which citizens and consumers could return messages to senders or gatekeepers through phone calls, e-mail, web postings, talk shows, or letters to the editor.

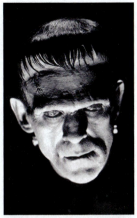

▲ Often, popular stories and characters evolve in our culture over time, acquiring new meaning. Consider the classic 1931 film *Frankenstein* (*top*) and the 1974 parody *Young Frankenstein* (*bottom*). How does each story reflect changes in cultural attitudes? © Photofest (top); © 20th Century Fox/Photofest (bottom)

The problem with the linear model is that in reality, media messages—especially in the digital era—do not usually move smoothly from a sender at point A to a receiver at point Z. Media messages and stories are encoded and sent in written and visual forms, but senders often have very little control over how their intended messages are decoded or whether the messages are ignored or misread by readers and viewers.

As an example, consider how the rise of the Internet and social media has complicated the communication and meaning-making process. The borderless, decentralized, and democratic nature of the Internet means that anyone can

▲ The cultural approach helps us understand media's role in shaping the debate over issues like gun violence. For example, a scholar might analyze media coverage of the student-led March for Our Lives demonstration in 2018. Or a scholar might examine how years of news coverage of school shootings has helped influence our attitudes and beliefs about the issue. Roger Kisby/Redux

become a sender of media messages—whether it's by uploading a video mash-up to YouTube or by writing a blog post. The Internet has also largely eliminated many gatekeepers. For example, some authors who are unable to find a traditional book publisher for their work turn to self-publishing on the Internet. And musicians who don't have deals with major record labels can promote, circulate, and sell their music online.

This is why another model—the *cultural model*—represents a more contemporary approach to understanding media. The cultural model recognizes that individuals bring diverse meanings to messages, given factors and differences such as gender, age, educational level, ethnicity, and occupation. In this more complex model of mass communication, audiences actively affirm, interpret, refashion, or reject the messages and stories that flow through various media channels. For example, take the *Harry Potter* book series. Some readers see the series as an innocent coming-of-age children's story. Others interpret it as more adult literature, containing pointed metaphors about good and evil that parallel current political events. Still others construe the series as a tool for luring children into a life of witchcraft. The cultural model suggests the complexity involved in transmitting a message from a sender to a receiver, as well as the lack of control that senders often have over how audiences receive messages and interpret their intended meanings.

Surveying the Cultural Landscape

Some cultural phenomena gain wide popularity, while others appeal only to certain groups of people. For example, some forms of music, such as rock and roll and jazz, are popular worldwide; other forms, such as Tejano and Cajun music, are popular primarily in certain regions or ethnic communities. Certain aspects of culture (e.g., opera) are considered elite in one place (the United States) and popular in another (Italy). Though categories may change over time and from one society to another, two metaphors offer contrasting views about the way culture operates in our daily lives: culture as a hierarchy, represented by a *skyscraper* model, and culture as a process, represented by a *map* model.

The "Culture as Skyscraper" Metaphor

Throughout the twentieth century, many Americans envisioned our nation's culture as consisting of ascending levels of superiority—like floors in a skyscraper. They identified **high culture** (the top floors of the building) as good taste, higher education, and fine art supported by wealthy patrons and corporate donors, and they associated **low** or **popular culture** (the bottom floors) with the questionable tastes of the masses, who lapped up the commercial junk circulated by the mass media, such as reality TV shows, celebrity gossip websites, and action films.

Some cultural researchers have pointed out that this high–low hierarchy has become so entrenched that it powerfully influences how we view and discuss culture today.[5] For example, people who subscribe to the hierarchy metaphor believe that low culture prevents people (students in particular) from appreciating fine art, exploits high culture by transforming classic works into simplistic forms, and promotes a throwaway ethic. These same critics accuse low culture of driving out higher forms of culture. They also argue that it inhibits political discourse and social change by making people so addicted to mass-produced media that they lose their ability to see and challenge social inequities (also referred to as the Big Mac Theory).[6]

▲ On Netflix's *Queer Eye*, five gay lifestyle experts provide advice and makeovers (or "make-betters") to participants looking to transform themselves. A reboot of Bravo's *Queer Eye for the Straight Guy*, which aired in the 2000s, the show won three Emmy Awards in 2018. Where do you think this show would fit on a "skyscraper" of high to low culture? Everett Collection, Inc

The "Culture as Map" Metaphor

Other researchers think of culture as a map. In this metaphor, culture—rather than being a vertically organized structure—is an ongoing process that accommodates diverse tastes. Cultural phenomena, including media—printed materials we read, movies and TV programs we watch, songs and podcasts we listen to—can take us to places that are conventional, recognizable, stable, and comforting. However, they can also take us to places that are innovative, unfamiliar, unstable, and challenging. Rather than elevating one type of media over another, the map metaphor flattens out the hierarchy and emphasizes the ways that ideas connect, like roads connecting towns and cities on a map.

Human beings are attracted to both consistency and change, and cultural media researchers have pointed out that most media can satisfy both of those desires. For example, a movie can contain elements that are familiar to us (such as particular plots) as well as elements that are completely new and strange (such as a cinematic technique we've never seen before).

Tracing Changes in Values

In addition to examining metaphors of culture that we use to understand media's role in our lives, cultural researchers examine the ways in which our values have changed along with changes in mass media. Researchers have been particularly interested in how values have shifted during the modern era and the postmodern period.

The Modern Era

From the Industrial Revolution to the mid-twentieth century—which historians call the **modern era**—four values came into sharp focus across the American cultural landscape. These values were influenced by developments that unfolded during the era and the media's responses to those developments:

- **Working efficiently.** As businesses used new technology to create efficient manufacturing centers and produce inexpensive products more cheaply and profitably, advertisers spread the word about new gadgets that could save Americans time and labor.
- **Celebrating the individual.** With access to novel ideas in the form of scientific discoveries communicated by the media, people began celebrating their power as individuals to pick and choose from ideas instead of merely following what religious and political leaders told them.
- **Believing in a rational order.** Being modern also meant valuing logic and reason and viewing the world as a rational place. In this orderly place, the printed mass media—particularly newspapers—served to educate the citizenry, helping build and maintain an organized society.[7] This belief in reason and scientific progress also lent itself to greater trust in experts and various institutions in society, from journalism to the government.
- **Rejecting tradition and embracing progress.** Within the modern era was a shorter phenomenon: the **Progressive Era**. This period of political and social reform lasted roughly from the 1890s to the 1920s and inspired many Americans—and mass media—to break with tradition and embrace change.

The Postmodern Period

In the **postmodern period**—from roughly the mid-twentieth century to today—cultural values changed shape once more, influenced again by developments in American society and the media's responses to those developments. Cultural researchers have identified the following dominant values in today's postmodern period:

- **Celebrating populism.** As a political idea, **populism** tries to appeal to ordinary people by setting up a conflict between "the people" and "the elite." For example, populist politicians often run ads criticizing big corporations and political favoritism. And many famous film actors champion oppressed groups, even though their work makes them wealthy global icons of consumerist culture.
- **Questioning authority.** Related to populism, a defining characteristic of the postmodern perspective is the questioning of the authority figures and institutions that were more widely trusted during the modern era. On the one

hand, this may be helping to advance social change, as women and minorities challenge existing power structures. On the other hand, the distrust of experts has fed climate change denial and anti-vaccination campaigns. This questioning of authority may also explain the popularity of movies like *Deadpool* and *Suicide Squad*, which feature gritty antiheroes as protagonists.
- **Embracing technology.** Even as some people question certain kinds of scientific knowledge, there seem to be fewer qualms about using the latest technology, such as computers and smartphones.

▲ Jessica Jones, a lesser-known hero from the Marvel comic books and the title character of a show adapted for television by streaming service Netflix, is an example of the kind of morally ambiguous antihero typified in the postmodern era.
Myles Aronowitz/©Netflix/courtesy Everett Collection Inc

Critiquing Media and Developing Media Literacy

In contemporary life, cultural boundaries are being tested; the arbitrary lines between information and entertainment have become blurred. Consumers now read newspapers on their smartphones and tablets. Media corporations do business globally. We are witnessing media convergence, in which everything from magazines to movies is channeled onto screens through the Internet, TV, tablets, and smartphones.

Considering the diversity of mass media, to paint them all with the same broad brush would be inaccurate and unfair. Yet that is often what we seem to do, which may in fact reflect the distrust many of us have of prominent social institutions, from local governments to daily newspapers. While revelations about phone hacking and government surveillance make this distrust understandable, it's ultimately more useful to replace cynicism with genuine criticism.

To deal with these shifts in how we experience media and culture, as well as their impact, we need to develop a profound understanding of the media, focused on what they offer or produce and what they downplay or ignore. To do this, we need to learn to critique media content ourselves in a methodical, disciplined way, and to keep in mind the benefits of a critical perspective.

Media Literacy and the Critical Process

Becoming truly *media literate*—attaining an understanding of mass media and how they construct meaning—requires following a **critical process** and applying it to everyday encounters with communication media. This process encompasses five steps: description, analysis, interpretation, evaluation, and engagement (see also "The Critical Process Behind Media Literacy" on page 23).

1. *Description* involves developing a working knowledge of the particular medium being addressed—whether it's a book, a TV show, a song, a movie, a video game, a magazine, a radio program, or some other form. What can we observe that is relevant to the question we are asking? For example, if we are looking at violence in a television program, background knowledge about common storytelling techniques and character types in television programming may be useful. We will also want to note the various acts we identify as violent, the characters who commit or suffer from the violence, the context of the violence, and the consequences of the violence within the program.

2. In the *analysis* phase, we start to look for patterns and make connections. Do certain kinds of things seem to repeat or follow a common sequence? If we are comparing more than one media artifact—for example, how different news outlets cover the same topic—we will want to note patterns in each and compare how those patterns are the same or different from source to source.

3. *Interpretation* involves deciding what we think those patterns mean. To do so, we need to ask ourselves why something happens in a certain way. For example, if we notice a pattern in the way a news outlet or outlets cover female athletes, why might that be happening? Does the gender of the reporter or the gender balance of the newsroom make a difference? Could it have something to do with the larger culture of sports and gender? As we move into this stage, it may be necessary to do more reading about existing research on these topics.

4. As we move into *evaluating* what we learned in the first three steps of the critical process, we make a critically informed value judgment. Done correctly, this moves beyond our personal tastes and biases, critiquing the piece of media on the way it interacts with society. For instance, we may like or dislike country, hip-hop, or pop music, but if we want to criticize the messages in one or more of those musical genres intelligently, we need to understand what they have to say and consider why their messages appeal to particular audiences.

5. The last stage of our process is *engagement*. Research and criticism does little good if it is only read in classrooms and by other researchers. By conducting a methodical and informed approach to gathering data,

THE CRITICAL PROCESS BEHIND MEDIA LITERACY

Becoming literate about communication media involves striking a balance between taking a critical stand (developing knowledgeable interpretations and judgments) and being tolerant of diverse forms of expression (appreciating the distinctive variety of cultural products and processes). Developing a media-literate critical perspective involves completing five overlapping stages that build on each other.

Stage One: Description
- Pay close attention, take notes, and research the subject under study.
- Develop descriptive skills associated with breaking down a story into character types and plot structure.
- Master the terms and understand the techniques of telling stories in a particular medium.

Examples
- Describe how the conventions of the documentary are used in sitcoms like *Modern Family* and *Parks and Recreation*.
- Describe the use of gritty or graphic content in a network show like *NCIS* and a cable series like *The Walking Dead*.

Stage Two: Analysis
- Focus on and discuss the significant patterns that emerged during the description stage.
- Make connections. How does this song or story connect with other items of popular culture?
- Decide how you want to focus your critique.

Examples
- How does the satirical approach of *Last Week Tonight* compare to that of *The Daily Show*?
- What are the similarities and differences between *Fox & Friends* and NBC's *Today*?

Stage Three: Interpretation
- Interpret findings; try to determine the meaning of the patterns you have analyzed.
- If there is a distinct pattern, what is the cause or reason? Consider whether comedy, irony, and satire complicate this stage.

Examples
- What does the presence of criminal protagonists mean for shows like *Orange Is the New Black* and *Better Call Saul*?
- What does it mean when Jeff Dunham fashions a comedy act around Achmed, the Dead Terrorist? Why do Dunham's fans find the "I keel you" line so funny?

Stage Four: Evaluation
- Arrive at an informed judgment about whether something is good, bad, or mediocre that goes beyond your personal tastes.
- Does the media product under analysis cause harm? Does it inspire thought? Does it perpetuate a dehumanizing view of a group? Does it promote active citizenship or passive consumerism?

Examples
- The action movies *Wonder Woman* and *Wonder Woman 1984* feature Gal Gadot as the tough Amazonian warrior. Should the movies be celebrated for challenging the normal roles of women in action films?
- *Captain America: Civil War* pits heroes against each other in a clash between the desire for freedom and the need for security. Is this film antigovernment propaganda?

Stage Five: Engagement
- Make your voice heard. Take action that connects your critical perspective to your role as a citizen.
- Become involved in doing your part to challenge media institutions and make them accountable.

Examples
- Write letters, e-mails, or online messages to media editors about blind spots in news coverage.
- Contact companies that perpetuate harmful images of women in their advertising and recommend more socially responsible ways of selling their products.

Media Literacy

CASE STUDY

Masculinity and the Media

There have been at least 110 mass shootings in the United States since 1982 (a number that is still climbing), and more than half of them have occurred since 2006.[1] What are the reasons? Our news media respond with a number of usual suspects: the easy availability of guns in the United States; influential movies, television shows, and video games; mental illness; bad parenting. But educator, author, and filmmaker Jackson Katz sees another major factor. The least talked about commonality in all the shootings is the one so obvious most of us miss it: Nearly all the mass murderers are male (and usually white).

"If a woman were the shooter," Katz says, "you can bet there would be all sorts of commentary about shifting cultural notions of femininity and how they might have contributed to her act."[2] But women were involved in only four of the 107 mass shootings; all the others had a man (or men) behind the trigger. "Because men represent the dominant gender, their gender is rendered invisible in the discourse about violence," Katz says.[3]

In fact, the dominance of masculinity is the norm in our mainstream mass media. Dramatic content is often about the performance of heroic, powerful masculinity (e.g., many action films, digital games, and sports). Similarly, humorous content often derives from calling into question the standards of masculinity (e.g., a man trying to cook, clean, or take care of a child). The same principles apply for the advertising that supports the content. How many automobile, beer, shaving cream, and food commercials peddle products that offer men a chance to maintain or regain their rightful masculinity?

Sociologists Rachel Kalish and Michael Kimmel analyzed the problem of mass shootings that usually end in suicide. In their research, they found that males and females generally have similar rates of suicide attempts. "Feeling aggrieved, wronged by the world—these are typical adolescent feelings, common to many boys and girls," they report. How these feelings play out, though, differs by gender. Female suicide behaviors are more likely to be a cry for help. Male suicide behaviors, informed by social norms of masculinity, often result in "aggrieved

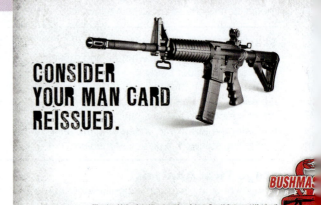

▲ AR-15-style rifles, like this Bushmaster model, were used in some of the biggest and bloodiest mass shootings in the United States, including those in Aurora, Colorado; Newtown, Connecticut; San Bernardino, California; Las Vegas, Nevada; and Pittsburgh, Pennsylvania. According to the *New York Times*, there are several million AR-15s in circulation in the United States.

⊙ **Visit LaunchPad** to watch a clip from a documentary featuring Jackson Katz. According to Katz, what is the relationship between media, masculinity, and violence? Do you agree with his assessment of this relationship?

launchpadworks.com

entitlement." Kalish and Kimmel define this as "a gendered emotion, a fusion of that humiliating loss of manhood and the moral obligation and entitlement to get it back. And its gender is masculine."[4]

There is some evidence that the gun industry understands this sense of masculine entitlement but uses that knowledge to sell guns, not to consider how they might be misused. A marketing campaign begun in 2010 for the Bushmaster .223-caliber semiautomatic rifle showed an image of the rifle with the large tagline "Consider Your Man Card Reissued." The Bushmaster was the same civilian assault rifle used by the shooter who massacred twenty-eight people at the Newtown elementary school in 2012.

How do we find a way out of this cultural cycle? "Make gender a central part of the national conversation about rampage killings," Katz says. "It means looking carefully at how our culture defines manhood, and how pressure to stay in the 'man box' not only constrains boys' and men's emotional and relational development, but also their range of choices when faced with life crises."[5]

APPLYING THE CRITICAL PROCESS

Investigate the way masculinity is portrayed in popular culture by reviewing a list of movies for men compiled by a top-selling men's magazine. For example, *Men's Journal* created a list of what they call the "Best Guy Movies"—a list that includes *Dirty Harry* (1972), *The Godfather* (1972), *Scarface* (1983), *Die Hard* (1988), and *The Terminator* (1984). Watch one of the movies from this or a similar list.

DESCRIPTION   Describe the main hero (or heroes) of the movie, his attributes, and the way he interacts with other characters.

ANALYSIS   What patterns emerge in the way the hero talks and acts throughout the movie? What emotions does the hero show, and how often? Does the hero use a weapon, and if so, under what circumstances? How are women represented in this movie, and how does the hero treat them?

INTERPRETATION   Does your analysis of the hero's behavior support or contradict the idea that masculinity is defined in the ways described in this case study?

EVALUATION   Lists of top "guy movies" tend to reflect the characteristics of what an ideal manly hero should look and act like. What does this suggest about how the lists' creators define what it means to be masculine? Is there much variation in how masculinity is portrayed from movie to movie (to the extent that you are familiar with these movies or can look up plot summaries online)? What might the portrayal of women in "guy movies" tell us about how the ideal manly type is "supposed" to interact with women?

ENGAGEMENT   Write a letter to the editor of a men's magazine (or another magazine that compiles such movie lists) in which you suggest creating an alternative list of movies with more nuanced and three-dimensional portrayals of masculinity.

▲ One way to critique the media is to analyze the highly stylized advertisements and information that appear before us. In the poster for the 2018 film *Black Panther*, what is being sold, and what does it reveal about American audiences? Everett Collection, Inc

recognizing patterns, and evaluating what we find, we should end up with conclusions that could benefit the larger world. So, for example, after conducting research about municipally owned Internet systems and developing a careful critique, we might craft a letter asking a congressperson to support or reject laws that would regulate those systems.

Benefits of a Critical Perspective

Developing an informed critical perspective on the media enables us to participate in a debate about media's impact on our democracy and culture. For instance, on the one hand, the media can be a force for strengthening our democracy and making the world a better place. Consider the role of television in documenting racism and injustice in the 1960s—coverage that encouraged the Civil Rights movement. Or consider how talk-show host Ellen DeGeneres's decision to publicly come out as a lesbian influenced the fight for LGBTQ equality.

On the other hand, media portrayals can have a negative impact. For example, consider how mass media portrayals of people of color might reinforce negative stereotypes and have real-world negative consequences. Or consider how mass media's portrayal of "ideal" male and female behavior might have problematic results for society (see "Media Literacy Case Study: Masculinity and the Media" on pages 24–25). Also consider that the media have helped create a powerful commercial culture in our nation—a culture in which fewer and fewer multinational corporations dominate our economy and generate more and more of the media messages we consume. A society in which only a few voices are telling us stories about what's important, what our values should be, and how we should behave is hardly a healthy democracy.

Because the media constitute forces for both good and ill, it's that much more important for each of us to think carefully about which media we consume; what messages we draw from those media; and how those messages affect our actions, the quality of our lives, and the health of our democracy. We also need to ask questions, such as the following:

- Why might some people continue clinging to either/or thinking about media (such as high-brow versus low-brow books or movies) when so many boundaries in our society have blurred? Does this either/or thinking reflect a desire to keep people in their "proper" socioeconomic class?

- What does it mean that public debate and news about everyday life now seem more likely to come from Facebook, *John Oliver*, or bloggers than from the *New York Times* or the *NBC Nightly News*? Can we no longer distinguish real news from entertainment? If so, does this affect how well informed we are?
- How can we hone our awareness of the economic interests fueling the messages delivered through the media we consume? For example, do you listen to a talk show on a radio station that survives on advertising revenue? If so, ask yourself how the host might distort information (e.g., by deliberately inciting conflict between guests) to attract more listeners and therefore bring in more advertising revenue. (Advertisers only want to spend money on ads that will reach as many people as possible.) If such distortion is taking place, how reliable is the information you're consuming by listening to the show?

▲ Powerful celebrities like Oprah Winfrey have a profound influence on popular opinion and people's beliefs. Developing an informed critical perspective on the media allows individuals to engage in discussions about their impact on the world. Don Arnold/WireImage/Getty Images

Unfortunately, we can't rely on professional media critics or watchdog organizations to do all the work of critiquing the media for us and analyzing their effects on our lives. Each of us is responsible for doing some of that work ourselves. As you read through the chapters in this book, you'll learn more about each type of media—and you'll hone your ability to examine each with a critical eye.

CHAPTER ESSENTIALS

Review

- **Media literacy** is an understanding of how the media work and what impact they have on our lives. It is important to acquire media literacy so that we have a say in the roles that media play around us.

- The mass media have their roots in mass communication. **Mass media** are the industries that create and distribute songs, novels, newspapers, movies, Internet services, TV shows, magazines, and other products to large numbers of people. **Mass communication** is the creation and use of symbols (such as languages, motion pictures, and binary computer codes) that convey information and meaning to large and diverse audiences through all manner of channels.

- We can trace the historical development of media through several eras: the oral and written eras (1000 BCE to the mid-fifteenth century), the print era (beginning in the mid-fifteenth century), and the electronic and digital eras (from the late nineteenth century to today).

- **Media convergence** can refer to the technological merging of media content across different media channels (such as the availability of a magazine article in print and online form) or to a business model in which media companies consolidate media holdings to reduce costs and maximize profits. This convergence, as well as the speed of communication made possible by an ever-faster Internet and more powerful personal devices, is an important characteristic of the **digital turn**.

- A new medium typically evolves through four stages: the development—or emergence or novelty—stage (inventors and technicians try to solve a particular problem), the entrepreneurial stage (inventors and investors determine a practical and marketable use for the new device), the mass medium stage (businesses figure out how to market the new device as a consumer product), and finally the convergence stage (older media are reconfigured in various forms into newer digital media).

- The cultural model is a way of studying the media that looks at how the media influence and shape **culture**, and how culture influences and shapes the media. This model also addresses the diverse ways in which an audience attaches meanings to a media message, actively affirming, interpreting, refashioning, or rejecting those messages.

LaunchPad

Visit LaunchPad for *Media Essentials* at **launchpadworks.com** for additional learning tools:

- **REVIEW WITH LEARNINGCURVE**
  LearningCurve adaptive quizzing helps you master the concepts you need to learn from this chapter.

- **VIDEO: THE MEDIA AND DEMOCRACY**
  This video traces the history of media's role in democracy, from newspapers and television to the Internet.

- **MEDIA LITERACY PRACTICE**
  This activity challenges you to develop a critical perspective and apply it to everyday encounters with communication media.

- Two metaphors offer contrasting views about the way culture operates in our daily lives: culture as a hierarchy, represented by a *skyscraper* model, and culture as a process, represented by a *map* model.

- Cultural researchers trace changes in values that accompany changes in mass media. The **modern era** saw the rise of four values: efficient work, celebration of the individual, belief in a rational order, and rejection of tradition and an embracing of progress. The **postmodern period** witnessed the emergence of its own values: celebration of **populism**, a questioning of authority, and an embracing of technology.

- Citizens can become media literate by following a **critical process** and applying it to everyday encounters with the media. This process consists of describing, analyzing, interpreting, evaluating, and engaging with mass media.

Study Questions

1. Explain the interrelationship between *mass communication* and *mass media*.

2. What are the stages a medium goes through before becoming a mass medium?

3. What are the hallmarks of the digital turn, and what makes it different from earlier stages of mass media development?

4. What are the strengths and weaknesses of the skyscraper and map models of culture?

5. What are the steps of the critical process behind media literacy, and why are they important?

Key Terms

media literacy, p. 5
mass media, p. 6
mass communication, p. 6
digital communication, p. 10
digital turn, p. 10
media convergence, p. 11
culture, p. 16
high culture, p. 18
low (popular) culture, p. 19
modern era, p. 20
Progressive Era, p. 20
postmodern period, p. 20
populism, p. 20
critical process, p. 22

Mass Media Industries

2

Books and the Power of Print

34
The Early History of Books: From Papyrus to Paperbacks

38
The Evolution of Modern Publishing

41
Trends in Contemporary Book Publishing

44
The Organization and Economics of the Book Industry

50
Books in a Democratic Society

Trade books are the largest segment of the book industry, and one of the fastest-growing segments within trade books are graphic novels and comics. According to global information provider the NPD Group, comics and graphic novels have had generally "robust" growth for more than five years.[1] Graphic novels now comprise 6 percent of the U.S. book market.[2]

Although adults sometimes lament that younger people don't read books, "buyers in the 13–29 age group account for 57 percent of purchasing of comics and graphic novels overall," NPD Group reports.[3] Manga, a graphic style originating in Japan, has the youngest and most racially diverse audience of the graphic novels and comics category, "with 76 percent of the purchasing being done by those ages 13–29."[4]

Overall, comics and graphic novels have made a big impact in the book industry and popular culture, especially as the stories have been transformed into television and movie narratives. Moreover, graphic novelists have received some of the highest honors and cultural acclaim. Graphic novelists Alison Bechdel and Gene Luen Yang have won MacArthur Fellowships, and for the first time a graphic novel won a National Book Award (*March: Book 3*, the third part of the memoir by Civil Rights leader Rep. John Lewis, awarded in 2016).[5]

◀ Despite their popularity, graphic novels got snubbed by the *New York Times*, which dropped its graphic novel best-seller lists in 2017. Mandel Ngan/AFP/Getty Images

Yet people in the graphic novel business have felt dismayed by the *New York Times*' decision in 2017 to drop its graphic novel best-seller lists, which had been in existence for eight years. The *Times*' lists of best sellers are the most influential in the industry and can increase sales by communicating what are the most important books of the week.

In the wake of the *Times* dropping its Hardcover Graphic Novel, Paperback Graphic Novel, and Manga best-seller charts in 2017, more than nine hundred people signed a letter in February 2018 asking the *Times*' publisher to "increase coverage of the comics medium and bring back the graphic novel bestseller list."[6]

The *New York Times* best-seller list is important to the graphic novel industry, argued Susana Polo at *Polygon*. "Historically, comics in newspapers belonged to the gutter of journalistic practices," she explained. The *New York Times* shunned comic strips, treating them as the stuff of sensationalistic newspapers. "The mere existence of *The New York Times* Graphic Novel bestseller lists was evidence of a sea change in the way its audience and its editors viewed sequential art (a fancy umbrella term for comics, comic strips, cartoons and the like)."[7] Yet graphic novels and comics, one of the brightest segments of the book industry, are again getting second-rate treatment from the *Times*.

According to Charlie Olsen, a literary agent for graphic novelists and the organizer of the letter to the *New York Times*, "Comics are a vibrant medium and shouldn't be on the sidelines of the book world."[8]

FOR HUNDREDS OF YEARS—before newspapers, radio, and film, let alone television and the Internet—books were the only mass medium. Books have fueled major developments throughout human history, from revolutions and the rise of democracies to new forms of art (including poetry and fiction) and the spread of various religions. When cheaper printing technologies laid the groundwork for books to become more widely available and more quickly disseminated, people gained access to knowledge and ideas that were previously reserved for the privileged few.

With the emergence of new types of mass media, some critics claimed that books would cease to exist. So far, however, that's not happening. In 1950, U.S. publishers introduced more than 11,000 new book titles; by 2014, that number had reached more than 200,000 (see Figure 2.1). Though books have adapted to technology and cultural change (witness the advent of e-books), our oldest mass medium still plays a large role in our lives. Books remain the primary repository of history and everyday experience, passing along stories, knowledge, and wisdom from generation to generation.

FIGURE 2.1 // ANNUAL NUMBERS OF NEW BOOK TITLES PUBLISHED, SELECTED YEARS

As each new mass medium was introduced, from film to the Internet, there were fears that it would result in the death of book publishing. As this graph shows, not only did book publishing survive each new major technological advance, but the number of books published has risen over time, most steeply in the last twenty-five years.

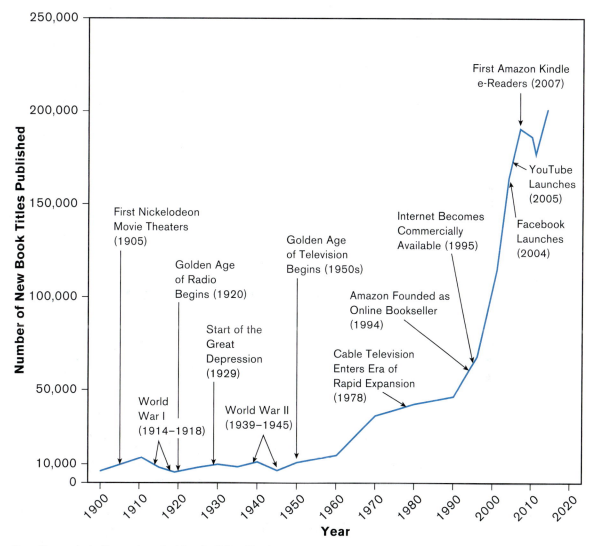

Note: Changes in the Almanac's *methodology in 1997 and for the years 2004–07 resulted in additional publications being assigned ISBNs and included in the count.

Data through 1945 from John Tebbel, A History of Book Publishing in the United States, 4 vols. (New York: R. R. Bowker, 1972–81); data after 1945 from various editions of the Library and Book Trade Almanac (formerly The Bowker Annual [Information Today, Inc.]) and Bowker press releases.

In this chapter, we will trace the history of this enduring medium and examine its impact on our lives today by:

- assessing books' early roots, including the inventions of papyrus (the first writing surface) and the printing press, as well as the birth of the publishing industry in colonial America

- exploring the unique characteristics of modern publishing, such as the formation of publishing houses and the many types of books that are available today

- discussing the major trends in book publishing and consumption in the digital age, including the impact of convergence and the influences of television and film

- examining the organization and economics of the book industry, including how players in the industry make money

- considering the role of books in our democracy today, as this mass medium confronts several challenges

launchpadworks.com

Use **LearningCurve** to review concepts from this chapter.

The Early History of Books: From Papyrus to Paperbacks

Books have traveled a unique path in their journey to mass medium status. They developed out of early innovations, including papyrus (scrolls made from plant reeds), parchment (treated animal skin), and codex (sheets of parchment sewn together along the edge and then bound and covered). They then entered an entrepreneurial stage, during which people explored new ways of clarifying or illustrating text and experimented with printing techniques, such as block printing and movable type. The invention of the printing press set the stage for books to become a mass medium, complete with the rise of a new industry: publishing.

Papyrus, Parchment, and Codex: The Development Stage of Books

The ancient Egyptians, Greeks, Chinese, and Romans all produced innovations that led up to what we think of today as a book. It all began some five thousand years ago, in ancient Sumer (Mesopotamia) and Egypt, where people first experimented with pictorial symbols called *hieroglyphics* or early alphabets. This writing was placed on wood strips or stones, or pressed into clay tablets. Eventually, these objects were tied or stacked together to form the first "books." Around 1000 BCE, the Chinese were using strips of wood and bamboo, tied together to make a booklike object.

In 2400 BCE, the Egyptians began turning plants found along the Nile River into a material they could write on, called **papyrus** (from which the word *paper* is derived). Between 650 and 300 BCE, the Greeks and Romans adopted the use of papyrus scrolls. Gradually, **parchment**—treated animal skin—replaced papyrus in Europe. Parchment was stronger, smoother, more durable, and less expensive than papyrus. Around 105 CE, the Chinese began making paper from cotton and linen, though paper did not replace parchment in Europe until the thirteenth century.

The first protomodern book was most likely produced in the fourth century by the Romans, who created the **codex**—sheets of parchment sewn together along one edge, then bound with thin pieces of wood and covered with leather. Whereas scrolls had to be rolled and unrolled for use, a codex could be opened to any page, and people could write on both sides of a page.

Writing and Printing Innovations: Books Enter the Entrepreneurial Stage

Books entered the entrepreneurial stage with the emergence of **manuscript culture**. In this stage, new rules about written language and book design were codified—books were elaborately lettered, decorated, and bound by hand. Inventors also began experimenting with printing as an alternative to hand lettering and a way to speed up the production and binding of manuscript copies.

Manuscript Culture

During Europe's Middle Ages (400 to 1500 CE), Christian priests and monks transcribed the philosophical tracts and religious texts of the period, especially versions of the Bible. These **illuminated manuscripts** featured decorative, colorful illustrations on each page and were often made for churches or wealthy clients. These early publishers developed certain standards for their works, creating rules of punctuation, making distinctions between small and capital letters, and leaving space between words to make reading easier. Some elements of this manuscript culture remain alive today in the form of design flourishes, such as the drop capitals occasionally used for the first letter in each chapter of a book.

▼Illuminated manuscripts were handwritten by scribes and illustrated with colorful and decorative images and designs. Fine Art Images/Heritage/The Image Works

Block Printing

If manuscript culture involved advances in written language and book design, it also involved hard work: Every manuscript was painstakingly copied one book at a time.

As early as the third century, Chinese printers developed **block printing**, an innovation that made mass production possible. Using this technique, printers applied sheets of paper to large blocks of inked wood, into which they had hand-carved a page's worth of characters and illustrations. The oldest dated block-printed book still in existence is China's *Diamond Sutra*, a collection of Buddhist scriptures printed by Wang Chieh in 868 CE.

Movable Type

The next significant step in printing came with the invention of movable type in China around the year 1000. This was a major improvement (in terms of speed) over block printing, because rather than carving each new page on a block, printers carved commonly used combinations of characters from the Chinese language into smaller, reusable wood (and later ceramic) blocks. They then arranged the pieces needed to represent a desired page of text, inked the small blocks, and applied the sheets of paper. This method enabled them to create pages of text much more quickly than before.

The Printing Press and the Publishing Industry: Books Become a Mass Medium

Books moved from the entrepreneurial stage to mass medium status with the invention of the printing press (which made books widely available for the first time) and the rise of the publishing industry (which arose to satisfy people's growing hunger for books).

The Printing Press

The **printing press** was invented by Johannes Gutenberg in Germany between 1453 and 1456. Drawing on the principles of movable type and adding a device adapted from the design of a wine press, Gutenberg's staff of printers produced the first so-called modern books, including two hundred copies of a Latin Bible—twenty-one of which still exist. The Gutenberg Bible (as it's now known) was printed on a fine calfskin-based parchment called **vellum**.

Printing presses spread rapidly across Europe in the late 1400s and early 1500s. Many of the early books being printed were large, elaborate, and expensive, but printers gradually reduced the size of books and developed less-expensive grades of paper. These changes made books cheaper to produce, so printers could sell them for less, making the books affordable to many more people.

The spread of printing presses and books sparked a major change in the way people learned. Previously, people followed the traditions and ideas framed by local authorities—the ruling class, clergy, and community leaders. But as books became more broadly available, people gained access to knowledge and viewpoints far beyond those of their immediate surroundings and familiar authorities, leading some to begin challenging the traditional wisdom and customs of their tribes and leaders.[9] This interest in debating ideas would ultimately encourage the rise of democratic societies in which all citizens had a voice.

The Publishing Industry

In the two centuries following the invention of the printing press, publishing—the establishment of printing shops to serve the public's growing demand for books—took off in Europe, eventually spreading to England and finally to the American colonies. In the late 1630s, English locksmith Stephen Daye set up the first colonial print shop in Cambridge, Massachusetts. By the mid-1760s, all thirteen colonies had print shops. Some publishers, such as Benjamin Franklin, grew quite wealthy in this profession.

However, in the early 1800s, U.S. publishers had to find ways to further lower the cost of producing books to meet the exploding demand. By the 1830s, machine-made paper replaced the more expensive handmade varieties, cloth covers supplanted costlier leather ones, and **paperback books** were made with cheaper paper covers (introduced in Europe), all of which helped to make books even more accessible to the masses. Further reducing the cost of books, publishers introduced paperback **dime novels** (so called because they sold for five or ten cents) in 1860. By 1885, one-third of all books published in the United States consisted of popular paperbacks and **pulp fiction** (a reference to the cheap, machine-made pulp paper that dime novels were printed on).

Meanwhile, the printing process itself also advanced. In the 1880s, the introduction of **linotype** machines enabled printers to save time by setting type mechanically using a typewriter-style keyboard. In addition, the introduction of steam-powered and high-speed rotary presses permitted the production of even more books at lower costs. With the development of **offset lithography** in the early 1900s, publishers could print books from photographic plates rather than from metal casts. This greatly reduced the cost of color illustrations and accelerated the production process, allowing publishers to satisfy Americans' steadily increasing demand for books.

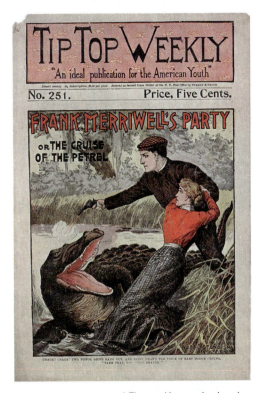

▲ The weekly paperback series *Tip Top Weekly*, which was published between 1896 and 1912, featured the most popular dime novel hero of the day, Yale football star and heroic adventurer Frank Merriwell.
The New York Public Library/Art Resource, NY

The Evolution of Modern Publishing

From the end of the Revolutionary War through the following century, the demand for books increased as literacy rates increased. This provided fertile soil for the early publishing houses, which were small and focused on offering the works of quality authors, as well as for the major publishing corporations that snapped up the houses over time. Today the publishing industry categorizes books into types, which include trade books, textbooks, reference books, and books targeting specific professions, such as law or medicine.

The Formation of Publishing Houses

The modern book industry in the United States developed gradually in the 1800s with the formation of "prestigious" publishing houses: companies that identified and produced the works of respected writers.[10] The oldest American houses include J. B. Lippincott (1792); Harper & Bros. (1817), which became Harper & Row in 1962 and HarperCollins in 1990; Houghton Mifflin (1832); Little, Brown (1837); G. P. Putnam (1838); Scribner's (1842); E. P. Dutton (1852); Rand McNally (1856); and Macmillan (1869).

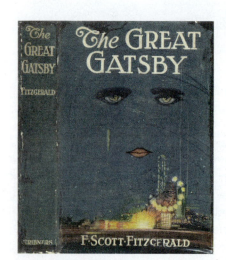

▲ Scribner's—known more for its magazine in the late 1800s than for its books—became the most prestigious literary house of the 1920s and 1930s, publishing F. Scott Fitzgerald (*The Great Gatsby*, 1925) and Ernest Hemingway (*The Sun Also Rises*, 1926). Photo by Princeton University Library. Rare Books Division. Department of Rare Books and Special Collections. Princeton University Library.

Between 1880 and 1920, as more people moved from rural areas to cities and learned to read, Americans became interested in reading all kinds of books: novels, historical accounts, reference materials, instructional resources. This caught the attention of entrepreneurs eager to profit by satisfying this demand. Thus, a savvy breed of publishing house, focused on marketing, was born. These firms included Doubleday & McClure Company (1897), McGraw-Hill Book Company (1909), Prentice Hall (1913), Alfred A. Knopf (1915), Simon & Schuster (1924), and Random House (1925).

Book publishing sputtered from the 1910s into the 1940s, as the two world wars and the Great Depression turned Americans' attention away from books. But as the U.S. economy recovered during the 1950s and 1960s, the industry bounced back. Major corporations and international media conglomerates began acquiring the smaller houses to expand their markets and take advantage of the **synergy** (the promotion and sale of different versions of a media product across the various subsidiaries of a conglomerate) between books and other media types.

Types of Books

Today, the publishing industry produces titles that fall into a wide variety of categories, including trade books, textbooks, professional books, mass market paperbacks, reference books, religious books, and university press books. These categories have been formally defined by various trade organizations, such as the Association of American Publishers (AAP), the Book Industry Study Group (BISG), and the American Booksellers Association (ABA).

Trade Books

One of the most lucrative markets in the industry, **trade books** include hardbound and quality paperback books aimed at general readers and sold at commercial retail outlets. The industry distinguishes among adult trade, juvenile trade, and comics and graphic novels. Adult trade books include hardbound and paperback fiction; current nonfiction and biographies; literary classics; books on hobbies, art, and travel; popular science, technology, and computer publications; self-help books; and cookbooks. Juvenile trade categories range from preschool picture books to young-adult or young-reader books, such as the Dr. Seuss books, the *Junie B. Jones* series, and the *Harry Potter* series.

Textbooks

Textbooks are divided into elementary through high school (el-hi) texts, college texts, and vocational texts. In about half the states in the country, local school districts determine which el-hi textbooks are appropriate for their students. The remaining states, including Texas and California, have statewide adoption policies governing which texts can be used.

Unlike el-hi texts, which are subsidized by various states and school districts, college texts are paid for by students (or their parents) and are sold primarily through college bookstores. The cost of textbooks has led some students to trade, resell, or rent textbooks, or to download less expensive e-book versions. Surveys indicate that college students spent an average of $484 during the 2017–18 academic year on required course material, which was down from $701 during the 2007–08 academic year.[11]

▼Even though they may not be as much fun to read for some students as, say, graphic novels, textbooks and learning materials are an important part of education today. Ariel Skelley/DigitalVision/Getty Images

Professional Books

Professional books target various occupational groups, not the general consumer market. This area of publishing capitalizes on the growth of professional specialization that has characterized the U.S. job market. Traditionally, the industry has subdivided professional books into the areas of law, business, medicine, and technology-science. These books are often bought by professional schools and university libraries; however, both stagnating and dwindling library budgets have led to a decline in professional book sales in recent years.

Mass Market Paperbacks

Unlike the larger-size trade paperbacks, which are sold mostly in bookstores, **mass market paperbacks** are sold on racks in drugstores, supermarkets, and airports, as well as in bookstores. Contemporary mass market paperbacks are paperback versions of hardcover trade books by such blockbuster authors as Stephen King and Veronica Roth. They are generally priced low (under $10) and printed on low-quality paper stock. Paperbacks first became popular back in the 1870s, when middle- and working-class readers popularized dime novels. All categories of paperbacks remain strong sellers for book publishers, with over a billion paperbacks sold in 2017.[12]

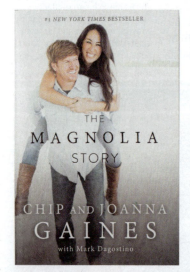

▲ Inspirational titles in the religious-book segment of the market—including *The Magnolia Story* (2016) from home designers and reality stars Chip and Joanna Gaines—have been top sellers in recent years.

Reference Books

Reference books include dictionaries, encyclopedias, atlases, almanacs, and volumes related to particular professions or trades, such as legal casebooks and medical manuals. Encyclopedias and dictionaries have traditionally accounted for the largest portion of reference book sales, but most of these reference works have moved to online formats since the 1990s, in response to competition from companies offering different formats. These rival formats include free online or built-in word-processing software dictionaries, search engines such as Google, and online resources like Wikipedia.

Religious Books

The best-selling book of all time is the Bible, in all its diverse versions. Over the years, the success of Bible sales has created a large industry for religious books, and many religious-book publishers have extended their offerings to include secular titles on such topics as war and peace, race, poverty, gender, and civic responsibility. Although revenue from religious books has been on a slow decline, these books still accounted for more than $416 million in U.S. sales in 2017.[13]

University Press Books

The smallest market in the printed-book industry is the nonprofit **university press**, which publishes scholarly works for small groups of readers interested in specialized areas, such as literary theory and criticism, art movements, and contemporary philosophy. Some of these presses are small, publishing only a few books a year, but the largest, Oxford University Press, publishes over six thousand titles annually. Whereas large commercial trade houses are often criticized for publishing only high-selling, mainstream books, university presses often suffer the opposite criticism: that they produce mostly obscure books that only a handful of scholars read.

Trends in Contemporary Book Publishing

Publishers are continually experimenting with alternatives to the printed-book format in order to remain competitive and to leverage the advantages of new technologies. The rise of the digital age saw a big increase in the sale of traditional print books online, as well as the development of the *e-book*, which became popular when retailers like Amazon and Barnes & Noble introduced electronic devices for reading (e-readers) and reading apps for smartphones, tablets, and laptops.

In addition to the e-book, trends in contemporary publishing include the rise of self-publishing, a focus on audio books, and the licensing of popular film and television programs based on books.

Convergence: Books in the Digital Age

The development of the **e-book**—a digital book read on a computer or a digital reading device—has been greatly affected by two defining elements of the digital turn: convergence and speed, made possible by advances in technology.

While efforts to digitize and share books via computer can be traced to the 1970s, the first attempts to market something recognizable as a forerunner of today's e-readers came from RCA and Sony in the early 1990s. Those early e-readers were heavy, offered few choices, had difficult-to-read screens, and were expensive. But when Amazon, already the largest online bookseller, introduced its Kindle e-reader in 2007, the long-predicted digital book market started to gain traction. Bookselling giant Barnes & Noble soon followed with a competing product called the Nook. Apple, already experiencing success with its iTunes online store, opened the iBookstore.

Since the first Kindle and Nook models were introduced, companies have delivered a steady stream of increasingly more

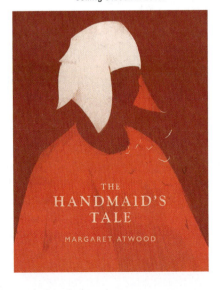

▼ *The Handmaid's Tale*, Margaret Atwood's classic from 1985, became an award-winning Hulu TV series in 2017. Atwood's dystopian novel tells the story of an authoritarian regime—one in which women have no rights—that has taken over the United States. Because of the show's popularity and the political climate following the 2016 election, it became the top-selling e-book in 2017.

versatile, powerful, and portable electronic devices that allow users to access the web and run a variety of reading and book-purchasing apps. Apple launched the first of several iPad tablet versions in 2010. Amazon responded by morphing its e-reader into a tablet, releasing the Kindle Fire in 2011. In addition, e-books have been fully adapted to smartphones. With the ability to connect multiple devices to a single account and to buy reading material with nothing more than an Internet connection, an avid reader is only mere moments away from a new book at any given time. This convergence of technology led to the rapid growth of e-books, with sales rising to a peak of more than $3 billion in 2013.[14]

E-book growth has slowed somewhat in recent years—sales fell over 35 percent from 2013 to 2017, and e-books account for just over $2 billion in sales.[15] Experts offer several ideas about why this decline may be happening. First, e-book prices went from an average of $5 a title to an average of $8 a title in 2015. Second, fewer people are buying dedicated e-readers, and people tend to purchase more e-books if they own these devices. Finally, some customers may be suffering from digital fatigue, seeking out print copies rather than electronic versions.[16]

Despite the slowdown of e-book sales, however, it's hard to imagine traditional publishers turning their backs on digital publishing. In the trade book market, e-books still account for 15 percent of sales; in addition, it's relatively inexpensive to produce an electronic version of a title. Paper books must be printed and distributed to commercial outlets or college bookstores. This means that publishers must monitor their warehouse inventories to ensure that enough copies of a book will be available to meet demand, while making sure they don't get stuck with copies of a book that doesn't sell. E-publishing, on the other hand, reduces much of this production and distribution overhead because there is no printing, storage, or shipping involved.

Self-Publishing

Another part of the book business that digital publishing has changed significantly is the practice of self-publishing. Once considered a vain enterprise, self-publishing has been equated with amateurism and work that is not worthy of the considerable expenses and promotional resources associated with the big publishing houses. But the commercial success of some authors who have self-published their own e-books—an undertaking that is easier and cheaper since the digital turn—is something big publishers can't ignore.

Self-published authors are upsetting the established business model because they need not pay 10 percent to a literary agency. In addition, self-publishing affects how much authors make on each copy of a book. If writers self-publish through Amazon, they receive between 35 and 70 percent of the e-book purchase price rather than the typical 5–15 percent royalty of paper-based book authors (though the purchase price of a self-published e-book is typically lower than the purchase price of a print book).[17] For this and other reasons, Amazon's business model has encouraged the growth of self-publishing.

Audio Books

Audio books are voice recordings of popular fiction and nonfiction trade books, generally read by actors or authors. Indispensable to sightless readers and older readers with diminishing vision, audio books are also popular among readers who have long commutes by car or train, or who want to listen to a book while doing something else, like exercising. Audio books became popular in the 1990s and early 2000s, by which time they were readily available on the Internet for downloading to iPods and other portable devices. More recently, audio-book sales have been the fastest growing part of the publishing industry, more than doubling from 2013 to 2017.[18]

▲ The audio version of *Born a Crime* (2016), comedian Trevor Noah's book about growing up in South Africa, won Audible's Best of 2016 award for celebrity memoirs and received the highest rating of new books that year by customers on the site. Noah narrated the audio book himself.

Influences of Television and Film in the Digital Age

Regardless of what channel a publisher sells its books through, trade publishers are constantly on the hunt for the next *best-seller*—a tradition dating back to the huge success of Harriet Beecher Stowe's abolitionist novel *Uncle Tom's Cabin*, which sold fifteen thousand copies in just fifteen days in 1852. Today that hunt is often closely tied to—or even relies on—convergence with both small and large screens.

There are two major facets in the relationship among books, television, and film: how TV and film can help sell books, and how books serve as ideas for TV shows and movies. TV exposure for books and authors on talk shows can boost sales, sometimes considerably. One of the most influential forces for promoting books on television was Oprah Winfrey. Beginning in 1996, each selection for Oprah's Book Club became an immediate best-seller, generating tremendous excitement within the book industry. *The Oprah Winfrey Show* ended in 2011, but the book club was revived online in 2012.

When a book becomes a movie or a television program, book sales soar. Publishers and authors also benefit by selling the rights to adapt a story from page to screen. But the real synergy happens when television and film adaptations spur interest in books and authors, which in turn can generate more interest in movies. This has proven exceptionally true—and exceptionally profitable—in the case of blockbuster book-film crossovers, like the *Harry Potter* series of films. The subgenre of comic books and graphic novels has also led to countless films, including several top box-office hits, like the *Wonder Woman* films and Marvel's interconnected Avengers series.

LaunchPad
launchpadworks.com

Based On: Making Books into Movies
Writers and producers discuss the process that brings a book to the big screen.

Discussion: How is the creative process of writing a novel different from that of making a movie? Which would you rather do, and why?

▲ Based on a 2013 novel by Kevin Kwan, *Crazy Rich Asians* was released as a film in 2018. Starring Constance Wu and Henry Golding, the film is about an American professor who goes to Singapore to meet her boyfriend's very rich family. Warner Bros. Pictures/Everett Collection, Inc

Other examples of classic and recent books that have been adapted into movies include Madeleine L'Engle's *A Wrinkle in Time* (1962), R. J. Palacio's *Wonder* (2012), Kevin Kwan's *Crazy Rich Asians* (2013), and Angie Thomas's *The Hate U Give* (2017).

One of the biggest book-to-TV success stories in recent years has been HBO's *Game of Thrones*, based on the Song of Ice and Fire series by George R. R. Martin. Other television programs adapted from books include *The Handmaid's Tale* on Hulu, based on the dystopian novel by Margaret Atwood; and *11.22.63* on Hulu, based on the novel by Stephen King. Comic books are also enjoying recent popular and even critical success on the small screen. *Arrow*, *Supergirl*, and *The Flash* are top performers for the CW, while Netflix original series like *Daredevil* and *Jessica Jones* have had success in this subgenre.

The Organization and Economics of the Book Industry

From an organizational and economic standpoint, book publishing looks a lot like other mass media industries: publishers are often global corporations, and ownership is concentrated in a small number of major players. But regardless of the size of the company or who owns them, publishing houses are structured similarly to carry out the processes involved in book publishing—attracting authors and acquiring new books; editing those books; and producing, distributing, and selling the books in either print or electronic form.

The Conglomerates

Today, book publishing is dominated by a handful of giant corporations. Looking globally and at all kinds of publishing (see Table 2.1), the top five book publishers in terms of revenue are Pearson (textbooks, educational materials), RELX Group (professional books), Thomson Reuters (professional books), Bertelsmann (trade books), and Wolters Kluwer (professional books).

Mergers and consolidations have driven the book industry. For example, the world's largest publisher is Pearson, based in the U.K. Pearson established

TABLE 2.1 // WORLD'S LARGEST BOOK PUBLISHERS (REVENUE IN BILLIONS OF DOLLARS), 2018

Rank/Publishing Company (Group or Division)	Home Country	Revenue in $Billions
1 Pearson	U.K.	$6.070
2 RELX Group	U.K./NL/U.S.	$5.609
3 Thomson Reuters	Canada	$4.941
4 Bertelsmann	Germany	$4.240
5 Wolters Kluwer	NL	$3.994
6 Hachette Livre (Lagardère)	France	$2.735
7 Grupo Planeta	Spain	$1.974
8 Springer Nature	Germany	$1.956
9 Scholastic	U.S.	$1.742
10 McGraw-Hill Education (tied)	U.S.	$1.719
Wiley (tied)	U.S.	$1.719

Data from: "The World's 54 Largest Publishers, 2018," Publishers Weekly, September 14, 2018, www.publishersweekly.com/pw/by-topic/industry-news/publisher-news/article/78036-pearson-is-still-the-world-s-largest-publisher.html.

its book business in the 1920s and at one point owned the *Financial Times*, a 50 percent share in the *Economist* magazine, and nearly half of Penguin Random House (PRH). But in 2015, Pearson committed its focus to the el-hi, college, and professional publishing business, and is deeply involved with publishing textbooks, digital materials, and assessment exams for the education market.

Germany's Bertelsmann shook up the book industry by adding Random House, the largest U.S. book publisher, to its fold for $1.4 billion. Bertelsmann's book-related subsidiaries include Ballantine Bantam Dell, Doubleday Broadway, Alfred A. Knopf, and the Random House Publishing Group. In 2013, Random House merged with Penguin Books (then owned by Pearson), creating Penguin Random House—the largest trade book publisher in the world—under the Bertelsmann umbrella. Bertelsmann also owns large European magazine and television divisions.

The consolidation of the book industry has raised concerns among observers who mourn the loss of the older houses' distinctive styles and their associations with renowned literary figures, like Mark Twain and Nathaniel Hawthorne. Moreover, the large corporations that now define the industry's direction have huge marketing budgets and can buy needed resources (such as paper, printing, and binding services) at a discount and thus charge less for their product. Few independent publishers have been able to compete against them.

The Structure of Book Publishing

Regardless of their size or the types of books they publish, publishing houses are structured similarly. For example, they have teams or divisions responsible for acquisitions and manuscript development; copyediting, design, and production; marketing and sales; and administration. Most publishing houses pay independent printers to produce their books.

The majority of publishers employ **acquisitions editors** to seek out authors and offer them contracts to publish specific titles. For fiction, this might mean discovering talented writers through book agents or reading unsolicited manuscripts. For nonfiction, editors might examine proposals and letters of inquiry or match a known writer to a project (such as a celebrity biography). Acquisitions editors work with authors to negotiate the royalty that they will be paid for each book, and sometimes they negotiate *advance money*, an up-front payment that will be subtracted from royalties later earned from book sales. Acquisitions editors also handle **subsidiary rights** for an author—that is, selling the rights to a book for use in other media, such as a mass market paperback, or as the basis for a screenplay.

After a contract is signed, the acquisitions editor may turn the book over to a **developmental editor**, who helps the author draft and revise the manuscript by providing feedback and soliciting advice from reviewers. If a book is to contain illustrations, the editor works with photo researchers to select photographs or find artists to produce the needed drawings or other graphics. At this point, the production staff enters the picture. While the **copy editor** fixes any spelling, punctuation, grammar, or style problems in the manuscript, the **design manager** determines the look and feel of the book, making decisions about type styles, paper, cover design, and layout of page spreads.

Simultaneously, the publishing house determines a marketing strategy for the book, including identifying which readers will be most interested in the title, deciding how many copies to print and what price to charge, and selecting advertising channels for reaching the target customers. Marketing budgets usually make up a large part of a publishing company's expenses, and marketing managers are often fairly high up in the organization. One advantage of traditional publishing houses over self-publishers is that they have the money and expertise to market books. For trade books and some scholarly books, publishing houses may send advance copies of a book to appropriate magazines and newspapers with the hope of receiving positive reviews. A house may also send well-known authors on book-signing tours and arrange radio and TV talk-show interviews, buy shelf space from major chains to assure prominent locations, and buy advertising across the spectrum of traditional and online media. (For a look at how popularity on social media can translate to book sales, see "The Digital Turn Case Study: The Epic Rise of Instapoets" on page 47.)

The Digital Turn

CASE STUDY

The Epic Rise of Instapoets

Poetry has been around for a very long time: *The Epic of Gilgamesh*, which dates back to around 2500 BCE, was written in cuneiform on clay tablets. While poetry has always been a popular literary form, poets typically enjoy more critical appreciation than they do commercial success. But that might be changing thanks to a new generation of young poets—and the popularity of Instagram.

When most people think of Instagram, they envision an online repository of countless selfies and images of beautiful sunsets. But for Canadian poet Rupi Kaur, the social media platform is much more: It's a carefully curated gallery of her poetry, gorgeously shot photographs, and videos starring celebrities such as Emma Watson. Kaur is one of a new group of "Instapoets"—poets who use platforms like Instagram to create shareable versions of their poetry, which are often paired with visual or video elements. These Instapoets have seen their efforts translate into millions of online followers, but that's not all: They've also helped make poetry collections one of the fastest growing categories in book sales.

Consider these numbers: From 2013 to 2017, print poetry sales in the United States more than doubled, and roughly 80 percent of that growth came from the work of Instapoets.[1] In addition, more than half of the twenty top-selling poets of 2017 were Instapoets.[2] Kaur herself sold more than two and a half million copies of her first poetry collection, *Milk and Honey*, which was released in 2014. Her follow-up book, *The Sun and Her Flowers*, debuted at number one on the *New York Times* paperback fiction best-seller list in October 2017.[3]

This new trend in poetry isn't making everyone happy. Some critics consider poets like Kaur to be too sentimental, accuse the work of being similar to that of a greeting card, and question how much depth can be included in poetry that is short enough to fit into an Instagram post. At the same time, however, some longtime poets and poetry critics consider Instapoets to be both a breath of fresh air and a way to make poetry relevant and interesting for a new generation.[4] And survey data shows that many readers are receptive: According to a 2018 National Endowment for the Arts study, the number of adults who reported reading poetry shot up from 6.7 percent in 2012 to 11.7 percent in 2017, while the comparable number for those between the ages of eighteen and twenty-four years old "more than doubled."[5]

Although debates about this work's value as a literary form may continue, then, one thing is clear: Instapoets are having an undeniable impact on the popularity of the medium—and on the economics of the book industry as a result.

> **▶ Web Clip**
>
> **YouTube.com** has many video interviews with Instapoets like Rupi Kaur. For example, do a search for "Poet Rupi Kaur reaches new audiences in a new way" posted by *PBS NewsHour*. How has making her work available on Instagram influenced this poet's career? How has it influenced how her readers experience this work?
>
>

Selling Books

Compared with other mass media industries, book publishing has adapted to the digital turn and has been able to avoid huge declines in revenue. From the mid-1980s to 2017, total revenues for U.S. book publishing went from $9 billion to over $26 billion (see Figure 2.2).[19] Worldwide, the book publishing industry accounted for well over $100 billion in sales and revenue as of 2017.[20] The most obvious source of revenue for publishers is sales of the books themselves, whether they're in print, audio, or e-book form. There are several main outlets for selling books.

Book Superstores and Independent Booksellers

Today, about fifteen thousand retail outlets, sometimes called "brick-and-mortar stores," sell books in the United States. These include traditional bookstores, department stores, drugstores, used-book stores, and toy stores. But the distribution of these outlets changed dramatically over the years with the arrival of major changes in business practices and technology.

In the late 1970s, independent bookstores dominated the bookselling scene. But beginning in the 1980s with book superstore Borders, and later with Barnes & Noble and competition from major box-store retailers, independent stores started closing their doors in droves. Then along came Amazon and other online booksellers, and brick-and-mortar stores took another hit. For example, Borders went bankrupt in 2011, and in 2018, the continuing decline of sales at Barnes & Noble led a *New York Times* columnist to write: ". . . the death of Barnes & Noble is now plausible."[21] Concerns that the chain might

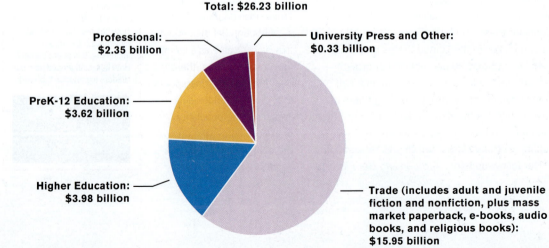

FIGURE 2.2 // ESTIMATED U.S. BOOK REVENUE, 2017

Total: $26.23 billion

Professional: $2.35 billion
University Press and Other: $0.33 billion
PreK-12 Education: $3.62 billion
Higher Education: $3.98 billion
Trade (includes adult and juvenile fiction and nonfiction, plus mass market paperback, e-books, audio books, and religious books): $15.95 billion

Data from: Jim Milliot, "2017 Sales Had Small Decline," Publisher's Weekly, July 23, 2018, www.publishersweekly.com/pw/by-topic/industry-news/financial-reporting/article/77552-2017-sales-had-small-decline.html; and American Association of Publishers, "Book Publisher Revenue Estimated at More Than $26 Billion in 2017," July 20, 2018, http://newsroom.publishers.org/book-publisher-revenue-estimated-at-more-than-26-billion-in-2017.

close persisted through 2018, but the sale of the company to a hedge fund in 2019 lessened those concerns to some degree.[22]

As the superstores fell on hard times, an amazing thing happened: Independent bookstores came back. From 2009 to 2018, there has been an almost 40 percent increase in the number of independent bookstores. A professor at Harvard Business School says that the success of independent bookstores lies in the three Cs: community (responding to the distinct local needs of the place), curation (providing a thoughtfully selected inventory for customers), and convening (making the store a place for meetings, reading groups, events, and even parties).[23]

Selling Books Online

Since the late 1990s, online booksellers have created an entirely new book-distribution system, in which consumers use websites to find and buy books. The strength of online sellers lies in their convenience and low prices, especially their ability to offer backlist titles and the works of less famous authors that even superstores don't carry on their shelves. The trailblazer is Amazon.com, established in 1995 by then thirty-year-old Jeff Bezos. Since then, others have followed suit, including Apple.

The shift from buying printed books in brick-and-mortar stores to ordering them online was only part of the way the digital turn changed book publishing's business model. Amazon's bigger objective was to transform the entire book industry from one based on bound-paper volumes to one based on digital files, and by 2017, Amazon had a 79.6 percent share of e-book sales in the United States (see Figure 2.3).[24] Moreover, Amazon also dominated in sales of printed books, selling 45.5 percent of U.S. print books in 2017.[25]

FIGURE 2.3 // AMAZON CORNERS THE E-BOOK MARKET

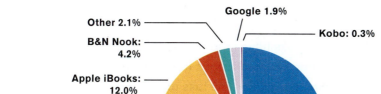

Data from: "February 2017 Big, Bad, Wide & International Report: Covering Amazon, Apple, B&N, and Kobo Ebook Sales in the US, UK, Canada, Australia, and New Zealand," Author Earnings, February 2017, http://authorearnings.com/report/february-2017. (Figures are rounded by the source.)

launchpadworks.com

Amazon's Brick-and-Mortar Bookstores

Bloomberg reports on the opening of Amazon Books in New York City.

Discussion: Why might a wildly successful online bookseller like Amazon choose to open physical bookstore locations?

With a publishing arm that can sign authors to book contracts, a distribution system in the form of the Amazon online store, and the potential to put millions of Kindle devices in the hands of readers and audio books on their smartphones (the company also owns audio-book site Audible.com), Amazon has become a vertically integrated company whose domination is unparalleled. Ironically, it has also become a brick-and-mortar bookseller: In late 2015, Amazon opened its first Amazon Books store in Seattle; and by 2018, it had opened almost twenty stores across the country (with additional pop-up stores in other locations).

Books in a Democratic Society

Books have played a vital role in our democracy—not only by spreading the notion of democracy itself but also by disseminating ideas that inspire people to drive change. For example, Harriet Beecher Stowe's *Uncle Tom's Cabin* sparked outrage over slavery, helping end the institution in the 1860s. Rachel Carson's *Silent Spring* exposed the perils of the pesticide industry in the 1960s, prompting the American public to demand reform. And, more recently, George Orwell's *1984*, a book about a dystopian, tyrannical government originally published in the mid-twentieth century, has surged in popularity as citizens consider issues of democracy and personal freedom.

Books have enabled people to share ideas freely, discuss those ideas' merits and flaws, and make informed choices—all key elements in any democracy. Indeed, the ability to write whatever one wants has its very roots in our founding documents: The First Amendment of the U.S. Constitution guarantees freedom of the press. But although books have long played this crucial role and will continue to do so, they face challenges that threaten to dilute their impact. These challenges include the loss of old books to physical deterioration and the persistence of censorship.

Physical Deterioration

Many older books, especially those from the nineteenth century printed on acid-based paper, gradually deteriorate. To prevent loss of the knowledge in these books, research libraries have built climate-controlled depositories for older books that have permanent research value.

The Google Books Library Project represents a different kind of effort. Begun in 2004, the project features partnerships with the New York Public Library and several major university research libraries to scan millions of books and make them available online and searchable through Google. The Authors Guild and the Association of American Publishers challenged Google's right to digitize books without permission. Google responded that displaying only a limited portion of the books was legal under "fair use" rules. After years of legal battles, a U.S. court of appeals sided with Google's fair-use argument in 2013 and dismissed the lawsuit. The Authors Guild appealed, but in April 2016, the U.S. Supreme Court refused to hear the appeal, so the lower court ruling stands.

Censorship

Throughout human history, rulers intent on maintaining their power have censored or banned books to prevent people from being exposed to alternative ideas and ways of living. For example, in various parts of the world, some versions of the Bible, Karl Marx's *Das Kapital* (1867), *The Autobiography of Malcolm X* (1965), and Salman Rushdie's *The Satanic Verses* (1989) have all been banned at one time or another. (For more on banned books, see "Media Literacy Case Study: Banned Books and 'Family Values'" on pages 52–53.)

In the United States, censorship and book banning are illegal. But citizens can sometimes force the removal of a particular book from public or school libraries if enough people file a formal complaint—a **book challenge**—about subject matter they find objectionable. The American Library Association (ALA) compiles a list of the most challenged books in the United States. Common reasons for challenges include sexually explicit passages, offensive language, occult themes, violence, homosexual themes, promotion of a religious viewpoint, nudity, and racism. The ALA defends the right of libraries to offer material with a wide range of views and does not support removing books on the basis of partisan or doctrinal disapproval.

This tension between citizens' desire to suppress printed materials they find objectionable and the desire to uphold freedoms guaranteed by the Constitution has long characterized our democracy—and will likely continue to do so.

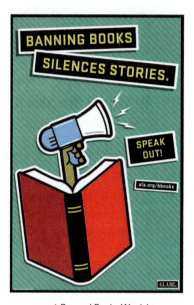

▲ Banned Books Week is an event sponsored by the American Library Association to raise awareness of challenges to reader freedoms and attempts to ban books. Used with permission from the American Library Association.

Resiliency of Reading

The physical deterioration of books and censorship present challenges to books as a mass medium essential to our democracy. But the good news is that books and their readers seem to be adapting quite well to new technology. Americans are reading books at roughly the same rate as they were in previous years—just not always in the same way. A Pew Research Center study found that 74 percent of Americans age eighteen and older had read at least one book in the past year, with the average American reading twelve books per year. Moreover, these readers experienced books across several formats: 67 percent read a book in print, 26 percent read an e-book, and 18 percent listened to an audio book.[26] The ultimate value of books is their ability to encourage the exchange and exploration of ideas among a broad audience. Clearly, despite the challenges and changes that have reshaped this oldest form of media, they are still serving this purpose.

Media Literacy

CASE STUDY

Banned Books and "Family Values"

When Raina Telgemeier's 2012 book *Drama* first made the American Library Association's list of the most challenged books in 2015, the ALA reported complaints that the book was too "sexually explicit." This news was surprising for one simple reason: The young-adult graphic novel about middle-school crushes doesn't actually have any sex. What it does have is one quick on-stage kiss between two characters who are part of the drama club. Because those two characters are both male, however, objections were raised.[1] When certain groups accused Telgemeier of having "an agenda," she explained that everyone involved worked to make sure that the book was age appropriate and the themes universal: "Finding your identity, whether gay or straight, is a huge part of middle school," said Telgemeier.[2]

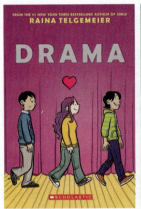

▲ Raina Telgemeier's *Drama* was one of the country's most challenged books in 2017, and Mark Twain's *Huckleberry Finn* is the most censored book in U.S. history. Uschi Gerschner/Newscom (right)

▶ Visit LaunchPad to watch a clip from a film adaptation of *Huckleberry Finn*. What audience does it seem to be aimed at?

launchpadworks.com

The American Library Association tracks challenges that are made against books, and in 2017, *Drama* was the third most challenged book in schools and libraries across the United States (see also Figure 2.4). It was second on the list the year before. These challenges typically come from a group or an individual in a community, who requests in writing that the book be removed from a library's shelves.

Drama is certainly not alone. Despite the constitutional guarantees regarding freedom of speech, there is a long history of books facing censorship in the United States, often in the name of protecting children and a community's "family values." *Ulysses* by James Joyce, *The Scarlet Letter* by Nathaniel Hawthorne, *Leaves of Grass* by Walt Whitman, *The Diary of a Young Girl* by Anne Frank, *Lolita* by Vladimir Nabokov, and *To Kill a Mockingbird* by Harper Lee have all been banned by a U.S. community, school, or library at one time or another. In fact, the most censored book in U.S. history is Mark Twain's *The Adventures of Huckleberry Finn*, the 1884 classic that still sells tens of thousands of copies every year.

FIGURE 2.4 // TOP TEN MOST CHALLENGED BOOKS OF 2017

1. *Thirteen Reasons Why* **written by Jay Asher**
   Reason: Discusses suicide
2. *The Absolutely True Diary of a Part-Time Indian* **written by Sherman Alexie**
   Reasons: Profanity; has situations that were deemed sexually explicit
3. *Drama* **written and illustrated by Raina Telgemeier**
   Reason: Includes LGBT characters; considered "confusing"
4. *The Kite Runner* **written by Khaled Hosseini**
   Reasons: Includes sexual violence; thought to "lead to terrorism" and "promote Islam"
5. *George* **written by Alex Gino**
   Reason: Includes a transgender child
6. *Sex Is a Funny Word* **written by Cory Silverberg and illustrated by Fiona Smyth**
   Reasons: Addresses sex education; believed to lead children to "want to have sex or ask questions about sex"
7. *To Kill a Mockingbird* **written by Harper Lee**
   Reasons: Violence; use of the N-word
8. *The Hate U Give* **written by Angie Thomas**
   Reasons: Considered "pervasively vulgar"; drug use, profanity, and offensive language
9. *And Tango Makes Three* **written by Peter Parnell and Justin Richardson and illustrated by Henry Cole**
   Reason: Features a same-sex relationship
10. *I Am Jazz* **written by Jessica Herthel and Jazz Jennings and illustrated by Shelagh McNicholas**
    Reason: Addresses gender identity

Information from: American Library Association, www.ala.org/bbooks.

APPLYING THE CRITICAL PROCESS

DESCRIPTION Identify two contemporary books that have been challenged in two separate communities. (Check the American Library Association website [www.ala.org] for information on the most frequently challenged books, or use the LexisNexis database.) Describe the communities involved and what sparked the challenges.

ANALYSIS Look at the patterns that emerge: the main arguments for censoring these books and for defending these books, and any middle-ground positions or unusual viewpoints brought up in the book controversies.

INTERPRETATION Why did these issues arise, and what do you think are the actual reasons why people would challenge a book? For example, does it seem as though people are genuinely concerned about protecting young readers, or do they just seem personally offended by particular books?

EVALUATION In your opinion, who is right and wrong in these controversies? How are First Amendment protections of printed materials significant here?

ENGAGEMENT Contact your local library, and ask what policies it has in place to respond to book challenges and whether it observes the ALA's annual Banned Books Week each September.

CHAPTER ESSENTIALS

Review

- Books first developed due to innovations made by the Egyptians, Greeks, Chinese, and Romans. Egyptians created **papyrus** in 2400 BCE. Gradually, people began writing on **parchment** because of its durability and cheaper cost; by the fourth century CE, Romans had created the **codex**—the first protomodern book.

- Books entered the entrepreneurial stage in the Middle Ages, at which time people explored new ways of writing. This led to the emergence of **manuscript culture**, whereby priests and monks advanced the art of bookmaking with **illuminated manuscripts**. At the same time, inventors experimented with new printing techniques, such as **block printing** and movable type.

- The invention of the **printing press** by Gutenberg between 1453 and 1456 allowed for the mass production of books, such as the Bible. This advancement marked books' move to the mass medium stage, complete with the rise of the publishing industry two centuries later.

- Initially, publishing houses were small and focused on offering the works of prestigious authors, but by the 1950s and 1960s, they were snapped up by major corporations with ties to international media conglomerates.

- The publishing industry produces titles that fall into a wide variety of categories, including **trade books**, **textbooks**, **professional books**, **mass market paperbacks**, **reference books**, religious books, and **university press** books.

- The convergence of books and digital technology has led to a rise in the use of **e-books**—digital books read on a variety of devices, ranging from dedicated e-readers to smartphones, tablets, and computers. Audio books can be downloaded digitally as well, and convergence has enabled the rise of self-publishing.

- Books serve as important source material for other forms of mass media—for example, they frequently provide material for films and television programs. TV and films can also help sell books.

- Regardless of their size or the types of books they publish, all publishing houses are structured similarly. Positions include **acquisitions editors**, **developmental editors**, **copy editors**, **design managers**, and marketing managers. Today, the book publishing industry is dominated by a handful of giant corporations.

LaunchPad

Visit LaunchPad for *Media Essentials* at **launchpadworks.com** for additional learning tools:

- **REVIEW WITH LEARNINGCURVE**
  LearningCurve adaptive quizzing helps you master the concepts you need to learn from this chapter.
- **MEDIA LITERACY PRACTICE**
  This activity challenges you to develop a critical perspective and apply it to everyday encounters with communication media.

- Books are sold through both brick-and-mortar stores and online stores.

- Books have played a vital role in democracy by spreading its very notion and disseminating ideas that have inspired people to drive change. Despite the crucial role of books, they face certain challenges. For example, censorship, which has played a role in book distribution throughout human history, prevents people from being exposed to alternative ideas or ways of living. In addition, the physical deterioration of books means that some works could be lost. The good news is that Americans are reading books at roughly the same rate as in previous years, although they now access books in digital and audio formats, as well as in print.

Study Questions

1. Why was the printing press such an important and revolutionary invention?
2. What does a publishing house do?
3. What are the main ways in which digital technologies have changed the publishing industry?
4. Why have book superstores experienced difficulty in the past decade, whereas independent bookstores have had a resurgence?
5. How do books play a vital role in our society?

Key Terms

papyrus, p. 35
parchment, p. 35
codex, p. 35
manuscript culture, p. 35
illuminated manuscripts, p. 35
block printing, p. 36
printing press, p. 36
vellum, p. 36
paperback books, p. 37
dime novels, p. 37
pulp fiction, p. 37
linotype, p. 37
offset lithography, p. 37
synergy, p. 38
trade books, p. 39
textbooks, p. 39
professional books, p. 40
mass market paperbacks, p. 40
reference books, p. 40
university press, p. 40
e-book, p. 41
acquisitions editors, p. 46
subsidiary rights, p. 46
developmental editor, p. 46
copy editor, p. 46
design manager, p. 46
book challenge, p. 51

Mass Media Industries

3

Newspapers to Digital Frontiers: Journalism's Journey

59
The Early History of American Journalism

65
The Evolution of Newspaper Journalism: Competing Models and the Rise of Professionalism

70
Journalism Evolves across Media

73
The Culture of News and Rituals of Reporting

82
The Economics of Journalism in the Twenty-First Century

87
Changes, Challenges, and Threats to Journalism Today

93
Journalism in a Democratic Society

In 1887, a young reporter left her job at the *Pittsburgh Dispatch* to seek her fortune in New York City. Only twenty-three years old, Elizabeth "Pink" Cochrane had grown tired of writing for the society pages and answering letters to the editor; she wanted to be on the front page. At that time, it was considered "unladylike" for women journalists to use their real names, so the *Dispatch* editors, borrowing from a Stephen Foster song, had dubbed her "Nellie Bly."

After four months of persistent job hunting and freelance writing, Nellie Bly earned a tryout at Joseph Pulitzer's *New York World*, the nation's largest paper. Her assignment: to investigate conditions at the Women's Lunatic Asylum on Blackwell's Island. Her method: to get herself committed to the asylum. After practicing the look of a disheveled lunatic in front of a mirror, she wandered the city's streets unwashed and seemingly dazed and acted strangely around her fellow boarders in a New York rooming house.[1] Her tactics worked: Doctors declared her mentally deranged and had her committed.

◄ Journalist Nellie Bly—real name Elizabeth Jane Cochrane—laid the groundwork for what we know today as investigative journalism. Her first undercover assignment exposed a need for reform in the care of the mentally ill. Granger—All rights reserved.

Ten days later, an attorney from the *World* went in to get her out. Her two-part story appeared in October 1887 and caused a sensation. Nellie Bly's dramatic first-person account documented harsh, cold baths; attendants who abused and taunted patients; and newly arrived immigrant women, completely sane, who had been dragged to the asylum simply because no one could understand them. Bly became famous. Pulitzer gave her a permanent job, and New York City committed $1 million toward improving its asylums. Through her courageous work, Bly pioneered what was then called *detective* or *stunt* journalism—a model that would pave the way toward the twentieth-century practice of investigative journalism.

JOURNALISM IS THE ONLY MEDIA ENTERPRISE that democracy absolutely requires—and is the only media practice and business specifically protected by the U.S. Constitution. However, with the decline in traditional news audiences, mounting criticism of "celebrity" journalists, the growth of partisanship in politics, the rise of highly opinionated twenty-four-hour cable news and Internet news blogs, and sustained attacks from high-profile politicians, mainstream journalists have found themselves facing distrust—and sometimes even violence—from the public.

To understand where journalism, in all its print and electronic forms, is today, it's useful to explore the often partisan and sensationalistic history of newspapers—the legacy form of journalism that still represents the bulk of local news coverage in many communities. Yet it's also important to look beyond the printed page to see how journalists took this craft and adapted it to the big screen, to the airwaves, and to the Internet.

In this chapter, we will look at how the profession of journalism, the technology of gathering and sharing news, and the economics of the news business have shaped one another over the last three hundred years by:

- **exploring journalism's early history, including the rise of the political-commercial press, penny papers, and yellow journalism**

- **assessing the modern era of print journalism, including the tensions between objective and interpretive journalism**

- **considering how journalism has evolved across media, including radio, television, and the Internet**

- **looking at the culture of news and the rituals of reporting, including changing definitions of *news*, the evolution of journalism's values, and journalistic ethics**

- **examining the business side of newspapers, including the economic impact of the digital turn**

- taking stock of the challenges facing journalism today, such as the digitization of content, the proliferation of propaganda and fake news (as well as the use of the "fake news" label), and violence against journalists

- considering how journalism's current struggles may affect the strength of our democracy

The Early History of American Journalism

Human beings have always valued **news**—the process by which people gather information and create narrative reports to help one another make sense of events happening around them. The earliest news was passed along *orally*—from family to family and from tribe to tribe—by community leaders and oral historians. Soon after moving from oral to written form, news shifted from an information source accessible only to elites and local leaders to a mass medium that satisfied a growing audience's hunger for information. In the earliest days of American newspapers (the late 1600s through the 1800s), written news took on a number of styles: political analyses in subscription-based publications; human-interest accounts in inexpensive, widely available papers; sensational stories with big headlines and bold designs; and the beginnings of investigative journalism. Each of these formats fulfilled Americans' "need to know," whether they wanted coverage of the political scene, exposés of corruption in business, or entertaining perspectives on current events.

LaunchPad
launchpadworks.com
Use **LearningCurve** to review concepts from this chapter.

Colonial Newspapers and the Partisan Press

Inspired by the introduction of the printing press in Europe, American colonists began producing their first newspapers in the late seventeenth century. Two main types of early papers developed: the **partisan press** and commercial shipping news. The partisan press got its name because unlike the business models we are familiar with today, these papers were increasingly being sponsored by political parties, politicians, and other partisan groups. They served a vital function before, during, and after the Revolutionary period, critiquing government and disseminating the views of political parties. Other papers were more focused on providing information on commercial markets and about ships that were coming in and out of colonial ports, or they reprinted news from European magazines and newspapers brought on board

▲ During the colonial period, *New-York Weekly Journal* printer John Peter Zenger was arrested for seditious libel. He eventually won his case, which established the precedent that today allows U.S. journalists and citizens to criticize public officials. Bettmann/Getty Images

those ships. In the partisan press, one can see a forerunner to today's editorial pages as well as partisan cable news channels, talk radio, and websites. In the commercial papers, one can see the ancestor of today's business sections, as well as numerous papers, cable news programs, and websites focused on business news.

The first newspaper, *Publick Occurrences, Both Forreign and Domestick*, was published on September 25, 1690, by Boston printer Benjamin Harris, but it was banned after just one issue for its negative view of British rule. In the early 1700s, other papers cropped up, including Benjamin Franklin's *Pennsylvania Gazette*, which many historians regard as the best of the colonial papers. The *Gazette* was also one of the first papers to make money by printing advertisements alongside news.

One significant colonial paper, the *New-York Weekly Journal*, was founded in 1733 by the Popular Party, a political group that opposed British rule. *Journal* articles included attacks on the royal governor of New York. The party had installed John Peter Zenger as printer of the paper, and in 1734 he was arrested for *seditious libel* when one of his writers defamed a public official's character in print. Championed by famed Philadelphia lawyer Andrew Hamilton, Zenger won his case the following year. The Zenger decision helped lay a foundation—the right of a democratic press to criticize public officials—for the First Amendment to the Constitution, adopted as part of the Bill of Rights in 1791.

By 1765, the American colonies boasted about thirty newspapers, all of them published weekly or monthly. In 1784, the first daily paper began operation. But even the largest of these papers rarely reached a circulation of fifteen hundred. Readership was largely confined to educated or wealthy men who controlled local politics and commerce (and who could afford newspaper subscriptions).

The Penny Press: Becoming a Mass Medium

During the 1830s, a number of forces transformed newspapers into an information source available to, valued by, and affordable to all—a true mass medium. For example, thanks to the Industrial Revolution, factories could make cheap machine-made paper to replace the expensive handmade paper previously in use. At the same time, the rise of the middle class, enabled by the growth of literacy, set the stage for a more popular and inclusive press. And with steam-powered presses replacing mechanical presses, publishers could crank out as many as four thousand copies of their newspapers every hour, which dramatically lowered their cost. Popular **penny papers** soon began outselling the six-cent elite publications previously available. The success of penny papers would change not only who was reading newspapers but also how those papers were written.

The First Penny Papers

In 1833, printer Benjamin Day founded the *New York Sun*, lowered the price of his newspaper to one penny, and eliminated subscriptions. The *Sun* highlighted local events, scandals, and police reports. It also ran fabricated and serialized stories, making legends of frontiersmen Davy Crockett and Daniel Boone and blazing the trail for Americans' enthusiasm for celebrity news. Within six months, the *Sun* had a circulation of eight thousand—twice that of its nearest competitor. The *Sun*'s success unleashed a barrage of penny papers that favored **human-interest stories**: news accounts that focused on the daily trials and triumphs of the human condition, often featuring ordinary individuals who had faced down extraordinary challenges.

In 1835, James Gordon Bennett founded another daily penny paper, the *New York Morning Herald*. Considered the first U.S. press baron, Bennett—rather than any one political party—completely controlled his paper's content, establishing an independent publication that served middle- and working-class

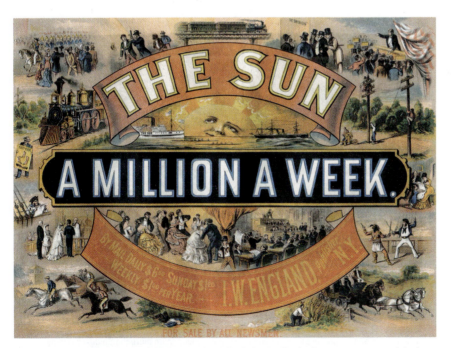

▲ Founded by Benjamin Day in 1833, the *New York Sun* helped usher in the penny press era, bringing news to the working and emerging middle class. © North Wind Picture Archives

readers. By 1860, the *Herald* had nearly eighty thousand readers, making it the world's largest daily paper.

Changing Business Models, Changing Journalism

As ad revenues and circulation skyrocketed, the newspaper industry expanded overall. In 1830, about 650 weekly and 65 daily papers operated in the United States, reaching a circulation of 80,000. Just ten years later, the nation had a total of 1,140 weeklies and 140 dailies, attracting more than 300,000 readers.

As they proliferated and gained new readers, penny papers shifted not just their business models but also the way the news was presented—and, in the process, changed the practice of journalism. Previously, papers had been funded primarily by the political parties that sponsored them, and their content emphasized overt political views. But as their readership grew, owners realized they could derive even more revenue from the market—that is, by selling space for advertisements and by hawking newspapers. Editors began putting their daily reporting on the front page, moving overt political viewpoints to the editorial page. In other words, as the business model relied more on selling to a mass audience, there was a financial incentive to appeal to customers with a wider range of political beliefs. This trend toward an "objective" style

▲ Children sold papers on the streets of New York in the 1890s. With more than a dozen dailies competing, street tactics were ferocious, and publishers often made young "newsies"—newsboys and newsgirls—buy the papers they could not sell. Library of Congress

would also be supported by services that provided content for several different newspapers.

The First News Wire Service

In 1848, the enormous expansion of the newspaper industry led six New York newspapers to form a cooperative arrangement and found the Associated Press (AP), the first major news wire service. **Wire services** began as commercial and cooperative organizations that relayed news stories and information around the country and the world using telegraph lines (and, later, radio waves and digital transmissions). In the case of the AP, which functioned as a kind of news co-op, the founding New York papers provided access to their own stories and those from other newspapers.

Such companies enabled news to travel rapidly from coast to coast, setting the stage for modern journalism in the United States. And because the papers still cost only a penny, more people than ever now had access to a widening array of news. Clearly, newspapers had moved from the entrepreneurial stage to the status of a mass medium.

As individual newspapers became aware of the financial rewards of not alienating readers with differing political viewpoints, wire services saw the need to offer material that as many newspapers as possible would buy. Based on this economic need, a journalistic style of writing called the **inverted pyramid** was developed.

Developed by Civil War correspondents working for individual papers or wire services, inverted-pyramid reports were often stripped of adverbs and adjectives and began—as they do today—with the most dramatic or newsworthy information.[2] They answered the questions who, what, where, when (and, less frequently, why and how) at the top of the story and then narrowed the account down to its less significant details. This approach offered an important advantage: If editors needed to shorten the story to fit the available space on the page, they could cut from the bottom up without affecting the main points of the story. Still a staple of introductory news-writing courses, this form tends to emphasize immediate events and facts over deeper discussions of context or partisan debate.

But the move from overt political partisanship on the front page wasn't the only way the economic desire for increasingly larger audiences changed the way journalism was practiced.

Yellow Journalism

Following the tradition established by the *New York Sun* and the *New York Morning Herald*, a new brand of paper arose in the late 1800s. These publications ushered in the era of **yellow journalism**, which emphasized exciting human-interest stories, crime news, large headlines, and

▲ Generally considered America's first comic-strip character, the Yellow Kid was created in the mid-1890s by cartoonist R. F. Outcault. The cartoon was so popular that newspaper barons Joseph Pulitzer and William Randolph Hearst fought over control of the character, giving yellow journalism its name. Dept. of Special Collections, Syracuse University Library

easy-to-digest copy. Generally regarded as the direct forerunner of today's tabloid papers, reality TV, and celebrity-obsessed websites like TMZ, yellow journalism featured two major characteristics:

- Overly dramatic—or sensational—stories about crime, celebrities, disasters, scandals, and intrigue
- News reports exposing corruption, particularly in business and government—the foundation for *investigative journalism*

The term *yellow journalism* has its roots in the press war that pitted Joseph Pulitzer's *New York World* against William Randolph Hearst's *New York Journal*. During their furious fight to win readers, the two papers competed by publishing versions of the first popular cartoon strip, *The Yellow Kid*, created in 1895 by artist R. F. Outcault. Pulitzer, a Jewish Hungarian immigrant, had bought the *New York World* in 1883 for $346,000. Aimed at immigrant and working-class readers, the *World* crusaded for improved urban housing, better treatment of women, and equitable labor laws, while railing against big business. It also manufactured news events and printed sensationalized stories on crime and sex. By 1887, its Sunday circulation had soared to more than 250,000—the largest anywhere.

The *World* faced its fiercest competition in 1895, when William Randolph Hearst bought the *New York Journal* (a penny paper founded by Pulitzer's brother Albert) and then raided Joseph Pulitzer's paper for editors, writers, and cartoonists. Hearst focused on lurid, sensational stories and appealed to immigrant readers by using large headlines and bold designs. To boost circulation, the *Journal* invented interviews, faked pictures, and provoked conflicts that might result in eye-catching stories. In 1896, its daily circulation reached 450,000. A year later, the circulation of the paper's Sunday edition rivaled the *World*'s 600,000.

Yellow journalism has been vilified for its sensationalism and aggressive tactics to snatch readers from competitors by appealing to their low-brow interests, but this unique era gave birth to several newspaper elements still valued by many readers today, including advice columns and feature stories. It even inspired the founding of the prestigious Pulitzer Prizes, which today recognize quality writing, reporting, and research in a variety of categories.

The Evolution of Newspaper Journalism: Competing Models and the Rise of Professionalism

In the late 1800s, as newspapers pushed to expand circulation even further, two distinct types of journalism emerged: the story-driven model, which dramatized important events and characterized the penny papers and the yellow press, and "the facts" model, an approach that seemed more impartial and had its roots in the early commercial newspapers.[3] Provocative questions arose: Could news accounts be entirely objective? Should reporters actively interpret the meaning of particular events for readers? In response to these questions, the 1920s saw the rise of *interpretive journalism*, which aimed to explain events and place them in context.

"Objectivity" and Professionalization in Modern Journalism

Throughout the mid-1800s, the more a newspaper appeared not to take sides on its front pages, the more readers it could attract. Also at this time, wire service organizations were serving a variety of newspaper clients in different regions of the country. To satisfy all their clients, newspapers strived for the appearance of impartiality, presenting the facts and leaving it up to readers to interpret the implications for their own lives. At the same time, the more sensational aspects of yellow journalism created an image problem for newspapers, with journalists seen as low-status tradespeople at best and as disreputable at worst. But with the approach of the twentieth century, newspapers and journalism were about to change.

Adolph Ochs and the New York Times

The ideal of an impartial, or purely informational, news model was reinvented by Adolph Ochs, who bought the *New York Times* in 1896. Through wise hiring, Ochs and his editors rebuilt the paper around substantial news coverage and provocative editorial pages. To distance the *Times* from the yellow press, the editors also downplayed sensational stories, favoring the documentation of major events or issues, and developed a powerful marketing message touting the *Times* as the higher-brow choice.

▼ Known for gathering information and presenting it in a straightforward way—without the opinion of the reporter—the *New York Times* was the first truly modern newspaper. It established itself as the official paper of record by the 1920s and maintains a venerable reputation today. Andrew Harrer/Bloomberg/Getty Images

With the Hearst and Pulitzer papers capturing the bulk of working- and middle-class readers, managers at the *Times* initially tried to use their straightforward, "no frills" reporting to appeal to more affluent and educated readers. In 1898, Ochs also lowered the paper's price to a penny. Soon middle-class readers gravitated to the paper as a status marker for the educated and well informed. Between 1898 and 1899, circulation soared from 25,000 to 75,000. By 1921, the *Times* had a daily circulation of 330,000 and a Sunday circulation of 500,000.

"Just the Facts, Please": Journalism Gets Professional

Early in the twentieth century, with reporters adopting a more scientific attitude to news- and fact-gathering, the ideal of objectivity took a firmer hold in journalism. In **objective journalism**, which distinguishes factual reports from opinion columns, reporters ideally strive to maintain a neutral attitude toward the issue or event they cover. They also search out competing points of view among the sources for a story in an effort to provide balanced coverage.

The early twentieth century was also a time when even the most notorious yellow journalists wanted to boost the respectability of the news business. That, combined with a broader cultural trend that favored a more scientific approach to the world, pushed the training of new journalists away

▲ *Cincinnati Enquirer* staff won the 2018 Pulitzer Prize for local reporting, "for a riveting and insightful narrative and video documenting seven days of greater Cincinnati's heroin epidemic, revealing how the deadly addiction has ravaged families and communities." Meg Vogel-Pool/Getty Images News/Getty Images

from apprenticeships and toward universities. Early in the century, Joseph Pulitzer approached Columbia University in New York about setting up the first journalism school. He wanted to see the status of journalists rise to that of other professionals, such as lawyers and doctors. But the reputation of journalism was such that it took several years for the directors of the school to accept the millions Pulitzer offered, finally founding the school in 1912. (In addition to offering graduate degrees, the school began awarding the coveted Pulitzer Prizes in journalism in 1917 and continues to do so to this day.) But the distinction of being the first journalism school in the United States goes to a different Columbia: the School of Journalism at the University of Missouri in Columbia, Missouri, founded in 1908.[4]

Interpretive Journalism

By the 1920s, people began wondering whether the impartial approach to news reporting was sufficient for helping readers understand complex national and global developments. As one news scholar contended, it was partly as a result of "drab, factual, objective reporting" that "the American people were utterly amazed when [World War I] broke out in August 1914, as they had no understanding of the foreign scene to prepare them for it."[5] Such concerns triggered the rise of **interpretive journalism**, which aims to explain the ramifications of key issues or events and place them in a broader historical or social context.

Editor and columnist Walter Lippmann insisted that although objectivity should serve as journalism's foundation, the press should do more. He ranked three press responsibilities: (1) "to make a current record"; (2) "to make a running analysis of it"; and (3) "on the basis of both, to suggest plans."[6]

The rise of radio in the 1930s intensified tensions between the objective and interpretive models of print journalism. As radio gained in popularity, broadcasters increasingly took their news directly from papers and wire services. Seeking to maintain their dominion over "the facts," some newspaper editors and lobbyists argued that radio should provide only interpretive commentary. Radio followed that path and developed a broad bench of well-known news commentators who reported stories with their own analysis.

It wasn't until the 1950s—with the outbreak of the Korean War, the development of atomic power, the deepening of the Cold War, and the U.S. anticommunist movement—that newspapers began providing more interpretive journalism. They did so in part to compete with the latest news medium: television, where former radio commentators like Edward R. Murrow of CBS were flourishing. By the 1970s, newspapers' interpretive material often took the form of an "op-ed" page, named after its position opposite the editorial page. The op-ed page offered a wider variety of columns, news analyses, and letters to the editor.

Media Literacy

CASE STUDY

Investigative Journalism: In the "Spotlight"

When the *Boston Globe* ran a series of stories about the Roman Catholic Church in the early 2000s, the paper's investigative reporters did more than challenge one of the most powerful institutions in Boston; they took on one of the most powerful institutions in the world. The *Globe*'s Spotlight team uncovered decades of sexual abuse of children by Catholic priests in and around Boston, as well as cover-ups by top church officials who allowed the abuse to continue. This reporting by the country's "oldest continually operating newspaper investigative unit" prompted criminal investigations and promises of church reform, which are ongoing.[1] The behind-the-scenes story of the investigation was also made into a movie, *Spotlight*, which won the 2015 Academy Award for best picture.

The Spotlight team's church investigation is indeed impressive, and it represents one small part of a much bigger story: that of investigative journalism's role in society and its function as a watchdog, digging up and exposing wrongdoing by the powerful—from local government officials to private corporations to religious institutions. Modern investigative journalism can trace its roots to the beginning of the twentieth century, when journalists like Nellie Bly (see chapter opener) exposed scandals and prompted reforms. And it was in the 1970s when another formative journalistic event took place, influencing future generations of investigative reporters: *Washington Post* reporters Bob Woodward and Carl Bernstein's investigation following the arrest of five men for breaking into Democratic National Committee headquarters at the Watergate office complex in Washington, D.C., on June 17, 1972. By the time they were done, Woodward and Bernstein had uncovered information connecting the break-in and a number of other illegal activities to President Richard Nixon and his staff. The House of Representatives started investigating, Nixon ultimately resigned, and the word *Watergate* became synonymous with the exposure of official misconduct and scandal.

Investigative reporting is vital for a functioning democracy. At the same time, it is a time- and labor-intensive enterprise, and it can take multiple reporters months—or even years—to uncover the secrets that powerful men and women work hard to keep hidden. That makes it an expensive

▲ *Washington Post* reporters Bob Woodward and Carl Bernstein investigated a plot to bug the Democratic National Committee headquarters at the Watergate building, unraveling a story that implicated President Richard Nixon and led to his resignation.
AP Photo

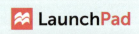

⏵ Visit LaunchPad to watch a clip from the movie *Spotlight*. If fewer news organizations are willing to invest in the type of investigative reporting depicted in this clip, what will the implications be for society?

launchpadworks.com

undertaking, and though some smaller local newspapers and even television stations have reporters who do this type of reporting, an investigative effort like that of the Spotlight team is something few papers can afford. Even so, communities need journalists who can act as watchdogs.

One organization that promotes and supports this kind of journalistic work is the nonprofit Investigative Reporters and Editors (IRE). IRE was formed in 1975 and provides training, resources, and a community for investigative journalists. The group works to promote ethical reporting and protect the rights of investigative reporters. The acronym of the organization, IRE, was intentional because, as one founder put it, "What most characterizes the investigative reporter is a 'sense of outrage.'"[2]

Other nonprofit groups also hope to fill the growing void of local investigative journalists. One example is Report for America (RFA). Borrowing ideas from Teach for America and the Peace Corps, RFA hopes to add more than one thousand reporters to local newsrooms by the early 2020s.[3] There are also organizations like IowaWatch at the Iowa Center for Public Affairs Journalism, where student reporters and newsroom veterans work together to conduct in-depth investigations and make their stories available to any outlets that want to use them.[4]

But while these efforts have already made an impact, the fact remains that there are tens of thousands of fewer reporters in newsrooms across the country today than there were two decades ago. That means that the kind of daily newspaper journalism exhibited by the Spotlight team is the exception rather than the rule, and there are fewer people holding the powerful institutions in our society accountable.

APPLYING THE CRITICAL PROCESS

DESCRIPTION Choose a newspaper, preferably one local to your school or your hometown. Search the newspaper's website looking for evidence of reporters or units within the paper who specialize in investigative work. Alternatively, use search engines to seek out stories from the paper that are promoted as investigative.

ANALYSIS How does the newspaper characterize its investigative-reporting efforts? Is there any indication that it has reporters or teams of reporters dedicated to investigative work? What kinds of investigative stories, if any, are featured on the paper's website?

INTERPRETATION Write a two- to three-paragraph critical interpretation of the information you've found. What do your findings suggest about the resources the paper dedicates to investigative reporting? Are there many such reports? Do they seem complicated? If the paper you are examining has investigative coverage on its website, does it feature stories only, or does it include online interactive features as well?

EVALUATION Based on what you've discovered, in what ways does this paper seem to serve (or *not* serve) a watchdog function for the surrounding community? Explain what that might mean for the community's ability to make decisions about local issues and politics.

ENGAGEMENT Contact an editor from the paper you examined, and conduct further research into how the paper handles investigative reporting. Ask if the paper's approach to investigative reporting has changed over time, considering that many newspapers have cut newsroom staff (some quite dramatically).

Journalism Evolves across Media

The rise of radio and the coming of television would give way to new forms of journalism. Nearly every new mass medium has eventually found a home for journalism of some kind, from radio and television in the first half of the twentieth century, to the addition of cable television in the 1980s, to the emergence and convergence of the Internet in the 1990s through the present day. Many mass media have coexisted with traditional print journalism, but the converged media offered by the Internet has been the catalyst for some of the biggest changes in the journalism world since its early days.

Journalism on the Airwaves

By the time America plunged into the Great Depression, the unique abilities of broadcasting were becoming apparent. For example, President Franklin Delano Roosevelt tapped this potential during his now-famous fireside chats. Later, news icon Edward R. Murrow made a name for himself and CBS News during World War II by broadcasting from rooftops during the Nazi bombing of London and by taking a recorder with him as he flew on B-17 bombing missions over Germany, taping commentary for later broadcast. This immediacy gave the audience a sense of being there and added a new dimension to reporting.

By the 1950s, the rules and rituals surrounding journalism would extend to the newest medium, television. Many radio news icons, including Murrow, would switch to TV. In 1951, his radio program *Hear It Now* was retitled *See It Now*, and from this venue, Murrow went on to challenge Senator Joseph McCarthy for his reckless abuse of power and disregard for evidence in labeling people as communists in the United States. He was also among the first to warn of the dangers of smoking tobacco. However, as much as Murrow and his work on radio and television are held in high esteem by broadcast journalists even to this day (one of the industry's highest awards is named after him), it's worth noting that his coverage of controversial subjects and the accompanying offense taken by advertisers often brought Murrow into conflict with CBS owner William S. Paley and ultimately doomed the program.

The Power of Visual Language

The shift from a print-dominated culture to an electronic-digital culture brings up the question of how the power of visual imagery compares with the power of the printed word. For the second half of the twentieth century, TV news dramatized America's key events visually. Civil rights activists, for instance, acknowledge that the movement benefited enormously from televised news and the evocative, moving images that documented the plight of southern blacks in the 1960s. Many people find visual images far more compelling and memorable than written descriptions of events or individuals. If listening to President Roosevelt on the radio was part of creating a shared national experience, the effect was amplified as a nation watched and celebrated milestones together, from the first man to walk on the moon to the inauguration of the first African American U.S. president.

▲ Major network morning news programs like *CBS Morning News*, *Good Morning America* (ABC), and NBC's *Today* (shown) are staples of the network lineup and have been since the 1950s. Combining a lot of "happy talk" and guest interviews with some news content, these shows typically fill several hours of programming every weekday morning. Chance Yeh/FilmMagic/Getty Images

But just as sound and moving pictures provide powerful communication tools, the technical requirements and styles that have developed also bring some shortcomings. TV news reporters share many values and conventions with their print counterparts, yet they also differ from them in significant ways:

- Whereas print editors fit stories around ads on the printed page, TV news directors have to time stories to fit between commercials, which can make the ads seem more intrusive to viewers.
- Whereas newspapers can increase or decrease their page counts, time is a finite commodity. This has often led commercial news operations to place strict limits on the length of individual news stories. In a half-hour newscast, about ten minutes goes to commercials and ten minutes goes to sports and weather, which leaves only ten minutes for the news.
- TV news reporters gain credibility from providing on-the-spot reporting, believable imagery, and an earnest, personable demeanor that makes them seem more approachable—and perhaps more trustworthy—than detached, faceless print reporters. As TV news reporting evolved, it developed a style of its own—one defined by attractive, congenial newscasters skilled at perky banter (sometimes called "happy talk"), and short, seven- to eight-second quotes (or "sound bites") from interview subjects.

Cable News Enters the Field

The transformation of TV news by cable—which began with the arrival of CNN in 1980—led to dramatic changes in TV news delivery at the national level. Before cable news (and the Internet), most people tuned to their local

▲ The popularity of 24/7 cable news has led to increased screen time for news anchors and television personalities. CNN's Christiane Amanpour was first hired as a desk assistant in the early 1980s and later served as chief international correspondent for the cable network. In 2018, she became host of a one-hour PBS interview show. Michael Kovac/WireImage/Getty Images

and national news late in the afternoon or evening on a typical weekday, with each program lasting just thirty minutes. Today, we can get TV news anytime, day or night, and the constant need for new content (sometimes called "feeding the beast") has led to major changes in what is considered news. Because it is expensive to dispatch reporters to document stories or to maintain foreign news bureaus, the much less expensive "talking head" pundit has become a standard for cable news channels.

Today's main cable channels have built their evening programs along partisan lines and follow the model of journalism as opinion and assertion: Fox News goes right with pundit stars like Sean Hannity; MSNBC leans left with Rachel Maddow; and CNN stakes out the middle with hosts who try to strike a more neutral pose, like Anderson Cooper. In the Trump era, ratings and revenue have gone up across cable news, but especially on those networks that are the most partisan. Whereas in 2018 Hannity and Maddow occasionally drew an audience of three million or more, CNN's Cooper had an average viewership of just under one million. Of the three, Cooper (by far) did the most actual reporting in the field.

With their (somewhat) traditional approach to television programming, broadcast and cable news organizations play an important role in society. Yet it's nearly impossible to describe or define the current state of journalism, from whatever source, without discussing its convergence with the Internet.

Internet Convergence Accelerates Changes to Journalism

For mainstream print and TV reporters and editors, online news has added new dimensions to journalism. Both print and TV news can continually update breaking stories online, and many reporters now post their online stories first and then work on the traditional versions. This means that readers and viewers no longer have to wait until the next day for the morning paper or for the local evening newscast for important stories. To enhance the online reports, which do not have the time or space constraints of television or print, newspaper reporters are increasingly required to provide video or audio for their stories. This allows readers and viewers to see and hear full interviews rather than just selected quotes or sound bites.

However, in the wake of the digital turn, online news comes with a special set of problems. For example, rather than leaving the office to question a subject in person, print reporters can now do e-mail interviews. Many editors discourage this practice because they think relying on e-mail gives interviewees too much control over how they shape their answers. Although some might argue that this provides more thoughtful answers, journalists say it takes the elements of surprise and spontaneity out of the traditional news interview, during which a subject might accidentally reveal important information—something less likely to occur in an online setting.

Another problem for journalists is, ironically, the wide-ranging resources of the Internet, including access to versions of stories from other papers and broadcast stations. The mountain of information available has made it all too easy for journalists to copy other journalists' work—whether intentionally or unwittingly. In addition, access to databases and other informational sites can keep reporters at their computers rather than out tracking down new kinds of information, cultivating sources, and staying in touch with their communities.

Most notable for journalists in the digital age, however, are the demands that convergence has made on their reporting and writing. Print journalists are expected to carry digital cameras so that they can post video along with their stories, and TV reporters are expected to write print-style news reports for their station's website to supplement their televised stories. In addition, most journalists today are expected to tweet and blog.

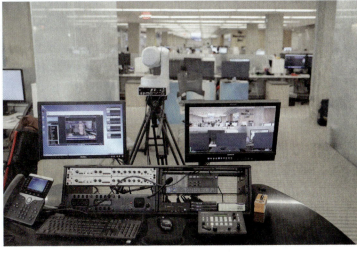

▲ Major newspapers like the *Washington Post* take convergence with digital storytelling and social media very seriously. In 2016, the *Post* inaugurated a new Washington, D.C., headquarters complete with a state-of-the-art multimedia suite, where reporters and producers can shoot, edit, and post videos.
Chip Somodevilla/Getty Images News/Getty Images

The Culture of News and Rituals of Reporting

Throughout the twentieth century, sets of beliefs and practices came to define what was accepted as news and what it meant to be a journalist reporting that news. Despite the technical and inherent stylistic differences among print, radio, and television, mainstream journalists in all media shared a similar mission, encountered similar ethical issues, and developed methods designed to get and share information. These concepts have proven invaluable for news operations trying to do the never-ending job of providing the information the public needs in order to make informed and intelligent decisions. They also provide a framework within which journalists say they are adhering to principles of unbiased truth-seeking and from which they derive a great portion of their authority. Critics suggest that these practices are just as likely to create biases, derail honest discussions about those biases, and paint a picture that distorts reality. But before one can discuss what is a useful tool and what is a potential pitfall, it's helpful to understand more about news culture and the common customs of gathering the news, beginning with the most basic question of journalism: What is news?

What Is News?

As discussed in the beginning of this chapter, news is the process of gathering information and making reports that use a narrative framework; in other words, news reports tell stories. But which stories do they tell? The first task of journalism is to decide what information is **newsworthy**—what merits transformation into a news story. The traditional criteria used to determine newsworthiness (criteria that help shape the culture of newsrooms) are timeliness, proximity, conflict, prominence, human interest, consequence, usefulness, novelty, and deviance:[7]

- Most issues and events that journalists cover are *timely* or *new*. Reporters, for instance, cover speeches, meetings, crimes, and court cases that have just happened.
- The bulk of these events usually occur close by, or in *proximity* to, the readers and viewers who will consume the news stories.
- In developing news narratives, reporters often seek contentious quotes from those with opposing or *conflicting* views. In theory, this helps create balance. In practice, it can lead to seeking out the most extreme positions, rather than a range of positions, to create drama.
- Surveys indicate that most people identify more closely with an individual than with an abstract issue. Therefore, the news media tend to report stories that feature *prominent*, powerful, or influential people.
- However, reporters also look for the *human-interest* story: extraordinary incidents that happen to "ordinary" people. In fact, reporters often relate a story about a complicated issue (such as unemployment, health care, or homelessness) by illustrating its impact on an "average" person or a "typical" family.
- Many editors and reporters believe that some news must also be of *consequence* to a majority of their readers or viewers. For example, they might include stories about new business regulations that affect credit cards or home mortgages.
- Likewise, many people look for *useful* stories: for instance, those offering hints on how to buy a used car or choose a college.

- When events happen that are outside the routine of daily life—that is, they are *novel*—they will likely generate news coverage. Examples might include a seven-year-old girl who tries to pilot a plane across the country or a bear that somehow got into a parked car.
- Reporters also cover events that appear to *deviate* from social norms, including murders, rapes, fatal car or plane crashes, fires, political scandals, and wars.

In producing news stories that meet many of these criteria, journalists influence our interpretations of what is going on around us and thus the decisions we make. For example, if we read a story in the newspaper emphasizing the consequences of failing to save for retirement, we may conclude that such saving is important—and that we'd better do more of it. If we see a lot of stories about crime and violence, even at a time when fewer violent crimes are actually being committed, we might conclude that the world is a more dangerous place than the facts actually suggest.

▲ While many people get their news online, there are still those who enjoy reading a physical newspaper in its traditional and instantly recognizable broadsheet format. Mark Edward Atkinson/Tracey Lee/Getty Images

Values in American Journalism

In addition to telling us how journalists define news, newsworthiness criteria begin to paint a picture of the values that came to define American journalism by the 1960s and 1970s. This was a time some refer to as the golden age of journalism, when newspapers enjoyed consistent profitability and NBC, CBS, and ABC hadn't yet encountered the competition from cable and online news. It was also a time when the journalism profession was enjoying a boost in prestige and popularity in the wake of big stories about the Watergate scandal and the Pentagon Papers. It was at this time that researchers began identifying and critiquing the values—not always recognized by the journalists themselves at the time—that influenced how stories were covered (or not).

Putting It in Neutral

Perhaps the most prominent and obvious of these values is neutrality, or the apparent lack of bias—a quality that remains prized even in a more polarized environment that has given rise to more opinionated forms of news. Many professional journalists believe strongly that their job is to gather and then present facts without judging them. That has led to the development of conventions like the following, which help reporters present their findings in a supposedly neutral way:

- The inverted-pyramid news lead: starting reports with the most important information
- The careful attribution of sources: favoring quoted interview subjects rather than the reporter's analysis
- The minimal use of adverbs and adjectives: getting rid of ornate, flowery language in order to appear factual
- The detached third-person point of view: using the omniscient, or all-knowing, authorial point of view favored by many novelists

Journalists argue that this dedication to neutrality (and the related concepts of fairness, balance, independence, objectivity, and so on) boosts their credibility and is an important part of what separates news from propaganda. Generations of journalists have spent their careers trying to live up to these ideals as part of what they see as their mission to serve their audiences and communities. At its best, a commitment by individual journalists to these traditional news values has helped them root out the news, hold the powerful to account, and resist manipulation by those who would deceive the public.

However, critics in and out of the profession say this approach also brings problems. In practice, total neutrality is itself an impossible goal. In deciding which stories to cover with limited resources, news operations make judgments about what is worthy of attention (or not) by the public. Merely by deciding which information and whose experience to include in a news story, journalists cannot help but present a point of view on the story's topic. And although the pursuit of personal detachment might have become part of a well-intentioned set of standards, it is still true that the origins of the shift from partisan to objective journalism in the 1800s had at least as much to do with economics as with ethics.

Another problem with the concept of "neutrality" for journalism might be the way in which believing one's judgment to be neutral can create dangerous blind spots, which ultimately undermine the ethical intentions of journalists. Assumptions about what is "normal" or "natural" often play a role when trying to find the neutral position, especially when dealing with social issues. Take, for example, the experience of the *New York Times* during the 1970s and 1980s and the way it covered—or, rather, often ignored—gay rights and the AIDS epidemic. The antigay positions of the paper's management and owners at the time became a target for critics, who said the silence of this "objective" newspaper slowed public attention and support for the fight against AIDS, contributing to the ultimate death toll from the disease. (The *Times* changed its policies in the late 1980s.)[8]

Diversity in the Newsroom

An important part of the critique of the ability of newsrooms to achieve neutrality or objectivity involves the ways in which the demographics of a newsroom reflect the demographics of the community it covers. For much of the twentieth century, mainstream news operations were dominated by white men and, as such, lacked the perspective that comes with the different lived experiences of other groups in society. This hurts the ability of a newsroom to question what it considers "normal" or "neutral," which is really based on a very non-neutral worldview.

Beginning in the 1970s, there was a push to make newsrooms more diverse. The good news is that from 1977 to 1994, the number of minority reporters in newspaper newsrooms nearly tripled, from 4 percent to 11 percent, and that number has slowly continued to climb.[9] The bad news is that white men are still disproportionally represented in newsrooms today. As of 2017, minority journalists made up about 16.6 percent of the total workforce at newspapers and digital-only newsrooms, and 39 percent of employees were women.[10] Results were similar for leadership and news management positions: just over 13 percent of newsroom leaders were minorities, and 39 percent of leaders were women.[11] The problem with these numbers is that they don't reflect what America actually looks like: just over 39 percent of all Americans are nonwhite, and just under 51 percent are women.[12]

▲ In June 2015, *NBC Nightly News* permanently promoted Lester Holt to the job of anchor, making him the first African American to be a solo anchor on a nightly network news program. D Dipasupil/Getty Images Entertainment/Getty Images

Television newsrooms seem to be faring somewhat better than their newspaper counterparts. In 2018, minority journalists made up 25 percent of television newsroom staff and 17 percent of news directors. Women, while still underrepresented, are making gains: In 2018, women made up 44 percent of television newsroom staff and 34 percent of news directors, both of which were record numbers. Radio fared the worst: 11 percent of newsroom staff were minorities, whereas just under 34 percent of newsroom staff were women.[13]

The resulting imbalance in the newsroom affects not just how the news is covered but also how the newsroom operates and how journalists are treated in the work environment. This issue received national attention in 2017 and 2018 with the rise of the #MeToo movement, when a number of powerful men in the news business—including Fox News's Bill O'Reilly, NBC's Matt Lauer, and

CBS/PBS's Charlie Rose—lost their jobs after being accused of sexual harassment. These high-profile cases reflect something that many journalists have known about male-dominated newsrooms for a long time: behind the scenes they can operate as a boys' club, which results in a number of negative consequences for women working in these environments.

Getting a Good Story

According to Don Hewitt, the creator and longtime executive producer of *60 Minutes*, "There's a very simple formula if you're in Hollywood, Broadway, opera, publishing, broadcasting, newspapering. It's four very simple words—tell me a story."[14] For most journalists, the bottom line is "Get the story"—an edict that overrides most other concerns. This is the standard against which many reporters measure themselves and their profession. At its best, it can provide inspiration to keep digging in order to gather perspectives that might be difficult to get or to uncover important information that someone might be trying to hide from public view. At its worst, it can lead to a variety of unethical and even criminal behaviors. It has also occasionally led journalists to make up stories, such as in the early 1980s, when former *Washington Post* reporter Janet Cooke won a Pulitzer Prize for a story she made up about a mother who contributed to the heroin addiction of her eight-year-old son (the prize was later revoked). Or in the early 2000s, when it came to light that *New York Times* reporter Jayson Blair had frequently plagiarized and fabricated stories. These more extreme cases are typically career ending and draw condemnation from the journalistic community.

Getting a Story First

In addition to getting a good story, one of the most valued achievements for a reporter is getting the story *first*. It is a badge of honor to be a reporter who can *scoop* the competition—that is, uncover and report a story before anyone else. Again, this creates a double-edged sword: It provides motivation for carrying out the necessary and sometimes difficult news-gathering tasks of reporting, but it also applies pressure that too often results in poorly researched stories, rampant misinformation, little or no fact-checking, and all-around sloppy reporting.

What's not always clear is how the public is better served by a journalist's claim to have gotten a story first. What *is* clear is that the problems that have always existed because of the pressure to get the story first have only intensified since the advent of 24/7 cable news channels, the Internet, and social media. We discuss this further later in the chapter, when we look more closely at how the entire journalism profession is changing and being challenged in the digital era.

Getting a Story "Right"

Although journalists certainly value being the first ones to uncover an interesting story and tell it in a compelling way, it would be a mistake to ignore the importance to professional journalists of getting the facts correct. Traditionally, serious journalists pride themselves on the results of careful news-gathering, ideally using multiple sources to confirm controversial information and allegations made in news stories. From the lessons learned in journalism schools to the awarding of top prizes for reporting, getting accurate information is the gold standard. More than just a professional standard, getting the truth also carries legal responsibilities. Journalists are taught that the best defense against a libel lawsuit is to be able to show that the report is factually true. However, critics are quick to point out that in practice, the gold standard isn't always met. Reasons for this can range from an honest mistake (journalists are human, after all), to deadline and workload pressures preventing adequate fact-checking, to outright lying or omission of important information due to a desire for self-promotion by sources—and sometimes by journalists themselves. In addition, journalists often face the task of sifting through information provided by public relations practitioners, who are paid (on average, 50 percent more than their journalistic counterparts) to make their clients look good to the public. As of 2016, U.S. labor statistics indicated that there were 5.2 public relations practitioners for every journalist.[15]

Other Values in Journalism

Some sociologists—including Herbert Gans, who studied the newsroom cultures of CBS, NBC, *Newsweek*, and *Time* in the 1970s—generalize that several basic "enduring values" have been historically shared by most American reporters and editors. These values include **ethnocentrism** (viewing other cultures through an American lens), **responsible capitalism** (the assumption that the main goal of business is to enhance prosperity for everyone), **small-town pastoralism** (favoring small, rural communities over big cities), and a major emphasis on **individualism** and personal stories over the operations of large institutions or organizations.[16] Many of these beliefs are still prevalent in today's more fragmented news culture, though they are undergoing shifts along with the rest of the industry.

When Values Collide: Ethics and the News Media

Up to this point, we have been talking about some of the common practices, values, and goals by which professional journalists tend to define who they are and what they do. As you might have noticed, these can sometimes conflict with one another and with the realities of gathering the news (deadlines, shrinking newsroom staffs, bigger demands on limited resources).

Journalists regularly face many such conflicts and ethical dilemmas. For example, they must decide when to protect government secrets and when to reveal those secrets to the public. They must consider whether it is ethically acceptable to use deception or invade someone's privacy in order to get information the public deserves to know, and they must guard against accepting gifts or favors in return for producing a news story or presenting a story's subject in a favorable light.

▲ Brian Williams lost his coveted spot as network anchor after he lied about coming under fire while covering the Iraq War, one of several instances in which Williams had been accused of exaggerating the truth. While this was a grave violation of journalistic ethics, NBC didn't fire him; after a six-month suspension, the network demoted him to cable news channel MSNBC. AP Photo/The Roanoke Times, Stephanie Klein-Davis

Professional Codes of Ethics

So how do journalists decide what to do in these cases? One way is to refer to sets of ethical guidelines produced by professional journalistic groups, such as the Society of Professional Journalists (SPJ), the Radio Television Digital News Association (RTDNA, formerly the Radio-Television News Directors Association), and the National Press Photographers Association (NPPA). Although each has a slightly different focus, all three instruct journalists to seek the truth, hold the powerful accountable, maintain integrity, and consider the consequences of each news report, especially for people who appear in the news. Journalism education programs typically contain stand-alone ethics courses or attempt to integrate ethics into other classes—or both. Each newsroom might have its own printed code of ethical guidelines or, more likely, might rely on veteran reporters and editors to pass along to newer journalists what's considered acceptable in that particular news department. It's also worth noting that the professional codes of ethical conduct are not etched in stone. All of these groups periodically review and update their ethics—especially now, with the new ethical dilemmas that have come with the Internet.

Applying Ethics and Values Inside the Job

Codes of ethics can be helpful, but they would be impossibly long if they were to cover every possible situation a reporter might encounter. There are even times when parts of a given code will come in conflict with one another. What's more, these dilemmas often happen when reporters are facing the crush of deadlines and daily duties. Many times, the necessity for making a quick decision means solving the dilemma in the way that has become established professional practice—that is, the way things have always been done. Although relying on the experience of the individual or the organization can be helpful and save time, it can also undermine careful critical examination of a given situation.

In addition to guidelines designed specifically for the profession, a journalist might borrow from other philosophical approaches to ethics when confronted with an ethical quandary. Although this isn't intended to be a complete list of those approaches, the next few paragraphs attempt to offer some useful examples.

The Greek philosopher Aristotle offered an early ethical concept, the "golden mean," as a guideline for seeking balance between competing positions. For Aristotle, the golden mean referred to the desirable middle ground between extreme positions. For example, Aristotle saw ambition as the golden mean between sloth and greed.

Another ethical principle entails the "categorical imperative," developed by German philosopher Immanuel Kant (1724–1804). This idea suggests that a society must adhere to moral codes that are universal and unconditional, applicable in all situations at all times. For example, the ideal to always tell the truth might lead a Kantian to argue that it's never okay to use deception to get a news story.

British philosophers Jeremy Bentham (1748–1832) and John Stuart Mill (1806–1873) promoted a general ethics principle derived from "the greatest good for the greatest number." This principle directs us "to distribute a good consequence to more people rather than to fewer, whenever we have a choice."[17]

Applying Ethics and Values Outside the Job

Although the Internet, bloggers, social media, and partisan cable stations and websites have blurred the lines between journalist and nonjournalist, most mainstream news organizations have ethical expectations of their journalists that extend beyond the hours spent on the job. The SPJ's code of ethics also warns reporters and editors not to place themselves in positions that create a **conflict of interest**—that is, situations in which journalists may stand to benefit personally from producing a story or from presenting the subject in a certain light. "Journalists should refuse gifts, favors, fees, free travel and special treatment," the code states, "and avoid political and other activities that may compromise integrity or impartiality, or may damage credibility."[18]

Many news outlets attempt to protect journalists from getting into compromising positions. For instance, in most cities, journalists do not actively participate in politics or support social causes. Some journalists will not reveal their political affiliations, and some have even declined to vote. If a journalist has a tie to any organization, and that organization is later suspected of involvement in shady or criminal activity, the reporter's ability to report fairly on the organization will be compromised—along with the credibility of the news outlet for which the reporter works. Conversely, other journalists believe that not participating in politics or social causes means abandoning one's civic obligations.

The Economics of Journalism in the Twenty-First Century

Ask almost any veteran reporter to list the challenges facing the profession of journalism, and either at or near the top will be a concern about rapidly shrinking numbers of reporters, editors, and photographers in the newsroom. Although the business models for broadcasters (see Chapters 6 and 8 for specifics on the radio and TV broadcasting industries) are not quite the same as those for print newsrooms, they do share this common concern: Budget cuts, for whatever reason, mean cuts to newsroom staff.

Back in 2001, reporters working at daily newspapers numbered over 56,000. In 2018, that number was less than 25,000, meaning a loss of more than half of the daily print news workforce. In 2017, the number of reporters working in TV news outnumbered those at daily papers for the first time, 27,100 to 25,000.[19] A closer look reveals that the number of journalists in both print and television newsrooms shrank between 2015 and 2017, but print declined faster. Yet even as print news staffs decline, the fact is that more people are reading news *from* newspapers than at any time in U.S. history; it's just that they are mostly reading the news online, delivered "free" from Google or Facebook, which rake in all the digital ad money.

Because newspapers are the legacy format for journalism and still represent the lion's share of reporting in many communities, it's important to spend some time in this chapter examining the business side of newspapers and considering what recent developments are doing to the ability of newspapers to fulfill their journalistic missions.

A Business Model in Transition

At the most basic level, the traditional business model for a commercial news enterprise looks like this: The business attracts an audience with its content (such as news) and, in turn, sells that audience's attention to advertisers, who pay for the chance to attract paying customers. If a newspaper can say it has a certain number of readers, or a broadcaster can say it has a certain number of viewers or listeners, it can attach a value to that audience. The bigger that number, the more the business providing the content can charge for an advertisement.

Although some newspapers also earn revenue by charging subscription fees, it became clear by the end of the nineteenth century that keeping subscription prices relatively low helped increase audience size (or *circulation*) and that the real money came from selling that larger audience to advertisers. Today, the majority of large daily papers devote as much as one-half to two-thirds of their pages to advertisements. What remains after the advertising department places the ads in the paper is called the **newshole**. This space is devoted to front-page news reports, special regional or topical sections, horoscopes, advice columns, crossword puzzles, and letters to the editor.

Although there were some ups and downs, this advertising-centered approach (supplemented with income from subscription fees and classified ads) worked well for newspaper businesses through the twentieth century. Around the year 2000, however, newspaper revenue began to weaken in conjunction with the digital turn: Audiences were seeking out free versions of news articles online, and people could place ads for free on sites like craigslist, rather than paying newspapers to run classified ads. Then, when the Great Recession hit in 2007, the advertising revenue bottom really fell out, as major advertisers cut back their ad spending. Since then, the numbers have continued to fall: In 2017, estimated ad revenue in the newspaper industry was $16.48 billion, the lowest it had been since 1980 (see Figure 3.1).[20]

While the digital turn has created significant challenges for the news industry, newspapers and other traditional news media are attempting to find ways to

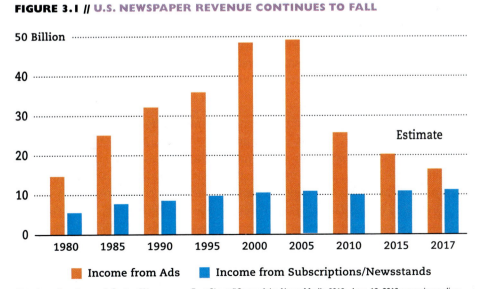

FIGURE 3.1 // U.S. NEWSPAPER REVENUE CONTINUES TO FALL

Data from: Pew Research Center, "Newspapers Fact Sheet," State of the News Media 2018, *June 13, 2018, www.journalism.org/fact-sheet/newspapers.*

▲ The *New York Times* is one of the papers trying to balance the need to generate income with the need to not anger readers who are accustomed to receiving free content on the Internet. The *Times* uses a hybrid paywall model, in which users can access a number of articles online each month for free, after which they would need to buy a subscription. By early 2019, the *Times* reported more than 3.3 million digital-only subscriptions for its news products.

generate revenue online. Though still a far cry from replacing traditional advertising dollars, digital revenue is increasing as a percentage of newspaper revenue (although that increase is due more to the precipitous fall of print ads than to a huge jump in online revenue). According to the Pew Research Center, among newspapers owned by publicly traded companies (which are required to publish revenue data), 31 percent of advertising revenue was coming from digital operations by 2017.[21]

In addition to online advertising, some news sites are trying to make money by using a **paywall**, a subscription fee that allows access to articles. Paywalls can be controversial and unpopular with potential readers who are used to getting free content online. To balance this, the *New York Times* and other newspaper operations have gone to a hybrid model, in which a person would be able to access a limited number of articles for free each month but need a paid subscription to access additional articles or other premium products.

News companies are also finding ways to cater to readers' increasingly digital lifestyles, developing material for platforms like tablets or smartphones. In some cases, digital subscription rates are also tailored, depending on the device (and app) the reader is going to use.

Newspaper Operations

Like any other enterprise, a newspaper has to spend money to fulfill its mission. Its costs include salaries and wages and any investments in wire services or feature syndication required to offer content for readers.

Salaries, Wages, and Shareholder Concerns

A major expense for most newspapers comes in the form of salaries and wages paid to the various editors and reporters working for the paper, although in the last fifteen years, newspapers have shrunk not only their newshole but the size of their reporting staffs. Traditionally, most large papers have a publisher and an owner, an editor in chief, a managing editor in charge of the daily news-gathering and writing processes, and assistant editors and news managers running different news divisions. These key divisions include features, sports, photos, local news, state news, and a wire service containing much of the day's national and international news reports.

Reporters work for editors. *General assignment reporters* handle all sorts of stories that might emerge (or break) on a given day. *Specialty reporters* are assigned to particular beats (police, courts, schools, local and national government) or topics (education, religion, health, environment, technology). On large dailies, *bureau reporters* file reports from other major cities. In addition, large daily papers feature columnists and critics who cover various aspects of culture, such as books, television, movies, and food. Since 2000, some newspapers have added staff solely responsible for online operations, although newsroom cuts have increasingly led to the shifting of these duties to on-staff reporters and editors.

In addition to paying the salaries and wages of employees, publicly traded companies have to consider how to pay dividends to keep shareholders happy, as well as how to compensate top executives. This can cause some troubling headlines for these companies. For example, newspaper powerhouse Gannett has repeatedly been criticized for giving out millions of dollars in executive pay packages after laying off thousands of reporters over the last decade.

Wire Services and Feature Syndication

To provide adequate coverage of important events from other places, many newspapers rely on wire services and syndicated feature services to supplement their own local coverage. A few major dailies, such as the *New York Times*, run their own wire services, selling their stories to other papers to reprint. Other agencies, such as the Associated Press (AP), United Press International (UPI), Reuters, and Agence France-Presse, have hundreds of staffers stationed throughout major U.S. cities and world capitals. These agencies submit stories, photos, and videos each day for distribution across the country, and sometimes internationally.

Daily papers generally pay monthly fees for access to all wire stories. Although they use only a fraction of what's available, editors carefully monitor wire services for important stories and ideas for local angles.

In addition, newspapers may contract with **feature syndicates**, such as Andrews McMeel Syndication and Tribune Content Agency, to provide work from the nation's best political writers, editorial cartoonists, comic-strip artists, and self-help columnists. These companies serve as brokers, distributing horoscopes and crossword puzzles as well as the columns and comic strips that appeal to a wide audience.

Consolidation and a Crash

As we saw earlier in this section, the 2007 economic crash had a serious impact on the newspaper industry's ability to raise ad revenue. But the recession also had another key impact on the industry—specifically, on the financial health of the country's newspaper chains.

launchpadworks.com

Newspapers and the Internet: Convergence

This video discusses the ways newspapers are adapting to online delivery of news.

Discussion: What kinds of skills are needed to be effective in the online world? What skills might remain the same?

Newspaper chains—newspapers in different cities owned by the same person or company—have been around since the late 1800s. By the 1980s, more than 130 chains owned an average of nine papers each, with the twelve largest chains accounting for 40 percent of total circulation in the United States. This trend continued to pick up steam through the end of the twentieth century, and by the early 2000s, the top ten chains controlled over half the nation's total newspaper circulation. Gannett, the nation's largest chain by circulation, owns over 100 daily papers in thirty-four states, as well as the national newspaper *USA Today*. In recent years, private equity firms—including Alden Capital, Citadel, Digital First Media, and GateHouse—have bought hundreds of U.S. newspapers, then cut jobs and journalism to increase short-term profit margins. Today, GateHouse (with newspapers such as the *Providence Journal*, the *Columbus Dispatch*, and the *Austin American-Statesman*) and Digital First Media (with the *San Jose Mercury News*, the *Denver Post*, and the *Boston Herald*) are the leading chains by number of newspapers owned.[22]

As large media corporations were adding up the numbers of newspapers (and often radio and television stations) they owned, they were also adding up the amount of money they were borrowing to make those purchases. Through the 1990s and the first few years of the 2000s, newspapers typically made enough money to make payments on these *leveraged* purchases. And then the economy started to tank in 2007.

As newspaper revenue from ads and subscriptions began to drop dramatically, large chains went from *leveraged* to *overleveraged*, no longer able to keep up with loan payments. In some cases, this meant filing bankruptcy; in other cases, it meant being forced to sell off newspapers or shutting down altogether. Although some smaller newspaper owners avoided being overleveraged, they still had to deal with the reality of shrinking revenues. Thus, the industry-wide reaction has been to cut costs by laying off huge numbers of editors, reporters, and photographers.

More than just bad news for the workers who lost their jobs, this trend raises concerns for the communities these papers are meant to serve. The newspaper industry as a whole lacks competition nationwide, as almost all the cities that once had multiple competing dailies have lost all but one of those daily papers. Critics and journalists worry about the ability of the remaining journalists to meet the information needs of local communities (see "Media Literacy Case Study: Investigative Journalism: In the 'Spotlight'" on pages 68–69). Additionally, the coverage of national and state politics has dropped, as bureaus at the national and state capitols were among the first victims of budget cuts.

Changes, Challenges, and Threats to Journalism Today

At the beginning of this chapter, we talked about how understanding the current state of journalism and the news media requires developing a sense of the history that got us to the present day. In this section, we discuss a series of recent developments that influence journalism today, affecting the ways that audiences consume and understand news as well as the ways that journalists do their jobs. Consider the meaning of these new developments—the impact of social media, the development of citizen journalism, the creation of satirical news, the proliferation of fake news, and attacks on journalists across the nation and the world—through the lens of this history. Does new technology change the core mission for journalists or their place in a democratic society? What does the history of journalism leading up to the present day suggest about the future of news? How might these changes and challenges affect the mission of journalists to cover their communities?

Social Media

One of the fastest-growing areas of research among those who study journalism involves trying to determine what the rise of social media sites means to journalism and journalists. This is because, in a little over a decade, it has become increasingly common for all types of news organizations—from high school newspapers to TV networks—to develop a comprehensive social media presence and strategy.

Using Social Media to Gather and Share News

The vast majority of news operations use social networking sites like Facebook, Twitter, and Instagram to promote their work, hoping readers will share articles and stories. Typically, journalists, reporters, anchors, and editors are required to have accounts at

▼News organizations like CNN use social media as part of their regular coverage, often combining photo and video elements and links to more detailed information. These organizations often require their journalists to have a public presence on social media platforms such as Twitter. There is an old saying in TV news: "Go where the eyeballs are."

these sites for use as part of their reporting duties, from sharing work to finding sources for stories. Social media has also changed the way people consume the news. Roughly 93 percent of Americans get at least some of their news online, and in 2017, 67 percent of Americans got at least some of that news from social media sites.[23]

Social media is also changing the way some nonjournalists contribute to news content. Because of the immediacy and accessibility of social media, users can post tweets, photos, and videos of protests, accidents, natural disasters, and even crimes, right as they happen. At the same time, this immediacy removes the ability to fact-check, as well as other benefits that come from thorough reporting. In addition, the accessibility of these platforms has contributed to the capacity for user manipulation. This was demonstrated throughout the 2016 U.S. presidential election, when *bots*—computer-generated accounts and pages on Twitter and Facebook—were used to advocate certain ideas, support campaigns, and promote propaganda, and may have had a direct hand in influencing the election.[24]

Finally, social media can be used by famous and influential people to drive the news narrative. A prominent example of this is the way President Trump's tweets make news on a daily basis. For the first two years of his presidency, he tweeted almost every morning, and for the rest of the day the national news media spent their time dissecting his tweets. As a number of media critics have noted, one result of the coverage of President Trump's tweeting habits has been that many important national news stories were neglected, overlooked, or under-covered.

Blogging and News Aggregation

Another digital-turn development for journalism is the rise of the blog. A form of social media, blogging (which derives its name from a combination of *web* and *log*) started out as the practice of writing a kind of journal that anyone could share online. But what began in the late 1990s and early 2000s as amateur sideline journalism has now become a major source of news. In fact, many reporters now write a blog in addition to their regular newspaper, television, or radio work. And some big-name newspapers, such as the *Washington Post* and the *New York Times*, even hire journalists to blog exclusively for their websites.

A close cousin of blogging is *news aggregation*, which occurs when sites (including blogs) gather and sometimes repackage news and information from more traditional news sources. This can take the form of sites like Google News or Apple News, which curate and constantly update the news, with multiple sources listed for big stories. Or it can involve sources that post a summary of a news story or an article by another reporter. News aggregation isn't always popular with the journalists who produce the original stories, who argue that aggregators benefit from advertising driven by viewer clicks, but pay little or nothing to the reporters or news outlets who did the actual work.

Citizen Journalism

The combination of the online news surge and traditional newsroom cutbacks has led to a phenomenon known as **citizen journalism** (also called *citizen media* or *community journalism*). As a grassroots movement, citizen journalism refers to people—activist amateurs and concerned citizens, not professional journalists—who use the Internet and blogs to disseminate news and information.

▲ One way technology has allowed citizens to become involved in the reporting of news is through smartphone photos and videos. Witnesses can now pass on what they have captured to mainstream news sources. Boris Roessler/picture alliance/Getty Images

Although the formal citizen journalism movement has cooled off since the early 2000s, social media and smartphones have made it easier than ever for average people to engage in citizen journalism, since anyone can take photos or record video if something newsworthy happens nearby. Sometimes these pictures and videos are shared first with traditional media outlets, who then disseminate them to the public. Other times the person who shot the video will upload it directly to social media, where it may go viral.

Some of the most notable videos of this kind document interactions between police officers and members of the public, who are often African American, as in the cases of Eric Garner, Sandra Bland, Walter Scott, and Philando Castile. In all these cases, smartphone videos created a different narrative from what was documented in police reports.

Satiric Journalism

In 2016, comedian Samantha Bee won the Television Critics Association award for Outstanding Achievement in News & Information with her satirical show *Full Frontal*, beating out traditional journalistic offerings from CNN and PBS. By 2018, the TCA had introduced a new category: Outstanding Achievement in Sketch/Variety Shows. The nominees in this category included Bee, as well as other comedians known for their emphasis on political content, including Stephen Colbert, Jimmy Kimmel, Seth Meyers, and John Oliver (who took home the award).

▲ Satirical news has become something of a cottage industry in recent years, stemming from *Saturday Night Live*'s Weekend Update segment and *The Daily Show*. After a successful stint as a *Daily Show* "correspondent," Samantha Bee has captured critical and popular praise for her solo effort *Full Frontal with Samantha Bee*. Everett Collection, Inc

As the TCA awards demonstrate, while the tradition of regularly satirizing news goes back at least to the mid-1970s with the sketch comedy program *Saturday Night Live*, more recently we've entered what journalist, historian, and author Malcolm Gladwell calls "the Golden Age of satire."[25] In America, this "golden age" hit its stride with the work of Jon Stewart on *The Daily Show with Jon Stewart* (now *The Daily Show with Trevor Noah*, after Noah took over in 2015). Using humor to criticize news conventions and the political system, *The Daily Show* employs a combination of monologue, reports from comedians acting as correspondents, and interviews. The show is also remarkable for having launched numerous variations on the theme of news satire, as well as the careers of the biggest names in this genre. Colbert (*The Colbert Report* and now *The Late Show with Stephen Colbert*), Oliver (*Last Week Tonight*), Hasan Minhaj (*Patriot Act with Hasan Minhaj*), Bee, and Noah himself are all past writers and "correspondents" who worked on the program.

These comedians repeatedly reject the label of "journalist," and as news court jesters, they display more amazement, irony, outrage, laughter, and skepticism than would be acceptable for real anchors. Still, they keep winning journalistic awards and garnering "serious" attention for their work.

This isn't to say that satirical news could, or even should, be considered a replacement for solid journalism. As Gladwell points out, satire can also undermine its own biting commentary through the laughs it generates. Media researchers have also noted that audiences can, and sometimes do, interpret satire in the opposite way from how it was intended. For example, Heather LaMarre and colleagues found that when Stephen Colbert was pretending to be an over-the-top right-wing talk-show host on the *Colbert Report* as a way to mock conservative narratives, some conservative audiences thought he was really poking fun at the left side of the political spectrum.[26]

Fake News

News sources like *The Daily Show* or *Full Frontal* aren't inherently designed to deceive: Their audiences are largely in on the joke and appreciate the programs' satirical messages. But another kind of fake news has a much darker purpose:

to intentionally mislead audiences for political or financial gain. In addition, the "fake news" label has been used to attack legitimate news outlets that dispute a particular version of the truth.

The Real Fakes

Though a growing problem for many years, fake news exploded into global consciousness during the 2016 U.S. presidential race. Countless online fake news articles attacking Democratic candidate Hillary Clinton were shared over social media sites like Facebook—articles that got hundreds of millions of views—leading to accusations that they played a role in tipping the election toward Republican candidate Donald Trump. These articles came from sites across the globe: More than one hundred pro-Trump sites were tracked to a single town in Macedonia, for example, while others were tracked to American sources intent on exploiting gullible readers to get advertising dollars.[27] (See also "The Digital Turn Case Study: Attacking Journalism: Trolls and State-Sponsored Troll Armies" on page 92.) One such source, Jestin Coler, told reporters that he makes between $10,000 and $30,000 a month from advertisers by getting people to click on and share his sites' invented stories.[28]

In addition to speculation that it influenced the presidential election, there have been other frightening consequences from the deluge of fake news. In December 2016, twenty-eight-year-old Edgar Maddison Welch entered a Washington, D.C., restaurant and opened fire with an assault rifle. (Luckily no one was hit, and Welch was arrested.) He did so because he believed a false conspiracy theory ("Pizzagate"), which accused Hillary Clinton of running a child sex ring out of the pizzeria.[29]

Giving Real News the "Fake" Label

As early as December 2016, media critics such as those at the *Columbia Journalism Review* were questioning the use of the phrase "fake news," fearing that it could too easily be co-opted and lose its meaning.[30] Indeed, following the election of Donald Trump, the phrase began to take on newer meanings. As the BBC reported, "All sorts of things—misinformation, spin, conspiracy theories, mistakes, and reporting that people just don't like—have been rolled into it."[31] In fact, as the BBC report suggests, President Trump managed to expand the definition to encompass any news report or news analysis—evidence based or not—that he did not like, especially those that portrayed his administration in a negative light (see also "The Troubled Future of Journalism" later in the chapter). Using the "fake news" label to refer to legitimate journalism can further muddy the already-murky online waters that contain actual fake news and propaganda. This alternate usage of "fake news" also helps undermine the public's already eroding trust in the news media, at a time when we need information sources we can count on—for example, as we face global problems ranging from climate change to the resurgence of fascism.

The Digital Turn

CASE STUDY

Attacking Journalism: Trolls and State-Sponsored Troll Armies

The prevalence of social media makes it necessary for today's reporters to have a robust online presence, but too often journalists find themselves experiencing an unpleasant element of the Internet's dark side: online harassment. "'I hope you get raped and killed,' one person wrote to me just this week," said MSNBC reporter Katy Tur. "And not just me, but a couple of my female colleagues as well."[1]

The harassment journalists experience can include threats via e-mail or Twitter, as well as more direct attacks, like the hacking of social media accounts and *doxxing*—the public release of personal information, such as addresses, social security numbers, and medical information. And while online attacks can happen to any reporter, recent research shows that women journalists face three times more online harassment than their male colleagues, and that this harassment tends to be much more graphic and sexualized.[2]

Where does this harassment come from? According to a 2018 report from Reporters Sans Frontières (Reporters Without Borders), some attacks arise from international state-sponsored systems of intimidation aimed directly at journalists. A number of authoritarian states have set up their own armies of *trolls* and *bots*—programs that use fake social media accounts to generate or share posts for a specific purpose. Regimes use nongovernmental groups and communities to work behind the scenes to discredit or attack journalists: "Among these new information mercenaries are the Vietnamese cyber-soldiers, the Russian troll-factories, the Chinese 'little pinks,' . . . 'white trolls' in Turkey, . . . [and] Iran's cyber-guardians."[3]

For these authoritarian regimes, using a troll army to target, discredit, and threaten journalists who work to expose wrongdoing is a relatively cheap and easy way to maintain control and undermine attempts at public scrutiny. For example, after Finnish investigative journalist Jessikka Aro wrote a story on the Russian "troll farms," she was targeted with threats and doctored photographs portraying her pornographically. Russia has also been caught using its troll army as a social media propaganda machine to interfere in elections, such as the 2016 U.S. presidential election.

However, this harassment is not just international—it can be domestic as well. President Trump has stoked the fires of anti-media resentment among his supporters, some of whom have begun to harass journalists in response. Tur explained why she believed this last scenario is what happened to her: "The most recent note I got ended with [Make America Great Again]," a popular Trump slogan.

When journalists face attacks, either domestically or abroad, the goal is usually the same: to discourage or silence those who work to report the facts. Ultimately, media experts worry about the chilling effect this could have on reporting: If journalists are intimidated into leaving the profession, or if they begin to avoid pursuing exposés that could get them targeted, how will the world's most important stories continue to be told?

Web Clip

YouTube.com has many videos that address attacks on journalism. For example, do a search for "World Press Freedom Day: Journalism Under Attack?" posted by Al Jazeera English. How might our understanding of the world change if journalists weren't willing to take risks for their reporting?

Journalism in a Democratic Society

Journalism is central to democracy: Both citizens and the media must have access to the information needed to make important decisions. Conventional journalists will fight ferociously for the principles that underpin journalism's basic tenets: questioning the government, freedom of the press, the public's right to know, and two sides to every story. However, they do not generally acknowledge any moral or ethical duty to improve the quality of daily civic life, leaving that work to political groups, nonprofit organizations, and individual citizens. Regardless of whether journalists should be observers or advocates, the profession is entering a new era marked by anti-journalism propaganda and threats of violence—challenges that ultimately serve to underscore journalism's crucial role in a functioning democracy.

Social Responsibility

Although reporters have traditionally thought of themselves primarily as observers and recorders, some journalists have acknowledged a social responsibility. Among them was James Agee in the 1930s. In his book *Let Us Now Praise Famous Men*, which was accompanied by the Depression-era photography of Walker Evans, Agee regarded conventional journalism as dishonest, partly because the act of observing intruded on people and turned them into story characters that newspapers and magazines exploited for profit.

Agee also worried that readers would retreat into the comfort of his writing—his narrative—instead of confronting what for many families was the horror of the Great Depression. For Agee, the question of responsibility extended not only to journalism and to himself but to the readers of his stories as well.

Professional conflicts over the ethical way to practice journalism remain. On one end of the spectrum, some journalists refuse to even vote in elections, lest it hurt their ability to remain detached from the politics they cover. These journalists value giving equal time to both sides of a controversial issue, and they argue that failing to remain vigilant against bias and partisanship will set journalism on a slippery slope that begins with sloppy reporting and ends with blatant lies and propaganda.

On the other end of the spectrum, there are those who believe that in addition to providing information, journalists should evaluate that information for the audience and put it into proper historical context. These journalists have increasingly voiced concern over what they call "false equivalency"—the idea that in order to remain balanced, opposing viewpoints should be presented as if they carry the same relative weight of supporting evidence or scientific consensus. For example, for decades most mainstream media covering climate change gave equal time to those who warned of the dangers of global warming and those who claimed it was a hoax. The problem isn't that news stories acknowledged climate change deniers but that their point of view was presented in a fashion that would lead the audience to believe it was equally valid—despite the fact that more than 97 percent of all climate experts say human behavior is causing the earth to warm at an alarming rate.[32]

As this example illustrates, reporters face challenges in informing the public about issues that may have enormous consequences for generations to come. Because citizens vote for political leaders who set public policy on issues like climate change, the importance of journalists getting the story right is clear.

The Troubled Future of Journalism

While pondering the future of journalism—and of our democracy—we must recognize that a free press isn't free, nor is its survival certain. As newsroom cutbacks accelerate; as state, national, and foreign bureaus close down; and as anti-journalism rhetoric grows stronger, we must ask ourselves where we will get the thorough reporting we need to make informed choices and present well-considered viewpoints—two hallmarks of a vibrant democracy.

Fewer Outlets, Concentrated Ownership

A host of current developments in print and broadcast journalism undermine the journalist's role as a bulwark of democracy. Many cities now have just one newspaper, which tends to cover only issues and events of interest to middle- and upper-middle-class readers. The experiences and events affecting poorer and working-class citizens get short shrift, and with the rise of newspaper chains, the chances that mainstream daily papers will publish a diversity of opinions, ideas, and information will likely decrease.

Moreover, chain ownership—often concerned first about saving money—has tended to discourage watchdog journalism, the most expensive type of reporting. And ownership issues have raised questions about editorial autonomy, as evidenced by the actions of Sinclair Broadcasting, the largest owner of local television stations in America. In April 2018, a viral video showed anchors from the company's stations across the country reciting, word for word, what appeared to be local independent commentary. In reality, the anchors were required by Sinclair to recite this copy, which echoed conservative talking points about bias and "false news." At the time, Sinclair owned 193 stations in more than 100 television markets.[33] Incidents like these mean that we, as citizens, must remain ever mindful of our news sources and not only consider the motivations and interests concealed behind the news we're receiving but also ask ourselves why we're receiving it.

Anti-journalism Propaganda and Threats of Violence

Journalists, historians, and others from America and abroad have also raised the alarm following a series of escalating attacks on news media critical of President Trump (see "The Digital Turn Case Study: Attacking Journalism: Trolls and State-Sponsored Troll Armies" on page 92). Of course, Trump didn't invent attacks on the press; the earliest political parties in America had their own partisan press and could be virulently critical of opposing parties and their newspapers. But in modern times, Trump's anti-media rhetoric is an unprecedented political tactic, where Trump-friendly media and commentators are deemed "good" and media that do critical or investigative reporting are attacked as "the enemy of the people."[34] Many media critics were alarmed by the demonization of journalism in a nation founded on a free press. "'Enemy of the people' is an incendiary phrase," said National Public Radio host Scott Simon in August 2018. "It's been uttered by some of history's most vicious thugs . . . to vilify their opponents, who were often murdered. President Trump must know that history by now when he calls the press the 'enemy of the people.'"[35]

This repeated vilification of the press was on many journalists' minds when a gunman walked into a newspaper in Annapolis, Maryland, in June 2018 and killed five people. While the shooter had an ongoing feud with the paper, some worried that the attack was partially fueled by the anti-journalism atmosphere.[36] Additional violent incidents against the press have continued, with a California man threatening to kill journalists at the *Boston Globe* in August 2018 ("You're the enemy of the people. . . . I'm going to shoot you in the head"), and a Florida man mailing pipe bombs to Democratic leaders, donors, and CNN's New York office in October 2018.[37] According to the U.S. Press Freedom Tracker, forty-two journalists were attacked and five were killed in 2018.[38] Critics have also argued that disparaging journalists in the United States emboldens other countries to act against critical journalists, such as the 2018 case in which Saudi Arabian journalist Jamal Khashoggi, a U.S. resident and writer for the *Washington Post*, was brutally murdered inside the Saudi consulate in Turkey.

That doesn't mean, however, that journalists have stopped reminding politicians and the public about the integral role of a free press in a democracy. In a statement released after a meeting with President Trump, *New York Times* publisher A. G. Sulzberger noted, "I made it clear repeatedly that I was not asking [Trump] to soften his attacks on the *Times* if he felt our coverage was unfair. Instead, I implored him to reconsider his broader attacks on journalism, which I believe are dangerous and harmful to our country."[39] Just three weeks into the Trump administration, after the president had said he was at war with the media, *Washington Post* editor Marty Baron argued that his newspaper was covering the president the same way it would cover any other president: "The way I view it is, we're not at war with the administration, we're at work. We're doing our jobs."[40]

Nevertheless, journalism needs to be mindful of addressing the concerns of all citizens as it moves forward. Many people feel cut off from major institutions, including journalism. As a result, some citizens are looking to take part in public conversations and civic debates—to renew a democracy in which many voices participate. Good journalism can help this key function of democracy work: It makes sense of key issues, documents events, keeps watch over our central institutions, and tells a community's significant stories. In the partisan era in which we now live, overloaded with decontextualized information and undocumented punditry, these skills are more important than ever. Good journalism and compelling stories will eventually save and sustain the profession, no matter how the marketplace continues to fracture.

CHAPTER ESSENTIALS

Review

- The social impact of **news**—the process by which people gather information and create narrative reports to make sense of events surrounding them—accelerated with the invention of the printing press, eventually making possible a **partisan press** in the American colonies, which helped spread different political ideas.

- An industrial revolution and a rising middle class helped transform American newspapers through the nineteenth century. **Penny papers** helped boost circulation, enabling newspapers to reach the status of mass medium, and **wire services** like the Associated Press used telegraph lines to relay information to multiple newspapers around the country and the world.

- As newspapers and their audiences grew larger from the nineteenth into the twentieth century, various styles of journalism emerged, including sensationalist **yellow journalism** and the **inverted pyramid** style of **objective journalism**. As the twentieth century progressed, some looked to **interpretive journalism** to help explain the complexities of an increasingly global society.

- Throughout the twentieth century and into the twenty-first, as radio, television, and later the Internet entered the scene, the practice of journalism moved into each new realm, drawing on and adapting previous practices for new platforms.

- Journalism has developed a professional culture and a set of criteria that help journalists decide what is **newsworthy** and therefore fit to fill the **newshole** in their papers. This culture comes with certain values, which include neutrality; newsroom diversity; and the drive to get a good story, to get the story first, and to get the story right. This culture also comes with ethical standards, such as the need to avoid **conflicts of interest**.

- Journalism, while a vital part of a functioning democracy, faces serious challenges in today's media landscape. One of the biggest challenges is the steady reduction in newsroom staffs, due in part to loss of revenue from traditional advertising. Some companies are using digital ad revenue and online **paywalls** to regain some of this income.

LaunchPad

Visit LaunchPad for *Media Essentials* at **launchpadworks.com** for additional learning tools:

- **REVIEW WITH LEARNINGCURVE**
  LearningCurve adaptive quizzing helps you master the concepts you need to learn from this chapter.
- **VIDEO: THE OBJECTIVITY MYTH**
  Pulitzer Prize–winning journalist Clarence Page and *Onion* editor Joe Randazzo explore how objectivity began in journalism and how reporter biases may nonetheless influence news stories.
- **MEDIA LITERACY PRACTICE**
  This activity challenges you to develop a critical perspective and apply it to everyday encounters with communication media.

- Other changes and challenges for journalism in the information age include the development of social media sites, citizen journalism, the proliferation of satirical and "fake" news, and attacks on journalists and the institution of journalism.

- As the fate of print journalism is called into question, we must continue to ask ourselves where we will get the information we need, based on strong reporting, to make informed choices and present thoroughly considered points of view.

Key Terms

news, p. 59
partisan press, p. 59
penny papers, p. 61
human-interest stories, p. 61
wire services, p. 63
inverted pyramid, p. 63
yellow journalism, p. 63
objective journalism, p. 66
interpretive journalism, p. 67
newsworthy, p. 74
ethnocentrism, p. 79
responsible capitalism, p. 79
small-town pastoralism, p. 79
individualism, p. 79
conflict of interest, p. 81
newshole, p. 83
paywall, p. 84
feature syndicates, p. 85
newspaper chains, p. 86
citizen journalism, p. 89

Study Questions

1. How did newspapers emerge as a mass medium during the penny press era? How did content changes make this happen?

2. What different models of journalism developed? What are their characteristics? What are their strengths and limitations?

3. What are some of the differences between the practices of print and broadcast journalism? How might the changes to journalism as it entered the broadcasting age be similar to or different from the changes currently happening to journalism in the Information Age?

4. Describe and discuss some of the business challenges faced by newspapers today.

5. How has the definition of *fake news* changed in recent years, and what meaning does that term have today?

6. What does it mean for a U.S. president to call journalists who are critical of him "enemies of the people"?

7. What is journalism's role in a democracy?

Mass Media Industries

4

Magazines in the Age of Specialization

101
The Early History of Magazines

103
The Evolution of Modern American Magazines

110
Types of Magazines: Domination of Specialization

115
The Organization and Economics of Magazines

120
Magazines in a Democratic Society

Considering that since the 1960s, *Cosmopolitan* has been effectively marketing itself to single women ages eighteen to thirty-four, it shouldn't be surprising that the publication is one of the most popular magazines among undergraduate college women. (Of the fourteen million women who read *Cosmopolitan* in 2018, almost two million were undergraduates.)[1] What might be surprising is that a college student reading today's *Cosmopolitan*, currently famous for revealing cover photographs and headlines like "67 New Sex Tricks," might have a subscription to the same magazine that her great-great-great grandmother subscribed to. Of course, other than the title, the two magazines don't have much in common.

The 1886 version of *Cosmopolitan* was also targeted to women—though more often to married women, with articles on cooking, child care, and household decoration. When it did feature fashion, it was of the high-collared Victorian-era variety.[2] The magazine struggled until it was rescued by journalist and entrepreneur John Brisben Walker, who turned it into an illustrated literary and journalistic magazine.

◀ Helen Gurley Brown was the editor in chief of *Cosmopolitan* magazine for over thirty years, beginning in 1965. Her vision—to create a magazine for young, single, professional women—helped make the publication an international success. Santi Visalli/Archive Photos/Getty Images

99

The magazine grew in prestige and earnings until it was sold at a profit in 1905 to powerful newspaper publisher William Randolph Hearst. The new owner turned *Cosmopolitan* into a muckraking magazine focused on digging up dirt against big business and corrupt politicians. Although this new focus didn't boost Hearst's political ambitions in the way that he'd hoped, it did help the magazine continue to grow and thrive. Despite this success, however, *Cosmopolitan* continued to change alongside the tastes of its readership. After 1912, the magazine returned to its literary past, featuring short stories and serialized novels largely targeted toward a female audience. This worked for a while, but by the 1960s, this format was losing interest among subscribers.

In 1965, the Hearst Corporation hired Helen Gurley Brown, who had recently written the best-selling book *Sex and the Single Girl*. Brown modeled the magazine on the book's vision of strong, sexually liberated women. The new *Cosmopolitan*, in its fifth iteration, helped spark a sexual revolution and was marketed to the "Cosmo Girl": women ages eighteen to thirty-four with an interest in love, sex, fashion, and their careers.[3]

Brown's vision of *Cosmo* lives on in the magazine's "fun fearless female" slogan, and today it's the top-selling women's fashion magazine. It also maintains a popular website and a mobile version for reading on smartphones. *Cosmopolitan*'s ability to reinvent itself repeatedly for over 130 years testifies to the remarkable power of magazines as a mass medium to both adapt to and shape American society and culture.

SINCE THE 1740s, magazines have played a key role in America, becoming a national mass medium even before newspapers, which at the time were mainly local and regional in scope. Magazines provided venues for political leaders and thinkers to offer their views on the broad issues and events of the day, including public education, abolition, women's suffrage, and the Civil War. Many leading literary figures also used magazines to gain public exposure for their essays or stories. Readers consumed the articles and fictional accounts offered in magazines, and snapped up the products and services advertised in each issue, hastening the rise of a consumer society. As consumerism grew, magazines themselves changed, with the most popular titles often focusing less on news and essays and more on fashion, celebrities, advice, and entertainment.

Today, more than twenty thousand magazines are published in the United States annually. And just like newspapers, these magazines—including *Cosmopolitan*—have met the digital turn by taking increasingly more content online and adapting that content for use on mobile devices.

In this chapter, we will track the shifting role of magazines in the United States by:

- tracing the early history of magazines, including their highly politicized purpose in colonial and early America and their transformation into the country's first national medium

- examining turning points in the evolution of modern American magazines, such as the emergence of muckraking as a magazine-reporting style and the rise and fall of general-interest magazines

- taking stock of the many types of magazines specialized for particular audiences (including men, women, sports fans, young people, and minorities)

- discovering how magazines are organized and how they operate economically, including how they make money

- considering how magazines today are affecting the health of our democratic society

The Early History of Magazines

launchpadworks.com

Use **LearningCurve** to review concepts from this chapter.

Magazines have changed extensively during their journey to mass medium status. They started out in Europe as infrequently published periodicals that looked like newspapers and contained mostly political commentary. They caught on slowly in colonial America and served mostly as vehicles for politicians (such as John Adams and Thomas Jefferson) and thinkers (including Thomas Paine) to convey their views. It wasn't until the nineteenth century that magazines really took off in America. During the 1800s, magazines took the form of specialized and general-interest periodicals that appealed to an increasingly literate populace, that could be published quickly through improved printing technologies, and that boasted arresting illustrations.

Today, the word **magazine** broadly refers to any collection of articles, stories, and advertisements published on a nondaily cycle (such as weekly or monthly) in the smaller tabloid style rather than the larger newspaper style.

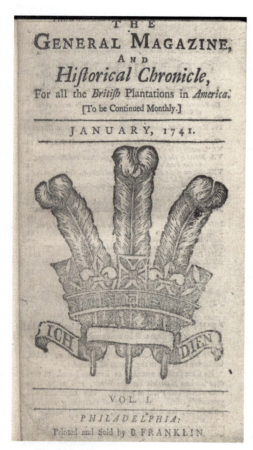

▲ The first issue of Benjamin Franklin's *General Magazine, and Historical Chronicle* appeared in 1741. Although it lasted only six months, Franklin found success with other publications, like his annual *Poor Richard's Almanack*, which appeared in 1732 and lasted twenty-five years. Library of Congress, Prints & Photographs Division, Reproduction number LC-USZ62-58140 (b&w film copy neg.)

The First Magazines: European Origins

The first magazines appeared in seventeenth-century France in the form of bookseller catalogues and notices that book publishers inserted in newspapers. (In fact, the word *magazine* derives from the French term *magasin*, meaning "storehouse.") Magazines soon became channels for political commentary and argument in Europe. They looked like newspapers of the time, but they were published less frequently. The first political magazine, called the *Review*, appeared in London in 1704 and was printed sporadically until 1713.

At around the same time, regularly published magazines such as the *Tatler* and the *Spectator* appeared, offering poetry, politics, and philosophy to London's elite. The first publication to use the term *magazine* was *Gentleman's Magazine*, which appeared in London in 1731 and consisted of articles reprinted from newspapers, books, and political pamphlets.

Magazines in Eighteenth-Century America: The Voices of Revolution

Without a substantial middle class, widespread literacy, or advanced printing technology, magazines took root slowly in America. Like the partisan newspapers of the time, colonial magazines served politicians, the educated, and the merchant class. However, they also served the wider purpose of conveying colonial leaders' thoughts about the big questions percolating during the era, such as how taxation should work, how much self-rule the colonies should have, how Indians should be treated, and who should have access to public education. Magazines thus gave voice to the people who ultimately decided to break away from England and create a new, independent nation.

The first colonial magazines appeared in Philadelphia in 1741, about fifty years after the earliest newspapers. Andrew Bradford started it all with *American Magazine, or A Monthly View of the Political State of the British Colonies*. Three days later, Benjamin Franklin launched his *General Magazine, and Historical Chronicle*. Though neither of these experiments was successful, they inspired other publishers to launch magazines in the remaining colonies.

Magazines in Nineteenth-Century America: Specialization and General Interest

As the nineteenth century dawned, the magazine industry remained somewhat unstable in the newly created United States. Between 1800 and 1825, about five hundred periodicals had cropped up and then withered. However, as the century progressed, the idea of specialized magazines devoted to certain categories of readers gained momentum, leading to the creation of religious magazines, literary periodicals that published the works of important writers of the day, and magazines devoted to professions such as law and medicine.

The nineteenth century also saw the birth of the first general-interest magazine aimed at a large national audience: the *Saturday Evening Post*, launched in 1821. Like most magazines of the day, the early *Post* included a few original essays but reprinted most of its pieces from other sources. Eventually, however, the *Post* grew to incorporate news, poetry, essays, play reviews, and the writings of popular authors.

The *Post* was also the first major magazine to appeal directly to women through its "Lady's Friend" advice column. This new device may have served as an inspiration; in 1828, Sarah Josepha Hale started the first magazine directed exclusively to a female audience: *Ladies' Magazine*. In addition to general-interest pieces such as essays and criticism, the periodical advocated for women's education, work, and property rights. Other women's magazines—including the hugely successful *Godey's Lady's Book*—would soon follow.

▲ Colorful illustrations first became popular in the fashion sections of women's magazines in the mid-1800s. The color for this fashion image from *Godey's* was added to the illustration by hand. North Wind Picture Archives

Going National as the Twentieth Century Approaches

Thanks to increases in literacy and public education, the development of faster printing technologies, and improvements in mail delivery (through rail transportation), demand for national (versus local) magazines soared. Whereas in 1825 a mere one hundred magazines struggled for survival, by 1850 nearly six hundred magazines were being published regularly, many of them with national readerships. Magazines were on their way to becoming a mass medium.

The advent of illustration further moved magazines toward mass medium status. By the mid-1850s, drawings, engravings, woodcuts, and other forms of illustration had become a major feature of magazines and greatly heightened their appeal for readers. During the 1890s, magazines (and newspapers) also began including photographs with printed articles, helping launch an entirely new profession: photojournalism.

The Evolution of Modern American Magazines

As the sun set on the nineteenth century, decreases in postage costs made it cheaper for publishers to distribute magazines, and improvements in production technologies lowered the costs of printing them. Now accessible and affordable to ever-larger audiences, magazines became a true mass medium. They also began reflecting the social, demographic, and technological changes unfolding within the nation as the twentieth century progressed. For example, a new interest in social reform sparked the rise of *muckraking*, or investigative journalism designed to expose wrongdoing.

The growth of the middle class initially heightened receptivity to general-interest magazines aimed at broad audiences, but then television's rising popularity put many general-interest magazines out of business. Some magazines struck back by focusing their content on topics not covered by TV programmers and by featuring short articles heavily illustrated with photos.

Distribution and Production Costs Plummet

In 1870, about twelve hundred magazines were being produced in the United States; by 1890, that number had reached forty-five hundred. By 1905, the nation boasted more than six thousand magazines. A reduction in postal rates and advances in mass-production printing, conveyor systems, assembly lines, and printing press speeds lowered production costs and made large-circulation national magazines possible.

This combination of reduced distribution and production costs enabled publishers to slash magazine prices. As prices dropped from thirty-five cents to fifteen cents to ten cents, people of modest means began subscribing to national publications, and magazine circulation skyrocketed. Even though publishers had dropped the price of an issue below the actual cost of producing it, they recouped the loss through ad revenue, guaranteeing large readerships to advertisers eager to reach more customers. By the turn of the twentieth century, advertisers increasingly used national magazines to capture consumers' attention and build a national marketplace.

Muckrakers Expose Social Ills

The rise in magazine circulation coincided with major changes in American society in the early 1900s. Americans were moving from the country to the city in search of industrial jobs, and millions were immigrating to the United States, hoping for new opportunities. Many newspaper reporters interested in writing about these and other social changes turned to magazines, for which they could write longer, more analytical pieces on such topics as corruption in big business and government, urban problems faced by immigrants, labor conflicts, and race relations. Some of these writers built their careers on crusading for social reform on behalf of the public good, often criticizing long-standing American institutions in the process.

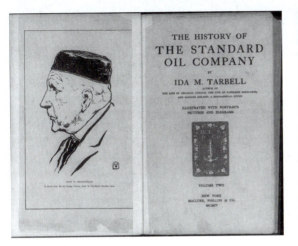 

▲ Muckrakers such as Ida Tarbell (1857–1944), who is best known for her "History of the Standard Oil Company," once remarked on why she dedicated years of her life to investigating the company: "They had never played fair, and that ruined their greatness for me." Everett Collection Inc/Alamy Stock Photo (left); Granger—All rights reserved (right)

In 1906, President Theodore Roosevelt dubbed these investigative reporters **muckrakers**, because they were willing to crawl through society's muck to uncover a story. Although Roosevelt wasn't always a fan, muckraking journalism led to some much-needed reforms. For example, influenced in part by exposés in *Ladies' Home Journal* and *Collier's* magazines, Congress in 1906 passed the Pure Food and Drug Act and the Meat Inspection Act. Reports in *Cosmopolitan*, *McClure's*, and other magazines led to laws calling for increased government oversight of business, a progressive income tax, and the direct election of U.S. senators. These reports included Ida Tarbell's "History of the Standard Oil Company" in *McClure's Magazine*, which took on John D. Rockefeller's oil monopoly.

General-Interest Magazines Hit Their Stride

The heyday of the muckraking era lasted into the mid-1910s, when America was drawn into World War I. During the next few decades and even through the 1950s, **general-interest magazines** gained further prominence. These publications were aimed at a broad national audience and covered a wide variety of topics, such as recent developments in government, medicine, or society. A key aspect of these magazines was **photojournalism**—the use of photographs to augment editorial content (see "Media Literacy Case Study: The Evolution of Photojournalism" on pages 106–107). High-quality photos gave general-interest magazines a visual advantage over radio, which was the most popular medium of the day. In 1920, about fifty-five magazines fit the general-interest category; by 1946, more than a hundred such magazines competed with radio networks for a national audience. Four giants dominated this magazine genre: the *Saturday Evening Post*, *Reader's Digest*, *Time*, and *Life*.

Media Literacy
CASE STUDY

The Evolution of Photojournalism
By Christopher R. Harris

What we now recognize as photojournalism started with the assignment of photographer Roger Fenton, of the *Sunday Times* of London, to document the Crimean War in 1856. Since then—from the earliest woodcut technology to halftone reproduction to the flexible-film camera—photojournalism's impact has been felt worldwide, capturing many historic moments and playing important political and social roles. For example, Jimmy Hare's photoreportage on the sinking of the battleship *Maine* in 1898 near Havana, Cuba, fed into growing popular support for Cuban independence from Spain and eventual U.S. involvement in the Spanish-American War. The documentary photography of Jacob Riis and Lewis Hine at the turn of the twentieth century captured the harsh working and living conditions of the nation's many child laborers; these shockingly honest photographs sparked a public outcry and resulted in new laws against the exploitation of children. In addition, *Time* magazine's coverage of the Roaring Twenties to the Great Depression and *Life*'s images from World War II and the Korean War changed the way people viewed the world.

With the advent of television, photojournalism continued to take on a significant role, bringing to the public coverage of the assassination of President John F. Kennedy in 1963 and its aftermath, as well as visual documentation of the turbulent 1960s, including aggressive photographic coverage of the Vietnam War and shocking images of the Civil Rights movement.

Into the 1970s and onward, the emergence of computer technologies raised new ethical concerns about photojournalism. These new concerns dealt primarily with the ability of photographers and photo editors to change or digitally alter the documentary aspects of a news photograph. By the late 1980s, computers could transform images into digital form, easily manipulated by sophisticated software programs. These days, any photographer can send images around the world almost instantaneously through digital transmission, and the Internet allows publication of virtually any image without censorship. Because of the absence of physical film, there is a resulting loss of proof, or veracity, of the authenticity of images. Digital images can be easily altered, and such alteration can be very difficult to detect.

A stark example of tampering with a famous image involved an Orthodox Jewish newspaper in Brooklyn that deleted then Secretary of State Hillary Clinton and Director for Counterterrorism

▶ Web Clip

YouTube.com features a number of videos about photojournalism. For example, search for "Power of Photojournalism 1/2" posted by the Reynolds Journalism Institute. How does the video define photojournalism as distinct from both regular photography and journalism in general?

Christopher R. Harris is a professor emeritus of the Department of Electronic Media Arts at Middle Tennessee State University.

"The Evolution of Photojournalism" by Christopher R. Harris. Reprinted by permission of Christopher R. Harris.

▲ Eddie Adams's Pulitzer Prize–winning photo of a general executing a suspected Vietcong terrorist during the Vietnam War is said to have turned some Americans against the war. Adams (1933–2004) later regretted the notoriety the image brought to the general, as the man he shot had just murdered eight people (including six children). AP Photo/Eddie Adams

Audrey Tomason from a photograph of President Barack Obama and other White House staff monitoring the Navy SEALs raid that killed Osama bin Laden. The paper does not publish images of women in accordance with Orthodox Jewish rules about modesty and ignored White House conditions that the supplied photo not be altered. The paper issued an apology shortly thereafter.

Have photo editors gone too far? Photojournalists and news sources are now confronted with unprecedented concerns over truth-telling. In the past, trust in documentary photojournalism rested solely on the verifiability of images as they were used in the media. Today, news sources have a variety of guidelines in place regarding image manipulation, ranging from vague requirements that the image not be changed in a misleading way to specific lists of acceptable Photoshop tools. Just as we must evaluate the words we read, we must now take a more critical eye to the images we view.

APPLYING THE CRITICAL PROCESS

DESCRIPTION Select three types of magazines (e.g., national, political, and alternative) that contain photojournalistic images. Look through these magazines, taking note of what you see.

ANALYSIS Document the patterns in each magazine. What kinds of images are included? What kinds of topics are discussed? Do certain stories or articles contain more images than others? Are the subjects generally recognizable, or do they introduce readers to new people or places? Do the images accompany an article, or are they stand-alone? Do the images appear with or without a caption?

INTERPRETATION What do these patterns mean? Talk about what you think the orientation is of each magazine based on the images. How do the photos work to achieve this view? Do the images help the magazine in terms of verification or truth-telling, or are the images there mainly to attract attention? Can images do both?

EVALUATION Do you find the motives of each magazine to be clear? Can you see any examples in which an image may have been framed or digitally altered to convey a specific point of view? What are the dangers in this? Explain.

ENGAGEMENT If you find evidence that a photo has been altered or has framed the subject in a manner that makes it less accurate, e-mail the magazine's editor and explain why you think this is a problem.

Saturday Evening Post

Although the *Post* had been around since 1821, it didn't become the first widely popular general-interest magazine until 1897. The *Post* printed popular fiction and romanticized American virtues through words and pictures. During the 1920s, it also featured articles celebrating the business boom of the decade. This reversed the journalistic direction of the muckraking era, in which magazines focused on exposing corruption in business. By the 1920s, the *Post* had reached two million in circulation, the first magazine to hit that mark.

Time

Begun in 1923, national newsmagazine *Time* developed its own brand of interpretive journalism, assigning reporter-researcher teams to cover newsworthy events, after which a rewrite editor would shape the teams' findings into articles presenting a point of view on the events covered. Newsmagazines took over photojournalism's role in news reporting by visually documenting national and international events. Today, *Time*'s print circulation stands at just over two million.

Life

More than any other magazine of its day, *Life*, an oversized pictorial weekly, struck back at radio's popularity by advancing photojournalism. Launched in 1936, *Life* satisfied the public's fascination with images by featuring extensive photo spreads. By the end of the 1930s, *Life* had a **pass-along readership**—the total number of people who come into contact with a single copy of a magazine—of more than seventeen million. This rivaled the ratings of even the most popular national radio programs.

▼ Margaret Bourke-White was a photojournalist of many firsts, including first female photographer for *Life* magazine and first female war correspondent. Bourke-White (*right*) was well known for her photos of World War II, as well as for her documentation of the India-Pakistan partition, including a photo of Gandhi at his spinning wheel (*left*).
Margaret Bourke-White/Time Life Pictures/Getty Images (left); Margaret Bourke-White/The LIFE Picture Collection/Getty Images (right)

Reader's Digest

Reader's Digest championed one of the earliest functions of magazines: printing condensed versions of selected articles from other magazines. With its inexpensive production costs, low price, and popular pocket-size format, the magazine saw its circulation climb to more than one million even during the Great Depression. By 1946, it was the nation's most popular magazine.

General-Interest Magazines Decline

In the 1950s, weekly general-interest magazines began to lose circulation after dominating the industry for thirty years. Following years of struggle, the *Saturday Evening Post* folded in 1969, *Look* (another oversized pictorial weekly) in 1971, and *Life* in 1972. Oddly, all three were in the Top 10 in paid circulation when they folded. Although some critics at the time attributed the problem to poor management, general-interest magazines were victims of several forces: high production costs, increased postal rates, and—most damaging—television. As families began spending more time gathered around their TVs, advertisers began spending more money on TV spots, which were less expensive than magazine ads and reached a larger audience.

Other magazines, however, were inspired by the birth of television. *TV Guide*, for example, started publishing TV listings in an array of regional editions beginning in 1953, transforming itself into a national entertainment magazine once newspapers started printing TV schedules and magazine circulation dropped. And *People* magazine, which features more photographs and shorter articles than what appears in a typical newsmagazine as a way to drive newsstand and supermarket sales, launched in 1974 to capitalize on the celebrity-crazed culture that accompanied the rise of television. (See Table 4.1 for the circulation figures of the Top 10 U.S. magazine print

▲ With large pages, beautiful photographs, and compelling stories on celebrities, *Look* entertained millions of readers from 1939 to 1971, emphasizing photojournalism to compete with radio. By the late 1960s, however, TV had lured away national advertisers, postal rates had increased, and production costs had risen, forcing *Look* to fold despite a readership of more than eight million. The Advertising Archives

TABLE 4.1 // THE TOP 10 MAGAZINES (RANKED BY PAID AND NONPAID U.S. CIRCULATION AND SINGLE-COPY SALES, 1972 VS. 2018)

1972		2018	
Rank/Publication	Circulation	Rank/Publication	Circulation
1 Reader's Digest	17,825,661	1 AARP The Magazine	24,099,602
2 TV Guide	16,410,858	2 AARP Bulletin	23,475,727
3 Woman's Day	8,191,731	3 Costco Connection	12,982,340
4 Better Homes and Gardens	7,996,050	4 Better Homes and Gardens	8,152,863
5 Family Circle	7,889,587	5 Game Informer	7,137,476
6 McCall's	7,516,960	6 Good Housekeeping	4,311,679
7 National Geographic	7,260,179	7 Family Circle	4,018,288
8 Ladies' Home Journal	7,014,251	8 People	3,423,322
9 Playboy	6,400,573	9 Woman's Day	3,255,790
10 Good Housekeeping	5,801,446	10 Cosmopolitan	3,040,285

Data from: "Total Paid, Verified and Analyzed Non-Paid Circulation," Alliance for Audited Media, June 30, 2018, http://abcas3.auditedmedia.com/ecirc/magtitlesearch.asp.

editions.) *People*'s success has inspired the launch of similar magazines, such as *InStyle* and *Hello*, and has influenced competing webzines like *TMZ* and *Wonderwall*.

Types of Magazines: Domination of Specialization

As television has commanded more of Americans' attention, many magazines have had to switch tactics to remain viable. General-interest publications have given way to highly specialized magazines that appeal to narrower audiences, which can entice advertisers seeking to tap into niche markets. These narrow groups of readers might be defined by profession (*CIO, Progressive Grocer*), lifestyle (*Dakota Farmer, Game Informer*), gender (*Men's Health, Woman's Day*), age (*AARP The Magazine, Highlights for Children*), ethnic group (*Ebony, Latina*), or membership in an organization (*Costco Connection*, a magazine just for Costco warehouse club members). There are also specialty magazines appealing to fans of specific interests and hobbies, such as hand-spinning, piloting, antique gun restoration, and poetry. These niche markets can be categorized under a few broader areas of specialization.

LaunchPad
launchpadworks.com

Magazine Specialization Today
Editors discuss motivations for magazine specialization and how the Internet is changing the industry.

Discussion: How have the types of magazines you read changed over the past ten years? Have their formats changed, too?

Men's and Women's Magazines

One way the magazine industry competed with television was to reach niche audiences that were not being served by that medium, including those interested in sexually explicit subject matter. *Playboy*, founded in 1953 by Hugh Hefner, was the first magazine to address this audience by emphasizing previously taboo topics and featuring pornographic photos. Newer men's magazines have broadened their focus to include health (*Men's Health*) and lifestyle (*Maxim*) in addition to titillating photos and stories.

Women's magazines had long demonstrated that targeting readers by gender was highly effective. Yet as the magazine industry grew more specialized, publishers stepped up their efforts to capture even more of this enormous market. *Better Homes and Gardens*, *Good Housekeeping*, *Ladies' Home Journal*, and *Woman's Day* focused on cultivating the image of women as homemakers and consumers in the conservative 1950s and early 1960s. As the women's movement advanced in the late 1960s and into the 1970s, these magazines and others, particularly *Cosmopolitan*, began including articles on sexuality, careers, and politics—topics magazine editors previously associated primarily with men.

Entertainment, Leisure, and Sports Magazines

In addition to *TV Guide* and *People*, the television age spawned a number of specialized entertainment, leisure, and sports magazines. Executives have developed multiple magazines for fans of soap operas, running, tennis, golf, hunting, quilting, antiquing, surfing, and gaming, to name only a few. Within categories, magazines specialize further, targeting older or younger runners, men or women golfers, duck hunters or bird-watchers, and midwestern or southern antique collectors.

The most popular sports and leisure magazine is *Sports Illustrated*, which took its name from a failed 1935 publication. Launched in 1954 by Henry Luce's Time Inc., *Sports Illustrated*'s circulation held fairly steady in 2018 at just under 2.8 million. It is now the most successful general sports magazine in history.

Another popular magazine type that fits loosely into this category comprises magazines devoted to music. The all-time circulation champ in this category is *Rolling Stone*, begun in 1967. Once considered an alternative magazine, *Rolling Stone* had become mainstream by 1982, with a circulation approaching 800,000. By 2018, that number was almost 1.3 million.

National Geographic is another successful publication in this category. Founded in 1888, the magazine promoted "humanized geography," and

▼ Specialized magazines target a wide range of interests, from mainstream sports to specific hobbies, such as making model airplanes. *Sports Illustrated* is one of the more successful specialized magazines. Joshua Mitchell

in 1910, it began featuring color photography. *National Geographic*'s circulation reached one million in 1935 and ten million in the 1970s. In the late 1990s, its circulation of paid subscriptions began to slide, down to just under 3.8 million in 2018. Still, many of *National Geographic*'s televised specials on nature and culture rank among the most popular programs in the history of public television.

Age-Specific Magazines

Magazines have sliced their target markets even more finely by appealing to ever-narrower age groups often ignored by mainstream television. For example, magazines such as *Boys' Life* (the Boy Scouts' national publication since 1912), *Highlights for Children*, and *Ranger Rick* have successfully targeted preschool and elementary-school children. The ad-free and subscription-only *Highlights for Children* boasts a circulation of about two million.

Leading female teen magazines have also shown substantial growth; the top magazine for thirteen- to nineteen-year-olds is *Seventeen*, with a circulation of just under two million in 2018.

Magazines that have had the most success with targeting audiences by age have set their sights on readers over fifty, America's fastest-growing age demographic. These publications have tried to meet the interests of older Americans, whom mainstream culture has historically ignored. By 2018, *AARP The Magazine*—established in 1958 as *Modern Maturity*—had a circulation of more than twenty-four million, far surpassing that of any other magazine besides its sister publication, *AARP Bulletin*, which has nearly as many subscribers (see Table 4.1).

Elite Magazines

Although they had long existed, *elite magazines* gained popularity as magazines began specializing. Elite magazines are characterized by their combination of literature, criticism, humor, and journalism and by their appeal to highly educated audiences, often living in urban areas. The most widely circulated elite magazine is the *New Yorker*. Launched in 1925 by Harold Ross, the *New Yorker* became the first city magazine aimed at a national upscale audience. Over the years, it featured many prominent biographers, writers, reporters, and humorists and introduced some of the finest literary journalism of the century. By the mid-1960s, the *New Yorker*'s circulation hovered around 500,000; by 2018, circulation stood at 1.3 million print-version subscribers.

Along with the *New York Times*, the *New Yorker* in 2017 broke the story of dozens of charges of sexual harassment, assault, and rape against film producer Harvey Weinstein. The

▼Ronan Farrow is the Pulitzer Prize–winning journalist whose exposé of film producer Harvey Weinstein in the *New Yorker* helped reignite and boost the #MeToo movement. He is the son of actress and activist Mia Farrow and film director and writer Woody Allen. Dimitrios Kambouris/Getty Images Entertainment/Getty Images

reports won Pulitzer Prizes for each publication and helped reignite the #MeToo movement, originally started in 2006 by activist Tarana Burke, which has prompted women around the world to share their personal stories of workplace harassment, assault, and rape.

Minority-Targeted Magazines

Minority-targeted magazines have existed since before the Civil War. One of the most influential early African American magazines, the *Crisis*, was founded by W. E. B. Du Bois in 1910 and is the official magazine of the NAACP (National Association for the Advancement of Colored People).

Since then, the major magazine publisher for African Americans has been John H. Johnson, a former Chicago insurance salesman. Johnson started *Negro Digest* in 1942, *Ebony* in 1945 (a picture-text magazine modeled on *Life* but serving black readers), and *Jet* in 1951 (*Jet* switched to a digital-only format in June 2014). *Essence*, the first major magazine geared toward African American women, debuted in 1969, and by 2018 it had more than one million subscribers.

Other magazines have served additional minority groups. For example, the *Advocate*, founded in 1967 as a twelve-page newsletter, was the first major magazine to address issues of interest to gay men and lesbians. Since its founding, it has published some of the best journalism on topics not covered by the mainstream press.

Magazines appealing to Spanish-speaking readers have proliferated since the 1980s, reflecting the growth of Hispanic populations in the United States. Some are Spanish-language versions of existing titles, and others were specifically created to serve a Hispanic audience. Today, *People en Español*, *Latina*, and *Vanidades* rank as the top three Hispanic magazines by ad revenue.

Although national magazines aimed at other minority groups were slow to arrive, there are now magazines targeting virtually every race, culture, and ethnicity, including *Asian Week*, *Native Peoples*, and *Tikkun* (published for Jewish readers).

Trade Magazines

Trade and professional magazines represent one of the most stable segments in the magazine industry. **Trade publications**—specialty magazines aimed at narrowly defined audiences—supply news; spot trends; share data; and disseminate expert insights relevant to specific manufacturing trades, professional fields, and business sectors. The trade press includes such diverse magazines as *Organic Matters* for organic farmers and *Coach and Bus Week*. Media industries, too, have relied on trade magazines like *Advertising Age* and

▲ *Selecta* is an upscale fashion magazine targeted to Hispanic women. The magazine is published in Spanish, although it maintains Twitter and Instagram feeds in English. Other popular magazines aimed at this audience include *Latina* and *People en Español*.

Variety. In addition to narrowly targeted advertising content, trade publications provide an invaluable venue for job notices related to a specific field.

Alternative Magazines

Only eighty-five of the twenty thousand American magazines now in existence have circulations that top one million. This means that most magazines serve relatively small groups of readers. Of these, many are alternative magazines. However, what constitutes an alternative magazine has broadened over time to include just about any publication considered "outside the mainstream," ranging from environmental magazines to alternative lifestyle magazines to punk zines—the magazine world's answer to punk rock. (**Zines**, pronounced "zeens," is a term used to describe self-published magazines.) Numerous alternative magazines have defined themselves in terms of politics—published by either the Left (the *Progressive*, *In These Times*, the *Nation*) or the Right (the *National Review*, *American Spectator*, the *Washington Examiner*).

Supermarket Tabloids

With headlines like "Meghan [Markle's] Drug Secret Exposed!" "Brad Wins Custody as 79-lb Angie Collapses," and "Stevie Wonder Can See Again!" **supermarket tabloids** push the limits of credibility. Although they are published on newsprint, the Alliance for Audited Media (formerly the Audit Bureau of Circulations)—which checks newspaper and magazine circulation figures to determine advertising rates—counts weekly tabloids as magazines. Tabloids have their historical roots in newspapers' use of graphics and pictorial layouts in the 1860s and 1870s. But the modern U.S. tabloid began with the founding of the *National Enquirer* by William Randolph Hearst in 1926. Its popularity inspired the founding of other tabloids, like *Globe* (1954) and *Star* (1974), as well as the adoption of a tabloid style by some general-interest magazines, such as *People* and *Us Weekly*. Today, tabloid magazine sales are down from their peak in the 1980s, but they continue to be popular.

▼ Online magazines like *Slate* have made the web their exclusive home. Since launching in 1996, *Slate* has won many awards, such as the National Magazine Award for General Excellence for Digital Media.

Online Magazines

Observers first viewed the Internet as the death knell for print magazines, but now the industry embraces it. Given the costs of paper, printing, and postage; the flexibility of the web, mobile devices, and social media; and the ability to reach new and larger audiences, many magazines are increasingly being distributed in both print and digital formats. For example, *Wired* magazine has a print circulation of about 880,000. It estimates its print edition reaches 2.8 million readers, but with its digital versions, social media pages, and video, it reaches nearly 62 million people monthly.[4] The magazine industry has adapted to the digital turn by thinking about magazines as not just paper publications but brands that find audiences across print and digital editions, desktop/laptop web, mobile web, and video. (For more on magazines and social media, see "The Digital Turn Case Study: Snapchats and Podcasts: Magazine Publishing Turns New Pages" on page 119.)

The web and app formats give magazines unlimited space—which is at a premium in their printed versions—and the opportunity to do things that cannot be done in print. Many online magazines now include blogs, original video and audio podcasts, social networks, games, virtual fitting rooms, and 3-D "augmented reality" components.

In addition to print magazines that publish digital versions and magazines that have moved from print to online only, other magazines have always been online only. *Slate* and *Salon*, for example, have made the web a legitimate arena for reporting breaking news and encouraging public debate about culture and politics.

launchpadworks.com

Narrowcasting in Magazines

Magazine editors explain the benefits and consequences of narrowcasting.

Discussion: Think of magazines that might be considered a good example of narrowcasting. What makes them a good example, and would you consider them successful? Why or why not?

The Organization and Economics of Magazines

Whatever their circulation size, specialty, or format (print or online), magazines must invest money to staff the departments and carry out the business practices that are essential to their operations. Magazines must also bring in money (e.g., from advertising revenues and subscription fees) to fulfill their mission and compete with other media. For instance, to combat loss of ad dollars to TV, many magazines began publishing special editions, which guaranteed advertisers access to their target markets. These competitive strategies fueled the massive growth of magazines despite the competition from television, but now magazines face new challenges from websites, blogs, and social media, all competing for audiences and ad dollars. To extend their reach, lower their costs, and beef up their budgets, many magazines have merged into large chains, often backed financially by major media conglomerates. Even large chains, however, are not immune to the economic reality that many well-known magazine titles have been forced to cease production entirely.

Magazine Departments and Duties

Unlike a broadcast station or a daily newspaper, a small newsletter or magazine can be created inexpensively on a computer, which enables an aspiring publisher-editor to write, design, lay out, and print or post online a modest publication. For larger operations, however, the work is divided into departments.

Editorial and Production

The lifeblood of any magazine is the *editorial department*, which produces its content, excluding advertisements. Like newspapers, most magazines have a chain of command that begins with a publisher and extends down to the editor in chief, the managing editor, and a variety of subeditors. These subeditors oversee various editorial functions, such as photography, illustrations, reporting and writing, and copyediting. Magazine writers generally include contributing staff writers, who are specialists in certain fields, and freelance writers—self-employed professionals assigned to cover particular stories or regions. Unlike newspapers, some magazines also rely on unsolicited manuscripts to fill their pages.

The *production and technology department* maintains the computer and printing hardware necessary to produce the magazine, though most of the actual printing is often outsourced. Large national magazines send digital copy to regional printers, who can insert local ads and distribute the finished product more quickly.

Advertising and Sales

Consumer magazines rely heavily on advertising revenue brought in by their *advertising and sales department*. The traditional display ad has been the staple of magazine advertising for more than a century, and the more successful the magazine (that is, the higher its circulation), the more it can charge for ad space. A top-rated consumer magazine like *People* might charge more than $371,500 for a full-page color ad and about $119,800 for a one-third-page black-and-white ad. The average magazine contains about 40 percent ad copy and 60 percent editorial content, a ratio that has remained fairly constant for the past decade.

As magazines have become digital brands, the advertising opportunities have become more creative. For example, Condé Nast offers multiple ways for advertisers to connect with audiences. In addition to traditional display ads in its print and digital magazine versions, Condé Nast offers data information about its digital readers to its customers, opportunities for **branded content** (specialized print, online, or video content produced and funded by individual advertisers), paid social media placements on platforms like Facebook and Instagram, and custom video stories and features. By offering these varied advertising opportunities, magazine publishers hope to generate new revenue to replace declining print display ad earnings.

The idea of tailoring content to specific subsets of an audience isn't exactly new to the magazine industry. As television stations began generating more national ad revenues in the 1950s, magazines started introducing different editions to guarantee advertisers a specific audience—and thus win them back. There are several types of special editions:

- **Regional editions** are national magazines whose content is tailored to the interests of specific geographic areas. For example, *Sports Illustrated* often prints several regional versions of its College Football Preview and March

Madness Preview editions, picturing a different local star on each of the covers.
- In **split-run editions**, the editorial content remains the same, but the magazines include a few pages of ads purchased by local or regional companies. Most editions of *Time* and *Sports Illustrated*, for example, contain a number of pages reserved for regional ads.
- **Demographic editions** target particular groups of consumers. In this case, market researchers identify subscribers primarily by occupation, class, and zip code. Time Inc., for example, developed special editions of *Time* magazine for high-income zip-code areas and ultrahigh-income professional/managerial households.

Whether they are placing ads in print or online, advertisers can sometimes influence editorial content. For example, some companies have canceled their ads after a magazine printed articles that were unflattering toward or critical of the firm or its industry.[5] For editors, the specter of a major advertiser taking its business elsewhere can present a dilemma: Should the magazine shift its editorial point of view to avoid offending advertisers? Or should it continue publishing the same types of articles, hoping that if some advertisers are driven away, others that agree with the magazine's viewpoint will come in and take their place?

▲ *Ms.* magazine, founded in 1972 as the first magazine to take the feminist movement seriously, made another bold move when it stopped carrying advertisements in 1990—except for ads from nonprofit and cause-related organizations. Although that choice has allowed the magazine to publish more thought-provoking articles, it has also led to continued financial instability.

Circulation and Distribution

Selling magazines (both paper and digital) to an audience is the focus of the *circulation and distribution department*. Currently, about 90 percent of magazines are sold through subscriptions rather than through other means, such as single-copy sales by retailers.

One tactic used by magazine circulation departments to increase subscription revenue is to encourage consumers to renew well in advance of their actual renewal dates. Magazines can invest and earn interest on early renewal money as a hedge against consumers who drop their subscriptions. Other strategies include **evergreen subscriptions**—those that automatically renew on a credit card account unless subscribers request that the automatic renewal be stopped—and *controlled circulations*, which provide readers with a magazine at no charge by targeting captive audiences, such as airline passengers or association members. These magazines' financial support comes solely from advertising and corporate sponsorship.

The biggest trend in magazine sales is the migration to digital distribution (see Figure 4.1). By 2017, combined print and digital editions accounted for 52 percent of the magazine audience. Mobile editions (usually via apps) attract 32 percent of the industry's audience, while web versions of magazines (via desktops and laptops) account for 12 percent.[6] Video remains a small

FIGURE 4.1 // MAGAZINE BRAND AUDIENCE BY DISTRIBUTION FORMAT, 2017

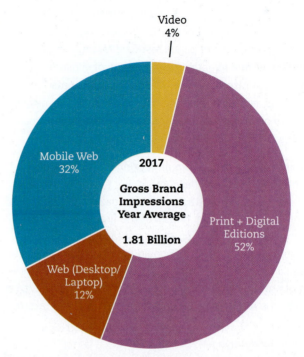

Data from: Magazine Media Factbook 2018/19, Association of Magazine Media, www.magazine.org/Magazine/Research_and_Resources_Pages/MPA_Factbook.aspx.

but growing dimension of magazine distribution (4 percent). (See also "The Digital Turn Case Study: Snapchats and Podcasts: Magazine Publishing Turns New Pages" on page 119.) Other models for magazine distribution, such as the Texture app, offer a Netflix-like plan, with more than two hundred titles accessible for a monthly fee. Apple bought Texture in 2018 and is reported to have plans to integrate the subscription service into its Apple News app.

Major Magazine Chains

To survive in an increasingly competitive marketplace, many magazines have merged into large, powerful chains, often backed by deep-pocketed media conglomerates. This strategy provides more funding for magazines and enables them to lower their costs—for example, by centralizing basic functions such as content development or production.

In the commercial magazine industry, large companies or chains have come to dominate the business. One example is the Meredith Corporation. Based in Des Moines, Iowa, it historically specialized in women's and home lifestyle–related

The Digital Turn

CASE STUDY

Snapchats and Podcasts: Magazine Publishing Turns New Pages

"This is where we are going to begin our journey . . . with the surprising sounds of lava." So began the introduction to the 2018 version of the *New York Times Magazine*'s annual Voyages edition.[1] Called "Listen to the World," the 2018 issue took readers on a tour of twelve locations around the globe, providing colorful images of each unique place. But that's not all. Readers of the print edition also received directions explaining how to access accompanying audio files, while online subscribers could view a thirty-minute slide show accompanied by narration and audio. From the sounds of a lava flow in Hawaii to rats singing in New York City to bats hunting in Mozambique, reader-listeners were treated to a multisensory experience—one that represents a new approach to magazine publishing, in which magazines harness the power of technology to enhance their content and build their readership.

Like the *New York Times Magazine*, *National Geographic* has also turned to digital technology in order to capture a bigger audience and more advertising dollars. The magazine has focused on photos, graphics, high-quality video, and social media as part of its growth strategy, and in just three months, it gained over three million followers on Snapchat. By 2018, *National Geographic* also had 86 million followers on Instagram, or roughly 11 percent of all Instagram users.[2] "A lot of what we changed is in our storytelling approach and also design—we went from a place of fragmented storytelling where we were pulling together a bunch of different content streams across the organization to a more cohesive experience," said *National Geographic*'s senior vice president of digital strategy, Jonathan Hunt. "We try to squeeze as much value out of a single item as possible."[3]

For both of these magazines, attempts to keep legacy brands relevant after the digital turn hinge on two factors: engaging visual content, and an approach to content delivery that connects with people who use online platforms—especially young people. That strong visual content gives an advantage to a magazine like *National Geographic*, which has decades of stunning images in its archives along with a steady stream of new content being shot for the magazine's print and online needs. Visual content is also very shareable, which is a hallmark of any successful social media strategy.

With magazines attracting roughly half of their audience through the mobile, web, and video segments of the business, it seems likely that magazine publishers will continue to emphasize the value of visual and digital experiences.[4] In the post–digital turn world, where media is converged and multimedia is the norm, we can see this trend as a window into magazines' future.

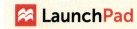

▶ Visit LaunchPad to watch a clip from *13 Going on 30*, set in a magazine office. What has changed in the fifteen years or so since this movie's release?

launchpadworks.com

▲ Launched in the United States by Condé Nast in 1914, *Vanity Fair* has a history of featuring top writers, including Dorothy Parker and P. G. Wodehouse. Known for its mix of social and political commentary, celebrity profiles, fiction, and arts coverage, *Vanity Fair* today includes contributions by noted photographer Annie Leibovitz and writers James Wolcott and Bethany McLean.

magazines (*Better Homes and Gardens*, *Family Circle*) and became the world's largest magazine publisher with its 2018 purchase of Time Inc. The $1.8 billion deal put Time's namesake newsweekly, *Time* magazine, and other popular titles, such as *People* and *Sports Illustrated*, under the same corporate umbrella as Meredith's magazine titles, if only briefly. Meredith's focus on women's and lifestyle-related magazines did not mesh with all of its new Time Inc. magazines, and within weeks of the purchase, Meredith announced that it had sold Time Inc. UK and *Golf* magazine. By mid-2019, it had also sold *Time* magazine to billionaires Marc and Lynne Benioff for $190 million, *Fortune* to executive Chatchaval Jiaravanon for $150 million, and *Sports Illustrated* to Authentic Brands Group for $110 million.

The Hearst Corporation is another formidable publisher, with titles like *Cosmopolitan*, *Esquire*, and *O: The Oprah Magazine*. In 2018, Hearst bought Rodale, which publishes health and wellness titles such as *Prevention* and *Men's Health*. A third major magazine publisher is Condé Nast. A division of Advance Publications, which operates the Newhouse newspaper chain, the Condé Nast group controls several upscale consumer magazines, including *Vanity Fair*, *GQ*, and *Vogue*.

Many of these large publishers have generated additional revenue by creating custom-publishing divisions that produce limited-distribution publications for client companies. These publications, sometimes called **magalogs**, combine the style of glossy magazines with the sales pitch of retail catalogues. For example, the car maker Subaru sends its customers the magalog *Drive*, which covers the travel and lifestyle interests of Subaru owners.

In addition, a number of major magazines (*Reader's Digest*, *Cosmopolitan*, *Time*) have further boosted revenues by launching international editions in several languages. Most U.S. magazines, however, are local, regional, or specialized and therefore not readily exportable to other countries.

Magazines in a Democratic Society

In the early days of the industry, individual magazines had a powerful national voice and united separate communities around important political and social issues, such as abolition and suffrage. Muckrakers promoted social reform in the pages of general-interest magazines.

Today, with so many specialized magazines appealing to ever-narrower groups of consumers, magazines no longer foster such a strong sense of national identity.

To be sure, contemporary commercial magazines still provide essential information about politics, society, and culture. Thus, they help us form opinions about the big issues of the day and make decisions—key activities in any democracy. However, owing to their increasing dependence on advertising revenue, some publications view their readers as consumers first (viewers of displayed products and purchasers of material goods) and citizens second. To keep advertising dollars flowing in, editorial staffs may decide to keep controversial content out of their magazine's pages, which constrains debate and thus endangers the democratic process.

There may also be legal ramifications when a magazine publishes unflattering or embarrassing content about powerful people or groups, as tabloid website *Gawker* found out firsthand. *Gawker's* problems began when the site publicly outed PayPal cofounder Peter Thiel as gay in 2007, then posted a sex tape of Terry Bollea (otherwise known as wrestler Hulk Hogan) with his friend's wife in 2012. Thiel secretly bankrolled Bollea's lawsuit against *Gawker*, and in 2016 Bollea was awarded $140 million after a jury agreed *Gawker* had invaded his privacy. *Gawker* filed for bankruptcy, went broke, shut down, and was ultimately sold to Univision, which decided not to resurrect the site. In a final twist, it was revealed that Thiel had been secretly bankrolling other lawsuits against *Gawker* for years. Some media watchers fear the fallout from this decision could affect more than just *Gawker* if Thiel's tactics encourage others—particularly those who are subjected to legitimate investigative journalism—to use a similar method of revenge by proxy.[7]

Despite these kinds of challenges, however, magazines have arguably had more freedom than other media to encourage and participate in democratic debate. More magazines circulate in the marketplace than do broadcast or cable television channels. And many new magazines are uniting dispersed groups of readers—for example, by giving cultural minorities or newly arrived immigrants a sense of membership in a broader community.

Amid today's swirl of images, magazines and their advertisements certainly contribute to the commotion. But good magazines—especially those offering carefully researched, thoughtful, or entertaining articles and photos—have continued to inspire lively discussion among readers. And if they're also well designed, they will maintain readers' connection to words—no small feat in today's image-driven and increasingly digital culture.

CHAPTER ESSENTIALS

Review

- The first **magazines**—collections of articles, stories, and advertisements published on a nondaily cycle in the smaller tabloid style—were influenced by seventeenth-century European newspapers. In the American colonies and during the Revolutionary period, magazines provided an important space for sharing ideas about politics and society. By the mid-nineteenth century, increases in literacy, faster printing technology, and improvements in mail delivery helped move magazines toward mass medium status.

- By the twentieth century, some magazines (like newspapers) became sources of investigative journalism aimed at social reform and exposing wrongdoings. Investigative reporters were called **muckrakers**.

- The growth of the middle class created a market for **general-interest magazines**, which covered a wide variety of topics aimed at a broad national audience. A key aspect of these magazines was **photojournalism**.

- General-interest magazines have now given way to highly specialized magazines appealing to narrower audiences and niche markets.

- Following the digital turn, the magazine industry began thinking about magazines as not just paper publications but brands that find audiences across print and digital editions, desktop/laptop web, mobile web, and video. Some magazines are published in both print and online versions, others have moved to online-only formats, and still others started up online and have remained there.

- Small independent magazines can be run by one or two people, but larger operations require a number of workers in various departments, including *editorial*, which is responsible for nonadvertising content; *production*, which maintains the computer and printing hardware necessary to produce the magazine; *advertising and sales*, which sells traditional display ads as well as newer types of advertising, like **branded content**; and *circulation and distribution*, which puts most of its focus on selling magazines through subscriptions (both paper and digital).

- National magazines sometimes run multiple versions of the same issue to target specific audiences and guarantee advertising revenue.

LaunchPad

Visit LaunchPad for *Media Essentials* at **launchpadworks.com** for additional learning tools:

- **REVIEW WITH LEARNINGCURVE**
  LearningCurve adaptive quizzing helps you master the concepts you need to learn from this chapter.

- **VIDEO: *ESSENCE* MAGAZINE**
  The president of Essence Communications, Michelle Ebanks, speaks about brand identity, advertising, and *Essence*'s leadership team.

- **MEDIA LITERACY PRACTICE**
  This activity challenges you to develop a critical perspective and apply it to everyday encounters with communication media.

Versions may include **regional editions**, whose content is tailored to the interests of specific geographic areas; **split-run editions**, which contain the same editorial content but include some regionally targeted ads; and **demographic editions**, which target specific groups of consumers.

- Early magazines had a powerful national voice and united separate communities around significant political and social issues. Today, with so much specialization, magazines no longer foster a strong sense of national identity, though they continue to have a strong influence on society.

Key Terms

magazine, p. 101
muckrakers, p. 105
general-interest magazines, p. 105
photojournalism, p. 105
pass-along readership, p. 108
trade publications, p. 113
zines, p. 114
supermarket tabloids, p. 114
branded content, p. 116
regional editions, p. 116
split-run editions, p. 117
demographic editions, p. 117
evergreen subscriptions, p. 117
magalogs, p. 120

Study Questions

1. How did magazines become national in scope?
2. What role did magazines play in social reform at the turn of the twentieth century?
3. What triggered the move toward magazine specialization?
4. How have the Internet and the digital turn changed the magazine industry? How have they changed magazine consumers?
5. How do magazines serve a democratic society?

Mass Media Industries

5

Sound Recording and Popular Music

127
The Early History and Evolution of Sound Recording

134
U.S. Popular Music and the Rise of Rock

140
The Evolution of Pop Music

146
The Economics of Sound Recording

152
Sound Recording in a Democratic Society

It was the 2017 Grammy Awards in Los Angeles, and a twenty-three-year-old rapper from Chicago, Chancellor Johnathan Bennett, walked out with awards for best new artist, best rap performance, and best rap album. Bennett, better known as Chance the Rapper, is now a major music artist, having emerged from a very untraditional path. As *Billboard* magazine put it in August 2016, "Chance the Rapper is one of the hottest acts in music, has a Top 10 album and his own festival—all without a label or physical release."

Other artists have paved the way for Chance's business approach. In 2007, British alternative rock group Radiohead decided to sell its album *In Rainbows* on its website for whatever price fans wished to pay. Adele and Rihanna record for independent labels, and Macklemore sells music under his own label. Chance the Rapper has gone one step further by not selling any music at all.

His recording career started with mixtapes *10 Day* (2012) and *Acid Rap* (2013), which he posted for free. Both were critically praised, and he had offers from multiple music labels. Chance decided to make a business deal that would make some money and also help promote his next release, *Coloring Book* (2016). He still didn't sign with a label but agreed to a short-term contract with a streaming service. Apple Music got exclusive streaming rights to *Coloring Book* for two weeks, a deal that Chance later disclosed was worth $500,000.[1] The Apple Music connection

◀ Artist Chance the Rapper shows off one of his signature "3" baseball caps at the 59th Annual Grammy Awards.
Mark Ralston/Getty Images

gave his work an even greater audience. His album became the first to debut on the *Billboard* 200 chart (at No. 8) based only on the number of streams.[2] All of his recordings remain available for free streaming on SoundCloud.

Why does Chance the Rapper remain independent and refuse to sell recordings? He sat down with journalist Katie Couric in 2017 to explain his approach to his career: "I get to choose how much my music costs. I get to choose when my music gets released. I choose when I go on tour...."[3]

Instead, Chance makes his money selling merchandise (including his ubiquitous "3" baseball cap) and concert tickets on his website ChanceRaps.com. In addition to merchandise and ticket sales and revenue-generating streams on Apple Music, Spotify, and YouTube, Chance and his manager have put together deals, such as sponsorship from Bud Light and Citibank for his sold-out 2016 Magnificent Coloring Day music festival.[4] In 2018, Chance bought the Chicago local-news-and-events website Chicagoist and announced that he would be teaming up with Cardi B and T.I. to host a music competition show on Netflix.[5]

"My dad taught me to work hard, and my mom taught me to work for myself," Chance told Couric. "And so now I work for myself really hard."[6]

The rise of new forms of distribution is one of the most significant developments in the music industry in the past two decades. The old route to success for musical artists was highly dependent on signing with a major label, which handled all the promotion to sell records. Now, with so many distribution forms for music—traditional CDs and vinyl; digital downloads and streaming; social media; music licensed for use in advertising, television, and film; and (of course) live, in-person concerts—there are multiple paths for talented artists to find an audience with an independent label or on their own.

THE INVENTION OF SOUND RECORDING TECHNOLOGY transformed our relationship with popular music and made sound recording a mass medium. Before recording, people had only one way to listen to music: attend a live performance. With the advent of sound recording, people could buy recordings and listen to their favorite music as often as they wanted in their own homes. As technological advances made it cheaper and easier for everyone to gain access to sound recordings, music began reshaping society and culture. But the recording industry itself has changed with the times. Consider what happened in the 1950s, after TV began capturing a bigger share of Americans' attention and time: Record labels and radio stations—previously adversaries—joined forces to create Top 40 (or "hit song") programming to attract more listeners and stimulate music sales. Many years later, the industry was forced to shift again in the face of technology, as the MP3 format made recorded music more accessible (and easier to duplicate) than ever. And just as the music industry began integrating digital music downloads into its business model, the digital turn brought a new wrinkle: streaming music.

In this chapter, we assess the full impact of sound recording and popular music on our lives by:

- examining the early history and evolution of sound recording, including the shift from analog to digital technology and the changing relationship between record labels and radio stations

- shining a spotlight on the rise of popular music (including jazz and rock) in the United States

- tracing the changes in the American popular music scene, such as rock's move into the mainstream and the proliferation of rock alternatives (including folk and punk)

- analyzing the economics of the sound recording industry, including how music labels, artists, and other participants make and spend money in an age when paying to *own* music is rapidly transforming into paying to *access* music

- considering sound recording's impact on our democratic society today by exploring such questions as whether the recording industry is broadening participation in democracy or constraining it

The Early History and Evolution of Sound Recording

Early inventors' work helped make sound recording a mass medium and a product that enterprising businesspeople could sell. The product's format changed with additional technological advances (moving from records and tapes to CDs, and then to online downloads and digital music streaming). Technology also enhanced the product's quality; for example, many people praised the digital clarity of CDs over "scratchy" analog recordings. However, the latest technology—online downloading and streaming of music—has drastically reduced sales of CDs and other physical formats, forcing industry players to look for other ways to survive.

LaunchPad
launchpadworks.com

Use **LearningCurve** to review concepts from this chapter.

From Cylinders to Disks: Sound Recording Becomes a Mass Medium

In the development stage of sound recording, inventors experimented with sound technology; and in the entrepreneurial stage, people sought to make money from the technology. Sound recording finally reached the mass medium stage when entrepreneurs figured out how to quickly and cheaply produce and distribute multiple copies of recordings.

The Development Stage

In the 1850s, French printer Édouard-Léon Scott de Martinville conducted the first experiments with sound recording. Using a hog's-hair bristle as a needle, he tied one end to a thin membrane stretched over the narrow part of a funnel. When he spoke into the wide part of the funnel, the membrane vibrated, and the bristle's free end made grooves on a revolving cylinder coated with a thick liquid. Although de Martinville never figured out how to play back the sound, his experiments ushered in the *development stage* of sound recording.

The Entrepreneurial Stage

In 1877, Thomas Edison helped move sound recording into its *entrepreneurial stage* by first determining how to play back sound, then marketing the machine that did it. He recorded his own voice by concocting a machine that played foil cylinders, known as the *phonograph* (derived from the Greek terms for "sound" and "writing"). Edison then patented his phonograph in 1878 as a kind of answering machine. In 1886, Chichester Bell and Charles Sumner Tainter patented an improvement on the phonograph, known as the *graphophone*, which played more-durable wax cylinders.[7] Both Edison's phonograph and Bell and Tainter's graphophone had only marginal success as a voice-recording office machine. Yet eventually these inventors began to produce cylinders with prerecorded music, and their inventions laid the foundation for others to develop more viable sound recording technologies.

▼ In addition to inventing the phonograph, Thomas Edison (1847–1931) ran an industrial research lab that is credited with inventing the motion-picture camera, the first commercially successful lightbulb, and a system for distributing electricity.
Bettmann/Getty Images

The Mass Medium Stage

Adapting ideas from previous inventors, Emile Berliner, a German engineer who had immigrated to America, made sound recording into a *mass medium*. Berliner developed a turntable machine that played flat disks, or "records," made of shellac. He called this device a *gramophone* and patented it in 1887. He also discovered how to mass-produce his records by making a master recording from which many copies could be easily duplicated. In addition, Berliner's records could be stamped in the center with labels indicating song title, performer, and songwriter.

By the early 1900s, record-playing phonographs were widely available for home use. Early record players, known as Victrolas, were mechanical and had to be primed with a crank handle. Electric record players, first available in 1925, gradually replaced Victrolas as more homes were wired for electricity.

Recorded music initially had limited appeal, owing to the loud scratches and pops that interrupted the music, and each record contained only three to four minutes of music. However, in the early 1940s, when shellac was needed for World War II munitions, the record industry began manufacturing records made of polyvinyl plastic. These vinyl records (called 78s because they turned at seventy-eight revolutions per minute, or rpms) were less noisy and more durable than shellac records. Enthusiastic about these new advantages, people began buying more records.

In 1948, CBS Records introduced the 33⅓-rpm *long-playing record* (LP), which contained about twenty minutes of music on each side. This created a market for multisong albums and classical music, which was written primarily for ballet, opera, ensemble, and symphony, and continues to have a significant fan base worldwide. The next year, RCA developed a competing 45-rpm record, featuring a larger, quarter-size hole in the middle that made these records ideal for playing in jukeboxes. The two new recording configurations could not be played on each other's machines; thus, a marketing battle erupted. In 1953, CBS and RCA compromised. The LP became the standard for long-playing albums, the 45 became the standard for singles, and record players were designed to accommodate both formats (as well as 78s, at least for a while).

LaunchPad
launchpadworks.com

Sound Recordings from a Century Ago
A museum curator demonstrates how to operate two hand-cranked working phonographs, one that plays wax cylinders and one that plays disks (an early version of records).

Discussion: If the phonograph was still the main method of music delivery, how might it change the way people consume music today?

From Records to Tapes to CDs: Analog Goes Digital

The advent of magnetic **audiotape** and tape players in the 1940s paved the way for major innovations, such as cassettes and—most significantly—digital recording. Audiotape's lightweight magnetized strands made possible sound editing and multiple-track mixing, in which instrumentals or vocals could be recorded at one location and later mixed onto a master recording in a studio. Audiotape also enabled stereophonic sound. Invented in 1931 by Alan Blumlein but not put to commercial use until 1958, **stereo** permitted the recording of two separate channels, or tracks, of sound. Using audiotape, recording-studio engineers could record many instrumental or vocal tracks, which they could then "mix down" to two stereo tracks, creating a more natural sound.

launchpadworks.com

Recording Music Today

Composer Scott Dugdale discusses technological innovations in music recording.

Discussion: What surprised you the most about song production as shown in the video?

By the mid-1960s, engineers had placed miniaturized (reel-to-reel) audiotape inside small plastic cases and developed portable cassette players. Listeners could now bring recorded music anywhere, which created a market for prerecorded cassettes. For a few years in the 1980s, cassettes became the leading music format. Audiotape also permitted home dubbing, which enabled music fans to create their own mixtapes.

The biggest recording advancement came in the 1970s, when electrical engineer Thomas Stockham made the first digital audio recordings on standard computer equipment. In contrast to **analog recording**, which captures the fluctuations of sound waves and stores those signals in a record's grooves or a tape's continuous stream of magnetized particles, **digital recording** translates sound waves into binary on–off pulses and stores that information in sequences of ones and zeros as numerical code. Drawing on this technology, in 1983 Sony and Philips began selling digitally recorded **compact discs** (CDs), which could be produced more cheaply than vinyl records and even audiocassettes. By 2000, CDs had rendered records and audiocassettes nearly obsolete except among deejays, hip-hop artists (who still used vinyl for scratching and sampling), and some audiophile loyalists. However, vinyl albums, once nearly extinct, have been making a comeback. Still a relatively small part of the overall market in music sales, vinyl sales have jumped to such an extent that many new albums are being pressed on vinyl, giving music fans a physical, collectible music format in a new digital era.

From Downloads to Streaming: Sound Recording Goes through the Digital Turn

In 1992, the **MP3** file format was developed as part of the MPEG video compression standard, enabling sound—including music—to be compressed into small, manageable digital files. Combined with the Internet, MP3 revolutionized sound recording. By the mid-1990s, computer users were swapping MP3 music files online. These files could be uploaded and downloaded in a fraction of the time it took to exchange noncompressed music, and they used up less memory.

Unfortunately for music companies and artists, this also meant that it was easy to get copies of songs without paying for them, especially as file-sharing sites like Napster grew in popularity. In 2001, the U.S. Court of Appeals sided with the music industry when it decided that free music file-swapping—music piracy—violated music copyrights. This decision led to Napster's quick demise.

The music industry still loses money to piracy and does its best to fight back. At the same time, music companies realize that MP3s are not going away and have embraced the format through legal music downloads. Launching in 2003 to accompany the iPod, Apple's iTunes Store became the first big success story in music downloading. By 2011, the music industry was making more money from digital downloads than from sales of CDs and other physical media. But just as the music industry was adapting to this approach, the digital turn served up another innovation that favored the music industry even more: streaming.

Today, streaming is the music industry's best means for controlling the music it sells, as music *ownership* has shifted to music *access*. The access model has been driven by the availability of streaming services such as the Sweden-based Spotify, which made its debut in the United States in 2011 and hit 87 million worldwide subscribers in 2018.[8] Other services include Apple Music, Google Play Music, Amazon Music, Pandora, Tidal, Deezer, and SoundCloud. With these services, listeners can choose from different options at different tiers of service. Some sites offer a free version with fewer features, which makes money by selling ads, similar to traditional radio. Alternatively, listeners can choose to pay a subscription fee (typically $5 to $10 per month) and instantly access millions of songs on demand via the Internet. YouTube and Vevo also supply ad-supported music streaming and have wide international use. (For more on music streaming services, see "Media Literacy Case Study: The New Masters of Music Modernization: Daniel Ek, Spotify, and Streaming Services" on pages 132–133. For more on streaming's free tier and its relationship to radio, see Chapter 6.)

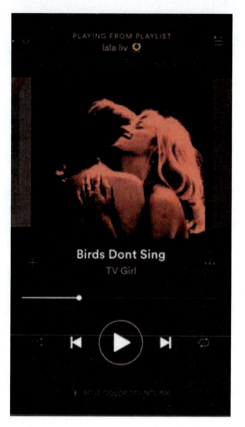

◀ Music streaming services like Spotify (seen here) and Pandora provide users with more opportunity to fully customize their listening experience. Free accounts may include ads or limit a user's selection, while a few dollars a month allow subscribers to search and stream any song.

Media Literacy

CASE STUDY

The New Masters of Music Modernization: Daniel Ek, Spotify, and Streaming Services

"When I started Spotify, I didn't actually know that I needed licenses from record labels," Spotify founder Daniel Ek admitted in a 2012 interview. "It took me two and a half years to get things started."[1] Ek chuckles now at his naiveté when he first entered the complicated world of international music copyrights and licensing.

Traditionally, licensing creates a way for those who play music, such as radio stations, to respect copyrights and pay the record labels, artists, and composers who created the music. When Ek was looking at starting a legal music streaming service, years of illegal file-sharing had cut the legs out from under the music industry, reducing worldwide revenue from $27 billion in 1999 to roughly half that amount by 2008.[2] Ek's idea was that if music lovers who were downloading songs illegally had a legal alternative that was just as convenient, they would do that instead. He launched Spotify in Europe in 2008 and in the United States in 2011, and by 2017, streaming accounted for 65 percent of U.S. music industry revenue.[3]

Coming up with this new business model was only one part of Ek's challenge; another part was negotiating copyright laws written before there was such a thing as digital streaming. If a music service wanted to stream a song, it needed to obtain a *mechanical* license, which compensated songwriters, and a *sound recording* license, which compensated recording artists. Getting any of this paperwork wrong could result in a lawsuit—a real risk, with streaming sites adding tens of thousands of new songs to their libraries in a single day.[4]

For the decade or so that streaming sites and the recording industry struggled to work under this system, there were lawsuits and accusations that songwriters and publishers of music and lyrics weren't getting fairly compensated. As each side fought for its own interests, it seemed the only thing they could agree on was that the system wasn't working—which may be why something unusual occurred in 2018: Most major streaming services, songwriters, major labels, and music publishers agreed to support a new U.S. copyright law called the Music Modernization Act (MMA).

▲ Sweden's Daniel Ek founded his first Internet business in 1997, when he was just fourteen years old. Nine years later, Ek started Spotify with Martin Lorentzon, who left the company in 2015. Michael Loccisano/Getty Images

Web Clip

YouTube.com has many videos about Spotify. For example, do a quick search for "Spotify CEO on going public, convincing Taylor Swift to rejoin" by *CBS This Morning*. As services like Spotify develop ever-more sophisticated song-recommendation algorithms based on personal preferences, how might this affect our exposure to new music?

The final version of the bill got unanimous approval—an impressive feat in the frequently contentious U.S. House and Senate—and was signed into law in October of that year.

According to the law, the U.S. Copyright Office will set up a new, nonprofit licensing agency that will provide blanket mechanical licensing services for musical compositions.[5] Streaming sites will be able to keep track of what songs get played and pay a periodic fee for this blanket license, rather than setting up licenses for each individual song. (The MMA doesn't address *sound recording* licenses; those will still be negotiated between streaming services and music labels. Performance rights organizations like ASCAP and BMI also will still handle royalties for *public performances* of music in places from concert halls to restaurants.) There is optimism about how this new legislation will streamline the licensing process, though there are also details that remain to be worked out. For example, some have expressed concerns that the new licensing agency—which will bring proceedings to copyright judges to establish royalty rates—will lack strong incentives to make sure the money gets to composers.[6]

In addition, there are concerns that established sites will use the legislation to maintain control of the streaming market. No longer an outsider or an upstart, Spotify—worth nearly $30 billion when the company went public in 2018[7]—is now as powerful as the record labels Ek had to petition for early licensing. Depending on how high the fees for a blanket license become, powerhouse services like Spotify may find themselves protected against competition from start-ups with fewer resources—start-ups just like Spotify and the others once were. A variety of interested parties—including labels, songwriters, and investors—will be watching.

APPLYING THE CRITICAL PROCESS

DESCRIPTION As the industry sorts out the relationship between streaming and licensing, most people just focus on accessing the music. Arrange to interview four to eight students on your campus who currently use a music streaming service. Include students who are not musicians and those who are majoring in music. Ask them which streaming site they use the most, if it is free or premium, and why they picked that service. Have they considered how their favorite site compensates the artists they listen to? Would they leave that site if they discovered that it didn't pay the artists at all?

ANALYSIS Chart and organize your results. Do you recognize any patterns emerging from the data? What influences your fellow students' selection of a music streaming site, and how important is the question of licensing and payment to artists? Do students who are music majors have different opinions than students who aren't majoring in music?

INTERPRETATION Consider the patterns you have charted. What does it mean if consumers are (or are not) concerned about how artists get paid?

EVALUATION Should consumers care about music licensing? Should streaming sites' business relationships with artists influence whether listeners continue to use these services?

ENGAGEMENT To expand on your findings, arrange to speak with a local professional musician. How does this person feel about streaming services? How often does this artist think about things like copyright and licensing? Consider how musicians today might navigate a world in which people buy and access music very differently than they did even a few years ago.

The Music Industry and Radio: A Rocky Relationship

We can't discuss the development of sound recording without also discussing radio (covered in detail in Chapter 6). Though each industry developed independently of the other, radio constituted recorded sound's first rival for listeners' attention. This competition triggered innovations both in sound recording technology and in the business relationship between the two industries.

In the mid-1920s, when the recorded-sound industry had just introduced electric record players, radio stations began broadcasting recorded music without compensating the music industry. The American Society of Composers, Authors and Publishers (ASCAP), founded in 1914 to collect copyright fees for music publishers and writers, accused radio of hurting the sales of records and sheet music. By 1925, ASCAP established music-rights fees for radio, charging stations between $250 and $2,500 a week to play recorded music. Many stations couldn't afford these fees and had to leave the air. Other stations countered by establishing their own live in-house orchestras, disseminating music free to listeners. Throughout the late 1920s and 1930s, record sales continued plummeting as the Great Depression worsened.

In the early 1950s, television became popular and began pilfering radio's programs, advertising revenue, and audience. Seeking to reinvent itself, radio turned to the recorded-music industry. Brokering a deal that gave radio a cheap source of content and record companies greater profits, many radio stations adopted a new hit-song format—dubbed "Top 40," for the typically small set of favorites bar patrons would repeatedly play on jukeboxes. Now when radio stations aired songs, record sales soared.

In the early 2000s, though, the radio and recorded-music industries were in conflict again. Upset by online radio stations' decision to stream music on the Internet, the recording industry began pushing for high royalty charges, hindering the development of Internet radio. The most popular online streaming services developed separately from traditional radio stations.

U.S. Popular Music and the Rise of Rock

As sound recording became a mass medium, it fueled the growth of popular music, or **pop music**, which appeals to large segments of the general population as well as sizable groups distinguished by age, region, or ethnic background. Pop music today includes numerous genres—rock and roll, jazz, blues, country, Tejano, salsa, reggae, punk, hip-hop, and dance—many of which evolved from a common foundation. For example, rock splintered off from blues (which originated in the American South), and hip-hop grew out of R&B, reggae, dance music, and rock. This proliferation of music genres created a broad range of products that industry players could package and sell, targeted to increasingly narrow listener groups.

It would be a mistake to think of the label "pop music" as an insult, somehow referring to music that is frivolous, unimportant, or unartistic. To be sure, some music is indeed just meant to entertain (or to separate consumers from their dollars). But from the folk music protests of Woody Guthrie to the blurring of racial lines in the development of rock music to the antiwar anthem "What's Going On" by Marvin Gaye, popular music has exerted a major influence on society, culture, and even politics.

The Rise of Pop Music

Though technological advancements made sound recording a mass medium and sparked the proliferation of pop music genres, this music had its earliest roots in something far less technical: sheet music. With mass production of sheet music in the nineteenth and early twentieth centuries, pop developed into a business fed by artists who set standards for the different genres, including jazz, rock, blues, and R&B.

Back in the late nineteenth century, a section of Broadway in Manhattan known as Tin Pan Alley began selling sheet music for piano and other instruments. (The name Tin Pan Alley referred to the way these quickly produced tunes supposedly sounded like cheap pans clanging together.) Songwriting along Tin Pan Alley helped transform pop music into a big business. At the turn of the twentieth century, improvements in printing technology enabled song publishers to mass-produce sheet music for a growing middle class. Previously a novelty, popular music was now becoming a major enterprise. With the emergence of the phonograph and recorded tunes, interest in and sales of sheet music soared. (These sales would eventually decline with the rise of radio in the 1920s, which turned audiences more into listeners of music than active participants playing instruments to sheet music in their living rooms.)

As sheet music gained popularity and phonograph sales rose, **jazz** developed in New Orleans. An improvisational and mostly instrumental musical form, jazz absorbed and integrated a diverse array of musical styles, including African rhythms, blues, and gospel. Groups led by Louis Armstrong, Tommy Dorsey, and others counted among the most renowned of the "swing" jazz bands, whose rhythmic sound dominated radio, recordings, and dance halls.

The first pop vocalists of the twentieth century came out of vaudeville—stage performances featuring dancing, singing, comedy, and magic shows.

By the 1930s, Rudy Vallée and Bing Crosby had established themselves as the first "crooners" by singing pop standards. Bing Crosby also popularized Irving Berlin's "White Christmas," which became one of the most recorded songs in history. Meanwhile, the bluesy harmonies of the Boswell Sisters—a New Orleans vocal trio—influenced the Andrews Sisters, whose boogie-woogie style sold more than sixty million records in the late 1930s and 1940s. Helped by radio, pop vocalists like Frank Sinatra in the 1940s were among the first singers to win the hearts of a large national teen audience. Indeed, Sinatra's early performances incited the kinds of audience riots that would later characterize rock-and-roll concerts.

Rock and Roll Arrives

Pop music's expanding appeal paved the way for **rock and roll** to emerge in the mid-1950s. Rock both reflected and shaped powerful societal forces (such as blacks' migration from the South to the North and the growth of youth culture) that had begun transforming American life. Rock also stirred controversy. Like the word *jazz*, the phrase *rock and roll* was a blues slang expression meaning "sex," which offended those with more conservative musical tastes and made them worry about their children's choice in music.

Rock grew out of a blending of numerous musical styles. For instance, early rock combined the vocal and instrumental traditions of pop with the rhythm-and-blues sounds of Memphis and the country twang of Nashville. As rock and roll developed, that fusion of musical styles contributed to both racial progress and fears reflecting the social unease of the 1950s and 1960s.

Blues and R&B Set the Stage for Rock

The migration of southern blacks to northern cities in search of better jobs during the first half of the twentieth century helped disseminate different popular music styles to new places. In particular, **blues** music traveled north. Blues became the foundation of rock and roll and was influenced by African American spirituals, ballads, and work songs from the rural South.

▼ Bessie Smith (1895–1937) is considered the best female blues singer of the 1920s and 1930s. Mentored by the famous Ma Rainey, Smith had many hits, including "Down Hearted Blues" and "Gulf Coast Blues." She also appeared in the 1929 film *St. Louis Blues*. Michael Ochs Archives/Getty Images

Influential blues artists included Robert Johnson, Ma Rainey, Bessie Smith, Muddy Waters, Howlin' Wolf, and Charley Patton. After the introduction of the electric guitar in the 1930s, blues-based urban black music began to be marketed under the name **rhythm and blues (R&B)**. This new music appealed to young listeners fascinated by the explicit (and forbidden) sexual lyrics in songs like "Annie Had a Baby," "Sexy Ways," and "Wild Wild Young Men." Although banned on some stations, R&B continued gaining popularity into the early 1950s. Still, black and white musical forms were segregated, and trade magazines in the 1950s tracked R&B record sales on "race" charts, separate from the white "pop" charts.

Rock Reflects and Reshapes Racial Politics

As artists began to produce music that borrowed from what mainstream society thought of as "black" and "white" musical traditions, American society as a whole was entering a tumultuous time of social and political change that would help fuel rock's popularity. By the early 1950s, President Truman's 1948 executive order integrating the armed forces was in full practice, bringing young men from very different ethnic and economic backgrounds together. Then, in 1954, the Supreme Court's *Brown v. Board of Education* decision declared unconstitutional the "separate but equal" laws that had segregated blacks and whites for decades. Mainstream America began to wrestle with the legacy of slavery and the unequal treatment of its African American citizens. And so rock music reflected the complicated changes happening at the time while also helping to influence those changes. On the one hand, the fusion of musical traditions made rock music popular among young people across racial lines and could be understood as "desegregating" in its own right. On the other hand, sometimes the rock-and-roll business of the 1950s and 1960s (and beyond) perpetuated racial inequalities and denied artists of color the fruits of their artistic efforts. White producers would often give cowriting credit to white performers like Elvis Presley (who never wrote songs himself) for the tunes they recorded. Many producers also bought the rights to potential hits from black songwriters, who seldom saw a penny in royalties or received songwriting credit.

By 1955, R&B hits regularly crossed over to the pop charts, but for a time the white **cover music** versions were more popular and profitable. For example, Pat Boone's cover of Fats Domino's "Ain't That a Shame" shot to No. 1 and stayed on the Top 40 pop chart for twenty weeks; Domino's original made it only to No. 10. A turning point, however, came in 1962, when Ray Charles covered "I Can't Stop Loving You," a 1958 country song by the Grand Ole Opry's Don Gibson. This marked the first time that a black artist covering a white artist's song had notched a No. 1 pop hit.

▲ A major influence on early rock and roll, Chuck Berry (1926–2017) scored big hits between 1955 and 1958, writing "Maybellene," "Roll Over Beethoven," "School Day," "Sweet Little Sixteen," and "Johnny B. Goode." At the time, he was criticized by some black R&B artists for sounding white and by some white conservative critics for his popularity among white teenagers. Berry's experience is another example of the complicated and sometimes contradictory nature of the relationship between race and popular music. Bettmann/Getty Images

Fear Fuels Censorship

Rock's blurring of racial and other lines alarmed enough Americans that performers and producers alike worried that fans would begin defecting. In an attempt to avoid this, they used various tactics to get people to accept the music. Cleveland deejay Alan Freed played original R&B recordings from the race charts and black versions of early rock on his radio program, while Philadelphia deejay Dick Clark took a different tactic: playing white artists' cover versions of black music. Still, problems persisted that further eroded rock's acceptance.

One particularly difficult battle rock faced was the perception among mainstream adults that the music caused juvenile delinquency. Such delinquency was statistically on the rise in the 1950s, owing to a variety of contributing factors, such as parental neglect, the rising consumer culture, and the burgeoning youth population after World War II. But adults sought an easier culprit to blame. It was far simpler to point the finger at rock—especially artists who blatantly defied rules governing proper behavior. Authorities responded by censoring rock lyrics.

Rattled by this and other developments, the U.S. recording industry decided it needed a makeover. To protect the enormous profits the new music had been generating, record companies began practicing some censorship of their own. In the early 1960s, the industry introduced a new generation of clean-cut white singers, including Frankie Avalon, Connie Francis, Ricky Nelson, Lesley Gore, and Fabian. Rock's explosive violations of racial, class, and other boundaries gave way to simpler generation gap problems, and the music—for a time—developed a milder reputation.

Rock Blurs Additional Boundaries

Although rock and roll was molded by powerful social, cultural, and political forces, it also shaped them in return. As we've seen, rock and roll began by blurring the boundary between black and white, but it broke down additional divisions as well—between high and low culture, masculinity and femininity, country and city, North and South, and the sacred and the secular.

▼Although his unofficial title, King of Rock and Roll, has been challenged by Little Richard and Chuck Berry, Elvis Presley remains among the most popular solo artists of all time. From 1956 to 1962, he recorded seventeen No. 1 hits, from "Heartbreak Hotel" to "Good Luck Charm." Bettmann/Getty Images

High and Low Culture

Rock challenged the long-standing distinction between high and low culture initially through its lyrics and later through its performance styles. In 1956, Chuck Berry's song "Roll Over Beethoven" merged rock and roll (which many people considered low culture) with high culture through lyrics that included references to classical music: "You know my temperature's risin' / And the jukebox's blowin' a fuse . . . Roll over Beethoven / And tell Tchaikovsky the news." Rock artists also defied norms governing how musicians should behave: Berry's "duck walk" across the stage, Elvis Presley's tight pants and gyrating hips, and Bo Diddley's use of the guitar as a phallic symbol not only shocked elite audiences but inspired additional antics by subsequent artists.

Masculinity and Femininity

Rock and roll was also the first pop music genre to overtly challenge assumptions about sexual identity and orientation. Although early rock and roll largely attracted males as performers, the most fascinating feature of Elvis Presley, according to the Rolling Stones' Mick Jagger, was his androgynous appearance.[9] Little Richard (Penniman) took things even further, sporting a pompadour hairdo, decorative makeup, and feminized costumes during his performances.[10]

Country and City

Rock and roll also blended cultural borders between white country and western music and early-twentieth-century black urban rhythms. Early white rockers such as Buddy Holly and Carl Perkins combined country or hillbilly music, southern gospel, and Mississippi delta blues to create a sound called **rockabilly**. Conversely, rhythm and blues spilled into rock and roll. Many songs first popular on the R&B charts, such as "Rocket 88," crossed over to the pop charts during the mid- to late 1950s, though many of these songs were performed by more widely known white artists.

Rock lyrics in the 1950s may not have been especially provocative or overtly political by today's standards, but soaring record sales and the crossover appeal of the music itself represented an enormous threat to long-standing racial and class divisions defined by geography. Distinctions at the time between traditionally rural white music and urban black music dissolved, as some black artists (such as Chuck Berry) strived to "sound white" to attract Caucasian fans, and some white artists (such as Elvis Presley) were encouraged by record producers to "sound black."

North and South

Not only did rock and roll blur the line between urban and rural but it also mixed northern and southern influences together. As many blacks migrated north during the early twentieth century, they brought their love of blues and R&B. Meanwhile, musicians and audiences in the North had claimed blues music as their own, forever extending its reach beyond its origins in the rural South. Some white artists from the South—most notably Carl Perkins, Elvis Presley, and Buddy Holly—further carried southern musical styles to northern listeners.

The Sacred and the Secular

Many mainstream adults in the 1950s complained that rock and roll's sexual overtones and gender bending constituted an offense against God, even though numerous early rock figures (such as Elvis Presley, Jerry Lee Lewis, and Little Richard) had strong religious upbringings. In the late 1950s, public outrage over rock proved so great that even Little Richard and Jerry Lee Lewis, both sons of southern preachers, became convinced that they were playing "the devil's music." Both changed course but later returned to rock and roll.

Throughout the rock era and even today, boundaries between the sacred and the secular continue to blur through music. For example, some churches use rock and roll to appeal to youth, and some Christian-themed rock groups record in seemingly incongruous musical styles, such as heavy metal.

The Evolution of Pop Music

As the volatile decade of the 1960s unfolded, pop music (including rock) changed to reflect the social, cultural, and political shifts taking place, while also continuing to influence these aspects of American life. Authorities made further attempts to "tame" rock, concerned about its influence on teenagers. These attempts sparked resistance from defiant young people, many of whom embraced rock musicians from Great Britain who hadn't toned down their style. As pop music continued to adapt, it spun off into several genres, including soul, folk, and psychedelic, as well as punk, indie, hip-hop, and country.

The British Are Coming!

Rock and roll proved so powerful that it transformed pop music across national borders. For instance, in England during the late 1950s, the young members of the Rolling Stones covered blues songs by American artists Robert Johnson and Muddy Waters. And the young Beatles imitated Chuck Berry and Little Richard.

Until 1964, rock-and-roll recordings had traveled on a one-way ticket to Europe. Even though American artists regularly reached the tops of charts overseas, no British performers had yet appeared on any Top 10 pop lists in

▼ British rock groups like the Beatles and the Rolling Stones first invaded American pop charts in the 1960s. Although the Beatles broke up in 1970, each member went on to work on solo projects. The Stones are still (mostly) together and touring years later. Paul Popper/Popperfoto/Getty Images (left); Dave Hogan/Getty Images (right)

the United States. This changed virtually overnight in 1964, when the Beatles came to America with their mop haircuts and delivered pop interpretations of American blues and rock. Within the next few years, more British bands—the Kinks, the Who, the Yardbirds—produced hits that climbed the American Top 40 charts. Ed Sullivan, who booked the Beatles several times on his TV variety show in the mid-1960s, helped promote the group's early success.

With the British invasion, the rock industry split into two styles of music. The Rolling Stones developed a style emphasizing gritty, chord-driven, high-volume rock, which would influence later bands that created glam rock, hard rock, punk, heavy metal, and grunge. Meanwhile, the Beatles presented a more accessible, melodic, and softer sound, which would eventually inspire new genres, such as pop rock, power pop, new wave, and alternative rock. The British groups' success also demonstrated to the recording industry that older American musical forms, especially blues and R&B, could be repackaged as rock and exported around the world.

Motown: The Home of Soul

As rock attracted more and more devotees, it resurrected interest in the styles of music from which it had originated. Throughout the 1960s, black singers like James Brown, Aretha Franklin, Wilson Pickett, Otis Redding, and Ike and

◀One of the most successful groups in rock-and-roll history, the Supremes recorded twelve No. 1 hits between 1964 and 1969, including "Where Did Our Love Go," "Baby Love," "Come See about Me," and "Stop! In the Name of Love." The group was inducted into the Rock and Roll Hall of Fame in 1988. Archive Photos/Getty Images

▼ Born Robert Allen Zimmerman in Minnesota, Bob Dylan took his stage name from Welsh poet Dylan Thomas. He led a folk music movement in the early 1960s with engaging, socially provocative lyrics, but later infused folk with the electric sounds of rock. He continues recording and touring today, typically spending most of April through November on the road. He was awarded the Nobel Prize in Literature in 2016. Andrew DeLory

Tina Turner picked up on this interest, transforming the rhythms and melodies of older R&B, pop, and early rock and roll into what would become known as **soul**. These artists attracted large and racially diverse audiences, countering the British invaders with powerful vocal performances.

The most prominent independent label supporting black songwriters' and performers' work was Motown, founded in 1959 by former Detroit autoworker and songwriter Berry Gordy. Motown signed many successful black artists and groups, including the Four Tops ("Baby I Need Your Loving"), the Marvelettes ("Please Mr. Postman"), Marvin Gaye ("What's Going On"), and the Jackson 5 ("I'll Be There"). But the label's most successful group was the Supremes, featuring Diana Ross, which scored twelve No. 1 singles between 1964 and 1969 (including "Where Did Our Love Go" and "Stop! In the Name of Love"). The Supremes' success showed Motown producers that songs emphasizing romance and featuring a danceable beat won far more young white fans than those trumpeting rebellion and political upheaval.

Folk and Psychedelic: Protest and Drugs

Popular music has always been both a product of and a shaper of its time. So it's not surprising that the social upheavals of the 1960s and early 1970s—over Civil Rights, women's rights, environmental protection, the Vietnam War, and the use of recreational drugs—found their reflections in rock music during these decades. By the late 1960s, many songwriters and performers spoke to their generation's social and political concerns through two music genres: folk and psychedelic rock.

Folk Inspires Protest

The musical genre that most clearly expressed pivotal political events of the time was folk, which had long served as a voice for social activism. **Folk music** exists in all cultures; it's usually performed by untrained musicians and passed down mainly through oral traditions. With its rough edges and amateur quality, folk is considered a democratic and participatory musical form. During the 1930s, the work of Woody Guthrie ("This Land Is Your Land") set a new standard for American folk music. Later, in the 1960s and 1970s, groups such as the Weavers, featuring labor activist and songwriter Pete Seeger, carried on Guthrie's legacy. These newer groups inspired yet another crop of singer-songwriters—Joan Baez; Arlo Guthrie; Peter, Paul, and Mary; Phil Ochs; Bob Dylan—who took a stand against worrisome developments of the day, including industrialization, poverty, racism, and war.

Rock Turns Psychedelic

With the increasing use of recreational drugs by young people and the availability of LSD (not illegal until the mid-1960s), more and more rock musicians experimented with and sang about drugs during rock's *psychedelic* era. Defining groups and performers of this era included newcomers like Jefferson Airplane, Big Brother and the Holding Company (featuring Janis Joplin), the Jimi Hendrix Experience, the Doors, and the Grateful Dead, as well as established artists like the Beatles and the Rolling Stones. These musicians believed they could enhance their artistic prowess by taking mind-altering drugs. They also saw the use of these drugs as a form of personal expression and an appropriate response to the government's failure to deal with social and political problems, such as racism and America's involvement in the Vietnam War.

After a surge of optimism that culminated in the historic Woodstock concert in August 1969, the sun set on the psychedelic era as some of psychedelic rock's greatest stars died from drug overdoses, including Janis Joplin, Jimi Hendrix, and Jim Morrison of the Doors.

Punk and Indie Respond to Mainstream Rock

As rock and roll moved from the edges of the American music scene into the mainstream, other genres arose to take its place on the fringes. While many people had considered rock a major part of the rebel counterculture in the 1960s, they increasingly viewed it as part of consumer culture in the 1970s. With major musical acts earning huge profits, rock had become just another product for manufacturers and retailers to promote, package, and profit from. According to critic Ken Tucker, this situation produced "faceless rock" performed by bands with "no established individual personalities outside their own large but essentially discrete audiences" of young white males.[11] To Tucker, these "faceless" groups—REO Speedwagon, Styx, Boston, Journey, Kansas—filled stadiums and entertained the maximum number of people while stirring up the minimum amount of controversy. It was only a matter of time before new types of music—like punk and indie rock—arose to challenge rock's mainstream once more.

Punk Revives Rock's Rebellious Spirit

Punk rock arose in the late 1970s to defy the orthodoxy and commercialism of the record business. Punk attempted to revive rock's basic defining characteristics: simple chord structures that anyone with a few guitar lessons could master, catchy melodies, and politically or socially defiant lyrics. Emerging in New York City around bands such as the Ramones, Blondie, and the Talking Heads, punk quickly spread to England, where a soaring unemployment rate and growing class inequality ensured the success of socially critical rock. Groups like the Sex Pistols, the Clash, the Buzzcocks, and Siouxsie and the Banshees sprang up and even scored Top 40 hits on the U.K. charts. Even so, the Sex Pistols—one of the most controversial groups in rock history—was eventually banned for offending British decorum.

▲ Joan Jett, of the punk-rock group the Runaways and later Joan Jett and the Blackhearts, was influential in breaking down the boys' club mentality of rock and roll. She was inducted into the Rock and Roll Hall of Fame in 2015. Mark Metcalfe/Getty Images

Punk didn't succeed commercially in the United States, in part because it was so hostile toward the commercialization of the mainstream music industry. However, it did help break down the boys' club mentality of rock, launching unapologetic and unadorned frontwomen like Patti Smith, Joan Jett, Debbie Harry, and Chrissie Hynde. It also introduced all-women bands whose members not only wrote but also performed their own music. Through these and other innovations, punk reopened the door to experimentation at a time when the industry had turned music into a purely commercial enterprise.

Indie Groups Reinterpret Rock

Taking the spirit of punk and updating it, **indie rock** groups emerged from the do-it-yourself approach of independent labels and created music that found its audience in live shows and on alternative-format college radio stations beginning in the 1980s. Groups often associated with early indie rock include R.E.M., the Cure, Sonic Youth, the Pixies, the Minutemen, and Hüsker Dü. In the Pacific Northwest, a subgenre called **grunge** emerged in the 1980s. After years of limited commercial success, grunge broke into the American mainstream with Nirvana's "Smells Like Teen Spirit" on the 1991 album *Nevermind*. Nirvana opened the floodgates to other "alternative" bands, such as Green Day, Pearl Jam, Soundgarden, Hole, and Sleater-Kinney.

Mainstream attention illustrates a key dilemma for successful indie artists: Their popularity results in commercial success, a situation that their music often criticizes. Still, independent acts like Arcade Fire and Vampire Weekend are among many that have launched and sustained successful recording careers built on independent labels, playing concerts and using the Internet and social media to promote their music and sell merchandise.

Hip-Hop Redraws Musical Lines

With the growing segregation of radio formats and the dominance of mainstream rock by white male performers, the place of black artists in the rock world diminished from the late 1970s onward. This trend—combined with the rise of "safe" dance music (or disco) by white bands (the Bee Gees), black artists (Donna Summer), and integrated groups (the Village People)—created space for a new sound to emerge beginning in the late 1970s: **hip-hop**, a term for the urban culture that includes *rapping*, *cutting* (or *sampling*) by deejays, breakdancing, street clothing, poetry slams, and graffiti art.

Similar to punk's opposition to commercial rock, hip-hop music stood in direct opposition to the polished, professional, and often less political world of soul. Its combination of social politics, swagger, and confrontational lyrics carried forward long-standing traditions in blues, R&B, soul, and rock and roll. Deejays, like the pioneering Jamaican émigré Clive Campbell (a.k.a. DJ Kool Herc), emerged first in New York, scratching and re-cueing old reggae, disco, soul, and rock albums.

The music industry initially saw hip-hop as a novelty, despite the enormous success of the Sugarhill Gang's "Rapper's Delight" in 1979. Then, in 1982, Grandmaster Flash and the Furious Five released "The Message" and forever infused hip-hop with a political take on ghetto life, a tradition continued by artists like Public Enemy and Ice-T. By 1985, hip-hop had exploded as a popular genre with the commercial successes of groups like Run-DMC, the Fat Boys, and LL Cool J. That year, Run-DMC's album *Raising Hell* became a major crossover hit, the first No. 1 hip-hop album on the popular charts (thanks in part to a collaboration with Aerosmith on a rap version of the group's 1976 hit "Walk This Way").

But because most major labels and many black radio stations rejected the rawness of hip-hop, the music spawned hundreds of new independent labels. Although initially dominated by male performers, hip-hop was open to women, and some—Salt-N-Pepa and Queen Latifah among them—quickly became major players.

On the one hand, the conversational style of rap makes it a forum in which performers can debate issues of gender, class, sexuality, violence, and drugs. On the other hand, hip-hop, like punk, has often drawn criticism for lyrics that degrade women, espouse homophobia, and applaud violence. Although hip-hop encompasses many different styles, one of its most controversial subgenres is **gangster rap**, which, in seeking to tell the truth about gang violence in American culture, has been accused of creating violence.

Another controversy in rap and hip-hop has been the place of white artists such as Eminem, Iggy Azalea, and Macklemore, who have found success emulating black artists. Some critics worry about a repeat of the appropriation of urban musical forms by white artists, robbing the original artists of opportunities and their artistic voice. These concerns over race and cultural appropriation will likely continue to be a source of controversy.

Today, hip-hop's stars include such artists as Vince Staples, who revisits the gangster genre, and artists like Kendrick Lamar, Chance the Rapper, Future, Drake, and Lizzo, who bring an old-school social consciousness to their

▲ Kendrick Lamar made history in 2018 when he became the first hip-hop musician—and, in fact, the first nonclassical or non-jazz musician—to win a Pulitzer Prize when his album *Damn* took home the award in April of that year. Theo Wargo/Getty Images

performances. By 2017, hip-hop/R&B surpassed rock to become the top music genre in the United States, with the majority of the top recordings and songs coming from that genre.[12]

The Country Road

Country music has attracted enough loyal listeners in its various forms to survive as a profitable sector of the recording industry since the early days of pop music. Though the many styles of **country** represent significant variations in the development of this musical form, they all share one element: the country voice, inflected by a twang or a drawl. In the late 1950s, the wilder honky-tonk sounds of country were tamed by a smoother style, inspired by the mellower songs of Elvis Presley. Replacing the fiddles, electric guitars, and nasal vocals of honky-tonk with symphonic strings, pitch-perfect background vocalists, and crooning stars like Jim Reeves and Patsy Cline, the emergent style would become known as the "Nashville sound." This laid-back and toned-down form of country music reigned throughout the 1960s.[13] In the 1970s, some singers and producers aimed for more mainstream acceptance. Lynn Anderson, Charley Pride, and Marie Osmond belted out hits that made the country idiom well liked in suburban America.[14] By the 1970s, country music saw two emerging trends: pop country, typified by artists like Glen Campbell, Dolly Parton, and Kenny Rogers, who appealed to a wider audience; and the edgier outlaw country, performed by artists like Waylon Jennings, Johnny Cash, Kris Kristofferson, and Willie Nelson. The mainstreaming of country music hit its stride in the 1990s, with Garth Brooks, Shania Twain, and other major crossover stars helping boost the popularity of the genre. Today's top country artists include Florida Georgia Line, Carrie Underwood, and Luke Bryan.

▲ "I feel like one of the things that sets country music apart from other types of music is the storyteller aspect," Grammy Award–winning singer-songwriter Carrie Underwood writes on her official website. "I want three-and-a-half-minute movies on the radio. You can follow the characters, and you can see it all playing out in your head." Jason Merritt/Getty Images

The Economics of Sound Recording

Sound recording is a complex business, with many participants playing a variety of roles and controlling numerous dimensions of the industry. Songwriters, singers, and musicians create the sounds. Producers and record labels sign up artists to create music and often own the artists' work. Promoters market artists' work, managers handle bands' touring schedules, and agents seek the best royalty deals for their artist-clients. And finally, the music reaches consumers via streaming services, digital downloads, CDs, and the radio.

Since its earliest days as a mass medium, the sound recording industry has made a lot of money through the sale of a physical product—until recently, the sales of records and CDs. But with the rise of online streaming, the traditional business model has broken down. The business has also changed through consolidation: Only three major labels remain (Universal Music Group, Sony Music Entertainment, and Warner Music Group), while streaming services like Spotify and Apple Music dominate the distribution of that music. But despite the *oligopoly* (few owners exerting great control over an industry), another big change in the music industry—also resulting from the digital turn—is the new energy surrounding independent music labels.

A Shifting Power Structure

Over the years, the U.S. recording industry has experienced dramatic shifts in its power structure. From the 1950s through the 1980s, the industry consisted of numerous competing major labels as well as independent production houses, or **indies**. Over time, the major labels began swallowing up the indies and then buying each other. By 1998, only six big labels remained: Universal, Warner, Sony, BMG, EMI, and Polygram. After a series of acquisitions and mergers, by 2012 only Universal Music Group, Sony Music Entertainment, and Warner Music Group remained. With their stables of stars, financial resources, and huge libraries of music to sell, these firms exert a great deal of control, and critics, consumers, and artists complain that this consolidation of power results in the labels supporting only major artists and styles that have large mainstream appeal. Together, these companies control about 70 percent of the global recording industry market share (see Figure 5.1). Although this is still a major

FIGURE 5.1 // GLOBAL MARKET SHARE OF THE MAJOR LABELS IN THE RECORDING INDUSTRY, 2017

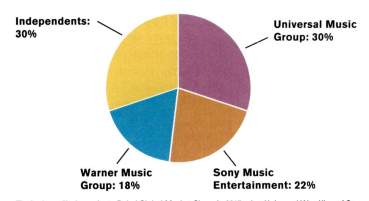

Independents: 30%
Universal Music Group: 30%
Warner Music Group: 18%
Sony Music Entertainment: 22%

Data from: Tim Ingham, "Independents Ruled Global Market Share in 2017—but Universal Was King of Streaming," *Music Business Worldwide*, April 25, 2018, www.musicbusinessworldwide.com/independents-ruled-global-market-share-in-2017-but-universal-was-king-of-streaming. Figures are rounded.

▲ Often many of the year's most acclaimed albums are released by artists on independent labels. Kishi Bashi is the stage name of singer, songwriter, and multi-instrumentalist Kaoru Ishibashi. A member of several indie bands—including Jupiter One and Of Montreal—Ishibashi has performed at major festivals, including SXSW and Austin City Limits. Scott Dudelson/Getty Images

portion of the market, the bigger news is that the slice of the pie for all indies combined equals the slice for the largest of the big three music companies.

The Indies Grow with Digital Music

The rise of rock and roll in the 1950s and early 1960s showcased a rich diversity of independent labels—including Sun, Stax, Chess, and Motown—all vying for a share of the new music. That tradition lives on today. In contrast to the three global players, some five thousand large and small independent production houses (indies) record music that appears to be less commercial. Often struggling enterprises, indies require only a handful of people to operate them.

For years, indies accounted for 10 to 15 percent of all music releases. But with the advent of downloads and streaming, the enormous diversity of independent-label music became much more accessible, and the market share of indies more than doubled in size. Indies often still depend on wholesale distributors to promote and sell their music, or they enter into deals with one of the three major labels to gain wider distribution for their artists. Independent labels have produced some of the best-selling artists of recent years: Big Machine Records (Florida Georgia Line, Rascal Flatts), Broken Bow Records (Jason Aldean), XL Recordings (Adele, Vampire Weekend), and Cash Money Records (Drake, Nicki Minaj).

Making, Selling, and Profiting from Music

Like most mass media, the music business is divided into several areas, each working in a different capacity. These areas are making the music, selling the music, and dividing the profits. All these areas are essential to the industry, yet there has always been a certain amount of conflict between business concerns and artistic concerns.

Making the Music

For major labels and indies, the process of producing music begins with **A&R (artist and repertoire) agents**, the talent scouts of the industry who discover, develop, and sometimes manage artists. A&R executives at the labels scout new talent and listen to demonstration recordings, or *demos*, from new artists, deciding whom to sign and which songs to record.

Recording is complex and expensive. A typical recording session involves the artist, the producer, the session engineer, and audio technicians. In charge of the overall recording process, the producer handles most nontechnical elements of the session, including reserving studio space, hiring session musicians if necessary, and making final decisions about the recording's quality. The session engineer oversees the technical aspects of the recording session, everything from choosing recording equipment to managing the audio technicians.

Selling the Music

Streaming services like Spotify, Apple Music, Google Play, and Amazon are the leading revenue generators in the music industry today, accounting for 65 percent of the music business in 2017 (see Figure 5.2) and on track to generate as much as 75 percent of revenue by the middle of 2018.[15]

As recently as 2011, physical recordings (CDs and some vinyl) accounted for almost 50 percent of U.S. music sales. But CD sales continue to decline and now constitute about 12 percent of the U.S. market (although in some countries, like Japan and Germany, CDs retain a much larger market share). Vinyl album sales have carved out a successful niche as a classic format in the United States and

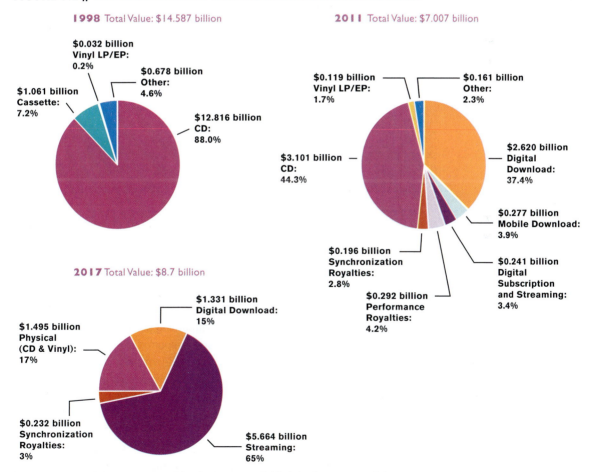

FIGURE 5.2 // THE EVOLUTION OF DIGITAL SOUND RECORDING SALES

Data from: Recording Industry Association of America, Annual Year-End Statistics. Figures are rounded.

Note: 1998 is the year before Napster arrived and the peak year of industry revenue. In 2011, digital product revenue surpassed physical product revenue for the first time. Synchronization royalties are those from music being licensed for use in television, movies, and advertisements.

account for about 4.5 percent of industry revenues. Digital downloads of singles and albums are about 15 percent of the market, down from the days in the early twenty-first century when the iTunes store was the dominant seller of music.

Total U.S. music sales hit a peak of $14.6 billion in 1998, but revenue started shrinking in 2000 as file-sharing began undercutting CD sales. Within about a decade, annual music industry revenue was only about half of what it had been, dropping to $7 billion by 2011. However, spurred by growth in the music streaming part of the business, revenues have started to bounce back, approaching $9 billion in 2017 in the United States and topping $17 billion worldwide in 2017 (up a billion dollars from 2016).[16]

Because it has become a key revenue source, the international recording industry has largely gotten over its original skepticism about streaming. (For more on other revenue sources, see "The Digital Turn Case Study: 360 Degrees of Music" on page 151.) Although **online piracy**—unauthorized online file-sharing—still exists, the advent of advertising-supported music streaming services has satisfied some consumer demand for free music and weakened interest in illegal file-swapping. That said, according to a 2018 report, a new—and common—form of piracy involves users ripping songs from online streaming services so they can listen offline without paying premium fees.[17]

Dividing the Profits

The digital upheaval in the music industry has shaken up the once-predictable sale of music through CDs or digital downloads, creating multiple digital venues for selling music and an equally large number of methods for dividing the profits.

With streaming as the leading music distribution format, figuring out what counts as a "sale" of a song or an album is important. The music industry developed an equivalency standard, with 1,500 song streams from an album equal to the sale of one album, and 150 song streams equal to the sale of one single.[18] The way in which songs are counted in music streaming has been similar, but compensation has varied widely by service. For example, the Recording Industry Association of America reports that Apple Music paid artists $12.50 per 1,000 streams, whereas Spotify paid $7.50 and YouTube paid only $1 per 1,000 streams.[19] This piecemeal approach to music licensing and royalties for streaming services—and a host of resulting problems, including numerous lawsuits—spurred major players in the music industry to push for a new law. The Music Modernization Act (MMA), which passed in late 2018, created a new nonprofit agency that would administer a blanket license with a more uniform fee structure to music streaming services. (For more on the MMA, see "Media Literacy Case Study: The New Masters of Music: Daniel Ek, Spotify, and Streaming Music" on pages 132–133.)

For CDs, profits get divided more transparently. Let's take the example of a CD that retails at $17.98. The wholesale price for that CD is about $12.50, leaving the remainder as retail profit. Discount retailers like Walmart and Best Buy sell closer to the wholesale price to lure customers in so that they will buy

The Digital Turn

CASE STUDY

360 Degrees of Music

It used to be that recording labels made most or all of their money by receiving a percentage of the money generated by the sale of physical media, such as CDs and records. But the arrival of the digital turn saw sales revenue cut in half in little over a decade; in response, the recording industry is turning to 360-degree agreements. Defined by legal scholar Sara Karubian as "a legal contract between a musical artist and one company incorporating components of an artist's career that have traditionally been handled by separate contracts with different companies," the 360-degree deal gives a single corporation control over everything, from merchandising and publishing to endorsements and touring.[1]

This means that in addition to the money a record company would make from sales of recordings, the company would also get a cut from concert tours, publishing (if the artist is also the songwriter), merchandise, endorsements, and television and movie appearances for the length of the contract. In theory, the record company would help organize, market, and cover the up-front costs of concert tours, merchandise production, and so on. The recording industry describes these deals as mutually beneficial, centralizing and maximizing revenue for the artist and the label at a time when both are suffering from the drop in recorded-music sales.

But in practice, critics worry that there may be downsides to these arrangements. Depending on the negotiated deal, a 360-degree arrangement might allow a record label to take a chunk of the profit from a concert tour or song sales even if the label didn't help fund or promote it. These deals also shift power back to conglomerates at a time when more indie labels have gained traction in the industry.

As an alternative to signing a 360-degree agreement, some artists are content to become "touring bands," making a little money off albums and singles but using them primarily to promote their live shows and accompanying merchandise. Musical acts with large enough fan bases may also follow the lead of British alternative rock group Radiohead, which handles its career without contracted-label backing, and independent hip-hop artist Chance the Rapper, who gives away his music but makes money by selling merchandise (see the chapter opener). But while few big artists can maintain a label-free career, many more are offering fans the option of buying their music directly through the artist's or the label's website, often selling exclusive packages that may include digital downloads, vinyl albums, T-shirts, limited-edition releases, and concert tickets. In these cases, artists are allowing multiple media to converge into their own hands. Whether through 360-degree deals, touring careers, or a self-releasing strategy, convergence is changing the way many musicians make money.

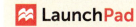

⊙ **Visit LaunchPad** to watch a clip showing Katy Perry on tour. *Forbes* magazine dubbed Perry the "highest paid woman in music" in 2018, thanks in part to an eighty-performance tour that grossed more than $1 million each night.[2] How might an expensive tour bring in additional money for an artist like Perry?

launchpadworks.com

▲ Solomon Linda (on far left, pictured with his singing group, the Original Evening Birds), the writer of the frequently covered hit song "The Lion Sleeps Tonight," signed over the copyright for the song for 10 shillings—the equivalent of 87 cents today—in 1952. After Linda's death in 1962, with only $22 to his name, his family fought for the royalties he should have received, resulting in a successful financial settlement for the family in 2006. Naashon Falk/Full Frame

other things (even if they make less profit on the CD itself). The wholesale price represents the actual cost of producing and promoting the recording plus the music label's profits. The music label reaps the highest revenue (close to $9.74 on a typical CD) but, along with the artist, bears the bulk of the expenses: manufacturing costs, packaging and CD design, advertising and promotion, and artists' royalties.

Let's also consider the costs and profits from a typical $1.29 iTunes digital download. iTunes gets 30 percent of every song sale, which equals about $0.40 per song. A standard $0.09 royalty for the song publisher and writer leaves about $0.60 for the record company. Artists at a typical royalty rate of about 15 percent would get $0.20 from the song download.

In addition to sales royalties, there are also performance and mechanical royalties that go to various participants in the industry. A *performance royalty* is paid to artists and music publishers whenever a song they created or own is played in any money-making medium or venue—such as on the radio, on television, in a film, or in a restaurant. Performance royalties are collected and paid out by the three major performance-rights organizations: ASCAP; the Society of European Stage Authors and Composers (SESAC); and Broadcast Music, Inc. (BMI). Songwriters also receive a *mechanical royalty* each time a recording of their song is sold. The mechanical royalty is usually split between the music publisher and the songwriter. However, songwriters sometimes sell their copyrights to publishers to make a short-term profit. In these cases, they forgo the long-term royalties they would have received by retaining the copyright.

Sound Recording in a Democratic Society

Of all the developments that have unfolded since sound recording became a mass medium, controversies sparked by some forms of popular music have raised the most provocative questions about music's role in our democracy. Battles over what artists should be allowed to say in a song and how they should behave on stage or in a video speak to the heart of democratic expression.

Are songs that express violent intent toward gay people, women, or ethnic or racial groups hate crimes? Are songs protected as free speech under the First Amendment of the U.S. Constitution? Moreover, will the ongoing consolidation of the industry by a few powerful music labels encourage them to "approve" lyrics and other forms of musical expression only if doing so will earn them maximum profits? Will the Internet and the shift to music streaming continue to create more spaces for independent music to grow and for alternative voices to be heard? Popular musical forms that push at cultural boundaries face a dilemma: how to uphold the right to free expression while resisting control by companies bent on maximizing profits. Since the 1950s, forms of rock music have arisen to break through boundaries, then have been reined in to create a successful commercial product, then have reemerged as new agents of rebellion—and on and on, repeating the cycle.

Still, this dynamic between popular music's innovation and capitalism's profit motive seems like an ongoing dance that has sustained—at least until the age of the Internet—the economic structure of the music industry. The major labels need indies to identify and develop new and fresh talent, and talent is fresh only if it seems alternative or less commercial and comes from nonmainstream origins, such as ethnic communities, backyard garages, dance parties, and neighborhood clubs. For a long time, it was taken as a given that musicians need the major labels if they want to distribute their work widely, become famous, and reach large audiences. But an examination of major label practices, in terms of both business and artist relations, may not reinforce this belief any longer, especially given the considerable success of several musical acts that have never been on a major label. A major component of media literacy as related to popular music involves evaluating the usefulness and pitfalls of the conglomerates that attempt to lead the industry. It also involves considering the ways in which the digital turn has changed this dynamic—and what is staying the same. The interdependence of artists and businesses presents alluring opportunities (and potential trade-offs) for participants in the industry as well as those who watch and analyze it.

CHAPTER ESSENTIALS

Review

- In the development stage of sound recording, inventors experimented with sound technology; in the entrepreneurial stage, people sought to make money from the developing technology; and, in the mass medium stage, entrepreneurs figured out how to cheaply produce and distribute multiple copies of recordings.

- The introduction of **audiotape** in the 1940s paved the way for commercial **stereo** recording.

- Records and tapes are examples of **analog recording**. **Digital recording**, which got its start in the 1970s, enabled the creation of **compact discs** and later the **MP3** file format, which would revolutionize sound recording and lead the way to digital downloading and music streaming.

- As sound recording became a mass medium, it fueled the growth of **pop music**, with numerous genres evolving from a common foundation (the first of which were **blues** and **jazz**). Pop led to the creation of major genres in modern American music, including **rhythm and blues (R&B)**, **rock and roll**, **soul**, **folk music**, psychedelic rock, **punk rock**, **indie rock**, **grunge**, **hip-hop**, **gangster rap**, and **country**.

- Rock and roll broke down many racial divisions in American culture, giving rise to genres like **rockabilly**. Yet the early rock and roll industry also promoted white **cover music** versions of black artists' songs, undermining black songwriters and performers.

- Over the years, the recording industry has gone from numerous competing labels and independent production houses, or **indies**, to a few major labels swallowing up the indies and buying each other out. Recently, however, indies have been growing again.

- The process of producing music often starts with **A&R (artist and repertoire) agents**, who find new talent for record companies to sign, then decide which songs to record.

- In the recording industry, artists and businesspeople divide profits in a variety of ways, depending on how the money is generated. Revenue is earned through the sales of digital downloads and recordings on CD and vinyl, as well as through fees and royalties paid by online music streaming services, online radio stations, and third parties who want to use a song in other media, like films. The 2018 Music Modernization Act (MMA) aims to make paying royalties for online streaming simpler and more uniform for all parties.

LaunchPad

Visit LaunchPad for *Media Essentials* at **launchpadworks.com** for additional learning tools:

- **REVIEW WITH LEARNINGCURVE**
  LearningCurve adaptive quizzing helps you master the concepts you need to learn from this chapter.
- **VIDEO: STREAMING SERVICES**
  This Bloomberg video discusses the financial impact that streaming has had on the music industry.
- **MEDIA LITERACY PRACTICE**
  This activity challenges you to develop a critical perspective and apply it to everyday encounters with communication media.

- Some forms of popular music have raised questions about music's role in our democracy, such as what artists should be allowed to say in a song and whether or not they are protected under the First Amendment. The challenge becomes how to support freedom of expression while resisting powerful control by companies whose profit motives are usually paramount.

Key Terms

audiotape, p. 129
stereo, p. 129
analog recording, p. 130
digital recording, p. 130
compact discs, p. 130
MP3, p. 130
pop music, p. 134
jazz, p. 135
rock and roll, p. 136
blues, p. 136
rhythm and blues (R&B), p. 136
cover music, p. 137
rockabilly, p. 139
soul, p. 142
folk music, p. 142
punk rock, p. 143
indie rock, p. 144
grunge, p. 144
hip-hop, p. 144
gangster rap, p. 145
country, p. 146
indies, p. 147
A&R (artist and repertoire) agents, p. 148
online piracy, p. 150

Study Questions

1. How did sound recording survive the advent of radio and the Great Depression?

2. How did rock and roll both challenge and perpetuate racial inequalities in the United States in the 1950s and 1960s?

3. Why did hip-hop and punk rock emerge as significant musical forms in the late 1970s and 1980s? What do their developments have in common, and how are they different?

4. What are some of the major changes the recording industry experienced as a result of the digital turn and the rise of music streaming as the biggest segment of music industry revenue? What have these changes meant for artists? For record labels? For consumers?

5. How does popular music push the boundaries of the First Amendment? Why might music be worthy of those constitutional guarantees of free speech?

Mass Media Industries

6

Popular Radio and the Origins of Broadcasting

159
The Early History of Radio

169
The Evolution of Radio

171
The Characteristics of Contemporary Radio

179
The Economics of Commercial Radio

182
Radio in a Democratic Society

The year 2017 was a breakthrough year for podcasting: one-third of Americans tuned into podcasts, and one-sixth listened to podcasts at least once a week.[1] Today, more than 500,000 podcast titles are available, and 1,000 more are added every week.[2] Just as listeners tuned in during the golden age of radio in the 1930s, when creative storytelling and sound effects transfixed American audiences, podcast listeners appreciate the simple pleasure they get from listening to stories. These listeners have embraced the fresh perspectives that made sensations out of investigative journalism podcasts *Serial* (2014) and *S-Town* (2017) and household names out of ongoing podcasts like *Pod Save America*, *2 Dope Queens*, and NPR's *Alt.Latino*.

Forty-five percent of all podcasts currently address society and culture, with true-crime podcasts tending to be the most popular. News and politics make up 34 percent of all podcast genres, followed by comedy (32 percent) and sports (23 percent).[3] Listeners have seamlessly integrated podcasts into their lives: while driving, exercising, working, or doing chores at home. And, not surprisingly, this new audio format has both challenged and invigorated radio broadcasting.

◀ Jasmine Garsd of NPR's podcast *Alt.Latino* interviews musician Ana Tijoux at the SXSW Music, Film + Interactive.
Heather Kennedy/Getty Images

Since podcasts are easy to make, they are flooding the listening market with inexpensive, accessible content. This new content tends to be less polished than radio, taking a casual approach that many listeners find appealing. Also, since podcasts are not required to play along with broadcast rules that limit indecent, obscene, or profane language, they offer flexible topics that broadcast radio isn't as easily able to explore and present an exhilarating mix of diverse voices.

"Podcasts bring you to places you've never been, they give you the impression of sharing an animated kitchen-table banter (or a loud bar argument) with a couple of friends," media scholar Juliette De Maeyer noted in the *Atlantic*.[4]

Perhaps most importantly, podcasts can be played at any time and on a variety of devices (especially mobile phones), are downloadable, and are not dependent on an on-air time slot. Because podcast listeners tend to be younger, college educated, digitally savvy, and well paid, the new format has been attracting advertising dollars away from radio.[5]

Radio has answered these challenges by creating podcasts out of its live programming. Perhaps National Public Radio (NPR) has been the most successful at making serious inroads in the podcasting space. NPR, and now the rest of the radio industry, has embraced podcasting as an extension of what it has been doing since the beginning of radio—creating intimate connections through sound. Radio conglomerates such as iHeartMedia now develop full podcasts with their biggest radio personalities.

The radio industry is also interested in exploring the expanding podcast environment to discover future broadcast radio personalities. It remains to be seen if podcast hosts will sacrifice their autonomy to join a broadcast network, or if radio content will change dramatically because of the podcasting challenge. Radio's biggest fear is that audiences will simply avoid radio altogether in search of new listening experiences that speak directly to their interests—a fear expressed succinctly by radio industry consultant Alan Burns: What if the increasing selection of podcasts create "infinite inventory, that is, too many audio avails chasing too few audio advertising dollars"?[6]

THE STORY OF RADIO—from its invention in the late nineteenth century to its current incarnation as a multitechnology mass medium—is one of the most remarkable in media history. In the United States, the early days of network radio gave Americans "a national identity" and "a chance to share in a common experience."[7] Even with the arrival of television in the 1950s, the recent "corporatization" of broadcasting, and the demographic segmentation of radio today, this medium has continued to play a powerful role in our lives. Likewise, the ways in which legislators a century ago wrote the first laws governing radio set the stage for later laws written to cover all forms of electronic mass media, from television to cable to the Internet. For people throughout the nation, the music and talk emanating daily from their radios, PCs, and handheld devices powerfully shape their political opinions, social mores, and (owing to advertisements) purchasing decisions. In this chapter, we will explore these themes by:

- examining radio's early history, including how its evolution from one-to-one to one-to-many communication led to new regulations and innovations in programming

- looking at how technological advances such as transistors and FM sparked the rise of format radio

- familiarizing ourselves with the array of characteristics defining radio today, such as format specialization, nonprofit business models, and digital radio technologies

- exploring the economics behind modern radio, including advertising and consolidation of ownership over the public airwaves

- considering radio's influence on American culture in an age when control of the public airwaves lies in fewer hands than ever

The Early History of Radio

Radio did not emerge as a full-blown mass medium until the 1920s, though its development can be traced to the introduction of the telegraph in the 1840s. As with most media, inventors tinkered in these earliest years with the technologies of the day to address practical needs. The telegraph and early experiments with wireless transmission set the stage for radio as a communication medium.

Inventors Paving the Way: Morse, Maxwell, and Hertz

The **telegraph**—the precursor of radio technology—was invented in the United States in the 1840s and was the first technology to enable messages to move faster than human travel. This meant that news and other messages could be transmitted from coast to coast within minutes, rather than the days required to

LaunchPad
launchpadworks.com

Use **LearningCurve** to review concepts from this chapter.

▲ A telegraphy class at Iowa State University, circa 1910. Sending messages using Morse code across telegraph wires was the precursor to radio, which did not fully become a mass medium until the 1920s. Like the Internet, radio was popularized through universities and high schools. Education-related clubs met to build radio transmitters and receivers, and teachers were among the first to develop radio content during the 1920s. Bettina Fabos/Fortepan Iowa

physically carry information from place to place. American artist and inventor Samuel Morse initially developed this practical system of sending electrical impulses from a transmitter through a cable to a reception device. Telegraph operators used what became known as **Morse code**—a series of dots and dashes that stood for letters of the alphabet and interrupted the electrical current along a wire cable. By 1844, Morse had set up the first telegraph line, which linked Washington, D.C., and Baltimore, Maryland. By 1861, telegraph lines stretched from coast to coast. Just five years later, the first transatlantic cable, capable of transmitting about six words a minute, ran between Newfoundland and Ireland along the ocean floor.

Though revolutionary, the telegraph had significant limitations. For one thing, it couldn't transmit the human voice. Moreover, because it depended on wires, it was useless for anyone seeking to communicate with ships at sea. The world needed a telegraph *without* wires. In the mid-1860s, Scottish physicist James Maxwell theorized the existence of **radio waves**, which could be harnessed to send signals from one place to another without wires. In the 1880s, German physicist Heinrich Hertz tested Maxwell's theory by using electrical sparks that emitted **electromagnetic waves**, invisible electronic impulses similar to light. The experiment was the first recorded transmission and reception of radio waves, and it would dramatically advance the development of wireless communication.

Innovators in Wireless: Marconi, Fessenden, and De Forest

As the nineteenth century unfolded, inventors building on the earlier technologies continued improving wireless communication. New developments took wireless from **narrowcasting** (person-to-person or point-to-point transmission of messages) to **broadcasting** (transmission from one point to multiple listeners; also known as one-to-many communication).

Marconi: The Father of Wireless Telegraphy

In 1894, a twenty-year-old, self-educated Italian engineer named Guglielmo Marconi read Hertz's work. He quickly realized that developing a way to send high-speed messages over great distances would transform communication, commercial shipping, and the military. The young engineer set out to make wireless technology practical. After successfully figuring out how to build a wireless communication device that could send Morse code from a transmitter to a receiver, Marconi traveled to England in 1896. There, he received a patent on **wireless telegraphy**, a form of voiceless *point-to-point communication.*

In London the following year, the Italian inventor formed the Marconi Wireless Telegraph Company, later known as British Marconi. He began installing wireless technology on British naval and private commercial ships. This left other innovators to explore the wireless transmission of voice and music, later known as **wireless telephony** and eventually **radio**. In 1899, Marconi opened a branch in the United States, commonly referred to as American Marconi. That same year, he sent the first wireless Morse code signal across the English Channel to France. In 1901, he relayed the first wireless signal from Cornwall, England, across the Atlantic Ocean to St. John's, Newfoundland.

History often cites Marconi as the "father of radio," but Russian scientist Alexander Popov accomplished similar feats in St. Petersburg at the same time. In addition, it's important to note that Nikola Tesla, a Serbian-Croatian scientist who immigrated to New York, invented and demonstrated a wireless electrical device ahead of both Marconi and Popov.[8] Tesla's work was overshadowed by Marconi's, though Marconi used much of Tesla's work in his own developments. However, in 1943 (a few months after Tesla died penniless in New York), the U.S. Supreme Court overturned Marconi's wireless patent and deemed Tesla the inventor of radio.[9]

▲ Nikola Tesla conceived the high-capacity alternating current systems that made worldwide electrification possible, and he invented a wireless system in 1892. Here, a double-exposed photograph combines the image of Tesla reading a book in his laboratory in 1899 with the image of his Tesla coil discharging several million volts. Bettmann/Getty Images

Fessenden: The First Voice Broadcast

Marconi had taken major steps in London and the United States. But it was Canadian engineer Reginald Fessenden who transformed wireless telegraphy into *one-to-many communication.* Fessenden is credited with providing the first voice broadcast. Formerly a chief chemist for Thomas Edison, he went to work for the U.S. Navy and eventually for General Electric (GE), where he focused on improving the frequency of wireless signals. Both the navy and GE were interested in the potential for voice transmission. On Christmas Eve in 1906, using a powerful transmitter built by GE, Fessenden gave his first public demonstration, sending his violin performance of "O Holy Night" and a reading of a Bible passage through the airwaves from his station at Brant Rock, Massachusetts, to an unknown number of shipboard operators off the Atlantic Coast.

De Forest: Birthing Modern Electronics

American inventor Lee De Forest improved the usefulness of broadcasting by greatly increasing listeners' ability to hear dots and dashes, and later speech and music, on a receiver. In 1906, he developed the Audion vacuum tube, which detected and amplified radio signals. The device was essential to the development of voice transmission, long-distance radio, and (eventually) television. Even though De Forest held the patent for the Audion, he was accused in court and by fellow engineers of stealing others' ideas, even after the court ruled in his favor.[10] Many historians consider the Audion—which powered radios until the arrival of transistors and solid-state circuits in the 1950s—the origin of modern electronics.

In 1907, De Forest demonstrated his invention's power and practical value by broadcasting a performance by Metropolitan opera tenor Enrico Caruso to his friends in New York. The next year, he and his wife, Nora, played records into a microphone from atop the Eiffel Tower in Paris; the signals were picked up by receivers up to five hundred miles away.

Early Regulation of Radio

By the turn of the twentieth century, radio had become a new force in American life. Recognizing radio's power to shape political opinion, economic dynamics, and military strategy and tactics, lawmakers moved to ensure U.S. control over the fledgling industry. With this goal in mind, legislators first defined radio as a shared resource for the public good. They then passed laws regulating how the public airwaves could be used and in what manner private businesses could take part in the industry.

Providing Public Safety

Because radio waves crossed state and national borders, legislators determined that broadcasting constituted a "natural resource"—a type of interstate commerce that should be regulated on the public's behalf in the public's best interests. Therefore, radio waves could not be owned, just licensed for use for a set period of time.

The first public safety rule came in 1910, when Congress passed the **Wireless Ship Act**. The law mandated that all major U.S. seagoing ships carrying more than fifty passengers and traveling more than two hundred miles off either coast be equipped with wireless equipment with a one-hundred-mile range. The importance of this act was underscored by the *Titanic* disaster in 1912, when over seven hundred passengers were saved by nearby ships responding to the passenger liner's radio distress signals. In the wake of the *Titanic* tragedy, Congress passed the **Radio Act of 1912**, which required all radio stations on land or at sea to be licensed and assigned special call letters. The act helped bring some order to the airwaves, which had been increasingly jammed with amateur radio operators. It also formally adopted the SOS Morse-code distress signal.

Ensuring National Security

By 1915, more than twenty American companies sold wireless point-to-point communication systems, primarily for use in ship-to-shore communication. American Marconi (a subsidiary of British Marconi) was the biggest of these companies. But with World War I erupting in Europe, the U.S. Navy questioned the wisdom of allowing a foreign-controlled company to wield so much power over communication. When the United States entered the war in 1917, the government closed down all amateur radio operations, took control of key radio transmitters, and blocked British Marconi from purchasing radio equipment from General Electric. In addition to addressing concerns about national security, these moves enabled the United States to reduce Britain's influence over communication and tightened U.S. control over the emerging wireless infrastructure. American corporations, especially GE and AT&T, capitalized on the navy's xenophobia and succeeded in undercutting Marconi's influence.

RCA: The Formation of an American Radio Monopoly

Some members of Congress, along with some business leaders, opposed federal legislation granting the government or the navy a radio monopoly. To secure a place in the fast-evolving industry, GE proposed a plan by which it would create a *private-sector monopoly*—a privately owned company that would have the government's approval to dominate the radio industry. In 1919, the plan was accepted by the powers that be at both GE and the U.S. Navy—the government branch most prominently fighting for control of the radio industry in America. GE founded the **Radio Corporation of America (RCA)**, which soon acquired American Marconi. RCA purchased and pooled patents from the navy, AT&T, GE, the former American Marconi, and other companies to ensure U.S. control over the manufacture of radio transmitters and receivers. Under the various agreements, AT&T made most of the transmitters; GE (and later Westinghouse) made radio receivers; and RCA administered patents, collected royalties, and redistributed them to the others.[11]

KDKA: The First Commercial Radio Station

With the advent of the United States' global dominance in mass communication, many people became intrigued by radio's potential. Amateur stations popped up in places like San Jose, California; Medford, Massachusetts; New York; Detroit; and Pierre, South Dakota. The best-known early station was begun by an engineer named Frank Conrad, who worked for GE's rival, Westinghouse Electric Company. In 1916, he set up a radio studio above his Pittsburgh garage by placing a microphone in front of a phonograph. Conrad broadcast music and news to his friends (whom he supplied with receivers) two evenings a week on experimental station 8XK. When a Westinghouse executive got wind of Conrad's activities in 1920, he established KDKA, generally regarded as the first commercial (profit-based, privately owned) broadcast station. The following year, the U.S. Commerce Department officially licensed five radio stations for operation; by early 1923, more than six hundred commercial and noncommercial stations were operating. Just two years later, a whopping 5.5 million radio sets were in use across America, made by companies such as GE and Westinghouse and costing about $55 ($664 in today's dollars). Radio was officially a mass medium.

The Networks

With the establishment of the private sector's involvement, the groundwork was laid for radio to take off as a business, which would enable commercial station owners to reach more listeners more efficiently than ever. The radio **network** arose: a cost-saving operation that links a group of affiliate or subsidiary broadcast stations that share programming produced at a central location. (At that time, stations were linked through special phone lines; today, they're linked through satellite relays.)

The network system enabled stations to control program costs and avoid unnecessary duplication of content creation. Simply put, it was cheaper to produce programs at one station and broadcast them simultaneously over multiple owned or affiliated stations than for each station to generate its own programs. Networks thus brought the best musical, dramatic, and comedic talent to one place, where programs could be produced and then distributed all over the country. This new business model concentrated control of radio in the hands of a few corporate players, all of whom jockeyed for additional power.

AT&T: Making a Power Grab

The shift toward networks began in 1922, when RCA's partnership with AT&T began to unravel. In a major power grab, AT&T, which already had a government-sanctioned monopoly in the telephone business, decided to break its RCA agreements in an attempt to monopolize radio. Identifying the new medium as the "wireless telephone," AT&T argued that broadcasting was merely an extension of its control over the telephone. The corporate giant complained that RCA had gained too much power. In violation of its early agreements with RCA, AT&T began making and selling its own radio receivers.

That same year, AT&T started WEAF (now WNBC) in New York, the first radio station to regularly sell commercial time to advertisers. Advertising, company executives reasoned, would ensure profits long after radio-set sales—the original motivator for Westinghouse's, GE's, and RCA's initial ventures into radio

▲ Westinghouse engineer Frank Conrad transformed his hobby into Pittsburgh's KDKA. Although this station is widely celebrated as the first broadcasting outlet, one can't underestimate the influence Westinghouse had in promoting this "historical first." Westinghouse saw the celebration of Conrad's garage studio as a way to market the company's radio equipment. The resulting legacy has thus overshadowed other individuals who also experimented with radio broadcasting. Bettmann/Getty Images

programming—had saturated the consumer market. AT&T claimed that under the RCA agreements, it had the exclusive right to sell ads, which AT&T called *toll broadcasting*. Most people in radio at the time recoiled at the idea of using the medium for advertising, viewing it instead as a public information service. But executives remained riveted by the potential of radio ads to enhance profits.

Still, the initial motivation behind AT&T's toll broadcasting idea was to dominate radio. Through its agreements with RCA, AT&T retained the rights to interconnect the signals between two or more radio stations via telephone wires. By the end of 1924, AT&T had interconnected twenty-two stations in a network to air a talk by President Calvin Coolidge. Some of these stations were owned by AT&T, but most simply consented to become AT&T "affiliates," agreeing to air the phone company's programs.

Seeing AT&T's success, GE, Westinghouse, and RCA launched a competing network. AT&T promptly denied them access to its telephone wires, so the new network used inferior telegraph lines to connect its stations. In 1925, the Justice Department, irritated by AT&T's power grab, redefined patent agreements. AT&T received a monopoly on providing the wires, known as *long lines*, to interconnect stations nationwide. In exchange, AT&T agreed to sell its network to RCA for $1 million and promised not to reenter broadcasting for eight years.

NBC: RCA Forms a Network

The commercial rewards of the network and affiliate system continued to excite executives' imaginations. For example, in September 1926, after RCA bought AT&T's telephone line–based radio network, David Sarnoff—RCA's general manager—created a new subsidiary called the National Broadcasting Company (NBC). NBC's ownership was shared by RCA (50%), General Electric (30%), and Westinghouse (20%). The former group of AT&T stations became known as NBC-Red. The network RCA, GE, and Westinghouse had already been building became NBC-Blue. By 1933, NBC-Red would have twenty-eight affiliates; NBC-Blue, twenty-four.

CBS: A Rival Network Challenges NBC

The network and affiliate system under RCA/NBC thrived throughout most of the 1920s and brought Americans together as never before to participate in the big events of the day. For example, when aviator Charles Lindbergh returned from the first solo

▼As a young man, David Sarnoff taught himself Morse code and learned as much as possible in Marconi's experimental shop in New York. Sarnoff ultimately created NBC and network radio, and his calculated ambition in the radio industry can be compared to Bill Gates's drive to control the computer software and Internet industries. Bettmann/Getty Images

▲ CBS helped establish itself as a premier radio network by attracting top talent from NBC, like Eddie Cantor. *The Eddie Cantor Show* featured lighthearted comedy and singers such as Ethel Merman (shown here). In 1934, Cantor introduced "Santa Claus Is Comin' to Town," and by the next day, the song was a hit.
Archive Photos/Getty Images

transatlantic flight in 1927, an estimated twenty-five to thirty million people listened to his welcome-home party on the six million radio sets then in use. At the time, it was the largest shared audience experience in the history of any mass medium.

During this decade, competition stiffened further within the industry. For instance, in 1928, William Paley, the twenty-seven-year-old son of a Philadelphia cigar company owner, bought the Columbia Phonograph Company and built it into a network later renamed the Columbia Broadcasting System (CBS). Unlike NBC, which actually charged its affiliates up to $96 a week for the privilege of carrying its programming, CBS paid affiliates as much as $50 an hour to carry its programs. By 1933, Paley's efforts had netted CBS more than ninety affiliates, many of which had defected from NBC. Paley also concentrated on developing news programs and entertainment shows, particularly soap operas and comedy-variety series. To that end, CBS raided NBC not just for affiliates but also for top talent, such as comedian Jack Benny and singer Frank Sinatra. In 1949, CBS finally surpassed NBC as the highest-rated network on radio.

The Radio Act of 1927

The growing concentration of power in the network and affiliate system raised a red flag for government leaders. From the 1920s through the early 1940s, lawmakers would enact many regulations aimed at regaining control over the industry. In particular, by the late 1920s, the government had become alarmed by RCA-NBC's growing influence over radio content. Moreover, as radio moved from narrowcasting to broadcasting, battles among various players over such issues as more frequency space and less channel interference heated up. Manufacturers, engineers, station operators, network executives, and the listening public demanded action to address their conflicting interests. Many wanted more sweeping regulation than the simple licensing function granted under the Radio Act of 1912, which gave the Commerce Department little power to deny a license or unclog the airwaves.

To restore order, Congress passed the **Radio Act of 1927**, which introduced a pivotal new principle: Licensees did not *own* their channels but could use them as long as they operated to serve the "public interest, convenience, or necessity." To oversee licenses and negotiate channel problems, such as too many stations trying to air on too few frequencies, the 1927 act created the **Federal Radio Commission (FRC)**, whose members were appointed by the president.

Although the FRC was intended as a temporary committee, it grew into a powerful regulatory agency. With passage of the **Federal Communications Act of 1934**, the FRC became the **Federal Communications Commission (FCC)**. Its jurisdiction covered not only radio but also the telephone and the telegraph (and later television, cable, and the Internet). More significantly, by this time Congress and the president had sided with the already-powerful radio networks and acceded to a system of advertising-supported commercial broadcasting as best serving the "public interest, convenience, or necessity," overriding the concerns of educational, labor, religious, and citizen broadcasting advocates.

In 1941, an activist FCC set out to break up what it saw as overly large and powerful networks, which led to a Supreme Court ruling forcing RCA to sell NBC-Blue. The divested enterprise became the American Broadcasting Company (ABC). Such government crackdowns brought long-overdue reforms to the radio industry. However, they came too late to prevent considerable damage to noncommercial radio.

The Golden Age of Radio

From the late 1920s to the 1940s, radio basked in a golden age, marked by a proliferation of informative and entertaining programs (such as weather forecasts, farm reports, news, music, dramas, quiz shows, variety shows, and comedies). This diversity of programming shaped—and was shaped by—American culture. It also paved the way for programs that Americans would later enjoy on television, as NBC, CBS, and ABC created television networks in the late 1940s and 1950s.

Early Radio Programming

In the early days of radio, only a handful of stations operated in most large radio markets. Through the networks they were affiliated with, these stations broadcast a variety of programs into listeners' homes (and in some cases, their cars). People had favorite evening programs, usually fifteen minutes long. After dinner, families would gather around the radio to hear comedies, dramas, public service announcements, and more. Popular programs included *Amos 'n' Andy* (a serial situation comedy), *The Shadow* (a mystery drama), *The Lone Ranger* (a western), *The Green Hornet* (a crime drama), and *Fibber McGee and Molly* (a comedy), as well as the fireside chats regularly presented by President Franklin D. Roosevelt.

◀ This bank of radio network microphones makes us wonder today how President Franklin D. Roosevelt managed to project such an intimate and reassuring tone in his famous fireside chats. Conceived originally to promote FDR's New Deal policies amid the Great Depression, these chats were delivered between 1933 and 1944 and touched on national topics. Roosevelt was the first president to effectively use broadcasting to communicate with citizens. Library of Congress, Prints & Photographs Division, Reproduction number LC-DIG-hec-47251 (digital file from original negative)

Variety shows featuring musical performances and comedy skits planted the seeds for popular TV variety shows that would come later, such as the *Ed Sullivan Show. Quiz shows* (including *The Old Time Spelling Bee*) introduced Americans to the thrill of competition. These radio programs set the stage for later competition-based TV shows, ranging from *The Price Is Right* and *Who Wants to Be a Millionaire* to reality-based shows such as *Survivor*, *Project Runway*, and *Top Chef*.

Dramatic programs, mostly radio plays broadcast live from theaters, would inspire later TV dramas, including soap operas. (The term *soap opera* came into use after Colgate-Palmolive began selling its soap products on the dramas it sponsored.) Another type of program, the *serial*, introduced the idea of continuing story lines from one day to the next—a format soon adopted by soap operas and some comedy programs.

Radio as Cultural Mirror

Radio programs powerfully reflected shifts in American culture, including attitudes about race and levels of tolerance for stereotypes. For example, the situation comedy *Amos 'n' Andy* was based on the conventions of the nineteenth-century minstrel show and featured black characters stereotyped as shiftless and stupid. Created as a blackface stage act by two white comedians, Charles Correll and Freeman Gosden, the program was criticized as racist by some at the time; however, NBC and the program's producers claimed that *Amos 'n' Andy* was as popular among black audiences as it was among white listeners.[12]

Early radio research estimated that the program aired in more than half of all radio homes in the nation during the 1930–31 season, making it the most popular radio series in history. In 1951, *Amos 'n' Andy* made a brief transition to television, after Correll and Gosden sold the rights to CBS for $1 million. It became the first TV series to have an all-black cast. But amid a strengthening Civil Rights movement and a formal protest by the NAACP, which argued that "every character is either a clown or a crook," CBS canceled the program in 1953.[13]

The Authority of Radio

In addition to reflecting evolving cultural beliefs, radio increasingly shaped them—in part by being perceived by listeners as the voice of authority. The adaptation of science-fiction author H. G. Wells's *War of the Worlds* (1898) on the radio series *Mercury Theatre on the Air* provides the most notable example of this. Considered the most famous single radio broadcast of all time, *War of the Worlds* was produced and hosted by Orson Welles, who also narrated it. On Halloween eve in 1938, the twenty-three-year-old Welles aired the Martian-invasion story in the style of a contemporary radio news bulletin. For people who missed the opening disclaimer, the program sounded like an authentic news report, with apparently eyewitness accounts of battles between Martian invaders and the U.S. Army.

◀ On Halloween eve in 1938, Orson Welles (*left*) broadcast a radio dramatization of *War of the Worlds* that created a panic up and down the East Coast, especially in Grover's Mill, New Jersey—the setting for the fictional Martian invasion that many listeners assumed was real. A seventy-six-year-old Grover's Mill resident (*right*) guarded a warehouse against alien invaders. Bettmann/Getty Images (left); Bettmann/Getty Images (right)

The program triggered a panic among some listeners. In New Jersey, some people walked through the streets with wet towels wrapped around their heads for protection against deadly Martian heat rays. In New York, young men reported to their National Guard headquarters to prepare for battle. Across the nation, calls from terrified citizens jammed police switchboards. The FCC called for stricter warnings both before and during programs imitating the style of radio news.

The Evolution of Radio

In the 1950s, a new form of mass media—television—came on the scene. TV snatched radio's advertisers, program genres, major celebrities, and large evening audiences. The TV set even physically displaced the radio as the living room centerpiece around which families gathered. To survive, players in the radio industry transformed their business model so that they could provide new forms of value for listeners.

Transistors: Making Radio Portable

The portability of radio proved to be a major advantage in the medium's struggle for survival. In the late 1920s, car radios had existed but were considered a luxury. But when Bell Laboratories invented the transistor in 1947, radios became more accessible than ever before—and portable. **Transistors** were small electrical devices that, like vacuum tubes, could receive and amplify radio signals. However, they used less power and gave off less heat than vacuum tubes and were more durable and less expensive. Best of all, they were tiny. The development of transistors let radio go where television could not—to the beach, to the office, into bedrooms and bathrooms, and into nearly all new cars.

The FM Revolution

To replace the shows radio had lost to TV, many people in radio switched the medium's emphasis to music, turning to the recording industry for content. However, making music sound good on radio would require some technological innovation. Until then, radio technology had centered on **AM** (amplitude modulation). This type of modulation was sufficient for talk, but it wasn't ideal for music. For that, radio needed **FM** (frequency modulation), which provided greater clarity as well as static-free radio reception.

FM radio existed for decades before it became the more dominant radio technology. American inventor Edwin Armstrong had discovered and developed FM radio during the 1920s and early 1930s, and between 1930 and 1933, Armstrong filed five patents on FM. The number of FM stations grew to 700 but then fell to 560 by the 1950s, as Armstrong was pulled into legal skirmishes over patents with such heavy hitters as RCA executive David Sarnoff, who had initially supported Armstrong's explorations into FM but then opted to throw his weight behind the development of TV. With the FCC allocating and reassigning scarce frequency spaces, RCA wanted to ensure that channels went to television before they went to FM. Most of all, however, Sarnoff wanted to protect RCA's existing AM empire. In 1954, weary from years of legal battles, Armstrong wrote a note apologizing to his wife and committed suicide. It wasn't until the early 1960s, when the FCC opened up more spectrum space for the superior sound of FM, that FM began to grow into the preferred radio band for music.

The Rise of Format Radio

Once radio became portable and FM was introduced, music began to dominate the medium more than ever. This eventually led to the creation of **format radio**, in which station managers (rather than disc jockeys) controlled the station's hour-by-hour music programming. Of course, in the late 1930s, music had been radio's single biggest staple, accounting for 48 percent of all programming. However, most music was live, which many people considered superior to recorded music. The first disc jockeys demonstrated that recorded music could attract just as many listeners as live music.

As early as 1949, station owner Todd Storz and his program manager in Omaha, Nebraska, noticed that bar patrons and waitstaff repeatedly played certain favorite songs from the records available in a jukebox. Drawing from jukebox culture, Storz hit on the idea of **rotation**: playing the top songs many times during the day. By the mid-1950s, the **Top 40 format** was born. Although the term *Top 40* derived from records frequently replayed on jukeboxes, this format came to refer to the forty most popular hits in a given week as measured by record sales.

As format radio grew, program managers combined rapid deejay chatter with the best-selling songs of the day and occasional oldies: popular songs from a few months earlier. Managers created a program log for deejays to follow and sectioned off blocks of roughly four hours throughout the day and night. Each block was designed to appeal to listeners' interests and thus attract more advertising dollars. For instance, a Top 40 station would feature its best deejays in the morning and afternoon periods, during listeners' commutes to and from school or work. Management also made savvy use of research. For example, if statistics showed that teenagers tended to listen to the radio mostly during evening hours and preferred music to news, then stations marketing to teens avoided scheduling news breaks during those hours.

The expansion of FM in the mid-1960s created room for stations to experiment, particularly with classical music, jazz, blues, and non–Top 40 rock songs. Many noncommercial stations broadcast from college campuses, where student deejays and managers rejected the commercialism associated with Top 40 songs and began playing lesser-known alternative music and longer album cuts.

▲ Jukeboxes often played the same songs over and over, as requested by patrons and waitstaff, who chose their favorite songs. This inspired the idea of rotation in the radio industry. WIN-Initiative/Getty Images

The Characteristics of Contemporary Radio

Contemporary radio differs markedly from its predecessor. In contrast to the few stations per market in the 1930s, most large markets today include more than forty stations vying for listener loyalty. In total, more than fifteen thousand radio stations now operate in the United States. With the exception of national network-sponsored news segments and nationally syndicated programs, most programming is locally produced (or made to sound like it) and heavily dependent on the music industry for content. In short, stations today are more specialized. Listeners are loyal to favorite stations, music formats, and even radio personalities, rather than to specific shows, and they generally listen to only four or five stations.

Format Specialization

Radio stations today use a variety of formats to serve diverse groups of listeners (see Figure 6.1). To please advertisers, who want to know exactly who is listening, formats usually target audiences according to their age, income, gender, or race/ethnicity. Radio's specialization enables advertisers to reach smaller target audiences at costs much lower than those for television. The most popular formats include the following:

- **Country.** The most popular format in the nation (except during morning drive time, when news/talk is number one), country is traditionally the default format for small communities with only one radio station. Country music has old roots in radio, beginning in 1925 with the influential Grand Ole Opry program on WSM in Nashville.
- **News/talk.** As the second most popular format in the nation, news and talk radio has been buoyed by the popularity of personalities like Howard Stern and Rush Limbaugh. This format tends to cater to adults over age thirty-five (except for sports talk programs, which draw mostly male sports fans of all ages). Though more expensive to produce than a music format, it appeals to advertisers seeking to target working and middle-class adult consumers (see "Media Literacy Case Study: How Did Talk Radio Become So One-Sided?" on pages 174–175).

FIGURE 6.1 // THE MOST POPULAR RADIO FORMATS IN THE UNITED STATES AMONG PERSONS AGE TWELVE AND OLDER

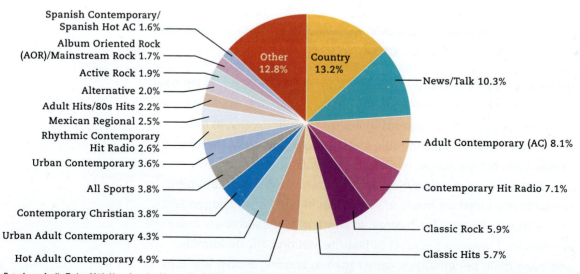

Data from: Audio Today 2018: How America Listens, April 2018, www.nielsen.com/content/dam/corporate/us/en/reports-downloads/2018-reports/audio-today-report-apr-2018.pdf.

- **Adult contemporary (AC).** This format, also known as middle of the road, or MOR, is among radio's oldest and most popular formats. It reaches about 8.1 percent of all listeners, most of them over the age of forty, with an eclectic mix of news, talk, oldies, and soft rock.
- **Contemporary hit radio (CHR).** Also called Top 40 radio, CHR encompasses everything from rap to pop rock and appeals to many teens and young adults. Since the mid-1980s, however, these stations have steadily lost ground, as younger generations turned first to MTV and then to online sources for their music, rather than to radio.
- **Urban contemporary.** In 1947, WDIA in Memphis was the first station to program exclusively for black listeners. This format targets a wide variety of African American listeners, primarily in large cities. Urban contemporary typically plays popular dance, rap, R&B, and hip-hop music.
- **Spanish-language radio.** One of radio's fastest growing formats, the Spanish-language format is concentrated mostly in large Hispanic markets, such as Miami, New York, Chicago, Las Vegas, and metro areas in California, Arizona, New Mexico, and Texas. Besides talk shows and news segments in Spanish, this format features a variety of Spanish, Caribbean, and Latin American musical styles.

In addition, today there are other formats that are spin-offs of **album-oriented rock (AOR)**, a format that hit its stride in the 1970s playing both popular and deeper cuts from albums by such artists as Pink Floyd, AC/DC, and Queen. Classic rock serves up rock favorites from the mid-1960s through the 1990s to the baby-boom generation and other listeners who have outgrown Top 40. The oldies format originally served adults who grew up on 1950s and early 1960s rock and roll. As that audience has aged, oldies formats now target younger audiences with the classic hits format, featuring songs from the 1970s, 1980s, and 1990s. The alternative format recaptures some of the experimental approach of the FM stations of the 1960s, although with much more controlled playlists, and has helped introduce such artists as Imagine Dragons and Billie Eilish.

Research indicates that most people identify closely with the music they listened to as adolescents and young adults. This tendency partially explains why classic hits and classic rock stations combined have surpassed Top 40 stations today. It also helps explain the recent nostalgia for music from the 1980s and 1990s.

Nonprofit Radio and NPR

Although commercial radio dominates the radio spectrum, nonprofit radio maintains a voice. Two government rulings, both in 1948, aided nonprofit radio. Through the first ruling, the government began authorizing noncommercial licenses to stations not affiliated with labor, religion, education, or civic groups.

Media Literacy

CASE STUDY

How Did Talk Radio Become So One-Sided?

For young adults, news/talk radio is in another universe. Radio listeners ages eighteen to thirty-four are all about music, with country, contemporary hit radio, and urban contemporary as their top radio formats.

It turns out that radio listeners ages fifty-five to sixty-four live in that other universe. Their top radio format is news/talk.[1] According to Nielsen research, the news/talk universe is also mostly white and male. The stars of that universe—the leading radio personalities—are Rush Limbaugh, Sean Hannity, Dave Ramsey, Michael Savage, Glenn Beck, Mark Levin, George Noory, Laura Ingraham, Mike Gallagher, and Hugh Hewitt. Although there are some moderates (e.g., Jim Bohannon) and progressives/liberals (e.g., Thom Hartmann and Stephanie Miller) among the top fifteen, their rarity suggests one other thing about the news/talk universe: it's predominantly politically conservative.[2]

▲ After the Fairness Doctrine was repealed, stations were free to air hours of partisan political programming—including that offered by Rush Limbaugh—without giving equal time to opposing viewpoints. Since the 1990s, radio stations have found Limbaugh's style of over-the-top conservative programming lucrative, though his attacks on women and minorities have resulted in some backlash against him, his advertisers, and the stations that carry him. shepard sherbell/Getty Images

 **Web Clip**

Being on the radio is not all there is for a successful news/talk operation like National Public Radio. In fact, NPR has its own dedicated YouTube Channel. How might a radio reporter or host vary his or her broadcast routine for a different medium?

How did one point of view come to dominate news/talk in the United States? Its roots were in the repeal of a little-known regulation that had been on the books of the Federal Communications Commission for decades. Since 1949, the FCC enforced what was called the Fairness Doctrine. This allowed "a station to editorialize, provided it made air time available for 'balanced presentation of all responsible viewpoints on particular issues.'"[3] The rationale behind the doctrine was that there were a limited number of stations on the public airwaves, and that broadcast stations should serve the public interest of the communities where they were located.

But by 1987, President Reagan was pushing business-friendly deregulation, and a chief target for the broadcasting industry was the Fairness Doctrine, since broadcasters did not like the demands of reporting contrasting positions on controversial issues. The National Association of Broadcasters (NAB) stated that broadcasters could report even-handedly without regulation. However, after its 1987 repeal, radio broadcasters did not continue to "report both sides of controversial issues," as the NAB had promised, but instead rolled out new programs that *created* controversy with very one-sided political opinions. As media historians Robert Hilliard and Michael Keith explain, the demise of the

Fairness Doctrine changed the tenor of talk radio. "Ostensibly this put no limits on any ideas, philosophies, or other political matter a station might wish to advocate. In reality, it swung the tide of radio and television political advocacy to the right."[4]

Limbaugh, still talk radio's biggest star, was the first conservative talk show host to go national in 1988. His show was a huge hit for ABC Radio, after which a host of conservative personalities flooded the airwaves. Limbaugh's support of conservative causes in his national radio program led to the Republicans gaining control of the House of Representatives in 1994, and Republicans named him an "honorary member of their class."[5]

There was an attempt at a liberal talk radio network with Air America from 2004 to 2010, yet Air America could never build the critical mass that conservative talk had. Rush Limbaugh has about 590 affiliate stations for his three-hour weekday show, while Air America could never get more than 70 affiliate stations to run its programs.

But another alternative to commercial news/talk has thrived: noncommercial news/talk. While Limbaugh's rise was meteoric, since the 1970s NPR has slowly built a broad base of listeners for its nonprofit, nonpartisan public radio network. Rush Limbaugh's audience is commercial talk radio's largest, at 14 million weekly listeners, but NPR's flagship *Morning Edition* program has a weekly audience of 14.2 million listeners at more than 800 affiliate stations.[6] As a noncommercial alternative, NPR does not focus on personalities and is heavily based in reporting, not commentary.

Still, commercial news/talk holds a significant edge on the airwaves, in politics, and in overall radio ratings: It has 8.3 percent of the U.S. listening audience, compared to 4 percent of the national listening audience for noncommercial news/talk—although, it's important to note, there are roughly four times as many commercial news/talk stations as there are noncommercial stations.[7]

APPLYING THE CRITICAL PROCESS

DESCRIPTION Listen to a typical morning or late-afternoon hour of a popular commercial news/talk radio station and a typical hour of noncommercial news/talk programming from an NPR station from the same time period for two to three days. Keep a log of what topics are covered and what news stories are reported.

ANALYSIS Look for patterns. What kinds of stories are covered? What kinds of topics are discussed? Create a chart to categorize the stories. How much time is given to *reporting* (clearly verified information) compared to time devoted to *opinion*? What kinds of interview sources are used?

INTERPRETATION What do these patterns mean? Is there a balance between reporting and opinion? Do you detect any bias, and if so, how did you determine this?

EVALUATION Do you agree with the 1949–1987 Fairness Doctrine rule that broadcasting should provide "reasonable, although not necessarily equal," attention to "controversial issues of public importance"? Why or why not? From which station did you learn the most, and which station did you find most entertaining? Explain. What did you like and dislike about each station?

ENGAGEMENT Contact the local general manager, program director, or news director at the stations you analyzed. Ask them what their goals are for their daily news/talk programming and what audience they are trying to reach. Incorporate their comments into a report on your findings. Finally, offer suggestions on how to make the programming at each station better.

▲ National Public Radio has created a variety of well-received podcasts, ranging from entertainment stories to hard news, to exist alongside its radio programming. The NPR Politics Podcast team (shown here) typically records a show once a week. Because podcasts aren't part of the set broadcasting schedule, however, the team can choose to record more frequently—for example, in the weeks leading up to an election. NPR

The first license went to Lewis Kimball Hill, a radio reporter and pacifist during World War II who started the **Pacifica Foundation** to run experimental public stations. Pacifica stations have often challenged the status quo in both radio and government. In the second ruling, the FCC approved 10-watt FM stations. Before 1948, radio stations had to have at least 250 watts to get licensed. A 10-watt station with a broadcast range of only about seven miles took very little capital to operate, so the ruling enabled many more people to participate in radio. Many of these tiny stations became training sites for students interested in a broadcasting career.

During the 1960s, nonprofit broadcasting found a new friend in Congress, which proved sympathetic to an old idea: using radio and television as educational tools. With the **Public Broadcasting Act of 1967**, Congress created the **Corporation for Public Broadcasting (CPB)**, the nonprofit parent organization to the first noncommercial networks: television's **Public Broadcasting Service (PBS)**, established in 1969, and **National Public Radio (NPR)**, established in 1970. With more than one thousand member stations, NPR draws over thirty-six million listeners each week to popular news and interview programs like *Morning Edition*, *All Things Considered*, and *Fresh Air*. In addition to traditional radio listeners, 8.1 million people download NPR podcasts each week.[14] NPR and PBS stations rely on a blend of private donations, corporate sponsorship, and a small amount of public funding.

Radio and Convergence

Like every other mass medium, radio has made the digital turn by converging with the Internet. Interestingly, this digital turn is taking radio back to its roots in some ways. Internet radio allows for much more variety, which is reminiscent of radio's earliest years, when nearly any individual or group with some technical skill could start a radio station. Moreover, podcasts have brought back such content as storytelling, instructional programs, and local topics of interest, which have largely been missing in corporate radio. And the portability of smartphones harks back to the compact transportability that first came with the popularization of transistor radios in the 1950s. When we talk about these kinds of convergences, we are talking about the blurring of lines between categories.

Even so, it's still possible to identify five particular ways radio is converging with digital technologies:

- **Internet radio.** Emerging in the 1990s with the popularity of the web, Internet radio stations come in two types. The first involves an existing AM, FM, satellite, or HD station "streaming" a simulcast version of its on-air signal over the web. Most radio stations stream programming over the web today and often facilitate the listening with an app. The other kind of Internet radio, which takes the form of a website created just for the purpose of streaming music (e.g., Pandora, and iHeartRadio, which streams live stations and Internet-only custom stations), offers "stations" with songs curated by the site based on an artist or a genre picked by the listener. (For more about the relationship between streaming and broadcast radio, see "The Digital Turn Case Study: Streaming Services Set Their Sights on Broadcast Radio" on page 178.)
- **Podcasting.** Developed in 2004, podcasting (the term marries *iPod* and *broadcasting*) refers to the practice of making audio files available on the Internet so that listeners can download and listen to them on their smartphones, iPods, tablets, or computers (see also the chapter opener). This popular distribution method quickly became mainstream as mass media companies created commercial podcasts to promote and extend existing content, such as news and reality TV, while independent producers kept pace with their own podcasts on niche topics like knitting, fly-fishing, and learning Russian. As noted earlier, by 2017, one in six Americans were listening to podcasts at least once a week.[15]
- **Portable listening.** For the broadcast radio industry, portability used to mean listening on a transistor or car radio. But with the digital turn to iPods and smartphones, broadcasters haven't been as easily available on today's primary portable audio devices. Some smartphones today come equipped with a chip that makes them able to receive FM radio signals, something that is used quite frequently in developing countries. In the United States, however, these chips have mostly been deactivated by cellular and smartphone companies that make money by charging customers for streamed data or music streaming services.

In the wake of the devastating hurricanes in Puerto Rico and the U.S. mainland in 2017, which knocked out cell phone towers, FCC chair Ajit Pai requested that all cell phone providers activate the FM chip.[16] As he and many others have pointed out, FM radio can offer lifesaving information during major emergencies to a public increasingly reliant on smartphones for all communication. By 2018, Sprint, Samsung, and LG had enabled these chips, but Apple declined to do so, responding that it no longer put the FM chips in its phones.[17] The NAB pushed back, claiming that engineering studies indicate that the chips are still part of the iPhone design, should the company wish to enable them, and pointing out that Apple has issued FM radio–capable

LaunchPad
launchpadworks.com

Going Visual: Video, Radio, and the Web
This video looks at how radio adapted to the Internet by providing multimedia on its websites to attract online listeners.

Discussion: If video is now important to radio, what might that mean for journalism and broadcasting students who are considering a job in radio?

The Digital Turn

CASE STUDY

Streaming Services Set Their Sights on Broadcast Radio

Music services like Spotify and Pandora have reshaped the sound recording industry, moving it from a business model based on CD sales and song downloads to one driven by streaming. Now these same streaming services are hoping to reshape another part of the way people enjoy music: They're taking on traditional broadcast (*terrestrial*) radio.

Most streaming companies offer different tiers of service: The premium tier gives users more control over song choice but includes a monthly fee, while the free tier carries ads but comes free to subscribers. According to *Billboard*, it's this second option—the free, ad-supported tier—that companies like Pandora and Spotify consider to be "direct competitors to terrestrial radio," meaning they consider their services compelling rivals for the ad dollars that companies are spending on broadcast radio. In fact, Spotify executive Troy Carter has called the free tier "the biggest radio station in the world."[1]

What might make ad-supported streaming attractive to advertisers? Streaming services are taking the following steps to snag listeners from traditional radio:

- Making their free services more flexible and attractive to further boost audience size.
- Capitalizing on changing consumer habits as more listeners get music from smartphones, cars connected to digital services, and "smart speakers"—services that don't always have AM/FM antennas.
- Appealing to younger listeners, who might be less interested in traditional radio.
- Using prepared playlists and enormous audiences of subscribers to drive the *Billboard* charts and cultivate more influence with the sound recording industry.[2]

In addition, artists and music labels receive revenue from streaming services, which isn't the case with terrestrial radio stations—an advantage that the streaming sites aren't shy about promoting in an effort to divert companies' ad dollars away from traditional radio.[3]

Music streaming services are telling investors and advertisers that traditional radio is vulnerable to their competition, but broadcasters are saying "not so fast." After a 2017 report from New York University detailed what it saw as radio's vulnerability to streaming services, both Nielsen (which measures ratings) and the National Association of Broadcasters issued heated replies, calling the study "silly" and citing ratings numbers that showed that "radio continues to have the broadest weekly reach among all media," even among teenage audiences.[4]

In his reply, the spokesperson for the NAB points out—correctly—that this wouldn't be the first time a new technology prompted predictions of radio's end. However, the digital turn has resulted in seismic shifts across the mediascape, and it remains to be seen whether this latest threat to traditional radio will be different. Those in the streaming business seem confident that it will: "[Right now Pandora has] only 10 percent of the listening that happens on terrestrial radio," said Pandora CEO Roger Lynch. "But that's a ratio that I think will flip over the next decade."[5]

> ### ▶ Web Clip
>
> **YouTube.com** features music videos from a wide variety of artists, and with its immediacy for finding popular music, it siphons off listeners from music-format radio stations. For example, you can search for "Thank U, Next," posted by Ariana Grande. Besides YouTube, what are some of the many ways a listener might seek out this track? Is simply turning on the radio still a popular option?
>
>

devices in the past, so the company could do so again if it chose to.[18] As of late 2018, the two sides had not reached a resolution.
- **Satellite radio.** Two companies, XM and Sirius, completed their introduction of nationwide satellite radio by 2002 and merged into a single provider in 2008. The merger was precipitated by their struggles to make a profit after building competing satellite systems and battling for listeners. SiriusXM offers about 174 digital music, news, and talk channels throughout the continental United States, with monthly prices starting at $15.99 and satellite radio receivers costing from $50 to $200. SiriusXM access is also available on mobile devices via an app, and U.S. automakers (investors in the satellite radio companies) now equip most new car radios with a satellite band, in addition to AM and FM. In 2018, SiriusXM announced it was buying streaming radio service Pandora in order to better compete with Spotify and Apple music services.[19] SiriusXM had about 33.7 million subscribers by 2018. (For comparison, on-demand streaming service Spotify had more than twice that number.)
- **HD radio.** Approved by the FCC in 2002, HD radio is a digital technology that enables AM and FM radio broadcasters to multicast two to three additional compressed digital signals within their traditional analog frequency. For example, KNOW—a public radio station at 91.1 FM in Minneapolis–St. Paul—runs its NPR news format on 91.1 HD1, Radio Heartland (acoustic and Americana music) on 91.1 HD2, and the BBC news service on 91.1 HD3. About twenty-two hundred radio stations now broadcast in digital HD.

The Economics of Commercial Radio

Radio today remains one of the most used mass media, reaching 93 percent of all Americans age twelve or older every week.[20] Because of this continued broad reach, the airwaves are still desirable real estate for advertisers and content programmers, who want to target people in and out of their homes; for record labels, who want their artists' songs played; and for radio station owners, who want to attract large groups of diverse listeners to dominate multiple markets.

Selling Ads and Paying for Programming

About 10 percent of all U.S. spending on media advertising goes to radio stations. Like newspapers, radio generates its largest profits by selling local and regional ads. Thirty-second radio ads range from $1,500 in large markets to

launchpadworks.com

Radio: Yesterday, Today, and Tomorrow

Scholars and radio producers explain how radio adapts to and influences other media.

Discussion: Do you expect that the Internet will be the end of radio, or will radio stations still be around decades from now?

just a few dollars in the smallest markets. Today, gross advertising receipts for radio are between $13.9 and $17 billion (about 75 percent of which are from local ad sales, with the remainder in national spot ads, network, and digital radio sales), down from an industry peak of $21.7 billion in 2006.[21] (The radio industry stopped reporting annual revenue in 2016, a signal that radio's revenue growth trend is declining; see "The Digital Turn Case Study: Streaming Services Set Their Sights on Broadcast Radio" on page 178 for some possible reasons why.) Nevertheless, the number of stations keeps growing, now totaling more than 2,000 broadcasting in HD and 15,493 broadcasting in analog. Of those analog stations, 4,626 are AM, 6,737 are FM commercial, and 4,130 are FM educational.[22]

Traditionally, local radio stations have received much of their content free from the recording industry. This is because for decades, radio broadcasters have paid royalties to songwriters and music publishers but not to the performing artists or record companies, arguing that the promotional value of getting songs played on the radio is sufficient compensation. The fact that broadcasters don't pay these royalties and satellite and streaming companies do has led to years of ongoing tension. Although in 2018 the Music Modernization Act restructured the royalty system for music played online or via satellite (see also Chapter 5), the act left traditional broadcast radio alone.[23]

When radio stations do want to purchase programming, they often turn to radio networks like Westwood One, which provides syndicated programs ranging from talk and news to entertainment and music. Stations can pay for this programming with money, receive the programming in exchange for time slots for national ads, or combine the two. In addition, some stations spend money on local programming. Although corporate consolidation and drastic local cutbacks have taken a toll on radio stations, some still hire staff to provide locally produced content and to play music.

Manipulating Playlists with Payola

Payola, the practice by which record promoters pay deejays to play particular records, was rampant during the 1950s, as record companies sought to guarantee record sales. In response, management took control of programming, arguing that if individual deejays had less control over which records would be played, the deejays would be less susceptible to bribery.

Despite congressional hearings and new regulations, payola persisted. Record promoters showered their favors on a few influential, high-profile deejays, whose backing could make or break a record nationally, or on key program managers in charge of Top 40 formats in large urban markets.

With the growth of music and radio streaming services, the practice of payola has again surfaced. But because streaming services aren't broadcasting, they fall outside the FCC's oversight. *Billboard* magazine reports that music promoters have been paying to influence playlists at services like Spotify, Deezer, and Apple Music. Playlists, used by hundreds of thousands of subscribers as a way to discover music, are created by the streaming services, influential individuals, or the music labels themselves. Spotify announced in 2015 that it would prohibit any playlists that had been influenced by money or other compensation (meaning that it wanted playlists to be based on honest opinion, not on payments to the person making the list). Yet the three major music corporations continue to influence streaming music: Universal Music Group features its music playlists on Digster, Sony showcases its music on Filtr, and Warner Music Group promotes its playlists on Topsify.[24]

Radio Ownership: From Diversity to Consolidation

From the 1950s through the 1980s, the FCC tried to encourage diversity in broadcast ownership—and thus programming—by limiting the number of stations a media company could own. The **Telecommunications Act of 1996** introduced a new age of consolidation in the industry, as the FCC eliminated most ownership restrictions on radio. As a result, some twenty-one hundred stations and $15 billion changed hands that year alone. From 1995 to 2005, the number of radio station owners declined by one-third, from sixty-six hundred to about forty-four hundred.[25]

The 1996 act allows individuals and companies to acquire as many radio stations as they want, with relaxed restrictions on the number of stations a single broadcaster may own in the same city. The larger the market or area, the more stations a company may own within that market.

This has reshaped the radio industry. Take, for example, the former Clear Channel Communications. It was formed in 1972 with one San Antonio station. Eventually, it gobbled up enough conglomerates to become the nation's largest radio chain owner, hitting a peak of 1,205 stations in 2005. Today, as iHeartMedia, it owns 849 radio stations and has branched out into other areas, owning about 600,000 billboard and outdoor displays in twenty countries, including 99,000 displays in forty-three of the fifty largest U.S. markets. iHeartMedia also distributes many of the leading syndicated programs, including *The Rush Limbaugh Show*, *The Glenn Beck Program*, *On Air with Ryan Seacrest*, and *Delilah* through its Premiere Networks business. iHeartMedia is also an Internet radio source with its iHeartRadio, which has more than 110 million registered users.

Combined, the top three commercial radio groups—iHeartMedia, Cumulus, and Townsquare Media—own over sixteen hundred stations, dominate the fifty largest markets in the United States, and control at least one-third of the entire radio industry's revenue. This expansion and the burden of billions of dollars in borrowing debt created problems for iHeartMedia and Cumulus, leading them to file for Chapter 11 bankruptcy in 2018, though both companies were set to emerge intact and with less debt.[26]

▲ Though much mainstream radio programming is now managed by corporations, with many more specific voices opting to produce podcasts rather than traditional radio shows, local college and community stations are still able to broadcast locally. Luisa Porter/The Commercial Dispatch, via AP Images

When large corporations regained control of America's radio airwaves in the 1990s, activists in hundreds of communities across the United States protested by starting up their own noncommercial "pirate" radio stations, capable of broadcasting over a few miles with low-power FM signals of 1 to 10 watts. The major complaint of pirate radio station operators was that the FCC had long since ceased licensing low-power community radio stations. In 2000, the FCC responded to tens of thousands of inquiries about the development of a new local radio broadcasting service: It approved a new noncommercial **low-power FM (LPFM)** class of 10- and 100-watt stations to give voice to local groups lacking access to the public airwaves. LPFM station licensees included mostly religious groups but also high schools, colleges and universities, Native American tribes, labor groups, and museums. Then FCC chair William E. Kennard, who fostered the LPFM initiative, explained: "This is about the haves—the broadcast industry—trying to prevent many have-nots—small community and educational organizations—from having just a little piece of the pie. Just a little piece of the airwaves which belong to all of the people."[27]

Radio in a Democratic Society

As the first national electronic mass medium, radio has powerfully molded American culture. It gave us soap operas, situation comedies, and broadcast news, and it helped popularize rock and roll, car culture, and the politics of talk radio. Yet for all its national influence and recent move toward consolidation, broadcast radio is still a supremely local medium. For decades, listeners have tuned in to hear the familiar voices of their community's deejays and talk-show hosts, and to enjoy the music of their cultural heritage.

The early debates over how radio should be used produced one of the most important and enduring ideas in communication policy for any democracy: a requirement to operate in the service of "public interest, convenience, or necessity." But as we've seen, the broadcasting industry has long chafed at this policy. Executives have maintained that because radio corporations invest heavily in technology, they should have more control over the radio frequencies on which they operate, and have no limit on the amount of stations they can own. Deregulation in the past few decades has moved the industry closer to that corporate vision. Today, nearly every radio market in the nation is dominated by a few owners, and those owners are required to renew their broadcasting licenses only every eight years.

This trend has begun moving radio away from its localism, as radio groups often manage hundreds of stations from afar. Given broadcasters' reluctance to openly discuss their own economic arrangements, public debate regarding radio as a natural resource has dwindled. Looking to the future, we face a big question: With a few large broadcast companies now permitted to dominate radio ownership nationwide, will the number and kinds of voices permitted to speak over the public airwaves be restricted? And if restrictions occur, what will happen to the democracy we live in, which is defined by local communities' having a say in how they're governed? To ensure that mass media, including radio, continue to serve democracy, we—the public—must play a role in developing the answers to these questions.

CHAPTER ESSENTIALS

Review

- With the invention of the **telegraph** in the 1840s, operators used **Morse code** to send electrical signals over wires. Then, experiments involving **radio waves** and **electromagnetic waves** dramatically advanced the development of wireless communication. As the nineteenth century unfolded, new developments—including inventions from Marconi, Fessenden, and De Forest—took wireless from **narrowcasting** (point-to-point transmission of messages) to **broadcasting** (one-to-many communication).

- A sharp increase in the number of radio stations and the growth of the radio **network**, such as NBC in 1926, prompted Congress to pass the **Radio Act of 1927**, which created the **Federal Radio Commission (FRC)** to oversee licenses and negotiate channel problems. Passage of the **Federal Communications Act of 1934** replaced the FRC with the **Federal Communications Commission (FCC)**, the agency that still oversees radio stations and other media.

LaunchPad

Visit LaunchPad for *Media Essentials* at **launchpadworks.com** for additional learning tools:

- **REVIEW WITH LEARNINGCURVE**
  LearningCurve adaptive quizzing helps you master the concepts you need to learn from this chapter.
- **MEDIA LITERACY PRACTICE**
  This activity challenges you to develop a critical perspective and apply it to everyday encounters with communication media.

- The late 1920s to the 1940s constituted a golden age of radio, but the massive popularity of television in the 1950s led to its decline—until **transistors** made radios portable and music-intensive **format radio** introduced the idea of **rotation** into its programming. The addition of better-sounding **FM** radio to the existing **AM** radio also served to strengthen the industry through the latter half of the twentieth century and into the twenty-first.

- Currently, commercial radio stations stick to a variety of formats, including **country**, **news/talk**, **adult contemporary (AC)**, **contemporary hit radio (CHR)**, **urban contemporary**, **Spanish-language radio**, and **album-oriented rock (AOR)**.

- Nonprofit radio stations and noncommercial networks, such as **National Public Radio (NPR)** and the **Public Broadcasting Service (PBS)**, were created to provide alternatives to commercial broadcasting. **Low-power FM (LPFM)** stations were also approved in 2000 as an alternative to corporate-controlled radio.

- Since the digital turn, alternative radio technologies have helped bring more diverse sounds and options for listening to radio audiences, including **Internet radio**, **podcasting**, portable listening, **satellite radio**, and **HD radio**.

- Commercial radio stations take in revenue from advertisers and spend money on assets such as content programming, often purchasing programming from national network radio.

- As control of the public airwaves consolidates into fewer and fewer hands, it's important to think about the impact this will have on local communities and the variety of voices that will be heard on those airwaves.

Key Terms

telegraph, p. 159
Morse code, p. 160
radio waves, p. 160
electromagnetic waves, p. 160
narrowcasting, p. 160
broadcasting, p. 160
wireless telegraphy, p. 161
wireless telephony, p. 161
radio, p. 161
Wireless Ship Act, p. 162
Radio Act of 1912, p. 162
Radio Corporation of America (RCA), p. 163
network, p. 164
Radio Act of 1927, p. 166
Federal Radio Commission (FRC), p. 166
Federal Communications Act of 1934, p. 166
Federal Communications Commission (FCC), p. 166
transistors, p. 170
AM, p. 170
FM, p. 170
format radio, p. 170
rotation, p. 171
Top 40 format, p. 171
country, p. 172
news/talk, p. 172
adult contemporary (AC), p. 173
contemporary hit radio (CHR), p. 173
urban contemporary, p. 173
Spanish-language radio, p. 173
album-oriented rock (AOR), p. 173
Pacifica Foundation, p. 176
Public Broadcasting Act of 1967, p. 176
Corporation for Public Broadcasting (CPB), p. 176
Public Broadcasting Service (PBS), p. 176
National Public Radio (NPR), p. 176
Internet radio, p. 177
podcasting, p. 177
portable listening, p. 177
satellite radio, p. 179
HD radio, p. 179
payola, p. 180
Telecommunications Act of 1996, p. 181
low-power FM (LPFM), p. 182

Study Questions

1. How did broadcasting, unlike print media, come to be federally regulated?
2. What is the significance of the Radio Act of 1927 and the Federal Communications Act of 1934?
3. How did radio adapt to the arrival of television?
4. What changes are currently happening to the radio business as a result of the digital turn?
5. What has been the main effect of the Telecommunications Act of 1996 on radio station ownership?
6. What is the relevance of localism to debates about ownership in radio?

Mass Media Industries

7

Movies and the Impact of Images

189
The Early History of Movies

193
The Evolution of the Hollywood Studio System

196
Hollywood's Golden Age: The Development of Style

204
The Transformation of the Hollywood Studio System

207
The Economics of the Movie Business

214
The Movies in a Democratic Society

In May 1977, a groundbreaking film took audiences to a galaxy far, far away. George Lucas's space epic *Star Wars* targeted young people, a new primary audience for Hollywood, and introduced massive promotion and lucrative merchandising tie-ins—all the now-typical characteristics of a blockbuster. Repeat attendance and positive buzz made the first *Star Wars* the most successful movie of its generation.

Star Wars marked a cultural shift in movies and a technological transformation, with each new film in the series pushing the boundaries of what was possible with special effects. From stop-motion models used in the 1977 movie to the seamless digital effects of *Star Wars: The Force Awakens* (2015), *Star Wars: The Last Jedi* (2017), and *Star Wars: The Rise of Skywalker* (2019), the franchise continues to push the envelope of how special effects can make the space fantasy seem ever more real—and audience grabbing. The trajectory of the *Star Wars* franchise is a prime example of how movie storytelling can be enhanced by new technology, a pattern that stretches back to the early days of film.

Another movie about space—made over a century ago with what was then state-of-the-art technology and special effects—also amazed audiences and captured imaginations. Georges Méliès's *A Trip to the*

◀ In its forty-year journey from sci-fi blockbuster to movie industry megalith, the *Star Wars* franchise has been at the forefront of moviemaking technology. The franchise has also set the bar for converged financial and cultural success: From prequels to sequels, from toys to theme park rides, from clothing to catchphrases, the box-office numbers have only been part of the *Star Wars* story. © Walt Disney Studios Motion Pictures/Lucasfilm Ltd./Courtesy Everett Collection Inc

launchpadworks.com

Storytelling in *Star Wars*

Visit LaunchPad to view a short clip from *Star Wars: The Last Jedi.*

Discussion: Based on this clip, how does the movie seem to use advanced technical tools to tell its story?

Moon, released in 1902, was an early example of how new techniques and technologies led filmmakers to make movies that heralded new eras in filmmaking. Along with *Star Wars*, Warner Brothers' *The Jazz Singer* in 1927, Orson Welles's *Citizen Kane* in 1941, and James Cameron's *Avatar* in 2009 all mark such changes in the art, craft, and business of filmmaking. Méliès pioneered the use of fantasy in film; Warner Brothers ushered in the sound era; Welles developed deep-focus cinematography and other technical milestones; and Cameron masterfully deployed the innovation of digital performance-capture technology to transform the 3-D movie from gimmick to potential art form. The movies, then, have always been a technological spectacle, a grand illusion that—like a magic act—uses smoke, light, and trickery to make marvelous illusions come to life. Since the early twentieth century, the movies have operated as one of the world's chief storytellers.

These movie narratives create community, too. We attend theaters or watch at home with family and friends. Movies distract us from our daily struggles: They evoke and symbolize universal themes of human experience (childhood, coming of age, family relations, growing older, coping with death); they help us understand and respond to major historical events and tragedies (for instance, the Holocaust and 9/11); and they encourage us to rethink contemporary ideas as the world evolves, particularly in terms of how we think about race, class, spirituality, gender, and sexuality. The best films can untether us from the reality of our daily lives, only to challenge us to try to reconnect with our world in a new way.

Of course, as cultural products, movies are subject to the same economic constraints as are other mass media forms. For example, major studios tend to roll out big-budget blockbusters in hopes of finding the next *The Force Awakens*, while narratives that break the standard mold can sometimes languish for lack of major studio backing. But in the emerging terrain of digital video and Internet distribution, the ability of moviemakers to find audiences without major studio support is increasing.

GIVEN THE FILM INDUSTRY'S LENGTHY AND COMPLEX ROLE in Americans' lives, along with its steady transformation in response to new technologies, cultural change, and other developments, it's vital to take a closer look at this unique mass medium. We need to ask big questions about what purposes movies serve for us today, compared to the past; how strong an impact the U.S. film industry has on society and culture in our own country and in others; and where the film industry may be headed in the future.

To these ends, we will use this chapter to examine the rich legacy and current role of movies by:

- considering film's early history, including the technological advances that made movies possible

- tracing the evolution of the Hollywood studio system, which arose to dominate the global film industry

- exploring how narrative styles developed in moviemaking, including the transition from silent film to "talkies" and the emergence of different camera techniques and movie genres

- examining the transformation of the Hollywood studio system in response to new forces, such as the birth of television and the rise of home entertainment

- analyzing the economics of the movie business—specifically, how it makes money following the digital turn

- weighing movies' role in our democracy today and in the diverse world around us

The Early History of Movies

Filmmaking has passed through several stages on its way to mass medium status. In the following pages, we trace those stages—including development (when inventors first made pictures move), entrepreneurial (when experimenters conducted movie demonstrations for a small number of paid viewers), and finally true mass medium (when movies became widely accessible and began telling coherent stories with specific meanings for viewers). Throughout these stages, creative and bold innovators have worked together to continually advance the medium, revealing the strongly collaborative nature of this industry.

LaunchPad
launchpadworks.com

Use **LearningCurve** to review concepts from this chapter.

Advances in Film Technology

The concept of film goes back to Leonardo da Vinci, who theorized in the late 1400s that a device could be created to reproduce reality. There were other early precursors to film as well. For example, in the 1600s, the *magic* lantern projected images painted on glass plates using an oil lamp as a light source. In 1824, the *thaumatrope* consisted of a two-sided card whose different images appeared to combine when the card was twirled. And the *zoetrope*, created in 1834, was a cylindrical device with slits cut into it that rapidly spun images on the inside, making it appear to viewers as if the images were moving.

But the true development stage of filmmaking began when inventors discovered a process for making a series of photographs appear to move while being projected on a screen.

Muybridge and Goodwin Make Pictures Move

Eadweard Muybridge, an English photographer living in America, is credited with being the first person to make images move. Muybridge studied motion by using multiple cameras to take successive photographs of humans and animals in motion. By 1880, he had developed a method for projecting the photographic images on a wall for public viewing.

Meanwhile, other inventors were also capturing moving images and projecting them. In 1884, George Eastman (founder of Eastman Kodak) developed the first roll film, a huge improvement over the heavy metal-and-glass plates previously used to make individual photos. Louis Aimé Augustin Le Prince, a Frenchman living in England, invented the first motion-picture camera using roll film. Le Prince is credited with filming the first motion picture, *Roundhay Garden Scene*, in 1888. Recorded at twelve frames per second, the film depicts several people strolling on a lawn and runs for just a few seconds.

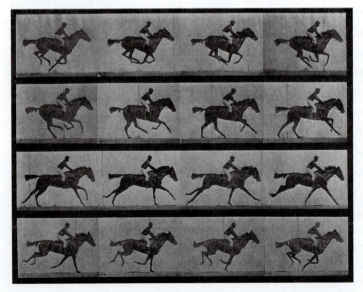

▼ Eadweard Muybridge's studies of horses in motion, like the one shown, proved that a horse gets all four feet off the ground during a gallop. *"A galloping horse and rider"* by Eadweard Muybridge and University of Pennsylvania/Wellcome Collection

In 1889, a New Jersey minister, Hannibal Goodwin, improved Eastman's roll film by using thin strips of transparent, pliable material called **celluloid**, which could hold a coating of chemicals sensitive to light. Goodwin's breakthrough enabled a strip of film to move through a camera and be photographed in rapid succession, producing a series of pictures.

Edison and the Brothers Lumière Create Motion Pictures

The early developers of film laid the groundwork for the shift to the entrepreneurial stage. During this stage, inventors came up with new projection and distribution technologies, enabling people to come together in a public place to view movies. The action began in the late 1800s, when American inventor and businessman Thomas Edison (with the help of his assistant, William Kennedy Dickson) combined his incandescent lightbulb, Goodwin's celluloid, and Le Prince's camera to create another early movie camera, the **kinetograph**, and a single-person viewing system, the **kinetoscope**. This small projection system required individual viewers to look through a small hole to see images moving on a tiny plate.

▲ Kinetoscopes allowed individuals to view motion pictures through a window in a cabinet that held the film. The first kinetoscope parlor opened in 1894 in New York City and was such a hit that many others quickly followed. Everett Collection, Inc

Meanwhile, in France, brothers Louis and Auguste Lumière developed the *cinematograph*—a combined camera, film development, and projection system. The projection system was particularly important, as it enabled more than one person at a time to see the moving images on a large screen.

With inventors around the world now dabbling in moving pictures, Edison continued innovating in film. He patented several inventions and manufactured a new large-screen system called the **vitascope**, through which longer filmstrips could be projected without interruption. This device hinted at the potential of movies as a future mass medium. Staged at a music hall in New York in April 1896, Edison's first public showing of the vitascope featured shots from a boxing match and waves rolling onto a beach. Some members of the audience were so taken with the realism of the images that they stepped back from the screen's crashing waves to avoid getting their feet wet.

At this point, movies consisted of movement recorded by a single continuous camera shot. Early filmmakers had not yet figured out how to move the camera itself or how to edit film shots together. Moreover, movies' content consisted simply of people or objects in motion, without conveying a story. Nonetheless, various innovators had spotted the commercial possibilities of film. By 1900, short movies had become part of the entertainment industry, used as visual novelties in amusement arcades, traveling carnivals, wax museums, and vaudeville theaters.

Telling Stories: The Introduction of Narrative

With the introduction in the late 1890s of **narrative films**—movies that tell stories through the series of actions depicted (later matched with sound)—the industry advanced from the entrepreneurial stage to mass

▲ *The Great Train Robbery* (1903) may have introduced the western genre, but it was actually filmed in New Jersey. This still is from a famous scene in which a bandit shoots his gun at the audience. Library of Congress

medium status. Film now promised to offer a far richer experience than other storytelling media—specifically, books and radio. Unlike those media, narrative films provided realistic moving images and compelling stories in which viewers became so immersed that they sometimes forgot they were watching a fictional representation.

Some of the earliest narrative films (which were silent) were produced and directed by French magician and inventor Georges Méliès, who opened the first public movie theater in France in 1896. Méliès began producing short fantasy and fairy-tale films, including *The Vanishing Lady* (1896), *Cinderella* (1899), and *A Trip to the Moon* (1902). He increasingly used editing and unique camera tricks and techniques, such as slow motion and cartoon animation, which would become key ingredients in future narrative filmmaking.

The first American filmmaker to adapt Méliès's innovations to narrative film was Edwin S. Porter. Porter shot narrative scenes out of order (for instance, some in a studio and some outdoors) and reassembled, or edited, them to tell a story. In 1902, he made what is regarded as America's first narrative film, *The Life of an American Fireman*, which included the first recorded close-up. Porter also introduced the western genre and the first chase scene in *The Great Train Robbery* (1903).

The Arrival of Nickelodeons

Another turning point in film's development as a mass medium was the 1907 arrival of the **nickelodeon**—a type of movie theater whose name combines the admission price (five cents) with the Greek word for *theater*. According to media historian Douglas Gomery, these small and uncomfortable makeshift theaters often consisted of converted storefronts redecorated to mimic vaudeville theaters.[1] Nickelodeons showed silent films, which typically transcended language barriers and provided workers and immigrants with an inexpensive escape from the challenges of urban life. Not surprisingly, nickelodeons flourished during the great European immigration at the dawn of the twentieth century. Between 1907 and 1909, the number of nickelodeons in the United States skyrocketed from five thousand to ten thousand. The craze peaked by 1910, when entrepreneurs began seeking more affluent spectators, attracting them with larger and more lavish movie theaters.

The Evolution of the Hollywood Studio System

By the 1910s, movies had become a major industry, and entrepreneurs developed many tactics for controlling it, including monopolizing patents on film-related technologies and dominating the "three pillars" of the movie business: production (making movies), distribution (getting films into theaters), and exhibition (playing films in theaters). Controlling all the parts of an industry's supply chain achieves **vertical integration**. In the film business, this means managing the entire moviemaking process—from the development of an idea to the screening of the final product before an audience. The resulting concentration of power gave rise to the **studio system**, in which creative talent was firmly controlled by certain powerful studios. Five vertically integrated movie studios, sometimes referred to as the Big Five, made up this new film **oligopoly** (a situation in which an industry is controlled by just a few firms): Paramount, MGM, Warner Brothers, Twentieth Century Fox, and RKO. An additional three studios, sometimes called the Little Three—Columbia, Universal, and United Artists—did not own chains of theaters but held powerful positions in movie production and distribution.

Edison's Attempt to Control the Industry

Among the first to try his hand at dominating the movie business and reaping its profits, Thomas Edison formed the Motion Picture Patents Company, known as the Trust, in 1908. A cartel of major U.S. and French film producers, the company pooled film-technology patents, acquired most major film distributorships, and signed an exclusive deal with George Eastman, who agreed to supply stock film only to Trust-approved theater companies.

However, some independent producers refused to bow to the Trust's terms. These producers abandoned film production centers in New York and New Jersey and moved to Cuba; Florida; and ultimately Hollywood, California.

In particular, two Hungarian immigrants—Adolph Zukor (who would eventually run Paramount Pictures) and William Fox (who would found the Fox Film Corporation, later renamed Twentieth Century Fox)—wanted to free their movie operations from the Trust's tyrannical grasp. Zukor's early companies figured out ways to bypass the Trust. A suit by Fox, a nickelodeon operator turned film distributor, resulted in the Trust's breakup for restraint-of-trade violations in 1917.

A Closer Look at the Three Pillars

Ironically, film entrepreneurs like Zukor who fought the Trust realized they could control the film industry themselves through vertical integration. The three pillars of vertical integration occur in a specific sequence: First, movies are produced. Next, copies are distributed to people or companies who get them out to theaters. Finally, the movies are exhibited in theaters. So, while power through vertical integration was becoming concentrated in just a few big studios, other studios were seeking to dominate one or another of the three pillars. This competition sparked tension between the forces of centralization and those of independence.

Production

A major element in the production pillar is the choice of actors for a particular film. This circumstance created an opportunity for some studios to gain control using tactics other than Edison's pooling of patents. Once these companies learned that audiences preferred specific actors to anonymous ones, they signed exclusive contracts with big-name actors. In this way, the studio system began controlling the talent in the industry. For example, Adolph Zukor hired a number of popular actors and formed the Famous Players Film Company in 1912. One Famous Players performer was Mary Pickford, who became known as "America's Sweetheart" for her portrayal of spunky but innocent heroines. Pickford so elevated film actors' status that in 1919, she broke from Zukor to form her own company, United Artists. Actor Douglas Fairbanks (her future husband) joined her, along with comedian-director Charlie Chaplin and director D. W. Griffith.

Although United Artists represented a brief triumph of autonomy for a few powerful actors, by the 1920s the studio system had solidified its control over all creative talent in the industry. Pioneered by director Thomas Ince and his company, Triangle, the system constituted a kind of assembly line for moviemaking talent: Actors, directors, editors, writers, and others all worked under exclusive contracts for the major studios. Ince also designated himself the first studio head, appointing producers to handle hiring, logistics, and finances so that he could

▼ With legions of fans, Mary Pickford became the first woman to earn a salary of $1 million in a year and gained the freedom to take artistic risks with her roles. She launched United Artists—a film distribution company—with Douglas Fairbanks, Charlie Chaplin, and D. W. Griffith. No woman since has been as powerful a player in the movie industry. Library of Congress, Prints & Photographs Division, Reproduction number LC-DIG-ggbain-36276 (digital file from original negative)

more easily supervise multiple pictures at once. The studio system proved so efficient that major studios were soon producing new feature films every week. Pooling talent, rather than patents, turned out to be a more ingenious tactic for movie studios seeking to dominate film production.

Distribution

Whereas there were two main strategies for controlling the production pillar of moviemaking (pooling patents or pooling talent), studios seeking power in the industry had more options open to them for controlling distribution. One early effort to do so came in 1904, when movie companies provided vaudeville theaters with films and projectors on a *film exchange* system. In return for their short films, shown between live acts in the theaters, movie producers received a small percentage of the vaudeville ticket-gate receipts.

Edison's Trust used another tactic: withholding projection equipment from theater companies not willing to pay the Trust's patent-use fees. However, as with the production of film, independent film companies looked for distribution strategies outside the Trust. Adolph Zukor again led the fight, this time through the development of **block booking**. Under this system, movie exhibitors who wanted access to popular films with big stars like Mary Pickford had to also rent new or marginal films featuring no stars. Although this practice was eventually outlawed as monopolistic, such contracts enabled the studios to test-market possible up-and-coming stars at little financial risk.

As yet another distribution strategy, some companies marketed American films in Europe. World War I so disrupted film production in Europe that the United States stepped in to fill the gap, eventually becoming the leader in the commercial movie business worldwide. After the war, no other nation's film industry could compete economically with Hollywood. By the mid-1920s, foreign revenue from U.S. films totaled $100 million. Even today, Hollywood dominates the world market for movies.

Exhibition

Companies could gain further control of the movie industry by finding ways to get more people to buy more movie tickets. Innovations in exhibition (such as construction of more inviting theaters) transformed the way people watched films and began attracting more middle- and upper-middle-class viewers.

Initially, Edison's Trust tried to dominate exhibition by controlling the flow of films to theater owners. If theaters wanted to ensure they had films to show their patrons, they had to purchase a license from the Trust and pay whatever price it asked. But after the Trust collapsed, emerging studios in Hollywood came up with their own ideas for controlling exhibition and making certain that the movies they produced were shown. When industrious theater owners began forming film cooperatives to compete with block-booking tactics, producers like Zukor conspired to buy up theaters. Zukor and the heads of

▲ This image depicts part of the ornate auditorium of the Ohio Theatre in Columbus, Ohio, which, after its deterioration and closing in 1969, would have been destroyed had it not been for three determined preservationists who literally stood in the way of a wrecking ball. Library of Congress, Prints & Photographs Division, Reproduction number LC-DIG-highsm-41843 (original digital file)

several major studios understood that they did not have to own all the theaters to ensure that their movies would be shown. Instead, the major studios needed to own only the first-run theaters (about 15% of the nation's theaters). First-run theaters premiered new films in major downtown areas and generated 85 to 95 percent of all film revenue.

The studios quickly realized that to earn revenue from these first-run theaters, they would have to draw members of the middle and upper-middle classes to the movies. With this goal in mind, they built **movie palaces**, full-time single-screen theaters that provided a more enjoyable and comfortable movie-viewing environment. In 1914, the three-thousand-seat Strand Theatre, the first movie palace, opened in New York.

Hollywood's Golden Age: The Development of Style

Once the Hollywood studio system was established as a profitable business model, studios had the luxury of developing a distinctive moviemaking style that ultimately marked Hollywood's Golden Age. This style began taking shape in 1915, characterized by the use of new narrative techniques (such as close-up camera shots and multiple story lines) in the silent era, the later introduction of sound, and the rise of movie genres. Hollywood's monopolization of this style produced numerous films that have since become treasured classics. Yet during Hollywood's Golden Age, other moviemaking models—including global cinema, documentaries, and independent films—provided alternatives to the classic style and shaped the medium just as powerfully.

Narrative Techniques in the Silent Era

Though telling stories in films occurred early on, moviemaking hit its stride as a viable art form when studios developed innovative narrative techniques, including the use of varied camera distances, close-up shots, multiple story lines, fast-paced editing, and symbolic imagery—even before sound was introduced. As these techniques evolved, making a movie became about more than just telling a story; it became about *how* to tell the story. For example, when filmed from different camera angles, the same sequence of events can affect viewers quite differently.

D. W. Griffith, among the earliest "star" directors, used nearly all these techniques simultaneously in *The Birth of a Nation* (1915)—the first *feature-length film* (more than an hour long) produced in America. Although considered a technical masterpiece and an enormous hit, the film glorified the Ku Klux Klan and stereotyped southern blacks. The NAACP campaigned against the film, and protests and riots broke out at many screenings.

Other popular films created during the silent era were historical and religious epics. The era also produced pioneering social dramas, mysteries, comedies, horror films, science-fiction movies, war films, crime dramas, and westerns.

Augmenting Images with Sound

Hollywood's Golden Age also saw the introduction of sound in 1927, which further established a distinctive narrative style and set new commercial standards in the industry. Technical breakthroughs in the 1910s at AT&T's research arm, Bell Labs, produced prototypes of loudspeakers and sound amplifiers. Experiments with sound continued during the 1920s, particularly at Warner Brothers. In 1927, the studio produced *The Jazz Singer*, a feature-length silent film interspersed with musical numbers and brief dialogue. Starring Al Jolson, a charismatic and popular vaudeville singer who wore blackface as part of his act, the movie further demonstrated racism's presence in the film industry. Warner Brothers' 1928 release *The Singing Fool*, which also starred Jolson, became the real breakthrough for **talkies** (sound pictures). Costing $200,000 to make, the film raked in a whopping $5 million and "proved to all doubters that talkies were here to stay."[2]

The availability of movies with sound pushed annual movie attendance in the United States from sixty million a week in 1927 to ninety million a week just two years later. By 1931, nearly 85 percent of America's twenty thousand theaters accommodated talkies. And by 1935, the rest of the world had adopted talkies as the commercial standard.

▼ *The Jazz Singer* (1927), one of the first commercially successful talkies, helped bring about Hollywood's transition from silent movies to movies with sound. The film stars Al Jolson as Jack Rabinowitz, a Jewish American who defies his family's wishes by putting on blackface and pursuing a career as a jazz musician.
Everett Collection, Inc

Warner Brothers was not the only studio exploring sound technology. Five months before *The Jazz Singer* opened, Fox premiered sound-film **newsreels** (weekly ten-minute compilations of news events from around the world). Fox's newsreel company, Movietone, captured the first film footage with sound of the takeoff and return of Charles Lindbergh, who piloted the first solo, nonstop flight across the Atlantic Ocean in May 1927. The Movietone sound system eventually became the industry standard.

Inside the Hollywood System: Setting the Standard for Narrative Style

By the time talkies had transformed the film industry, Hollywood had established firm control over narrative style: the recognizable way in which directors told stories through the movies they made. The model serves up three ingredients that give Hollywood movies their distinctive flavor: the narrative (story), the genre (type of story), and the author (director). The right blend of these ingredients—combined with timing, marketing, and luck—has enabled Hollywood to create a long string of hit movies, from 1930s and 1940s classics like *Gone with the Wind* and *Casablanca* to recent successes like *Incredibles 2* and *Avengers: Infinity War*.

Hollywood Narratives

As we've seen, storytelling had long existed in movies, even in the silent era. But it was Hollywood's Golden Age that saw the emergence of a distinctive narrative style that movie viewers soon associated with American filmmaking. *Narrative* always includes a story (what happens to whom) and discourse (how the story is told). Most movies feature a number of stories that play out within the film's larger, overarching narrative. These narratives also present recognizable character types (protagonist, antagonist, romantic interest, sidekick) and have a clear beginning, middle, and end. The plot is usually propelled by the main character's decisions and actions to resolve a conflict by the end of the movie. Nowadays, filmmakers also use computer-generated imagery (CGI) or digital remastering to augment narratives with special effects, providing a powerful experience that satisfies most audiences' appetite for both the familiar and the distinctive.

Hollywood Genres

In addition to establishing a unique narrative style in its Golden Age, Hollywood gave birth to movie **genres**, categories in which conventions regarding characters, scenes, and themes recur in combination. Familiar genres include comedy, drama, romance, action/adventure, mystery/suspense, gangster, western, horror, fantasy/science fiction, musical, and film noir (French for "black film")—a genre developed in the United States after World War II that explores unstable characters and the sinister side of human nature.

▲ Hollywood genres help us categorize movies. Alfred Hitchcock's *Psycho* (1960) is a classic example of horror, *Frozen* is an animated musical, and *Sorry to Bother You* (2018) crosses multiple genres: comedy, fantasy, and science fiction. Everett Collection, Inc (left); © Walt Disney Pictures/Everett Collection, Inc (middle); Everett Collection, Inc (right)

Grouping films by category enabled the movie industry to achieve both *product standardization* (a set of formulas for producing genres) and *product differentiation* (a diverse set of movie-watching experiences for viewers to choose from).

Hollywood "Authors"

As another defining characteristic of Hollywood's Golden Age, movie directors gained significant status. In commercial filmmaking, the director serves as the main "author" of a film. Sometimes referred to by the French term, *auteurs*, successful directors develop a particular cinematic style or an interest in specific topics that differentiates their narratives from those of other directors. During Hollywood's Golden Age, notable directors included Alfred Hitchcock, Howard Hawks, and Sam Goldwyn, each famous for his defining moviemaking style. Today, directors are just as distinctive: When you hear that a new movie is a "Spielberg film," a "Tarantino project," a "Spike Lee joint," or "the latest from the Coen brothers," you have a good idea of what to expect.

As the 1960s and 1970s unfolded, the films of Francis Ford Coppola (*The Godfather*), Brian De Palma (*Carrie*), William Friedkin (*The Exorcist*), George Lucas (*Star Wars*), Martin Scorsese (*Taxi Driver*), and Steven Spielberg (*Jaws*) signaled the start of a period that Scorsese has called "the deification of the director." Through this development, a handful of talented directors gained the kind of economic clout and celebrity standing that had previously belonged only to top movie stars. Though directors lost power in the 1980s and 1990s, the tradition carries on with well-known directors like Tim Burton, Quentin Tarantino, Alfonso Cuarón, Hayao Miyazaki, Kathryn Bigelow, and Christopher Nolan.

Even today, most well-known film directors are white men. Only five women have ever received an Academy Award nomination for directing a feature film: Lina Wertmüller in 1976 for *Seven Beauties*, Jane Campion in 1994 for *The Piano*, Sofia Coppola in 2004 for *Lost in Translation*, Kathryn Bigelow in 2010 for *The Hurt Locker* (she won), and Greta Gerwig in 2018 for *Lady Bird*.

A recent study finds that women were hired to direct only 3.4 percent of major Hollywood releases, calling attention to the film industry's gender problem.[3] In light of women's persistently low status in Hollywood, and the

▲ Women directors have long struggled in Hollywood, but some, like Ava DuVernay, are making a name for themselves. DuVernay, who directed the acclaimed film *Selma* (2014), about Martin Luther King Jr., went on to direct the film version of Madeleine L'Engle's popular novel *A Wrinkle in Time* (2018). Everett Collection, Inc

dozens of charges of sexual harassment, assault, and rape against producer Harvey Weinstein (spurring the #MeToo movement of women sharing similar stories), a number of powerful women in the entertainment industry formed Time's Up in 2018. The advocacy group, which established a legal defense fund for those who have experienced sexual harassment or retaliation in the workplace, had more than three hundred signers to its founding letter, including Oprah Winfrey, Reese Witherspoon, and Constance Wu.[4]

Directors from other groups have also struggled for recognition in Hollywood, and a few have been successful. Well-regarded African American directors include John Singleton (*Abduction*, 2011), Barry Jenkins (*Moonlight*, 2017), Ryan Coogler (*Black Panther*, 2018), Ava DuVernay (*A Wrinkle in Time*, 2018), and Spike Lee (*BlacKkKlansman*, 2018). (For more, see "Media Literacy Case Study: Breaking through Hollywood's Race Barrier" on pages 202–203.) Asian Americans Wayne Wang (*Snow Flower and the Secret Fan*, 2011), Ang Lee (*Billy Lynn's Long Halftime Walk*, 2016), and M. Night Shyamalan (*Glass*, 2019) have also built accomplished directing careers.

Outside the Hollywood System: Providing Alternatives

Despite Hollywood's dominance of the film industry, viewers have long had alternatives to the feature-length, hugely attended, big-budget movies offered by the studio system. These alternatives include global cinema, documentaries, and independent films.

Global Cinema

Films made in other countries constitute less than 2 percent of motion pictures seen in the United States today. Yet foreign films did well in 1920s America, especially in diverse neighborhoods in large cities. These films' popularity has waxed and waned since the Great Depression, in response to such developments as assimilation of immigrants, postwar prosperity, and the rise of the home video market.

To be sure, the modern success in the United States of movies like *Amélie* (France, 2001), *The Girl with the Dragon Tattoo* (Sweden, 2009), and *Instructions Not Included* (Mexico, 2013) suggests that American audiences are willing to watch subtitled films with non-Hollywood perspectives. But foreign films have continued losing screen space to the expanding independent American film market. Today, the largest film industry is in India, out of Bollywood (a play on

launchpadworks.com

Breaking Barriers with *12 Years a Slave*

Visit LaunchPad to view a short clip from the Oscar-winning movie from director Steve McQueen.

Discussion: How do you think *12 Years a Slave* differs from previous depictions of black history in America?

words combining city names Bombay—now Mumbai—and Hollywood), where close to two thousand films a year are produced—mostly romance or adventure musicals in a distinct style.[5] In comparison, U.S. moviemakers release more than seven hundred films a year, and the growing film industry in China produced more than six hundred movies annually. (The United States and China are first and second in terms of film revenue.) Japan, France, and Nigeria are also major film-producing nations.

▲ *Wolf Warrior 2* (2017), about realizing the "Chinese Dream" of cultural power and international dominance, is the current highest-grossing Chinese film of all time, having made over $870 million (U.S.) at the box office. Everett Collection, Inc

Documentaries

Documentaries, through which directors interpret reality by recording real people and settings, evolved from several earlier types of nonfictional movies: *interest films* (which contained compiled footage of regional wars, political leaders, industrial workers, and agricultural scenes), *newsreels*, and *travelogues* (depictions of daily life in various communities around the world).

Over time, documentaries developed a unique identity. As educational, noncommercial presentations, they usually required the backing of industry, government, or philanthropy to cover production and other costs. By the late 1950s and early 1960s, the development of portable cameras led to a documentary style known as **cinema verité** (French for "truth film"). Portable cameras enabled documentarians (such as Robert Drew, for *Primary*, 1960) to go where cameras could not go before and record fragments of everyday life unobtrusively.

Perhaps the major contribution of documentaries has been their willingness to tackle controversial subject matter or bring attention to issues about which the public might not be aware. For example, American documentary filmmakers Kirby Dick and Amy Ziering address complex topics about sex and power. Their films include *The Invisible War*, about sexual assault in the military; *The Hunting Ground*, about campus assault at Harvard University; and their yet-to-be-named documentary about Harvey Weinstein and the reality of sexual assault and harassment in Hollywood. "What our film will capture," Dick explains, "especially at this pivotal turning point in Hollywood history, is the underlying current of abuse and manipulation at the hands of power."[6]

Independent Films

The success of some documentary films dovetails with the rise of **indies**, another alternative to the Hollywood system. As opposed to directors who

Media Literacy

CASE STUDY

Breaking through Hollywood's Race Barrier

The problem of the term *black cinema* is that such a term needs to exist. (Do we, for example, talk about a *white cinema* in the United States?) But there is a long history of blacks' exclusion from the industry as writers, directors, and actors—and even as audience members at theaters—so when a film like *Dope* (2015) by director Rick Famuyiwa gets praised as "revolutionary" and "subversive," it's because this teen coming-of-age story dares to feature a cast that for the most part isn't white.

Despite African Americans' long support of the film industry, their moviegoing experience has not been the same as that of whites. From the late 1800s until the passage of Civil Rights legislation in the mid-1960s, many theater owners discriminated against black patrons. In large cities, blacks often had to attend separate theaters, where new movies might not appear until a year or two after white theaters had shown them. In smaller towns and in the South, blacks were often not allowed to patronize local theaters before midnight. In addition, some theater managers required black patrons to sit in less desirable areas of the theater.[1]

Changes took place during and after World War II, however. With the "white flight" from central cities during the suburbanization of the 1950s, many downtown and neighborhood theaters began catering to black customers in order to keep from going out of business. By the late 1960s and early 1970s, these theaters had become major venues for popular commercial films such as *Guess Who's Coming to Dinner?* (1967).

Based on the popularity of these films, black photographer-turned-filmmaker Gordon Parks—who'd directed *The Learning Tree* (1969), adapted from his own novel—started making commercial action/adventure films, including *Shaft* (1971), remade by John Singleton in 2000. Popular in urban theaters, especially among black teenagers, the movies produced by both Parks and his son, Gordon Parks Jr. (*Super Fly*, 1972), spawned a number of commercial imitators. These films, labeled blaxploitation movies, were the subjects of heated cultural debates in the 1970s, both praised for their realistic depictions of black urban life and criticized for glorifying violence. Nevertheless, they reinvigorated urban movie attendance.

Opportunities for black film directors expanded in the 1980s, 1990s, and 2000s, with work from such notable directors as Spike Lee, Tyler Perry, and Julie Dash, who in 1991 was the first black female director to get a general theatrical film release. But only recently have black filmmakers achieved a measure of mainstream success. Lee Daniels received only the second Academy Award nomination for a black director for *Precious: Based on the Novel "Push" by Sapphire* in 2009 (the first was John Singleton, for *Boyz N the Hood* in 1991). In 2013, *12 Years a Slave*, a film adaptation of Solomon Northup's 1853 memoir by black British director Steve McQueen, won three Academy Awards, including best picture, and a best director nomination for McQueen. McQueen became the first black director to win a best picture award. The overall lack of recognition of nonwhite actors, writers, and directors during the 2016

⊙ **Visit LaunchPad** to watch a clip from the Ryan Coogler film *Black Panther* and a video from Bloomberg about the impact of the film. Do you agree with the analysis? Why or why not?

launchpadworks.com

▲ Spike Lee's many films include *Do the Right Thing* (1989), *Malcolm X* (1992), and *BlacKkKlansman* (2018), for which he received a best director Academy Award nomination. Julie Dash directed *Daughters of the Dust* (1991) and *Travel Notes of a Geechee Girl* (2017), among other films. Everett Collection, Inc (left); The Washington Post/Getty Images (right)

Academy Awards, however, led to much discussion and a trending #OscarsSoWhite hashtag. In 2017, *Moonlight*, a coming-of-age drama with an all-black cast and a black director, Barry Jenkins, won the best picture award.

But in Hollywood, nothing speaks more loudly than a blockbuster. In less than a month after its February 2018 release, Marvel/Disney's *Black Panther* (directed by Ryan Coogler) generated more than $1.1 billion in global box-office revenue and over $570 million in domestic box-office receipts.[2] More important was what that success represented. As Jamil Smith of *Time* magazine noted, "It may be the first mega-budget movie—not just about superheroes, but about anyone—to have an African American director and a predominantly black cast. Hollywood has never produced a blockbuster this splendidly black."[3] *Black Panther* went on to receive a nomination for best picture at the 2019 Academy Awards.

APPLYING THE CRITICAL PROCESS

DESCRIPTION Consider a list of the all-time highest-grossing movies, such as the one on Box Office Mojo at www.boxofficemojo.com/alltime/world/.

ANALYSIS Note patterns in the list. For example, of the top fifty or so, pay attention to how many films are from African American directors or have major roles with African American actors. Note what the most popular genres are.

INTERPRETATION What do the patterns mean? Economically, it's clear why Hollywood likes to have successful blockbuster movie franchises. But what kinds of films and representations get left out of the mix?

EVALUATION It is likely that we will continue to see an increase in youth-oriented, animated/action movie franchises that are heavily merchandised and intended for wide international distribution. Indeed, Hollywood does not have a lot of motivation to put out movies that don't fit these categories. Is this a good thing?

ENGAGEMENT Watch a film by an African American director and consider what's missing from most theater marquees. Visit aafca.com or browse imdb.com to find more films that feature African American directors and actors. See if Netflix, Hulu, or your campus library carries any of these titles, and request them if they don't. Spread the word on notable African American films by reviewing them online or in a college newspaper.

work within the Hollywood system, independent filmmakers typically operate on a shoestring budget and show their movies in campus auditoriums, small film festivals, and—if they're lucky—independent theaters. Successful independents like Kevin Smith (*Clerks*, 1994), Sofia Coppola (*Lost in Translation*, 2003; *The Beguiled*, 2017), and Robert Rodriguez (*El Mariachi*, 1992; *Spy Kids* franchise, 2001–2011; *Alita: Battle Angel*, 2019) continue to find substantial audiences in theaters and through online services like Netflix, which promote, feature, and produce work from outside the studio system.

The rise of independent film festivals in the 1990s also helped Hollywood rediscover low-cost independent films as alternatives to the standard big-budget blockbusters. Big studios looked to these festivals as ways to discover new talent, which sometimes led them to purchase independent film companies or set up deals to help with distribution for a cut of the profits. This feeder system has since declined somewhat, but indie films are increasingly turning to digital platforms, video streaming sites, and social media to find audiences (see "The Digital Turn Case Study: Attracting an Audience in a Digital Age" on pages 212–213).

The Transformation of the Hollywood Studio System

Beginning in the late 1940s, a number of forces began reshaping how people viewed movies and what they expected to see when they watched a film. These forces stemmed from new regulations seeking to break up studios' hold over the film industry, social developments (e.g., massive migrations of city dwellers to the suburbs), and competing mass media (namely, the increasing popularity of TV). Together, these changes forced the Hollywood studio system to adapt in an effort to remain viable and profitable, even after national weekly movie attendance peaked in 1946.

The Paramount Decision

An important force reshaping the Hollywood system took form in the wake of the **Paramount decision**. This 1948 court ruling (fueled by the government's discomfort with the movie industry's power) forced the big, vertically integrated studios to break up their ownership of movie production, distribution, and exhibition. As a result, the studios eventually gave up their theater businesses.

The ruling never really changed the oligopoly structure of the Hollywood film industry, because it failed to weaken the industry's control over movie distribution. However, it did open up opportunities in the exhibition pillar of the industry for new players outside Hollywood. For instance, art houses began showing more documentaries and foreign films, and thousands of new drive-in theaters sprang up in farmers' fields, all of which offered alternative fare to moviegoers.

Flight to the Suburbs

After World War II, waves of Americans experienced a severe case of pent-up consumer demand after years of wartime frugality. Thus, they migrated from cities to the suburbs to purchase their own homes and spend their much-increased discretionary income on all manner of newly available luxuries. These changes badly hurt the Hollywood studio system, as suburban neighborhoods were located far from downtown movie theaters, and people's leisure-time preferences had shifted from watching movies to shopping for material goods, such as cars, barbecue grills, and furniture.

To make matters worse for studios, the average age of couples entering marriage dropped from twenty-four to nineteen after the war. Thus, there were significantly fewer young couples going on movie dates.

Television Changes Hollywood

As Hollywood responded to the regulatory and social changes transforming 1940s and 1950s America, it also sought to strike back at the major technological force emerging at that time: television. Studios used several strategies in their efforts to compete with TV.

First, with growing legions of people gathering around their living room TV sets, studios shifted movie content toward more serious themes, including alcoholism (*The Lost Weekend*, 1945), racism (*Pinky*, 1949), sexuality (*Peyton Place*, 1957; *Butterfield 8*, 1960; and *Lolita*, 1962), adult–teen relationships (*Rebel without a Cause*, 1955), and other topics from which television stayed away. Ironically, such films challenged the authority of the industry's own Motion Picture Production Code, adopted in the early 1930s to restrict film depictions of violence, crime, drug use, and sexual behavior. (For more on the Code, see Chapter 13.) In 1967, the Motion Picture Association of America initiated the current ratings system, which rates films for age appropriateness rather than censoring all adult content.

Second, the film industry introduced a host of technological improvements designed to lure Americans away from their TV sets. These innovations included Technicolor, a series of color film processes that was all the more alluring in a world where TV screens showed only black-and-white images. Movie theaters

▶ *Rebel Without a Cause* (1955), starring James Dean and Natalie Wood, was marketed in movie posters as "Warner Bros.' Challenging Drama of Today's Teenage Violence!" James Dean's memorable portrayal of a troubled youth forever fixed his place in movie history. He was killed in a car crash a month before the movie opened. Everett Collection, Inc

also began offering wide screens, stereophonic sound, and sharper film quality, which was a huge improvement over previously fuzzy images. But although these developments may have drawn some people back to downtown movie theaters, they weren't enough to surmount the studios' core problem: the middle-class flight to the suburbs.

Hollywood Adapts to Home Entertainment

Things got even more challenging for the studio system in the 1970s, when the introduction of cable television and the videocassette gave rise to the home entertainment movement. Despite some worries that this trend would be a blow to the studios, Hollywood managed to adapt, developing a new market for renting and selling movies—first on VHS, then on DVD and Blu-ray, and most recently via Internet streaming.

Studios and indies alike are looking toward Internet distribution for the future of the video business. Movie fans can rent or purchase from services like Netflix, Amazon, Hulu, Google Play, and the iTunes store and view on smart TVs or with devices like Roku, Apple TV, Amazon Fire TV Stick, Google Chromecast, TiVo Premiere, or video game consoles. As people invest in wide-screen TVs and sophisticated sound systems, home entertainment is getting bigger and keeping pace with the movie theater experience. Interestingly, home entertainment is also getting smaller: Movies are increasingly becoming available to stream and download on portable devices like tablets, laptop computers, and smartphones.

The Economics of the Movie Business

Despite the many changes transforming the movie business, the Hollywood studio system continues to make money. In fact, since 1963, Americans have purchased roughly 1 billion movie tickets each year. In addition, gross revenues from North American box-office sales have climbed to nearly $11.9 billion, and global box-office revenues continue to grow, hitting a record high of $41.7 billion in 2018.[7]

The growing global market for Hollywood films has helped cushion the industry as it undergoes a significant transformation, brought on by the demise of the video rental business and the rise of video streaming. In order to flourish, the movie industry has had to continually revamp its production, distribution, and exhibition systems and consolidate its ownership.

Making Money on Movies Today

The cost of producing films has risen, and studios have had to find ways to generate more revenue in order to produce movies profitably. On top of that, with 80 to 90 percent of newly released films failing to break even at the domestic box office, studios need a couple of major hits each year to offset those losses. Studios have multiple revenue sources to make money on films:

- **Box-office sales.** Studios get about 40 percent of the theater box-office take in this first "window" for movie exhibition (the theater gets the rest).
- **Sales to the home-viewing market** (video-on-demand, subscription streaming, DVD/Blu-ray sales and rentals). These sales typically start about three to four months after a theatrical release (sometimes sooner), generating more revenue than domestic box-office income for major studios.
- **Cable and television outlets.** This includes premium cable (such as HBO and Showtime), and network and basic cable showings. The syndicated TV market also pays the studios on a negotiated film-by-film basis.
- **Foreign distribution.** Studios earn revenue from distributing films in foreign markets. In fact, at a record-breaking $29.8 billion in 2018 (about 71 percent of worldwide box-office revenues of $41.7 billion), international box-office gross revenues are more than double those of the United States and Canada ($11.9 billion in 2018), and they continue to climb annually, even as other countries produce more of their own films.
- **Independent-film distribution.** Studios make money by distributing the work of independent producers and filmmakers, who hire the studios to gain wider

circulation. Independents pay the studios 30 to 50 percent of the box-office and home-viewing revenue they make from their movies.

- **Licensing and product placement.** Studios earn revenue from licensing merchandise to retailers. In addition, companies pay studios to place their products in movies so that actors and characters will be shown using those products. Famous product placements include Reese's Pieces in *E.T.: The Extra-Terrestrial* (1982), Pepsi-Cola in *Back to the Future II* (1989), and *The Lego Movie 2* (2019)—an entire movie built around the popular toy line.

Conglomerations and Synergy in the Movie Industry

Already heavily concentrated in terms of ownership, the list of Hollywood's commercial film business leaders shrunk yet again in 2019, when Disney finalized its purchase of 21st Century Fox. That leaves just the **Big Five**—Disney (including Fox), Warner Brothers, Universal, Columbia Pictures, and Paramount—in control of nearly 87 percent of the revenue generated by commercial films in the United States (see Figure 7.1) and more than half of the movie market in Europe and Asia.

FIGURE 7.1 // MARKET SHARE OF U.S. FILM STUDIOS AND DISTRIBUTORS, 2018 (IN MILLIONS)

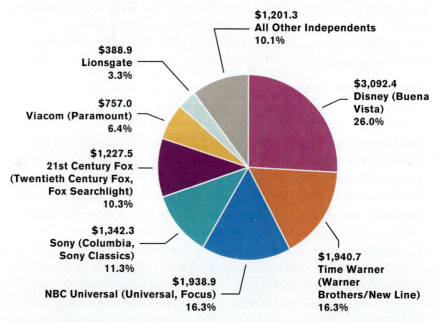

Data from: Box Office Mojo, "Studio Market Share, 2018," www.boxofficemojo.com/studio/?view=company&view2=yearly&yr=2018&p=.htm.

Note: Based on gross box-office revenue, January 1, 2018–December 31, 2018. Overall gross for period: $11.889 billion.

Note: Disney's plan to acquire 21st Century Fox was pending in 2018.

Synergy—the promotion and sale of a product throughout the various subsidiaries of a media conglomerate—provides a powerful advantage to large movie studios. Companies like Disney promote the new movies produced by its studio division as well as books, soundtracks, calendars, T-shirts, and toys based on these movies. This synergy also helps explain why a company like Disney has been snapping up other studios, including Pixar (purchased for $7.6 billion in 2006), Marvel (purchased for $3.96 billion in 2009), Lucasfilm (purchased for $4.06 billion in 2012), and 21st Century Fox (purchased for $71.3 billion in 2019):[8]

▲ *Avengers: Infinity War* cost an estimated $300 million to produce, which was the second highest budget of any film when it was made. Why is Hollywood willing to take risks on big blockbusters like this one? Because the payoff can be enormous. It took *Avengers: Infinity War* roughly one month to earn $665 million in box-office revenue—and that's not counting its other lucrative income streams, such as merchandising. Photofest

- Pixar has created some of the most successful animated movies of the past two decades, such as *Up* (2009), *Toy Story 3* (2010), *Coco* (2017), and the *Incredibles 2* (2018).
- Disney-produced films from the Marvel cinematic universe include *Iron Man 3* (2013), *Captain America: The Winter Soldier* (2014), *Guardians of the Galaxy 2* (2017), and *Avengers: Infinity War* (2018).
- After acquiring Lucasfilm, Disney released *Star Wars: Episode VII: The Force Awakens* (2015), which became the highest-earning film in U.S. box-office history. That was followed by *Rogue One: A Star Wars Story* (2016), *Star Wars: Episode VIII: The Last Jedi* (2017), and *Solo: A Star Wars Story* (2018).
- By purchasing Fox, Disney gathered even more rights to popular Marvel characters, including the X-Men and Deadpool.

Theater Chains Consolidate Exhibition

Film exhibition is also heavily concentrated in terms of ownership, with the five leading theater chains operating more than 50 percent of U.S. screens. The major chains—AMC Entertainment, Regal Entertainment Group, Cinemark USA, Cineplex Entertainment, and Marcus Theatres—own thousands of screens in suburban malls and at highway crossroads, and most have expanded into international markets as well.

By the 1990s, **multiplex** theaters, which had several screens in the same facility, were giving way to **megaplex** theaters, containing fourteen or more screens, upscale concessions, stadium-style seating, and digital surround sound. By 2017, growth of the movie exhibition business had leveled off at 39,651 indoor screens, most of them at megaplex locations.

To remain competitive with ever-more-sophisticated home entertainment systems, theaters have started experimenting with a number of innovations in exhibition. These include bigger screens, responsive 4-D seating (which feature seats with "sway" and "twist" options), virtual reality experiences, and catered food options.

Convergence: Movies Adjust to the Digital Turn

The biggest challenge the movie industry faces today is the Internet. After witnessing the difficulties that illegal file-sharing brought on the music labels (some of which share the same corporate parent as film studios), the movie industry has more quickly embraced the Internet for movie distribution through outlets like Amazon and Netflix.

The popularity of Netflix's streaming service (added in 2008 to its DVD-rental-by-mail service) opened the door to other similar services (see Figure 7.2). That same year, NBC Universal (Universal Studios), News Corp. (21st Century Fox), and Disney launched Hulu. Since then, others—including Comcast (Xfinity TV), Google (YouTube), Walmart (Vudu), and Amazon (Amazon Video)—have gotten into online digital movie distribution. By 2019, Disney was planning to launch its own streaming service and remove its titles from Netflix.

The year 2012 marked a turning point: For the first time, movie fans accessed more movies through digital online media than through physical copies, like DVDs or Blu-rays.[9] For the movie industry, this shift to Internet distribution has had mixed consequences. On the one hand, the industry needs to offer movies where people want to access them, and digital distribution is a growing market. On the other hand, although providing streaming is less expensive than producing physical DVDs, the revenue is still much lower compared to DVD sales; thus, this shift has had a large impact on the major studios, which had grown reliant on healthy DVD revenue. Of course, as major studios like Disney explore their own dedicated streaming services, they may find a way to boost revenue rather than sharing with other streaming services.

The Internet has also become an essential tool for movie marketing—one that studios are finding less expensive than traditional methods,

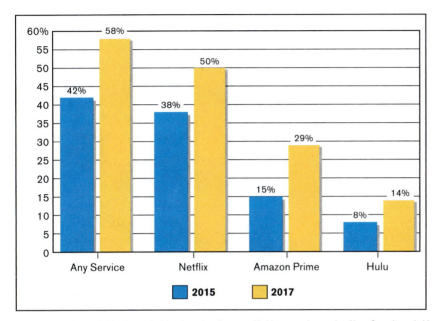

FIGURE 7.2 // ONLINE VIDEO STREAMING MARKET SHARE, 2015 AND 2017

Percentage of U.S. households with a television that subscribe to a paid video streaming service. Note: Some households may subscribe to more than one.

Data from: Christine Wang, "Overwhelming Majority of People Watching Streaming Services Still Choose Netflix," CNBC, July 21, 2016, www.cnbc.com/2016/07/21/overwhelming-majority-of-people-watching-streaming-services-still-choose-netflix.html; "Share of Consumers Who Have Subscriptions to an On-Demand Video Service in the United States in 2017," Statista, www.statista.com/statistics/318778/subscription-based-video-streaming-services-usage-usa.

like television ads or billboards. Many studios now use a full menu of social media to promote films in advance of their release (see also "The Digital Turn Case Study: Attracting an Audience in a Digital Age" on pages 212–213).

In addition to distribution and promotion, special effects and digital video have led to dramatic changes in the film industry. Powerful computer-generated imagery (CGI) makes the fantastic seem common, whether it be a superhero fighting aliens or elves fighting orcs. But while top-end CGI can be expensive, filmmakers of the last decade cut costs by switching from expensive and bulky 16-mm and 35-mm film cameras to **digital video**, which eliminates the need to buy and pay to develop film. Between digital video and computer-based desktop editors like Adobe Premiere Pro, it's possible to make movies for a few thousand dollars and post them on venues like YouTube and Vimeo.

The Digital Turn

CASE STUDY

Attracting an Audience in a Digital Age

"I bet you're wondering why I'm wearing this red suit," the costumed superhero says, looking straight into the camera while sitting on the edge of a busy highway overpass. "It's so the bad guys don't see me bleed," he continues, and gestures with his head toward some approaching vehicles. "Let's hope these guys are wearing their brown pants." He jumps from his perch, free-falling several stories before plunging through the sunroof of an SUV and attacking the villainous henchmen inside.

These opening lines of leaked test footage for the movie *Deadpool* hint at the fourth-wall-breaking vulgar irreverence that this comic book character is known for. These lines also illustrate screenwriters Rhett Reese and Paul Wernick's understanding of just how well a self-aware, wise-cracking, visually stimulating antihero would appeal to an Internet audience in a post–digital turn world.

In fact, it was the character's appeal to scores of fans on the Internet that helped the movie get made in the first place. In a 2016 interview with talk-show host Jimmy Fallon, actor Ryan Reynolds explained that the test footage he and three friends created sat on a shelf for four years at Fox Studios. Then someone leaked it to the Internet. "The Deadpool fans freaked out and overwhelmed Fox, and Fox basically had to green-light the movie," said Reynolds. "The problem was, this footage was owned by Fox and was sort of illegal that it got leaked. I know that one of us [who made the test footage] did it, but I'm 70 percent sure it wasn't me."[1]

There are many ways digital technology has changed movies, from technical advances in 3-D and high definition to ever-more-powerful computer-generated special effects. But as the story of *Deadpool*'s Internet appeal suggests, the digital

▲ Thanks in part to a digital marketing campaign that played up the main character's tendency for absurdity, dark humor, and irreverence, *Deadpool* broke several box-office records when it opened on Valentine's Day weekend in 2016. The film's success quickly ensured a sequel, *Deadpool 2*, which also broke box-office records in 2018, and a PG-13 rerelease, *Once Upon a Deadpool*. Everett Collection, Inc

▶ Web Clip

YouTube.com has many video examples of digital marketing. For example, search for "Team Thor—Official Marvel," posted by Marvel UK, to watch a clip from a tongue-in-cheek video with superheroes Thor and the Hulk. How might a clip like this help franchises capture viral video buzz in between theatrical releases?

212

turn also presents new ways for studios to fill seats when a film hits the theater. *Deadpool*'s adept use of digital marketing started with the leaked trailer, but it didn't stop there; the movie's digital media blitz included more short videos, a Deadpool Tinder profile, actor Ryan Reynolds's Deadpool-esque tweets, and even Deadpool emojis.

It also didn't stop after the first movie: For the film's sequel, *Deadpool 2*, another irreverent digital marketing campaign—which included a video of Deadpool as popular painting show host Bob Ross and a website with downloadable paper dolls—helped build excitement with fans before the film's successful May 2018 release.[2] The franchise also took another big chance in December 2018, releasing a re-edited PG-13 version of the sequel as a "Christmas family film" (the original movies were rated R) under the name *Once Upon a Deadpool*. The marketing campaign included easily shareable videos, teasing visuals, and a strong social media presence—as well as references to the 1987 fairy-tale comedy *The Princess Bride*.

The traditional approach to most marketing efforts is to focus on print and TV ads four to six weeks before a movie is released. But as the *Deadpool* and *Deadpool 2* examples illustrate, studios also invest in a variety of digital strategies before a movie hits theaters, and these strategies can pay off at the box office. For example, NBC Universal accumulated millions of followers on Facebook for its *Fifty Shades of Grey* and *Fast and Furious* franchises long before the films were released.[3] In addition, marketing across multiple digital platforms helps studios retain a level of buzz about upcoming movies set in increasingly complex cinematic universes, like those of the *X-Men* (Fox); *Star Wars* and *Avengers* (Disney); and Superman, Batman, and the Justice League (Warner Brothers/Time Warner).

These efforts help keep audiences interested as they wait for the next film installment to hit theaters.

And it's not just big film studios that have found success using online marketing. One of the first independent films that turned online buzz into box-office success was 1999's *The Blair Witch Project*, which used now-archaic message boards and newsgroups to help gross over $140 million in ticket sales, despite its tiny budget of just $22,500. These days, indies use an even bigger array of online platforms to help attract an audience, investors, and major studios. For example, a filmmaker might use a site like YouTube or Vimeo to upload all or part of a film, recruit the film's cast and crew to post about the film on social media, and hope to get featured on a site like Gizmodo's io9.com to boost publicity.[4] And unlike film festivals, which have long been used to promote indie films but which can cost hundreds or thousands of dollars in registration fees, this online exposure can reach a large audience at no additional cost to the filmmaker.

At the same time, social media and other digital marketing efforts can be nerve-racking for studio public relations because online conversations are unpredictable and uncontrollable. For example, when Amber Heard filed for divorce from Johnny Depp, saying the actor had abused her, the hashtag #ImWithAmber went viral along with calls to boycott Depp's *Alice through the Looking Glass*, a sequel to the very successful *Alice in Wonderland*. The negative publicity is believed to have contributed to disappointing ticket sales for the Disney film.

Publicity has always been important to movies. But marketing films after the digital turn, and having audiences interact with marketing campaigns in ways that are beyond studio control, might feel a little like jumping off a freeway overpass into heavy traffic—and not being sure where you'll land.

The Movies in a Democratic Society

From the earliest days of film, there were questions about how the medium would fit into society and how First Amendment free-speech protections would—or wouldn't—apply to movies. As community and political leaders increasingly realized how powerful movies could be, they became concerned about the power of film to upset existing social norms. But a mid-twentieth-century government crackdown on movies and those who made them would destroy lives and alter Hollywood for decades to come.

In 1947, in the wake of the unfolding Cold War with the Soviet Union, some members of Congress began investigating Hollywood for alleged subversive and communist ties. During the investigations, the House Un-American Activities Committee (HUAC) coerced prominent people from the film industry to declare their patriotism and to give up the names of colleagues suspected of having politically unfriendly tendencies. Upset over labor union strikes and outspoken writers, many film executives were eager to testify and provide names. For instance, Jack L. Warner of Warner Brothers suggested that film writers whose work made fun of the wealthy or America's political system or was sympathetic to "Indians and the colored folks" were engaging in communist propaganda.[10] Many other prominent actors and directors also "named names," either out of a belief that it was their patriotic duty or out of fear of losing their jobs.

Eventually, HUAC subpoenaed ten unwilling witnesses who were questioned about their memberships in various organizations. The so-called **Hollywood Ten**—nine screenwriters and one director—refused to discuss their memberships or to identify communist sympathizers. Charged with contempt of Congress in November 1947, they were eventually sent to prison. Jailing the Hollywood Ten clearly violated their free-speech rights, but in the atmosphere of the Cold War, many people worried that "the American way" could be sabotaged via unpatriotic messages planted in films. Upon release from jail, the Hollywood Ten found themselves *blacklisted*, or boycotted, by the major studios, and their careers in the film industry were all but ruined. The national fervor over communism continued to plague Hollywood well into the 1950s.

When HUAC made sure to include the film industry in its communist witch hunts, it was reacting to the way it saw film as a powerful cultural tool that could threaten the status quo. That's because movies function as **consensus narratives**—popular cultural products that provide

▼ While many studio heads, producers, and actors "named names" to HUAC, others, such as the group shown here, held protests to demand the release of the Hollywood Ten. Everett Collection, Inc

us with shared experiences. Whether they are dramas, romances, westerns, or mysteries, movies communicate values, hopes, and dreams through accessible language and imagery that can reinforce some cultural norms, challenge others, and even bridge cultural differences. This can be a double-edged sword.

As the American film industry has continued to dominate the movie-watching experience in many other nations, observers have begun questioning this phenomenon. Some have wondered whether American-made films are helping create a kind of global village, where people around the world share a universal culture. Others have asked whether these films stifle local cultures worldwide.

With the rise of international media conglomerates, public debate over such questions has ebbed. This is worrisome, as movies exert a powerful impact on people's beliefs, values, and even actions. As other nations begin to view the American film industry as an interloper in their people's culture, they may develop a resentment against the United States overall.

Likewise, the continuing power of the movie industry within our own nation raises questions about movies' role in our democracy. It's vital that those of us who consume movies do so with a critical eye and a willingness to debate these larger questions about this mass medium's cultural, political, and social significance. The political significance of film is easy to see in movies that strike a political chord with many members of the audience, such as Michael Moore's *Capitalism: A Love Story* (a director and film that surely would have drawn the wrath of HUAC) or Spike Lee's *BlacKkKlansman*. But that's not to say that viewers need only watch serious, issue-based films closely or critically. If anything, a consensus narrative is more powerful when audiences accept it without even really knowing that's what they are doing.

For instance, most mainstream audiences see Disney's movies as harmless forms of entertainment. But a critical look at the images of femininity in Disney films, from *Snow White* to *Pirates of the Caribbean*, reveals a consistent view of beauty that hews close to a Barbie-doll ideal. What's more, inner beauty is typically reflected by an attractive outward appearance. Other Disney films (like *The Lion King* and *Pocahontas*) verge on racial stereotyping or xenophobia, as when the heroes of *Aladdin* look less Middle Eastern than the villains. A media-literate viewer, then, must recognize that part of the cultural power of broad entertainments like Disney movies is bound up in packaging potentially questionable messages about gender, race, and class in stories that seem transparently wholesome. Given the expanded viewing options and the increasing access to independent, foreign, and otherwise nonmainstream films, viewers can seek out various alternatives to mass-marketed Hollywood films. With an entity as large as the U.S. film industry producing compelling messages about what we should value, how we should live, and how we should act, it's vital for those of us who consume movies to do so with a critical, media-literate eye—and to seek out other cinematic voices.

More Than a Movie: Social Issues and Film

Independent filmmakers are using social media to get moviegoers involved.

Discussion: Do you think digital media converging with social-issue films helps those films make a larger impact? Why or why not?

CHAPTER ESSENTIALS

Review

- Major advances in film technology took place in the late nineteenth century. Eadweard Muybridge created a method for making images move, and George Eastman developed the first roll film, capable of capturing moving images and projecting them. Soon after, Hannibal Goodwin improved roll film by using strips of transparent, pliable material called **celluloid**, enabling a strip of film to move through a camera and be photographed in rapid succession, producing a series of pictures.

- Film moved to the entrepreneurial stage with the invention of new projection and distribution technologies, such as Thomas Edison's **kinetograph**, **kinetoscope**, and **vitascope**.

- Movies advanced to the mass medium stage beginning in the late 1890s with the introduction of **narrative films** and the arrival of early movie theaters, called **nickelodeons**.

- The "three pillars" of the movie business are production (making movies), distribution (getting films into theaters), and exhibition (playing films in theaters). In the early days, studios attempted to achieve **vertical integration** by controlling all three of these parts. The resulting concentration of power gave rise to the **studio system**. Five film studios made up the early twentieth century's film **oligopoly**.

- Once the Hollywood studio system established itself as a profitable business, the Golden Age of Hollywood began to take shape, beginning with the introduction of new narrative techniques in 1915. Over the next decades, the Golden Age would be marked by the introduction of sound pictures (**talkies**) and later sound-film **newsreels**, movie **genres**, and the rise in status of the movie director.

- Outside the Hollywood system, many alternatives to the feature-length film exist, such as global cinema, **documentaries**, and independent films (or **indies**).

- Beginning in the late 1940s, a number of regulatory, social, and cultural forces reshaped how people viewed movies, forcing the Hollywood studio system to adapt. For example, the **Paramount decision** in 1948 and the migration of Americans from the cities to the suburbs changed the way movies were consumed.

LaunchPad

Visit LaunchPad for *Media Essentials* at **launchpadworks.com** for additional learning tools:

- **REVIEW WITH LEARNINGCURVE**
  LearningCurve adaptive quizzing helps you master the concepts you need to learn from this chapter.

- **VIDEO: THE THEATRICAL EXPERIENCE AND THE HOBBIT**
  Watch a clip from one of Peter Jackson's *Hobbit* films, then discuss how technology can enhance (or detract from) the viewing experience.

- **MEDIA LITERACY PRACTICE**
  This activity challenges you to develop a critical perspective and apply it to everyday encounters with communication media.

- Filmmakers make money from box-office sales, sales to the home-viewing market, cable and television outlets, foreign distribution, independent-film distribution, and licensing and product placement.

- Big media conglomerates like the **Big Five**—Disney, Warner Brothers, Universal, Columbia Pictures, and Paramount—also make money through **synergy**.

- The dawn of the digital age is forcing studios to rethink their business models. The movie industry has embraced the Internet more quickly than did the music industry, distributing movies online through outlets like Amazon and Netflix.

- The continuing power of the movie industry raises questions about movies' role in society—both internationally and within the United States. Therefore, it's vital for those who consume movies to do so with a critical eye.

Key Terms

celluloid, p. 190
kinetograph, p. 191
kinetoscope, p. 191
vitascope, p. 191
narrative films, p. 191
nickelodeon, p. 192
vertical integration, p. 193
studio system, p. 193
oligopoly, p. 193
block booking, p. 195
movie palaces, p. 196
talkies, p. 197
newsreels, p. 198
genres, p. 198
documentaries, p. 201
cinema verité, p. 201
indies, p. 201
Paramount decision, p. 204
Big Five, p. 208
synergy, p. 209
multiplex, p. 210
megaplex, p. 210
digital video, p. 211
Hollywood Ten, p. 214
consensus narratives, p. 214

Study Questions

1. How did film go from the development stage to the mass medium stage?

2. Why did Thomas Edison and the Trust fail to shape and control the film industry, and why did Adolph Zukor of Paramount succeed?

3. Why are genres and directors important to the film industry?

4. What regulatory, social, and cultural forces changed the Hollywood system in the 1950s?

5. What are the various ways in which major movie studios make money in the film business?

6. Do films contribute to a global village in which people throughout the world share a universal culture, or do U.S.-based films overwhelm the development of other cultures worldwide? Discuss.

Mass Media Industries

8

Television, Cable, and Specialization in Visual Culture

222
The Early History of Television

226
The Evolution of Network Programming

234
The Evolution of Cable Programming

236
Regulatory Challenges Facing Television and Cable

239
Technology and Convergence Change Viewing Habits

242
The Economics of Television, Cable, and Streaming Video

248
Television in a Democratic Society

On a Friday night in early November 2017, 361,000 viewers binge-watched all nine episodes of the just-released second season of *Stranger Things*, an homage to 1980s horror and science fiction and one of Netflix's biggest hits. The audience ratings service Nielsen called this a "significant viewing experience." On that night, the second season's first episode alone drew an estimated 15.8 million viewers.[1] By contrast, the second season premiere of *Big Bang Theory*, a perennial Top 5 network show, drew 10 million viewers back in 2008.

Many media analysts and traditional network executives consider Netflix—which had amassed more than 137 million subscribers around the world by the third quarter of 2018—a disruptive force that has turned the TV and cable programming business on its head. What makes streaming services like Netflix so different? For one thing, Netflix and its competitor Amazon are mostly financed by inexpensive monthly subscription packages, which means they are not subject to the TV ratings game or to advertiser pressure that dictates what is available on network television. In addition, Netflix has a stable of executives authorized to find good stories all over

◀ The first eight-episode season of *Stranger Things* was such an enormous hit for Netflix in 2016 that the streaming service ordered a third season before the second season had even been released. Netflix/Photofest

the world, which means they don't have to wait for company approval to sign promising new projects. And finally, in creating original programming, Netflix is not locked into the traditional network standard of making twenty-two to twenty-four shows per season. With an approach that's more akin to the cable model of HBO and Showtime, Netflix produces series with as few as six and usually no more than ten or twelve episodes per season. This kind of production schedule promotes quality, with fewer shows and more time to create each show.

On the heels of this disruption, it's perhaps unsurprising that, in a classic case of "if you can't beat 'em, join 'em," the traditional television networks (ABC, CBS, NBC, and FOX) are taking steps to get themselves a piece of the streaming pie. Disney, which bought the ABC network in 1996, announced in 2018 that it would launch Disney+, a streaming service designed to go head to head with Netflix. With an enormous library of movies and television shows, Disney has a significant advantage heading into this new venture.

Meanwhile, Disney is already a part of the streaming service Hulu, which was created in 2007 in partnership with Comcast (NBC Universal), 21st Century Fox, and AT&T. After purchasing Fox in 2019, Disney gained 60 percent control of Hulu and plans to consolidate this control by buying out the other partners. CBS, not a partner in the Hulu venture, has its own stand-alone streaming service called CBS Access, which features only CBS programming. AT&T, which bought Time Warner in 2018, also plans to start a streaming service with its huge cache of Warner Media programming.

But even as the disruption continues and networks and streaming services jockey for position, it is important to note that one crucial element of the television experience remains unchanged: High-quality stories resonate with enthusiastic audiences. Whether accessed through streaming, cable, or network TV, good shows can still draw a range of viewers—everyone from younger fans who grew up with the Internet to older fans who embrace programs that capture their nostalgia for a time before this technology existed.

FOR A LONG TIME AFTER ITS INCEPTION, television brought millions of American viewers together to share major turning points in U.S. history. For example, people gathered around their sets to watch coverage of Civil Rights struggles, the moon landing, the Watergate scandal, the explosion of a space shuttle, the 9/11 attacks, Hurricane Katrina, and the wars in Iraq and Afghanistan. Television also united people around more enjoyable activities, such as movie, television, and music awards shows (the Oscars, the Emmys, or the CMA Awards), or major sporting events like the Super Bowl. Throughout the country, Americans watched the latest episode of their favorite TV comedy or drama at home, then discussed it with friends and colleagues the next day.

The invention of cable and then satellite television resulted in more channels and programming options than ever to choose from, each of them appealing to narrow niches of viewers. New platforms keep attracting more users, as the ways we experience television continue to change. In 1977, only 14 percent of all American homes received cable service (which at that time carried just twelve channels). By 1999, that number had grown to 70 percent (with many times more channels). However, that number has been slipping due to competition from Internet-based streaming and direct broadcast satellite (DBS) services, leading to an increase in "cord-cutting" (the practice of canceling cable and relying on the Internet to access programs). Even traditional cable-television customers no longer rely on the same services, with digital cable, DVR, and video-on-demand providing more options for what we watch and how we watch it.

These technologies have changed the way we watch television and modified the role it plays in our lives. It's become easier to watch only what we want—when and where we want. But it's also harder to capture that sense of community that comes from watching a program together in our living rooms and talking about it with others afterward.

In this chapter, we will examine television's impact on American life—yesterday, today, and tomorrow—by:

- **considering television's early history, including its foundational technological innovations, the development of program content, and the arrival of cable**

- **tracing turning points in the evolution of network programming, such as the development of daily news broadcasts, the arrival of new entertainment forms (comedy, drama, talk shows, reality television), and the creation of public television**

- **exploring the evolution of cable programming, including the emergence of basic and premium services**

- **assessing the regulatory challenges network television and cable have faced, such as the government's attempts to restrict networks' control over content and limit cable's growth**

- **examining network television and cable in the digital age, including the impact of home video; the Internet, smartphones, and mobile video; and direct broadcast satellite**

- analyzing the economics of television, cable, and streaming video by considering how industry players make money and what they spend it on to stay in business

- raising questions about television's role in our democratic society, such as whether it is uniting us or fragmenting us

LaunchPad
launchpadworks.com
Use **LearningCurve** to review concepts from this chapter.

The Early History of Television

In 1948, only 1 percent of American households had a television set. By 1953, more than 50 percent had one, and by the early 1960s, more than 90 percent had one. During these early years, several major developments shaped television and helped turn it into a dominant mass medium. Others, especially an infamous scandal over corrupt TV quiz shows, brought its potential and promise into question.

Becoming a Mass Medium

Inspired by the ability to transmit audio signals from one place to another, inventors had long sought to send "tele-visual" images. For example, in the 1880s, German inventor Paul Nipkow developed the *scanning disk*, a large flat metal disk perforated with small holes organized in a spiral pattern. As the disk rotated, it separated pictures into pinpoints of light that could be transmitted as a series of electronic lines. Subsequent inventors improved on this early electronic technology. Their achievements pushed television from the development stage to the entrepreneurial stage to the mass medium stage, complete with technical standards, regulations, and further innovation (such as the move from black-and-white to color television).

▼ Philo Farnsworth, one of the inventors of television, experiments with an early version of an electronic TV set. Bettmann/Getty Images

The Development Stage: Establishing Patents
Television's development and commercialization were fueled by a battle over patents between two independent inventors—Vladimir Zworykin and Philo Farnsworth—each seeking a way to send pictures through the air over long distances.

In 1923, after immigrating to America and taking a job at RCA, the Russian-born Zworykin invented the *iconoscope*, the first TV camera tube to convert light rays into electrical signals. Zworykin received a patent for his device in 1928.

Around the same time, Farnsworth—an Idaho teenager—transmitted the first electronic TV picture by rotating a straight line scratched on a square of painted glass by 90 degrees. RCA accused Farnsworth of patent violation, but in 1930, after his high school teacher provided evidence of his original drawings from 1922, Farnsworth received a patent for the first electronic television and later licensed his patents to RCA and AT&T, which used them to commercialize the technology. He also conducted the first public demonstration of television at the Franklin Institute in Philadelphia in 1934—five years before RCA's much more famous public demonstration at the 1939 World's Fair.

The Entrepreneurial Stage: Setting Technical Standards

Turning television into a business required creating a coherent set of technical standards for product manufacturers. In the late 1930s, the National Television Systems Committee (NTSC)—a group representing engineers, inventors, network executives, and major electronics firms—began outlining industry-wide manufacturing practices and defining technical standards. In 1941, the Federal Communications Commission (FCC) adopted an **analog** standard (based on radio waves) for all U.S. TV sets, which at that time could show only black-and-white images. About thirty countries adopted this system, though most of Europe and Asia eventually adopted a system with slightly better image quality and resolution.

The Mass Medium Stage: Assigning Frequencies and Introducing Color

TV signals are part of the same electromagnetic spectrum that carries light waves and radio signals. In the early days of television (before the advent of cable), the number of TV stations a city or region could support was limited because airwave frequencies interfered with one another (so you could have a Channel 5 but not a Channel 6 in the same market). In the 1940s, the FCC began assigning certain channels in specific geographic areas to prevent interference. In 1952, after years of licensing freezes due to World War II, the FCC created a national map in which it attempted to evenly distribute all available channels throughout the country. By the mid-1950s, the nation had more than four hundred television stations in operation. Television had become a mass medium.

Television's new status led to additional standards. In 1952, the FCC tentatively

▼ Shown here on the assembly line, this 1954 RCA CT-100 was the first mass-produced electronic color TV set. Only affluent customers could afford these early sets, priced at $1,000 or more. AP Photo/Thomson Consumer Electronics

approved an experimental color system developed by CBS; however, its signal could not be received by black-and-white sets. In 1954, RCA's color system, which sent TV images in color but allowed older sets to receive the images as black-and-white, became the color standard.

Controlling TV Content

As a mass medium, television had become big business, and broadcast networks began jockeying for increased control over its content. As in radio during the 1930s and 1940s, early television programs were developed, produced, and supported by a single sponsor—often a company, such as Goodyear, Colgate, or Buick. This arrangement gave the companies that controlled brand-name products extensive power over what was shown on television. But then newly emerging broadcast networks wanted more control and, using several strategies, set out to diminish sponsor and ad agency control.

One strategy involved lengthening program times. Sylvester "Pat" Weaver, president of NBC, took the lead. A former advertising executive used to controlling radio content for his clients, Weaver increased TV program length from fifteen minutes (standard for radio programs) to thirty minutes and even longer. This substantially raised program costs for advertisers, discouraging some from sponsoring programs.

In addition, NBC introduced two program types to gain more control over content. The first type was the magazine format, which featured multiple segments, including news, talk, comedy, and music. (These early-1950s programs—*Today* and the *Tonight Show*—are still attracting morning and late-evening audiences.) By running daily rather than weekly, these programs made studio production costs much more prohibitive for a single sponsor. Thus, instead of sponsoring, an advertiser would pay the network for thirty- or sixty-second time slots during the show. Now the network, not the sponsor, owned such programs or bought them from independent producers.

For the second new program type—the "television spectacular"—networks bought programs on special topics from producers and sold ad spots to multiple advertisers. Early spectaculars (which came to be called "specials") included decades of Bob Hope Christmas shows and the 1955 TV version of *Peter Pan*, which drew over sixty-five million viewers—more than double the audience for a typical episode of *American Idol* at its peak in the early 2000s.

Staining Television's Reputation

In the late 1950s, corruption in an increasingly popular TV program format—the quiz show—tainted television's reputation and further altered the power balance between broadcast networks and program sponsors. Quiz shows had become huge business. They were (and remain) cheap to produce, with inexpensive sets and amateurs as guests. For each show, the corporate sponsor—such as Revlon or Geritol—prominently displayed its name on the set throughout the program.

As it turned out, many quiz shows were rigged. To heighten the drama and get rid of unappealing guests, sponsors pressured TV executives to give their favorite contestants answers to the quiz questions and allow them to rehearse their responses. The most notorious rigging occurred on *Twenty-One*, a quiz show owned by Geritol, whose profits had climbed by a whopping $4 million a year after it began sponsoring the program in 1956.

When investigations exposed the rigging, the fraud undermined Americans' belief in television's democratic promise: to bring inexpensive, honest information and entertainment into every household. The scandals had magnified the separation between the privileged, powerful few (wealthy companies) and the general public. For the next forty years, the broadcast networks kept quiz shows out of **prime time**—the block of time (7:00–11:00 P.M. EST) with large viewer audiences.

▲ In 1957, the most popular contestant on the quiz show *Twenty-One* was college professor Charles Van Doren (*left*). Congressional hearings on rigged quiz shows revealed that Van Doren had been given answers to help him defeat opponents whom the show's producers and sponsors deemed less appealing than Van Doren. Everett Collection, Inc

Introducing Cable

Despite the quiz-show scandals, broadcast television continued to grow in popularity in the late 1950s; however, some communities remained unable to receive traditional over-the-air TV signals, often because of their isolation or because mountains or tall buildings blocked transmission. The first small cable systems—called **CATV**, or community antenna television—originated in Oregon, Pennsylvania, and New York City in the late 1940s as an attempt to solve this problem. New cable companies ran wires from relay towers that brought in broadcast signals from far away. The cable companies then strung wire from utility poles and sent the signals to individual homes, stimulating demand for TV sets in those communities.

These early systems served only about 10 percent of the country and typically contained only twelve channels because of early technical and regulatory limits. Yet cable offered big advantages. First, it routed each channel in a separate wire, thereby eliminating the over-the-air interference that sometimes happened with broadcast transmissions. Second, it ran signals through *coaxial cable*, a core of aluminum wire encircled by braided wires that provided the option of adding more channels. Initially, many small communities with CATV received twice as many channels as were available over the air in much larger cities. Eventually, the cable industry would pose

launchpadworks.com

Television Networks Evolve

Insiders discuss how cable and satellite have changed the television market.

Discussion: How might definitions of a TV network change in the realm of new digital media?

FIGURE 8.1 // A BASIC CABLE TELEVISION SYSTEM

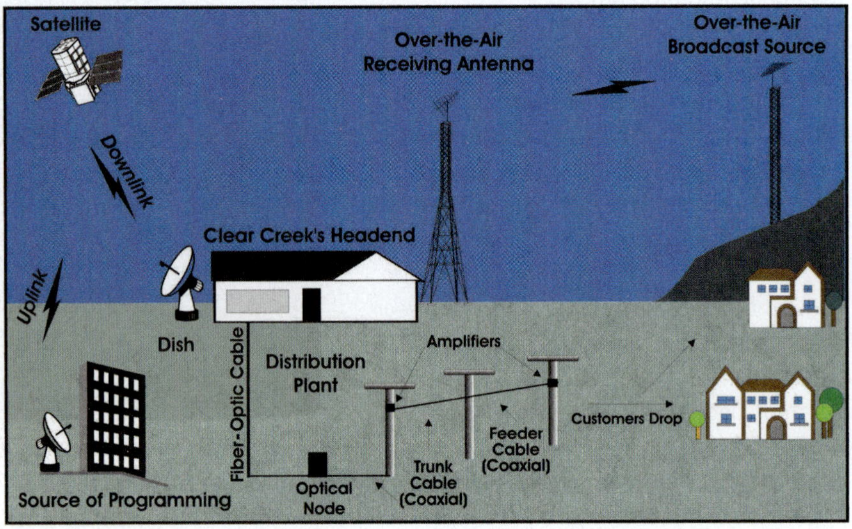

Data from: Clear Creek Telephone & TeleVision.

a major competitive threat to conventional broadcast television. But cable would also encounter new challenges (and opportunities) with the invention of satellite television, which uses large dishes to "downlink" signals from communication satellites in order to transmit cable TV services like HBO and CNN (see Figure 8.1).

The Evolution of Network Programming

Even with the emergence of mostly small-town cable operations, broadcast networks still controlled most TV programming in the 1950s. They began specializing in many types of programming (much of it "borrowed" from radio), including early-evening newscasts, variety shows, sitcoms, and soap operas. Eventually, additional genres and services emerged, including talk shows, newsmagazines, reality television, and public television. Television's powerful cultural presence has meant that its portrayals of women, African Americans, and other groups have had profound implications for those groups (see "Media Literacy Case Study: Race, Gender, and Sexual Orientation in TV Programming" on pages 232–233).

Information: Network News

Over time, many Americans abandoned their habit of reading an afternoon newspaper and began following the network evening news to catch coverage of the latest national and international events. By the 1960s, NBC, CBS, and ABC offered their thirty-minute versions of the evening news, dominating national TV news coverage until the emergence of CNN and the 24/7 cable news cycle in the 1980s. The network news divisions have been responsible for a number of milestones. The *CBS-TV News*, which premiered on CBS in May 1948, became in 1956 the first news show videotaped for rebroadcast in central and western time zones on **affiliate stations** (local TV stations that contract with a network to carry its programs; each network has roughly two hundred affiliates around the country), while NBC's weekly *Meet the Press* (1947–) remains the oldest show on television.

As with entertainment programming, the ever-broadening competition from cable and online sources of news has siphoned off network viewers. In 1980, the Big Three evening news programs had a combined audience of more than fifty million viewers on a typical weekday evening. By late 2018, that weekday evening news viewership hovered around twenty-two million.[2]

▲ In 1968, after the popular CBS news anchor Walter Cronkite visited Vietnam, CBS produced the news special *Report from Vietnam by Walter Cronkite*. Most political observers said that Cronkite's opposition to the war—along with his reputation as "the most trusted man in America"—influenced President Lyndon Johnson's decision not to seek reelection. CBS Photo Archive/Getty Images

Entertainment: Comedy

Originally, many new programs on television were broadcast live and are therefore lost to us today. The networks did sometimes manage to save early 1950s shows through poor-quality **kinescopes**, made by using a film camera to record live TV shows off a studio monitor (which today would be like saving a *Big Bang Theory* episode by shooting the TV screen in our living room with a video camera). However, the producers of *I Love Lucy* decided to preserve their comedy series by filming each episode, like a movie. This produced a high-quality version of each show that could be played back as a rerun. In 1956, videotape was invented, and many early comedies were preserved this way, allowing networks to create a rerun season in late spring and summer, thereby reducing the number of episodes produced each year from thirty-nine live broadcasts to about twenty-four taped programs.

In capturing *I Love Lucy* on film for future generations, the program's producers understood the enduring appeal of comedy. Although a number of comedy programs and ideas were stolen from radio, television eventually developed its own history with comedy, which became a central programming strategy for both the networks and cable. Throughout its history, TV comedy has been delivered to audiences through sketch comedy and situation comedy (sitcom).

Sketch Comedy

Most current audiences are familiar with **sketch comedy** thanks to NBC's long-running *Saturday Night Live* (1975–). In the early days of television, variety shows drew heavily from vaudeville-style performers, such as singers, dancers, acrobats, animal acts, stand-up comics, and ventriloquists. These shows typically required new ideas for sketches and other acts each week, along with new characters and new sets. This is still somewhat true of *Saturday Night Live* (many *SNL* alums have written about the all-consuming demands of working on the show), but other sketch comedy is often pretaped and delivered without variety elements, such as on *Portlandia* and *Drunk History*, which offer more diverse and specific viewpoints than the earlier mass-appeal variety shows.

Situation Comedy

In contrast, **situation comedy (sitcom)** is at least in some ways a simpler story form than sketch comedy. In sitcoms, you have the same characters in the same places from week to week, dealing with an increasingly complicated situation (often at home or at work) that is usually resolved in some way at the end of the half-hour program.³ From early hits like *I Love Lucy* and *The Honeymooners* to *Brooklyn Nine-Nine* and *The Good Place*, the programs developed more grounded character development. Other shows take this development further, adding more serious elements to create a *dramedy*. *M*A*S*H* was an early example of this form, which has become more common with shows like *Orange Is the New Black* and *Atlanta*.

▼ The critically acclaimed *Brooklyn Nine-Nine* was canceled by Fox after five seasons but quickly picked up by NBC. The sitcom is set in an NYPD precinct and stars an ensemble cast, including Andy Samberg, Andre Braugher, Terry Crews, Stephanie Beatriz, and Melissa Fumero. Photofest

Entertainment: Drama

Television's drama programs, which also came from radio, developed as another key genre of entertainment programming. Because production of TV entertainment was centered in New York in its early days, many of the sets, technicians, actors, and directors came from the New York theater world. Young stage actors often worked in the new television medium if they couldn't find stage work. The TV dramas that grew from these early influences fit roughly into two categories: anthology dramas and episodic series.

Anthology Drama

Although the subject matter, style, and storytelling are very different, **anthology dramas** share some of the same challenges as sketch comedy. Both essentially start from scratch each week, requiring new stories, new characters, and new sets. And like the variety programs of early television, the anthology dramas of the early 1950s borrowed heavily from live theater, first with stage performances and later with *teleplays* (scripts written for television).

But by the 1960s, networks were moving away from anthologies. This shift was due not only to the demands of producing a completely new story each week but also to the fact that anthologies mimicked the stage tradition of dealing with heavy, complicated, and controversial topics. This increasingly contrasted both with the goal of producing less challenging programming and with advertising itself, which tended to claim products could offer quick and easy fixes to life's problems. These factors combined to make the programs less appealing to advertisers, and thus to networks, regardless of the artistic, cultural, and social contributions anthologies could make. Despite having mostly disappeared from network television, anthology drama's legacy continues with such programs as the British import PBS drama *Masterpiece Theatre* (1971–), now known as *Masterpiece*, and the dystopian British science-fiction series *Black Mirror* (2016–) on Netflix.

Episodic Series

Abandoning anthologies, network producers and writers developed **episodic series**, first used on radio in the late 1920s. In this format, main characters continue from week to week, sets and locales remain the same, and technical crews stay with the program. Story concepts are broad enough to accommodate new adventures each week, establishing ongoing characters with whom viewers can regularly identify. Such episodic series come in two general types: chapter shows and serial programs.

Chapter shows are self-contained stories that feature a problem, a series of conflicts, and a resolution. Often reflecting Americans' hopes, fears, and values, this

LaunchPad
launchpadworks.com

Television Drama: Then and Now

Head to LaunchPad to watch clips from two drama series: one several decades old and one more recent.

Discussion: What kinds of changes in storytelling can you see by comparing and contrasting the two clips?

▼ *Empire*—a soapy Fox drama series about the music industry, featuring big-name actors Terrence Howard and Taraji P. Henson—quickly became one of TV's biggest hits after it debuted in 2015. The show has been nominated for numerous awards, and Henson won a best actress Golden Globe in 2016 for her portrayal of Cookie Lyon. Everett Collection, Inc

structure has been used in a wide range of dramatic genres, including network medical dramas like *ER* and *Grey's Anatomy*; police/crime network shows like *CSI: Crime Scene Investigation* and *Lethal Weapon*; family dramas like *This Is Us*; and fantasy/science fiction programs like *Dr. Who*. **Serial programs** are open-ended episodic shows, meaning that most story lines continue from episode to episode. Among the longest-running and most familiar serial programs in TV history are daytime *soap operas*, which typically run five days a week; however, by 2018, just four soap operas remained on network television.

Over the years, the lines between traditionally separate chapter and serial approaches have blurred. Although many dramas are written to tell a more-or-less self-contained story in each episode, they also commonly incorporate serial elements, with story arcs that carry over several episodes, or even from season to season. Many dramas today somewhat resemble the television *miniseries*, a form that is less common now but has a notable place in broadcast television history. A miniseries typically ran during prime time over a few nights or perhaps over a week or two and then was over. Perhaps the most famous example was when ABC turned Alex Haley's novel *Roots: The Saga of an American Family* into an award-winning miniseries in 1977. Current shows like HBO's *True Detective* and FX's *Fargo* have positioned themselves as a hybrid of miniseries and serial drama, with one season covering a full serialized story before starting over with a new (if sometimes related) set of characters in subsequent seasons.

Talk Shows and TV Newsmagazines

Many other programming genres have arisen in television's history, both inside and outside prime time. Talk shows like the *Tonight Show* (1954–) emerged to satisfy viewers' curiosity about celebrities and politicians, and to offer satire on politics and business. Variety programs like the *Ed Sullivan Show* (1948–1971) have introduced new comedians as well as musicians, including Elvis Presley and the Beatles. **TV newsmagazines** like CBS's long-running *60 Minutes* (1968–) usually feature three stories per episode, alternating hard-hitting investigations of corruption or political intrigue with softer feature stories about Hollywood celebrities and cultural trends.

Reality Television

Reality television dominated programming from the late 1990s through much of the first decade of the twenty-first century. Inspired by MTV's longest-running program, *The Real World* (1992–), the genre's biggest success was probably Fox's *American Idol*, which was the nation's top-rated show from 2004 to 2009. The popularity of the genre meant variations showed up on many of the niche channels up and down the broadcast and cable lineups. One could (and largely still can) find offerings ranging from network programs like *The Bachelor* to cooking-based shows like *Hell's Kitchen* to talent contests like *Dancing with the Stars*.

Featuring non-actors, cheap sets, and limited scripts, reality shows (like quiz shows) are much less expensive to produce than are sitcoms and dramas. For a time, critics worried the combination of popularity with cheap overhead would spell the doom of scripted television programs. However, no reality programs made it into the 2017–18 Top 10 rated shows.[4]

Public Television

In the 1960s, public television was created by Congress to serve viewers whose interests were largely ignored by ad-driven commercial television. Much of this noncommercial television was targeted to children, older Americans, and the well educated. Under President Lyndon Johnson, Congress passed the Public Broadcasting Act of 1967. The act created the Corporation for Public Broadcasting (CPB), which in 1969 established the Public Broadcasting Service (PBS). The act led to the creation of children's series like *Mister Rogers' Neighborhood*, *Sesame Street*, and *Barney*. Public television also broadcasts more adult fare, such as *Sherlock* and other imported British programs.

In the early 2000s, despite the continued success of such staples as *Sesame Street*, government funding of public television was slashed. The Obama administration restored some of it, but with the rise of cable and satellite, people who have long watched PBS now often get their favorite kinds of content from sources other than network and public television. For example, the BBC—historically a major provider of British programs to PBS—also sells its shows to cable channels (including its own BBC America) and to streaming video services, such as Netflix. In 2015, Sesame Workshop reached a deal with cable channel HBO to produce more new episodes of *Sesame Street*, to air exclusively on HBO for six months before being provided to PBS stations for free. Though some were upset by HBO's exclusive window, money from HBO will keep *Sesame Street* on the air (and at a lower cost to PBS stations) for the foreseeable future.

▼ The most influential children's show in TV history, *Sesame Street* (1969–) has been teaching children their letters and numbers for fifty years. Photofest

Media Literacy
CASE STUDY

Race, Gender, and Sexual Orientation in TV Programming

From the first days of television, the America portrayed across all genres of programming was far whiter than the country's actual population. It was rare for actors of color to appear at all, and if they did, it was often in minor roles, like someone holding a door or waiting a table. Members of other minority groups experienced similar marginalization: They were largely treated as if they didn't exist, and when they were represented, the portrayals were often deeply rooted in stereotypes. People of color and members of the LGBTQ community were often cast as villains or clownish caricatures—either objects to be feared or the butt of the joke.[1] For example, *Amos 'n' Andy* drew criticism, first as a radio show and later as a TV program, for representing blacks as lower class and unintelligent. In addition, women were often depicted as mothers, homemakers, or trophies to be won by amorous men, as well as overly emotional and less competent than men.

There was also the problem of assimilated representation: minority characters that were made acceptable because they behaved like the white characters on white shows. In the 1980s, *The Cosby Show* drew praise for challenging many stereotypical portrayals of African Americans and for proving that a show about a black family could be a ratings success. Still, some critics argued that the Huxtable family reflected a version of black success that seemed tied to adopting a white middle-class vision of the American Dream.

As programs like *The Cosby Show* illustrate, a study of race, gender, and sexual orientation representations on television is a complicated undertaking, but it is also an important one. We can critique television's portrayal of various minority groups, but we can also consider ways in which programs have challenged racism, misogyny, and bigotry in society.

For example, African American characters in the 1970s—in sitcoms like *Sanford and Son* and dramas like the mini-series *Roots*—laid the groundwork for current representations in sitcoms and dramas like *Black-ish* and *Empire*. Similarly, the change in what we consider "normal" or "acceptable" roles for women—from the housewives in programs like *Leave It to Beaver* in the late 1950s to the superhero stars in shows like *Supergirl* (2015–)—shows improvements in gender representation. We can also examine the way gay and lesbian characters started coming out of the closet in the 1990s on programs like *Ellen*, *Will & Grace*, and *Roseanne*. We can consider differences and similarities in how actors like Desi Arnaz (*I Love Lucy*) and Gina Rodriguez (*Jane the Virgin*) portrayed members of the Latino community a half-century apart. And we can compare the historic depictions of Asian men, often as evil villains or sexless helpers, and Asian women, often as cunning sexual "dragon ladies" or submissive concubines (the original *Hawaii Five-O*, 1968–1980), with more nuanced portrayals in modern programs (*Fresh Off the Boat*).

Many media scholars have also looked at news programming and what it means for the information industry to be dominated by straight white males. Whereas newsrooms are more diverse now than they were during the golden age of network TV news (1960s–1980s), scholars argue that problems remain, including a lack of understanding about alternative points of view. According to media scholar Edward Alwood,

LaunchPad

▶ **Visit LaunchPad** to watch a clip from the sitcom *Black-ish*. How does this program use humor to address complex topics like race, parenting, and relationships?

launchpadworks.com

▲ *Amos 'n' Andy* (*left*) began as a radio program, with both characters voiced by white men. When it switched to television in 1951, the show hired African American actors, but it was criticized by the NAACP for promoting negative stereotypes. *Black-ish* (*right*) tells the story of a successful advertising executive who worries that he and his family have become too assimilated into white culture.
CBS Photo Archive/Getty Images (left); ABC/Photofest (right)

who has researched how mainstream news covers LGBTQ issues, "For many years, newsrooms have been almost exclusively controlled by white, middle-class, heterosexual men who have relied on a common set of assumptions to guide them in how they reflect the world through their work. Although bias is traditionally regarded as an intentional distortion of the facts, another form of bias results from unwitting ignorance."[2]

Critics worry that the more television programming ignores or misrepresents groups of Americans, the more distorted our understanding of the world around us will be. For this reason, it's especially important to produce programs that preserve cultural and narrative authenticity—and to do so without reducing characters to one-dimensional stereotypes.

APPLYING THE CRITICAL PROCESS

DESCRIPTION Watch an episode of a current television program and one of an older show from a similar genre. For example, you could watch episodes of *The Big Bang Theory* (current) and *Friends* (1990s), both sitcoms about groups of friends living in a city; *Black-ish* (current) and *Sanford and Son* (1970s), both family sitcoms starring black actors; or *Transcendent* (current) and *Queer Eye for the Straight Guy* (2000s and a current reboot), reality television programs featuring members of the LGBTQ community.

ANALYSIS Make a list of each show's characters, and describe them in detail. Note which characters play major and minor roles, and how they are portrayed (as a stereotype or in a positive or negative light). Jot down three of each character's defining characteristics. Take note of which groups described in this case study do *not* appear in each program.

INTERPRETATION What do these representations mean? Are the characters fully formed and three-dimensional or shallow and one-dimensional?

EVALUATION According to popular wisdom, our society—and the TV programming that acts as a mirror of that society—is generally becoming more inclusive. Do the shows you viewed from different eras support this idea? Why or why not?

ENGAGEMENT Organize a watch party with a group of friends to view the two programs you examined for this activity. Discuss how each program portrays men, women, people of color, and members of the LGBTQ community. Consider how these portrayals might be empowering, problematic, or both.

The Evolution of Cable Programming

As network programming evolved, so did cable programming, offering a greater variety of content and services thanks in part to satellite technology. For instance, in 1975, the HBO (originally called Home Box Office) premium cable service began delivering uncut, commercial-free movies and exclusive live coverage of major boxing matches via satellite for a monthly fee. The following year, WTBS—an independent Atlanta broadcast station then owned by future media mogul Ted Turner—was uplinked to a satellite and made available to cable companies, becoming the first cable "superstation." In 1980, Turner, who had become a major player in cable, established CNN (originally the Cable News Network) as a 24/7 news operation. Such efforts gave more people greater and more convenient TV access to movies, news, sports, and other content, presenting a direct challenge to traditional over-the-air broadcast television.

With the advent of satellite TV, cable companies could excel at **narrowcasting**—the delivery of specialized programming, such as the History Channel or the Food Network, for niche viewer groups—which cut into broadcasting's large mass audience. Narrowcasting gave rise not only to different types of cable stations offering various content but also to cable providers offering various service options: Viewers could choose basic cable services with just a few channels for a modest monthly fee or add more niche channels and premium cable services for a higher monthly or per-use fee.

Basic Cable

Basic cable offers numerous channels, covering a variety of specific interests, that the broadcast networks don't offer, such as ESPN (sports), CNN (news), MTV and VH1 (music), Nickelodeon (new children's programs and older TV series reruns), Lifetime (movies), BET (Black Entertainment Television), the Weather Channel, and QVC (home shopping). Basic cable also traditionally offers **superstations**—independent broadcast TV stations uplinked to a satellite—such as WPIX (New York).

Typically, local cable companies pay each satellite-delivered service anywhere from $.06 cents per month per subscriber (for low-cost, low-demand channels like C-SPAN) to over $7 per month per subscriber (for ESPN, the most expensive channel by far). Most channels charge between $.50 cents and $1.25 per subscriber. Those fees are passed along to consumers as part of their basic monthly bill.

In 1992, eighty-seven cable networks were in business. By 2014, that number had grown to over nine hundred.[5] This dramatic increase was made possible in part due to better technology, such as fiber-optic cable and *digital cable* signals. Even more than broadcast network programming, cable services evolved far beyond the old limited categories of news information and fictional entertainment. Satisfied with smaller niche audiences, cable became much more specialized than its broadcast counterpart.

Premium Cable

Besides basic programming, cable offers special **premium channels**, which feature recent and classic Hollywood movies as well as original movies and popular series—all with no advertising, as subscribers pay fees in addition to charges for basic cable.

HBO—the oldest premium cable channel—pioneered original, uncut movies and series on cable. Its most successful and acclaimed shows include *The Sopranos*, *True Detective*, *Curb Your Enthusiasm*, and *Game of Thrones*. Other premium channels have also found success creating their own series. Showtime's most recent successes have been *Homeland* and *Ray Donovan*, while Starz's *Outlander* and *American Gods* both tap into existing cult followings—one for a popular romance novel and the other for a popular fantasy novel.

In addition to presenting fresh types of programming, premium cable has introduced innovative viewing options to customers. **Pay-per-view (PPV)** channels came first. These offered recently released movies or special one-time sporting events

▼ *Westworld* is an HBO series about a futuristic amusement park in which rich human guests can act out consequence-free fantasies with lifelike androids. As in the 1973 movie of the same name, the dream vacations become nightmares when the androids begin to malfunction.
Pictorial Press Ltd/Alamy Stock Photo

to subscribers who paid a designated charge to their cable company. In the early 2000s, U.S. cable companies introduced **video-on-demand (VOD)**. This service enables customers to choose among hundreds of titles and watch their selection whenever they want in the same way as a video, pausing and fast-forwarding when desired—features later copied by streaming services.

Regulatory Challenges Facing Television and Cable

Though cable cut into broadcast TV's viewership, both types of programming came under scrutiny from the U.S. government. Initially, thanks to extensive lobbying efforts, cable growth was suppressed to ensure that ad-revenue streams of local broadcasters and traditional TV networks were not harmed by the emergence of cable. Later, as cable developed, FCC officials worried that power and profits were growing increasingly concentrated in fewer and fewer industry players' hands. Therefore, the commission set out to mitigate the situation through the implementation of a variety of rules and regulations.

Restricting Broadcast Networks' Control

From the late 1950s to the end of the 1970s—the **network era**—CBS, NBC, and ABC dominated prime-time TV programming. By the late 1960s, the FCC, viewing the three networks as a quasi-monopoly, passed a series of regulations to undercut their power. The Prime Time Access Rule (PTAR), introduced in April 1970, reduced networks' control of prime-time programming from four to three hours in an effort to encourage more local news and public affairs programs, usually slated for the 6:00–7:00 P.M. EST time block. However, most stations simply ran thirty minutes of local news at 6:00 P.M. and then acquired syndicated quiz shows (*Wheel of Fortune*) or **infotainment** programs (*Entertainment Tonight*) to fill up the remaining half hour.

In 1970, the FCC also created the Financial Interest and Syndication Rules—called **fin-syn**—which banned the networks from running their own syndication companies and thus reduced their ability to reap profits from syndicating old TV series. Five years later, the Department of Justice limited the networks' production of non-news shows, requiring them to seek most of their programming from independent production companies and film studios.

With the rise of cable and home video in the 1990s, the FCC gradually phased out fin-syn, arguing that by then, the TV market had grown more competitive. Beginning in 1995, the networks were once again allowed to syndicate and profit from rerun programs, but only those they had produced in-house.

Buoyed by the spirit of deregulation in the 1980s and 1990s, the elimination of fin-syn and other rules opened the door for major merger deals (such as Disney's acquisition of ABC in 1995), which have constrained independent producers from creating new shows and competing for prime-time slots. Many independent companies and TV critics complain that the corporations that now own the networks—Disney, CBS, Fox, and Comcast—have historically exerted too much power and control over broadcast television content.

The digital turn, however, has changed that picture, with the explosion of available entertainment in a constantly shifting mix of services and producers. For example, companies like Amazon and Netflix are engaged in producing significant amounts of original scripted programming for a streaming audience, and their investment is significant. Netflix announced it would spend $8 billion on new programming in 2018, a move that came just as Disney prepared to yank all of its content from Netflix to start its own streaming service (see the chapter opener). One effect of the fluctuations in the television, cable, and streaming industry is a big demand for scripted programming. In 2002, 182 new scripted shows debuted; in 2018, that number had risen to 495, with 32 percent of those shows airing on streaming services.[6]

▲ *Seinfeld* (1989–1998) was not an immediate hit, but it was in the ratings top three for the final five of its nine seasons. Now, thirty years after its first episode, the show can still be seen in heavy syndication. Produced by Sony Pictures Television and NBC, *Seinfeld* is the type of successful show the fin-syn rules targeted to keep out of the networks' hands.
© Castle Rock Entertainment/Everett Collection

Reining in Cable's Growth—for a While

Throughout the 1950s and 1960s (before the broadcast networks accumulated extensive power), the FCC blocked cable companies from bringing distant TV stations into cities and towns that had local channels. The National Association of Broadcasters (NAB), the main trade organization for over-the-air television, lobbied Congress to restrict cable's growth so that it would not interfere with broadcast station interests and local TV ad sales. However, by the early 1970s, particularly with the advent of communication satellites, cable had the capacity for more channels and better reception—and the potential to expand beyond small isolated communities. In 1972, new FCC rules allowed cable to start expanding while still protecting broadcasters.

Through the **must-carry rules**, the FCC required cable operators to carry all local TV broadcasts on their systems. This ensured that local network affiliates, independent stations (those not carrying network programs), and public television channels would benefit from cable's clearer reception. The FCC also mandated **access channels** in the nation's top one hundred TV markets, requiring cable systems to provide free nonbroadcast channels for local citizens, educators, and governments to use.

Because the Communications Act of 1934 had not anticipated cable, the industry's regulatory status was unclear at first. As a result, there was uncertainty in the 1970s about whether cable should be treated like print and broadcast media (with cable receiving First Amendment protections of its content choices). Cable operators argued that they should be considered **electronic publishers**, able to choose which channels and content to carry. However, some FCC officials and consumer groups maintained that cable systems were really more like **common carriers**—services, like phone companies, that do not get involved in monitoring channel content. Thus, access to content should be determined by whoever paid the money to lease or use the channel (like a telephone company that does not interfere with the content of a phone call). In 1979, this debate ended in the landmark *Midwest Video* case, in which the U.S. Supreme Court upheld cable companies' right to dictate their own content and defined the industry as a form of electronic publishing.[7] With cable's regulatory future secured, competition to obtain franchises to supply local cable services intensified.

Through the 1980s and early 1990s, Congress approved several cable acts before rewriting the nation's communications laws in the **Telecommunications Act of 1996**, which took away a number of ownership restrictions from radio and television and also brought cable fully under federal oversight, treating the industry like broadcasting. In its most significant move, Congress used the Telecommunications Act to knock down regulatory barriers. By allowing regional phone companies, long-distance carriers, and cable companies to enter one another's markets, lawmakers hoped to spur competition and lower rates for consumers. Instead, cable and phone companies have merged operations in many markets, keeping prices at a premium. In fact, broadcast networks are now bundled together with cable networks under larger corporate ownership, as discussed later in this chapter. The Telecommunications Act of 1996 laid the legal groundwork necessary for these mergers to happen.

Technology and Convergence Change Viewing Habits

Thanks to new technologies, Americans can now watch all the visual content they want (whether it's movies, broadcast TV shows, or cable programming) whenever and wherever they want (on a TV set, on their laptop, on a handheld mobile device). What's more, with video streaming on the Internet, we are in the middle of a transformation in how programs are produced, distributed, and watched.

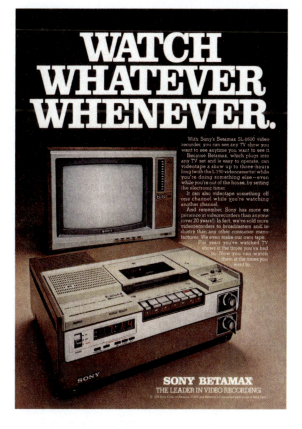

▼The emergence of home recording technology, such as Sony's Betamax VCR in 1975, changed American viewing habits. The Advertising Archives

Home Video and Recording

The introduction of videocassettes and **videocassette recorders (VCRs)** in the mid-1970s changed television viewing in two key ways. First, it enabled **time shifting**: Viewers could suddenly tape-record TV programs and play them back later. Even though the picture quality of the new VHS (Video Home System)—the industry standard—was much lower than that of the actual TV screen in real time, liberation from a time-locked TV schedule was a life changer for many viewers. Beginning in 1999, the **digital video recorder (DVR)** rapidly replaced the VCR, and viewers started recording shows on hard drives or DVDs instead of on VHS tapes. Today, with so much content available via streaming at any time, time shifting has switched to online viewing.

Second, home video spurred a booming video rental business. Video rental, formerly the province of walk-in video stores like Blockbuster, has since given way to streaming services like Amazon, Hulu, and Netflix (which started as a mail service and later added streaming); movie rental kiosks like Redbox; or online services like iTunes. Both time shifting and rentals/streaming have threatened the TV industry's advertising-driven business model: When viewers watch on DVRs or stream TV shows, they often skip the ads.

The Internet, Smartphones, and Mobile Video

The way traditional television has converged across so many digital platforms is perhaps one of the most striking examples of how fast these changes can take place—and how dramatic they can be. The first part of this picture is the Internet, which has fueled convergence with other technologies as high-speed connections and Wi-Fi have become more common.

Many new TV sets are Internet ready out of the box. For those that aren't or for older-model televisions, there are a wide variety of options for consumers who want to connect their TV to the Internet, from laptops and high-end video game consoles to dedicated devices such as Roku, Google Chromecast, or Amazon Fire TV Stick. The advantage is the ability to watch streaming content on whatever has the biggest screen and best sound in the home (see also the discussion of home entertainment in Chapter 7).

On the other end of the screen-size spectrum, consumers can take their TV viewing with them using smartphones and tablets capable of accessing the Internet via Wi-Fi systems or with faster cellular technology commonly called 4G LTE (Long-Term Evolution).

Once consumers have the hardware in place, the next piece is identifying the service they will use to find whatever show they want to watch. Some programs will stream episodes directly from their websites (like Comedy Central's *The Daily Show*) or make segments available via YouTube (like HBO's *Last Week Tonight with John Oliver*). Other programs and networks keep tighter control of their programs and try to earn money by selling them via services like Apple's iTunes Store or on Amazon, or through fee-based streaming services such as Hulu or Netflix. And streaming services these days no longer rely solely on showing films and shows created by others: Sites like Netflix, Amazon, and Hulu now produce their own programs with their own fan bases (see also the chapter opener).

The final piece of the convergence puzzle is understanding that the streaming services can link all of an audience member's devices together. So, for example, using a combination of apps for smartphones and tablets as well as devices like a Roku box at home, a person might use the same Netflix account on any of these devices anywhere there is Internet service (see also "The Digital Turn Case Study: Bingeing Purges Traditional Viewing Habits" on page 241).

The Digital Turn

CASE STUDY

Bingeing Purges Traditional Viewing Habits

Why settle for just one show at the same time every week when you can watch two episodes any time you want? Or three? Or a dozen? Binge viewing, or bingeing, means watching multiple episodes of a program one after another. Although bingeing has been around since the emergence of DVDs and Blu-ray discs, it wasn't until streaming video services gained a significant foothold that it became a cultural phenomenon.

Binge watching is most common among millennials: In a 2017 survey, 31 percent of viewers who reported heavy (daily) binge watching were eighteen to twenty-four years old. But bingeing is not just for younger generations. The same survey showed that viewers ages fifty-five to sixty-five made up 7 percent of heavy bingers, 13 percent of medium bingers (who binge on a monthly basis), and 29 percent of light bingers (who binge less than once a month).[1]

In addition, a study commissioned by Netflix showed that an increasing number of users will watch an entire season of a TV show within a week. This study also found that almost two-thirds of self-identified binge viewers use their mobile phones (or another second screen) while bingeing, and that this use complements their viewing instead of competing with it.[2] For that matter, smartphones and tablets mean that binge watching can happen practically anywhere, and the ability to view programs on demand means that it can happen anytime.

But what are the larger implications for television viewing now that bingeing has become so popular? On the business side of the industry, media giants like Comcast, which want to charge websites more for faster Internet connections, are butting heads with net neutrality advocates and companies like Netflix, which see the Comcast proposal of a tiered Internet system as nothing more than a shakedown (see the section on net neutrality in Chapter 9).

On the creative side of the business, critics note a positive trend in the number of high-quality dramatic and comedic television programs being produced, which they see as a welcome change after reality television meant less demand for scripted productions.

The social implications of binge viewing are still the subject of some debate. Some critics worry that bingeing could lead to loss of productivity or social interaction, while others argue that the flexibility offered by streaming makes it easier to be productive, because viewers don't have to adjust personal schedules to accommodate TV schedules. Still others point out that simultaneous engagement with social media can encourage conversations that might not have happened in years past. Binge watchers are watching TV differently than did people in other eras, but they may also be learning to engage with TV more actively than ever before.

▶ **Visit LaunchPad** to view a clip from frequently binge-watched program *Stranger Things*. What might the success of this series, which was produced for a streaming service rather than a broadcast or cable network, mean for the future of TV production and consumption?

launchpadworks.com

DBS

Direct broadcast satellite (DBS) was the biggest challenger to the cable industry—at least until digital streaming appeared on the scene. In its early days, DBS transmission was especially efficient in regions with rugged terrain or isolated farmland, where it was difficult or cost prohibitive to install cable wiring. DBS differs from cable in that it allows individual consumers to downlink satellite-transmitted signals into their homes without having them relayed through cable companies, which process these same signals and then send them out to the homes of cable customers via wires.

Japanese companies launched the first satellite TV system in Florida in 1978, but the early receiving dishes, which dotted the rural landscape in the 1980s, were ten to twelve feet in diameter and expensive ($3,000). By 1994, however, full-scale DBS service was available, and consumers would soon be able to buy satellite dishes the size of a large pizza. Today, there are two U.S.-based DBS companies: DirecTV (now owned by AT&T) and Dish (formerly the Dish Network). These companies offer consumers most of the same channels and tiers of service that cable companies carry, often at a slightly lower monthly cost. While DBS and cable have long competed against each other with prices and bundles of services, both are now facing competition from streaming video.

The Economics of Television, Cable, and Streaming Video

It is not much of a stretch to define TV programming as a system that mostly delivers viewers to merchandise displayed in blocks of ads. And with more than $60 billion at stake in advertising revenues each year, networks and cable services work hard to attract the audiences and subscribers that bring in the advertising dollars. To understand the TV economy today, we need to examine the production, distribution, and syndication of programming; the rating systems that set advertising rates; and the ownership structure that controls programming and delivers content to our homes. We also need to understand how streaming services are reshaping the business model for TV and cable, offering challenges and potential opportunities.

Production

Key players in the TV industry—networks, producers, and film studios—spend fortunes creating programs that they hope will keep viewers captivated for a long time. *Below-the-line* costs, which account for roughly 40 percent of a new program's production budget, include the "hardware" side of production: equipment, special effects, cameras and crews, sets and designers, carpenters, electricians, art directors, wardrobe, lighting, and transportation. *Above-the-line*, or "software," costs include the creative talent: actors, writers, producers, editors, and directors. These costs account for about 60 percent of a program's budget, except in the case of successful long-running series, in which salary demands by actors can drive these costs to more than 90 percent.

Most prime-time programs today are developed by independent production companies that are owned or backed by a major film studio, such as Sony or Disney. In addition to providing and renting production facilities, these film studios serve as a bank, offering capital to producers. In television, programs are funded through **deficit financing**: the production company leases the show to a network or cable channel for a license fee that is actually lower than the cost of production. (The company hopes to recoup this loss later in lucrative rerun syndication, which we will discuss in a moment.)

Because of smaller audiences and fewer episodes per season, costs for original programs on cable channels are usually lower than those for network broadcasts.[8] And unlike networks, cable channels air far fewer programs each year and have two revenue streams to pay for original programs—monthly subscription fees and advertising. By 2017, however, competition from HBO and Netflix had driven production costs up, especially for cable programs. While an average hour-long cable drama might cost between $3 and $4 million, Netflix was paying $8 million per episode for season two of *Stranger Things*, and roughly $10 million an episode for *The Crown*. But the most expensive show might be *Game of Thrones*, which cost HBO around $15 million per episode in its final season.[9]

Distribution

Programs get from production studios to viewers in a variety of ways, each with different financial arrangements. Cable service providers (e.g., Comcast or Charter) and satellite services rely mostly on customer subscriptions to pay for distributing their channels, but they also have to pay the broadcast networks **retransmission fees** to carry network channels and programming. While broadcast networks do earn carriage fees from cable and satellite providers, they pay *affiliate stations* license fees to carry their programs. In return, the networks sell the bulk of advertising time to recoup their fees and their investments in these programs. In this arrangement, local stations receive national programs that attract large local audiences and are allotted some local ad time to sell to generate their own revenue.

Streaming services operate on different models, which vary from service to service. Some are strictly fee based, whereas others sell advertising. Netflix, for example, earns money through monthly subscriptions, while YouTube's video streaming contains ads. In order to distribute programming, services either own their own content or negotiate licensing deals in order to show a

▲ *The Walking Dead* has been enormously successful for AMC, the cable channel that produces and airs the hit zombie-apocalypse program. The show's high ratings mean AMC can charge advertisers a premium rate. An edited-for-broadcast-TV version of the show entered syndication in 2014, and AMC also has agreements with streaming services like Netflix. Photofest

movie or program—or do some of both. For a service like Netflix, the licensing is a big cost, reportedly exceeding $7.5 billion in 2018.[10]

Syndication Keeps Shows Going and Going . . .

Syndication—leasing TV stations or cable networks the exclusive right to air TV shows—is a critical component of the distribution process. Each year, executives from thousands of local TV stations and cable firms gather at the National Association of Television Program Executives (NATPE) convention to acquire the exclusive local market rights to game shows, talk shows, and **evergreens**—popular old network reruns, such as *Cheers*. Networks might make cash deals or give a program to a local station in exchange for a split in the advertising revenue—usually called a **barter** deal, as no money changes hands.

Syndication plays a large role in programming for broadcast and cable networks, as well as for streaming services. For local network-affiliated stations, syndicated programs are often used during **fringe time**—programming immediately preceding the evening's prime-time schedule and following the local evening news or a network late-night talk show. Cable channels also syndicate network shows, airing them at a variety of times, including during prime time. And syndication is also important to streaming services like Hulu, which started as a partnership of major networks, and Netflix, which has long been a place to discover episodes of TV series old and new. And as Netflix becomes more established as a source of original production, syndication may become a two-way street. In 2018, Netflix struck a deal with cable network Comedy Central to show previous seasons of its animated comedy *BoJack Horseman*.[11]

There are different types of syndication. In off-network syndication, older programs that had long runs during network prime time are made available as reruns. Rerun, or off-network, syndication is the key to erasing the losses generated by deficit financing. With a successful program, the profits can be enormous. First-run syndication relates to any program specifically produced for sale into syndication markets, including *Wheel of Fortune* and *The Ellen DeGeneres Show*.

Measuring Television Viewing

Primarily, TV shows live or die based on how satisfied advertisers are with the quantity and quality of the viewing audience. Since 1950, the major organization that tracks and rates prime-time viewing has been the Nielsen Corporation, which estimates what viewers are watching in the nation's major markets. Ratings services like Nielsen provide advertisers, broadcast networks, local stations, and cable channels with considerable details about viewers—from race and gender to age, occupation, and educational background.

The Impact of Ratings and Shares on Programming

In TV measurement, a **rating** is a statistical estimate expressed as the percentage of households that are tuned to a program in the market being sampled. Another audience measure is the **share**, a statistical estimate of the percentage of homes that are tuned to a specific program but expressed as a percentage of households that are actually using their sets at the time of the sample.

The importance of ratings and shares to the survival of TV programs cannot be overestimated. Audience measurement tells advertisers not only how many people are watching but, more important, what kinds of people are watching. Prime-time advertisers on the broadcast networks want to reach relatively affluent eighteen- to forty-nine-year-old viewers, who account for most consumer spending. If a show is attracting those viewers, advertisers will compete to buy time during that program. (See Figure 8.2 for costs for a thirty-second commercial during prime-time programs.)

FIGURE 8.2 // PRIME-TIME NETWORK TV PRICING

Average costs are shown for a thirty-second commercial during prime-time programs on Monday and Thursday nights in 2018.

Monday

	8:00 P.M.	8:30 P.M.	9:00 P.M.	9:30 P.M.	10:00 P.M.
ABC	Dancing with the Stars ($113,977)				The Good Doctor ($155,916)
CBS	The Neighborhood ($84,417)	Happy Together ($98,261)	Magnum, P.I. ($99,430)		Bull ($102,620)
NBC	The Voice ($212,618)				Manifest ($167,311)
FOX	The Resident ($108,593)		911 ($173,854)		No network programming

Thursday

	8:00 P.M.	8:30 P.M.	9:00 P.M.	9:30 P.M.	10:00 P.M.
ABC	Grey's Anatomy ($204,792)		Station 19 ($120,301)		How to Get Away with Murder ($126,951)
CBS	The Big Bang Theory ($285,934)	Young Sheldon ($213,536)	Mom ($126,395)	Murphy Brown ($120,734)	S.W.A.T. ($105,103)
NBC	Superstore ($106,487)	The Good Place ($125,498)	Will & Grace ($161,373)	I Feel Bad ($99,902)	Law & Order: SVU ($105,030)
FOX	Thursday Night Football ($434,078)				No network programming

Data from: "Cost for a 30-Second Commercial," Advertising Age: Marketing Fact Pack, 2019, pp. 18–19.

Cable, in contrast, targets smaller audiences, so programs that do not attract a large audience might survive on cable because most of cable's revenues come from subscription fees rather than advertising. Most basic cable channels block out time for local and regional ads, such as those for restaurants or car dealerships in the area. These ads are cheaply produced compared with national network ads, and they reach a smaller audience.

Assessing Today's Converged and Online Markets

To account for the rise of DVRs, Nielsen now offers three versions of its ratings: live; live plus twenty-four hours, counting how many DVR users played shows within a day of recording; and live plus seven days, adding in how many viewers played the shows within a week.

In its efforts to keep up with TV's move to smaller screens, Nielsen is also using special software to track TV viewing on computers and mobile devices. But this method is also being challenged by streaming services, such as Netflix. While Netflix can instantly see its own data on which shows were viewed and how often, it doesn't typically release those numbers. While this doesn't affect Netflix advertising rates—because there aren't any—it makes it hard to fully understand in specific terms the impact of the service on viewing habits.

Some other streaming sites—such as those run by the networks and YouTube—do use advertising as a revenue stream, although the way advertising works online differs substantially from the way it works on network TV. Online advertisers pay a rate per one thousand *impressions*—which is a single ad shown to a person visiting an online site. So, if a product company or ad agency purchases one thousand online impressions at a $1 rate, the company or agency would need to spend $10 to have its advertisement displayed ten thousand times.

The Major Programming Corporations

After deregulation began in the 1980s, many players in TV and cable consolidated to broaden their offerings, expand their market share, and lower expenses. For example, Disney now owns both ABC and ESPN and can spread the costs of sports programming over its networks and its various ESPN cable channels. This business strategy has produced an *oligopoly* in which just a handful of media corporations now controls programming.

The Major Broadcast Networks

Despite their declining reach, the traditional networks have remained attractive business investments. In 1985, General Electric, which once helped start RCA-NBC, bought back NBC. In 1995, Disney bought ABC for $19 billion; in 1999, Viacom acquired CBS for $37 billion but split off from the company in 2005. In January 2013, Comcast completed its purchase of NBC Universal from GE—a deal valued at $30 billion. More recently, Disney completed its purchase of 21st Century Fox in 2019.

To combat audience erosion in the 1990s, the major networks began acquiring or developing cable channels to recapture viewers. Thus, what appears to be competition between TV and cable is sometimes an illusion. NBC, for example, operates MSNBC, CNBC, and Bravo; Disney's ABC owns ESPN and its many spin-offs, along with portions of Lifetime, A&E, and History; and Disney now owns Fox cable channels like FX and National Geographic (but not Fox Sports, Fox News, or the Fox television network).

Major Cable and DBS Companies

In the late 1990s, cable became a coveted investment, not so much for its ability to carry TV programming as for its access to households connected with high-bandwidth wires. Today, there are about 5,000 U.S. cable systems, down from 11,200 in 1994. Since the 1990s, thousands of cable systems have been bought by large **multiple-system operators (MSOs)**—corporations like Comcast and Charter, which own many cable systems. For years, the industry called its major players **multichannel video programming distributors (MVPDs)**, a term that included DBS providers like DirecTV and Dish. By 2014, cable's main trade organization had moved away from the MVPD classification and started using the term **video subscription services**, which now also includes Netflix and Hulu (see Table 8.1).

TABLE 8.1 // TOP 10 VIDEO SUBSCRIPTION SERVICES

Rank	Video Subscription Service	Subscribers (in millions)
1	Netflix	57.4
2	Amazon	26.0
3	DirecTV (AT&T)	25.5
4	Comcast	22.1
5	Hulu	20.0
6	Charter Communications	16.7
7	Dish	10.7
8	Verizon FiOS	4.6
9	Cox Communications	3.8
10	Altice	3.4

Data from: National Cable & Telecommunications Association, "Industry Data," Q2 2018, www.ncta.com/chart/top-10-video-subscription-services.

In the cable industry, Comcast became the top player after its takeover of NBC and move into network broadcasting. Back in 2001, AT&T had merged its cable and broadband business in a $72 billion deal with Comcast, then the third-largest MSO. The new Comcast instantly became the cable industry leader. Along with Comcast, the other large MSO is Charter Communications, which became the nation's second largest cable company with its 2016 acquisition of Time Warner Cable and Bright House Networks.

In the DBS market, DirecTV and Dish control virtually all the DBS service in the continental United States. In 2008, News Corp. sold DirecTV to cable service provider Liberty Media, which also owned the Encore and Starz movie channels. AT&T bought DirecTV in 2015 and Time Warner in 2018. The independently owned Dish was founded as EchoStar Communications in 1980.

Television in a Democratic Society

The development of cable, home video, DVRs, the Internet, and smartphone services has fragmented television's audience by appealing to viewers' individual and special needs. And by providing more specialized and individual choices, these changes have altered television's former role as a national unifying cultural force, potentially de-emphasizing the idea that we are all citizens who share the culture of a larger nation and world. Moreover, as cable and streaming services like Netflix are creating an increasing amount of quality original programming, the definition of what we call TV is expanding. New generations that grow up on cable and the Internet rarely make a distinction between a broadcast network, a cable service, and a streaming service. In addition, tablets, smartphones, and Internet services that now offer or even create our favorite programs are breaking down the distinctions between mobile devices and TV screens; TV today isn't necessarily consumed on a TV set.

The bottom line is that television, despite the audience fragmentation, still provides a gathering place for friends and family at the same time that it provides anytime access to a favorite show. Like all media forms before it, television is adapting to changing technology and shifting economics. As the technology becomes more portable and personal, television-related industries continue to search for less expensive ways to produce stories and more channels on which to deliver them. But what will remain common ground on this shifting terrain is that television will continue as our nation's chief storyteller, whether those stories come in the form of news bulletins, sporting events, cable dramas, network sitcoms, binge-worthy streaming series, or YouTube vignettes.

TV's future will be about serving smaller rather than larger audiences. As more sites develop original programming and as niche cable services like the Weather Channel produce reality TV series about storms, no audience seems too small and no subject matter too narrow for today's TV world. An overwhelming number of programming choices now exist for big and small TV screens alike. How might this converged TV landscape, with its volatile ups and downs in viewer numbers, change how audiences watch—and pay for—television? With hundreds of shows available, will we adopt à la carte viewing habits, in which we download or stream only the shows that interest us, rather than pay for cable (or DBS) packages containing hundreds of channels we don't watch?

▲ Kanopy is an effort to bring the democratic function of public libraries to video streaming. Patrons of any of the hundreds of participating U.S. libraries can use their library card to stream from three to ten videos per month—for free.

CHAPTER ESSENTIALS

Review

- In the development stage of television, early inventors (Zworykin and Farnsworth) competed to establish a patent for the first electronic television. In the entrepreneurial stage, television developed technical standards and turned into a business, and the FCC adopted **analog** (broadcast signals made of radio waves) for all U.S. TV sets. In the mass medium stage, the FCC began assigning channels throughout the country and later introduced the color standard.

- The introduction of cable provided access for communities that couldn't receive over-the-air broadcast signals, but it also posed a major competitive threat to broadcast television. The first small cable systems originated in the late 1940s.

- Beginning in the 1950s, broadcast networks began specializing in different types of programming, ranging from news to entertainment in such genres as **situation comedy (sitcom)** and drama.

- With the advent of satellite TV, cable companies could excel at **narrowcasting**—delivering specialized programming for niche viewer groups on **basic cable, premium channels, pay-per-view (PPV), video-on-demand (VOD)**, and later streaming video.

- During the **network era**—from the late 1950s to the end of the 1970s—CBS, NBC, and ABC dominated prime-time TV programming. To undercut the networks' power, the FCC passed a series of regulations, such as one that banned the networks from running their own syndication companies. These rules have since been eliminated.

- The FCC and cable operators went back and forth for many years about how much legal authority the federal agency had to regulate the industry. The **Telecommunications Act of 1996** eventually brought cable fully under federal jurisdiction.

- Home video technologies challenged traditional television, beginning with the introduction of **videocassette recorders (VCRs)** in the mid-1970s. **Digital video recorders (DVRs)** started replacing VCRs in 1999, and today, **time shifting** has switched to online viewing.

- Traditional and cable television have converged across multiple platforms and joined with video streaming services to make content available via many sources, including the Internet, TV sets, and smartphones.

LaunchPad

Visit LaunchPad for *Media Essentials* at **launchpadworks.com** for additional learning tools:

- **REVIEW WITH LEARNINGCURVE**
  LearningCurve adaptive quizzing helps you master the concepts you need to learn from this chapter.

- **VIDEO: CHANGES IN PRIME TIME**
  Television industry experts discuss shifts in programming, including the fading influence of the prime-time block.

- **MEDIA LITERACY PRACTICE**
  This activity challenges you to develop a critical perspective and apply it to everyday encounters with communication media.

- **Direct broadcast satellite (DBS)** allows individual consumers to downlink hundreds of satellite channels and services for a monthly fee.

- Networks and producers spend money on the production and distribution of programs.

- Broadcast networks, cable programmers, and some streaming sites make money from **syndication** and advertising; cable providers and some video streaming services also collect subscription fees.

- Since the 1990s, thousands of cable systems have been bought by **multiple-system operators (MSOs)**. Cable systems are now classified as **video subscription services**, which also include streaming services like Netflix.

- Even with niche programming and increasingly fragmented audiences, television still provides a forum where friends and family can gather. Though television is adapting to changing technology and shifting economics, it will continue to be our nation's chief storyteller.

Key Terms

analog, p. 223
prime time, p. 225
CATV, p. 225
affiliate stations, p. 227
kinescopes, p. 227
sketch comedy, p. 228
situation comedy (sitcom), p. 228
anthology dramas, p. 229
episodic series, p. 229
chapter shows, p. 229
serial programs, p. 230
TV newsmagazines, p. 230
narrowcasting, p. 234
basic cable, p. 234
superstations, p. 234
premium channels, p. 235
pay-per-view (PPV), p. 235
video-on-demand (VOD), p. 236
network era, p. 236
infotainment, p. 236
fin-syn, p. 236
must-carry rules, p. 238
access channels, p. 238
electronic publishers, p. 238
common carriers, p. 238
Telecommunications Act of 1996, p. 238
videocassette recorders (VCRs), p. 239
time shifting, p. 239
digital video recorder (DVR), p. 239
direct broadcast satellite (DBS), p. 242
deficit financing, p. 243
retransmission fees, p. 243
syndication, p. 244
evergreens, p. 244
barter, p. 244
fringe time, p. 244
rating, p. 245
share, p. 245
multiple-system operators (MSOs), p. 247
multichannel video programming distributors (MVPDs), p. 247
video subscription services, p. 247

Study Questions

1. What were the major factors that shaped the early history of television?
2. Why did cable and its programming pose a challenge to broadcasting?
3. How has streaming video posed a challenge to cable and broadcasting?
4. What role has the FCC taken in regulating networks and cable?
5. What are the technological challenges that network television and cable face?
6. How has television served as a national cultural center or reference point?

Mass Media Industries

The Internet and New Technologies: The Media Converge

256
The Early History of the Internet

259
The Evolution of the Internet: Going Commercial, Getting Social, Making Meaning

268
The Economics of the Internet

274
Security and Appropriateness on the Internet

277
The Internet in a Democratic Society

It was like something out of a horror movie. In the middle of the night in December 2018, a Houston-area couple was startled awake by the sound of someone swearing—from their four-month-old's bedroom. When they clicked on their own light, the security camera in their bedroom turned on and a man's voice told them to turn the light off. "I'm going to kidnap your baby. I'm in your baby's room," the couple remembered the voice saying. They ran to the baby's room, where the child was still sleeping, alone and unharmed.¹

A few months earlier, a South Carolina couple realized that someone had hacked their baby monitor when they saw the monitor's lens moving, but nobody in the home was controlling it. The couple believes the hacker may have been spying on them for months.²

In both of these cases, hackers invaded private homes using products that are part of the *Internet of things*—appliances and devices with new features allowing them to connect to the Internet. In theory, these connected devices enable greater convenience and efficiency by working with smartphones and special apps. For example, a person sitting at work can use his or her smartphone to "talk" to Wi-Fi enabled devices at home,

◀ The Internet touches nearly every aspect of modern life. Even the most intimate of family tasks, like watching over infant children, can be augmented, assisted, and even threatened by devices that use the Internet. Jinxy Productions/Getty Images

doing things like adjusting the thermostat, unlocking the front door to let in a visiting friend, making sure the lights are off, checking security cameras, and even using those cameras to speak to someone in the house.

In practice, however, these devices can make people's homes more vulnerable to hacking, even while they provide increased convenience and connectivity. While computers, tablets, and smartphones have gotten steadily better with security and anti-virus software, experts warn that many of the devices that make up the Internet of things lack this level of security. What's more, in a home where several devices are interconnected, there is a risk that one poorly protected device might give hackers a back door to other devices.

In the case of baby monitors and home security cameras, we expect them to allow us to watch and listen on our own terms—and not leave us vulnerable to being watched and listened to by others. However, our growing tapestry of personal devices includes products that we *do* buy specifically for the purpose of having them listen to us. Siri (Apple), Alexa (Amazon), Google Assistant, and Cortana (Microsoft) function as voice-controlled assistants through smartphones or smart speakers.

These devices are only supposed to listen when they hear a key word or phrase, at which point they send a recording of the user command to the parent company's cloud and respond with an answer or action. But while devices like Amazon Echo only have room to store a few recordings at a time, Amazon itself may have hundreds or even thousands of these recorded commands and snippets of conversation for each user—much like how your Internet search history is saved. This means that companies may know a lot about you based on your audio commands. According to one privacy expert, "Even if you think you're not saying anything very interesting or worthwhile, the data gets married and mingled with lots of other kinds of data that can create a very detailed picture of you."[3]

Making connections is part of the Internet's DNA, so creating an Internet of things was a logical next step in technology's ongoing push toward innovation, convenience, and connection. But these devices also introduce new threats to our privacy and personal security. As consumers caught in this web of interconnectivity, we would be well served to demand that manufacturers and regulators require ever-stronger safeguards as we do our best to be smart users of our smart devices.

THE INTERNET—the vast network of telephone and cable lines, wireless connections, and satellite systems that link and carry computer information worldwide—was described early on as the *information superhighway*. This description suggests that people envisioned a new system for conveying information that would replace the old one (books, newspapers, television, and radio). Created in the 1950s, the Internet was a government-sponsored technology enabling military and academic researchers in different locations to share information and findings by computer. Drawing on the technology used to build the first computer (the ENIAC, invented in 1946), the Internet exploited the power of digitization. Through **digitization**, information in analog form (such as text or pictures) is translated into binary code: a series of ones and zeros that can be encoded in software and transmitted between computers.

In many ways, the original description of the Internet has turned out to be accurate. This medium has expanded dramatically from its initial incarnation into a vast entity that encompasses all other media today (video and audio content in addition to text). Since becoming a mass medium in the mid-1990s, the Internet has transformed the way we do business, communicate, socialize, entertain ourselves, and get information; in short, it has profoundly touched the way most of us interact with media across all aspects of our lives.

Unlike other mass media, the Internet seems to have no limits. An increasing amount of content is being made accessible on it, more and more types of media are converging on it, and more people are gaining access to it all the time. But one thing is certain: As governments, corporations, and public and private interests vie to shape the Internet so that it suits their needs, questions of who will have access to it and who will control it are taking on more urgency.

In this chapter, we will explore these questions, along with the Internet's impact on various aspects of our lives, by:

- examining the early history of the Internet, including its initial uses as a military-government communication tool

- tracing the evolution of the Internet to a mass medium with multimedia capability

- analyzing the economics of the Internet, including the new business models it has inspired and the noncommercial entities that use it

- considering concerns that have arisen regarding the security of personal information on the Internet and the appropriateness of content now accessible through this medium

- weighing the negative and positive implications of the Internet for our democratic society

> **LaunchPad**
> launchpadworks.com
>
> Use **LearningCurve** to review concepts from this chapter.

The Early History of the Internet

After World War II, the United States entered the Cold War against the Soviet Union, pitting the two great powers in a decades-long battle of military and economic superiority. The space race was a symbolic part of the Cold War, and when the Soviet spacecraft *Sputnik* became the first to orbit the earth in 1957, the United States was shocked at being beaten. The event ushered in a new era of U.S. government spending on technological, scientific, and military developments. The United States would later make its first successful space launch with *Explorer* in 1958, but perhaps more important to our world today was the creation that same year of a U.S. Defense Department research agency that would eventually develop the Internet. In the decades that followed, new technologies such as microprocessors and fiber-optic cable increased the commercial viability of data transmission, paving the way for the Internet to become a mass medium.

Military Functions, Civic Roots

Created in 1958, the U.S. Defense Department's Advanced Research Projects Agency (ARPA) assembled a team of computer scientists around the country to develop and test technological innovations. Computers were relatively new at this time, and there existed only a few expensive mainframe computers, each large enough to fill an entire room. The scientists working on ARPA projects wanted access to these computers, and so they came up with a way to allow people to share computer-processing time: They created a wired network system in which users from multiple locations could log onto a computer whenever they needed it. To prevent logjams in data communication, the network used a system called packet switching, which broke down messages into easily routable pieces and reassembled them on the other end. This system provided multiple paths linking computers to one another, thereby allowing communication to continue if one of the paths got clogged or disrupted—much like the national highway system supported by President Dwight Eisenhower. This computer network became the original Internet—called **ARPAnet** and nicknamed the Net—and it enabled military

▲ Unveiled on April 7, 1964, the IBM 360 was considered one of the most influential computer rollouts. Programmers could use the special typewriter to talk to the mainframe. Van D Bucher/Getty Images

FIGURE 9.1 // DISTRIBUTED NETWORKS
Paul Baran, a computer scientist at the Rand Corporation during the Cold War era, worked on developing a national communications system. Centralized networks (*a*) lead all the paths to a single nerve center. Decentralized networks (*b*) contain several main nerve centers. In a distributed network (*c*), which resembles a net, there are no nerve centers; if any connection is severed, information can be immediately rerouted and delivered to its destination. But is there a downside to distributed networks when it comes to the circulation of network viruses?

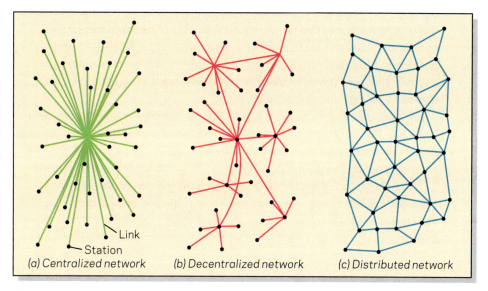

Information from: Katie Hafner and Matthew Lyon, *Where Wizards Stay Up Late* (New York: Simon & Schuster, 1996).

and academic researchers to communicate on a distributed network system (see Figure 9.1).

With only a few large research computers in the country, many computer scientists were suddenly able to access massive (for that time) amounts of computer power. The first Net messages ever were sent in 1969, when ARPAnet connections linked four universities: the University of California–Los Angeles, the University of California–Santa Barbara, Stanford, and the University of Utah. By 1970, another terminal was in place in Cambridge, Massachusetts, at the computer research firm Bolt, Beranek and Newman (BBN), and by late 1971, there were twenty-three Internet hosts at university and government research centers across the United States. That same year, Ray Tomlinson of BBN came up with an essential innovation to help researchers communicate—**e-mail**—and decided to use the "@" sign to separate the user's name from the computer name, a convention that has been used ever since.

During this development stage, the Internet (still called ARPAnet at this time) was used primarily by universities, government research labs, and corporations involved in computer software and other high-tech products. These users exchanged e-mail and posted information on computer *bulletin boards*—sites that listed information about particular topics, such as health, technology, and employment services.

The Net Widens

From the early 1970s to the late 1980s, the Internet moved from the development stage to the entrepreneurial stage, in which it became a marketable medium. With the introduction in 1971 of **microprocessors**—miniature circuits that could process and store electronic signals—it became possible to build the first *personal computers* (*PCs*), which were smaller, cheaper, and more powerful than the bulky systems that had occupied entire floors of buildings during the 1960s.

In 1986, the National Science Foundation sponsored the development of a high-speed communications network (NSFNET) and established supercomputer centers on the campuses of Princeton, the University of Illinois, the University of California–San Diego, and Cornell, and a fifth in Pittsburgh—jointly operated by Carnegie Mellon, the University of Pittsburgh, and Westinghouse—which were designed to speed up access to research data and encourage private investment in the Net. This government investment triggered a dramatic rise in Internet use and opened the door to additional commercial possibilities.

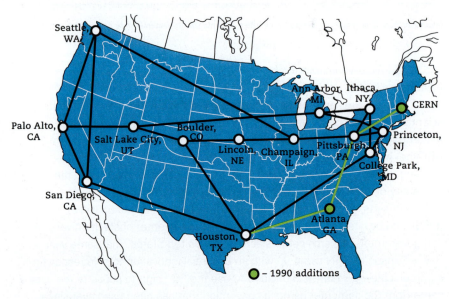

▲ The National Science Foundation (NSF) developed NSFNET in 1986 to promote research and education. As part of this effort, the NSF funded several university supercomputing centers and linked them with a high-speed network, which became the basis for the commercial Internet of the 1990s.

Also in the mid-1980s, **fiber-optic cable**—thin bundles of glass capable of transmitting thousands of messages simultaneously (via laser light)—had become the standard for conveying communication data speedily, making the commercial use of computers even more viable than before. Today, thanks to this increased speed, the amount of information that digital technology can transport is nearly limitless.

In 1990, ARPAnet officially ended, and in 1991, the NSF opened its network fully to commercial use. By this time, a growing community of researchers, computer programmers, amateur hackers, and commercial interests had already tapped into the Internet. These tens of thousands of participants in the network became the initial audience for the Internet's emergence as a mass medium.

The Evolution of the Internet: Going Commercial, Getting Social, Making Meaning

During the 1990s and early 2000s, the Internet's primary applications were e-mail (one-to-one communication) and web page display (one-to-many communication). By 2005, it had evolved into a far more powerful commercial and social network, becoming a many-to-many tool as an increasing number of applications led to the creation of new content and navigational possibilities for users. Today, users can make purchases; engage in real-time conversations with others; write, read, and comment on blogs and wikis; share photos and videos; and interact within virtual 3-D environments. And as the Internet gets more commercial and more social, the next phase of web development is already starting. This so-called Semantic Web takes connectivity beyond people and websites to other machines—from cars to refrigerators.

The Commercialization of the Internet

The introduction of the World Wide Web and the first web browsers in the 1990s helped transform the Internet into a mass medium. Soon after these developments, the Internet quickly became commercialized, leading to battles between corporations vying to attract the most users and those who wished to preserve the public, nonprofit nature of the Net.

The World Begins to Browse
Internet use before the 1990s consisted mostly of people transferring files, accessing computer databases from remote locations, and sending e-mails

▲ The GUI (graphical user interface) of the World Wide Web changed overnight with the release of Mosaic in 1993. As the first popular web browser, Mosaic unleashed the multimedia potential of the Internet—even if its interface seems rudimentary by today's standards. Mosaic was the inspiration for the commercial browser Netscape, which was released in 1994. Courtesy of the National Center for Supercomputing Applications and the Board of Trustees of the University of Illinois

through an unwieldy interface. The **World Wide Web** (or the web) changed all of that. Developed in the late 1980s by software engineer Tim Berners-Lee at the CERN particle physics lab in Switzerland to help scientists better collaborate, the web enabled users to access texts through clickable links rather than through difficult computer code. Known as *hypertext*, the system allowed computer-accessed information to associate with, or link to, other information on the Internet—no matter where it was located. **HTML (hypertext markup language)**, the written code that creates web pages and links, can be read by all computers. Thus, computers with different operating systems (Windows, Macintosh, Linux) can communicate easily through hypertext. After CERN released the World Wide Web source code into the public domain in 1993, many people began to build software to further enhance the Internet's versatility.

The release of **web browsers**—software applications that help users navigate the web—brought the web to mass audiences for the first time. Computer programmers led by Marc Andreessen at the University of Illinois (a supercomputer center that was part of NSFNET) released Mosaic in 1993, the first user-friendly browser to load text and graphics together in a magazine-like layout. With its attractive fonts and easy-to-use navigation buttons, Mosaic was a huge improvement over previous technology. In 1994, Andreessen joined investors in California's Silicon Valley to introduce another major advance: a commercial browser called Netscape. Together, the World Wide Web, Mosaic, and Netscape gave the Internet basic multimedia capability, enabling users to transmit pictures, sound, and video.

As the web became the most popular part of the Internet, many became convinced that the key to commercial success on the Net would be through a web browser. In 1995, Microsoft released its own web browser, Internet Explorer, which overtook Netscape as the most popular web browser. Today, Internet Explorer has been replaced by Microsoft's Edge, and Google Chrome, Safari, and Firefox remain leading web browsers.

Users Link In through Telephone and Cable Wires

In the first decades of the Internet, most people connected to "cyberspace" through telephone wires. In 1985, AOL began connecting home users to its proprietary web system through dial-up access, and it quickly became the United States' top **Internet service provider (ISP)**. AOL's success was so great that by 2001, the Internet start-up bought the world's largest media company, Time Warner—a deal that shocked the industry and signaled the Internet's economic significance as a vehicle for media content. As **broadband** connections—which can quickly download multimedia content—became more available, users moved away from the slower telephone dial-up service to high-speed service from cable, telephone, and satellite companies.[4] By 2007, both AT&T (offering DSL and cable broadband) and Comcast (offering cable broadband) surpassed AOL in numbers of customers. Today, the major ISPs in the United States are AT&T, Comcast, Verizon, Spectrum (owned by Charter Communications), and Cox.

People Embrace Digital Communication

In **digital communication**, an image, a text, or a sound is converted into electronic signals (represented as a series of binary numbers—ones and zeros) that are then reassembled as a precise reproduction of the image, text, or sound.

E-mail, a type of digital communication, was one of the earliest services of the Internet, and people typically used the e-mail services connected to their ISPs before major web corporations such as Google, Microsoft (Hotmail), and Yahoo! began to offer free web-based e-mail accounts to draw users to their sites. Today, all the top e-mail services include advertisements in their users' e-mail messages, one of the costs of the "free" e-mail accounts. Google's Gmail goes one step further by scanning messages to dynamically match a relevant ad to the text each time an e-mail message is opened. Such targeted advertising has become a hallmark feature of the Internet.

Although e-mail remains a standard for business-related text communications in the digital era, it has been surpassed in popularity by social apps, which include Facebook, Instagram, Snapchat, and Twitter.

▲ Snapchat allows users to send one another photos, videos, and text that will disappear after a certain amount of time. Like a lot of popular apps, the program gained a large following from a young audience and expanded from there. Hundreds of millions of photos are sent through the application every day. Bettina Fabos

Search Engines Organize the Web

As the number of websites on the Internet quickly expanded, companies seized the opportunity to provide ways to navigate this vast amount of information by providing directories and search engines. One of the more popular search engines, Yahoo!, began as a directory. In 1994, Stanford University graduate students Jerry Yang and David Filo created a web page to organize their favorite websites, first into categories, then into increasingly more subcategories as the web grew.

Eventually, though, cataloging individual websites became impractical. **Search engines** offer a more automated route to finding content by allowing users to enter key words or queries to locate related web pages. Search engines are built on mathematical algorithms. Google, released in 1998, became a major success because it introduced a new algorithm that ranked a page's "popularity" on the basis of how many other pages linked to it. By the end of 2018, Google remained the dominant search engine, with a global market share across all platforms of approximately 92.3 percent of searches, with Microsoft's Bing at 2.4 percent, Yahoo! at 2.1 percent, Baidu (based in China) at 1.0 percent, and Russia's Yandex at 0.6 percent.[5]

The Web Gets Social

As the Internet has developed, it has focused more intently on *media convergence*: different types of content created by different types of sources coming together on a variety of devices. Whereas the early Internet was primarily a medium for computer-savvy users to deliver text-and-graphic content, it has since been transformed into a place where people can access and share all manner of media content. And whereas the signature products of the early Internet were increased content access and accompanying dot-com consumerism, the iconic achievement of the web in recent years has been social media. In a little over a decade, a number of different types of social media have evolved, offering multiple platforms for the creation of user-generated content.

Types of Social Media Sites

Social media sites are among the most popular places on the Internet. Though varied, these sites share certain characteristics that make them "social"—most commonly some combination of the ability to share information, pictures, videos, jokes, memes, news articles, and other kinds of content with a network of friends or with the public.

- On sites like Facebook and LinkedIn, users present information about themselves in an ever-evolving personal web page that allows others to read, communicate, share, and often debate different posts, while also keeping users updated on their friends' activities.
- Video sites like YouTube, Vimeo, and Twitch specialize in video content generated by users and shared with others, as well as content created by large media companies.
- Microblogs like Twitter allow only short messages, which means that users can quickly scroll through posts, then easily share and respond.

LaunchPad
launchpadworks.com

The Rise of Social Media

Media experts discuss how social media platforms are changing traditional media.

Discussion: Some consider the new social media an extension of the very old oral form of communication. Do you agree or disagree with this view? Why?

- Sites like Snapchat, Instagram, and TikTok are largely focused on pictures and videos. Snapchat is famous for its use of filters, which make images look strange or funny.
- Blogs are typically forums used for longer written pieces. They sometimes function like journals and can include multimedia content. WordPress, Wix, and Weebly are common blogging sites.
- Hobby or interest sites combine a magazine niche appeal with social media styles of communicating. Pinterest and Etsy, for example, allow users to share ideas for crafts, fashion, recipes, and design.

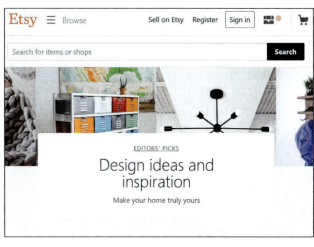

▲ Etsy is principally a commerce site, but the way it connects crafters with potential buyers has a social component, creating a sense of community even in the business of buying and selling goods.

The popularity of these various types of social media sites, combined with the explosion of mobile devices, has altered our relationship with the Internet. In a world in which the small screens of smartphones are becoming the preferred medium for going online, we don't typically get the full open Internet, one represented by the vast searches brought to us by Google. Instead, we get a more managed Internet—what some call a closed Internet or a walled garden[6]—brought to us by apps or platforms that carry out specific functions via the Internet.

Are you looking for a nearby restaurant? Don't search online—use this app especially designed for that purpose. The distributors of these apps act as gatekeepers; Apple, for example, has more than 2.2 million apps in its App Store, and Apple approves every one of them. Facebook offers a similar walled garden experience: the interface and the user experience on the site are highly managed by CEO Mark Zuckerberg and his staff. Facebook has installed measures to stop search engines from indexing users' photos, Wall posts, videos, and other data. The effect of both Apple's devices and the Facebook interface is a clean, orderly, easy-to-use environment but one in which we are "tethered" to the Apple App Store or to Facebook.[7]

Social Media and Democracy

In just a decade, social media has changed the way we consume, relate to, and even produce media, as well as the way we communicate with others. It has also proven to be an effective tool for democratic action, bringing to light repressive regimes that thrive on serving up propaganda and hiding their atrocities from view. This has led to some profound changes in national and world politics and in society.

One of the earliest instances of democratic action was the wave of protests taking place in more than a dozen Arab nations in North Africa and the Middle East that began in late 2010 and resulted in four rulers' being forced from power by mid-2012. The period called Arab Spring began in Tunisia. Young activists, using mobile phones and social media, organized marches and protests across the country. As satellite news networks spread the story and protesters' videos to the rest of the world, Tunisia's dictator of nearly twenty-four years fled the country. In the following spring, pro-democracy protests spread to other countries, including Egypt, Bahrain, Syria, Libya, Yemen, Algeria, Iraq, Jordan, Morocco, and Oman. In Libya and Yemen, it resulted in civil war, and in Syria, an ongoing civil war with multiple warring factions has so far left at least 500,000 dead and more than five million displaced, causing the greatest global humanitarian crisis in decades.[8]

The events of the Arab Spring inspired the Occupy Wall Street movement in the United States in September 2011, in which hundreds of people occupied a park in New York's financial district and made encampments in hundreds of other cities to protest economic inequality. The physical occupations didn't last, but the movement changed the language of economic inequality with the chant, "We are the 99 percent."[9] The Occupy Wall Street movement became the model for another social movement in 2013, Black Lives Matter. After the acquittal of George Zimmerman in the shooting of unarmed African American teenager Trayvon Martin in Florida, #BlackLivesMatter helped change the conversation on race in America (see also the Chapter 1 opener).

Although social media has proven to be an effective tool for democracy, its effectiveness for evil purposes has also become clear. One of the warring parties in Syria and Iraq was the terrorist organization ISIS, which had a lot of success using the Internet and social media to recruit naïve young men and women from other countries to Syria and Iraq, and to inspire others to commit terrorism in their home countries.[10]

In addition, unscrupulous con artists and fake news operations have learned how to make money by getting people to share their lies on social media, generating clicks that result in advertising dollars but degrade the sharing of reliable information that is so important in a democracy. What's worse, political parties and dictatorial nations exploit social media to spread their own lies and disrupt or change the outcome of democratic elections in other countries (see also "The Digital Turn Case Study: Social Media Fraud and Elections" on pages 266–267 and "The Digital Turn Case Study: Attacking Journalism: Trolls and State-Sponsored Troll Armies" on page 92).

The Next Era: The Semantic Web

Many Internet visionaries talk about the next generation of the Internet as the *Semantic Web*, a term that gained prominence after hypertext inventor Tim Berners-Lee and two coauthors published an influential article in a 2001 issue of *Scientific American*.[11] Semantics is the study of meaning, so a Semantic Web refers to a more meaningful—or organized—web. Essentially, the future promises a layered, connected database of information that software will sift through and process automatically for us. Whereas the search engines of today generate relevant web pages for us to read, the software of the Semantic Web will make our lives easier as it places the basic information of the web into meaningful categories and makes significant connections for us.

One early example of the Semantic Web is Apple's voice recognition assistant, Siri, which first shipped with its iPhone 4S in 2011. Siri uses conversational voice recognition to answer questions, find locations, and interact with various iPhone functionalities, such as the calendar, reminders, the weather app, the music player, the web browser, and the maps function.

The next generation of this trend is already launching with the Internet of things (see chapter opener). Appliances, lights, air-conditioning, heating, window shades, and home entertainment systems can now be controlled via wireless (**Wi-Fi**) home networks and synced to smartphones via apps. In addition, a new breed of devices boasting voice-control capabilities—including Google Home and Amazon Echo—can control home devices connected to this Internet of things. According to projections, there will be 20.4 billion of these smart devices in use by 2020.[12]

While they come with many conveniences, it's important to note that devices on the Internet of things may also have a downside. For example, these devices currently lack the security software used on computers, smartphones, and tablets. Security experts warn that devices that "talk" to each other—from lightbulbs to door bells to baby monitors—could let a hacker turn off a house's alarm system or tap into the Wi-Fi and steal sensitive data.[13] (For more, see the chapter opener.)

The Internet in 1995

In a clip from the 1995 thriller *The Net*, Sandra Bullock's character communicates using her computer.

Discussion: How does this movie from over two decades ago portray online communication? What does it get right, and what seems outdated now?

▼This high-tech refrigerator uses cameras, a tablet-style interface, and wireless Internet to help its owner keep track of grocery needs. Some security experts have noted that devices like these lack the firewalls and anti-virus protection of most computers, smartphones, and tablets. Bloomberg/Getty Images

The Digital Turn

CASE STUDY

Social Media Fraud and Elections

In the early years of social media, it seemed as if democracy had a new friend. Ideally, social media sites like Facebook, Twitter, and YouTube would open up political conversation, enabling democratic discourse to flourish. In 2010, the London newspaper the *Guardian* optimistically called Facebook "the election's town square" and hoped "that people [were] prepared to let their politics show online."[1] The *Guardian* was right: People *did* let their politics show online, and many of them posted relevant news stories, offered thoughtful discussion, and organized friends to become more politically involved. It turned out, however, that there were a lot of jerks hanging out in the election's town square: people posting nasty political memes, heated arguments, and insults. It all came to a head with the 2016 presidential election. "What had been simmering all year suddenly boiled over as [the] presidential election cycle made online friends hostile and prompted many to mute or unfriend those whose political rantings were creating stress," the *Dayton Daily News* wrote.[2]

Unfortunately, that wasn't the worst of it. There were also criminals in the election's town square, as foreign countries infiltrated social media to spread political disinformation and disrupt America's 2016 presidential election. The assistant director of the FBI's Counterintelligence Division testified before a U.S. Senate committee in June 2017 regarding a report, "Assessing Russian Activities and Intentions in Recent Elections." He said, in part:

> Russia's 2016 presidential election influence effort was its boldest to date in the United States. Moscow employed a multi-faceted approach intended to undermine confidence in our democratic process. . . . This Russian effort included the weaponization of stolen cyber information, the use of Russia's English-language state media as a strategic messaging platform, and the mobilization of social media bots and trolls to spread disinformation and amplify Russian messaging.[3]

The extent of disinformation has been shocking. On Facebook, an estimated 126 million users might have been exposed to the fake ads and event posts produced by a Russian troll farm between 2015 and 2017. According to a Facebook official, "Many of the ads and posts we've seen so far are deeply disturbing—seemingly intended to amplify societal divisions and pit groups of people against each other."[4] By 2018, Twitter had identified more than 3,100 Russian-linked troll accounts spreading divisive information during the 2016 election, and said it had notified more than 677,000 people exposed to the fake messages.[5] Google also found at least two phony Russian accounts and eighteen fake YouTube channels with forty-three hours of content.[6]

In addition, a December 2018 report revealed that Russian operatives created social media accounts on sites like Instagram and YouTube that seemed to support equality for African Americans, when in fact they were working to get African Americans following these accounts so disgusted

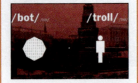

▶ Web Clip

YouTube.com has a number of videos about social media fraud during the 2016 election. For example, search for "How Russian Bots Invade Our Elections," posted by the *New York Times* in 2017. How has this type of manipulation affected early dreams that the Internet would be a "friend" to democracy? What can users of social media do to help stop the spread of misinformation?

▲ Russian government trolls meddling in the 2016 U.S. presidential election took advantage of social media to spread inflammatory posts and ads like these, while disguising themselves as American religious or equal rights advocacy groups. Whether explicitly targeting political candidates or fanning the flames of existing tensions and distrust in the government, the goal was the same: to support a particular outcome by mobilizing or discouraging targeted groups of voters.

by all politicians that they would, among other things, decide to skip voting altogether. As one of the authors of the report, Renee DiResta, told the *New York Times*, "Very real racial tensions and feelings of alienation exist in America, and have for decades. . . . The [Russian effort] didn't create them. It exploits them."[7]

This is what is known so far, as the U.S. Department of Justice continues its investigation. Russian trolls have also attempted to disrupt elections in the United Kingdom, where they tried to spread discord during the Brexit campaign; in France; and in several other European countries.

Because Europe has been dealing with Russian propaganda for decades, most of its nations have a head start on strategies to combat such disinformation:

- In Sweden, there is a school literacy program to teach young people to identify Russian propaganda.
- Lithuania has citizen volunteers in the "Elves vs. Trolls" battle, with the good citizen investigators (elves) researching and revealing Russian trolls.
- Britain and France monitor Facebook closely and pressure the social media company to close down fake accounts.
- In Germany, political candidates all agreed not to use bots—fake accounts (mostly on Twitter) that make automated posts in an effort to boost a topic's profile—in their social media campaigns.
- In Slovakia, fourteen hundred advertisers have pulled their business from websites identified by researchers as the work of trolls.
- In Brussels, a European Union task force has published thousands of phony stories to reveal their deception.

In nearly all European countries affected, fact-checking and investigative journalism are additional countermeasures to the Russian troll offensive.[8] What ideas do you think would work best in America to combat political social media fraud?

The Economics of the Internet

One of the unique things about the Internet is that no one owns it. But that hasn't stopped some corporations from trying to control it. Companies have realized the potential of dominating the Internet business through access to phone and broadband wires, search engines, software, social networking, and original content, all in order to sell the essential devices that display the content or to amass users who become an audience for advertising. In addition, companies that provide Internet services have realized that they can make more money by setting up tiers of service based on Internet speed (see also "Media Literacy Case Study: Net Neutrality" on pages 272–273). However, there remain those who want to keep the spirit of the Internet's independent early days alive, and alternative voices still have a home on the noncommercial web.

Ownership: Controlling the Internet

By the end of the 1990s, four companies—AOL, Yahoo!, Microsoft, and Google—had emerged as the leading forces on the Internet. In today's converged world, in which mobile access to digital content prevails, Microsoft and Google still remain powerful. Those two, along with Apple, Amazon, and Facebook, constitute the leading companies of digital media's rapidly changing world. Of the five, all but Facebook operate proprietary cloud services and encourage customers to store all their files in the company's walled garden for easy access across all devices. This ultimately builds brand loyalty and generates customer fees for file storage.[14]

Microsoft

Microsoft, the oldest of the dominant digital firms (established by Bill Gates and Paul Allen in 1975), is an enormously wealthy software company that struggled for years to develop an Internet strategy. As its software business declined, its flourishing digital game business (Xbox) helped it continue to innovate and find a different path to a future in digital media. The company finally found moderate success on the Internet with its search engine Bing in 2009. With the 2012 release of the Windows Phone 8 mobile operating system and the Surface tablet, Microsoft made headway in the mobile media business. In 2014, Microsoft brought its office software to mobile devices, with Office for iPad and Office Mobile for iPhones and Android phones, all of which work with OneDrive, Microsoft's cloud service. Microsoft is also developing its next generation of the HoloLens, a holographic computer operated with a headset.

Apple

Apple, Inc., was founded by Steve Jobs and Steve Wozniak in 1976 as a home computer company. Apple had been only moderately successful and was near bankruptcy in 1997, when Jobs, having been forced out of the company for a decade, returned. Apple introduced the iPod and iTunes in 2001, two innovations that led the company to become the number one music retailer in the United States. Then, in 2007, Jobs introduced the iPhone, transforming the mobile phone industry. The company further redefined wireless computing with the iPad in 2010, the Apple Watch in 2015, and the Siri-controlled Apple HomePod in 2018.

With the iPhone and iPad now at the core of Apple's business, the company expanded to include providing content—music, television shows, movies, games, newspapers, magazines—to sell its media devices. The next wave of Apple's innovations was the iCloud, a storage and syncing service that enables users to access media content anywhere (with a wireless connection) on its mobile devices. The iCloud helps ensure that customers purchase their media content through Apple's iTunes store, further tethering users to its media systems. Apple also announced its own streaming service, which is set to launch in 2019.

Amazon

Amazon started its business in 1995 in Seattle, selling the world's oldest mass medium (books) online. Amazon has since developed into the world's largest e-commerce store, selling not only books but also electronics, garden tools, clothing, appliances, and toys. Yet by 2007, with the introduction of its Kindle e-reader, Amazon was following Apple's model of using content to sell devices. The Kindle became the first widely successful e-reader, and by 2010, e-books were outselling hardcovers and paperbacks at Amazon. In 2011, in response to Apple's iPad, Amazon released its own color touchscreen tablet, the Kindle Fire, giving Amazon a device that can play all the media—including music, TV, movies, and games—it sells online and in its Appstore.

Like Apple, Amazon has a Cloud Player for making media content portable. In addition, Amazon is now competing with television, cable networks, and Netflix by producing Amazon Original television series for its streaming service and even branching into feature films. In addition, Amazon's Alexa-controlled Echo speakers have become the best-selling voice-assisted home digital assistant.

▼After years in the retail business, Amazon has been experimenting with content creation. Successful shows include *Transparent*, *The Man in the High Castle*, and *The Marvelous Mrs. Maisel* (pictured). Amazon Studios was the first streaming service to receive an Academy Award nomination for best picture—for *Manchester by the Sea* in 2017. Everett Collection, Inc

Google

Google, established in 1998, had instant success with its algorithmic search engine and now controls over 90 percent of the global search market, generating billions of dollars of revenue yearly through the pay-per-click advertisements that accompany key-word searches. Google has also branched out into a number of other Internet offerings, including Google Shopping, Google Maps, Gmail, Blogger, the Chrome browser, YouTube, and the Chromecast television device. Google has also challenged Microsoft's Office programs with Google Apps, a cloud-based bundle that includes word-processing, spreadsheet, calendar, messaging, and e-mail software. Google competes against Apple's iTunes with Google Play, an online media store, and vies with Amazon's voice-controlled Echo speakers with its own Google Home digital assistant.

Facebook

Facebook was established in 2004 by then-twenty-three-year-old Harvard psychology major and avid computer programmer Mark Zuckerberg. Facebook's immense, socially dynamic audience (about two-thirds of the U.S. population and more than 2.1 billion users around the globe) is its biggest resource. Like Google, it has become a data processor as much as a social media service, collecting every tidbit of information about its users—what we "Like," where we live, and what we want—and selling this information to advertisers. Because Facebook users reveal so much about themselves in their profiles and the messages they share with others, Facebook can offer advertisers exceptionally tailored ads: A user who recently got engaged gets ads like "Vacation in Hawaii," while a teenage girl sees ads for prom dresses.

Facebook has focused on becoming more mobile with its purchase of Instagram in 2012 for $1 billion and its 2014 purchase of WhatsApp, a global instant messaging service. Facebook made its first major investment in hardware with the Oculus VR, a virtual reality technology company, for $2 billion in 2014. The purchase set off a flurry of investments, as companies aimed to compete with Facebook in the new virtual reality market.

▼ An attendee at a Facebook developer conference tries out the Oculus VR system. Josh Edelson/Getty Images

Targeted Advertising and Data Mining

In the early years of the web, advertising took the form of traditional display ads placed on pages, but because they reached small general audiences, they weren't very profitable. In the late 1990s, web advertising began to shift to search engines. Paid links started to appear as "sponsored links" at the top, bottom, and side of a search engine result list and even, depending on the search engine, within the "objective" result list itself. Now, every time a user clicks on a sponsored link, the advertiser pays the search engine for the click-through. For online retailers, having paid placement in searches can be a good thing.

Advertising has since spread to other parts of the Internet, including social networking sites, e-mail, and mobile apps. These activities make advertising easy to track, effective in reaching the desired niche audience, and relatively inexpensive, since ads get wasted less often on uninterested parties. For example, Google scans the contents of Gmail messages; Facebook uses profile information, status updates, and "Likes" to deliver individualized, real-time ads to users' screens; and Apple targets users through in-app ads.

While TV, radio, and newspapers have seen advertising dollars stagnate or decline, Internet advertising has seen double-digit growth over the last few years. In 2018, it was the single biggest recipient of ad dollars, raking in $78.3 billion.[15] Much of that increase was in mobile advertising delivered via devices such as the smartphone, which jumped from $3.4 billion in 2012 to $40 billion in 2017, and is predicted to reach $65 billion by 2020.[16]

Gathering users' location and purchasing habits has been a boon for advertising, but these data-collection systems also function as consumer surveillance and data mining operations. The practice of **data mining**—searching through electronic files to identify trends—also raises issues of Internet security and privacy. Millions of people have embraced the ease of **e-commerce**: the buying and selling of products and services on the Internet. What many people don't know is that their personal information may be used without their knowledge for commercial purposes—such as **targeted advertising**, which sends ads to consumers based on information websites have gathered about them. For example, in 2011, the Federal Trade Commission charged Facebook with eight violations in response to the company's having told consumers their information would be private but making it public to both advertisers and third-party applications. Facebook settled with the FTC by fixing the problems and agreeing to submit to privacy audits through the year 2031.[17] But Facebook came under fire again in 2018 after it revealed that a political consulting firm, Cambridge Analytica, had gained access to 87 million Facebook user accounts, and after reports that Facebook had also given phone and device makers access to data on users and their friends. Some have suggested that this data was later used to help target a Russian online propaganda campaign (see also "The Digital Turn Case Study: Social Media Fraud and Elections" on pages 266–267).

One common method that commercial interests use to track the browsing habits of computer users is **cookies**, or information profiles that are automatically collected and transferred between computer servers whenever users access websites.[18] The legitimate purpose of a cookie is to verify that a user has been cleared for access to a particular website, such as a library database that is open only to university faculty and students. However, cookies can also be used to create marketing profiles of web users to target them for advertising. Most commercial websites require users to accept cookies in order to gain access to the site.

Media Literacy
CASE STUDY

Net Neutrality

For more than a decade, the debate over net neutrality has framed the potential future of the Internet, and it continues to be a back-and-forth fight. **Net neutrality** refers to the principle that every website and every user—whether a multinational corporation or a private citizen—has the right to the same Internet network speed and access. The idea of an open and neutral network has existed since the origins of the Internet, but there had never been a legal, formal policy until 2015, when the Federal Communications Commission reclassified broadband Internet service and approved net neutrality rules. Still, as we will see, this battle is far from over.

▲ Without a net neutrality policy, ISPs may make the Internet into a two-tiered system: a fast lane reserved for the companies able to afford it, and a slow lane for all others. Steve Sack/Cagle Cartoons

The opposition to net neutrality is dominated by some of the biggest communications corporations. These major telephone and cable companies—including Comcast, AT&T, Spectrum, Verizon, and Cox—control 98 percent of broadband access in the United States through DSL and cable modem service. These companies want to offer faster connections and priority to clients willing to pay higher rates, and provide preferential service for their own content or for content providers who make special deals with them—in other words, to eliminate net neutrality. For example, tiered Internet access might mean that these companies would charge customers more for data-heavy services like Netflix, YouTube, and Hulu. These companies argue that the profits they could make with tiered Internet access would allow them to build expensive new networks, benefiting everyone.

But supporters of net neutrality—bloggers, video gamers, educators, religious groups, unions, small businesses—argue that the cable and telephone giants actually have incentive to rig their services and cause net congestion in order to force customers to pay a premium for higher-speed connections. They claim that an Internet without net neutrality would hurt small businesses, nonprofits, and Internet innovators, who might be stuck in the "slow lane" and not be able to afford the fast connections that large corporations can afford. Large Internet corporations like Google, Amazon, eBay, Microsoft, Skype, and Facebook also support net neutrality because their businesses depend on their millions of customers having equal access to the web.

In 2015, the FCC under Barack Obama reclassified broadband Internet service as a telecommunications service and put net neutrality rules into place.[1] Specifically, the FCC made rules that

▶ Visit LaunchPad to view a video discussing net neutrality. Do you support net neutrality? Why or why not?

launchpadworks.com

disallow **blocking** (broadband providers prohibiting access to legal content and services), **throttling** (intentionally impairing or degrading Internet performance based on content or source), and **paid prioritization** (favoring some Internet traffic over other lawful traffic in exchange for payment, thereby creating "fast lanes").[2]

When Donald Trump became president in 2017, however, he appointed a new chair of the FCC, former Verizon lawyer Ajit Pai. On December 14, 2017, the FCC voted to repeal the 2015 FCC net neutrality policy on a 3–2 party-line vote, with Republicans rejecting the earlier safeguards. Yet even then, the battle continued. In January 2018, attorneys general from twenty-one states and the District of Columbia filed lawsuits to challenge the decision, stating that the FCC vote to repeal net neutrality was "arbitrary, capricious, and an abuse of discretion." The governor of Montana went one step further and ordered ISPs that have contracts with the state to follow net neutrality principles.[3]

After the FCC's actions in 2017, Tim Wu, the legal scholar who coined the term *net neutrality* in 2003, argued that the policy is necessary and should be reinstated. "There is a long history of anticompetitive throttling and blocking—often concealed—that the FCC has had to stop to preserve the health of the internet economy," he said. "Services like Skype and Netflix would have met an early death without basic net neutrality protections."[4] Now, more than fifteen years and counting into the debate and tangle of lawsuits over net neutrality, it's likely that it will take legislation or a decision by federal courts—and not just an FCC regulation—to provide a more conclusive answer to this question.

APPLYING THE CRITICAL PROCESS

DESCRIPTION Interview a sample of people about their views on net neutrality. Would they be willing to pay higher rates for faster connections? Do they think every website should have the same network speed and access?

ANALYSIS What sorts of patterns emerge from your interviews? Are there common views on the way the Internet should be accessed? Do your interviewees seem to be concerned or unconcerned about the issue of net neutrality? Do your questions make them think about this issue for the first time?

INTERPRETATION What do these patterns mean? Is the idea of net neutrality better or worse for democracy?

EVALUATION Is the concept of net neutrality a benefit of the Internet? Should net neutrality rules be restored? What should the standards of speed and access to the Internet be? How should they be enforced?

ENGAGEMENT Learn about and take action for or against net neutrality. Share your knowledge with your peers.

▲ With hundreds of billions of web pages and tens of millions of other digital files ranging from books to video and audio, the Internet Archive is a free-to-use site run by a nonprofit organization. The massive archive was established in 1996, as the Internet was in the midst of transforming from a tool used by research universities and the government to a public mass medium.

The Noncommercial Web

Despite powerful commercial forces dictating much of the content we access online, the pioneering spirit of the Internet's early days endures, and the Internet continues to be a participatory medium where anyone can be involved. Two of the most prominent areas in which alternative voices continue to flourish are in open-source software and digital archiving.

Open-Source Software

Microsoft has long dominated the software industry, requiring users to pay for both its applications and its upgrades, and keeping its proprietary code protected from changes by outsiders. Yet independent software creators persist in making alternatives through **open-source software**, in which code can be updated by anyone interested in modifying it. One example is the open-source operating system Linux, introduced in 1991 by Linus Torvalds and shared with computer programmers and hobbyists around the world, who have avidly participated to improve it. Today, even Microsoft acknowledges that Linux is a credible alternative to expensive commercial programs.

Digital Archiving

Librarians have worked tirelessly to build digital archives that exist outside any commercial system. One of the biggest and most impressive digital-preservation initiatives is the Internet Archive (www.archive.org), established in 1996. The Internet Archive aims to ensure that researchers, historians, scholars, and all U.S. citizens have access to digitized content. This content comprises all the text, moving images, audio, software, and more than 330 billion archived web pages reaching back to the earliest days of the Internet. The Internet Archive—whose mission states its belief in universal access to all knowledge—has also worked with academic institutions and libraries to scan and archive digital copies of twenty million books and texts, as well as millions of audio recordings, videos, and images.

Security and Appropriateness on the Internet

When we watch television, listen to the radio, read a book, or go to a movie, we don't need to provide personal information to get access to the media content we're consuming. However, when we use the Internet—whether it's to sign up for an e-mail account, comment on a blog, or shop online—we give away personal information, even if we don't mean to. This has raised concerns about the security of information, personal safety, and the appropriateness of content available on the web.

Information Security: What's Private?

Government surveillance, online fraud, unethical data gathering, and malicious programs have become common, making the Internet a potentially treacherous place.

- *Government Surveillance.* Since the inception of the Internet, government agencies around the world have obtained the communication logs, web browser histories, and online records of users who thought their Internet activities were private. In the United States, for example, the USA PATRIOT Act (which became law about a month after the September 11 attacks in 2001, with most provisions renewed in 2006, 2011, and 2015) grants sweeping powers to law-enforcement agencies to intercept individuals' online communications, including e-mail messages and browsing records. The act was intended to allow the government to more easily uncover and track potential terrorists and terrorist organizations, but many now argue that it is too vaguely worded, allowing the government to unconstitutionally probe the personal records of citizens without probable cause and for reasons other than preventing terrorism. Moreover, searches of the Internet permit law-enforcement agencies to gather huge amounts of data, including the communications of people who are not targets of an investigation. Documents leaked to the news media in 2013 by former CIA employee and former National Security Agency (NSA) contractor Edward Snowden revealed that the NSA had continued its domestic spying program for more than a decade, collecting bulk Internet and mobile phone data on millions of Americans.
- *Online Fraud.* The Internet has increasingly become a conduit for online robbery and *identity theft*, the illegal obtaining of someone's credit and identity information to fraudulently spend his or her money. One particularly costly form of Internet identity theft is **phishing**. Through this tactic, scammers send phony e-mail messages that appear to be from official websites—for example, eBay, PayPal, and Chase—asking customers to enter or update their credit card details and other personal information (such as bank account numbers). Once scammers have this information, they can go on a shopping spree using the victim's credit card or siphon funds out of the victim's bank account.
- *Unethical Data Gathering.* As discussed in an earlier section on the economics of the Internet, companies use cookies to collect information and tailor marketing messages, as well as for targeted advertising and data mining.

▲ In March 2018, journalists revealed a huge unauthorized use of Facebook user data by British firm Cambridge Analytica. The firm bought a data set and scraped information from those people's friends, ultimately accessing information on about 87 million Facebook users. Facebook founder and CEO Mark Zuckerberg was called to testify before the U.S. Congress and the European Parliament. Is Facebook's business model of profiting from our personal data also an ever-present problem for data security?

Some companies, like Facebook, have gotten into hot water over gathering but failing to protect various kinds of personal data (see page 271). Unethical data gathering also includes **spyware**—software that is often secretly bundled with free downloaded software and that sends pop-up ads to users' computer screens.

- *Malicious Programs.* Spyware is just one kind of **malware** (malicious software) that hackers sneak onto computers, tablets, smartphones, and high-tech household appliances. Other types of malware, such as worms and Trojan horses, can do more than just spy on a device: They can actually take control. For example, malware can tell infected computers and devices to contact a particular website at a preprogrammed time, overwhelming and crashing the site in a distributed denial-of-service (DDoS) attack.

In 1998, the FTC developed fair information principles to combat the unauthorized collection of personal data online. Unfortunately, the FTC had no power to enforce these principles, and most websites didn't enforce them.[19] As a result, consumer and privacy advocates called for stronger regulations, such as opt-in or opt-out policies. **Opt-in policies**, favored by consumer and privacy advocates, require websites to obtain explicit permission from consumers before the sites can collect browsing-history data. **Opt-out policies**, favored by data-mining corporations, allow for the automatic collection of browsing-history data unless the consumer requests to "opt out." In 2012, the FTC approved a report recommending that Congress adopt Do-Not-Track legislation to limit tracking of user information and to enable users to easily opt out of data collection. Several web browsers now offer Do-Not-Track options.

On May 25, 2018, the European Union's General Data Protection Regulation (GDPR) became effective, requiring informed consent before data is collected on any user. The GDPR also has new, stronger penalties for violations. Although the GDPR applies only to EU citizens, the rules became the default standard for global Internet companies, and many companies operating in the United States sent out notices to customers about their updated privacy policies.

Personal Safety: Online Predators, Spreading Hate, and Deciding What's Appropriate

In addition to the various kinds of scams and malware that target electronic devices, predators use the Internet to cause harm. One predatory behavior is called **catfishing**, which is the practice of pretending to be another person, even a person of a different gender, to trick someone into having an online relationship. One of the scariest forms of catfishing happens when a child molester poses as a friendly person on social networking sites, with the goal of forming relationships with naïve young people. Once a relationship takes root online, the predator suggests a face-to-face meeting, with the intent of exploiting the young person sexually. These incidents have provoked an outcry from parents and demands for better mechanisms for protecting Internet users' safety.

There are also concerns about controversial online content that can be harmful to users or to society as a whole, such as sites that cultivate hate, feature sexually explicit content, or provide instructions on making weapons or drugs. Because of their controversial nature, sites that carry potentially dangerous information have incited calls for Internet censorship. The terrorist attacks of September 11, 2001, along with the mass shootings in schools, churches, and other public places, have intensified debate about whether hate speech and other dangerous information should be available on the Net. The Southern Poverty Law Center, which identifies and tracks white supremacists and other hate groups, warns that some websites, including 4chan and Reddit, can be used to spread bigotry and recruit new members.

Public objection to indecent and obscene Internet content has led to various legislative efforts to tame the web. For example, the Children's Internet Protection Act of 2000 was passed and upheld in 2003. This act requires schools and libraries that receive federal funding for Internet access to use software that filters out any visual content deemed obscene, pornographic, or harmful to minors unless disabled at the request of adult users. Yet regardless of laws, pornography continues to flourish on commercial sites, individuals' blogs, and social networking pages.

The Internet in a Democratic Society

Despite concerns over some online content, many tout the Internet as the most democratic social network ever conceived. But this same medium has also presented threats to our democracy—in the form of a division between people who can afford to use the Internet and those who can't, and the Internet's increasing commercialization.

Access: Closing the Digital Divide

Coined to echo the term *economic divide* (the disparity of wealth between the rich and the poor), the term **digital divide** refers to the contrast between the information haves (those who can afford to pay for Internet services) and the information have-nots (those who can't).

About 89 percent of U.S. households are connected to the Internet, but there are gaps in access to advanced broadband service, which typically offers the best downloading and uploading speeds. For example, about 65 percent of Americans have home broadband service, but these numbers vary considerably by income: 87 percent of adults with household incomes of more than $75,000 have home broadband, while only 45 percent of adults with household incomes of less than $30,000 have it (see Figure 9.2). There is also a difference when it comes to education: 85 percent of adults with a college degree have home broadband, while only 24 percent of adults with less than a high school diploma have home broadband.[20]

Although not a perfect substitute for a home broadband connection, smartphones are helping narrow the digital divide. In fact, the total number of broadband users dropped by 8 percent from 2016 to 2018, while the number of adults who use a smartphone and cell service only grew by the same amount.[21] Meanwhile, the mobile phone industry forecasts that smartphone use in North America will increase from 84 percent in 2017 to 86 percent by 2025, bringing more small-screen data connections to users.[22] In addition, while broadband continues to have advantages in speed and capacity, in 2018 the industry began rolling out the next generation of mobile phone data speeds—5G—in major cities, which is projected to account for nearly half of smartphone connections by 2025.[23]

Globally, however, the have-nots face even greater obstacles in crossing the digital divide. Although the web claims to be worldwide, the most economically powerful countries—such as the United States, Sweden, Japan, South Korea, Australia, and the United Kingdom—account for much of its activity and content. In nations such as Jordan, Saudi Arabia, Syria, and Myanmar (Burma), the government permits limited or no access to the web. In other countries, an inadequate telecommunications infrastructure hampers access to the Internet. However, as mobile phones become more popular in the developing world, they could provide one remedy to the global digital divide.

Ownership and Customization

Some people have argued that the biggest threat to democracy on the Internet is its increasing commercialization. Similar to what happened with radio and television, the growth of commercial channels on the Internet has far outpaced the emergence of viable nonprofit channels, as a few corporations have gained more control over this medium. Although there was much buzz about lucrative Internet start-ups in the 1990s, it has been large corporations that weathered the crash of the dot-coms in the early 2000s and maintained their dominance.

As we've seen, the Internet's booming popularity has tempted commercial interests to gain even more control over the medium. It has also sparked debate between defenders of the digital age and those who want to regulate the Net. Defenders argue that newer media forms—digital music, online

FIGURE 9.2 // DIGITAL DIVIDE BASED ON DEMOGRAPHICS AND INTERNET SPEED

The digital divide is as much about speed and volume of data as it is about simple access; Internet via cellular connection can be slower than broadband, and getting unlimited smartphone data often involves paying a premium price.

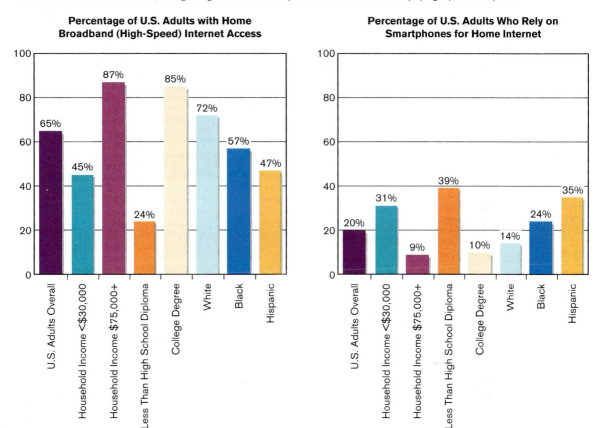

Data from: "Internet/Broadband Fact Sheet," Pew Research Center, February 5, 2018.

streaming, blogs—have made life more satisfying and enjoyable for Americans than has any other medium. Further, they maintain that **mass customization**, whereby individual consumers can tailor a web page or another media form, has enabled us to express our creativity more easily than ever. For example, if we use a service like Facebook or WordPress, we get the benefits of creating our own personal web space without having to write the underlying code. On the other hand, we're limited to the options, templates, and other platform features provided by the media company. So (the dissenters ask), how free are we, really, to express our true creative selves? And how much are we being controlled by the big Internet firms?

CHAPTER ESSENTIALS

Review

- The **Internet**—the vast central network of telephone and cable lines, wireless connections, and satellite systems that link and carry computer information worldwide—was created in the late 1960s as the U.S. Defense Department's **ARPAnet** and used as a military-government communication tool. **E-mail** enabled researchers to communicate from separate locations.

- Innovations in the 1970s and 1980s took the Internet from the development stage to the entrepreneurial stage. **Microprocessors** led to the introduction of the first personal computers (PCs), and **fiber-optic cable** helped make the commercial use of computers even more viable.

- The introduction of the **World Wide Web** and the first **Web browsers** in the 1990s helped transform the Internet into a mass medium. Soon after these developments, the Internet quickly became commercialized. Key features of the commercial Internet include **Internet service providers (ISPs)**, which bring web access to customers; e-mail services and messaging via social apps; and **search engines**, which are capable of searching and retrieving information and linking to websites based on a few key words.

- As it's developed, the Internet has become more converged and more social. **Social media** sites provide a place for people to share information, pictures, videos, jokes, and other kinds of content with a network of friends or with the public. Social media has also proven to be an effective tool for democratic action, though foreign countries have also used these sites to spread political disinformation and disrupt America's elections.

- The next generation of the Internet is referred to as the Semantic Web, which features a connected database of information that software will sift through and automatically process for us. Included in this is the Internet of things, which takes connectivity beyond people and websites to other devices, which can be controlled via **Wi-Fi** or voice commands.

- Although no one owns the Internet, a number of corporations have tried to control it. Microsoft, Apple, Amazon, Google, and Facebook are currently the leading Internet companies.

- Advertising is big business, and companies like Google have become models of how to generate dollars through **targeted advertising**, or ads targeted to a consumer based on information various websites have gathered about that individual.

LaunchPad

Visit LaunchPad for *Media Essentials* at **launchpadworks.com** for additional learning tools:

- **REVIEW WITH LEARNINGCURVE**
  LearningCurve adaptive quizzing helps you master the concepts you need to learn from this chapter.

- **VIDEO: USER-GENERATED CONTENT**
  Editors, producers, and advertisers discuss the varieties of user-generated content and how it can contribute to the democratization of media.

- **MEDIA LITERACY PRACTICE**
  This activity challenges you to develop a critical perspective and apply it to everyday encounters with communication media.

The biggest area of online advertising is now targeted at mobile devices and their apps.

- Noncommercial entities on the web do not make a profit from the Internet. **Open-source software** is shared freely and developed collectively, whereas digital archiving aims to ensure that data is stored and preserved digitally, so that all people have access to it.

- Government surveillance; online fraud, such as **phishing**; unethical data gathering, such as **spyware**; and the use of **malware** have raised questions about information security on the web and what should be considered private. At the same time, the issues of online predators, hate speech, and deciding what constitutes appropriate content on the web—particularly regarding sexually explicit material—have sparked public concern.

- The Internet has made it easier for more people to voice opinions and become involved in a wide range of topics, but it has also revealed a **digital divide** between those who have access to information and those who do not.

Key Terms

digitization, p. 255
ARPAnet, p. 256
e-mail, p. 257
microprocessors, p. 258
fiber-optic cable, p. 259
World Wide Web, p. 260
HTML (hypertext markup language), p. 260
web browsers, p. 260
Internet service provider (ISP), p. 260
broadband, p. 261
digital communication, p. 261
search engines, p. 262
social media, p. 262
Wi-Fi, p. 265
data mining, p. 271
e-commerce, p. 271
targeted advertising, p. 271
cookies, p. 271
net neutrality, p. 272
blocking, p. 273
throttling, p. 273
paid prioritization, p. 273
open-source software, p. 274
phishing, p. 275
spyware, p. 276
malware, p. 276
opt-in policies, p. 276
opt-out policies, p. 276
catfishing, p. 276
digital divide, p. 277
mass customization, p. 279

Study Questions

1. How did the Internet originate? How did it evolve? What does its development have in common with earlier mass media?

2. How have social media sites been used to manipulate elections and other democratic processes, and what should we be doing as a society to fight back?

3. How have major companies tried to control the Internet? Which failed, and why?

4. What are the central concerns about the Internet regarding security and appropriateness?

5. What is the digital divide? In modern society, what are the implications of being on the "have-not" side of that divide?

Mass Media Industries

10

Digital Gaming and the Media Playground

285
The Early History of Digital Gaming

288
The Evolution of Digital Gaming

295
Trends and Issues in Digital Gaming

304
The Economics of Digital Gaming

307
Digital Gaming in a Democratic Society

College scholarships, competitions to make the team, grueling practice sessions, matches in arenas drawing thirty thousand people or more, huge television audiences for championships, profiles in *Sports Illustrated*, and hopes to one day compete in the Olympics . . .

This is not swimming, track and field, soccer, hockey, or skiing. These "athletes" have no incentive to cheat with steroids, although they might fail a test for Mountain Dew and Doritos. These are eSports athletes: athletes who competitively play video games at the highest levels.

In the past two decades, eSports have followed the trajectory of traditional sports, with an increasing number of colleges and universities recruiting scholarship athletes, major sponsors underwriting teams and tournaments, big media corporations offering contracts, and, perhaps in the near future, the International Olympic Committee including them in the Olympic Games.

Stanford University's Artificial Intelligence Laboratory hosted the first video game tournament in October 1972, in which about two dozen people

◀ Video game tournaments can draw huge audiences, with some eSports events matching or even surpassing the viewership of traditional professional sports. AFP Contributor/Getty Images

competed against each other in the game *Spacewar!*[1] At this time, however, video games were still in their infancy; the breakthrough arcade game *Pong* wouldn't be released until the following month.

More organized eSport leagues and tournaments developed in the late 1990s, as the Internet became a mass medium. *Quake* and *Counter-Strike* were among the leading games for league play.[2] By the early 2000s, *StarCraft* and *Warcraft III* became the dominant eSports games, and South Korea fostered eSports with the first twenty-four-hour cable gaming channels.

Dozens of colleges and universities have had club eSports teams for years. In 2014, Robert Morris University, a small private school, became the first university in the country to offer college scholarships to eSports athletes. In 2016, the University of California–Irvine became the first public research university to do so, and in 2017, the University of Utah established the first eSports program at a university belonging to one of the power five athletic conferences.[3]

With such a marked increase in college eSports, professional eSports athletes sound increasingly plausible. Just like traditional sports, growing audience size has drawn media coverage, which has drawn big money into eSports. According to one report, the eSports TV-streaming audience had already surpassed that of Major League Soccer (MLS) and the National Hockey League (NHL) by 2018. It is predicted that by 2021, eSports will have exceeded the National Basketball Association (NBA) and Major League Baseball (MLB) in viewership, trailing only the National Football League (NFL), and will have more than $5 billion in annual revenue.[4]

Not surprisingly, a number of media corporations have invested in platforms to stream game competitions and content, including Amazon (with Twitch), Google (YouTube Gaming), and Disney (BAMTech). In early 2018, Facebook became the latest entry, signing a contract with ESL (the largest eSports company) to carry tournaments and gameplay for *Dota 2* and *Counter-Strike: Global Offensive* on its Facebook Watch platform.[5] Riot Games (maker of *League of Legends*) and Activision Blizzard (maker of *Overwatch*) are two of the biggest forces behind professional eSports leagues. The leagues have team franchise fees of between $10 million and $20 million; interestingly, some of the leading investors in American eSports teams are owners of NFL, NBA, MLB, and NHL teams.[6]

And the Olympics? First, eSports will be a medal event at the 2022 Asian Games, the world's largest multisport event besides the Olympics. After that comes the 2024 Summer Olympic Games. The International Olympic Committee co-chair held open the possibility: "The youth, yes they are interested in eSport[s]. . . . Let's look at it. Let's meet them. Let's try if we can find some bridges."[7]

DIGITAL GAMES offer play, entertainment, and social interaction. Like the Internet, they combine text, audio, and moving images. But they go even further than the Internet by enabling players to interact with aspects of the medium in the context of the game—from deciding when an on-screen character jumps or punches to controlling the direction of the "story." This creates an experience so compelling that vibrant communities of fans have cropped up around the globe. And the games have powerfully shaped the everyday lives of millions of people worldwide.

Players can now choose from a massive range of games designed to satisfy almost any taste. Today, digital gaming and the media playground encompass classic video games like *Super Mario Bros.*, virtual sports-management games like ESPN's *Fantasy Football*, and more physically interactive games like those found on *Wii Fit*—to say nothing of massively multiplayer online role-playing games like *Fortnite* and casual games like *slither.io*. Indeed, for players around the world, digital gaming has become a social medium—one just as compelling and distracting as other social media. The U.S. Supreme Court has even granted digital gaming First Amendment freedom-of-speech rights, ensuring its place as a mass medium.

In this chapter, we will take a look at the evolving mass medium of digital gaming by:

- examining the early history of digital gaming, including its roots in penny arcades

- tracing the evolution of digital gaming from arcades and bars to living rooms and hands

- discussing the rise of gaming as a social medium that forms communities of play

- analyzing the economics of gaming, including the industry's various revenue streams

- raising questions about the role of digital gaming in our democratic society

The Early History of Digital Gaming

When the Industrial Revolution swept Western civilization two centuries ago, the technological advances involved weren't simply about mass production. They also promoted mass consumption and

LaunchPad
launchpadworks.com

Use **LearningCurve** to review concepts from this chapter.

the emergence of *leisure time*—both of which created moneymaking opportunities for media makers. By the late nineteenth century, the availability of leisure time sparked the creation of mechanical games like pinball. Technology continued to grow, and by the 1950s, computer science students in the United States had developed early versions of the video games we know today.

Mechanical Gaming

In the 1880s, the seeds of the modern entertainment industry were planted via a series of coin-operated contraptions devoted to cashing in on idleness. First appearing in train depots, hotel lobbies, bars, and restaurants, these leisure machines (also called "counter machines") would find a permanent home in the first thoroughly modern indoor playground: the **penny arcade**.[8]

Arcades were like nurseries for many fledgling forms of amusement, which would mature into mass entertainment industries during the twentieth century. Arcades offered fun even as they began shaping future media technology. For example, automated phonographs used in arcade machines evolved into the jukebox, and the kinetoscope (see Chapter 7) set the stage for the coming wonders of the movies. But the machines most relevant to today's digital gaming were more interactive and primitive than either the phonograph or the kinetoscope. Some were strength testers, which dared young men to show off their muscles by punching a boxing bag or arm-wrestling a robotlike Uncle Sam. Others required more refined skills and sustained play, such as those that simulated bowling, horse racing, or football.[9]

Another arcade game, the bagatelle, spawned the **pinball machine**, the most prominent of the mechanical games. In pinball, players score points by manipulating the path of a metal ball on a play field enclosed in a glass case. In the 1930s and 1940s, players could control only the launch of the ball. For this reason, pinball was considered a sinister game of chance, which—like the slot machine—fed the coffers of the gambling underworld. As a result, pinball was banned in most American cities, including New York, Chicago, and Los Angeles.[10] However, pinball gained mainstream acceptance and popularity after World War II with the addition of the **flipper bumper**, which enables players to careen the ball back up the play table. This innovation transformed pinball into a challenging game

▼ This image shows pinball players in a Pennsylvania steelworkers' club in 1941. Today, pinball machines remain in many bars and arcades, and pinball expos are held all over the country. Library of Congress, Prints & Photographs Division, Reproduction number LC-USF34-043121-D (b&w film neg.)

of skill, touch, and timing—all of which would become vital abilities for video game players years later.

The First Video Games

The postwar popularity of pinball set the stage for the emergence of video games; the first video game patent was issued on December 14, 1948. It went to Thomas T. Goldsmith and Estle Ray Mann for what they described as a "Cathode-Ray Tube Amusement Device." The invention, which was never marketed or sold, featured the key component of the first video games: the **cathode ray tube (CRT)**.

CRT-type screens provided the images for analog television and for early computer displays, on which the first video games appeared a few years later. Computer science students developed these games as novelties in the 1950s and 1960s, but because computers consisted of massive mainframes at the time, the games were not readily available to the general public.

However, more and more people owned televisions, and this development provided a platform for video games. Ralph H. Baer, a German immigrant and television engineer, developed the first home television gaming console, a system called Odyssey. Released by Magnavox in 1972 and priced at a whopping $100, Odyssey used player controllers that moved dots of light around the screen in a twelve-game inventory of simple aiming and sports games. From 1972 until Odyssey's replacement by a simpler model (the Odyssey 100) in 1975, Magnavox sold roughly 330,000 of the consoles.[11]

In the next decade, a ripped-off version of one of the Odyssey games brought the delights of video gaming into the modern **arcade**, an establishment that gathered multiple coin-operated games together in a newer version of the penny arcade. The same year that Magnavox released the Odyssey console, a young American computer engineer named Nolan Bushnell and a friend formed a video game development company called **Atari**. The enterprise's first creation was *Pong*, a simple two-dimensional tennis-style arcade game featuring two vertical paddles that bounced a white dot back and forth. Unlike the Odyssey version, *Pong* made blip noises when the ball hit the paddles or bounced off the sides of the court. *Pong* quickly became the first video game to hit it big in arcades.

In 1975, Atari began successfully marketing a home version of *Pong* through an exclusive deal with Sears. This arrangement established the home video game market.

▼ The Atari 2600 was followed by the Atari 400, the Atari 800, and the Atari 5200, but none matched the earlier success of the 2600 model. Interfoto/Alamy Stock Photo

Just two years later, Bushnell (who also started the Chuck E. Cheese pizza-arcade restaurant chain) sold Atari to Warner Communications for an astounding $28 million. Although Atari folded in 1984, plenty of companies—including Nintendo, Sony, and Microsoft—followed its early lead, transforming the video game business into a full-fledged industry.

The Evolution of Digital Gaming

In their most basic form, digital games involve users in an interactive computerized environment where they strive to achieve a desired outcome. These days, most digital games go beyond a simple competition like *Pong*; they often entail sweeping narratives and offer imaginative and exciting adventures, sophisticated problem-solving opportunities, and multiple possible outcomes.

But the boundaries were not always so far-reaching. Digital games have evolved over time, from their simplest arcade forms into four major formats: television, handheld devices, computers, and finally the Internet. As the form evolved and graphics advanced, distinctive types of games emerged and became popular. These include classically structured games played in arcades and on consoles and mobile devices, computerized versions of card games, online role-playing games, fantasy sports leagues, and virtual social environments. Together, these varied forms constitute an industry that now generates $135 billion in annual revenues worldwide—and that has become a socially driven mass medium.

▼ Though home consoles have become widespread, some gaming fans still enjoy playing in arcades, which have evolved from their earliest counterparts and provide a different social experience from today's Internet-enabled home systems. Marilynn K. Yee/The New York Times/Redux Pictures

Arcades and Classic Games

By the late 1970s and early 1980s, games like *Asteroids*, *Pac-Man*, and *Donkey Kong* filled arcades and bars, competing with traditional pinball machines. Arcade games still attract fun-seekers to amusement parks, malls, and casinos, as well as to businesses like Dave & Buster's—a gaming–restaurant chain operating in more than ninety locations.

To play the classic arcade games, as well as many of today's popular console games, players use controllers like joysticks and buttons to interact with graphical elements on a video screen. With a few notable exceptions (puzzle games like *Tetris*, for instance), these types of video games require players to identify with a position on the screen. In *Pong*, this position is represented by an electronic paddle; in *Space Invaders*, it's an earthbound shooting position. After *Pac-Man*, the **avatar** (a graphic interactive "character" situated within the world of the game) became the most common figure of player control and position identification.

Consoles Power Up

Home **consoles** have become more powerful since the appearance of the early Atari consoles in the 1970s. One way of charting the evolution of consoles is to track the number of bits (binary digits) they can process at one time. The bit rating of a console is a measure of its power at rendering computer graphics. The higher the bit rating, the more detailed and sophisticated the graphics. The Atari 2600, released in 1977, used an 8-bit processor, as did the wildly popular Nintendo Entertainment System, first released in Japan in 1983. Sega Genesis, the first 16-bit console, appeared in 1989. In 1992, 32-bit computers appeared on the market; the following year, 64 bits became the new standard. The 128-bit era dawned with the marketing of Sega Dreamcast in 1999. With the current generation of consoles, 256-bit processors are the standard.

But more detailed graphics have not always replaced simpler games. Nintendo's NES Classic Edition, with thirty built-in classic games mostly from the 1980s, and the Atari Flashback series, with built-in Atari games from the

▲ In the 1970s and 1980s, simple two-dimensional games with straightforward goals were popular, like driving a race car *(left)*, destroying asteroids, or gobbling up tiny dots. Today, most video games have more complex story lines based in fully fleshed-out worlds *(right)*.
Left: ArcadeImages/Alamy Stock Photo; Right: ZCHE/Newscom/WENN/

same era, have been hot commodities in recent years. Perhaps the best example of enduring games is the *Super Mario Bros.* series. Created by Nintendo mainstay Shigeru Miyamoto in 1983, the original *Mario Bros.* game began in arcades. The 1985 sequel—*Super Mario Bros.*, developed for the 8-bit Nintendo Entertainment System—became the best-selling video game of all time. Considered an action game (see Table 10.1 for examples of this and other video game genres), *Super Mario Bros.* held this title until as recently as 2009, when it was unseated by Nintendo's *Wii Sports*. Graphical elements from the *Mario Bros.* games, like the "1-Up" mushroom that gives players an extra life, remain instantly recognizable to gamers of all ages.

The Big Three: Sony, Microsoft, and Nintendo

Through decades of ups and downs in the digital gaming industry (Atari closing down, Sega no longer making video consoles), three major home console makers emerged: Sony, Microsoft, and Nintendo. Nintendo has been making consoles since the 1980s; Sony and Microsoft came later, but both companies were already major media conglomerates and thus well positioned to support and promote their interests in the video game market.

- Sony introduced its PlayStation series in 1994, and its current console is the PlayStation 4 (PS4). There are currently eighty million active PlayStation users, about 43 percent of which are paid online subscribers.[12]
- Microsoft's first foray into video game consoles was the Xbox, released in 2001 and linked to the Xbox Live online service in 2002. Xbox Live allows its nearly sixty million subscribers to play online and enables users to download new content directly to the console—the Xbox One S or the Xbox One X.[13]
- Nintendo released a new kind of console, the Wii, in 2006. The device supported traditional video games like the *New Super Mario Bros.* However, its unique wireless motion-sensing controller took the often-sedentary nature out of video gameplay. Games like *Wii Sports* require the user to mimic the full-body motion of bowling or playing tennis, while *Wii Fit* uses a wireless balance board for interactive yoga, strength, aerobic, and balance games. In 2017, Nintendo started selling the Switch—a hybrid of a television console, traditional game controllers, and a tablet.

Since 2014, Sony's PlayStation 4 has been the most popular of the new generation of consoles, yet Nintendo has recently begun to catch up: In 2018, Sony sold eighteen million PlayStations worldwide, Nintendo sold just over seventeen million of the Switch, and Microsoft sold just under seven million Xboxes.[14] All three of the major consoles develop games for their own proprietary systems, and although some game content is released on all three platforms, game offerings become a major selling point for a particular system. For example, Xbox One has exclusive rights to *Forza Motorsport 7*; PS4 has *Uncharted: The Lost Legacy*; and Nintendo Switch has *Splatoon 2*.

TABLE 10.1 // MAJOR VIDEO GAME GENRES

Genre		Gameplay	Examples
Action		Player uses hand-eye coordination and motor skills to overcome physical challenges. Player controls most of the action to:	
	Platform games	— move character(s) between various platform levels in order to avoid or chase adversaries	Super Mario Bros., Never Alone, Canabalt, Super Mario Odyssey, Celeste
	Shooter	— use a range of weapons to obliterate the enemy	Call of Duty: Advanced Warfare, Halo, Half-Life
	Fighting	— work in close-range combat against a small number of equally powerful opponents	Street Fighter, Dragon Ball FighterZ, Soulcalibur
	Stealth	— engage in subterfuge and precision strikes to beat the enemy	Dishonored, Mark of the Ninja
	Survival	— learn to survive in a hostile environment	Paladins: Battlegrounds, Fortnite, PlayerUnknown's Battlegrounds (PUBG)
	Rhythm	— challenge him- or herself in terms of rhythm, coordination, and musical precision	Dance Dance Revolution, Guitar Hero, Rock Band
Adventure		Player solves puzzles by interacting with people or the environment.	Myst, Tomb Raider, Lumino City, Monument Valley, Limbo, Hidden Folks
Action-Adventure		Player navigates horror-fiction elements or other obstacles (e.g., doors) and acquires special tools or abilities to get through them.	Zelda, Metroid, Castlevania, Resident Evil
Role-Playing		Player takes on specific characteristics and skill sets, goes on "adventures," and often amasses treasure; the most popular setting is a fantasy world.	Final Fantasy, Fallout, Grand Theft Auto, Minecraft
MMORPG (Massively Multiplayer Online Role-Playing Game)		Similar to role-playing games but distinguished by the high number of players interacting together	World of Warcraft, Star Wars: The Old Republic
Simulation		Player simulates a real or fictional reality to:	
	Construction/ Management	— expand or manage fictional communities or projects with limited resources	SimCity
	Life	— "realistically" live the life of a person or being (e.g., a wolf), possibly in a strange world	SimLife, Spore, Creatures
	Vehicle	— experience flight, race-car driving, train travel, combat vehicles, and so on	FlightGear, Microsoft Flight Simulator, NASCAR Racing
Strategy		Player carefully plots out tactics to achieve a goal, usually military or world domination.	Master of Orion, Hogs of War, Starcraft
	MOBA (Multiplayer Online Battle Arena)	Player on a team competes against another team to destroy the opposing team's main structure; similar to role-playing games but distinguished by the high number of players.	League of Legends, Data 2, Heroes of the Storm, Overwatch
Sports		Player takes either a player's or management's perspective in simulating a sport, such as soccer, football, or fighting.	Pong, FIFA, Fight Night, Championship Manager, Madden NFL
Casual Games		Player makes progress toward a simple reward, increasing the challenge if he or she feels like it; the rules are simple, and there is no long-term commitment.	Tetris, Candy Crush Saga, Run Sausage Run

Console Convergence: More Than Just a Game

Once used exclusively for games, video game consoles also work as part computer, part cable box. They've become powerful entertainment centers, with multiple forms of media converging in a single device. For example, the Xbox One and PS4 offer access to Twitter, Facebook, blogs, and video chat, and can function as DVD and Blu-ray players and digital video recorders. PS4, Xbox, and Wii all offer connections to stream programming from sources such as Netflix and Hulu. Microsoft's Xbox—which has Kinect's voice recognition system, allowing viewers to communicate with the box—has been the most successful in becoming a converged device for home entertainment.

Portable Consoles Compete with Smartphones and Tablets

Advances in graphics and gameplay have also enhanced smaller handheld devices dedicated to playing video games. Nintendo's Game Boy was an early success, launching in 1989. The early handhelds gave way to later generations of devices offering increasingly converged portable gaming experiences. For example, the Nintendo DS, released in 2004, and the PlayStation Portable (PSP), released in 2005, allowed owners to link up with other players on the Internet via built-in Wi-Fi capabilities.

In 2011, Nintendo released the 3DS as a successor to the DS. When Nintendo released its Wii U console the following year, it came with the GamePad controller, which is a hybrid of a console controller and a portable game device. The company took the concept a step further in 2017 with the Switch, which features a hybrid console that incorporates a touchscreen tablet.

Portable players are big business, with each upgrade spurring new sales. For example, globally, Nintendo has sold 118 million Game Boys, more than 81 million Game Boy Advances, 154 million DS players, and almost 75 million 3DS players.[15] Sony sold over 76 million PSPs before the device was discontinued in 2014.[16] The company also launched the PlayStation Vita portable in 2012 but discontinued production in 2019.[17]

▼ The 3-D platform action-adventure game *Super Mario Odyssey* was created by Nintendo for the Nintendo Switch. It features Mario in his never-ending quest to save Princess Peach from his evil archenemy, Bowser.
Bettina Fabos

One of the biggest challenges to these portable game consoles is the widespread use of smartphones and touchscreen tablets. These devices are not typically designed principally for games, but their capabilities bring casual gaming to customers who might not have been interested in the handheld consoles of the past. Portable and mobile gaming convergence is changing the way people look at digital games and their systems.

Computer Gaming

Early home computer games, like the early console games, often mimicked (and sometimes ripped off) popular arcade games like *Frogger*, *Centipede*, *Pac-Man*, and *Space Invaders*. But for a time in the late 1980s and much of the 1990s, personal computers held some clear advantages over console gaming. The versatility of keyboards, compared with the relatively simple early console controllers, allowed for ambitious puzzle-solving games, like *Myst*. Moreover, faster processing speeds gave some computer games richer, more detailed 3-D graphics. Many of the most popular, early first-person shooter games (like *Doom* and *Quake*) were developed for home computers rather than consoles.

As consoles caught up with greater processing speeds and disc-based games in the late 1990s, elaborate computer games attracted less attention. But due to the advent of Internet-based free-to-play games (*Spelunky*, *League of Legends*), subscription games (*World of Warcraft*, *Diablo III*), social media games (*Candy Crush Saga* on Facebook), and the Steam PC game platform, PC gaming has experienced a resurgence. With powerful processors for handling rich graphics, and more stable Internet connectivity for downloading games or playing games via social media and other gaming sites, personal computers can adeptly handle a wide range of activities.

The Internet and Social Gaming

The connectivity of the Internet has opened the door to social gaming and enabled the spread of video games to converged devices—such as tablets and mobile phones—making games more portable and creating whole new segments in the gaming industry. This connectivity has also opened the door to virtual worlds, multiplayer online battle arenas, and massively multiplayer online games.

MMORPGs and MOBAs

It is one of the longest acronyms in the world of gaming: **massively multiplayer online role-playing games (MMORPGs)**. These games are set in virtual worlds that require users to play through an avatar of their own design. The "massively multiplayer" aspect of MMORPGs indicates that digital games—once designed for solo or small-group play—have expanded to reach large groups, like traditional mass media do. One well-known MMORPG is *World of Warcraft*, which made a big splash when it launched in 2004 and had about 5.5 million subscribers in 2016 (down from a peak of 12 million in 2010). The game's producer, Blizzard Entertainment, hit it big again in 2016 with MMORPG *Overwatch*, which had more than 40 million players as of 2018.[18]

MOBAs (*multiplayer online battle arenas*) like *League of Legends*, *War Robots*, and *Fortnite* are a variation on the MMORPG theme. Rather than open-ended quests or story lines, MOBAs tend to feature short discrete

◤ *Overwatch*, a popular team-based multiplayer first-person shooter game created by Blizzard Entertainment, won 102 separate Game of the Year awards when it came out in 2016. Sari ONeal/Shutterstock.com

matches between individuals or teams matched up with as many as a hundred different opponents (also being controlled by live humans). Usually the goal is to be the last player or team left in the game. One advantage of MOBAs is that facing human-controlled opponents tends to keep the game fresher than if the opponents were controlled by an artificial intelligence (AI) program, since AI-controlled gameplay tends to follow predictable patterns.

Online Fantasy Sports

Online fantasy sports games also reach a mass audience with a major social component. Players—real-life friends, virtual acquaintances, or a mix of both—assemble teams and use actual sports results to determine scores in their online games. But rather than experiencing the visceral thrills of, say, the most recent release of *Madden NFL*, fantasy football participants take a more detached, managerial perspective on the game—a departure from the classic video game experience.

Fantasy sports' managerial angle makes it fun to watch almost any televised game, since players are focused more on making strategic investments in individual performances scattered across the various professional teams than they are in rooting for specific teams. In the process, players become statistically savvy aficionados of the game overall, rather than rabid fans of a particular team.

In 2017, over 59.3 million people played fantasy sports in the United States and Canada; the Fantasy Sports Trade Association estimates that fantasy sports players spend an average of $566 a year on single-player challenge games and league-related costs and materials.[19]

Games on Social Networking Sites

The increasingly social nature of video games has made them a natural fit for social networking sites. Games like *Candy Crush Saga*, *Clash of Clans*, and *Farm Heroes Saga* attract millions of players on Facebook every day, while Snapchat—a site built around funny filters on photos—has Snappables: games that use facial recognition to let players control gameplay. For example, *Cucumbers Biting* lets players "chomp" virtual cucumbers in a set amount of time, then allows users to challenge friends to beat their scores.

The Children's Market

The children's market is another big area in online gaming. For example, toy maker Ganz developed the online Webkinz World to revive its stuffed-animal sales. Each Webkinz stuffed animal comes with a code that lets players access the online world, play games, and care for the virtual version of their plush pets.

It's notable that games that are marketed to teens—including *Fortnite* and sports-related games—are also very popular among preteens. However, parents of younger children should take note of the 12 and over age rating of a game like *Fortnite*, which, despite the cartoon look, features players stalking and shooting other players.

Trends and Issues in Digital Gaming

To fully explore the larger media playground, we need to look beyond digital gaming's technical aspects and consider the human faces of gaming. The attractions of this interactive playground validate digital gaming's status as one of today's most powerful social media. Players can interact socially within the games themselves; they can also participate in communities outside the games, organized around gaming-related interests.

At the same time, however, there are a number of issues to consider. For example, the powerful attraction of immersive gameplay can lead to addictive behaviors, games can be violent, and the interactive playground can be filled with misogynistic bullies.

Communities of Play: Inside the Game

Virtual communities often crop up around online video games and fantasy sports leagues. Indeed, players may get to know one another through games without ever meeting in person, interacting in two basic types of groups: PUGs and guilds or clans. PUGs (short for "pick-up groups") are temporary teams usually assembled by matchmaking programs integrated into the game. The members of a PUG may range from noobs (clueless beginners) to elite players and may be geographically and generationally diverse. PUGs are notorious for harboring ninjas and trolls: two universally despised player types (not to be confused with ninja or troll avatars). Ninjas are players who snatch loot out of turn and then leave the group; trolls are players who delight in intentionally spoiling the gaming experience for others.

Because of the frustration of dealing with noobs, ninjas, and trolls, most experienced players join organized groups called guilds or clans. These groups can be small and easygoing or large and demanding. Guild members can usually avoid PUGs and team up with guildmates to complete difficult challenges requiring coordinated group activity. As the terms *noob*, *ninja*, and *troll* suggest, online communication is often encoded in gamespeak—a language filled with jargon, abbreviations, and acronyms relevant to gameplay. The typical codes of text messaging (OMG, LOL, ROFL, and so forth) form the bedrock of this language system.

Players communicate in two forms of in-game chat: voice and text. Xbox Live, for example, uses three types of voice chat that allow players to socialize and strategize, either in groups or one-on-one. Other in-game chat systems are text-based, with chat channels for trading in-game goods or coordinating missions within a guild. These methods of communicating with fellow players who may or may not know one another outside the game create a sense of community around the game's story. Some players have formed lasting friendships or romantic relationships through game playing.

Communities of Play: Outside the Game

Communities also form outside games, through websites and even face-to-face gatherings dedicated to digital gaming in its many forms. This is similar to when online and in-person groups form to discuss other mass media, such as movies, TV shows, and books. These communities of play fit into three categories:

- **Collective intelligence.** Gamers often come together to collect and share user-generated **collective intelligence**—advice, tips, and "cheats" related to gameplay.[20] Many collective intelligence sites have popped up online for a wide range of digital games. The most advanced form of collective intelligence in gaming is **modding**, slang for "modifying game software or hardware." In many mass communication industries, modifying hardware or content would land someone in a copyright lawsuit. In gaming, modding is often encouraged, as it is yet another way players become more deeply invested in a game, and it can improve the game for others. Today, many games have active modding communities.
- **Gaming sites.** Gaming sites and blogs are among the most popular external communities for gamers. IGN (owned by Ziff Davis), GameSpot (CBS Interactive), and Kotaku (Gizmodo Media Group) are three of the leading

◀ Penny Arcade is perhaps the best known of the independent community-building sites. The site, which started out as a webcomic focused on video game culture, has since expanded to include forums, podcasts, and a web series called *Penny Arcade: The Series*, which documents behind-the-scenes work at Penny Arcade. Since 2003, Penny Arcade has organized a game industry charity called Child's Play, which benefits hospitalized children.

websites for gaming. Steam, the PC gaming software site, also has an active community, as does the blog at Twitch, the gameplay streaming site.
- **Conventions and expos.** Conventions and expos are gatherings where video game enthusiasts can come together in person to test out new games and other new products, play old games in competition, and meet video game developers. One of the most significant is the Electronic Entertainment Expo (E3), held annually in Los Angeles. Formerly known as the Penny Arcade Expo, PAX is a series of conventions created by gamers for gamers. PAX is held each year in Seattle, Boston, San Antonio, Philadelphia, and Melbourne.

Immersion and Addiction

As games and their communities have grown more elaborate and alluring, many players have spent an increasing amount of time immersed in them—a situation that can feed addictive behavior in some people. These deep levels of involvement are not always considered negative, especially within the media playground, but they are nonetheless issues to consider as gaming continues to evolve.

Immersion

Gaming technology of the future promises experiences that will be more immersive. For example, some games involve a player's entire body in the gameplay rather than just a few fingers on a control pad. The Nintendo Wii system successfully harnessed user-friendly motion-control technology in handheld controllers and, for some games, a balance board in order to open up gaming to nontraditional players. Microsoft's Kinect system uses sensor cameras and microphones to translate a player's movements and commands into actions by on-screen avatars.

Some game systems aim to transport players to new worlds from the comfort of their homes, using various combinations of special goggles, helmets, vests, and gloves embedded with visual and audio functions, haptic feedback capabilities, and sensors. Examples of these types of virtual reality (VR) devices include the Oculus Rift, Sony PlayStation VR, HTC Vive VR, and Samsung Gear VR. And in a combination of low and high tech, Google Cardboard turns a smartphone into an old-fashioned stereoscope or View-Master through a cardboard viewer and accompanying app.

There are other new approaches to immersion as well. A company called the VOID has nearly a dozen virtual reality play parks around the world that feature VR games played out like laser tag in a real space: 60-by-60-foot rooms with digital overlays of different types of scenes, including movie tie-ins like *Star Wars* and *Ghostbusters*. Participants can "feel" laser and creature attacks through the interactive VR gear that they wear during the experience.

Enhanced reality games like *Pokémon Go* take immersion in a different direction, moving the gaming experience out of living rooms and arcades and into the world. Using smartphone screens to reveal "hidden" characters and rewards, the game requires players to walk around outside (see "The Digital Turn Case Study: Games in the Great Wide Open: *Pokémon Go* and the Future of Mobile Gaming" on page 299).

But digital gaming technologies aren't just for entertainment. Games get used in workforce training, in military recruiting, for social causes, in classrooms, and as part of multimedia journalism. For instance, dementia researchers used a game called *Sea Hero Quest* as part of a massive research project to chart the spatial navigation abilities of 2.4 million people ranging in age from nineteen to seventy-five. Another group of game designers created a game called *Before I Forget* to help illustrate the experience of early-onset dementia.[21] Developments like these continue to make games an ever-larger part of our media experiences—even for people who may not consider themselves avid gamers.

▶ In the summer of 2016, *Pokémon Go* captured the attention of gamers around the globe. For several weeks, players were out pursuing Pokémon at locations of all kinds, from public parks to shopping malls. While that intense level of excitement has since faded, the game continues to be popular. Christopher Martin

The Digital Turn

CASE STUDY

Games in the Great Wide Open: *Pokémon Go* and the Future of Mobile Gaming

The unique thing about the release of the digital game *Pokémon Go* on July 6, 2016, is that everyone played in open view. Millions of people were trying to catch wild Pokémon, not on consoles or computers in their living rooms or bedrooms but outdoors, in public, where individuals and groups of people scoured neighborhoods to locate PokéStops and Pokémon Gyms.

In a matter of hours, *Pokémon Go*—developed by Nintendo, the Pokémon Company, and Niantic Labs—became the most popular mobile game app ever in America, and over the course of the month, it expanded into a global sensation, with over 100 million downloads in more than seventy countries. By early 2018, it had been downloaded more than 800 million times and had earned almost $2 billion.[1] Although the game is free to play, in-game purchases and sponsorships helped it earn its revenue.

Pokémon Go is an augmented-reality, geo-based game—the type of game made possible by the many technological advances that came with the digital turn. Players create their own avatars and use their phone cameras as they walk through neighborhoods. The augmented-reality technology overlays the game's map on a player's phone, and the map follows the real-world geography of the place where the player is walking. Niantic Labs uses computer servers around the world to operate the game and locate Pokémon, PokéStops, and Pokémon Gyms, where teams can battle for control of the site. (Niantic received complaints about some of their initial Gym sites, which sent people into graveyards, a hospital delivery room, and even the 9/11 Memorial in New York; these days, Gyms are mostly located in public parks and sponsored locations.)[2]

Although play of *Pokémon Go* peaked in summer 2016, it still remains popular, especially with worldwide *Pokémon Go* promotional events. For example, events like *Pokémon Go* Safari Zone in Sentosa, Singapore, in 2019 and the *Pokémon Go* Fest 2019 in Chicago offer geo-based play, where bonus encounters and catch rates occur for a limited period of time, drawing thousands of players.[3]

Niantic continues to expand and refine *Pokémon Go*, even as it prepares to launch another augmented-reality geo-hunt game: *Harry Potter: Wizards Unite*. According to author J. K. Rowling's Pottermore website, "The game encourages you to step outside with your phone, explore your local surroundings and take part in a series of adventures, such as searching for magical creatures and bumping into iconic wizarding world characters."[4] If the gameplay is immersive and authentic to Harry Potter's wizarding world, it is likely that millions more people will get on board with this new game as well.

> ### ▶ Web Clip
>
> **YouTube.com** has many videos about augmented-reality, geo-based games. For example, search for "Pokémon GO Travel: Research Tour—Trading Challenge, Pokémon GO Fest, and Celebi! (Ep. 2)," posted by Pokémon GO. What does this video tell us about the type of gamer the company is trying to reach? How does the gaming experience being marketed here differ from a console or a PC-based gaming experience?
>
>

Addiction

No serious—and honest—gamer can deny the addictive qualities of digital gaming. In a 2011 study of more than three thousand third through eighth graders in Singapore, one in ten were considered pathological gamers, meaning that their gaming addiction was jeopardizing multiple areas of their lives, including school, social and family relations, and psychological well-being. Children with stronger addictions were more prone to depression, social phobias, and increased anxiety, which led to poorer grades in school. Singapore's high percentage of pathological youth gamers is in line with studies from other countries, including the United States (8.5%), China (10.3%), and Germany (11.9%).[22]

Experts and researchers do debate the criteria being used to distinguish gaming addiction—sometimes called Internet gaming disorder (IGD)—from someone devotedly pursuing a much-loved hobby. For example, some critics consider the American Psychiatric Association's definition too vague (meaning it could describe someone who is "engaged" with a hobby but not addicted to it).[23] That being said, most experts do generally agree that IGD is a problem, and that gamers cross the line from hobbyist to addict when their physical and mental health is affected and they exhibit a reduced ability to cope with life's challenges.[24] One 2018 study found that all genders with IGD experience symptoms such as depression, anxiety, and feelings of isolation, but that males were more susceptible to IGD in the first place.[25] This makes sense, given that the most popular games—action and shooter games—are heavily geared toward male players.

These addiction-related findings are not entirely surprising, given that many digital games are not addictive by accident but rather by design. Just as habit formation is a primary goal of virtually every commercial form of digital media, from newspapers to television to radio, cultivating obsessive play is the aim of most game designs. From recognizing high scores to embedding levels that gradually increase in difficulty, designers provide constant in-game incentives for obsessive play. This is especially true of multiplayer online games—such as *League of Legends*, *Call of Duty*, and *World of Warcraft*—which make money from long-term engagement by selling expansion packs or charging monthly subscription fees. These games have elaborate achievement systems with hard-to-resist rewards, including military ranks like "General" or fanciful titles like "King Slayer," as well as special armor, weapons, and mounts (creatures your avatar can ride), all aimed at turning casual players into habitual ones.

Violence and Misogyny

The Entertainment Software Association (ESA)—the main trade association of the gaming industry—likes to point out that nearly half of game players are women and that more than three-quarters of games sold are rated in the family- and teen-friendly categories. While these statements are true, they also mask a troubling aspect of some of the industry's most popular games: their violent and sexist imagery.

Most games involving combat, guns, and other weapons are intentionally violent, with representations of violence becoming all the more graphic as game visuals reach cinematic hyperrealism. The most violent video games, rated M for "Mature," often belong to the first-person shooter, dark fantasy, or survival horror genres and cast players in sinister roles, in which they earn points by killing and maiming their foes in horrendous ways.

In addition, critics such as Anita Sarkeesian—herself an avid gamer—point to troubling stereotypes of women that are enmeshed in video games. Sarkeesian notes the tendency of games to portray women as damsels in distress, as rewards for successful male avatars, or as hypersexualized representations—even when they're the heroes (see also "Media Literacy Case Study: Fighting the Dark Side of Gaming Culture: Anita Sarkeesian and Feminist Frequency" on pages 302–303).

That some games can be violent and misogynistic is not a point of dispute. But the possible effects of such games have been debated for years, and video games have been accused of being a factor in violent episodes, such as mass shootings. Earlier research linked playing violent video games to aggressive thoughts or hostility, but those effects don't necessarily transfer to real-world environments. Instead, more recent studies suggest that the personality traits of certain types of players should be of greater concern than the violence of video games. For example, a study in the *Review of General Psychology* notes that individuals with a combination of "high neuroticism (e.g., easily upset, angry, depressed, emotional, etc.), low agreeableness (e.g., little concern for others, indifferent to others' feelings, cold, etc.), and low conscientiousness (e.g., break rules, don't keep promises, act without thinking, etc.)" are more susceptible to the negative outcomes measured in studies of violent video games.[26] For the vast majority of players, the study concluded, violent video games have no adverse effects.

There is less research on misogyny (hatred of women) in video games. One of the most extreme game narratives is from the hugely successful *Grand Theft Auto* series, in which male characters earn points by picking up a female prostitute, paying money for sex, and then beating up or killing the hooker to get their money back. This problem may result from the male insularity of the game development industry; for reasons that are unclear, few women are on the career path to be involved in game development: "In 2009, just 18% of undergraduate Computing and Information Sciences degrees were awarded to women; in 1985, women earned 37% of these degrees."[27]

Media Literacy

CASE STUDY

Fighting the Dark Side of Gaming Culture: Anita Sarkeesian and Feminist Frequency

Anita Sarkeesian has a well-documented love of playing video games, from *Mario Kart* to *Half-Life 2*. But that hasn't stopped her from becoming one of the most outspoken—and targeted—critics of how video games depict and treat women. In 2012, a successful Kickstarter campaign helped her launch the *Tropes vs. Women in Video Games* video series on her Feminist Frequency YouTube channel. As Sarkeesian explains, she was moved to examine video games because she recognized at a young age—as a girl growing up and playing those games—the many troubling stereotypes about women that were enmeshed in games and gaming culture.

"The games often reinforce a similar message, overwhelmingly casting men as heroes and relegating women to the roles of damsels, victims or hypersexualized playthings," Sarkeesian explains in a 2014 *New York Times* op-ed. "The notion that gaming was not for women rippled out into society, until we heard it not just from the games industry, but from our families, teachers and friends. As a consequence, I, like many women, had a complicated, love-hate relationship with gaming culture."[1]

"Love-hate" is probably also a good way to describe the reaction to Sarkeesian's critique of games. On the one hand, she has gained critical acclaim and visibility for her videos and writing, appearing in the *New York Times*, *Bloomberg Businessweek*, and *Rolling Stone*. On the other hand, since she began releasing her videos on digital games, she has been the target of incredibly graphic and violent threats of rape, torture, and murder on social media. This ongoing online harassment reached a new low in the fall of 2014, when another of her Feminist Frequency video releases coincided with the #GamerGate controversy.

The #GamerGate firestorm started when a computer programmer, Eron Gjoni, had a bad breakup with game designer Zoë Quinn. Gjoni then went online with their breakup, claiming that Quinn had had an affair with a writer at Kotaku, an influential gamers' website that had given Quinn's newest game a positive review. Gjoni's supporters pointed to this as indicative of a larger trend of shady journalistic ethics in the gaming press, and they organized their criticisms under the hashtag #GamerGate. Very quickly, however, the attacks on journalistic ethics were overshadowed by those focused on slut-shaming Quinn, as well as anonymous threats of rape, torture, and death to a number of women.[2]

It was at this point that Sarkeesian (and other critics) spoke up and pointed out that the threats against many female gamers proved her point about a deeper problem in the gaming culture, which in turn reflected broader cultural misogyny. Unfortunately, instead of the situation getting better as a result, Sarkeesian and others began experiencing vicious harassment. In one instance,

launchpadworks.com

▶ **Visit LaunchPad** to view a clip from one of Sarkeesian's videos. Do you agree with her analysis? Why or why not?

▲ Feminist Frequency maintains an active Twitter presence, using its tweets to share video game reviews, link to commentary, and promote its videos and podcasts.

before a speech Sarkeesian was scheduled to deliver at Utah State University, an anonymous person threatened to carry out a school shooting if she was allowed to speak. Sarkeesian canceled her speech after campus police said Utah's gun laws prohibited them from turning away any audience member who showed up with a gun. Sarkeesian also went into hiding for a time, afraid to return to her home because of various threats.

Despite the harassment and hatred she has faced, however, Sarkeesian is far from giving up. In an ironic twist, the flood of harassment has also brought many supporters her way and helped her reach a bigger audience. When Sarkeesian started, she made her videos with the help of a friend and a DSLR (digital single-lens reflex) camera. Today, Feminist Frequency is a nonprofit entity with a staff and the ability to take on bigger projects. As Sarkeesian explained in a 2016 interview in the *Daily Beast*, she stays focused on the fact that taking action is what helps create change: "In the *Tropes* episodes we're identifying patterns—we're not saying your one game is *the* problem. . . . We all have the responsibility . . . to start *changing* those patterns and not reinforcing them."[3]

APPLYING THE CRITICAL PROCESS

DESCRIPTION   Look up a current list of popular video games using a site like Kotaku. Read through the description of the top five games, then try playing them yourself or look up related gameplay videos on YouTube. Who are the main characters in these games, and what are their genders? How are these characters represented? What roles do they play, and how do they interact with other players?

ANALYSIS   What patterns do you notice in how characters of various genders are portrayed? In their roles in the game? In how they interact with one another?

INTERPRETATION   Describe what you think those patterns mean. What do they suggest about the cultural messages this game is sending? What do they suggest about the cultural messages that have shaped these games?

EVALUATION   What are the implications of your findings for gamers and, more broadly, for men and women in our society? Does your interpretation suggest something harmful, something beneficial, or something more nuanced?

ENGAGEMENT   Communicate your findings by creating a blog post, a video, or a podcast about this topic. Share your creation with friends on your social network, and encourage them to enter into the conversation about gender representation in video games.

The Economics of Digital Gaming

Today, 64 percent of American households have someone at home who regularly plays video games, with 41 percent of the gamers playing on a personal computer, 36 percent playing on smartphones, and 36 percent playing on dedicated game consoles.[28] The entire U.S. video game market, including portable and console hardware and accessories, added up to $43.4 billion in 2018, and the global market is projected to earn $134.9 billion in 2018—almost half of which will come from sales of games for mobile devices.[29]

Digital gaming companies can make money selling not just consoles and games but also online subscriptions, companion books, and movie rights. In addition to the costs of production, shipping, and marketing, digital gaming companies also pay writers, artists, and programmers to create the games.

Selling Digital Games

Traditionally, the primary source of revenue in the digital gaming industry is the sale of games and the consoles on which they can be played. But just as the digital turn has altered the distribution relationships between other mass media and their audiences, it has also transformed the selling of electronic games. Although the selling of $60 AAA (top of the line) console games at retail stores is an enduring model, many games are now free (with opportunities for hooked players to pay for additional play features), and digital stores are making access to games almost immediate.

Pay Models

There are three main pay models in the electronic game industry: the boxed game/retail model, the subscription model, and the free-to-play model.

- The *boxed game/retail model* is the most traditional, dating back to the days of cartridges on Atari, Sega, and Nintendo console systems. By the 1990s, games began to be released on CD-ROMs and later DVDs, to better handle the richer game files. Many boxed games are now sold with offers of additional downloadable content.
- With the *subscription model*, gamers pay a monthly fee to play. Notable subscription games include *World of Warcraft* and *Star Wars: The Old Republic*. At its height of popularity, *World of Warcraft* earned more than $1 billion a year for Activision Blizzard.[30] Yet with so many free-to-play games, the subscription

model hasn't expanded widely, and both *World of Warcraft* and *Star Wars: The Old Republic* shifted to the free-to-play model, with premium play as an option.
- *Free-to-play* (or *freemium*) is common with casual and online games, such as *100 Balls*. Free-to-play games are offered online or downloadable for free to gain or retain a large audience. These games make money by selling extras (like power boosters to aid in gameplay) or in-game subscriptions for upgraded play. In addition to free casual games (e.g., *Angry Birds Seasons* and *Clash of Clans*), popular MOBA games like *League of Legends* are free-to-play and generate revenue through in-game purchases.

Video Game Stores vs. Digital Distribution

Several brick-and-mortar stores sell boxed game titles (Walmart, Best Buy, Target), but there is only one major video game store chain: GameStop, which operates more than 7,200 stores in fourteen countries. The biggest challenge to gaming stores, regardless of size, is digital distribution. All three major consoles are Wi-Fi capable, and each has its own digital store: Xbox Games Store, Nintendo eShop, and PlayStation Store. Using these platforms, customers can purchase and download games, get extra downloadable content, and buy other media—such as television shows and movies—as the consoles compete to be the sole entertainment center of people's living rooms.

Although the three major console companies control digital downloads to their devices, several companies compete for the download market in PC games. The largest is Steam, which carries more than fifteen thousand games from a variety of game publishers. Of course, the most ubiquitous digital game distributors are Apple's App Store and Google Play, where users can purchase games on mobile devices. Although Google's Android system has surpassed the iPhone in market penetration, Apple customers are more likely to purchase apps, including games—a situation that has drawn more independent developers to work in the Apple operating system.

▼Milla Jovovich stars as Alice in the popular *Resident Evil* film series, including *Resident Evil: The Final Chapter* (2017). However, not all game adaptations have been so successful; film versions of *Super Mario Bros.*, *Doom*, and *Prince of Persia* disappointed at the box office—though gaming companies were still paid for the rights. Entertainment Pictures/Alamy Stock Photo

Digital Gaming Tie-Ins and Licensing

Beyond the immediate industry, digital games have had a pronounced effect on media culture. Fantasy league sports have spawned a number of draft specials on ESPN as well as a regular podcast, *Fantasy Focus*, on ESPN Radio. Like TV shows, books, and comics before them, digital games have inspired movies, such as *Tomb Raider* (2018), *Assassin's Creed* (2016),

launchpadworks.com

Video Games at the Movies

Alice, the hero of the game-based *Resident Evil* film series, fights zombies in this clip.

Discussion: In what ways does this clip replicate the experience of gameplay? In what ways are films inherently different?

and the *Resident Evil* series (2002–2017). For many Hollywood blockbusters today, a video game spin-off is a must-have item. Recent box-office hits—like *Spider-Man: Homecoming* (2017) and installments from the *Star Wars* franchise (1977–present)—have companion video games for consoles and portable players. Japanese manga and anime (comic books and animation) have also inspired video games, such as *Akira*, *Astro Boy*, and *Naruto*.

Whereas game adaptations of other media can serve partly as advertising for a cross-media franchise, some games also include direct advertising. In-game advertisements are ads for companies and products that appear as billboards or logos on products in the game environment, as components of the game, or as screen-blocking pop-up ads.

Making Digital Games

Development, marketing, and licensing constitute the major expenditures in game publishing, and AAA game titles (games that represent the current standard for technical excellence) can cost even more than a blockbuster film to make and promote.

The **development budget** pays for writers to create the concept and story line of a game, artists to design characters and scenery, actors to voice characters, and programmers to turn the ideas and images into computer code. Each new generation of gaming platforms doubles the number of people involved in designing, programming, and mixing digitized images and sounds.

But as costly as development can be, big game releases spend even more on marketing. The successful launch of a game involves online promotions, banner ads, magazine print ads, in-store displays, and—the most expensive of all—television ads. In many ways, the marketing blitz associated with introducing a major new franchise title, including cinematic television trailers, resembles the promotional campaigns surrounding the debut of a blockbuster movie. For example, several video game titles have cost $100 million or more to develop—and in some cases, at least as much to market. A few of these blockbuster games include *Destiny*, *Call of Duty 2*, *Grand Theft Auto V*, *Final Fantasy 7*, and *Star Wars: The Old Republic*.

Independent gamemakers must also deal with two types of licensing. First, they have to pay royalties to console manufacturers (Nintendo, Sony, or Microsoft) for the right to distribute a game using their system. These royalties vary from $3 to $10 per unit sold. The other form

▼ Producers of big blockbuster games pay close attention to initial sales, the digital game equivalent of a movie's opening weekend. The game *Destiny* reportedly cost $500 million to produce, but it racked up as much in initial global orders when it hit the market in 2014.

of licensing involves **intellectual properties**—stories, characters, personalities, and music that require licensing agreements. In 2005, for instance, John Madden reportedly signed a $150 million deal with EA Sports that allowed the company to use his name and likeness for the following ten years.[31]

Digital Gaming in a Democratic Society

Though many people view gaming as a simple leisure activity, the digital gaming industry has sparked controversy. Parents and politicians have expressed concern about the content of some games, whereas other critics say the portrayal of women and minorities in games is either nonexistent or troubling. Meanwhile, the gaming industry has argued that it qualifies for free-speech protection, and that its ratings and regulations should not necessarily bear the force of law.

Self-Regulation

Back in 1976, an arcade game called *Death Race* prompted the first public outcry over violence in digital gaming. The primitive graphics of the game depicted a blocky car running down stick-figure gremlins that, if struck, turned into grave markers. Described as "sick and morbid" by the National Safety Council, *Death Race* inspired a *60 Minutes* report on the potential psychological damage of playing video games. Since then, violent video games have prompted citizens' groups and politicians to call for government regulation of digital game content.

In 1993, after the violence of *Mortal Kombat* and *Night Trap* attracted the attention of religious and educational organizations, Senator Joe Lieberman conducted a hearing that proposed federal regulation of the gaming industry. Following a pattern established in the movie and music industries, the gaming industry implemented a self-regulation system enforced by an industry panel. The industry founded the **Entertainment Software Rating Board (ESRB)** to institute a labeling system designed to inform parents of sexual and violent content that might not be suitable for younger players. Currently, the ESRB sorts games into five categories: E (Everyone), E 10+ (Everyone 10+), T (Teen), M (Mature 17+), and AO (Adults Only 18+).[32]

Free Speech and Video Games

Though 80 percent of retail outlets voluntarily chose to observe the ESRB guidelines and not sell M- and AO-rated games to minors, the ratings did not have the force of law. In 2005, California tried to make renting or selling an M-rated game to a minor an offense enforced by fines. The law was immediately challenged by the industry and struck down by a lower court as unconstitutional. California petitioned the Supreme Court to hear the case. In a landmark decision handed down in 2011, the Supreme Court granted digital games speech protections afforded by the First Amendment. According to the opinion written by Justice Antonin Scalia, video games communicate ideas worthy of such protection:

> Like the protected books, plays, and movies that preceded them, video games communicate ideas—and even social messages—through many familiar literary devices (such as characters, dialogue, plot, and music) and through features distinctive to the medium (such as the player's interaction with the virtual world).[33]

Scalia even mentions *Mortal Kombat* in footnote 4 of the decision:

> Reading Dante is unquestionably more cultured and intellectually edifying than playing *Mortal Kombat*. But these cultural and intellectual differences are not constitutional ones. Crudely violent video games, tawdry TV shows, and cheap novels and magazines are no less forms of speech than *The Divine Comedy*. . . . Even if we can see in them "nothing of any possible value to society" . . . they are as much entitled to the protection of free speech as the best of literature.[34]

However, as in the music, television, and film industries, First Amendment protections will not make the rating system for the gaming industry go away. Parents continue to have legitimate concerns about the games their children play. Game publishers and retailers understand that it is still in their best interests to respect those concerns, even though the ratings cannot be enforced by law.

Alternate Voices

While much of the concern over video games has historically focused on portrayals of general violence, in recent years there has been a growing criticism about the portrayals of women and minorities in gaming and gaming culture. This has prompted pointed questions from gaming critics, including avid female gamers: Why aren't more games created to appeal to women? Why are some portrayals of women so deeply disturbing? (see also "Media Literacy Case Study: Fighting the Dark Side of Gaming Culture: Anita Sarkeesian and Feminist Frequency" on pages 302–303). Other critics point to the lack of heroic representations of nonwhite characters.

That's not to say there aren't games being written from other perspectives. Paradoxically, as the costs of the biggest blockbuster games skyrocket into the hundreds of millions of dollars, mobile gaming has provided a new entry point for independent game developers. Online funding sites like Kickstarter and Patreon are also helping independent game artists write and develop their own games. Some examples include *Depression Quest*, a nontraditional game that uses a multiple-choice text adventure to simulate the experience of having depression, or *Gone Home*, which deals with LGBT issues.³⁵ These games—although nowhere near as well-known as top-tier box games or casual games—have received good reviews in the gaming press. In addition, other games have found success by offering a gaming experience that differs from the shoot-'em-up or action-packed fare that tends to dominate the lists of top-selling games. For example, *Lumino City* is an award-winning puzzle-adventure game that uses elements like hand-painted scenery made out of paper to set itself apart from the smoother, hyperrealistic graphics of many modern games.

▲ *Lumino City*, a handcrafted puzzle video game that took three years to make, has received many awards and recognition, including four awards for best indie game. Bettina Fabos

Decades ago, groundbreaking critical cultural scholar Stuart Hall wrote that even though popular television wasn't considered "high culture" by many social critics and academics of the time, it was still very important to study and understand the cultural messages contained in television, because so many people spent so much time engaged with it. He argued that when looking at an entire nation, relatively few people in a society had the time or resources required to frequent museums or attend the opera. But they did own and watch televisions.³⁶

Perhaps a similar argument can be made about digital games. In one form or another, they are growing in popularity across ages and genders. Both serious and casual gamers spend many hours engaging with these virtual worlds, absorbing what they see and hear. Once considered a distraction, these games are now a prominent part of the mass media landscape.

CHAPTER ESSENTIALS

Review

- Coin-operated contraptions first appeared in train depots, hotel lobbies, bars, and restaurants in the 1880s, before finding a permanent home in the **penny arcade**. The most prominent of the mechanical machines, the **pinball machine** gained mainstream acceptance and popularity after World War II with the addition of the **flipper bumper**, which made the game more interactive.

- **Cathode ray tube (CRT)** screens provided the images for analog television as well as the displays for early computers, on which the earliest video games appeared.

- Magnavox released Odyssey, the first home television gaming system, in 1972. That same year, computer engineer Nolan Bushnell and a friend formed a video game development company called **Atari**. Atari's first creation was *Pong*, which became the first big **arcade** video game. In 1975, Atari began successfully marketing a home version of *Pong*, thus establishing the home video game market.

- By the late 1970s and early 1980s, games like *Asteroids*, *Pac-Man*, and *Donkey Kong* filled arcades and bars, competing with traditional pinball machines. After *Pac-Man*, the **avatar** became the most common figure of player control and position identification in a video game.

- Through decades of ups and downs in the digital gaming industry, three major home **console** makers emerged: Sony, Microsoft, and Nintendo.

- With multiple players joining in digital gaming through the Internet, gaming has become a contemporary social medium. The social dimension of gaming is especially apparent in **massively multiplayer online role-playing games (MMORPGs)** and MOBAs (multiplayer online battle arenas) and in **online fantasy sports**.

- Virtual communities often crop up around online video games and fantasy sports leagues, and players get to know one another online. There are also communities of play outside the game, including sites where players share **collective intelligence** about specific games, gaming sites with information and forums, and conventions and other physical gatherings.

- As games and their communities have grown more elaborate and alluring, many players have spent an increasing amount of time immersed

LaunchPad

Visit LaunchPad for *Media Essentials* at **launchpadworks.com** for additional learning tools:

- **REVIEW WITH LEARNINGCURVE**
  LearningCurve adaptive quizzing helps you master the concepts you need to learn from this chapter.

- **VIDEO: TABLETS, TECHNOLOGY, AND THE CLASSROOM**
  Tech experts discuss the use of handheld electronic devices (such as tablets) in the classroom.

- **MEDIA LITERACY PRACTICE**
  This activity challenges you to develop a critical perspective and apply it to everyday encounters with communication media.

in them—a situation that can feed addictive behavior in some people. Critics have also expressed concerns about the violent and misogynistic imagery present in some games and the effects this imagery might have on players.

- There are three main pay models for the video game industry: the boxed game/retail model, the subscription model, and the free-to-play (freemium) model.

- Development, marketing, and licensing constitute the major expenditures in game publishing. The marketing costs often equal or exceed the development costs.

- In response to a threat of regulation, the digital game industry founded the **Entertainment Software Rating Board (ESRB)** to institute a labeling system designed to inform parents of sexual and violent content that might not be suitable for younger players.

- In a landmark decision handed down in 2011, the Supreme Court granted digital games First Amendment free-speech protections.

- More critics and gaming journalists are speaking out about the need for improvement in the portrayal of women and minorities in games and gaming culture, which has led to some online backlash against these critics, including threats of violence. However, it has also led to the development of games from other perspectives.

Key Terms

penny arcade, p. 286
pinball machine, p. 286
flipper bumper, p. 286
cathode ray tube (CRT), p. 287
arcade, p. 287
Atari, p. 287
avatar, p. 289
consoles, p. 289
massively multiplayer online role-playing games (MMORPGs), p. 293
online fantasy sports, p. 294
collective intelligence, p. 296
modding, p. 296
development budget, p. 306
intellectual properties, p. 307
Entertainment Software Rating Board (ESRB), p. 307

Study Questions

1. What were the socioeconomic changes in American society that led to the rise of mechanical arcade games, the predecessors of digital games?

2. What are some of the positive—and negative—aspects of the social part of online gaming?

3. What different types of communities are created around video games?

4. What do psychiatrists and researchers say about issues of addiction and violence in video games?

5. On what grounds did the Supreme Court grant video games First Amendment protections?

Media Framing Industries

11

Advertising and Commercial Culture

315
The Early History of American Advertising: 1850s to 1950s

319
The Evolution of U.S. Advertising: 1950s to Today

329
Persuasive Techniques in Contemporary Advertising

335
Commercial Speech and Regulating Advertising

340
Advertising in a Democratic Society

You stop for gas on your way to school, and as you fill your tank, a video pops up on the gas pump screen advertising the two-for-one donut deal available at the convenience store inside. You continue driving, and as you sit behind a bus, a sign on the back invites you to buy the local paper before flipping to show the score from last night's big game. As you finish your commute, you pass a billboard of a child pointing upward, and as a real plane flies over the sign, the sign announces which flight it is and where it's heading.

These are examples of what's known as *digital out-of-home* (DOOH) marketing, which is a digitally converged form of billboard advertising—a type of advertising that can be traced back to posters in ancient Rome advertising gladiatorial games. Regular billboards are still a large part of the outdoor marketing picture, but digital screens are becoming more common (especially in large urban areas) as LED technology gets less expensive. And these days, we don't just see large digital screens on the sides of roads and highways; we also see digital signs of all sizes inside

◀ Advertising is around us all the time, helping define us as consumers rather than just citizens. Outdoor signs like these increasingly use digital technology and LED screens to create more-dynamic ads. Some signs are even being tested that use cameras and other technology to interact with people passing by. Gabe Ginsberg/Getty Images

and on the sides of buses, taxis, subway entrances, sidewalks, and stores. What's more, companies can tailor messages to target specific locations in real time. For example, a sign next to a bus stop that advertises breakfast sandwiches in the morning might advertise happy hour at a nearby tavern in the afternoon. One Chicago company even updated its signs during a snowstorm to advertise snow shovels at a nearby Kmart.[1]

There are also efforts to make these signs more interactive. For example, Google is working on ways to use data from Android phones to help target ads on digital billboards, converging smartphone data and cookies with advertising. As another example, in August 2018, signs in a New York neighborhood were equipped with cameras and an artificial intelligence program that spotted "stylish" passersby and displayed their pictures.[2] And some businesses, like McDonald's, are experimenting with digital screens that do double duty as advertising signs and kiosks that let customers place orders.[3]

While DOOH advertising is not where the most ad dollars are spent, it is the only form of traditional (non-Internet) media that is increasing its piece of the overall ad-dollar pie, as TV, radio, newspapers, and magazines continue to take smaller slices. In 2017, outdoor advertising hit $5 billion in the United States, and it is expected to keep growing.[4] Interestingly, some of the biggest tech companies are also some of the biggest customers for traditional marketing, such as billboards and newer forms of DOOH. Apple, Google, Amazon, and Netflix were four of the ten biggest spenders on this kind of advertising in 2018.[5]

While all this spending might be good news for billboard companies like iHeartMedia, what does it mean for the rest of us? Is there a downside to having our attention bombarded with even more ads—and having those ads use our own devices to target us more effectively? Given the billions of dollars that go into convincing us what to watch, what to read, and what to buy, it's worth considering how we can best navigate the advertising-saturated spaces that so frequently surround us.

ADVERTISING COMES IN MANY FORMS—from classified ads to business-to-business ads to those providing detailed information on specific consumer products. However, in this chapter, we will concentrate on the more conspicuous consumer advertisements that shape product images and brand-name identities. So much of consumer advertising intrudes into daily life, causing many people to routinely complain about it. And people are increasingly finding ways to avoid ads—for example, by using digital DVRs to zip through them or by blocking pop-ups with web browsers. However, because advertising shows up in most media—the Internet, TV, radio, books, newspapers, magazines, and movies—it serves as a kind of economic glue holding these industries together. Without consumer advertisements, most media businesses would cease to function in their present forms. The good news for these media businesses is that the advertising industry has been growing for the last several years, and in 2019, global advertising spending was on track to hit $563 billion.⁶

In this chapter, we will take a close look at advertising's evolving role in our lives by:

- examining the early history of American advertising, including the rise of ad agencies, brand-name recognition, advertising's power to create new markets and build a consumer culture, and regulation to control that power

- tracing the evolution of U.S. advertising, including the shift to emphasizing visual design in ads, specialization and restructuring of advertising agencies, and the impact of the Internet on this medium

- assessing persuasive techniques in contemporary advertising, such as using testimonials, playing on people's fears, and placing products in movie scenes or on TV shows

- considering the nature of commercial speech and regulation of such speech—for example, to combat deception in advertising

- exploring advertising's impact on our democracy

The Early History of American Advertising: 1850s to 1950s

Before the Industrial Revolution, most Americans lived in isolated areas and produced much of what they needed—tools, clothes, food—themselves. There were few products for sale, other than those by merchants who offered additional goods and services in their own communities, so anything like modern advertising simply wasn't necessary.

All that began changing in the 1850s with the Industrial Revolution and the linking of American villages and towns through railroads, the telegraph, and new print media. Merchants (such as patent medicine makers and cereal producers) wanted to advertise their wares in

LaunchPad
launchpadworks.com

Use **LearningCurve** to review concepts from this chapter.

newspapers and magazines, giving rise to advertising agencies, which could manage these deals. These first national ads introduced the notion that it was important for sellers to differentiate their product from competing goods—which inspired more and more businesspeople to adopt advertising to drive sales.

Over the coming decades, these practices fueled the growth of a consumer culture, in which Americans began desiring specific products and giving their loyalty to particular brands. Critics began decrying advertising's power to seemingly dictate values and create needs in people, triggering the formation of watchdog organizations and more vigilant consumers.

The First Advertising Agencies

The first American advertising agents were newspaper **space brokers**: individuals who purchased space in newspapers and then sold it to various merchants. Newspapers, accustomed to advertisers' not paying their bills (or paying late), welcomed the space brokers, who paid up front. Brokers usually received discounts of 15 to 30 percent, then sold the space to advertisers at the going rate. In 1841, Volney Palmer opened the first ad agency in Philadelphia; for a 25 percent commission from newspaper publishers, he sold space to advertisers.

The first full-service modern ad agency, N. W. Ayer, introduced a different model: Instead of working for newspapers, the agency worked primarily for companies—or clients—that manufactured consumer products. Opening in 1869 in Philadelphia, N. W. Ayer helped develop, write, produce, and place ads in selected newspapers and magazines for its clients. The agency collected a fee from its clients for each ad placed, which covered the price that each media outlet charged for placement of the ad, plus a 15 percent commission. According to this model, the more ads an agency placed, the larger its revenue. Today, while the commission model still dominates, some advertising agencies now work for a flat fee, and some are paid based on how well the ads they create drive sales for the client.

▼ Originally called the Joseph Campbell Preserve Co. back in 1869, the Campbell Soup Company introduced its classic red-and-white soup can labels in 1897. This ad shows the brand sometime between 1920 and 1930. Today, the label is updated, but Campbell's red-and-white cans remain one of the most recognized brands in the country. Library of Congress, Prints & Photographs Division, Reproduction number LC-DIG-ppmsca-42023 (digital file from original item)

Retail Stores: Giving Birth to Branding

During the mid-1800s, most manufacturers sold their goods directly to retail store owners, who usually set their own prices by purchasing products in large quantities. Stores would then sell these loose goods—from clothing to cereal—in large barrels and bins, so customers had no idea who made them. This arrangement shifted after manufacturers began using newspaper advertising to create brand names—that is, to differentiate their offerings and their company's image from those of their competitors in the minds of consumers and retailers, even if the goods were basically the same. For example, one of the earliest brand names, Quaker Oats (the first cereal company to register a trademark in the 1870s), used the image of William Penn, the Quaker who founded Pennsylvania in 1681, in its ads to project a company image of honesty, decency, and hard work.

Convinced by the ads, consumers began demanding certain products—and retail stores felt compelled to stock the desired brands. This enabled the manufacturers, not the retailers, to begin setting the prices of their goods, confident that they'd prevail over the stores' anonymous bulk items. Indeed, product differentiation in brand-name packaged goods represents advertising's single biggest triumph. Though most ads don't trigger a large jump in sales in the short run, over time they create demand by leading consumers to associate particular brands with qualities and values that are important to them.

Patent Medicines: Making Outrageous Claims

As the nineteenth century marched on, patent medicine makers, excited by advertising's power to differentiate their products, invested heavily in print ads developed and placed by ad agencies. But many patent medicines (which consisted of mostly water and high concentrations of ethyl alcohol) made outrageous claims about the medical problems they could cure. The misleading ads spawned public cynicism. As a result, advertisers began to police their own ranks and developed industry codes to restore consumers' confidence. Partly to monitor patent medicine claims, Congress passed the Pure Food and Drug Act in 1906.

Department Stores: Fueling a Consumer Culture

Along with patent medicine makers, department stores began advertising heavily in newspapers and magazines in the late nineteenth century. By the early 1890s, more than 20 percent of ad space in these media was devoted to department stores.

By selling huge volumes of goods and providing little individualized service, department stores saved a lot of money—and passed these savings on to customers in

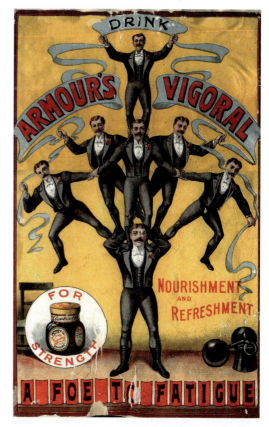

▼ Unregulated patent medicines, such as the one represented in this ad for Armour's Vigoral, created a bonanza for nineteenth-century print media in search of advertising revenue. After several investigative (or "muckraking") magazine reports about deceptive patent medicine claims, Congress created the Food and Drug Administration (FDA) in 1906.
The Advertising Archives

the form of lower prices (as Target and Walmart do today). The department stores thus lured customers away from small local stores, making even more money, which they could reinvest in advertising. This development further fueled the growth of a large-scale consumer culture in the United States.

Transforming American Society

By the dawn of the twentieth century, advertising had become pervasive in the United States. As it gathered force, it began transforming American society. For one thing, by stimulating demand among consumers for more and more products, advertising helped manufacturers create whole new markets. The resulting brisk sales also enabled companies to recover their product development costs quickly. In addition, advertising made people hungry for technological advances by showing how new machines—vacuum cleaners, washing machines, cars—might make daily life easier or better. All this encouraged economic growth by increasing sales of a wide range of goods.

Advertising also began influencing Americans' values. As just one example, ads for household-related products (mops, cleaning solutions, washing machines) conveyed the message that "good" wives were happy to vanquish dirt from their homes. By the early 1900s, business leaders and ad agencies believed that women, who constituted as much as 70 to 80 percent of newspaper and magazine readerships, controlled most household purchasing decisions. Agencies developed simple ads tailored to supposedly feminine characteristics—that is, ads featuring emotional and even irrational content. For instance, many such ads portrayed cleaning products and household appliances as "heroic" and showed grateful women gushing about how the product "saved" them from the shame of a dirty house or the hard labor of doing laundry by hand.

Early Regulation of Advertising

During the early 1900s, advertising's growing clout—along with revelations of fraudulent advertising claims and practices—catalyzed the formation of the first watchdog organizations. For example, advocates in the business community in 1913 created the nonprofit Better Business Bureau, whose mission included keeping tabs on deceptive advertising. The following year, the government established the Federal Trade Commission (FTC), in part to help monitor advertising abuses. Alarmed by government's willingness to step in, players in the advertising industry urged self-regulation to keep government interference at bay.

At the same time, advertisers recognized that a little self-regulation could benefit them in other ways as well. They especially wanted a formal service that tracked newspaper and magazine readership, guaranteed accurate audience measures, and ensured that newspapers didn't overcharge agencies and their clients. To that end, publishers formed the Audit Bureau of Circulations (ABC) in 1914 to monitor circulation figures. (In 2012, the group changed the name of its North American operations to the Alliance for Audited Media, a rebranding partly aimed at staying relevant in a time of emerging digital newspaper and magazine business.)

But it wasn't until the 1940s that the industry began to deflect the long-standing criticisms that advertisers created needs that consumers never knew they had, dictated values, and had too strong a hand in the economy. To promote a more positive self-image, the ad industry developed the War Advertising Council. This voluntary group of ad agencies and advertisers began organizing war bond sales, blood donor drives, and scarce-goods rationing. Known today by a broader mission and its postwar name, the Ad Council chooses a dozen worthy causes annually and produces pro bono *public service announcements* (PSAs) aimed at combating social problems, such as illiteracy, homelessness, drug addiction, smoking, and AIDS.

With the advent of television in the 1950s, advertisers had a brand-new visual medium for reaching consumers. Critics complained about the increased intrusion of ads into daily family life. They especially decried what was then labeled **subliminal advertising**. Through this tactic, TV ads supposedly used hidden or disguised print and visual messages (often related to sex, like the shape of a woman's body in an ice cube for a vodka ad) that allegedly register only in viewers' subconscious minds, fooling them into buying products they don't need. However, research has reported over the years that subliminal ads are no more powerful than regular ads. Demonstrating a willingness to self-regulate, though, the National Association of Broadcasters banned the use of anything resembling a subliminal-type ad in 1958.

▲ During World War II, government offices around the world engaged the advertising industry to create messages supporting the war effort. Advertisers promoted the sale of war bonds, conservation of natural resources such as tin and gasoline, and even the saving of kitchen waste so that it could be fed to farm animals. Bettmann/Getty Images

The Evolution of U.S. Advertising: 1950s to Today

As the twentieth century progressed, U.S. advertising changed in several ways. Visual design began to play a more prominent role in ads, reflecting people's growing interest in imagery. This trend helped spark the growth of new types of ad agencies, which began dominating the field: large global firms serving a broad range of clients, and small companies working for a select group of clients. Ad agencies of all types developed a distinctive organizational structure, which included specialized departments responsible for such activities as account planning and creative development. But that, too, began changing with the advent of the Internet in the 1990s. The new medium presented fresh possibilities for designing and placing ads, giving rise to entirely new types of players in the advertising sector, including search engine giant Google.

Visual Design Comes to the Fore

Visual design began playing a more central role in advertising during the 1960s and 1970s. This revolution was influenced in part by overseas design schools and European designers, whom agencies hired as art directors and who were not tied to word-driven print and radio advertising. The new emphasis on imagery also drew inspiration from changes in television and cable content. By the early 1970s, agencies had developed teams of writers and visual artists, thus granting equal status to images and words in the creative process. Video-style ads featuring prominent performers (Ray Charles, Michael Jackson, Madonna) soon saturated TV.

Today, thanks to technologies such as mobile phones, tablet computers, and incredibly crisp digital displays, visual design has reached new levels of sophistication. For example, ads on mobile phones feature full-motion 3-D animation and high-quality audio. At the same time, designers have had to simplify the imagery they create so that ads and logos can show up clearly and scroll vertically on small digital screens. Finally, to appeal to the global audience, many ad agencies are hiring graphic designers who can capture a diversity of visual styles from around the world.

New Breeds of Advertising Agencies Are Born

The increasing prominence of visual design in advertising led to the development of two specialized types of advertising agencies: **mega-agencies**, large firms that are formed from the merging of several individual agencies and that maintain worldwide regional offices, and **boutique agencies**, smaller companies that devote their talents to a handful of select clients. Both types of agencies wield great control over the kinds of advertising we see daily.

Mega-Agencies

Mega-agencies provide a full range of services—from handling advertising and public relations to operating their own in-house radio and TV production studios. In 2017, the four largest mega-agencies were WPP, Omnicom Group, Publicis Groupe, and the Interpublic Group of Companies, with a combined revenue

FIGURE 11.1 // GLOBAL REVENUE FOR THE WORLD'S LARGEST AGENCIES IN 2017 (IN BILLIONS OF DOLLARS)

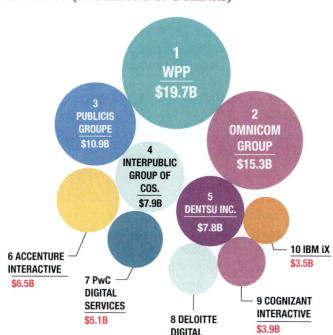

Data from: Advertising Age Marketing Fact Pack 2019, 24.

of almost $54 billion (see Figure 11.1). Four global business consulting firms—Accenture Interactive, PwC Digital Services, IBM iX, and Deloitte Digital—have recently assumed so much of their clients' advertising activities that they have joined the Top 10 of global mega-agencies.

The mega-agency trend has stirred debate among consumer and media watchdog groups. Some have considered large agencies a threat to the independence of smaller firms, which were slowly bought up in the 1990s. Others warn against having a few firms control much of the distribution of advertising dollars globally. According to these critics, with such a concentration of power, the cultural values depicted in U.S. and European ads (such as an obsession with youth or appearance) intrude upon developing countries or regions with markedly different values.

Boutique Agencies

The visual revolution in advertising during the 1960s elevated the standing of the creative side of the ad business, particularly the designers, writers, and graphic artists who became closely identified with the look of specific ads.

Breaking away from bigger agencies, many of these individuals formed small boutique agencies. Offering more personal services, the boutiques prospered—thanks to innovative ad campaigns developed to popularize such brands as Nike, ESPN, and Target.

Throughout the 1980s and 1990s, large agencies bought up many of the boutiques. Nevertheless, some boutiques continue to operate as fairly independent subsidiaries of multinational corporations.

Ad Agencies Develop a Distinctive Structure

Regardless of type (mega or boutique), most ad agencies have a similar organizational structure, comprising four main functions: account planning, creative development, media coordination, and account management.

Account Planning

The account planner's role is to develop an effective advertising strategy by combining the views of the client, the creative team, and consumers. Consumers' views are the most difficult to understand, so account planners coordinate **market research** to assess consumers' behaviors and attitudes concerning particular products long before the agency develops any ads. Researchers test consumers' preferences on a wide range of options, such as possible names for a new product, the size of text in a possible print ad, or potential features of a product in development.

Agencies have increasingly employed scientific methods to study consumer behavior. The earliest type of market research, **demographics**, mainly documented audience members' age, gender, occupation, ethnicity, education, and income, and then looked for patterns between these characteristics and consumers' purchasing choices. (For example, what types of clothing and skin-care products do high-earning women over forty years of age generally purchase?) Today, demographic data have become even more specific, enabling marketers to identify consumers' economic status and geographic location (usually by zip code) and compare their consumption behaviors, lifestyles, and attitudes.

By the 1960s and 1970s, advertisers and agencies began using **psychographics**, a research approach that attempts to categorize consumers according to their attitudes, beliefs, interests, and motivations. Psychographic analysis often relies on **focus groups**, a small-group interview technique in which a moderator leads a discussion about a product or an issue, usually with six to twelve participants. For instance, a focus group moderator might ask participants what they think of several possible names for a new brand of beer, why they like or dislike each of the names proposed, and what role beer plays in their lives.

In 1978, this research grew even more sophisticated when Strategic Business Insights (formerly SRI International) developed its **Values and Lifestyles (VALS)** strategy. Using questionnaires, VALS researchers today divide respondents into eight types associated with certain behaviors and preferences of interest to clients: thinkers, innovators, achievers, strivers, survivors, believers, makers, and experiencers. For example, an automaker considering which vehicle models to advertise during which types of TV shows might be told that *achievers* watch a lot of sports programs and prefer luxury cars, whereas *thinkers* enjoy TV dramas and documentaries and like minivans and hybrids.

VALS research assumes that not every product suits every consumer and encourages advertisers to pitch various sales slants to particular market niches. Ultimately, VALS (and similar research techniques) provides advertisers with microscopic details suggesting which consumers may be most likely to buy which products, but it also stereotypes people as consumers, reducing them to eight manageable categories.

Creative Development

Teams of writers and artists—many of whom regard ads as a commercial art form—make up the nerve center of the advertising business. They outline the rough sketches for print and online ads and then develop the words and graphics. For radio, "creatives" prepare a working script, generating ideas for everything from choosing the narrator's voice to determining background sound effects. For television, they develop a **storyboard**, a roughly drawn comic-strip version showing each scene in the potential ad. For digital media, the creative team may develop websites, interactive tools, games, downloads, social media campaigns, and **viral marketing**—short videos or other forms of content that they hope will swiftly capture an ever-widening circle of attention as users share the content with friends online or by word of mouth.

Creatives often lock horns with researchers over what will appeal most to consumers and how best to influence target markets. However, both sides acknowledge that they can't predict with absolute certainty which ads will succeed, especially in a competitive economy in which eight out of ten products introduced to market typically fail. Agencies say ads are at their best if they slowly create and then hold brand-name identities by associating certain products over time with quality and reliability in the minds of consumers. Famous brands like Coca-Cola, Budweiser, Toyota, and Microsoft spend millions of dollars each year just to maintain their brand-name aura. However, some economists believe that much of the money spent on advertising—especially to promote new products—is ultimately wasted, since it just encourages consumers to change from one well-known brand name to another (see Figure 11.2).

▲ The New York ad agency Doyle Dane Bernbach created a famous series of print and television ads for Volkswagen beginning in 1959, helping usher in an era of creative advertising that combined a single-point sales emphasis with bold design, humor, and apparent honesty.

FIGURE 11.2 // TOP U.S. ADVERTISERS IN 2017 (IN BILLIONS OF DOLLARS)

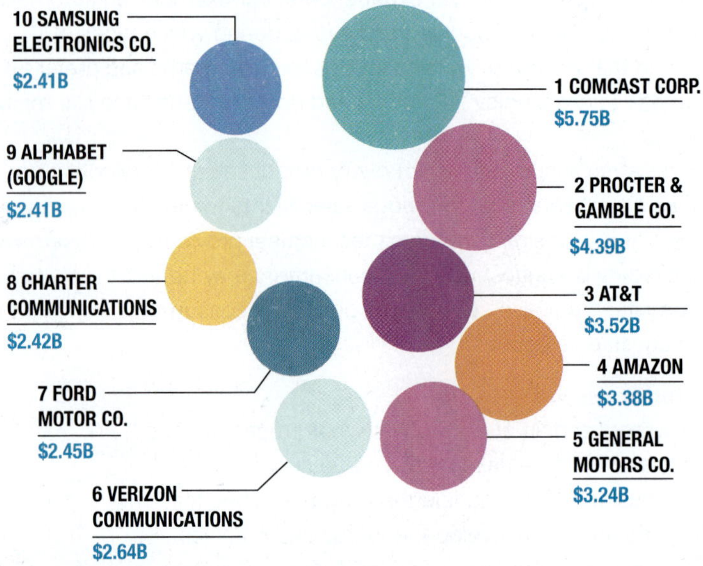

- 1 COMCAST CORP. $5.75B
- 2 PROCTER & GAMBLE CO. $4.39B
- 3 AT&T $3.52B
- 4 AMAZON $3.38B
- 5 GENERAL MOTORS CO. $3.24B
- 6 VERIZON COMMUNICATIONS $2.64B
- 7 FORD MOTOR CO. $2.45B
- 8 CHARTER COMMUNICATIONS $2.42B
- 9 ALPHABET (GOOGLE) $2.41B
- 10 SAMSUNG ELECTRONICS CO. $2.41B

Data from: Advertising Age Marketing Fact Pack 2019, *8.*

Media Coordination: Planning and Placing Advertising

An ad agency's media coordination department is staffed by media planners and **media buyers**: people who choose and purchase the types of media that are best suited to carry a client's ads and reach the targeted audience. For instance, a company like Procter & Gamble, always among the world's top purchasers of advertising, displays its hundreds of major brands—most of them household products like Crest toothpaste, Ivory soap, and Pampers diapers—on TV shows viewed primarily by women, who still do the majority of household cleaning and shopping.

Client companies usually pay an ad agency a commission or fee for its work, but they might also add incentive clauses to their contracts with the agency. For example, they might pay a higher fee if sales reach a specific target after an ad is aired—or pay a lower fee if sales fall short of the target. Incentive clauses can sometimes encourage agencies to conduct repetitive **saturation advertising**, by which they inundate a variety of media with ads aimed at target audiences. The initial Miller Lite beer campaign ("Tastes great, less filling"), which used humor and retired athletes to reach its male audience, ran from 1973 to 1991 and became one of the most successful saturation campaigns in media history.

Of course, such efforts are expensive. And indeed, the cost of advertising—especially on network television—increases each year. The Super Bowl remains the most expensive program for purchasing television advertising, and Sunday Night Football is the most expensive weekly program, costing $665,677 for a thirty-second ad. During a national prime-time non-sports program, thirty seconds of ad time can cost anywhere from just under $16,000 to almost $434,000, depending on the program's popularity and ratings.[7] Thus, cost strongly influences where and when media buyers place ads.

Account Management

An agency's **account executives** are responsible for bringing in new business. For example, if a potential new client has requested bids for an upcoming ad campaign, the account executive might coordinate the presentation of a proposed campaign, complete with cost estimates. Account executives also manage relationships with established clients, including overseeing project budgets, market research, creative work, and media planning done on their campaigns. Account executives thus function as liaisons between the client firm and the agency's creative team.

The advertising business is volatile, and account-management departments are especially vulnerable to upheavals. Clients routinely conduct **account reviews**, in which they assess an existing ad agency's campaign and sometimes even invite several other agencies to submit campaign strategies.

Online and Mobile Advertising Alter the Ad Landscape

When the Internet made its appearance as a new mass medium in the 1990s, it presented a host of new decisions for companies to grapple with—such as what kinds of ads to invest in and where to place them. It also opened the door for new giants (such as Google) to dominate the online advertising industry. Building on the popularity of smartphones and tablets, mobile advertising exploded, helping drive huge increases in Internet ad spending. Back in 2005, television dominated the advertising game, raking in roughly a third of all U.S. ad dollars; Internet advertising lagged behind at around 6 percent of ad spending. By 2017, however, Internet advertising was on top for the first time, earning 35 percent of all U.S. ad revenue. By 2021, the Internet is projected to get 48 percent of all ad dollars spent in the United States.[8] (See "The Digital Turn Case Study: Does the Digital Turn Spell Doom for Network TV?" on page 328.)

launchpadworks.com

Advertising in the Digital Age

This video discusses how ads evolve to overcome resistance to advertising.

Discussion: Do you recall many ads from the last few times you used the Internet? What do you think this might mean for advertisers?

The Rise of Web Advertising

The earliest form of web advertising appeared in the mid-1990s and featured *banner ads*, the printlike display ads that load across the top or side of a web page. Since that time, web advertising has grown in sophistication. Other formats have emerged, including pop-up ads, pop-under ads, multimedia ads, and video ads. Internet advertising now also includes classified-ad sites—the most prominent is craigslist—and e-mail ads. By 2016, unsolicited commercial e-mail—known as **spam**—made up 86 percent of all e-mails in the world's Internet traffic, with over 400 billion spam messages sent each day.⁹

Online ads are generally placed by advertising agencies and served to hundreds of client sites by the agencies' computers. The agencies track **ad impressions** (how often ads are seen) and **click-throughs** (how often users land briefly on a site before clicking through to the next site). They also develop consumer profiles that direct targeted advertisements to website visitors. Online agencies gather information about Internet users through *cookies* (code that tracks users' activity on the web) and online surveys.

Search Engines and Mobile Ads Drive Growth

Search engines led the way in the Internet advertising revolution, and today, paid search advertising dominates sites such as Google, Yahoo!, and Bing. These search engines have morphed into online advertising companies, selling sponsored links associated with search terms and distributing online ads to affiliated web pages.¹⁰

Consider Google's track record. On the cusp of the digital turn in 2001, Google earned roughly $70 million in ad revenue. In five years, that number had jumped to more than $10 billion, and by 2017, Google's ad revenue approached $95.4 billion.¹¹ To put that number in perspective, the biggest broadcast network advertising haul in 2017 (by CBS) was $7 billion, and the largest ad agency—WPP—made just under $20 billion.¹² Facebook, another Internet giant, reported $39.9 billion in advertising revenue in the same year.¹³

The meteoric rise of Internet advertising has also been driven by ads delivered on mobile devices. In 2012, mobile's share of Internet advertising was only 11 percent; by 2019, mobile was forecasted to be 65 percent of all Internet advertising, and by 2021, it is projected to account for nearly three-quarters of all Internet ads.¹⁴ Once again, Google and Facebook rode, and drove, that wave: By 2018, media analysts estimated that Google earned more than $60 billion through worldwide net mobile advertising, and Facebook earned roughly 90 percent of its total ad revenue, which was estimated at just under $34 billion in 2018, through mobile.¹⁵

Mining for Data

Social media, such as Facebook, Twitter, Snapchat, and Instagram, provide a wealth of data for advertisers to mine. These sites and apps create an unprecedented public display of likes, dislikes, locations, and other personal information, which advertisers use to further refine their ability to send targeted ads. The information users provide goes straight back to advertisers, so they can revise their advertising and better engage their viewers. With this better understanding of individual users, companies and organizations can choose between buying traditional paid advertisements on social media sites and sending ads micro-targeted to those individual users.

The type of social media advertising varies by—and is often tailored to—what the site actually does. For example, an ad on Facebook will typically appear as a clickable image next to the newsfeed. On Twitter, a sponsored tweet will usually appear in the feed. On YouTube, a user will most likely have to watch a commercial—or at least the first few seconds of a commercial—before or during a video.

In the current age of "big data," there is an enormous incentive to use individuals' online behavior to identify them as likely consumers for different products. One method of working with this information is called *deterministic identity*, which involves taking information customers provide about themselves (like a registration e-mail address) and connecting it with things like cookies, location data, and devices.[16] For example, if a user logs into his or her Facebook account from a laptop, a phone, and a tablet, Facebook can be reasonably certain that the same person is using each device; the company can then pool data gathered from all those devices and send back ads accordingly.[17] Another method is called *probabilistic identity*, and it uses statistical analysis of online behavior (rather than customer-provided data) to work out which sets of information apply to which customers.[18] Instead of relying on things like login information, this approach looks for patterns in other data—such as similar web browsing habits and shared locations of Internet use—to identify individual Internet users. Some suggest that a combination of these two approaches works best for targeted online advertising.

▲ Companies can create consumer profiles that are influenced by what sites you visit, what you "Like" on social media, and what you click on. For example, if you see an ad tied to the D.C. Comics character Aquaman, it is quite possible that you recently watched a trailer for the film on Facebook, looked up showtimes or bought tickets online, or even checked in via social media to a showing of the 2018 movie.

Word of Mouth, Earned Media, and Endorsements in the Digital Age

According to an old adage in marketing, the most effective form of advertising is word of mouth—a recommendation from a friend or family member. In today's post–digital turn world, defined by social media, word-of-mouth recommendations are referred to as "earned media," and they are every bit as valuable as the original.

Earned media can be passive or active on the part of the social media user. Say, for example, that you "Like" a page for a company, product, or person on Facebook, which causes that particular product to pop up on your friend's wall with a notification saying that you're a fan. This is a passive endorsement on your part, because the social media account has done the promotion for you. An active endorsement, on the other hand, occurs when you share a post on Facebook or issue a retweet on Twitter—with or without some kind of personal message that goes along with the repost or retweet.

The Digital Turn

CASE STUDY

Does the Digital Turn Spell Doom for Network TV?

Over the last several years, the digital turn has dramatically changed the way that products and advertising are bought, sold, and consumed. By 2016, television was one of the only older, or "legacy," mass media industries whose global advertising revenue was not totally disrupted by the Internet. However, Internet advertising surpassed TV advertising for the first time in the United States in 2017 and in the global media market in 2018. Projections show that the Internet will continue to dominate in 2019, with 41.6 percent of U.S. media ad spending versus television's 32 percent. Ad spending on radio, newspapers, magazines, outdoor signs, and movies will make up the remaining 26.4 percent.[1]

Analyzing data from Ad Age's yearly *Marketing Fact Pack* reveals what's happening. In 2013, "time spent using digital media overtook time spent watching television" for the first time. Back in the first half of 2015, traditional TV viewing in the United States declined almost 10 percent, with Netflix's digital streaming services accounting for almost half that decline.[2] And, of course, we are often watching ads on TV and texting on our smartphones at the same time.

ABC, CBS, Fox, and NBC are worried about these trends. While these once-dominant TV networks have started their own digital streaming services—including Hulu—they trail Netflix and Amazon Prime, which remain ad-free, subscription-only services. The drop in the network audience is reflected in the drop in price for ads during some of the most popular network programs. For example, CBS's long-running *Big Bang Theory* earned $348,000 per thirty-second ad in 2015 but just under $286,000 in 2018.[3]

Traditional TV has managed to hold on to roughly a third of the advertising pie because in a fragmented marketplace, the "mass" prime-time TV audience—only a quarter of what it was in the 1980s—still remains significantly larger than the audience a YouTube video or a Netflix series can generate. Once in a while, a brief hit the size of Fox's *Empire* will come along and instill faith in the networks' ability to capture a mass audience. However, the great-grandchildren of baby boomers who grew up on TV in the 1950s and 1960s will be raised on smartphones and tablets, with no loyalty to (or patience for) ad-based broadcast networks and no memory of gathering around the electronic hearth to watch a "must-see" network sitcom—and the ads that accompany it.

But people will always want stories. Thus, the challenge for the advertising industry is to figure out how its ads can be tied into the consumption of those stories. What will networks do to get younger viewers to watch those stories on their smartphones? Will Netflix look to advertising for another revenue stream? Will some of the ad budgets for the biggest U.S. advertisers shift from TV to digital platforms? In short: What will advertisers do to keep people watching ads, especially in a world of digital devices that either let us skip ads or offer ad-free story services, like HBO, Amazon Prime, and Netflix?

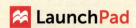

▶ **Visit LaunchPad** to view a video about the rise in Internet ad spending. Now that Internet spending has actually surpassed TV spending, do the conditions discussed in the video lead you to believe this trend will continue? Why or why not? What might this mean for TV and other legacy media?

FACEBOOK & GOOGLE DOMINATE ONLINE ADS

launchpadworks.com

But sometimes these endorsements can enter unethical—and possibly illegal—territory. One controversy in online advertising is whether people have to disclose if they are being paid to promote a product. For example, bloggers often review products or restaurants as part of their content, and some bloggers have been paid to give positive reviews or promote products on their site. When these instances—dubbed "blog-ola" by the press—came to light in 2008 and 2009, the bloggers argued that they did not have to reveal that they were being compensated. At the time, they were right. In 2009, however, the FTC released new guidelines requiring bloggers to disclose when an advertiser is compensating them for discussing a product.

In 2010, a similar controversy erupted when the FTC revealed that celebrities were being paid to tweet about their "favorite" products. In 2016, the FTC found Lord & Taylor in violation of the disclosure rules when the clothing company hired fifty bloggers (or "influencers") to wear the same designer dress within days of one another. The bloggers did not disclose that their posts were sponsored, and the FTC fined Lord & Taylor an undisclosed amount.[19]

Persuasive Techniques in Contemporary Advertising

In addition to using a similar organizational structure, most ad agencies employ a wide variety of persuasive techniques in the ad campaigns they create for their clients. Indeed, persuasion—getting consumers to buy one company's products and services and not another's—lies at the core of the advertising industry. Persuasive techniques take numerous forms, ranging from conventional strategies (such as having a famous person endorse a product) to not-so-conventional strategies (for instance, showing video game characters using a product).

Do these tactics work—that is, do they boost sales? This is a tough question, because it's difficult to distinguish an ad's impact on consumers from the effects of other cultural and social forces. But companies continue investing in advertising on the assumption that without the product and brand awareness that advertising builds, consumers just might go to a competitor.

▲ Major stars used to be somewhat wary of appearing in ads (at least in the United States), but many brands now use celebrity endorsements. This Revlon campaign, for example, features actress **Emma Stone.** Image Courtesy of The Advertising Archives

Using Conventional Persuasive Strategies

Advertisers have long used a number of conventional persuasive strategies to sell their products:

- **Famous-person testimonial:** A product is endorsed by a well-known person. For example, Serena Williams has become a leading sports spokesperson, having appeared in ads for such companies as Nike, Kraft Foods, and Procter & Gamble.
- **Plain-folks pitch:** A product is associated with simplicity. For instance, General Electric ("Imagination at work") and Microsoft ("Your potential. Our passion") have used straightforward slogans stressing how new technologies fit into the lives of ordinary people.
- **Snob appeal:** An ad attempts to persuade consumers that using a product will maintain or elevate their social status. Advertisers selling jewelry, perfume, clothing, and luxury automobiles often use snob appeal.
- **Bandwagon effect:** The ad claims that "everyone" is using a particular product. Brands that refer to themselves as "America's favorite" or "the best-selling" imply that consumers will be "left behind" if they ignore these products.
- **Hidden-fear appeal:** A campaign plays on consumers' sense of insecurity. Deodorant, mouthwash, and shampoo ads often tap into people's fears of having an embarrassing personal-hygiene problem if they don't use the suggested product.
- **Irritation advertising:** An ad creates product-name recognition by being annoying or obnoxious. (You may have seen one of these on TV, in the form of a local car salesman loudly touting the "unbelievable bargains!" available at his dealership.)

Associating Products with Values

In addition to the conventional persuasive techniques just described, ad agencies draw on the **association principle** in many campaigns for consumer products. Through this technique, an agency associates a product with a positive cultural value or image—even if that value or image has little connection to the product. For example, many ads displayed visual symbols of American patriotism in the wake of the 9/11 terrorist attacks in an attempt to associate products and companies with national pride.

Yet this technique has also been used to link products with stereotyped caricatures of targeted consumer groups, such as men, women, or specific ethnic groups. For example, many ads have sought to appeal to women by portraying men as idiots who know nothing about how to use a washing machine or heat up leftovers for dinner. The assumption is that portraying men as idiots will make women feel better about themselves—and thus be attracted to the advertised product (see "Media Literacy Case Study: Idiots and Objects: Stereotyping in Advertising" on pages 332–333).

Another popular use of the association principle is to claim that products are "real" and "natural"—possibly the most common adjectives used in advertising. For example, Coke sells itself as "the real thing." The cosmetics industry offers synthetic products that make us look "natural." And "green" marketing touts products that are often manufactured and not always environmentally friendly.

In the 1950s and 1960s, Philip Morris used the association principle to transform the image of its Marlboro filtered cigarette brand (considered a product for women in the 1920s) into a product for men. Ad campaigns featured images of active, rugged males, particularly cowboys. (Three of the men who appeared in these ad campaigns eventually died of lung cancer caused by cigarette smoking.) The branding consultancy BrandZ (a division of WPP) dropped Marlboro from the world's tenth "most valuable global brand" in 2015 to the world's thirteenth in 2018, citing the rise in technology/digital-based brands as one of the main reasons for the dip.[20] Google, Apple, and Amazon were the three top brand names in 2018 (see Table 11.1).

TABLE 11.1 // THE TOP 10 GLOBAL BRANDS

Rank	Brand	Brand Value ($Billions)	Brand Value Change, 2018 vs. 2017 (%)
1	Google	302.1	+23
2	Apple	300.6	+28
3	Amazon	207.6	+49
4	Microsoft	201.0	+40
5	Tencent	179.0	+65
6	Facebook	162.1	+25
7	Visa	145.6	+31
8	McDonald's	126.0	+29
9	Alibaba Group	113.4	+92
10	AT&T	106.7	−7

Data from: "Global Top 100 Brands 2018," BrandZ, http://brandz.com/charting/54.

Media Literacy
CASE STUDY

Idiots and Objects: Stereotyping in Advertising

Over the years, critics and consumers alike have complained about stereotyping in mainstream advertising. *Stereotyping* refers to the process of assigning people to abstract groups whose members are assumed to act as a single entity—rather than as individuals with distinct identities—and to display shared characteristics, which often have negative connotations.

Today, particularly in beer ads, men are often stereotyped as inept or stupid, incapable of negotiating a routine day or a normal conversation unless fortified—or dulled—by the heroic product. Throughout advertising history, men have often been portrayed as doofuses and idiots when confronted by ordinary food items or a simple household appliance.

On the other hand, in the early history of product ads on television, women were often stereotyped as emotional, naïve, brainless, or helpless, or offered as a man's reward for drinking a particular beer or smoking the right cigarette. Worst of all, women, or even parts of women—with their heads cut from the frame—have been used as objects, merely associated with a particular product (e.g., a swimsuit model holding a new car muffler). Influenced by the women's movement and critiques of advertising culture, such as Betty Friedan's *The Feminine Mystique* (1963), ads depicting women have changed to some degree. Although many sexist stereotypes still persist in advertising, women today are portrayed in a variety of social roles.

In addition to ads that have stereotyped men and women, there is also invisible stereotyping. This occurs when whole segments of the population are ignored—particularly African, Arab, Asian, Latin, and Native Americans. Advertising—especially in its early history—has often faced criticism that many segments of the varied and multicultural U.S. population have been missing or underrepresented in the ads and images that dominate the landscape.

In the last several years, however, conscious of how diverse the United States has become, some ad campaigns have been making changes. A notable shift began in 2013, when Cheerios featured an ad with a white mom, a black father, and a biracial daughter. The next year, the same family was featured in a Super Bowl commercial.[1] The company later launched a campaign featuring two gay white dads talking about the adoption of their black daughter.

Since then, a variety of major brands—including Old Navy, Gillette, State Farm, Coors Light, Cadillac, and Macy's—have begun using more racially and socially diverse advertising as a way to signal to customers that inclusivity is a brand value.[2] These ads have drawn a fair amount of backlash. For example, comments had to be disabled on a YouTube version of the Cheerios commercial because of the racist reactions it generated. But as the cofounder of marketing strategy firm Metaforce explains, there has been

> ### ▶ Web Clip
> YouTube.com includes many commercials—and commercial parodies. One good option to search for is "Totino's Activity Pack Super Bowl Commercial—SNL," posted by Saturday Night Live, which parodies football-themed snack ads. What do you think the ad is saying about stereotyping in advertisements?
>
>

▲ Once considered too shocking for advertising, more companies are showing interracial couples and families, as well as families with two dads or two moms.

a shift in the country that makes more inclusive advertising a good business decision: "Most marketers have come to realize that no matter what they do, a certain segment is going to be offended," Allen Adamson told the *New York Times* in 2018. "But the upside—seeming inclusive— outweighs the risk of ruffling feathers."[3]

Interestingly, it's not just America that seems to be focused on addressing negative stereotypes in advertising. Great Britain's Committee of Advertising Practice (CAP) announced that beginning in the summer of 2019, it would ban ads deemed "likely to cause harm, or serious or widespread offense" due to gender stereotypes.[4] Ella Smillie, the lead on the project, issued a statement explaining the committee's reasoning, which echoes critiques of advertising going back decades: "Harmful gender stereotypes in ads contribute to how people see themselves and their role in society. They can hold some people back from fulfilling their potential, or from aspiring to certain jobs and industries, bringing costs for individuals and the economy."[5]

APPLYING THE CRITICAL PROCESS

DESCRIPTION Gather four to six advertisements from various newspapers, magazines, or Internet sites that feature individuals (not just products).

ANALYSIS Examine the content of each ad: What product is being sold? What are the demographic profiles of the people who appear in the ad (or are the identities of the people in the ad ambiguous)? What are they doing? Be sure to note the source of each ad. What patterns emerge?

INTERPRETATION What do the patterns that you've identified mean? How are the people in each ad helping sell the product? What is the message that each ad is trying to portray? Why did the advertiser choose the specific newspaper, magazine, or Internet site to advertise the product?

EVALUATION Do any of the ads foster existing stereotypes? Explain how they do or do not. Do you think these ads are effective? How might the stereotypes in these ads convey a distorted or mixed message to the consumer?

ENGAGEMENT Choose one ad from your selection to revise. How might you redesign this ad to remove existing stereotypes? Compose a draft. Do you think your ad is more or less effective than the original? Explain your answer.

Telling Stories

Many ads also tell stories that contain elements found in myths (narratives that convey a culture's deepest values and social norms). For example, an ad might take the shape of a mini-drama or sitcom, complete with characters, settings, and plot. Perhaps a character experiences a conflict or a problem of some type. The character resolves the situation by the end of the ad, usually by purchasing or using the product. The product and those who use it emerge as the heroes of the story.

But brands can play a variety of roles in commercial storytelling. Besides emerging as the solution to a problem, a brand sometimes *becomes* the character, as in M&M commercials in which animated versions of the candies exhibit their own distinct personalities and find themselves in a number of silly scenarios. In addition, some commercials are one-time stories, while others take the form of a running gag. In a series of Snickers commercials, for example, a cranky person (played by a celebrity) transforms into someone who is happy and calm after taking a bite of the candy bar.

Although most of us realize that ads telling stories create a fictional world, we often can't help but get caught up in them. That's because they reinforce our values and assumptions about how the world works. And they reassure us that by using familiar brand names—packaged in comforting mini-stories—we can manage the everyday tensions and problems that confront us.

Placing Products in Media

Product placement—strategically placing ads or buying space in movies, TV shows, comic books, and video games so that they appear as part of a story's set environment—is another persuasive strategy ad agencies use. For example, the film *Get Out* (2017) prominently featured Windows products, such as Bing, the Windows Phone, and the Surface Pro in multiple scenes; the TV show *The Biggest Loser*, which was sponsored by Subway, took contestants on field trips to the sandwich shop; and Instagram hired thirty "influencer dudes" to use Axe hair-styling products and create their own "Instagroom" videos.

Many critics argue that product placement has gotten out of hand. In 2005, watchdog organization Commercial Alert asked both the FTC and the FCC to mandate that consumers be warned about product placement in television shows. The FTC rejected the petition, and by 2018, the FCC had still made no formal response to the request. Most defenders of product placement argue that there is little or no concrete evidence that this practice harms consumers. The 2011 documentary *POM Wonderful Presents: The Greatest Movie Ever Sold* takes a satirical look at product placement—and filmmaker Morgan Spurlock financed the film's entire budget using that very strategy.

Commercial Speech and Regulating Advertising

Advertisements are considered **commercial speech**—defined as any print or broadcast expression for which a fee is charged to organizations and individuals buying time or space in the mass media. Though the First Amendment protects freedom of speech and of the press, it doesn't specify whether advertisers can say anything they want in their commercial speech; thus, the question of whether commercial speech is protected by the Constitution is tricky. In some critics' view, certain forms of advertising can have destructive consequences and should therefore be regulated. These include ads that target children, that tout unhealthy products (such as alcohol and tobacco), that prompt people to adopt dangerous behaviors (such as starving themselves to look like models in magazines), and that hawk prescription medications directly to consumers.

To be sure, no one has figured out just how much power such ads have to actually influence targeted consumers. Indeed, studies have suggested that 75 to 90 percent of new consumer products fail because the buying public doesn't embrace them, suggesting that advertising isn't as effective as some critics might think.[21] Nevertheless, serious concerns over the impact of advertising persist.

Targeting Children and Teens

Because children and teenagers may influence billions of dollars each year in family spending—on everything from snacks to cars—advertisers have increasingly targeted them, often viewing young people as "consumers in training." When ads influence youngsters in a good way (for example, by getting them interested in reading books), no one complains about advertising's power. It's when ads influence kids and teens in what is perceived as a dangerous way (such as tempting them with unhealthy foods) that concerns arise.

For years, groups such as Action for Children's Television (ACT) worked to limit advertising aimed at children (especially ads promoting toys associated with a particular show and those that promoted unhealthy products, like sugar-coated cereals). Congress responded weakly, hesitant to question the First Amendment's protection of commercial speech and pressured by determined lobbying from the advertising industry. The Children's Television Act of 1990 mandated that networks provide some educational and informational

launchpadworks.com

Advertising and Effects on Children

Scholars and advertisers analyze the effects of advertising on children.

Discussion: In this video, some argue that using cute, kid-friendly imagery in alcohol ads can lead children to begin drinking, while others dispute this claim. What do you think, and why?

children's programming, but the act has done little to restrict advertising aimed at kids. These days, subscription television services like Netflix offer an alternative to ad-supported broadcast television, with a wide range of ad-free children's television programs.

In addition to trying to control TV advertising aimed at young people, critics have complained about advertising that has encroached on school property. The introduction of Channel One into thousands of schools during the 1989–90 school year was one of the most controversial cases of in-school advertising. Channel One offered free video and satellite equipment (tuned exclusively to Channel One) in exchange for a twelve-minute package of current events programming that included two minutes of commercials. Many parent and teacher groups objected to Channel One because it required teens to watch commercial messages in a learning environment. The service ended in 2018, an event celebrated by groups opposed to children's advertising.

Over the years, the National Dairy Council and other organizations have also used schools to promote products—for example, by providing free filmstrips, posters, magazines, folders, and study guides adorned with member companies' logos. Many teachers, especially in underfunded districts, have been grateful for these free materials. Another way commercials and marketing reach teens, tweens, and even younger kids is through their mobile devices, including smartphones and tablets. With mobile advertising exploding and an increasing number of kids having access to these devices, monitoring the ads children see is becoming even more difficult.

Medical organizations such as the Ontario Medical Association seek to warn consumers about the dangers of obesity through powerful ads like the one seen here.

Triggering Anorexia and Overeating

Some critics accuse ads of contributing to anorexia among girls and women. To be sure, companies have long marketed fashions and cosmetics by showing ultrathin female models using their products. Through such campaigns, advertising strongly shapes standards of beauty in our culture. Many girls and women apparently feel compelled to achieve those standards—even if it means starving themselves or having repeated cosmetic surgeries.

At the same time, advertising has been blamed for the tripling of obesity rates in the United States since the 1980s. Corn-syrup-laden soft drinks, fast food, junk food, and processed food are the staples of media advertising. Critics maintain that advertisements for fattening products have directly contributed to widespread obesity in the United States. The food and restaurant industry has denied this connection. Industry advocates claim that people have the power to decide what they eat—and many individuals are making poor choices, such as eating too much fast food.

Promoting Smoking

One of the most sustained criticisms of advertising is its promotion of tobacco consumption. Each year, an estimated 400,000 Americans die from diseases related to nicotine addiction and poisoning. Tobacco ads disappeared from television in 1971 under pressure from Congress and the FCC. Still, tobacco companies continued to crank out ad campaigns designed to win over new customer segments, which often included teenagers.

The government's position regarding the tobacco industry began changing in the mid-1990s. At that time, new reports revealed that tobacco companies had known that nicotine was addictive as far back as the 1950s and had withheld that information from the public. Settlements between the industry and states have put significant limits on advertising and marketing of tobacco products. For example, ads cannot use cartoon characters such as Joe Camel, because such characters appeal to young people. And companies can't show ads on billboards or in subway or commuter trains, where young people might be vulnerable to them. Despite these restrictions, tobacco companies still spend $9.5 billion annually on U.S. advertisements—more than twenty times the amount spent on anti-tobacco public service spots.[22]

Promoting Drinking

In 2016, about ninety thousand people in the United States died from alcohol-related or alcohol-induced diseases; another ten-thousand-plus lost their lives in car crashes involving drunk drivers. Many of the same complaints regarding tobacco advertising are being leveled at alcohol ads. For example, critics have protested that one of the most popular beer campaigns of the late 1990s—featuring a trio of frogs croaking *Budweis-errrr*—used cartoon-like animal characters to appeal to young viewers. Some alcohol ads, such as Pabst Brewing Company's ads featuring Snoop Dogg for Blast by Colt 45 (a strong flavored malt beverage that the Massachusetts attorney general called "binge-in-a-can"), have specifically targeted young minority populations.

The alcohol industry has also heavily targeted college students with ads, especially for beer. The images and slogans in alcohol ads often associate the products with power, romance, sexual prowess, or athletic skill. In reality, though, alcohol is a depressant: It diminishes athletic ability and sexual

▼ Budweiser, a heavy spender on ads during the Super Bowl and throughout the year, came under fire in 2015 for advertising on a Bud Light bottle that called it "the perfect beer for removing 'no' from your vocabulary"—a tagline that, as many pointed out, carried connotations of coercion, acting without considering consequences, and even sexual assault. © Bill Aron/PhotoEdit—All rights reserved

performance, triggers addiction in as much as 10 percent of the U.S. population, and factors into many domestic-abuse cases. Thus, many ads present a false impression of what alcohol products can do for consumers.

Hawking Drugs Directly to Consumers

New advertising tactics by the pharmaceutical industry—such as marketing directly to consumers rather than doctors—have drawn fire from critics worried about vulnerable groups of consumers. A study by the Kaiser Family Foundation found that from 1994 to 2007, spending on direct-to-consumer advertising for prescription drugs soared from $266 million to $5.3 billion. By 2017, that number was up to $5.8 billion.[23] About two-thirds of such ads are shown on television, and they've proved effective for the pharmaceutical companies that invest in and use them. A survey found that nearly one in three adults has talked to a doctor about a particular drug after seeing an ad for it on TV, and one in eight subsequently received a prescription.[24] The tremendous growth of prescription drug ads brings with it the potential for misleading or downright false claims. That's because a brief TV advertisement can't effectively communicate all the cautionary information consumers need to know about these medications. Meanwhile, the money spent marketing to patients is dwarfed by the $24 billion drug companies spend to market directly to doctors.[25]

Drug companies are also following the trend of advertising on the Internet. Companies today invite people to take online quizzes to see if they need a prescription eye medication, offer phone consultations and help prospective patients set up doctor's appointments, and give patients ideas about how to ask their doctor for a particular medication.[26]

Monitoring the Advertising Industry

Worried about advertising's power over vulnerable consumers, a few nonprofit watchdog and advocacy organizations, such as Commercial Alert and the Truth Initiative, have emerged. Such groups strive to compensate for some of the shortcomings of the FTC and other government agencies in monitoring false and deceptive ads and the excesses of commercialism. At the same time, the FTC is still trying to combat the negative impact of advertising, though its effectiveness remains questionable—especially in light of cutbacks at the agency, which have been going on since the 1980s.

Commercial Alert

Since 1998, Commercial Alert has worked to "limit excessive commercialism in society." Founded in part with help from longtime consumer advocate Ralph Nader, Commercial Alert became a project of Public Citizen, a nonprofit consumer protection organization based in Washington, D.C. In addition to its efforts to check commercialism, Commercial Alert has challenged specific marketing tactics that allow corporations to intrude into civic life. For example, in the past, Commercial Alert has worked to oppose ads disguised as regular posts on Instagram and advocated to keep hospital obstetrics wards free of ads for infant formula and other products. In constantly questioning the role of advertising in our democracy, Commercial Alert has aimed to strengthen noncommercial culture and limit the amount of corporate influence on publicly elected government officials and organizations.

The Truth Initiative®

Some nonprofit organizations have used innovative advertising of their own to offset the effects of ads for dangerous products, including the Truth Initiative, which launched the truth® campaign—an antismoking/anti–tobacco industry ad campaign—in 2000. The Truth Initiative has seen real results by reaching out to teens online (specifically offering them an opportunity to engage online with the website, volunteer, and become informed) and through a grassroots approach with summer tours and events. Additionally, the truth campaign has won multiple awards for creative ads like "Body Bags" and "Singing Cowboy," and in 2014, Ad Age—a global media brand that analyzes marketing and media—named truth one of the top fifteen campaigns of the twenty-first century. The truth campaign at least partly explains the reported decline in teen smoking.[27]

◀ In 2005, truth, the national youth smoking prevention campaign, won an Emmy Award in the National Public Service Announcement category. Truth Initiative

The FTC

Through its truth-in-advertising rules, the FTC plays an investigative role in substantiating the claims of various advertisers. Thus, the organization contributes to some regulation of the ad industry. The FTC usually permits a certain amount of *puffery*—ads featuring hyperbole and exaggeration—particularly when an ad describes a product as "new and improved." However, the FTC defines ads as deceptive when they are likely to mislead reasonable consumers through statements made, images shown, or omission of certain information. (For example, in Campbell Soup ads featuring images of a bowl of soup, marbles had been placed in the bottom of the bowl to push bulkier ingredients to the surface. This was deceptive advertising because it made the soup look less watery than it really was.) Moreover, when an advertiser makes comparative claims about a product, such as it's "the best," "the greatest," or "preferred by four out of five doctors," FTC rules require statistical evidence to back up the claims.

When the FTC discovers deception in advertising, it usually requires advertisers to change or remove the ads from circulation, though it can also impose monetary civil penalties to be paid to consumers. Occasionally, the FTC requires an advertiser to run spots correcting the deceptive ads.

Advertising in a Democratic Society

Advertising has had both creative and destructive effects on our democratic society. With its ability to "produce" not products but actual consumers, it became the central economic support system for American mass media industries, powerfully fueling our economy. Yet in creating a consumerist society, the ad industry has also widened divisions between those who can afford to buy all the alluring products it promotes and those who cannot (or, alternatively, those who go into debt buying the alluring products on credit). When some people can participate in an economy and others are unable to, democracy is undermined. Moreover, advertising's ubiquity intrudes on our privacy and subjects us to corporate efforts to gather our personal information (such as income and spending habits).

Equally worrisome, fewer and fewer large media conglomerates are controlling an increasing amount of commercial speech, especially in mainstream, traditional media. This raises the question of whether we're getting all the information we need to make well-reasoned choices—a key characteristic of any democratic society.

Advertising's role in politics offers an apt example. Since the 1950s, political consultants have adopted market-research and advertising techniques to

◀ Eye-catching logos and short, simple slogans have long been an important part of selling a candidate to the public. During the 2016 presidential election, the "Make America Great Again" slogan became an instantly recognizable symbol of then candidate Donald Trump. Trump and his supporters have continued to reference the slogan since he was elected president. Spencer Platt/Getty Images

"sell" their candidates to the electorate. **Political advertising**—the use of ad techniques to promote a candidate's image and persuade the public to adopt a particular viewpoint—is the most popular form of this. Many political ads are shown on television in the form of thirty-second spots paid for by candidates from the two main parties or largely unregulated political action committees (PACs) and Super PACs, made legal by the 2010 Supreme Court case *Citizens United v. Federal Elections Commission* (see also Chapter 13). The *Citizens United* decision is already having a huge impact on political ad spending. For example, the total money spent on presidential and congressional campaigns was $5.28 billion in 2008. In 2012, it jumped to $6.28 billion; and in 2016, $6.51 billion. Even in off-year federal elections in which there isn't a presidential race, political expenditures have soared, reaching a record $5.73 billion in 2018.[28] The Center for Responsive Politics notes that the "biggest driver of the leap is spending by outside groups," the kind of unregulated political action committees aided by the *Citizens United* decision.[29]

One result of this political system is that only very wealthy candidates, or those with the wealthiest patrons, have typically been able to afford these expensive promotional strategies. Thus, citizens who rely on television for their information don't get a complete picture of the options available and may never learn about obscure but qualified third-party candidates who can't afford to pay for TV spots. (The Internet has helped level that playing field to some degree, as any compelling content—whether purchased by wealthy interests or not—has the potential to go viral.)

Moreover, critics have raised probing questions about the unintended consequences of political ads aired on television or the Internet. For example, can serious information about complex political issues really be conveyed in a thirty-second spot? If not, viewers aren't getting a full understanding of the issues and can't make informed voting decisions. And do repeated attack ads, which assault another candidate's character, undermine citizens' confidence in the electoral process? If so, people may stop voting entirely—a *really* bad thing for a democracy.

Political ads most often appear during traditional televised commercial breaks, but other forms of advertising can be more subtle, especially in the digital world of promotion-paid Twitter accounts, product placement, and ads woven into search engine results. During the 2016 election, for example, we saw how extensive media coverage—though not advertising in the strictest sense—can provide free publicity for a candidate's campaign and drive the broader political narrative. During his candidacy, Donald Trump parlayed decades in the public spotlight, his status as a reality TV star, and his growing Twitter following into an unprecedented amount of free media coverage. From his extensively covered role in the "birther" movement (which questioned the authenticity of then president Obama's birth certificate) to regular appearances on Fox News, attention from a wide range of news sources before he even made a dent in the polls, and accommodating coverage in the *National Enquirer,* Trump obtained, by some estimates, billions of dollars' worth of free air time and mentions across the media spectrum—in part because his controversial and bombastic rhetoric translated into ratings for the news organizations that covered him so extensively.[30] In early 2016, then chair and CEO of CBS Les Moonves said of Donald Trump's place in the election and his network's resulting ratings bump: "It may not be good for America, but it's damn good for CBS."[31]

Despite these and other concerns about advertising's potential negative consequences for our democracy, it maintains its hold on American culture for several reasons. Without advertising, many mass media industries—television, the Internet, movies—would have to entirely reinvent their business models, as newspapers and magazines are doing right now in the face of losing so much of their ad revenue over the last decade. Leaders in these industries continue to embrace advertising as an economic necessity. Consumers themselves hold conflicting views of the ad industry. Some dismiss advertising as trivial and ineffective; as a result, these individuals don't typically support strong monitoring of the industry. Others find ads entertaining, decorating their rooms or clothing with their favorite product posters or company logos and happily identifying with the images certain products convey. These individuals, too, remain oblivious to advertising's less-than-positive effects on our society. Advertising can be enjoyable—think of those viewers who watch the Super Bowl primarily to see the new ads—but if we consider it just entertainment, we misunderstand its ultimate purpose.

What does all this mean for advertising's future in the United States? As with any other mass medium, it's important that we remember what advertising's purpose is, understand how it both benefits and costs our society, and "consume" commercial culture and its ads with a critical eye.

Think about it: In what ways are our own behaviors, values, and decisions—in all aspects of our life—affected by advertising? How might we consume and respond to ads more critically? And in what ways could we all participate in efforts to monitor the advertising landscape?

CHAPTER ESSENTIALS

Review

- The first American advertising agents were newspaper **space brokers**. The first full-service modern ad agencies worked mainly for companies that manufactured consumer products.

- As a result of manufacturers using newspaper stories and ads to create brand names, consumers began demanding specific products, and retail stores began stocking desired brands, ushering in product differentiation.

- By the twentieth century, advertising had transformed American society, creating new markets, shaping values, and influencing the rising consumer culture. This influence catalyzed the first watchdog organizations, including the Better Business Bureau and the Federal Trade Commission (FTC).

- Beginning in the 1960s and 1970s, visual design began playing a more prominent role in advertising. This trend sparked the growth of new types of advertising agencies: **mega-agencies** and smaller **boutique agencies**.

- Regardless of the type of ad agency, most have similar organizational structures, consisting of departments for account planning (including **market research**), creative development, media coordination, and account management.

- The growth of the Internet in the 1990s changed—and continues to change—the advertising industry considerably. Internet advertising now captures more ad dollars than any other medium, led by major tech companies like Google and Facebook. Online marketing includes a variety of different and increasingly targeted ads, as well as other methods of outreach, such as **spam** e-mails.

- Ad agencies use a number of persuasive strategies, including the **famous-person testimonial**, the **plain-folks pitch**, the **snob appeal**, the **bandwagon effect**, the **hidden-fear appeal**, and **irritation advertising**.

- In addition, advertisers draw on the **association principle** and tell stories that convey a culture's deepest values and social norms. They also use **product placement**, or strategically placing ads or buying space in movies, TV shows, comic books, and video games so that they appear as part of a story's environment.

- Advertisements are considered **commercial speech**, and the question of whether advertisers are fully protected by the First Amendment remains controversial.

LaunchPad

Visit LaunchPad for *Media Essentials* at **launchpadworks.com** for additional learning tools:

- **REVIEW WITH LEARNINGCURVE**
  LearningCurve adaptive quizzing helps you master the concepts you need to learn from this chapter.

- **VIDEO: BLURRING THE LINES: MARKETING PROGRAMS ACROSS PLATFORMS**
  An executive for MTV explores how recent television programs blur the line between scripted and reality shows.

- **MEDIA LITERACY PRACTICE**
  This activity challenges you to develop a critical perspective and apply it to everyday encounters with communication media.

- Serious concerns exist over the impact of advertising on children and teens and on those susceptible to eating disorders, obesity, smoking, alcohol abuse, or inappropriate prescription-drug use, leading to the creation of nonprofit watchdog and advocacy organizations such as Commercial Alert.

- Advertising has helped fuel the economy while also creating a consumer society with divisions between those who can afford to buy certain products and those who cannot. It has also raised concerns about the impact of a handful of large media conglomerates controlling commercial speech.

- The enormous amount of cash required to pay for **political advertising** raises concerns about who can afford to run for office and who gets to be heard by the electorate.

- Despite these issues, without advertising, many mass media industries would not survive. Given its pervasiveness, it's important for the public to be critical consumers of advertising.

Key Terms

space brokers, p. 316
subliminal advertising, p. 319
mega-agencies, p. 320
boutique agencies, p. 320
market research, p. 322
demographics, p. 322
psychographics, p. 322
focus groups, p. 322
Values and Lifestyles (VALS), p. 322
storyboard, p. 323
viral marketing, p. 323
media buyers, p. 324
saturation advertising, p. 324
account executives, p. 325
account reviews, p. 325
spam, p. 326
ad impressions, p. 326
click-throughs, p. 326
famous-person testimonial, p. 330
plain-folks pitch, p. 330
snob appeal, p. 330
bandwagon effect, p. 330
hidden-fear appeal, p. 330
irritation advertising, p. 330
association principle, p. 330
product placement, p. 334
commercial speech, p. 335
political advertising, p. 341

Study Questions

1. What role did advertising play in transforming the United States into a consumer society?

2. What are the major divisions at most ad agencies? What is the function of each department?

3. How can companies use the power and sophistication of Internet advertising and data mining to target consumers who access the Internet on multiple devices?

4. How do the common persuasive techniques used in advertising work?

5. What are the effects of advertising on a democratic society?

Media Framing Industries

12

Public Relations and Framing the Message

350
Early History of Public Relations

353
The Evolution of Public Relations

364
Tensions between Public Relations and the Press

367
Public Relations in a Democratic Society

America's biggest sport is having major public relations problems. While the NFL continues to deal with the fallout from incidents and research findings related to concussion and chronic traumatic encephalopathy (CTE), the league has also had to react to public scrutiny from the #MeToo and Black Lives Matter movements. The NFL has often responded to bad press by downplaying the incidents or covering them up, which has led critics to call the NFL's public relations (PR) strategy a fiasco.

The first PR problem is CTE, a serious head-trauma disease afflicting a number of players and former players. After linebacker Junior Seau committed suicide in 2012, it seemed as though the NFL was committed to taking head trauma seriously. A few months after the suicide, the NFL pledged $30 million to the National Institutes of Health (NIH) toward independent CTE research led by top neuropathologists. But when one of these researchers designed a study to find CTE in living patients, the NFL moved to veto the research and withdrew the $16 million the NIH had earmarked for it.[1]

In August 2017, the NFL funded another NIH study of deceased players' brains, which found that 99 percent of NFL players' brains and 91 percent of college players' brains had CTE.[2] The NFL downplayed the damning results as

◀ San Francisco 49ers players Eli Harold and Colin Kaepernick take a knee during the national anthem to protest the oppression of black people and people of color in the United States. Kirby Lee-USA TODAY Sports/Newscom

insignificant or misleading.[3] Part of the tepid response, critics suggested, was influenced by the $1 billion concussion settlement between players and the NFL, which was being finalized around the time the new CTE study came out. The lawsuit in question alleged that the NFL had concealed the link between football and brain damage, clearing the way for payouts to retired players. The NFL's response, critics supposed, was aimed at avoiding any challenges to the settlement or new lawsuits.[4]

The NFL's most recent PR strategy was to pledge $100 million toward its Play Smart, Play Safe initiative, which funds newly engineered headgear and "medical and neuroscience research."[5] Significantly, this new research will be done in-house, not by NIH's top neuropathologists. In addition, the NFL has issued only one study—about horse jockeys and CTE—and that study was headed up by a researcher who was critical of CTE media coverage and a doctor who minimized the importance of CTE.[6]

Meanwhile, the NFL had to field stories throughout the 2017 season about numerous players who chose to publicly support the Black Lives Matter movement by kneeling, sitting, or raising their fists during the national anthem, a moment when players and spectators are expected to stand and visibly honor the American flag. In the early stages of the controversy, the NFL issued a statement: "Players are encouraged but not required to stand during the playing of the national anthem." The next year, the NFL pledged $89 million over the next seven years toward social justice causes. But before the 2018 season, the NFL reversed itself, with the owners voting to require players on the field to stand for the anthem. The owners made an even larger symbolic statement by continuing their refusal to offer a contract to quarterback Colin Kaepernick, who had initiated the protests. In February 2019, the NFL relented and settled its case with Kaepernick for an undisclosed sum.

The NFL Network was also plagued by sexual harassment and assault lawsuits from women in 2018, as the #MeToo movement came to sports television. Five former NFL players and a former NFL Network executive were suspended by three media organizations after a former network employee brought a lawsuit against them, alleging sexual harassment;[7] an NFL Network executive was forced to resign because of a stream of sexually explicit tweets;[8] and a former NFL cheerleader filed an antidiscrimination suit against the New Orleans Saints.[9] Then, about two weeks after his team won the 2019 Super Bowl, New England Patriots owner Robert Kraft was charged with two counts of soliciting prostitution. The NFL, and football itself, swings from bad PR to bad PR.

THE STORY OF THE NFL illustrates a major difference between advertising and public relations: Advertising is controlled publicity that a company or an individual buys; public relations attempts to secure favorable media publicity (which is more difficult to control) to promote a company or a client.

Public relations covers a wide array of practices, such as shaping the public image of a politician or a celebrity, establishing or repairing communication between consumers and companies, and promoting government agencies and actions, especially during wartime. Broadly defined, **public relations** refers to the total communication strategy conducted by a person, a government, or an organization attempting to reach and persuade an audience to adopt a point of view.[10] While public relations may sound very similar to advertising, which also seeks to persuade audiences, it is a different skill in a variety of ways. Advertising uses simple and fixed messages (e.g., "our appliance is the most efficient and affordable") that are transmitted directly to the public through the purchase of ads. Public relations involves more complex messages that may evolve over time (e.g., a political campaign or a long-term strategy to dispel unfavorable reports about "fatty processed foods") and that may be transmitted to the public indirectly, often through the news media.

The social and cultural impact of public relations has been immense. In its infancy, PR helped convince many American businesses of the value of nurturing the public, whose members became purchasers rather than producers of their own goods after the Industrial Revolution. PR set the tone for the corporate image-building that characterized the economic environment of the twentieth century and for the battles of organizations taking sides on today's environmental, energy, and labor issues. Perhaps PR's most significant effect, however, has been on the political process, in which individuals and organizations—on both the Right and the Left—hire spin doctors to shape their media images.

In this chapter, we examine the workings and the impact of public relations in more detail by:

- looking at the early days of public relations, including the emergence of press agents and the birth of modern PR

- considering how the PR profession has evolved in terms of the structure of public relations firms and the functions that PR practitioners perform (such as formulating messages about their clients and conveying those messages to the public)

- exploring the tensions that have arisen between public relations professionals and the press, and the causes behind those tensions

- considering the role PR plays in our democratic society by focusing on the impact of public relations on the political process in particular

LaunchPad

launchpadworks.com

Use **LearningCurve** to review concepts from this chapter.

Early History of Public Relations

Public relations traveled an interesting path in its journey toward becoming a profession. The first PR practitioners were **press agents**, people who conveyed favorable messages to the public about their clients, often by staging stunts that reporters described in newspapers. As the United States became industrialized and people began purchasing more goods and services, larger companies—impressed by press agents' power to shape public opinion—began hiring these early practitioners to further their interests. Some PR tactics proved deceitful, but when journalists and citizens complained, PR agencies began policing themselves to foster more ethical practices in the profession.

Age of the Press Agent: P. T. Barnum and Buffalo Bill

The earliest press agents excelled at **publicity**—a type of PR communication that uses various media messages to spread information and interest (or buzz) about a person, a corporation, an issue, or a policy. The most effective publicity efforts not only excited people's imagination but also helped establish enduring national values.

In the 1800s, some publicity tactics could also border on the outrageous. Consider press agent Phineas Taylor (P. T.) Barnum, who used gross exaggeration, fraudulent stories, and staged events to secure newspaper coverage for his clients, for his American Museum, and (later) for his circus, which he dubbed "The Greatest Show on Earth."

William F. Cody was another notorious publicity hound. From 1883 to 1916, Cody, who once killed buffalo for the railroads, used press agents to promote himself and his traveling show: "Buffalo Bill's Wild West and Congress of Rough Riders of the World." The show employed sharpshooter Annie Oakley and Lakota holy man Sitting Bull, whose legends were partially shaped by Cody's press agents. These agents were led by John Burke, one of the first to use an array of media channels to generate publicity. Burke promoted Cody's show through a heady mix of newspaper stories, magazine articles and ads, dime novels, theater marquees, poster art, and early films. Burke and Buffalo Bill fired up Americans' love of rugged individualism and frontier expansion—a national mythology that later showed up in books, radio programs, and Hollywood films about the American West.

▼ "Buffalo Bill's Wild West and Congress of Rough Riders of the World" show, depicted here, was internationally popular as a touring show for more than thirty years. Library of Congress Prints & Photographs Division, Reproduction number LC-USZC4-3169 (color film copy transparency) LC-USZ62-24458 (b&w film copy neg.)

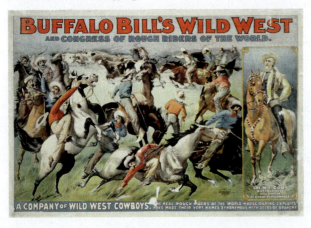

Business Adopts Press Agent Methods

The successes enjoyed by P. T. Barnum, Buffalo Bill, John Burke, and others demonstrated that publicity could not only stimulate business but also help any individual or organization (such as not-for-profit groups and government agencies) spread the word about its value and fulfill its mission. For businesses, press agentry became an important mechanism for generating profits and (in some cases) bringing in the government funding needed to achieve their mission. However, in the early days of press agents, some of the tactics used were especially deceptive.

Around 1850, for example, the railroads began hiring press agents to help them obtain federal funds, which hinged on positive public perceptions of the railroads' value. These agents' tactics included bribing reporters to write favorable news stories about the railroads. Agents also engaged in **deadheading**—giving journalists free rail passes with the tacit understanding that they would write glowing reports about traveling by rail. Finally, the larger railroads used **lobbyists**—professionals who seek to influence lawmakers' votes—to gain federal subsidies and establish policies (such as rate reductions) that made it harder for smaller regional lines to compete. Thanks to such efforts, a few large rail companies gained dominance over the industry.

Utility companies such as Chicago Edison and AT&T also used press agent strategies in the late 1800s for similar ends. Again, some of their tactics were deceptive. For instance, they, too, bought votes of key lawmakers, and they hired third-party editorial services to produce written pieces in their favor. These services sent articles touting the utilities to newspapers, produced ghostwritten articles lauding the utilities' value, and influenced textbook authors to write historical accounts that put the utilities in a positive light.[11]

Professional Public Relations Emerges

By the early 1900s, journalists began investigating and reporting on the questionable promotional practices businesses were using, which helped increase awareness of these tactics among the public. Facing a more informed citizenry, businesses were finding it harder to buy favorable press and use it to mislead people. Two PR pioneers—Ivy Ledbetter Lee and Edward Bernays—realized that public relations needed to be more professional. To that end, they ushered in new approaches that emphasized honesty, directness, and an understanding of psychology and sociology.

Ivy Ledbetter Lee: More Than One Side to Every Story

Press agent Ivy Ledbetter Lee counseled his corporate clients that honesty and directness were better PR devices than the deceptive practices of the 1800s, which had given big business a bad name. Lee opened one of the first PR firms

▶ Ivy Lee, a founding father of public relations, did innovative crisis work with John D. Rockefeller Jr., staging photo opportunities at the Ludlow mines. Bettmann/Getty Images; Rockefeller Archive Center

in the early 1900s with George Parker. Following a rail accident in late 1906, the Pennsylvania Railroad hired the firm to help downplay the resulting unfavorable publicity. Lee advised the railroad to admit its mistake, vow to do better, and let newspapers in on the story, rather than trying to cover up the accident or deny responsibility. In 1912, Lee quit the PR firm to work for the Pennsylvania Railroad.

In 1914, Lee went to work for John D. Rockefeller Jr., who by the 1880s controlled 90 percent of the nation's oil industry. Rockefeller and his Standard Oil Company already had image problems, beginning when journalists published a powerful muckraking series about his business tactics, running from 1902 to 1904. In 1913–14, strikebreakers at one of Rockefeller's mining companies and members of the state militia battled striking coal miners trying to win recognition for their union. Fifty-three workers and their family members were killed in Ludlow, Colorado. In response, the oil magnate hired Lee to contain the damaging publicity fallout. Lee immediately distributed a series of "fact sheets" to the press, telling the company's side of the story and discrediting the tactics of the United Mine Workers, who had organized the strike. Working under the premise that there were several sides to every story, Lee understood that decisions about which facts to present to the public—and which to leave out—could strongly shape public perception. Lee also brought in the press and staged photo opportunities at Rockefeller's company, which helped rehabilitate the Rockefeller family's image. While certainly effective, his efforts earned him the nickname "Poison Ivy" Lee from his enemies.

Edward Bernays: Public Relations Counselor

Edward Bernays was the first person to apply the findings of psychology and sociology to the public relations profession. Bernays, who opened his own PR office in 1919, described the shaping of public opinion through PR as the "engineering of consent." That is, he believed that skilled experts, leaders, and PR professionals could shape messages and ideas in ways people could rally behind.[12]

Indeed, Bernays referred to himself as a "public relations counselor" rather than a "publicity agent." Over the years, his client list included such big-name companies as the American Tobacco Company, which is now R. J. Reynolds Tobacco (see "Media Literacy Case Study: The Invisible Hand of PR" on pages 354–355); General Electric; and General Motors. Bernays also worked for the Committee on Public Information during World War I. In that role, he developed propaganda that supported the U.S. entry into the war and promoted the image of President Woodrow Wilson as a peacemaker.

Bernays also demonstrated that women could work in the PR profession. His business partner and later wife, Doris Fleischman, collaborated with him on many of his campaigns as a researcher and coauthor. PR later became one of the few professions accessible to women who chose to work outside the home. Today, more than 60 percent of PR professionals are women.

The Evolution of Public Relations

The Public Relations Society of America (PRSA) offers this simple and useful definition of PR: "Public relations is a strategic communication process that builds mutually beneficial relationships between organizations and their publics." As the PR profession evolved, two major types of public relations organizations developed to carry out this mutual communication process: PR agencies, whose sole job is to provide outside clients with PR services, and in-house PR staffs, which operate within companies or organizations. Practitioners in both of these settings began excelling at specific functions, such as researching target audiences and formulating messages conveyed to them.

▲ Edward Bernays and his business partner and wife, Doris Fleischman, creatively influenced public opinion. Bettmann/Getty Images

As media has developed, so has public relations. From print and film to radio and television, public relations practitioners were quick to adapt their techniques to make use of the media that would attract the most people. With the rise of the Internet, practitioners have faced a whole host of new tools and challenges.

Media Literacy

CASE STUDY

The Invisible Hand of PR

When you hear the phrase "Torches of Freedom," what type of image comes to mind? The Statue of Liberty? A candlelight vigil at the nation's capital? A Lucky Strike cigarette? If this last option is what pops into your head, you may have one of the earliest and most successful PR campaigns of all time to thank.

Back in the early part of the twentieth century, it was deemed unsavory—or even illegal in some places—for women to smoke in public. In an effort to target this untapped market, the owner of Lucky Strike and other cigarette brands hired Edward Bernays to make smoking socially acceptable for women. In April 1929, a woman and several friends stepped into an Easter Parade, lit cigarettes, and declared to reporters—whom Bernays had tipped off ahead of time—that smoking was part of the fight for women's rights. The stunt was front-page news in papers from coast to coast, even garnering an article with photos in the *New York Times*, and cigarettes were ultimately dubbed "torches of freedom."[1] In addition, Bernays later worked with the fashion industry to declare green the "in-style" color of the season, so it would match the Lucky Strike packaging.

One of the most notable things about Bernays's approach to this campaign—and something that is still characteristic of many public relations practitioners and campaigns today—is how invisible his involvement was to everyday people. John Stauber, founder of the Center for Media and Democracy (CMD) and its publication *PRWatch*, has described the PR industry as "a huge, invisible industry . . . that's really only available to wealthy individuals, large multinational corporations, politicians

▲ Edward Bernays worked on behalf of the American Tobacco Company to make smoking socially acceptable for women. Later, Bernays was asked to change public attitudes toward the color green, as women were apparently not buying Lucky Strike cigarettes because the forest green package clashed with their wardrobes. In response, Bernays and Doris Fleischman organized green fashion shows and sold the idea of a new trend in green to the press. By 1934, green had become the fashion color of the season. Image Courtesy of The Advertising Archives

> ▶ **Web Clip**
>
> **YouTube.com** has many videos related to PR. For example, search for "Edward Bernays 1: Torches of Freedom" by Stuff They Don't Want You to Know—HowStuffWorks. Bernays explored the idea that people's beliefs and opinions could be influenced without them being aware of that influence. Do you think that *you* have ever been influenced without your knowledge? Why or why not?
>
>

354

and government agencies."[2] Most major companies, organizations, politicians, and celebrities today use professional public relations services, but the public rarely hears about what these organizations actually do, not to mention how they influence our own perceptions of products and people. While most people have heard of A-list movie stars, prominent politicians, and major corporations such as McDonalds and Apple, few would recognize the name of public relations agencies, such as Edelman or FleishmanHillard, who might be carefully crafting the public images of those people and corporations behind the scenes.

In an interesting bit of connection to the Lucky Strike campaign, some of the most notable public relations campaigns of 2018 also featured major corporate brands connecting their image with equality for women. For example, airline easyJet launched a campaign aimed at promoting women becoming airline pilots, and Burger King offered a free Whopper (renamed the "WhoppHER") to any woman in Saudi Arabia who visited the drive-up window after the country passed a law allowing women to drive.

Considering campaigns like these, do you think Stauber is correct that the PR industry is doing billions of dollars' worth of work at changing our thoughts and attitudes, and that this is happening without us knowing who is doing it—or perhaps even realizing that it is happening to begin with? Are there other modern equivalents to the "torches of freedom" PR campaign?

APPLYING THE CRITICAL PROCESS

DESCRIPTION Test the so-called invisibility of the PR industry by seeing how often, and in what way, PR firms are discussed in the print media. Using LexisNexis, search U.S. newspapers—over the last six months—for any mention of three prominent PR firms: Edelman, Weber Shandwick, and FleishmanHillard.

ANALYSIS What patterns emerge from the search? Possible patterns may have to do with personnel: Someone was hired or fired. Or these personnel-related articles may reveal connections between politicians or corporations and the PR industry. What specific PR campaigns are discussed or articles written that quote "experts" who work for Edelman, Weber Shandwick, or FleishmanHillard?

INTERPRETATION What do these patterns tell you about how the news media covers the PR industry? Was the coverage favorable? Was it critical or analytical? Was the industry itself, and its influencing strategies, visible in your search?

EVALUATION PR firms have enormous power when it comes to influencing the public image of corporations, government bodies, and public policy initiatives in the United States and abroad. Do your findings support the idea that there is an "invisible hand of PR"? If so, what might this mean for a healthy democracy?

ENGAGEMENT Visit the Center for Media and Democracy's website (prwatch.org) and begin to learn about the unseen operations of the public relations industry. (You can also visit SpinWatch.org for similar critical analyses of PR in the United Kingdom.) Follow the CMD's Twitter feed. Visit the organization's wiki site, SourceWatch (sourcewatch.org), and if you can, do some research of your own on PR and contribute an entry.

PR Agencies and In-House PR Staffs

As of early 2019, LinkedIn maintained a list of more than ten thousand public relations companies. Many of the largest PR companies are owned by, or are affiliated with, multinational communications holding companies, such as WPP, Omnicom, and Interpublic (see Table 12.1). Other PR firms are independent. These companies tend to be smaller than the conglomerate-owned ones and to have just local or regional operations. New York– and Chicago–based Edelman, the largest independent PR agency, is an exception, boasting global operations and clients around the world.

Many corporations, professional organizations, and nonprofit entities retain PR agencies to provide a range of services. Large organizations of all types—particularly in the manufacturing and service industries—often have their own in-house PR staffs as well. These departments handle numerous tasks, such as writing press releases, managing journalists' requests for interviews with company personnel, staging special events, updating web and social media sites, and dealing with internal and external publics.

A Closer Look at Public Relations Functions

Regardless of whether they work at a PR agency or on staff at an organization's in-house PR department, public relations professionals pay careful attention to the needs of their clients and to the perspectives of their targeted audiences. They provide a multitude of services, including developing publicity campaigns and formulating messages about what their clients are doing in such areas as government relations, community outreach, industry relations, diversity initiatives, and product or service development.

Some PR professionals also craft **propaganda**. This is communication that is presented as advertising or publicity and that is intended to gain (or undermine) public support for a special issue, program, or policy—such as a nation's

TABLE 12.1 // THE TOP 5 PUBLIC RELATIONS FIRMS, 2017 (BY WORLDWIDE REVENUE IN MILLIONS OF U.S. DOLLARS)

Rank	Agency	Parent Firm	Headquarters	Revenue
1	Edelman	Independent	Chicago & New York	$894
2	Weber Shandwick	Interpublic	New York	$719
3	Burson Cohn & Wolfe	WPP	New York	$670
4	FleishmanHillard	Omnicom	St. Louis	$598
5	Ketchum	Omnicom	New York	$510

Data from: "Public Relations Worldwide," *Advertising Age, April 30, 2018*, p. 19.

war effort (see "The Digital Turn Case Study: Military PR in the Digital Age" on page 358). Because the term *propaganda* carries with it connotations of deception and manipulation, it is generally considered different from persuasion.

In addition, PR practitioners might work to produce employee newsletters, manage client trade shows and conferences, conduct historical tours, appear on news programs, organize damage control after negative publicity, or analyze complex issues and trends affecting a client's future.

Research: Formulating the Message

An essential practice of the PR profession is doing research. Like advertising, PR makes use of mail, telephone, and Internet surveys; focus groups; and social media analytics tools—such as Google Analytics, Klear, Keyhole, Sprout Social, and Twitter Analytics—to get a fix on an audience's perceptions of an issue, a policy, a program, or a client's image. This research also helps PR firms focus their campaign messages.

Communication: Conveying the Message

Once a PR group has formulated a message, it conveys that message through a variety of channels. With advances in digital technology, these channels have become predominantly Internet based in recent years. **Press releases**, or news releases, are announcements written in the style of news reports that provide new information about an individual, a company, or an organization, now typically issued via e-mail. In issuing press releases, PR agents hope that journalists will pick up the information and transform it into news reports about the agents' clients. Twitter has also become a popular format for releasing information to the news media. More than half of journalists follow Twitter to get news tips. A tweet can be just as successful as a complete press release in gaining news media coverage.

Since the introduction of portable video equipment in the 1970s, PR agencies and departments have also been issuing **video news releases (VNRs)**—thirty- to ninety-second visual press releases designed to mimic the style of a broadcast news report. Although networks and large TV news stations do not usually broadcast VNRs, news stations in small TV markets regularly use

▲ World War II was a time when the U.S. government used propaganda and other PR strategies to drum up support for the war. One of the most iconic posters at the time asked women to join the workforce. MPI/Getty Images

The Digital Turn

CASE STUDY

Military PR in the Digital Age

Public relations has a long connection with the military and wartime communication. After all, one of the founders of modern public relations, Edward Bernays, got his start developing propaganda promoting U.S. military involvement in World War I. Gaining and keeping public support has long been a key to any military endeavor, and public relations and wartime propaganda have played a major role in shaping public opinion.

But as media technology has changed over the last century, so have the PR efforts of governments looking for support for various wars. By the time the United States invaded Afghanistan and Iraq in 2002 and 2003, convergence had begun to alter the military PR game. Video games, for example, have become an important PR tool for the American military. The U.S. Army funded the creation of a downloadable game called *America's Army*, which promotes the organization with young gamers, and the army now fields eSports teams that compete together while recruiting for the organization.[1]

Social media has also had a significant impact. On the positive side, troops and their families use social media to stay in touch with each other, an important way to boost morale. Some of these messages home have even gone viral, including a 2010 YouTube video of soldiers in Afghanistan blowing off steam by dancing to a Lady Gaga song. Military bloggers also helped connect the home front with the front lines in ways that carried more authenticity than any press release.

On the other hand, some of the posts shared by soldiers on social media have had the opposite effect. From pictures and videos of inappropriate or dishonorable behavior while in uniform (including a video of U.S. Marines urinating on Taliban corpses in Afghanistan) to sites that make crude and threatening posts about female soldiers, the military has struggled to come up with a useful and enforceable social media policy. Complicating the task even further are social media sites by former military members or civilians, whom the Department of Defense has no control over or ability to punish.[2]

Still another dimension to converged military public relations is that it's a tool that anyone can use—including our enemies. Terrorist groups have taken advantage of the global reach of the Internet to post videos ranging from propaganda statements to executions. This new reality of waging war after the digital turn was the subject of a 2009 report published by the U.S. Army War College. The report argues that "terrorist attacks ought to be understood as consciously crafted *media events*": "Their true target is not that which is blown up . . . that is merely a stage prop. The goal, after all, is to have a psychological effect (to terrorize), and it isn't possible to have such an effect on the dead."[3]

The U.S. military's public relations effort, then, must contend with the way converged and viral media make its job trickier and more difficult to control. Part of fighting a war in an era of converged media involves recognizing that public perceptions matter—and because of this, images matter. And these images are more accessible and easier to disseminate than ever before.

Web Clip

YouTube.com has an array of videos of soldiers dancing to popular songs. For example, search for "Telephone Remake" posted by malibumelcher. How might videos like this one affect a viewer's thoughts about war and the military?

material from these releases—and in the case of stations owned by Sinclair Broadcasting, they may be required to air political VNRs supporting their corporate owner's ideology. As with press releases, VNRs give PR firms some control over what constitutes "news" and a chance to influence the public's opinion about an issue.

PR firms can also bring attention to nonprofits by creating **public service announcements (PSAs)**: usually fifteen- to sixty-second audio or video reports that promote government programs, educational projects, volunteer agencies, or social reform.

Managing Media Relations

Some PR practitioners specialize in media relations. These specialists promote a client or an organization by securing publicity or favorable coverage in the various news media. In an in-house PR department, media-relations specialists will speak on behalf of their organization or direct reporters to experts inside and outside the company who can provide information about whatever topic the reporter is writing about.

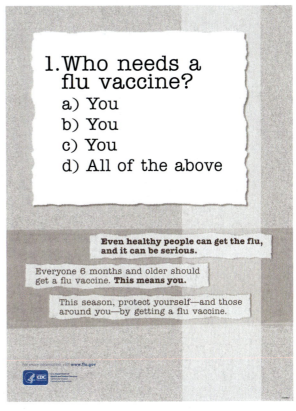

▲ Public service announcements also include print and web components (not just TV and radio ads). CDC/Centers for Disease Control

Media-relations specialists may also recommend advertising to their clients when it seems that ads would help focus a complex issue or enhance a client's image. In addition, they cultivate connections with editors, reporters, freelance writers, and broadcast news directors to ensure that their press releases or VNRs are favorably received.

If a client company has had some negative publicity (for example, one of its products has been shown to be defective or dangerous, or a viral video on the Internet has spread disinformation about the company), media-relations specialists perform damage control or crisis management. In fact, during a crisis, these specialists might be the sole source of information about the situation for the public. How PR professionals perform this part of their job can make or break an organization. The handling of the 2010 BP oil rig explosion and Tylenol tampering deaths in the 1980s offer two contrasting examples.

BP's *Deepwater Horizon* oil rig exploded on April 10, 2010, killing eleven workers. The oil gushed from the ocean floor for months, spreading into a vast area of the Gulf of Mexico and killing wildlife. BP's many public relations missteps included its multiple underestimations of the amount of oil leaking, the chairman's reference to the "small people" of the Gulf region, the CEO's wish that he could "get his life back," and the CEO's attendance at an elite yacht race in England even as the oil leak persisted. BP tried to salvage its reputation by vowing to clean up the damaged areas, establishing a fund to reimburse those economically affected by the spill, and creating a campaign of TV commercials to communicate its efforts. Nevertheless, harsh criticism persisted, and BP's ads were overwhelmed by online parodies and satires of its efforts. In 2016, claims against BP were resolved in a federal court settlement of more than $20 billion, the largest civil penalty for an environmental disaster. Projects to restore the Gulf Coast from Texas to Florida remain in progress.

A decidedly different approach was taken in the 1982 tragedy involving Tylenol pain-relief capsules. Seven people in the Chicago area died after consuming capsules that someone had laced with poison. The parent company, Johnson & Johnson, and its PR representatives discussed whether to pull all Tylenol capsules from store shelves. Some participants in these discussions worried that this move might send the message that corporations could be intimidated by a single deranged person. Nevertheless, Johnson & Johnson's chairman and the company's PR agency, Burson-Marsteller (now Burson Cohn & Wolfe), opted to fully disclose the tragedy to the media and to immediately recall all Tylenol capsules across the nation. The recall cost the company an estimated $100 million and cut its market share in half.

Burson-Marsteller tracked public opinion about the crisis and about its client nightly through telephone surveys. It also organized satellite press conferences

▶ Starbucks suffered a major PR crisis in April 2018 after a manager at a Philadelphia store called the police on two African American men waiting for a business meeting who had not yet ordered anything. A video of the men being arrested went viral, and Starbucks faced an irate public. The company's damage control campaign included apologies from top management, meetings with the two men, and the closing of eight thousand Starbucks locations for a day of mandatory anti-bias training. Christopher Martin

to debrief the news media. In addition, it set up emergency phone lines to take calls from consumers and health-care providers who had questions about the crisis. When the company reintroduced Tylenol three months later, it did so with tamper-resistant bottles that almost every major drug manufacturer soon copied. According to Burson-Marsteller, which received PRSA awards for its handling of the crisis, the public thought Johnson & Johnson had responded admirably to the situation and did not hold Tylenol responsible for the deaths. In fewer than three years, Tylenol had recaptured its dominant share of the market.

Coordinating Special Events and Pseudo-Events

Another public relations practice involves coordinating *special events* to raise the profile of corporate, organizational, or government clients. Through such events, a corporate sponsor aligns itself with a cause or an organization that has positive stature among the public. For example, John Hancock Financial has been the primary sponsor of the Boston Marathon since 1986 and provides the race's prize money.

In contrast to a special event, a **pseudo-event** is any circumstance created for the sole purpose of gaining coverage in the media. Pseudo-events may take the form of press conferences, TV and radio talk-show appearances, or any other staged activity aimed at drawing public attention and media coverage. Clients and sometimes paid performers participate in these events, and their success is strongly determined by how much media attention the event attracts. For example, during the 1960s, antiwar and Civil Rights activists staged protest events only if news media were assembled.

Fostering Positive Community and Consumer Relations

Another responsibility of PR practitioners is to sustain goodwill between their clients and the public. Many public relations professionals define "the public" as consisting of two distinct audiences: communities and consumers. Thus, they carefully manage relations with both groups.

PR specialists let the public know that their clients are valuable members of the communities in which they

▼The intense media coverage at awards shows drums up ad revenue for broadcasts and seemingly endless magazine coverage. Can we consider the Oscars or Golden Globes a pseudo-event? Frazer Harrison/Getty Images

operate by designing opportunities for them to demonstrate that they are good citizens. For example, they arrange for client firms to participate in community activities, such as hosting plant tours and open houses, making donations to national and local charities, participating in local parades and festivals, and allowing employees to take part in community fund-raising drives for good causes.

PR strategists also strive to show that their clients care about their customers. For example, a PR campaign might send the message that the business has established product-safety guarantees, or that it will answer all calls and mail from customers promptly. These efforts result in satisfied customers, which translates into repeat business and new business as customers spread the word about their positive experiences with the organization.

Cultivating Government Relations

PR groups working for or in corporations also cultivate connections with the government agencies that have some say in how companies operate in a particular community, state, or nation. Through such connections, these groups can monitor the regulatory environment and determine new laws' potential implications for the organizations they represent. For example, a new regulation might require companies to provide more comprehensive reporting on their environmental safety practices, which would represent an added responsibility.

Government PR specialists monitor new and existing legislation, look for opportunities to generate favorable publicity, and write press releases and direct-mail letters to inform the public about the pros and cons of new regulations. In many industries, government relations has evolved into **lobbying**: the process of trying to influence lawmakers to support legislation that would serve an organization's or industry's best interests. In seeking favorable legislation, some lobbyists contact government officials on a daily basis. In Washington, D.C., alone, there are more than eleven thousand registered lobbyists, and lobbying expenditures targeting the federal government amounted to $3.42 billion in 2018 (see Figure 12.1). Over the last ten years, lobbying spending has held fairly steady, after more than doubling from 1998 to 2008.[13]

The billions of dollars that lobbyists inject into the political process—treating lawmakers to special events and making campaign contributions in return for legislation that accommodates their clients' interests—is viewed by many as unethical. Another unethical practice is **astroturf lobbying**, which consists of phony grassroots public affairs campaigns engineered by unscrupulous public relations firms. Through this type of lobbying, PR firms deploy blogs, social media campaigns, massive phone banks, and computerized mailing lists to drum up support and create the impression that millions of citizens back their client's side of an issue—even if the number is much lower.

FIGURE 12.1 // TOTAL LOBBYING SPENDING AND NUMBER OF LOBBYISTS* (2000–2018)

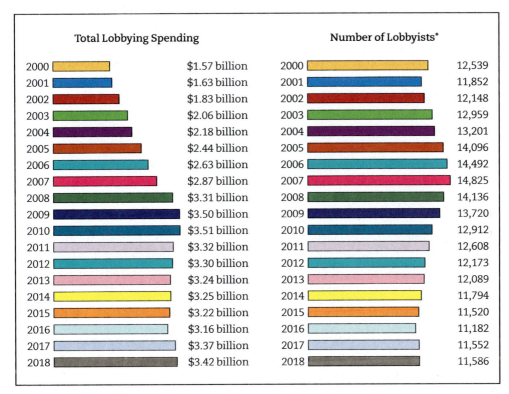

Year	Total Lobbying Spending	Number of Lobbyists*
2000	$1.57 billion	12,539
2001	$1.63 billion	11,852
2002	$1.83 billion	12,148
2003	$2.06 billion	12,959
2004	$2.18 billion	13,201
2005	$2.44 billion	14,096
2006	$2.63 billion	14,492
2007	$2.87 billion	14,825
2008	$3.31 billion	14,136
2009	$3.50 billion	13,720
2010	$3.51 billion	12,912
2011	$3.32 billion	12,608
2012	$3.30 billion	12,173
2013	$3.24 billion	12,089
2014	$3.25 billion	11,794
2015	$3.22 billion	11,520
2016	$3.16 billion	11,182
2017	$3.37 billion	11,552
2018	$3.42 billion	11,586

Note: Figures are calculations by the Center for Responsive Politics based on data from the Senate Office of Public Records, accessed March 4, 2019, www.opensecrets.org/lobby.
*The number of unique registered lobbyists who have actively lobbied.

Just as corporations use PR to manage government relations, some governments have used PR to manage their image in the public's mind. For example, following the September 11, 2001, terrorist attacks on the United States, the Saudi Arabian government hired the PR firm Qorvis Communications to help repair its image with American citizens after it was revealed that many of the 9/11 terrorists were from Saudi Arabia.[14]

Public Relations in the Internet Age

Historically, public relations practitioners have tried to earn news media coverage (as opposed to buying advertising) to communicate their clients' messages to the public. Although that is still true, the Internet, with its instant accessibility, offers public relations professionals a number of new routes for communicating with the public.

A company's or an organization's website has become the home base of public relations efforts. Companies and organizations can upload and maintain their media kits (including press releases, VNRs, images, executive bios, and organizational profiles), giving the traditional news media access to the information at any time. And because everyone can access these corporate websites, the barriers between the organization and the groups that PR professionals ultimately want to reach have been broken down.

The web also enables PR professionals to have their clients interact with audiences on a more personal, direct basis through social media tools like Facebook, Twitter, YouTube, Instagram, Wikipedia, and blogs. Now people can be "friends" and "followers" of companies and organizations. Corporate executives can share their professional and personal observations and seem downright chummy through a blog (e.g., *The Counterintuitive CEO* blog by George Colony, the CEO of Forrester Research). Executives, celebrities, and politicians can seem more accessible and personable through a Twitter feed. But social media's immediacy can also be a problem, especially for those who send messages into the public sphere without considering the ramifications.

Another concern about social media is that sometimes such communications appear without complete disclosure, which is an unethical practice. For example, some PR firms have edited Wikipedia entries for their clients' benefit, a practice Wikipedia founder Jimmy Wales has repudiated as a conflict of interest. A growing number of companies also compensate bloggers to subtly promote their products, unbeknownst to most readers. Public relations firms and marketers are particularly keen on working with "mom bloggers," who appear to be independent voices in discussions about consumer products but may receive gifts in exchange for their opinions. In 2009, the Federal Trade Commission instituted new rules requiring online product endorsers to disclose their connections to companies.

Tensions between Public Relations and the Press

The relationship between PR and the press has long been antagonistic. This tension has several sources, including the complex interdependence of the two professions as well as the press's skepticism about PR practices. Some of the press's complaints about PR have led public relations practitioners to take steps to enhance their profession's image.

Elements of Interdependence

Journalists have historically viewed themselves as independent professionals providing a public service: gathering and delivering the facts about current events to the public. Some have accused PR professionals of distorting the facts to serve their clients' interests. Yet journalists rely heavily on public relations practitioners to provide the information used in creating news reports. Many editors, for instance, admit that more than half of their story ideas each day originate from PR work, such as press releases. In the face of newspaper staff cutbacks and television's growing need to cover local news events, professionals in the news media need PR story ideas more than ever. This doesn't sit comfortably with some journalists.

As another example of the two professions' interdependence, PR firms often raid news media's workforces for new talent. Because most press releases are written in the style of news reports, the PR profession has always sought skilled writers who are well connected to sources and knowledgeable about the news business. But although many reporters move into the PR profession, few public relations practitioners—especially those who started their careers as journalists—move back into journalism.

PR practitioners, for their part, maintain that they make reporters' jobs easier—supplying the kinds of information reporters used to gather themselves. Some members of the news media criticize their own ranks for being lazy. Others, grateful for the help, have hesitated to criticize a particular PR firm's clients—which brings up questions of journalistic ethics.

▲ The manipulation of scientific facts by "experts" trying to promote a specific agenda is addressed in a series of books by Sheldon Rampton and John Stauber.

Journalists' Skepticism about PR Practices

In addition to the uncomfortable interdependence characterizing the journalism and PR professions, several specific complaints about PR from journalists have heightened the tension between the two groups. Specifically, some journalists maintain that PR professionals undermine the facts and block reporters' access to information. Journalism's most prevalent criticism of public relations is that it counters the truths reporters seek to bring to the public by selectively choosing which facts to communicate or by delivering deceptive information. To be sure, outright deception is unethical, and the PR profession has worked to eradicate it in its own ranks. But deciding which facts to present is something that journalists do, too. After all, a reporter cannot say everything about a particular event, so he or she must choose which information to include and which to leave out. Journalists have also accused PR professionals of blocking the press's access to business leaders, political figures, and other newsworthy people. This strategy, reporters explain, attempts to manipulate reporters by giving exclusives to those most likely to write a favorable story, or cutting off a reporter's access to a newsworthy client if the reporter has written unfavorably about that person.

launchpadworks.com

Give and Take: Public Relations and Journalism

This video debates the relationship between public relations and journalism.

Discussion: Are the similarities between public relations and journalism practices a good thing for the public? Why or why not?

Others dislike the PR field's tendency to present publicity as news, claiming that this practice takes media space and time away from organizations and individuals who do not have the money or sophistication required to attract the public eye. These critics also complain that by presenting client information in a journalistic context, PR gains credibility for its clients that the purchase of advertising does not offer.

The friction between some political PR professionals and journalists escalated early in President Trump's administration when one spokesperson greatly exaggerated crowd sizes at the presidential swearing-in, and another spokesperson defended the lie by calling it "alternative facts." The suggestion that "alternative facts" are a legitimate source of truth did not sit well with journalists or with the Public Relations Society of America (PRSA), which issued the following statement in early 2017: "PRSA strongly objects to any effort to deliberately misrepresent information. Honest, ethical professionals never spin, mislead or alter facts."[15] PRSA chair Jane Dvorak also wrote on Twitter: "We can't stand by & allow others to imply these unethical behaviors apply to #PR pros. It diminishes ALL of us. #ethicsmatter."[16]

Shaping PR's Image

Questionable PR moves in the past and journalism's hostility toward PR prompted some public relations practitioners to direct their skills toward improving their profession's image. In 1948, the PR industry formed the PRSA, its own professional organization. The PRSA functions as an internal watchdog group that accredits PR agents and firms, maintains a code of ethics, and probes its own practices, especially those pertaining to its influence on the news media. In addition to the PRSA, independent organizations devoted to uncovering shady or unethical public relations activities publish their findings in periodicals like *PRWeek* and *PR Watch*. In particular, the Center for Media and Democracy's PR Watch seeks to serve the public by discussing and investigating PR practices. Indeed, ethical issues have become a major focus of the PR profession (see Table 12.2).

PR practitioners have also begun using different language—such as *strategic communication*, *institutional relations*, *corporate communications*, *crisis communications*, and *news and information services*—to describe what they do. Their hope is that the new language will signal a more ethically responsible industry. Public relations' best strategy, however, may be to point out the shortcomings of the journalism profession itself. Journalism organizations only occasionally examine their own practices, and journalists have their own vulnerability to manipulation by public relations. Thus, by not publicly revealing PR's strategies to influence their news stories, many journalists have allowed PR professionals to interpret "facts" to their clients' advantage.

TABLE 12.2 // PUBLIC RELATIONS SOCIETY OF AMERICA ETHICS CODE

In 2000, the PRSA approved a completely revised Code of Ethics, which included core principles, guidelines, and examples of improper conduct. Here is an excerpt from the Code.

PRSA MEMBER STATEMENT OF PROFESSIONAL VALUES

This statement presents the core values of PRSA members and, more broadly, of the public relations profession. These values provide the foundation for the Member Code of Ethics and set the industry standard for the professional practice of public relations. These values are the fundamental beliefs that guide our behaviors and decision-making process. We believe our professional values are vital to the integrity of the profession as a whole.

ADVOCACY

We serve the public interest by acting as responsible advocates for those we represent. We provide a voice in the marketplace of ideas, facts, and viewpoints to aid informed public debate.

HONESTY

We adhere to the highest standards of accuracy and truth in advancing the interests of those we represent and in communicating with the public.

EXPERTISE

We acquire and responsibly use specialized knowledge and experience. We advance the profession through continued professional development, research, and education. We build mutual understanding, credibility, and relationships among a wide array of institutions and audiences.

LOYALTY

We are faithful to those we represent, while honoring our obligation to serve the public interest.

FAIRNESS

We deal fairly with clients, employers, competitors, peers, vendors, the media, and the general public. We respect all opinions and support the right of free expression.

Data from: PRSA Code of Ethics at www.prsa.org.

Note: Adherence to the PRSA Code of Ethics is voluntary; there is no enforcement mechanism.

Public Relations in a Democratic Society

PR's most significant impact on our democracy may be its involvement in the political process, especially when organizations hire public relations specialists to favorably shape or reshape a candidate's image. As with military propaganda (see also "The Digital Turn Case Study: Military PR in the Digital Age" on page 358), the history of modern public relations goes hand in hand with political campaigns. In fact, Edward Bernays, who literally wrote the book on propaganda in 1928, is believed to have staged the first presidential publicity stunt: a pancake breakfast for Calvin Coolidge with vaudevillian performers.

The need to handle a candidate's image has become increasingly important, as technology has allowed images of the candidates to be broadcast into America's living rooms. In 1952, Dwight D. Eisenhower became the first presidential candidate to hire a marketing agency to produce his "Eisenhower Answers America" television commercials, whereas John F. Kennedy set the bar for future presidential candidates with his ease and charisma on screen.[17]

By the end of the twentieth century, no president or major presidential candidate could exist without an immense PR effort. Sometimes that effort takes the shape of a well-crafted traditional PR push, as with the presidential campaign run by David Axelrod in 2008 that put Barack Obama in the White House. Other times, as in the case of Donald Trump's successful 2016 presidential campaign, it involves leveraging social media and a larger-than-life media personality into billions of dollars' worth of media coverage. Trump's social media tool of choice has been his Twitter account, which he and his PR team used to obtain publicity and influence the stories that were covered by the news media throughout the campaign and into his presidency.

Political public relations efforts don't end after an election, however. PR is in play when candidates take office, govern, or participate in or react to political movements—like the Tea Party or Occupy Wall Street. Many journalism outlets cover the news in permanent twenty-four-hour cycles, so PR agencies must stay involved with political, social, and media processes.

In addition, as discussed earlier in the chapter, the role of public relations efforts and lobbying is about more than presidential candidates and other politicians. From railroad companies looking for money from federal, state,

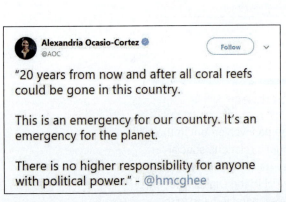
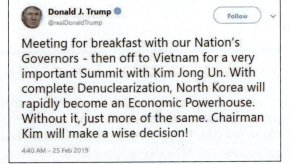

▲ Politicians across the political spectrum, including Representative Alexandria Ocasio-Cortez and President Donald Trump, use tools like Twitter to stay in touch with the public, disseminate their views, and promote the issues that are important to them.

and local governments to the explosion in the lobbying profession (see Figure 12.1), outside groups wanting to influence the government's actions have an enormous and not always easy-to-understand impact on how our democracy functions.

Though public relations often provides political information and story ideas, the PR profession bears only part of the responsibility for "spun" news; after all, it is the job of a PR agency to get favorable news coverage for the individual or group it represents. PR professionals to some extent police their own ranks for unethical or irresponsible practices, but the news media should also monitor the public relations industry, as they do other government and business activities. Journalism also needs to be more conscious of how its own practices play into the hands of spin strategies. As a positive example of change on this front, many major newspapers and TV networks now offer regular assessments of the facts and falsehoods contained in political advertising. Such media vigilance should be on behalf of citizens, who are entitled to robust, well-rounded debates on important social and political issues.

Like advertising and other forms of commercial speech, PR campaigns that result in free media exposure raise a number of questions regarding democracy and the expression of ideas. Large companies and PR agencies, like well-financed politicians, have money to invest in figuring out how to obtain favorable publicity. The question is not how to prevent that but how to ensure that other voices—those less well financed and less commercial—also receive an adequate hearing. To that end, journalists need to become less willing conduits in the distribution of publicity. PR agencies, for their part, need to show clients that participating as responsible citizens in the democratic process can serve them well and enhance their image. But in the end, all citizens bear the responsibility of understanding that the public relations industry surrounds us, regardless of what sides of issues we favor. It is a part of the media experience and, as such, part of our daily lives. Therefore, media literacy must also include awareness and knowledge of PR and all the ways it can affect us.

CHAPTER ESSENTIALS

Review

- **Public relations** refers to the total communication strategy conducted by a person, a government, or an organization attempting to reach and persuade an audience to adopt a point of view. The first PR practitioners were **press agents**, who focused on **publicity**.

- In the early days of press agents, some of the tactics used were deceptive. Agents bribed journalists to write favorable stories and engaged in **deadheading**, or giving reporters free rail passes.

- Big companies began using **lobbyists**, professionals who seek to influence lawmakers' votes—a practice that continues to this day.

- By the early 1900s, journalists began investigating some of the questionable PR practices being used, precipitating the professionalization of public relations. This effort was spearheaded by PR pioneers Ivy Ledbetter Lee and Edward Bernays.

- As the PR profession grew, two major types of public relations organizations took shape: PR agencies and in-house PR staffs.

- Many large PR agencies are owned by or affiliated with multinational holding companies, such as WPP, Omnicom, and Interpublic. Other firms are independent, such as Edelman.

- Both PR agencies and in-house PR staffs have many functions. They sometimes craft **propaganda**, and they research, formulate, and issue messages on behalf of clients, often via **press releases**, **video news releases (VNRs)**, or **public service announcements (PSAs)**.

- Some PR practitioners manage media relations, which includes responding to negative images or crisis situations. PR agents may also coordinate special events and staged **pseudo-events** in an effort to raise the profile of corporate, organizational, or business clients.

- PR practitioners foster positive community and consumer relations and cultivate government relations, which is sometimes accomplished via **lobbying**. **Astroturf lobbying** is a kind of lobbying that consists of phony grassroots public affairs campaigns engineered by unscrupulous PR firms.

- The tense relationship between public relations and the press consists of a complex interdependence of the two professions as well as

LaunchPad

Visit LaunchPad for *Media Essentials* at **launchpadworks.com** for additional learning tools:

- **REVIEW WITH LEARNINGCURVE**
  LearningCurve adaptive quizzing helps you master the concepts you need to learn from this chapter.

- **VIDEO: GOING VIRAL: POLITICAL CAMPAIGNS AND VIDEO**
  Online video has changed political campaigning forever. In this video, Peggy Miles of Intervox Communications discusses how politicians use the Internet to reach out to voters.

- **MEDIA LITERACY PRACTICE**
  This activity challenges you to develop a critical perspective and apply it to everyday encounters with communication media.

journalists' skepticism about PR practices. PR practitioners maintain that they make journalists' jobs easier by supplying stories and information, whereas journalists argue that PR agents selectively choose which facts to bring forward. Interestingly, many PR practitioners are former journalists.

- The industry formed its own professional organization, the Public Relations Society of America (PRSA), in 1948, which functions as a watchdog group.

- PR's impact on the political process is significant, as many organizations hire public relations specialists to shape or reshape a candidate's image.

- The fact that most affluent people and corporations can afford the most media exposure through PR raises questions about whether this restricts the expression of ideas from other, less affluent sources.

Study Questions

1. Who were the individuals who conducted the earliest type of public relations in the nineteenth century? How did they contribute to the development of modern public relations in the twentieth century?

2. What are the two organizational structures for a PR firm? What are some of the ways these structures conduct business for their clients?

3. Explain the antagonism between journalism and public relations. Can and should the often-hostile relationship between the two be mended? Why or why not?

4. In what ways does the profession of public relations serve the process of election campaigns? In what ways can it impede such campaigns?

Key Terms

public relations, p. 349
press agents, p. 350
publicity, p. 350
deadheading, p. 351
lobbyists, p. 351
propaganda, p. 356
press releases, p. 357
video news releases (VNRs), p. 357
public service announcements (PSAs), p. 359
pseudo-event, p. 361
lobbying, p. 362
astroturf lobbying, p. 362

Media Expressions

13

Legal Controls and Freedom of Expression

376
The Origins of Free Expression and a Free Press

388
Film and the First Amendment

391
The First Amendment, Broadcasting, and the Internet

396
The First Amendment in a Democratic Society

Politicians and their constituents can talk, but money as speech speaks much louder. Aspects of our present political system amount to a legal pay-to-play system in which the wealthiest can leverage indirect influence over elections (manipulating issues by buying lots of advertising) and more direct influence over legislation (manipulating politicians who desperately want money to pay for campaign advertising).[1] There is plenty of evidence that a majority of Americans dislike this system. For example, a 2018 survey found that 77 percent of Americans think we should limit money flowing from individuals and groups into political campaigns.[2] Yet the oversized influence of wealthy contributors and businesses is protected by the First Amendment as a form of speech, even though the First Amendment says nothing explicitly about money. So how did we end up here?

Ironically, it began with Congress's intention to control the amount of money in elections. In 1974, Congress amended federal election law to further limit campaign contributions. Two years later, in *Buckley v. Valeo* (1976), the U.S. Supreme Court suggested for the first time that political contributions count as speech. The court argued that restrictions on campaign

◀ Protesters here are speaking out against the 2010 Supreme Court decision in the *Citizens United v. Federal Election Commission* case. This ruling protects corporations and labor unions, allowing them to spend unlimited amounts of money on TV and radio advertising during elections. Alex Wong/Getty Images

money "necessarily reduce[d] the quantity of expression by restricting the number of issues discussed, the depth of the exploration, and the size of the audience reached. This is because virtually every means of communicating ideas in today's mass society requires the expenditure of money."

Over the ensuing years, Congress has tried to again rein in campaign finance with new laws, but federal courts, beholden to the idea that money equals speech, have always struck them down. This brings us to the current state of our national elections: The two main political parties and their supporters spent $6.5 billion on campaign advertising for the 2016 presidential and congressional elections, more than ever before. And in the 2018 off-year congressional election, spending topped $5.7 billion, more than one-third greater than the previous (2014) off-year election.[3]

The main explanation for why corporations and rich individuals can now spend extraordinary amounts lies in another decision by the Supreme Court, *Citizens United v. Federal Election Commission* (2010). The five-to-four decision said that it was a violation of First Amendment free-speech rights for the federal government to limit spending for TV and radio advertising, usually done through organized Super PACs (political action committees), which are most often sponsored by corporate interests or super-rich donors.

While the Supreme Court decision ran counter to public opinion, many advocates on the political Right and some on the Left offered that the First Amendment means what it says: "Congress shall make no law . . . abridging the freedom of speech." According to Gene Policinski of the First Amendment Center, the "good intentions" behind the idea of limiting campaign spending "don't justify ignoring a basic concept that the Supreme Court majority pointed out in its ruling: Nothing in the First Amendment provides for 'more or less' free-speech protection depending on who is speaking."[4]

An advantage in spending is only one of many variables, yet those with limited means are at a clear disadvantage when it comes to buying expensive commercial speech. Law professor Lawrence Lessig argues that money corrupted American politics long before the *Citizens United* ruling. "Politicians are dependent upon 'the funders,'" he wrote. "But 'the funders' are not 'the People'. . . . .01 percent [of Americans]—the 1 percent of the 1 percent—give more than $10,000 in an election cycle; and .0000063 percent have given close to 80 percent of the super PAC money spent in this election so far."[5]

Given the *Citizens United* ruling, what can be done to give all citizens a voice in the campaign finance system and make them "patrons" of the political process?

DEBATES OVER WHAT CONSTITUTES "free speech" or "free expression" have defined American democracy. Supreme Court Justice William Brennan Jr. captured this idea in 1989 when asked to comment on his favorite part of the Constitution: "The First Amendment, I expect. Its enforcement gives us this society. The other provisions of the Constitution really only embellish it." Of all the issues that involve the mass media and popular culture, none is more central—or explosive—than freedom of expression and the First Amendment.

The current era is as volatile a time as ever for free-speech issues. Contemporary free-speech debates include copyright issues, hate-speech codes on college and university campuses, explicit lyrics in music, violent images in film and television, the swapping of media files on the Internet, and the right of the press to publish government secrets. These debates have intensified as technological advances like the Internet have enabled easy creation of new types of media content, allowed politicians to bypass journalists, and revolutionized the speed and method by which people share information—and misinformation.

In this chapter, we examine a number of key First Amendment issues in more detail by:

- exploring the origins of free expression and a free press, taking a closer look at the First Amendment to the U.S. Constitution, identifying four models of free expression, tracing the evolution of censorship, examining five forms of unprotected expression, and comparing the First Amendment with the Sixth Amendment

- shining a spotlight on film and its relationship with the First Amendment by taking a look at the social and political pressures that affected moviemaking in its early days, self-regulation in the film industry, and the emergence of the film rating system

- taking stock of free expression in broadcast and online media, including examining the Federal Communications Commission (FCC) regulation of broadcasting, definitions and regulation of indecent speech, laws governing political broadcasts, the legacy of the Fairness Doctrine, and communication policy regarding the Internet

- considering the First Amendment's role in our democracy today, including such questions as who (journalists? citizens? both?) should fulfill the civic role of watchdog

LaunchPad
launchpadworks.com

Use **LearningCurve** to review concepts from this chapter.

The Origins of Free Expression and a Free Press

In the United States, freedom of speech and freedom of the press are protected by the First Amendment in the Bill of Rights, developed for our nation's Constitution. Roughly interpreted, these freedoms suggest that anyone should be able to express his or her views, and that the press should be able to publish whatever it wants, without prohibition from Congress. But there's always been a tension between the notion of "free expression" and the idea that some expression (such as sexually explicit words or images) should be prohibited or censored. Many people have wondered what free expression really means.

In this section, we examine several aspects of free speech and freedom of the press. We explore the roots of the First Amendment and different interpretations of *free expression* that have arisen in modern times. We look at evolving notions of censorship and forms of expression that are not protected by the U.S. Constitution. And we consider ways in which the First Amendment has clashed with the Sixth Amendment, which guarantees accused individuals the right to speedy and public trials by impartial juries.

A Closer Look at the First Amendment

To understand how the idea of free expression has developed in the United States, we must understand how the notion of a free press came about. The story goes back to the 1600s, when various national governments in Europe controlled the circulation of ideas through the press by requiring printers to obtain licenses from them. Their goal was to monitor the ideas published by editors and writers and swiftly suppress subversion. However, in 1644, English poet John Milton published his essay *Areopagitica*, which opposed government licenses for printers and defended a free press. Milton argued that in a democratic society, all sorts of ideas—even false ones—should be allowed to circulate. Eventually, he maintained, the truth would emerge. In 1695, England stopped licensing newspapers, and most of Europe followed suit. In many democracies today, publishing a newspaper, magazine, or newsletter requires no license.

Less than a hundred years later, the writers of the U.S. Constitution were ambivalent about the idea of a free press. Indeed, the version of the Constitution ratified in 1788 did not include such protection. The states took a different tack, however. At that time, nine of the original thirteen states had charters defending freedom of the press. These states pushed to have federal guarantees of free speech and the press approved at the first session of the new Congress. Their efforts paid off: The Bill of Rights, which contained the first ten amendments to the Constitution, won ratification in 1791.

However, commitment to freedom of the press was not yet tested. In 1798, the Federalist Party, which controlled the presidency and the Congress, passed the Sedition Act to silence opposition to an anticipated war against France. The act was signed into law by President John Adams and resulted in the arrest and conviction of several publishers. However, after failing to curb opposition, the Sedition Act expired in 1801, during Thomas Jefferson's presidency. Jefferson, a Democratic-Republican who had challenged the act's constitutionality, pardoned all defendants convicted under it.[6] Ironically, the Sedition Act—the first major attempt to constrain the First Amendment—ended up solidifying American support behind the notion of a free press.

Interpretations of Free Expression

Americans are not alone in debating what constitutes free expression and whether constraining expression is ever appropriate. In the middle of the twentieth century, mass communication researchers living in the midst of the Cold War created four models to describe the different approaches to "free expression."[7] We can think of these as the authoritarian, state, libertarian, and social responsibility models. These models, which are outlined in Table 13.1, are distinguished by the degree of freedom their proponents advocate, and by the ruling classes' attitudes toward the freedoms granted to average citizens.

▲ John Milton's *Areopagitica* is one of the most significant early defenses of freedom of the press. The British Library

The Evolution of Censorship

In the United States, the First Amendment theoretically prohibits censorship. Over time, Supreme Court decisions have defined censorship as **prior restraint**—meaning that courts and governments cannot block any publication or speech before it actually occurs. The principle behind prior restraint is that a law has not been broken until an illegal act has been committed. However, the Court left open the idea that the judiciary could halt publication of news in exceptional cases—for example, if such publication would threaten national security. In the 1970s, two pivotal court decisions tested the idea of prior restraint.

The Pentagon Papers Decision

In 1971, with the Vietnam War still raging, Daniel Ellsberg, a former Defense Department employee, stole a copy of the forty-seven-volume report "History of U.S. Decision-Making Process on Vietnam Policy." A thorough study of U.S.

TABLE 13.1 // MODELS OF EXPRESSION

Type of Model	Description
Authoritarian Model	• Developed in sixteenth-century England at around the time the printing press first arrived. • Criticism of government and public dissent are not tolerated, especially if such speech undermines "the common good"—an ideal defined by elites and rulers. • Although media outlets are owned by private citizens, government actively censors, threatens, or bureaucratically oppresses media outlets it considers oppositional, and rewards media outlets aligned with its political objectives. • Exists today in countries like Russia, Hungary, and Turkey, and developing countries where journalism's job is deemed to support government and business efforts to foster economic growth, minimize political dissent, promote social stability, and keep the current regime in power.
State Model	• Government "owns" the press and directly controls what it reports. Leaders believe that the press should serve the goals of the state. • Although the government tolerates some criticism, it suppresses ideas that challenge the basic premises of state authority. • Exists today in a few countries, including China, Cuba, and North Korea.
Libertarian Model	• Flip side of both the state and the authoritarian models; encourages vigorous criticism of government and supports the highest degree of individual and press freedoms. • Proponents argue that *no* restrictions should be placed on the mass media or on individual speech. • Exists today at many alternative newspapers and magazines in North America and Europe, which often emphasize the importance of securing rights for sidelined populations and follow an ethic that absolute freedom of expression is the best way to fight injustice and arrive at the truth.
Social Responsibility Model	• Captures the ideals of mainstream journalism in the United States and most other democracies. • Press is usually privately owned (although the government technically operates the broadcast media in most European democracies) and is free to function as a **Fourth Estate**—an unofficial branch of government that watches for abuses of power by the legislative, judicial, and executive branches. • Press supplies information about any abuses to citizens so that they can make informed decisions about political and social issues.

involvement in Vietnam since World War II, the report was classified by the government as top secret. Ellsberg and a friend leaked the report—nicknamed the Pentagon Papers—to the *New York Times* and the *Washington Post*. In June 1971, the *Times* began publishing excerpts of the report. To block any further publication, the Nixon administration applied for and received a federal court injunction against the *Times* to halt publication of the documents, arguing that it posed "a clear and present danger" to national security by revealing military strategy to the enemy.

In a 6–3 vote, the Supreme Court sided with the newspaper. Justice Hugo Black, in his majority opinion, attacked the government's attempt to suppress publication: "Both the history and language of the First Amendment support the view that the press must be left free to publish news, whatever the source, without censorship, injunctions, or prior restraints."[8] The Pentagon Papers case came back into discussion more recently with the government leak cases of Edward Snowden and Chelsea Manning, both of whom Ellsberg publicly defended.[9]

▲ In 1971, Daniel Ellsberg, a former Pentagon researcher, turned against America's military policy in Vietnam and leaked information to the press. The federal case against him was dropped in 1973 when illegal government-sponsored wiretaps of Ellsberg's psychoanalyst came to light during the Watergate scandal. Bettmann/Getty Images

The Progressive Magazine Decision

The conflict between prior restraint and national security resurfaced in 1979, when the U.S. government issued an injunction to block publication of the *Progressive*, a national left-wing magazine. The editors had planned to publish an article titled "The H-Bomb Secret: How We Got It, Why We're Telling It." The dispute began when the magazine's editor sent a draft to the Department of Energy to verify technical portions of the article. Believing that the article contained sensitive data that might damage U.S. efforts to halt the proliferation of nuclear weapons, the department asked the magazine not to publish it. When the magazine said it would proceed anyway, the government sued the *Progressive* and asked a federal district court to block publication.

In an unprecedented action, Justice Robert Warren sided with the government, deciding that "a mistake in ruling against the United States could pave the way for thermonuclear annihilation for us all. In that event, our right to life is extinguished and the right to publish becomes moot."[10] Warren was seeking to balance the *Progressive*'s First Amendment rights against the possibility that the article, if published, would spread dangerous information and undermine national security. During appeals, several other publications printed their own stories about the H-bomb, and the U.S. government eventually dropped the case. None of the articles, including one ultimately published by the *Progressive*, contained precise details on how to design a nuclear weapon. But Warren's decision represented the first time in American history that a prior-restraint order imposed in the name of national security stopped initial publication of a news report.

Unprotected Forms of Expression

Despite the First Amendment's provision that "Congress shall make no law" restricting speech and the press, the federal government, state laws, and even local ordinances have on occasion curbed some forms of expression. And over the years, the U.S. court system has determined that some kinds of expression do not merit protection under the Constitution. These forms include sedition, copyright infringement, libel, obscenity, and violation of privacy rights.

Sedition

For more than a century after the Sedition Act of 1798, Congress passed no laws prohibiting the articulation or publication of dissenting opinions. But sentiments that fueled the Sedition Act resurfaced in the twentieth century, particularly in times of war. For instance, the Espionage Acts of 1917 and 1918—enforced during the two world wars—made it a federal crime to utter or publish "seditious" statements, defined as anything expressing opposition to the U.S. war effort.

For example, in the landmark *Schenck v. United States* (1919) appeal case, taking place during World War I, the Supreme Court upheld the conviction of a Socialist Party leader, Charles T. Schenck, for distributing leaflets urging American men to protest the draft. Justices argued that Schenck had violated the recently passed Espionage Act.

In supporting Schenck's sentence—a ten-year prison term—Justice Oliver Wendell Holmes noted that the leaflets were entitled to First Amendment protection, but only during times of peace. In establishing the "clear and present danger" criterion for expression, the Supreme Court demonstrated the limits of the First Amendment.

Copyright Infringement

Appropriating a writer's or an artist's words, images, or music without consent or payment is also a form of expression not protected by the First Amendment. A **copyright** legally protects the rights of authors and producers to their published or unpublished writing, music, lyrics, TV programs, movies, or graphic art designs. Congress passed the first Copyright Act in 1790, which gave authors the right to control their published works for fourteen years, with the opportunity to renew copyright protection for another fourteen years. After the end of the copyright period, the work would enter the **public domain**, which would give the public free access to the work. (For example, a publisher could reprint a written work that had entered the public domain.) The idea was that a period of copyright control would give authors financial incentive to create original works, and that moving works into the public domain would give others incentive to create works derived from earlier accomplishments.

But in time, artists, as they began to live longer, and corporations, which could also hold copyrights, wanted to prolong the period in which they could profit from creative works. In 1976, Congress extended the copyright period to the life of the author plus fifty years (seventy-five years for a corporate copyright owner). In 1998, as copyrights on works such as Disney's Mickey Mouse were set to expire, Congress again extended the copyright period for an additional twenty years. There were no last-minute extensions of that copyright period, however, and on January 1, 2019, a number of works of music, art, and literature from 1923 entered the public domain. More are scheduled to do so on the first day of subsequent years.

Today, nearly every innovation in digital culture creates new questions about copyright law. For example, is a video mash-up that samples copyrighted sounds and images a copyright violation or a creative accomplishment protected under the concept of *fair use* (the same standard that enables students to legally quote attributed text in their research papers)? Should news aggregators like Google News and Facebook pay something to financially strapped newspapers when they link to their articles? One of the laws that tips the debates toward stricter enforcement of copyright is the Digital Millennium Copyright Act of 1998, which outlaws technology or actions that circumvent copyright systems. In other words, it may be illegal merely to create or distribute technology that enables someone to make illegal copies of digital content, such as a movie.

▲ The iconic album art for the Velvet Underground's 1967 debut—a banana print designed by artist Andy Warhol—has been a subject of an ongoing copyright dispute between the Andy Warhol Foundation for the Visual Arts and the rock band. The most recent disagreement occurred when the Warhol Foundation, which had previously accused the Velvet Underground of violating its claim to the print, announced plans to license the banana design for iPhone cases. The band, in turn, filed a copyright claim to the design, which a federal judge later dismissed. Richard Stonehouse/Camera Press/Redux

Libel

The biggest legal worry haunting editors and publishers today is the possibility of being sued for libel, a form of expression that, unlike political speech, is not protected under the First Amendment. **Libel** is defamation of someone's character in written or broadcast form. It differs from **slander**, which is spoken defamation. Inherited from British common law, libel is generally defined as a false statement that holds a person up to public ridicule, contempt, or hatred, or that injures a person's business or livelihood. Examples of potentially libelous statements include falsely accusing someone of professional incompetence (such as medical malpractice), falsely accusing a person of a crime (such as drug dealing), falsely stating that someone is mentally ill or engages in unacceptable behavior (such as public drunkenness), and falsely accusing a person of associating with a disreputable organization or cause (such as being a member of the Mafia or a neo-Nazi military group).

Since 1964, *New York Times v. Sullivan* has served as the standard for libel law. The case stems from a 1960 full-page advertisement placed in the

New York Times by the Committee to Defend Martin Luther King and the Struggle for Freedom in the South. Without naming names, the ad criticized the law-enforcement tactics used in southern cities to break up Civil Rights demonstrations. L. B. Sullivan—the city commissioner of Montgomery, Alabama—sued the *Times* for libel, claiming the ad defamed him indirectly. Alabama civil courts awarded Sullivan $500,000, but the *Times*' lawyers appealed to the Supreme Court. The Court reversed the ruling, holding that Alabama libel law violated the *Times*' First Amendment rights.[11]

Private individuals (such as city sanitation employees, undercover police informants, and nurses) must prove three things to win a libel case:

1. that the public statement about them was false;
2. that damages or actual injury occurred (such as loss of a job or mental anguish); and
3. that the publisher or broadcaster was negligent in failing to determine the truthfulness of the statement.

In the *Sullivan* case, the Supreme Court asked future civil courts to distinguish whether plaintiffs in libel cases are "public officials" or "private individuals." To win libel cases, the Court said, public officials (such as movie or sports stars, political leaders, and lawyers defending a prominent client) are held to a tougher standard and must prove falsehood, damages, negligence, and **actual malice** on the part of the news media. *Actual malice* means that the reporter or editor either knew the statement was false and printed or broadcast it anyway, or acted with a reckless disregard for the truth. Because actual malice against a public official is hard to prove, it is difficult for public figures to win libel suits.

Historically, the best defense against a libel lawsuit in American courts has been the truth. In most cases, if libel defendants can demonstrate that they printed or broadcast true statements, plaintiffs will not recover any damages—even if their reputations were harmed. There are other times when a person cannot sue for libel, even when damaging public statements against them are later found to be false. For example, prosecutors are granted *absolute privilege* in a court of law, so they can freely make accusatory statements toward defendants—a key part of their job. Reporters who print or broadcast statements made in court are also protected against libel.

Another defense against libel is the rule of **opinion and fair comment**, the notion that libel consists of *intentional* misstatements of factual information, not expressions of opinion. However, the line between fact and opinion is often blurry. For instance, one of the most famous tests of opinion and fair comment

▲ A 1960 *New York Times* advertisement triggered one of the most influential and important libel cases in U.S. history by criticizing law-enforcement tactics used against Martin Luther King (pictured above) and the Civil Rights movement. The behind-the-scenes machinations of King's later Alabama demonstrations are the subject of the film *Selma*. Howard Sochurek/The LIFE Picture Collection/Getty Images

came with a case pitting conservative minister and political activist Jerry Falwell against Larry Flynt, publisher of *Hustler*, a pornographic magazine. The case developed after a spoof ad in the November 1983 issue of *Hustler* suggested that Falwell had had sex with his mother. Falwell sued for libel, demanding $45 million in damages. The jury rejected the libel suit but found that Flynt had intentionally caused Falwell emotional distress—and awarded Falwell $200,000. Flynt's lawyers appealed, and the U.S. Supreme Court overturned the verdict in 1988, explaining that the magazine was entitled to constitutional protection.

Libel laws also protect satire, comedy, and opinions expressed in reviews of books, plays, movies, and restaurants. However, such laws do not protect malicious statements in which plaintiffs can prove that defendants used their free-speech rights to mount an uncalled-for, damaging personal attack.

Obscenity

For most of this nation's history, legislators have argued that **obscenity** is not a form of expression protected by the First Amendment. However, experts have not been able to agree on what constitutes an obscene work, especially as definitions of obscenity have changed over the years. For example, during the 1930s, novels (such as James Joyce's *Ulysses*) were judged obscene if they contained "four-letter words."

The current legal definition of *obscenity*, derived from the 1973 *Miller v. California* case, states that obscene materials meet three criteria:

1. the average person, applying contemporary community standards, finds that the material as a whole appeals to prurient interest (that is, incites lust);
2. the material depicts or describes sexual conduct in a patently offensive way; and
3. the material as a whole lacks serious literary, artistic, political, or scientific value.

▲ Actor Johnny Depp was accused of assault by his ex-wife Amber Heard, right. In 2018, Depp brought a £200,000 libel lawsuit against the tabloid newspaper the *Sun* for calling him a "wife-beater." Then, in 2019, Depp filed a $50 million lawsuit directly against Heard for libel, charging she defamed him in a December 2018 *Washington Post* opinion piece by implying he was a domestic abuser. John Phillips/Getty Images

The *Miller* decision acknowledged that different communities and regions of the country have different standards with which to judge obscenity. It also required that a work be judged *as a whole*. This was designed to keep publishers from simply inserting a political essay or literary poem into pornographic materials to demonstrate that their publication contained redeeming features.

Since the *Miller* decision, major prosecutions of obscenity have been rare (most have been aimed at child pornography), and most battles now concern the Internet, for which the concept of community standards has been eclipsed by the medium's global reach. A new complication in defining pornography has emerged with cases of "sexting," in which minors produce and send sexually graphic images of themselves via cell phones or the Internet (see "The Digital Turn Case Study: Is 'Sexting' Pornography?" on page 385).

Violation of Privacy Rights

Whereas libel laws safeguard a person's character and reputation, the right to privacy protects an individual's peace of mind and personal feelings. In the simplest terms, the **right to privacy** addresses a person's right to be left alone, without his or her name, image, or daily activities becoming public property. The most common forms of privacy invasion are unauthorized tape recording, photographing, or wiretapping of someone; making someone's personal records, such as health and phone records, available to the public; disclosing personal information, such as religious or sexual activities; and appropriating (without authorization) someone's image or name for advertising or other commercial purposes.

In general, the news media have been granted wide protections under the First Amendment to do their work, even if it approaches or constitutes violation of privacy. For instance, journalists can typically use the names and pictures of private individuals and public figures without their consent in their news stories. Still, many local municipalities and states have passed "anti-paparazzi" laws protecting public individuals from unwarranted scrutiny and surveillance on their private property.

In a recent test of the boundaries of privacy for public figures, a Florida jury in 2016 ordered gossip entertainment blog *Gawker* to pay more than $140 million to Terry G. Bollea, better known as the former professional wrestler Hulk Hogan. In 2012, *Gawker* posted a brief excerpt of a grainy sex tape that showed Bollea having sex with his best friend's wife. *Gawker* argued that its actions were protected by the First Amendment, and that Bollea was a public figure who had often talked about his sex life in media interviews. But the jury determined that Bollea's privacy had been violated, causing both emotional and economic distress. Ultimately, *Gawker* and Bollea reached a settlement of $31 million, but the litigation shattered *Gawker*, which declared bankruptcy and then sold itself to Univision for $135 million.

The Digital Turn

CASE STUDY

Is "Sexting" Pornography?

According to U.S. federal and state laws, when someone produces, transmits, or possesses images with graphic sexual depictions of minors, it is considered child pornography. Digital media have made the circulation of child pornography even more pervasive, according to a 2006 study on child pornography on the Internet. About one thousand people are arrested each year in the United States for child pornography, and according to a U.S. Department of Justice guide for police, they have few distinguishing characteristics other than being "likely to be white, male, and between the ages of 26 and 40."[1]

Now a social practice made quick and easy by the technology of the digital turn has challenged the common wisdom of what is obscenity and who are child pornographers: What happens when the people who produce, transmit, and possess images with graphic sexual depictions of minors are minors themselves? The practice in question is "sexting," the sending or receiving of sexual images via mobile phone text messages, social media apps like Snapchat, or the Internet. Sexting occupies a gray area of obscenity law—yes, the images are of minors, but they do not fit the intent of child pornography laws, which are designed to stop the exploitation of children by adults.

While such messages are usually meant to be private, technology makes it otherwise. And given the endless archives of the Internet, such images never really go away but can be accessed by anyone with enough skills to find them.

According to research published in 2018, 14.8 percent of teenagers sent sexts, and 27.4 percent received them. In addition, 12 percent of teens forwarded a sext without consent, and 8.4 percent had a sext of them forwarded without consent.[2] Various cases illustrate how young people have gotten caught up in a legal system designed to punish pedophiles.

In 2008, eighteen-year-old Florida resident Phillip Alpert sent nude images of his sixteen-year-old girlfriend to friends after they got in an argument. Alpert was convicted of child pornography and thus required by Florida law to be registered as a sex offender for the next twenty-five years. In 2009, three Pennsylvania girls took seminude pictures of themselves and sent the photos to three boys. All six minors were charged with child pornography. A judge later halted the charges in the interest of freedom of speech and parental rights. In Colorado, a 2015 sexting scandal involving middle and high school students exchanging hundreds of nude photos resulted in student suspensions, a canceled high school football game, and a criminal investigation (no charges were filed). A school in Iowa faced a similar situation in 2016.[3]

Twenty-five states have responded with new sexting laws, making it so that teens involved in sexting will generally face misdemeanor charges rather than be subject to the harsher felony laws against child pornography.[4] In the states without such laws, however, charges are often at the discretion of prosecutors and the courts and could be as harsh as a felony crime, with the accompanying fine, jail time, and permanent criminal record. How do you think sexting should be handled by the law?

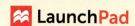

▶ **Visit LaunchPad** to watch a video clip about sexting. What legal and social consequences did the teenager in this clip face after sharing nude images? Were those consequences fair? Unfair? Why?

launchpadworks.com

▶ Hulk Hogan's successful lawsuit against the entertainment blog *Gawker* set an important precedent for celebrities and other public figures, who are normally not protected against invasions of privacy. Pool/Getty Images

A number of laws also protect regular citizens' privacy. For example, the Privacy Act of 1974 protects individuals' records from public disclosure unless they give written consent. In some cases, however, private citizens become public figures—for example, rape victims who are covered in the news. In these situations, reporters have been allowed to record these individuals' quotes and use their images without permission.

The Electronic Communications Privacy Act of 1986 extended the law regarding private citizens to include computer-stored data and the Internet, such as employees' e-mails composed and sent through their employer's equipment. However, subsequent court decisions ruled that employees have no privacy rights in electronic communications conducted on their employer's equipment. The USA PATRIOT Act of 2001 further weakened the earlier laws, giving the federal government more latitude in searching private citizens' records and intercepting electronic communications without a court order.

New technology has also created new legal questions. For example, in early 2016, there was a brief but significant standoff between the FBI and Apple over the FBI's getting access to an iPhone. The phone in question was recovered from one of the terrorists in the December 2015 attack in San Bernardino, California. A court ordered Apple to create a software key to allow the FBI to unlock the iPhone. Apple responded that writing such software would make all iPhones subject to FBI scrutiny and could make them more susceptible to other hackers. The day before a court hearing on the matter, the FBI withdrew its case, saying that it had already cracked the code needed to access the iPhone itself. In 2018, Apple announced it would close the software loophole that enabled the FBI to gain access to the iPhone.

First Amendment versus Sixth Amendment

First Amendment protections of speech and the press have often clashed with the Sixth Amendment, which guarantees an accused individual in "all criminal prosecutions . . . the right to a speedy and public trial, by an impartial jury." Gag orders, shield laws, and laws governing the use of cameras in a courtroom all put restrictions on speech and other forms of expression for the sake of Sixth Amendment rights.

Gag Orders

In recent criminal cases, some lawyers have used the news media to comment publicly on cases that are pending or in trial. This can make it difficult to assemble an impartial jury, thus threatening individuals' Sixth Amendment rights. In the 1960s, the Supreme Court introduced safeguards for ensuring fair trials in heavily publicized cases. These included placing speech restrictions, or **gag orders**, on lawyers and witnesses. In some countries, courts have issued gag orders to prohibit the press from releasing information or giving commentary that might prejudice jury selection or cause an unfair trial. But in the United States, especially since a Supreme Court review in 1976, gag orders have been struck down as a prior-restraint violation of the First Amendment.

Shield Laws

Shield laws state that reporters do not have to reveal the sources of the information they use in news stories. The news media have argued that protecting sources' confidentiality maintains reporters' credibility, protects sources from possible retaliation, and serves the public interest by providing information citizens might not otherwise receive. Forty-nine states and the District of Columbia now have some type of shield law or reporter protection from legal decisions. However, there is no federal shield law in the United States, leaving journalists exposed to subpoenas from federal prosecutors and courts.

Laws Governing the Use of Cameras in a Courtroom

Debates over limiting electronic broadcast equipment and photographers in courtrooms date back to the Bruno Hauptmann trial in the mid-1930s. Hauptmann was convicted and executed for the kidnap-murder of the nineteen-month-old son of Anne and Charles Lindbergh (the aviation hero who made the first solo flight across the Atlantic Ocean in 1927). During the trial, Hauptmann and his attorney complained that the circus atmosphere fueled by the presence of radio and flash cameras prejudiced the jury and turned the public against him. After the trial, the American Bar Association amended its professional ethics code, stating that electronic equipment in the courtroom detracted "from the essential dignity

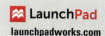
launchpadworks.com

Bloggers and Legal Rights

Legal and journalism scholars discuss the legal rights and responsibilities of bloggers.

Discussion: What are some of the advantages and disadvantages of the audience turning to blogs, rather than traditional sources, for news?

▲ An early 1980s Supreme Court ruling opened the door for the debut of Court TV in 1991 and the televised O. J. Simpson trial in 1994 (the most publicized case in history). VINCE BUCCI/AFP/Getty Images

of the proceedings." For years after the Hauptmann trial, almost every state banned photographic, radio, and TV equipment from courtrooms.

But as broadcast equipment became more portable and less obtrusive, and as television became the major news source for most Americans, courts gradually reevaluated the bans. In the early 1980s, the Supreme Court ruled that the presence of TV equipment did not make fair trials impossible. The Court then left it up to each state to implement its own system. Today, all states allow television coverage of some cases (some just trial courts, some just appellate courts, some both), though most also allow presiding judges to place certain restrictions on coverage of their courtrooms. The state courts are now dealing with questions about the use of other electronic devices, such as smartphones and tablets, and whether or not to allow reporters to tweet or send blog posts live from the courtroom. In some places, the decision about whether to allow tweeting and live-blogging is left up to the judge in each particular case.[12] In other circumstances, a judge may sidestep the tweeting problem by simply banning all cell phones and similar electronic devices from the courtroom.[13]

The Supreme Court continues to ban TV from its proceedings, although it broke its anti-radio rule in 2000 by permitting delayed broadcasts of the hearings on the Florida vote recount case that determined the winner of the 2000 presidential election.

Film and the First Amendment

Back when the Bill of Rights was ratified, our nation's founders could not have predicted the advent of visual media. Film, which came into existence in the late 1890s, presented new challenges for those seeking to determine whether expression in film should be protected. The First Amendment said nothing explicit about film, so lawmakers, courts, society, and industry began an ongoing struggle over exactly how to apply it. As new communication technologies emerged, so did concerns over the impact of films on the values and morals of the public—especially children. It's useful to understand how these ongoing battles over the limits of free speech have played out over the last century, inasmuch as the model of self-regulation and self-censorship developed in the movie industry is often invoked in discussions of the regulation of video games, the Internet, and similar technologies (see also discussions about regulation in technology-specific chapters).

Citizens and Lawmakers Control the Movies

During the early part of the twentieth century, civic leaders in individual towns and cities formed local *review boards*, which screened movies to determine their moral suitability for the community. By 1920, more than ninety cities in the United States had such boards, which were composed of vice squad officers, politicians, and other citizens. By 1923, twenty-two states had such boards.

Meanwhile, lawmakers seeking to please their constituencies introduced legislation to control films. For example, after African American heavyweight champion Jack Johnson defeated white champion Jim Jeffries in 1910, the federal government outlawed transportation of boxing movies across state lines. The move reflected racist attitudes (a fear of images of a black man defeating a white man) more than a distaste for violent imagery, as legislators pandered to white constituents who saw Johnson as a threat.

The idea of film as free speech took a big hit in 1915, when the Supreme Court decided in the *Mutual v. Ohio* case that films were "a business pure and simple" and thus not protected by the First Amendment. The Court further described the film industry as a circus, a "spectacle" for entertainment with "a special capacity for evil."¹⁴

The Movie Industry Regulates Itself

In the early 1920s, a series of scandals—including the rape and murder of an aspiring actress at a party thrown by silent-film comedian Fatty Arbuckle—rocked Hollywood and pressured the movie industry to regulate itself before public review boards or the government could force regulations on it (or before audiences were driven away from movie theaters by the scandals). Over the next few decades, the industry set up its own way of policing not only the content of films but also the personal lives of actors, directors, and others involved in the moviemaking process.

▼ Jack Johnson (1878–1946) was the first black heavyweight boxing champion, holding the title from 1908 to 1914. His stunning victory over former undefeated white champion Jim Jeffries in 1910 resulted in race riots across the country and led to a ban on the interstate transportation of boxing films. Bettmann/Getty Images

The Motion Picture Producers and Distributors of America

In the 1920s, industry leaders hired Will Hays, a former Republican National Committee chair, as president of the Motion Picture Producers and Distributors of America (MPPDA). Under Hays, promising actors or movie extras who had even minor police records were **blacklisted**, meaning they were put on a list of people who would subsequently not be hired by any of the movie studios. Hays also developed a public relations division for the MPPDA, which promptly squelched a national movement to create a federal law censoring movies.

The Motion Picture Production Code

In the early 1930s, the MPPDA—also known as the Hays Office—established the Motion Picture Production Code. The Code stipulated that "no picture shall be produced which will lower the moral standards of those who see it. Hence the sympathy of the audience shall never be thrown to the side of crime, wrong-doing, evil or sin." The Code also dictated which phrases, images, and topics producers and directors had to avoid. For example, "excessive and lustful kissing" and "suggestive postures" were not allowed. The code also prohibited negative portrayals of religion or religious figures. Anyone who broke these rules was blacklisted.

Almost every executive in the industry adopted the Code, viewing it as better than any regulation that would have come from the government, and it influenced most commercial movies for the next twenty years. However, the level of control Hays and his organization achieved under this "voluntary" self-censorship and blacklisting was arguably greater than anything the government could have achieved on its own. Not only did it stifle creativity and critique, but it expanded with the anticommunist hysteria in the mid-twentieth century, when individuals could get blacklisted for the merest suspicion of communist sympathies.

This ideologically based blacklisting, inherently a violation of a citizen's First Amendment rights, hit its peak in the 1950s, just as the grip of Hays's Motion Picture Production Code was about to crumble. In 1952, the Supreme Court decided in *Burstyn v. Wilson* that New York could not ban the Italian film *The Miracle* under state regulations barring "sacrilegious" films. The Court had decided that movies were an important vehicle for public opinion, putting American movies on the same footing as books and newspapers in terms of protection under the First Amendment.

The Rating System and Forced Self-Censorship

In the wake of the 1952 *Miracle* case and the demise of the Production Code, renewed discontent over sexual language and imagery in movies pushed the MPPDA (renamed the Motion Picture Association of America, or MPAA) in the late 1960s to establish a movie-rating system to help concerned viewers avoid offensive material (see Table 13.2). Eventually, G, PG, R, and X ratings emerged

TABLE 13.2 // FIFTY YEARS OF MPAA RATINGS, 1968–2018

Rating	Number of Films with This Rating	Examples
G	1,574	*Frozen II, Ralph Breaks the Internet*
PG	5,578	*How to Train Your Dragon: The Hidden World, The Kid Who Would Be King*
PG-13	4,913	*Captain Marvel, Glass*
R	17,202	*Us, What Men Want, Deadpool 2*
X/NC-17	524	*Showgirls, Crash* (1996)

Data from: Anna Thompson et al., "MPAA Turns 50: Here Are 12 of the Biggest Ratings Controversies, from 'Basic Instinct' to 'Blue Valentine,'" IndieWire, October 29, 2018, www.indiewire.com/2018/10/mpaa-ratings-controversies-50-anniversary-1202016148.

as guideposts for films' suitability for various age groups (X is no longer used by the MPAA but as a promotional tool by adult filmmakers). In 1984, the MPAA added the PG-13 rating to distinguish slightly higher levels of violence or adult themes in movies that might otherwise qualify as PG, and later the NC-17 rating (no children under 17) for films with strong content that aren't deemed pornographic.

Ratings have an important relationship to the ability of a film to make money. An R can sometimes have a negative effect, but an NC-17 in most cases is seen as a kiss of death, not least because several major theater chains refuse to screen films rated NC-17, and many outlets won't run ads for them. Most films that receive the rating are recut to get an R rating for wider distribution.

Critics have attacked the system for being secretive (in theory, the identities of ratings board members are kept anonymous) and for applying standards arbitrarily and unequally. For example, violence is generally more acceptable than nudity or sexual content, and often similar sex scenes can earn films wildly different ratings, depending on the scene's point of view. The controversy about the MPAA system stretches back a number of years, and it was the topic of the 2006 documentary *This Film Is Not Yet Rated*. These concerns have raised important free-speech questions regarding not only the movie industry but also industries that look to the film industry as a model of self-regulation (and self-censorship).

The First Amendment, Broadcasting, and the Internet

As the film industry developed, the lack of clarity regarding the First Amendment's protection of expression in movies prompted the industry to regulate itself. And with the rise of additional new media that our nation's founders could not have envisioned—namely, broadcasting and the Internet—legislators and industry players once again began debating the question of how free these media are under the First Amendment. Different types of protections and levels of regulation developed in broadcast and cyberspace. Whereas film received protections similar to those of print in the 1952 Supreme Court ruling, broadcast is subject to fewer protections, and the Internet is so new that people are still debating how First Amendment rights might apply to it.

The FCC Regulates Broadcasting

Drawing on the argument that limited broadcast signals constitute a scarce national resource, Congress passed the Communications Act of 1934 (see Chapter 6 on radio). The act mandated that radio broadcasters operate in "the public interest, convenience, or necessity," suggesting that they were not free to air whatever they wanted. Since that time, station owners have challenged the "public interest" statute and argued that because the government is not allowed to dictate newspaper content, it similarly should not be permitted to control licenses or mandate broadcast programming. But the U.S. courts have outlined major differences between broadcast and print, as demonstrated by two precedent-setting cases.

The first case—*Red Lion Broadcasting Co. v. FCC* (1969)—began when WGCB, a small-town radio station in Red Lion, Pennsylvania, refused to give airtime to author Fred Cook. Cook wrote a book criticizing Barry Goldwater, the Republican Party's presidential candidate in 1964. On a syndicated show aired by WGCB, a conservative radio preacher and Goldwater fan verbally attacked Cook on the air. Cook asked for response time from the stations that carried the attack. Most complied, but WGCB snubbed him. He appealed to the FCC, which ordered the station to give Cook free time. The station refused, claiming the First Amendment gave it control over its programming content. The Supreme Court sided with the FCC and ordered the station to give Cook airtime, arguing that the public interest—in this case, the airing of differing viewpoints—outweighs a broadcaster's rights. (However, as we'll see later in the chapter, judicial support for what became known as the Fairness Doctrine was ultimately undermined in the mid-1980s.)

The second case—*Miami Herald Publishing Co. v. Tornillo* (1974)—centered on the question of whether the newspaper in this case, the *Miami Herald*, should have been forced to give political candidate Pat Tornillo Jr. space to reply to an editorial opposing his candidacy. In contrast to the *Red Lion* decision, the Supreme Court sided with the paper. The Court argued that forcing a newspaper to give a candidate space violated the paper's First Amendment right to decide what to publish. Clearly, print media had more freedom of expression than did broadcasting.

Dirty Words, Indecent Speech, and Hefty Fines

Like the Supreme Court's rulings in the *Red Lion* and *Miami Herald* cases, regulators' actions regarding indecency in broadcasting reflected the idea that broadcasters had less freedom of expression than did print media. In theory, communication law says that the government cannot censor (prohibit before the fact) broadcast content. However, the government may punish broadcasters *after* the fact for **indecency**.

Concerns over indecent broadcast programming cropped up in 1937, when the FCC scolded NBC for airing a sketch featuring sultry comedian-actress Mae West. After the sketch, which West peppered with sexual innuendos, the networks banned her from further radio appearances for "indecent" speech. Since then, the FCC has periodically fined or reprimanded stations for indecent programming, especially during times when children might be listening. For example, after an FCC investigation in the 1970s, several stations lost their licenses or were fined for broadcasting *topless radio*, which featured deejays and callers discussing intimate sexual subjects in the afternoon. (Topless radio would reemerge in the 1980s, this time with doctors and therapists, rather than deejays, offering intimate counsel to listeners.)

The current precedent for regulating broadcast indecency stems from a complaint to the FCC that came in 1973. In the middle of the afternoon, WBAI, a nonprofit Pacifica network station in New York, aired George Carlin's famous comedy sketch about the "seven dirty words" that can't be said on TV. A man riding in a car with his fifteen-year-old son heard the program and complained to the FCC, which sent WBAI a letter of reprimand. Although no fine was issued, the station challenged the warning on principle—and won its case in court. The FCC promptly appealed to the Supreme Court. Though no court had legally defined indecency

▼ Often drawing criticism for its crass and abrasive humor, *Family Guy* has won several Emmys and other awards since its debut in 1999. One of its most famous episodes, which received an Emmy nomination, parodied the FCC's indecency rules. Everett Collection Inc

(which remains undefined today), the Supreme Court sided with the FCC in the 1978 *FCC v. Pacifica Foundation* case. The decision upheld the FCC's authority to require broadcasters to air adult programming only at times when children are not likely to be listening. The FCC banned indecent programs from most stations between 6:00 A.M. and 10:00 P.M.

Political Broadcasts and Equal Opportunity

In addition to indecency rules, another law affecting broadcasting but not the print media is **Section 315** of the Communications Act of 1934. This section mandates that during elections, broadcast stations must provide equal opportunities and response time for qualified political candidates. In other words, if broadcasters give or sell time to one candidate, they must give or sell the same opportunity to others. Local broadcasters and networks have fought this law for years, claiming that because no similar rule applies to newspapers or magazines, the law violates their First Amendment right to control content. Many stations decided to avoid political programming entirely, ironically reversing the rule's original intention. The TV networks managed to get the law amended in 1959 to exempt newscasts, press conferences, and other events—such as political debates—that qualify as news. For instance, if a senator running for office appears in a news story, opposing candidates cannot invoke Section 315 and demand free time.

Supporters of the equal opportunity law in broadcasting argue that it enables lesser-known candidates representing views counter to those of the Democratic and Republican parties to add their perspectives to political dialogue. It also gives less wealthy candidates a more affordable channel than newspaper and magazine ads for getting their message out to the public.

The Demise of the Fairness Doctrine

Considered an important corollary to Section 315, the **Fairness Doctrine** was to controversial issues what Section 315 is to political speech. Initiated in 1949, this FCC rule required stations to air programs about controversial issues affecting their communities and to provide competing points of view during those programs. Broadcasters again protested that the print media did not have similar requirements. And, like before, many stations simply avoided airing controversial issues. The Fairness Doctrine ended with little public debate in 1987 after a federal court ruled that it was merely a regulation, not an extension of Section 315 law. The end of the Fairness Doctrine opened up the floodgates to partisan talk radio, since there was no longer a requirement that stations needed to air competing points of view. Rush Limbaugh, still talk radio's biggest star, took his show nationwide in 1988 and inspired a multitude of imitators (see Chapter 6).

Since 1987, however, support for reviving the Fairness Doctrine has surfaced periodically. Its advocates argue that broadcasting is fundamentally different from—and more pervasive than—print media. Thus, it should be more accountable to the public interest.

Communication Policy and the Internet

Many have looked to the Internet as the one true venue for unlimited free speech under the First Amendment. The Internet's global expansion is comparable to that of the early days of broadcasting, when economic and technological growth outweighed laws and regulations. At that time, noncommercial experiments by amateurs and engineering students provided a testing ground that commercial interests later exploited for profit.

Public conversations about the Internet have not typically revolved around ownership. Instead, the debates have focused on First Amendment issues, such as civility and pornography. However, as we watch the rapid expansion of the Internet, an important question confronts us: Will the Internet continue to develop as a democratic medium? In late 2010, the FCC created net neutrality rules for wired broadband providers (such as Verizon, Comcast, AT&T, and Charter, who control nearly all broadband access in the United States through DSL and cable modem service), requiring that they provide the same access to all Internet services and content. The FCC's net neutrality rules were rejected by federal courts twice. The courts argued that because the FCC had not defined the Internet as a utility, it could not regulate it in this manner.

However, citizens and entrepreneurs opposed an unregulated system, arguing that the cable and telephone giants have an incentive to rig their services and cause net congestion in order to force customers to pay a premium for higher-speed connections. The debate generated a record four million comments to the FCC, the vast majority in favor of net neutrality.[15] In February 2015, the FCC reclassified broadband Internet as a Title II utility and voted to approve net neutrality rules. However, the FCC reversed course two years later under the leadership of Ajit Pai, who was appointed to head the agency by President Trump after the 2016 election. In December 2017, the FCC voted to repeal the 2015 FCC net neutrality policy on a 3–2 party-line vote, effective June 2018 (see Chapter 9).

▼ In 2017, President Trump appointed FCC chair Ajit Pai, who led the panel in reversing net neutrality safeguards. Bill Clark/Getty Images

The First Amendment in a Democratic Society

Ultimately, questions about the First Amendment's implications for freedom of expression in mass media are really about democracy. And when it comes to our democracy, the news media—whether print, TV, radio, or the Internet—play a particularly important role.

For most of our nation's history, citizens have counted on journalists to alert them to abuses in government and business. But during and after the 2016 election, journalists dealt with historically unique challenges, as top public officials targeted the press and challenged the veracity of verifiable facts in a way not seen even during the Nixon administration. In this climate, fake news gained new life on the Internet, thanks in part to social media and the ease with which false stories could be shared (see "Media Literacy Case Study: Fake News, the First Amendment, and Fighting Propaganda" on pages 398–399).

But there are other forces that have eroded public confidence in the news media as well. For example, as newspapers, TV stations, radio stations, and Internet corporations merged into larger entertainment corporations, and as jobs in the news industry dwindled as a result of outsourcing, consolidation, and budget cuts, it has become more difficult for journalists to adequately cover and lead critical discussions about media ownership, media regulation, and business practices in general. There are fewer journalists available, and the very companies journalists work for are the prime buyers and sellers of major news-media outlets and are often participants in a political system rife with advertising money during the campaign season.

For these reasons, it has become more important than ever for citizens to share the watchdog role with journalists. Citizens not only need to think critically about the news they consume to avoid believing and sharing fake news but also need to support local and national outlets that provide accurate and complete coverage of important ongoing topics. They also need to be aware of how media ownership can undermine even the best newsrooms—those filled with ethical and dedicated journalists. Citizen action groups like Free Press, the Media Access Project, and the Center for Digital Democracy have worked to bring media ownership issues into the mainstream. These groups remind us that the First Amendment protects not only the news media's free-speech rights but also the rights of all of us to speak out.

As we struggle to determine the future of converging print, electronic, and digital media, we need to take part in spirited public debates about media ownership and control, about the differences between commercial speech and free expression, and about what constitutes "speech" in the first place. As citizens, we must pay attention to who is included and excluded from opportunities not only to buy products but also to voice their views and thereby shape our nation's cultural and political landscape. To accomplish this, we need to challenge our journalists and our leaders. More important, we need to challenge ourselves to become watchdogs—critical consumers and engaged citizens—who learn from the past, care about the present, and map mass media's future.

Media Literacy

CASE STUDY

Fake News, the First Amendment, and Fighting Propaganda

Shortly after the 2016 election, news and entertainment website BuzzFeed released the disturbing results of a study on Facebook traffic: Top fake news stories from fake news sites got more online engagement (shares, reactions, and comments) leading up to the election than real news stories from legitimate news operations.[1] Fake news is not new. But as this data shows, whereas it was once mostly relegated to outlandish tabloids in grocery store checkout lines, fake news in the digital age has transformed into an influential force affecting the highest levels of our political process. (See also Chapter 3.)

One way we can understand the impact of fake news is to consider philosopher Jürgen Habermas's theory of the public sphere. This theory outlines how open discussion, disagreement, and debate should work so that members of a society can evaluate different ideas in order to make wise decisions on issues like public policy. According to this model, one key element of debate is that participants argue "in good faith." This means that while people may disagree on how to interpret and respond to evidence, they should not employ dishonesty to win over others to their point of view. Fake news—and those who knowingly or unknowingly share it—poisons these public-sphere discussions as well as the decisions based on these debates. Complicating the issue further is the mountain of data showing Russia and other hostile foreign powers as the source of much "fake news" propaganda.

If fake news is so potentially harmful to democracy and society, how is it allowed in the first place? The short answer is that it is protected under the freedom-of-speech guarantees of the First Amendment. Yet the growing concern over Internet-based disinformation will eventually put it on a collision course with the rights of the First Amendment. As the *Harvard Journal of Law and Technology* has noted, "Social media is now rife with false speech, and it is only a matter of time before those who use social media to spread misinformation are prosecuted in the United States. If that were to happen, a First Amendment challenge will be inevitable."[2]

For now, as with much of the Internet, fake news lives in the realm of caveat emptor, or "buyer beware." In other words, it is up to consumers to build up their media literacy and critical thinking skills so that they can avoid fake news sources and recognize credible news sources. Luckily, there are groups who are willing to help with this task.

Various library groups have provided online resources to help the public sort out the real stories from the fake, including Indiana University East and *School Library Journal*.[3] Highly regarded fact-checking and hoax-debunking sites—such as Snopes.com, FactCheck.org, PolitiFact.com, and the *Washington Post*'s Fact Checker—can also provide valuable help. Some have also tried crowd-sourcing and compiling informal but extensive lists of websites with varying degrees of reliability, such as Dr. Melissa Zimdars's Google doc called "False, Misleading, Clickbait-y, and/or Satirical 'News' Sources."[4] For basic tips from these resources

Web Clip

YouTube.com has many videos related to fake news. One good option to search for is "WhatsApp Takes on Fake News" from TicToc by Bloomberg. Do you think that limiting how many people can receive the same forwarded message will help stop the spread of fake news? Why or why not?

TABLE 13.3 // PRACTICAL TIPS FOR EVALUATING NEWS SOURCES

Tip	Explanation
1. Read past the headline.	Even legitimate news organizations can write poorly worded or intentionally sensational headlines.
2. See if you recognize the news outlet featuring the story.	If the source isn't familiar, search for it online—or look for it on Dr. Zimdars's list.
3. Double-check the date and time the article was published.	Sometimes old articles are shared again, and people mistakenly believe they are new.
4. Consider whether you recognize the author/reporter.	Conduct an online search to see if that person exists and whether he or she has a reputation.
5. Look for links and sources.	Be wary of stories that lack these elements, and follow any links that are included to see if they go somewhere reputable.
6. Look for reports on the same story in other news outlets.	If it is a big story, it will almost certainly be covered by more than one source.

about ways to separate fake news from real news, see Table 13.3.

And, of course, some basic rules of critical thinking also apply. If an article elicits a powerful emotional reaction from its readers, it might be reporting on a legitimate injustice, or it might be designed to cloud your thinking with emotion. Also, the more extraordinary the claim is, the greater should be the evidence provided to back up that claim. And finally, remember that when you share something on social media, it will seem to others that you have in some way endorsed the information you are sharing—whether you have looked into the source's legitimacy or not.

APPLYING THE CRITICAL PROCESS

DESCRIPTION Visit the Facebook page of the acquaintance, friend, or relative you feel is most likely to share stories that might be false or otherwise misleading. Select three memes or links to articles that seem to make extraordinary or inflammatory claims presented as factual.

ANALYSIS Using the six tips for separating real news from fake news and propaganda, list memes or articles that should be investigated further to determine if they are credible.

INTERPRETATION Research the components of the memes/articles you identified.

EVALUATION Based on your analysis and interpretation, are these memes/articles most likely to be credible sources or fake news? What are the key factors that made you reach that decision?

ENGAGEMENT Share your findings, either with classmates or as part of a blog. By sharing your process and your findings, you may help others become more critical consumers of information on social media.

CHAPTER ESSENTIALS

Review

- In the United States, freedom of speech and freedom of the press are protected by the First Amendment in the Bill of Rights. However, Americans have long debated what constitutes "free expression."

- Around the globe, four different models of press systems emerged in the twentieth century: the **authoritarian model**, the **state model**, the **libertarian model**, and the **social responsibility model**.

- The First Amendment theoretically prohibits censorship, which is defined as **prior restraint**—meaning that courts and governments cannot block any publication or speech before it actually occurs.

- Some forms of expression are not protected under the Constitution. These forms include sedition, **copyright** infringement, and **libel**. To win a libel case, public officials must prove falsehood, damages, negligence, and **actual malice**. Defenses against libel include the truth and the rule of **opinion and fair comment**—the notion that opinions are protected from libel.

- Other forms of expression not protected by the Constitution are **obscenity** and violations of the **right to privacy**.

- The First Amendment has clashed with the Sixth Amendment, which guarantees accused individuals the right to speedy and public trials by impartial juries. **Gag orders** (speech restrictions) and laws governing the use of cameras in the courtroom put restrictions on speech and other forms of expression for the sake of Sixth Amendment rights, whereas **shield laws** protect reporters from revealing confidential sources of information used in news stories.

- For the first half of the twentieth century, citizen groups and the Supreme Court failed to recognize movies as protected speech. The movie industry began regulating itself to safeguard its profits and avoid further government oversight.

- Because it uses the public airwaves, broadcasting receives fewer protections than do film and print. Although the government cannot censor broadcast content, it may punish broadcasters after the fact for **indecency**.

LaunchPad

Visit LaunchPad for *Media Essentials* at **launchpadworks.com** for additional learning tools:

- **REVIEW WITH LEARNINGCURVE**
  LearningCurve adaptive quizzing helps you master the concepts you need to learn from this chapter.

- **VIDEO: THE FIRST AMENDMENT AND STUDENT SPEECH**
  Legal and newspaper professionals explain how student newspapers are protected by the First Amendment.

- **MEDIA LITERACY PRACTICE**
  This activity challenges you to develop a critical perspective and apply it to everyday encounters with communication media.

- **Section 315** of the Communications Act of 1934 mandates that during elections, broadcast stations must provide equal opportunities and response time for qualified political candidates. From 1949 to 1987, the **Fairness Doctrine**—a corollary to Section 315—required stations to air programs about controversial issues affecting their communities and to provide equal time to competing points of view.

- Many consider the Internet a true venue for free speech, though debates exist about net neutrality and what forms of expression should be allowed.

- Questions about the First Amendment's influence over freedom of expression in mass media are centered on democracy, and when it comes to our democracy, the news media play a particularly important role. As various forces have eroded public confidence in the news media, however, it has become more important than ever for citizens to share the watchdog role with journalists.

Key Terms

prior restraint, p. 377
authoritarian model, p. 378
state model, p. 378
libertarian model, p. 378
social responsibility model, p. 378
Fourth Estate, p. 378
copyright, p. 380
public domain, p. 380
libel, p. 381
slander, p. 381
actual malice, p. 382
opinion and fair comment, p. 382
obscenity, p. 383
right to privacy, p. 384
gag orders, p. 387
shield laws, p. 387
blacklisted, p. 390
indecency, p. 393
Section 315, p. 394
Fairness Doctrine, p. 394

Study Questions

1. What is the basic philosophical concept that underlies America's notion of free expression?

2. What is libel? What are the legal defenses against libel suits? How is libel protection different for public figures and private citizens?

3. What is the legal test that the government is supposed to use to decide if something should be considered obscene? How does that definition of pornography and obscenity apply to sexting?

4. How did both the Motion Picture Production Code and the current movie-rating system come into being?

5. Why does "fake news" enjoy First Amendment protection?

Media Expressions

14

Media Economics and the Global Marketplace

406
The Transition to an Information Economy

412
Analyzing the Media Economy

418
Specialization and Global Markets

424
Social Issues in Media Economics

426
The Media Marketplace in a Democratic Society

"From the start, we've always strived to do more, and to do important and meaningful things with the resources we have," Google cofounder Larry Page wrote in a 2015 letter explaining the decision to move the Google empire under a new umbrella multinational corporation called Alphabet. "We did a lot of things that seemed crazy at the time. Many of those crazy things now have over a billion users, like Google Maps, YouTube, Chrome, and Android."[1]

The move to create a new parent company for Google allowed the company to put some distance between established parts of the business and its riskier experimental ventures (sometimes called "moonshots").[2] One of Google's moonshot ventures, called Waymo, is the development of a self-driving car. Another is Project Loon, which launches groups of high-altitude balloons equipped to act like floating cell phone towers, thereby providing Internet access to areas that otherwise lack the infrastructure to get online.[3] And while it may not please investors that initiatives like Waymo and Loon have yet to make money, Google wouldn't be one of the

◄ One of Google's "moonshot" ventures, called Project Loon, uses high-altitude balloons carrying cellular technology to supply Internet access to places that lack the physical infrastructure to get online. Project Loon is just one of the ways Google is experimenting with technology. Another example is Waymo, a self-driving car that is currently undergoing testing. CB2/ZOB/Supplied by WENN.com/Newscom

biggest companies in the world without its innovating spirit.

Google traces its origins to 1995, when Stanford student Sergey Brin was assigned to show prospective student Larry Page around campus. A year later, the pair were collaborating on a prototype search engine, and in 1997, they registered the domain name "Google.com"—a play on the mathematical word *googol* (the number written as a one followed by a hundred zeros). In 1998, the pair officially registered the company as an entity and hired their first employee. The company proceeded to grow at a startling pace, adding more services every few months.

One of those services—YouTube—has its own dizzyingly fast success story. The three founders, Chad Hurley, Steve Chen, and Jawed Karim, say they got the idea for a video-sharing site during a dinner party, and on Valentine's Day 2005 they registered the trademark, name, and logo for YouTube. The first video (of Karim at the zoo) was posted on April 23, and by September the site got its first million-hit video (a Nike ad). By December, the company was getting major investment attention, and the site was more widely available after upgrading its bandwidth and servers. Google bought YouTube in October 2006, just a year and a half after the first video was posted, for $1.65 billion. Since then, YouTube has been run as a subsidiary of Google and continues to grow in popularity.

Google and YouTube exemplify the kinds of Internet-driven mass media companies of the post–digital turn. But that doesn't mean older media corporations have gone away. Some of today's biggest mass media players have long histories, which they've built on and adapted through various technological changes. These giants—such as Comcast and Disney—exist and compete with relative upstarts like Amazon, Apple, Facebook, and Google. Though these newer companies are giving them a run for their money, there can be big advantages to having the resources, name recognition, and established political connections that come with being a longtime member of the mass media.

For either type of company, the key to future success is investing in fresh ideas, which becomes harder to do as a company becomes more established. According to Larry Page, "As you 'age'—even when you're still a teenager like Google—you have to work hard to stay innovative."[4] Alphabet, it seems, is structured to help the company do just that.

COMPARING GOOGLE WITH OLDER MEDIA GIANTS like Disney and Comcast, we see two types of media success: one based on an idea that could have happened only in the Internet age (a need for a better search engine), and the other, legacy entertainment conglomerates that have survived years of leadership changes and power struggles to enter the twenty-first century with massive resources. Of course, not all of the mergers, takeovers, and acquisitions that have swept through the global media industries in the last twenty years have capitalized on the histories and reputations of the corporations involved. Take, for instance, the ill-timed purchase of Myspace by News Corp. in 2005. Paying $580 million for what was then the world's most popular social media site, Rupert Murdoch would watch a newcomer named Mark Zuckerberg (and his site Facebook) reduce the value of Myspace to $35 million, the price Justin Timberlake and Specific Media, Inc., paid for the service in 2011.

Despite such spectacular exceptions, many cases of ownership convergence have provided even more economic benefit to the massive multinational corporations that dominate the current media landscape. As a consequence, we currently find ourselves enmeshed in an immense media economy characterized by consolidation of power in just a few corporate hands. This phenomenon, combined with the advent of the Internet, has made our modern media world markedly distinct from that of earlier generations—at least in economic terms. Not only have a handful of media giants—from Apple to Google—emerged, but the Internet has permanently transformed the media landscape. The Internet has dried up newspapers' classified-ad revenues; altered the way music, movies, and TV programs get distributed and exhibited; and forced almost all media businesses to rethink the content they will provide—and how they will provide it.

In this chapter, we explore the developments and tensions shaping this brave new world of mass media by:

- **examining the transition our nation has made from a manufacturing to an information economy by considering how the media industries' structures have evolved, the impact of deregulation, and the rise of media powerhouses through consolidation**

- **analyzing today's media economy, including how media organizations make money and formulate strategies within a climate of larger business trends that include the decline of labor unions, a widening wage gap, and the influence of hegemony**

- **assessing the specialization and use of synergy currently characterizing media, using the history of the Walt Disney Company as an example**

- **taking stock of the social challenges the new media economy has raised, such as subversion of antitrust laws, consumers' loss of control in the marketplace, and American culture's infiltration into other cultures**

- **evaluating the media marketplace's role in our democracy by considering such questions as whether consolidation of media hurts or helps democracy, and what impact recent media-reform movements might have on society**

> **LaunchPad**
> launchpadworks.com
> Use **LearningCurve** to review concepts from this chapter.

The Transition to an Information Economy

In the first half of the twentieth century, the U.S. economy was built on mass production, the proliferation of manufacturing plants, and intense rivalry with businesses in other nations. By midcentury, this manufacturing-based economy began transitioning into an economy fueled by information (which new technologies made easier to generate and exchange anywhere) and by cooperation with other economies. Offices displaced factories as major work sites; centralized mass production declined in the United States and other developed nations; and American firms began outsourcing manufacturing work to developing countries, where labor was cheap and environmental standards were lax.

Mass media industries seized the opportunity to expand globally. They began marketing music, movies, television programs, and computer software overseas. And the media mergers-and-acquisitions (M&A) drive that had begun in the United States in the 1960s expanded into global media consolidation by the 1980s.

This transition from a manufacturing-based to an information-based economy had several defining points: Early regulation designed to break up monopolies in manufacturing-related industries such as oil, railroads, and steel gave way to deregulation, which ultimately catalyzed the M&A drive that created media powerhouses. These information-based corporations in turn fueled new trends in the industry (including a decline of unionized labor and a growing wage gap). Soon a new society took shape—one in which the biggest media companies defined the values that dominated culture not only in the United States but also around the globe.

How Media Industries Are Structured

Most industries that make up the media economy have one of three common structures: monopoly, oligopoly, or limited competition (see Figure 14.1).

Monopoly

A **monopoly** arises when a single firm dominates production and distribution in a particular industry—nationally or locally. For example, at the national level, AT&T ran a rare government-approved and government-regulated monopoly—the telephone business—for more than a hundred years before the government broke it up in the mid-1980s. And Microsoft currently dominates the worldwide market for business computer operating systems.

On the local level, monopolies are more plentiful, arising in any city that has only one newspaper or one cable company. The federal government has encouraged owner diversity since the 1970s by prohibiting a newspaper from operating a broadcast or cable company in the same city. But since 2003, the Federal Communications Commission (FCC) has made several efforts to relax cross-ownership rules, arguing that the Internet and cable and satellite television provide sufficient informational diversity for citizens. Media activists have countered that the large traditional media are still the dominant news media in any market, and that when they merge, it results in fewer independent media voices.

Oligopoly

In an **oligopoly**, just a few firms dominate an industry. For example, in the late 1980s, the production and distribution of the world's music was controlled by only six corporations. By 2004, after a series of acquisitions, the "big six" had been reduced to the "big four"—Warner Music Group (United States), Sony (Japan), Universal (France), and EMI (Great Britain). In late 2011, Universal purchased EMI at auction, and by 2012, three companies controlled nearly two-thirds of the recording industry market. The Internet is also changing the music game, enabling companies like Apple to gain new dominance with innovative business models such as the iTunes store, and then Apple Music. Time will tell whether the "big three" maintain their status as an oligopoly.

▲ In 1911, John D. Rockefeller Sr., considered the richest industrialist in the world, saw his powerful monopoly, Standard Oil, busted into more than thirty separate companies. Bettmann/Getty Images

Firms that make up an oligopoly face little economic competition from small independent firms. However, many oligopolies choose to purchase independent companies in order to nurture the fresh ideas and products those companies generate. Without the financial backing of an oligopoly, many of those ideas and products could have a tough time making it to market.

Limited Competition

Limited competition characterizes a media market that has many producers and sellers but only a few products within a particular category.[5] For instance, hundreds of independently owned radio stations operate in the United States. However, most of these commercial stations feature just a few formats—such as country, classic rock, news/talk, or contemporary hit radio. Fans of other

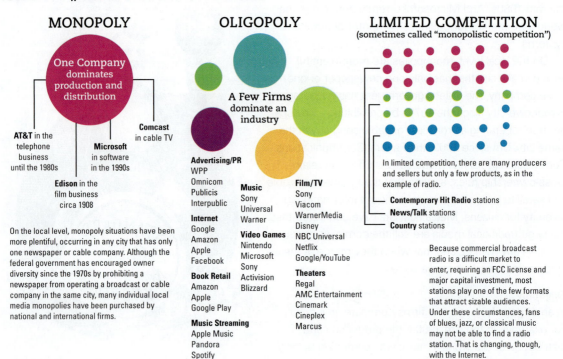

FIGURE 14.1 // MEDIA INDUSTRY STRUCTURES

formats—including blues, alternative country, and classical music—may not be able to find a radio station that matches their interests. Of course, as with music, the Internet is changing radio, too, enabling companies like Pandora and Spotify to offer streaming audio for a huge array of formats.

From Regulation to Deregulation

Beginning in the early twentieth century, Congress passed several acts intended to break up corporate trusts and monopolies, which often fixed prices to force competitors out of business. But later in the century, many business leaders began complaining that such regulation was restricting the flow of capital essential for funding business activities. President Jimmy Carter (1977–1981) initiated deregulation, and President Ronald Reagan (1981–1989) dramatically weakened most controls on business (e.g., environmental and worker safety rules). Many corporations in a wide range of industries flourished in this new pro-commerce climate. Deregulation also made it easier for companies to merge, to diversify, and—in industries such as the airlines, energy, communications, and financial services—to form oligopolies.[6]

In the broadcast industry, the Telecommunications Act of 1996 (under President Bill Clinton) lifted most restrictions on how many radio and TV stations one corporation could own. The act further permitted regional telephone companies to buy cable firms. In addition, cable operators regained the right to raise their rates with less oversight and to compete in the local telephone business. What prompted this shift to deregulation in the communications industry? With new cable channels, DBS, and the Internet, lawmakers no longer saw broadcasting as a scarce resource—once a major rationale for regulation as well as government funding of noncommercial and educational stations.

Not surprisingly, the 1996 act unleashed a wave of mergers in the industry, as television, radio, cable, telephone, and Internet companies fought to become the biggest corporations in their business sector and acquire new subsidiaries in other media sectors. The act also revealed legislators' growing openness to make special exemptions for communications companies. For example, despite complaints from NBC, News Corp. in 1995 received a special dispensation from the FCC and Congress that allowed it to continue owning and operating the Fox network and a number of local TV stations.

Today, regulation of the communications industry is even looser. In late 2007, the FCC relaxed its rules further when it said that a company located in a Top 20 market (ranging in size from New York to Orlando, Florida) could own one TV station and one newspaper as long as there were at least eight TV stations in that market. Previously, a company could not own a newspaper and a broadcast outlet (a TV or radio station) in the same market. In 2009, a U.S. federal court struck down the FCC's regulation limiting a cable company's holdings to not more than 30 percent of the U.S. cable market, a precursor to a wave of mergers and proposed mergers among Internet service providers.

Sinclair Broadcast Group is just one corporation that took advantage of increasing deregulation, using a variety of FCC regulation waivers and loopholes to become the biggest owner of local TV stations in the United States. The company now owns and operates network-affiliated local television stations that used to compete against one another in dozens of markets, growing from 62 stations in 2004 to 191 stations by 2019.[7]

Among other concerns, this type of consolidation is negatively affecting the number of media companies owned by people of color, who, along with women, are already at a great historic disadvantage. For example, the distribution of U.S. airwaves in the 1930s went only to white male owners. The situation has hardly improved since; according to media journalist Kristal Brent Zook, "African American ownership remains particularly low, hovering at less than 1 percent of all television properties, and less than 2 percent of radio."[8]

The Rise of Media Powerhouses

Into the 1980s, antitrust laws attempted to ensure diversity of ownership among competing businesses. In the mid-1980s, for instance, the Justice Department broke up AT&T's century-old monopoly, creating competition in the telephone industry. But with the gradual erosion of these laws came much more consolidation and much less competition in the world of mass media.

Besides just being relaxed, the antitrust laws have been unevenly applied in media industries, forcing competition in some industries while allowing consolidation in others. For example, whereas the Justice Department attempted to create competition in the telephone industry by breaking up AT&T, it also authorized several mass media mergers that concentrated power in the hands of a few behemoths. These included General Electric's purchase of RCA/NBC in the 1980s, Disney's acquisition of ABC for $19 billion in 1995, and Time Warner's purchase of Turner Broadcasting for $7.5 billion in 1996. In 2001, AOL acquired Time Warner for $165 billion—the largest media merger in history at the time. In 2011, cable giant Comcast purchased a majority share of NBC Universal once the deal was approved by regulatory agencies.

More recently, there have also been a number of high-profile mergers. In June 2018, Time Warner and AT&T beat a government lawsuit attempting to block their $85 billion deal, and the companies merged. In August 2018, the Trump administration filed an appeal trying to undo the merger, but by February 2019, a federal court decided in favor of the merger.[9] The Justice Department said it would not appeal, likely ending the fight. At the same time this merger was happening, Disney was at work on its merger with 21st Century Fox, which we will discuss later in the chapter.

As traditional mass media corporations have grown, we've also seen the rise of new media powerhouses in the twenty-first century (see the chapter opener and "The Digital Turn Case Study: Are the Big Digital Companies Too Big?" on page 411). Companies like Google, Amazon, and Facebook first grew to dominate their respective niches (search engines, online retail, and social media) and then branched out into new areas of the mass media. Apple and Microsoft have been around much longer but are still relatively young when compared to traditional mass media giants.

These five companies have envisioned new ways for us to experience media content: We buy content from their retail stores (e.g., the iTunes store and Amazon.com); benefit from their original content (e.g., Amazon film productions and Microsoft Office software, which is now available on mobile devices); consume content on their innovative devices (e.g., the iPad, Kindle Fire, Google Pixel phone, and Xbox); and are linked to other media content (via Google search and our friends on Facebook). Imagine experiencing the mass media without using a product or service of one of these companies and you begin to understand how the digital turn—with these five companies leading the way—has transformed the mass communication environment in less than a decade.

The Digital Turn

CASE STUDY

Are the Big Digital Companies Too Big?

In the past few years, Americans have come to the realization that Apple, Google, Amazon, Microsoft, and Facebook structure much of our everyday lives. Can one imagine living without these five companies? But perhaps that is the problem. As CNN reporter Dylan Byers said of the biggest tech companies, "It's their century. We're just living in it."[1]

With that realization comes reminders that all is not good with our big digital companies. Over the course of their relatively brief histories, all these companies have been under fire for a number of problems: deploying anticompetitive practices (Microsoft and Amazon), recording users' private conversations on home digital assistants (Amazon), gobbling up too much of the advertising industry (Google and Facebook), being manipulated by trolls during the 2016 presidential election (Google and Facebook), violating user privacy (Facebook), and slowing down mobile phone performance to spur sales (Apple).

But Amanda Lotz, a professor of media studies at the University of Michigan, warns us not to lump these companies together like we do for Big Oil, Big Pharma, and Big Tobacco: "Because all of these companies provide services relating to computers, there is a tendency to lump them together, calling them 'Big Tech' or the 'Frightful Five.'" However, she continues, "Lumping them together hides the fact they're very separate and distinct—not just as companies, but in terms of their business models and practices."[2]

In fact, some analysts are differentiating between the Big Five in terms of which ones might actually be too big. There is evidence that three of these companies have far too much dominance in their industries. The *Wall Street Journal* notes that "Facebook Inc., Google parent Alphabet Inc. and Amazon.com Inc. are enjoying profit margins, market dominance and clout that, according to economists and historians, suggest they're developing into a new category of monopolists."[3] Consider that Google and Facebook together raked in over $135 billion in digital ad revenue in 2017, or that Amazon controls 44 percent of U.S. online sales. Google and Facebook's ability to corner the market on digital advertising has decimated the newspaper industry as it has moved online. Local advertisers that once supported local newspapers with their ads now often just place ads with one or both of these companies.

Yet there can be an impermanence to seemingly powerful companies. For example, Amazon's powerful control over book sales online first devastated the big bookstore chains (which themselves had earlier hurt small independent bookstores). Amazon now sells everything and threatens brick-and-mortar grocery stores and department stores, including Walmart (whose superstores earlier shattered many small-town business districts). It is also important to remember that in the 1990s, it seemed that Microsoft had completely beaten its main rival, Apple, yet Apple came back. However, the Justice Department's scrutiny of Microsoft during the 1990s resulted in the company avoiding any engagement in anticompetitive practices, which cleared a path for Apple and other competitors.[4]

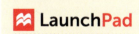

Visit LaunchPad to watch a video about the impact of media ownership. This video argues that it is the drive for bottom-line profits that leads to conglomerates. What solution(s) might you suggest to make the media system work better?

launchpadworks.com

Analyzing the Media Economy

The immense reach and heft of the mass media economy raises some complicated questions, beginning with the role government should play in regulating media ownership. Should citizens step up demands for more accountability from media? Is American culture, expressed through our mass media, hurting other cultures? And is concentration of ownership in the media damaging our democracy? To explore possible answers to these questions, we examine how media companies operate, how the Internet is transforming the media economy, the impact of different business trends, and the ways that people are persuaded to support media rules that may not be in the public's best interests.

How Media Companies Operate

Media organizations develop or distribute content, set prices, and generate profit. They are often asked to live up to society's expectations as well—that is, to operate with a sense of social responsibility in their role as mass communicators. These two main activities—maximizing profits while being socially responsible—are sometimes contradictory functions.

Maximizing Profits

Media companies make money in two main ways. The most obvious way revenue generation occurs is when consumers buy a book, song, game, movie, newspaper, magazine, or subscription—whether directly through the company or through a retailer. This monetary transaction once meant buying things like magazines or CDs in brick-and-mortar stores or through the mail. Now we buy much of our media online, often through the devices of media companies themselves (such as a Kindle).

The other way media companies generate revenue is through advertisements that support their products, such as those appearing on TV and radio shows, in most magazines, in newspapers, and on many websites. These media products might seem free to us, but advertisers are paying for our attention as we engage with the content. As consumers of advertising-based media, we actually have to work for the "free" content by giving our time and attention to commercial sponsors. Advertisers pay more or less depending on how many of us are being exposed to the ads and our potential buying power as an audience. Media companies similarly make money through product placement advertising in movies, television, and video games.

Media corporations generate the most money when they can get us to buy a media product or pay for a subscription (like a cable TV package or a newspaper or magazine subscription) and thus make us a target of the advertising that comes with that media product.

Balancing Profits and the Public Good

The harshest critics of capitalism suggest that running a business is all about maximizing profits, which often means keeping wages low and production high. The resulting impact on social responsibility for media corporations is twofold. First, should they compensate the workers within their own operations with a fair and sustaining wage? Second, should they produce media content—such as stories about fair wages—that are more than just profitable and contribute to society in some positive way?

Many business executives have argued that there is an obligation in flourishing democracies to balance earning profits with serving the larger public. Decisions by billionaires like Warren Buffett of Berkshire Hathaway and Jeff Bezos of Amazon to buy struggling newspapers resonate with the founders' belief that a robust free press has a central role in helping democracy work well. Media corporations can also serve the public good in not only providing information necessary for democracy but also creating content that reflects the full diversity of their audience. For example, television producers in recent years have increased the diversity of their stories and representations both to make more money by attracting younger audiences and "because it's the right thing to do," as one television critic put it.[10]

At the same time, companies that may do something positive in one part of their massive business may also draw criticism in other parts of that business. For example, labor activists have targeted Amazon for what they say is inequality between the overwhelming profits the company makes for owner Bezos and top executives, and the fact that employees in the warehouses and other parts of the behemoth struggle to earn a living on their wages. Meanwhile, Buffett and Berkshire Hathaway have come under fire for preying on those who live in mobile homes.[11]

▼ Labor activists argue that the current minimum wage is not a "living wage." As described by President Franklin D. Roosevelt in the wake of the Great Depression, a living wage means that after working a forty-hour week, a person would be able to provide necessities for a family—food, shelter, clothing, health care—and have something left over for leisure-time pursuits. Scott Olson/Getty Images

How the Internet Is Changing the Game

Historically, media companies have operated in separate industries. That is, the newspaper business functioned separately from book publishing, which operated independently of radio, which worked autonomously from the film industry.

The Internet has changed all that. This medium has not only provided a whole new portal through which people can consume older media forms but also pressured virtually all older media companies to establish an online presence. Today, newspapers, magazines, book publishers, music companies, radio and TV stations, and film studios all have websites or mobile apps marketing digital versions and ancillaries of their products.

This development has provided new opportunities for some media organizations. For example, it has enabled noncommercial public broadcasters to bring in ad revenue. Public radio and TV stations, which are prohibited by FCC regulations from taking advertising, face no such prohibitions online. As a result, many have begun raising money by posting advertisements on their websites.

However, the Internet has also posed new challenges for some older media companies, which must now navigate the realm of less established payment models. For instance, Internet sites like YouTube often display content from traditional broadcast and cable services; the companies selling those services lose direct-payment revenue every time someone consumes content on the Internet rather than paying for the service. Yet this availability may also create exposure for media companies' offerings. Traditional companies must then ask whether that new awareness translates into an increase in *paying* customers.

Business Trends in Media Industries

Consolidation and digitization are not the only trends redefining the mass media business landscape. Trends that shape business overall have further affected the media economy. These include the growth of flexible markets and the decline of labor unions, as well as downsizing and a growing wage gap.

Flexible Markets and the Decline of Labor Unions
In today's economy, markets are flexible—that is, business and consumer needs and preferences change continuously and quickly. Companies seeking to increase profitability alter their products, services, and production processes as needed to satisfy specialized, ever-shifting demands. Making niche products for specialized markets is expensive, and most new products fail in the marketplace. To offset their losses from product failures, companies need to score a few major successes—such as a blockbuster movie or a game-changing handheld device. Large companies with access to the most capital—such as media powerhouses—can more easily absorb losses than can small businesses with limited capital. Thus, the powerhouses stand the best chance of surviving in today's flexible markets.

To lower their costs and earn back their investments in product development, companies have begun relying heavily on cheap labor—sometimes exploiting poor workers in domestic and international sweatshops—and on quick, high-volume sales. Many U.S. companies now export manufacturing work, such as production of computers, TV sets, and mobile phones, to avoid the more expensive unionized labor at home. (Today, many companies outsource even technical and customer support services for their products.) As U.S. firms have gained access to alternative sources of labor, American workers' power has decreased. Since the early 1980s, membership in labor unions has declined dramatically and remains at a seventy-year low. Because one of the main functions of organized labor is to negotiate for better wages and employment stability and security, the drop in union membership has meant a reduction in the bargaining power of unions on behalf of workers. Many economists point to this as a major contributing factor in the dramatic growth in the wage gap between workers and the people who run the companies.

The Wage Gap and Downsizing

Since the 1980s, real wages (wages adjusted for things like inflation) have stagnated for most American workers. This means that as productivity has increased, pay for many has effectively not. Consider also that the pay of chief executives of major companies grew from about 20 times the pay of the average worker in 1965 (a peak time for union membership and overall economic prosperity) to 312 times the pay of the average worker in 2017 (see Figure 14.2).[12] Chief executive officers of major media companies like CBS, Discovery Communications, and Disney often show up in annual lists of the highest-paid CEOs.

Not only have wages stagnated and inequality in wages increased, but many workers have lost their jobs to downsizing as companies strive to become "more productive, more competitive, [and] more flexible."[13] Many people today scramble for paid work, often working two or three part-time and low-wage jobs. In his 2006 book *The Disposable American*, Louis Uchitelle noted unintended side effects of downsizing, including companies' difficulty in developing innovative offerings after gutting their workforces. The news media in particular has felt the pinch from this double jeopardy of downsizing and stagnant wages. Newsrooms have faced steep cuts since the 1990s, which has often meant more work for no additional pay and continued fears that workers will get a pink slip in the next round of layoffs.

The Age of Hegemony

As media corporations have grown larger, they have also been able to manage public debate and dissent about their increasing power. How? One explanation is their ability to exercise **hegemony** in our society. In hegemony, society's least powerful members are persuaded (often without realizing any persuasion has taken place) to accept the values defined by its most powerful members.

In his 1947 article "The Engineering of Consent," Edward Bernays, the father of modern public relations (see Chapter 12), expressed the core concept behind hegemony: Companies cannot get people to do what they want until the people consent to what those companies are trying to do—whether it is

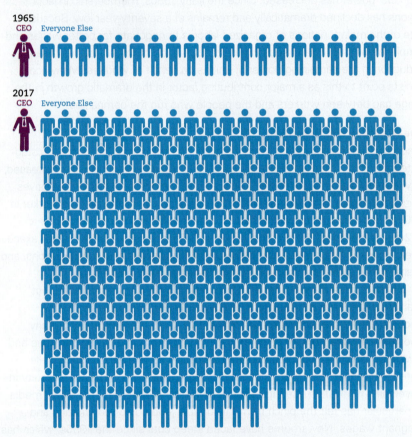

FIGURE 14.2 // CEO-TO-WORKER WAGE GAP, 1965 AND 2017

In 1965, the CEO-to-worker ratio at a major American company was 20:1—that is, the typical CEO earned twenty times the salary of the typical worker in that industry. By 2017, that ratio had climbed to 312:1.

Data from: Lawrence Mishel and Jessica Schieder, "CEO Compensation Surged in 2017," *Economic Policy Institute*, August 16, 2018, www.epi.org/publication/ceo-compensation-surged-in-2017.

getting more people to smoke cigarettes or persuading more of them to go to war. To win people's consent to his clients' goals, Bernays tried to convince Americans that his clients' interests were "natural" and "common sense."

Framing companies' goals in this way makes it unlikely that anyone will challenge or criticize those goals. After all, who is going to argue with common sense? Yet definitions of common sense change over time. For example, it was once common sense that the world was flat and that women and others who did not own property shouldn't be allowed to vote. When people buy uncritically into common sense, they inadvertently perpetuate the divisions that some common sense can create, and they shut out any viewpoints suggesting that these divisions are *not* natural.

◀ American Dream stories are distributed through our media. Early television shows in the 1950s like *The Donna Reed Show* idealized the American nuclear family as central to the American Dream. Everett Collection, Inc

The mass media—through the messages they convey in their products—play a powerful role in defining common sense and therefore setting up hegemony in society. Every time we read an article in a newspaper; read a book or magazine; or watch a movie, TV show, or video clip on YouTube, we absorb messages suggesting what is important and how the world works. If we consume enough of these "stories," we might conclude that what we are seeing in these media products reflects the way things are. And if we believe this is just "the way things are," we probably won't challenge these trends or come up with other, better possibilities.

The reason the narratives work is that they identify with a culture's dominant values. In the United States, Middle American virtues dominate our culture and include allegiances to family, honesty, hard work, religion, capitalism, health, democracy, moderation, and loyalty. These Middle American virtues are the ones that our politicians most frequently align themselves with in the political ads that tell their stories.

These virtues lie at the heart of powerful American Dream stories that for centuries have told us that if we work hard and practice such values, we will triumph and be successful. Hollywood, too, distributes these shared narratives, celebrating characters and heroes who are loyal, honest, and hardworking. Through this process, the media (and the powerful companies that control them) provide the commonsense narratives that keep the economic status quo relatively unchallenged, leaving little room for alternatives. In the end, hegemony helps explain why we sometimes support economic plans and structures that may not be in our best interest.

Specialization and Global Markets

The outsourcing and offshoring of many jobs and the breakdown of global economic borders were bolstered by trade agreements made among national governments in the mid-twentieth century. These included NAFTA (North American Free Trade Agreement) in 1994 and the WTO (World Trade Organization) in 1995. Such agreements enabled the emergence of transnational media corporations and stimulated business deals across national borders. Technology helped, too, making it possible for consumers around the world to easily swap music, TV shows, and movies on the Internet (legally and illegally). All of this has in turn accelerated the global spread of media products and cultural messages.

As globalization gathered momentum, companies began specializing to enter the new, narrow markets opening up to them in other countries. They also began seeking ways to step up their growth through synergies—opportunities to market different versions of a media product.

The Rise of Specialization and Synergy

As globalization picked up speed, several mass media—namely, the magazine, radio, and cable industries—sought to tap specialized markets in the United States and overseas, in part to counter television's mass appeal. For example, cable channels such as Nickelodeon and the Disney Channel serve the under-eighteen market, History draws older viewers, Lifetime and Bravo seek women, and BET targets young African Americans.

In addition to specialization, media companies sought to spur growth through **synergy**—the promotion and sale of different versions of a media product across a media conglomerate's various subsidiaries. An example of synergy is NBC's *Today Show* interviewing an actor from an action movie produced by Universal Pictures, which may then be turned into a ride at a Universal amusement park, with all of these entities owned by parent corporation Comcast. Another example is Sony, which owns a major Hollywood studio and record labels and makes content for its electronic devices (which are often prominently displayed in its movies). But of all the media conglomerates, the Walt Disney Company perhaps best exemplifies the power of both specialization and synergy.

Disney: A Postmodern Media Conglomerate

After Walt Disney's first cartoon company, Laugh-O-gram, went bankrupt in 1922, Disney moved to Hollywood and found his niche. He created Mickey Mouse (originally named Mortimer) for the first sound cartoons in the late

◄ Released in the fall of 2013, the animated hit film *Frozen* provided a big boost for Disney. Not only did it break records at the box office, but it also boosted company profits through all of 2014 and into 2015 with *Frozen*-themed toys, DVDs, soundtracks, and a *Frozen*-themed *Disney on Ice*. The sequel, *Frozen 2*, comes out in 2019. © Walt Disney Collection/Everett Collection, Inc

1920s. He later began development on the first feature-length cartoon, *Snow White and the Seven Dwarfs*, which he completed in 1937.

For much of the twentieth century, the Disney Company set the standard for popular cartoons and children's culture. Nonetheless, the studio barely broke even because cartoon projects took time (four years for *Snow White*) and commanded the company's full array of resources. Moreover, the market for the cartoon film shorts that Disney specialized in was drying up, as fewer movie theaters were showing the shorts before their feature films.

Driving to Diversify

With the demise of the cartoon film short in movie theaters, Disney expanded into other specialized areas. The company's first nature documentary short, *Seal Island*, came in 1949; its first live-action feature, *Treasure Island*, in 1950; and its first feature documentary, *The Living Desert*, in 1953. Also in 1953, Disney started Buena Vista, a distribution company. This was the first step on the studio's path toward becoming a major player in the film industry.

Disney also counted among the first film studios to embrace television. In 1954, the company launched a long-running prime-time show, and television became an even more popular venue than theaters for displaying Disney products. Then, in 1955, the firm added another entirely new dimension to its operations: It opened its Disneyland theme park in Southern California. (Walt Disney World in Orlando, Florida, would begin operation in 1971.) Eventually, Disney's theme parks would produce the bulk of the company's revenues.

Capturing Synergies

Walt Disney's death in 1966 triggered a period of decline for the studio. But in 1984, a new management team, led by Michael Eisner, initiated a turnaround. The company's newly created Touchstone movie division reinvented the live-action–animation hybrid for adults and children in *Who Framed Roger Rabbit?* (1988). A string of hand-drawn animated hits followed, including *The Little Mermaid* (1989) and *Beauty and the Beast* (1991). By the mid-1990s, Disney was well on its way to changing from a media company to a media conglomerate with

FIGURE 14.3 // EXAMPLES OF SYNERGY AT DISNEY

its purchase of ABC and ESPN properties in 1995. At the same time, animation remained an important business and cultural touchstone for the company. In a rocky partnership with Pixar Animation Studios, Disney distributed a series of computer-animated blockbusters—including *Toy Story* (1995) and *Finding Nemo* (2003)—and then Disney bought Pixar outright in 2006.

Since then, Disney has come to epitomize the synergistic possibilities of media consolidation (see Figure 14.3). It can produce an animated feature or regular film for theatrical release, DVD distribution, and streaming video. Characters and stories from blockbuster films like *The Avengers*, *Black Panther*, and the *Iron Man* franchise can become television series on ABC, Hulu, and new streaming service Disney+, with story lines that intersect with the movies. (Disney owns Marvel, ABC, Disney+, and a controlling interest in Hulu.) Book versions can be released through Disney's publishing arm, Disney Publishing Worldwide, and "the-making-of" versions can appear on cable's Disney Channel, FX, or Freeform (formerly ABC Family). Characters can become attractions at Disney's theme parks, which themselves have spawned lucrative Hollywood blockbusters, like the *Pirates of the Caribbean* series. Some Disney films have had as many as seventeen thousand licensed products—from clothing to toys to dog-food bowls. Disney has hundreds of retail stores in malls across the United States, and in New York City, Disney renovated several theaters and launched versions of *Mary Poppins*, *The Lion King*, *Aladdin*, and *Frozen* as successful Broadway musicals.

Expanding Globally

Building on the international appeal of its cartoon features, Disney extended its global reach by opening a successful theme park in Japan in 1983. Three years later, the company started marketing cartoons to Chinese television—attracting an estimated 300 million viewers per week. Disney also launched a magazine in

Chinese. In 1997, Orbit—a Saudi-owned satellite relay station based in Rome—introduced Disney's twenty-four-hour cable channel to twenty-three countries in the Middle East and North Africa, as well as a new nationwide Disney channel in Russia in 2010. Disney also started expanding its theme parks and resorts, opening EuroDisney (now Disneyland Paris) in the 1990s, a theme park in Hong Kong in 2005, and a Disney resort in Shanghai in 2016. Disney's fifth, sixth, and seventh international cruise ships will be added in 2021, 2022, and 2023.

Disney Today

Even as Disney grew into the world's No. 2 media conglomerate by the beginning of the twenty-first century, the cartoon pioneer experienced the multiple shocks of a recession, failed films and Internet ventures, and declining theme-park attendance. By 2005, Disney had fallen to No. 5 among movie studios in U.S. box-office sales—down from No. 1 in 2003. The new course for Disney was to develop (through acquisitions) new stories for movies and its other corporate offerings. In 2006, new CEO Robert Iger merged Disney and Pixar. In 2009, Disney purchased Marvel Entertainment for $4 billion, bringing Iron Man, Spider-Man, and the Avengers into the Disney family; in 2012, it purchased Lucasfilm and, with it, the rights to the *Star Wars* and *Indiana Jones* movies and characters.

In 2017, Disney announced it intended to purchase 21st Century Fox, which included rights to more Marvel properties (X-Men, Deadpool) and the Fox film and TV studios and cable channels. The deal was finalized in March 2019. In 2019 Disney also announced a new streaming service, Disney+, and indicated plans to consolidate its control of Hulu by buying out that service's other partners.

The Growth of Global Audiences

As Disney's story shows, international expansion has afforded media conglomerates key advantages, including access to profitable secondary markets and opportunities to advance and leverage technological innovations. As media technologies have become cheaper and more portable (from the original Walkman to the iPad), American media have proliferated both inside and outside U.S. boundaries.

Today, greatly facilitated by the Internet, media products flow easily into the eyes and ears of people around the world. Netflix, for example, leveraged the success of an online streaming platform to become a global giant (see "Media Literacy Case Study: Netflix and Change: The Streaming Revolution and the Business of Content Creation" on pages 422–423). And thanks to satellite transmission, North American and European television is now available at the global level. Cable services such as CNN and BBC World News deliver content to more than two hundred countries.

This growth of global audiences has permitted companies that lose money on products at home to profit in overseas markets. Roughly 80 percent of American movies, for instance, do not earn back their costs in U.S. theaters; they depend on foreign circulation as well as video revenue to make up for early losses. The same is true for the television industry.

LaunchPad
launchpadworks.com

Disney's Global Brand
Watch a clip from *Frozen*, one of Disney's biggest movies ever.

Discussion: What elements of *Frozen* might have contributed to its global popularity?

Media Literacy

CASE STUDY

Netflix and Change: The Streaming Revolution and the Business of Content Creation

In May 2018, Netflix moved closer to joining the select group of the world's top digital companies. Netflix's stock-market value surged to $153 billion, surpassing at that time traditional media companies Disney and Comcast (NBC Universal). Although just over twenty years old and a streaming company for only about ten years, Netflix has revolutionized television in the United States and around the world.

Netflix began as a modest idea in 1997. Two software engineers in California founded the company to rent movie DVDs online and ship them through the mail. In this model, customers would pay a flat monthly fee, rent and return as many videos as they liked each month, and incur no late fees (unlike at its biggest competitor, Blockbuster video stores). By its own admission, the company struggled for the first five years, even unsuccessfully offering to sell itself to Blockbuster and Amazon during that time.[1]

Eventually, though, DVD-rental-by-mail caught on, and Netflix continued to grow its customer base. Then, in 2007, Netflix developed Internet streaming—a better movie distribution system that proved to be immensely popular. In 2010, Netflix began expanding to a number of global markets, which now include Canada, Latin America, Europe, Japan, and Australia.

Web Clip

Netflix has its own channel on YouTube, where you can preview clips, trailers, and digital exclusives from Netflix programs. How is Netflix using this other platform—which also streams videos and includes original programming—to promote its own brand?

In 2013, Netflix came up with another significant innovation when it began creating its own original series. Some of the company's biggest and most critically acclaimed hits include *House of Cards*, *Orange Is the New Black*, *BoJack Horseman*, *Master of None*, *Unbreakable Kimmy Schmidt*, and *Big Mouth*.

By 2018, Netflix was generating about $15.8 billion in annual revenue, making it "the world's leading internet entertainment service with over 139 million paid memberships in over 190 countries enjoying TV series, documentaries and feature films across a wide variety of genres and languages."[2]

Netflix has changed TV culture. By releasing entire seasons of its own original programming and licensing series such as *Breaking Bad*, *The Walking Dead*, *Nurse Jackie*, *Mad Men*, and *The Office*, Netflix gave rise to the practice of binge-watching.[3] (See also Chapter 8.)

The key to Netflix's success has been providing excellent content and a superior user experience (easy access, reasonable price) that is being continuously improved. In doing so, not only did Netflix kill the video store, but it and the other video streaming services that have entered the fray are threatening to kill traditional television.

As media citizens, we have witnessed these kinds of transformations before. For example, in 1999, Napster offered a better way to access music: on the Internet, with a quick (and illegal) download. The new format marked the beginning of the death of the CD album. Apple improved the user experience a few years later, with a large (and legal) music catalog on the iTunes store and new iPod devices on which to play the music. Now,

▲ At the Netflix headquarters—based in Los Gatos, California, about an hour south of San Francisco—employees enjoy many perks, including free breakfast, lunch, and popcorn daily; a car-borrowing service; and a flexible vacation schedule. Jim Bennett, left, vice president of recommendation systems, and Reed Hastings, CEO, are seen here in a screening room at headquarters. Jim Wilson/The New York Times/Redux

music streaming and Internet radio businesses like Spotify and Apple Music have offered better user experiences for accessing music.

Netflix's leading position in the transition from linear to Internet TV puts the company in position to join the top five digital conglomerates: Amazon, Apple, Facebook, Google, and Microsoft. With its $15.8 billion in annual revenue in 2018, Netflix is still much smaller than the largest, Apple, with $265.6 billion in annual revenue in 2018.[4] Yet Netflix has enormous potential for growth over the next decade, as new generations of global binge-watchers emerge, demanding TV and movies on small digital screens—and on their own time.

However, the company will also face new challenges now that Disney has merged with 21st Century Fox, moved to consolidate its control of Hulu, and prepared to yank all Disney-owned programming from Netflix as it launches its own streaming service, Disney+. Netflix will still have other partners, its own content, and an established base of customers, but both opportunity *and* the potential for change are in the air as the company moves into the 2020s.

APPLYING THE CRITICAL PROCESS

DESCRIPTION To get an idea of how other streaming services (Hulu, Amazon) have affected Netflix's success and strategy, look up news stories from the past few years on this topic.

ANALYSIS What patterns do you notice in the content of these articles? What topics have journalists focused on most?

INTERPRETATION Based on what you have discovered, what do these patterns mean? How do they reflect larger trends in the media?

EVALUATION Rapid change is a hallmark of the mass media landscape following the digital turn. Have the changes with Netflix and other streaming services like Hulu been good or bad for consumers, both in the United States and around the globe? For the kinds of programming that gets made and shared?

ENGAGEMENT Think about which video streaming services you use, how often, and why you pick the one(s) you pay for. Ask two or three people around you to do the same, and compare your responses.

Social Issues in Media Economics

Mergermania has sparked criticism in some quarters. Some opponents lament the limits of antitrust laws. Others decry consumers' loss of control in the marketplace when just a few companies determine what messages and media content are produced. Still others warn against the infiltration of American culture and media messages into every corner of the globe.

The Limits of Antitrust Laws

Despite the intent of antitrust laws to ensure diversity of corporate ownership, companies have easily avoided these laws since the 1980s by diversifying their holdings and by forming local monopolies—especially in newspapers and cable. To accomplish this local control combined with megamedia mergers, media corporations developed well-polished and effective public relations and lobbying campaigns to get the public and lawmakers to back wave after wave of deregulation, thus weakening or stripping antitrust protections. These efforts have resulted in fewer voices in the marketplace and less competition among industry players.

Expanding through Diversification

Diversification, consolidation, and media partnerships promote oligopolies in which a few large companies control the majority of production and distribution of media content. Most media companies diversify among different media products (such as television stations and film studios), never fully dominating one particular media industry. WarnerMedia (formerly Time Warner), which is now owned by AT&T, for example, spreads its holdings among television programming, film, cable channels, and digital games. Meanwhile, parent company AT&T is already a vast telecommunications empire. However, WarnerMedia/AT&T competes directly with only a few other big companies, such as Disney, Comcast, and Viacom. And Comcast, following a series of mergers, not only has become the cable and broadband company that controls the path by which so many media products are streamed into the home but also, after buying NBC Universal, controls a big portion of the media products on that path.

One prime example of a media partnership is Hulu.com, started as a joint venture of NBC Universal TV (Comcast), Fox Broadcasting, Disney–ABC Television, and Time Warner. Not only did these four owners of the video streaming service offer content from the pantheon of networks they own, but they had several other "content partners" as well, including the BBC network. However, Disney's merger with Fox gave it majority control of Hulu, and in 2019, the company announced that it planned to buy the streaming service outright from its other partners.

Media partnerships can make it difficult for companies outside the oligopoly to compete in the marketplace. For example, an independent film production company may be unable to attract enough investors to get its movies distributed nationwide.

Building Local Monopolies

Antitrust laws aim to curb *national* monopolies, so most media monopolies today operate locally. Nearly every cable company has been granted monopoly status in its local community. These firms alone decide which channels are made available and what rates are charged. Independent voices have little opportunity or means to raise the questions that regulatory groups—such as the Justice Department and the FCC—need to hear in order to shape the laws.

The Fallout from a Free Market

Despite the concerns expressed by some critics, there has been little public debate overall about the tightening oligopoly structure of international media. Experts have identified two forces behind this vast hegemonic silence: citizens' reluctance to criticize free markets because they equate them with democracy, and the often unclear distinction between how much choice and how much control consumers have in the marketplace.

Equating Free Markets with Democracy

Throughout the Cold War period in the 1950s and 1960s, many Americans refused to criticize capitalism, which they saw as synonymous with democracy. Any complaint about capitalism was viewed as an attack on the free marketplace, and attacks on the free marketplace in turn sounded like criticism of free speech. This was in part because business owners saw their right to operate in a free marketplace as an extension of their right to buy commercial speech in the form of advertising. This line of thinking, which originated in corporate efforts to equate capitalism with democracy, still casts a shadow over American culture, making it difficult for many people to openly question the advertising-supported economic structure of the mass media.

Debating Consumer Choice versus Consumer Control

In discussing free markets, economists distinguish between *consumer control* over marketplace goods and freedom of *consumer choice*: "The former requires that consumers participate in deciding what is to be offered; the latter is satisfied if [consumers are] free to select among the options chosen for them by producers."[14] Most Americans and the citizens of other economically developed nations clearly have *choice*: options among a range of media products. Yet the choices sometimes obscure the fact that consumers have limited *control*: power in deciding what kinds of media get created and circulated. Consumers thus have little ability to shape the messages conveyed through media products about what is important and how the world should work. Instead, they can only react to those messages.

Yet independent and alternative producers, artists, writers, and publishers have provided a ray of hope. When their work becomes even marginally popular, big media companies often capitalize on these innovations by acquiring it—which enables the work to get out to the public. Moreover, business leaders "at the top"

▲ Ever since Hollywood gained an edge in film production and distribution, U.S. movies have dominated the box office in Europe, Asia, and the rest of the world. Worldwide grosses are thus more important to Hollywood than ever. © Walt Disney Movie Studios Motion Pictures/Lucasfilm Ltd./Everett Collection, Inc

depend on independent ideas "from below" to generate new product lines. Fortunately, a number of transnational corporations encourage the development of promising local artists.

Cultural Imperialism

The increasing dominance of American popular culture around the world has sparked heated debate in international circles. On the one hand, people in other countries seem to relish the themes of innovation and rebellion expressed in American media products, and the global spread of access to media (particularly the ease of digital documentation via mobile devices) has made it harder for political leaders to secretly repress dissident groups. On the other hand, American styles in fashion and food, as well as media fare, dominate the global market—a situation known as **cultural imperialism**. Today, numerous international observers contend that consumers in countries inundated by American-made movies, music, television, and images have even less control than American consumers. Even the Internet has a distinctively American orientation. The United States got a head start in deploying the Internet as a mass medium and has been the dominant force ever since. Although the Internet is worldwide and in many languages, the majority of the web's content is still in English; the United States has long controlled the top domains, including .com and .org (without the requirement of having a nation-identifying domain name, such as .jp for Japan or .fr for France); and leading global sites like Google, Facebook, Amazon, YouTube, and Wikipedia are all American in design.

Defenders of American popular culture's dominance argue that a universal culture creates a *global village* and fosters communication and collaboration across national boundaries. Critics, however, point out that two-thirds of the world's population cannot afford most of the products advertised on American, Japanese, and European television. Yet they see, hear, and read about consumer abundance and middle-class values through TV and other media, including magazines and the Internet. Critics worry that the obvious disparities in economic well-being and the frustration that must surely come from not having the money to buy advertised products may lead to social unrest.

The Media Marketplace in a Democratic Society

Multinational giants are controlling more and more aspects of production and distribution of media products. This is particularly worrisome when it comes to news media: Media conglomerates that own news companies have the capacity to use those resources to promote their products and determine

◀ Amy Goodman is cohost of *Democracy Now!*, a radio and TV newscast airing daily on more than eight hundred public and college radio stations, satellite television, and the Internet. *Democracy Now!* argues that it maintains editorial independence by accepting funding only from listeners, viewers, and foundations, and rejecting government funding, corporate underwriting, and advertisers. MONTEMAGNI/SIPA/Sipa Press/Brentwood California United States

what news receives national coverage. When news coverage is determined by fewer decision makers, citizens cannot be certain they are receiving sufficient information with which to make decisions. That's bad news for any democracy.

Media powerhouses are also increasingly shaping the regulatory environment. Politicians in Washington, D.C., regularly accept millions of dollars from media conglomerates and their lobbying groups to finance their campaigns. Companies that provide such financial support stand a better chance of influencing regulatory decisions. Indeed, they have successfully pushed for more deregulation, which has enabled them to grow even more and come under fewer constraints. This is also bad news for our democracy, especially because the journalism subsidiaries of major media conglomerates are not completely independent of the powerful corporate and political forces on which they report. Who will tell us the news about big media and their political allies?

Despite the forces we have examined that are discouraging energetic debate about these realities, some grassroots organizations have arisen to challenge the power and reach of media behemoths. Such movements—like the organization Free Press—are typically united by geographic ties, common political backgrounds, or shared concerns about the state of the media. The Internet has also enabled media reform groups to form globally, uniting around such efforts as fostering independent media, contesting censorship, or monitoring the activities of multinational corporations.

This development is encouraging news: It suggests that we consumers—whether in America or elsewhere—might be willing to look more closely at the media marketplace's impact on our lives. And we may start demanding that media companies take more responsibility for fulfilling one of their key missions: making democratic life better for those of us consuming their products and absorbing their messages.

CHAPTER ESSENTIALS

Review

- By the mid-twentieth century, the United States shifted from a manufacturing-based economy to one fueled by information and cooperation with other economies, causing mass media industries to expand globally. Although early regulation was designed to break up monopolies, deregulation of the industries won out, leading to a growth in mergers and acquisitions.

- Media industries have one of three common structures: **monopoly**, **oligopoly**, or **limited competition**.

- Today's media powerhouses avoid monopoly charges by purchasing diverse types of media rather than controlling just one medium.

- Media companies make money from selling media content (e.g., physical or digital versions of books, music, films, video games, software, and apps), subscriptions to streaming content, devices on which to use that content (e.g., smartphones, tablets, e-readers, and video game consoles), and advertising.

- In addition to generating profit, media companies are often asked to operate with a sense of social responsibility in their role as mass communicators. These are sometimes contradictory functions.

- Historically, media companies have operated in separate industries; however, the Internet has changed the way people consume media. This development has presented new opportunities for some media organizations while posing challenges for some older media companies.

- Other trends that have affected the media economy include flexible markets and the decline of unionized labor, as well as downsizing and a growing wage gap.

- All these trends take place, in part, because mass media play a powerful role in establishing **hegemony**, in which a society's least powerful members are persuaded to accept the values defined by its most powerful members.

- With the rise of globalization, companies began specializing to enter the new, narrow markets in other countries. They also sought to spur growth through **synergy**.

- The Walt Disney Company is an example of a media conglomerate that has excelled at specialization and synergy. Following Disney's model,

> **LaunchPad**
>
> Visit LaunchPad for *Media Essentials* at **launchpadworks.com** for additional learning tools:
>
> - **REVIEW WITH LEARNINGCURVE**
>   LearningCurve adaptive quizzing helps you master the concepts you need to learn from this chapter.
> - **VIDEO: THE MONEY BEHIND THE MEDIA**
>   Producers, advertisers, and advocates discuss how ownership systems and profits shape media production.
> - **MEDIA LITERACY PRACTICE**
>   This activity challenges you to develop a critical perspective and apply it to everyday encounters with communication media.

many media conglomerates look to international expansion as a way to access markets.

- Critics of mergers and media consolidation argue that antitrust laws are too limited, resulting in fewer voices in the marketplace, less competition among industry players, and loss of consumer control.

- Others warn against the infiltration of American culture and media messages into every corner of the globe—a situation known as **cultural imperialism**.

- Democracy suffers when news coverage is determined by fewer decision makers and when media powerhouses increasingly shape the regulatory environment. Grassroots organizations and the Internet have enabled media reform groups to form globally, suggesting that consumers might be willing to look more closely at the media marketplace's impact on our lives.

Key Terms

monopoly, p. 406
oligopoly, p. 407
limited competition, p. 407
hegemony, p. 415
synergy, p. 418
cultural imperialism, p. 426

Study Questions

1. How are the three basic structures of mass media organizations—monopoly, oligopoly, and limited competition—different from one another? How is the Internet changing everything?

2. Why has the federal government emphasized deregulation at a time when so many media companies are growing so large? How have media mergers changed the economics of mass media?

3. How do global and specialized markets factor into the new media economy? Using the Walt Disney Company as an example, what is the role of synergy in the current climate of media mergers?

4. What are the differences between consumer control over marketplace goods and freedom of consumer choice? What is cultural imperialism, and what does it have to do with the United States?

5. What do critics and activists fear most about the concentration of media ownership? What are some promising signs regarding the relationship between media economics and democracy?

Media Expressions

15

Media Effects and Cultural Approaches to Media Research

433
Early Media Research Methods

438
Research on Media Effects

446
Cultural Approaches to Media Research

452
Media Research in a Democratic Society

In October 2018, gunman Robert D. Bowers murdered eleven people and wounded half a dozen more when he stormed a Pittsburgh synagogue armed with an AR-15 style assault rifle.[1] In April 2018, Alek Minassian rammed a van into a Toronto crowd of mostly women, killing ten people and wounding over a dozen more.[2] In February 2018, Nikolas Cruz killed seventeen in a shooting spree at Marjory Stoneman Douglas High School in Parkland, Florida.[3] Shocking in their seeming randomness and scale of destruction, these and other cases like them are tied together by a common element: evidence the perpetrators were self-radicalized online after seeking out contact with white supremacist, alt-right, and related hate groups. Bowers, for example, frequented white nationalist social networks and "found a like-minded community, reposting messages from Nazi supporters," the *New York Times* reported.[4]

◄ Robert Bowers had a long history of activity in the world of online white supremacist hate before murdering eleven people in a Pittsburgh synagogue in 2018. His case is just one in recent years that connects mass murderers with a form of online self-radicalization. Here, Rabbi Jeffrey Myers is interviewed near the scene of the shooting. Brendan Smialowski/Getty Images

The Southern Poverty Law Center, which has spent decades tracking hate groups, said in a spring 2019 report that these groups are able to reach out in new ways via the Internet and social media, and—perhaps more importantly—that unbalanced and violent individuals find it easier to reach out to these hate groups in return.[5] While rallies, meetings, and other events used to be the main way groups recruited and spread their ideologies, online self-radicalization means that the perpetrators in the incidents described here sought out their own deeply racist communities and accompanying propaganda.

Media-influenced incidents like these raise important questions: Is this kind of online radicalization truly something new, enabled by new media pathways? What is social media's role in this surge in hate-related violence? The Internet's role? These are the types of questions that media researchers—scholars who study the media and its effects—can explore through rigorous investigation and analysis. But they are far from the only issues that interest these researchers; throughout this book we have discussed a series of other questions that scholars grapple with, including the importance of diversity in television (Chapter 8) and video games (Chapter 10); the role of economic forces on the production and distribution of media products (Chapter 14); and how journalists cover the news and how that shapes the way we see the world (Chapter 3).

Because mass media touches our lives on a daily basis, media studies research is relevant to each of us. Our society has a vested interest in using the best information available to guide our public policy decisions, and much of the information we consider—everything from the psychological effects of FOMO (Chapter 1) to the complicated connections between mass killings and hate groups—is generated from media research.

THE IDEA THAT MEDIA HAVE A SIGNIFICANT IMPACT on society has fueled the development of two types of research in the study of mass communication: media effects research and cultural studies research.

Media effects research, which has connections to a social scientific tradition of research, attempts to understand, explain, and predict the effects of mass media on individuals and society. The typical approach of this type of research is to define the problem with a testable hypothesis, collect data through one of various methodologies, and draw conclusions based on the data.

Researchers who focus on **cultural studies** explore how people make meaning, understand reality, articulate values, and interpret their experiences through the use of cultural symbols in media. Cultural studies scholars also examine how groups such as corporate and political elites use media to circulate their messages and serve their interests. Such research focuses on daily cultural experience, examining the subtle intersections among mass communication, history, politics, and economics.

In this chapter, we look at how these two forms of media research have evolved over time by:

- examining early media research methods, including propaganda analysis, public opinion research, social psychology studies, and marketing research

- assessing media effects research, including theories about how media influence people's behaviors and attitudes, and the benefits and limitations of such research

- taking stock of cultural approaches to media research, including early and contemporary cultural studies approaches and the strengths and limitations of such research

- considering the role of media research in our democracy and exploring how effectively such research addresses real-life problems

Early Media Research Methods

During most of the nineteenth century, philosophers such as Alexis de Tocqueville based their analysis of news and print media on moral and political arguments.[6] More scientific approaches to mass media research did not emerge until the late 1920s and 1930s. In 1920, Walter Lippmann's *Liberty and the News* called on journalists to operate more like scientific researchers in gathering and analyzing facts. Lippmann's next book, *Public Opinion* (1922), was the first to apply the principles of psychology to journalism. Considered by many academics to be "the founding book in American media studies,"[7] *Public Opinion* deepened Americans' understanding of the effects of media, emphasizing data collection and numerical measurement. According to media historian Daniel Czitrom, by the 1930s "an aggressively empirical spirit, stressing new and increasingly sophisticated research techniques, characterized the study of

launchpadworks.com

Use **LearningCurve** to review concepts from this chapter.

▲ Propaganda analysis researchers studied the impact of war posters and other government information campaigns to determine how audiences could be persuaded through stirring media messages about patriotism and duty. Alexander Liberman/National Archives and Records Administration [NWDNS-44-PA-370]

modern communication in America."[8] Czitrom traces four trends between 1930 and 1960 that contributed to the rise of modern media research: propaganda analysis, public opinion research, social psychology studies, and marketing research.

Propaganda Analysis

Propaganda analysis was a major early focus of mass media research. After World War I, some researchers began studying how governments used propaganda to advance the war effort. They found that during the war, governments routinely relied on propaganda divisions to spread "information" to the public. Though propaganda was considered important for mobilizing public support during the war, these postwar researchers criticized it as "partisan appeal based on half-truths and devious manipulation of communication channels."[9] Harold Lasswell's 1927 study *Propaganda Technique in the World War* defined propaganda as "the control of opinion by significant symbols, . . . by stories, rumors, reports, pictures and other forms of social communication."[10]

Public Opinion Research

After World War II, researchers went beyond the study of wartime propaganda and began examining how the mass media filter information and shape public attitudes. Social scientists explored these questions by conducting *public opinion research* through citizen surveys and polls.

Public opinion research on diverse populations has provided insight into how different groups view major national events, such as elections, and how those views affect their behavior. Journalists, however, have become increasingly dependent on polls, particularly for political insight.

Today, some critics argue that this heavy reliance on measured public opinion adversely affects Americans' participation in the political process. For example, people who read poll projections and get the sense that only a small number of people will be voting for their favored candidate may not bother casting a ballot. "Why should I vote," they tell themselves, "if my vote isn't going to make a difference?" Some critics of incessant polling argue that polls mainly measure opinions on topics of interest to business, government, academics, and the mainstream news media. The public responds passively to polls, without getting anything of value in return. Professional pollsters object to **pseudo-polls**—typically call-in, online, or person-in-the-street polls that the news media use to address a "question of the day." Such polls, which do not use a random sample of the population and are therefore not representative of the population as a whole, nevertheless persist on news and entertainment websites, radio, and television news programs.

Social Psychology Studies

Whereas opinion polls measure public attitudes, *social psychology studies* measure the behavior, attitudes, and cognition of individuals. The Payne Fund Studies—the most influential early social psychology media studies—comprised thirteen research projects conducted by social psychologists between 1929 and 1932. Named after the private philanthropic organization that funded the research, the Payne Fund Studies were a response to a growing national concern about the effects of motion pictures on young people. The studies, which some politicians later used to attack the movie industry, linked frequent movie attendance to juvenile delinquency, promiscuity, and other problematic behaviors, arguing that movies took "emotional possession" of young filmgoers.[11]

The conclusions of this and other Payne Fund Studies contributed to the establishment of the Motion Picture Production Code, which tamed movie content from the 1930s through the 1950s (see Chapter 13). As forerunners of today's research into TV violence and aggression, the Payne Fund Studies became the model for media research, although social psychology is also used to study the mass media's relationship to body image, gender norms, political participation, and a wide range of other topics. (See Figure 15.1 for one example of a contemporary policy that has developed from media research.)

Marketing Research

Marketing research emerged in the 1920s, when advertisers and consumer product companies began conducting surveys on consumer buying habits and other behaviors. For example, rating systems arose that measured how many people were listening to commercial radio on a given night. By the 1930s, radio networks, advertisers, large stations, and advertising agencies all subscribed to ratings services. However, compared with print media, whose circulation departments kept track of customers' names and addresses, radio listeners were more difficult to trace. The problem prompted experts to

FIGURE 15.1 // TV PARENTAL GUIDELINES

The TV industry continues to study its self-imposed rating categories, promising to fine-tune them to ensure that the government keeps its distance. These standards are one example of a policy that was shaped in part by media research.

The following categories apply to programs designed solely for children:

 All Children
This program is designed to be appropriate for all children. Whether animated or live-action, the themes and elements in this program are specifically designed for a very young audience, including children from ages 2–6. This program is not expected to frighten young children.

Directed to Older Children—Fantasy Violence
For those programs where fantasy violence may be more intense or more combative than other programs in this category, such programs will be designated TV-Y7-FV.

 Directed to Older Children
This program is designed for children age 7 and above. It may be more appropriate for children who have acquired the developmental skills needed to distinguish between make-believe and reality. Themes and elements in this program may include mild fantasy violence or comedic violence, or may frighten children under the age of 7. Therefore, parents may wish to consider the suitability of this program for their very young children.

The following categories apply to programs designed for the entire audience:

 General Audience
Most parents would find this program suitable for all ages. Although this rating does not signify a program designed specifically for children, most parents may let younger children watch this program unattended. It contains little or no violence, no strong language, and little or no sexual dialogue situations.

Parental Guidance Suggested
This program contains material that parents may find unsuitable for younger children. Many parents may want to watch it with their younger children. The theme itself may call for parental guidance and/or the program may contain one or more of the following: some suggestive dialogue (D), infrequent coarse language (L), some sexual situations (S), or moderate violence (V).

 Parents Strongly Cautioned
This program contains some material that many parents would find unsuitable for children under 14 years of age. Parents are strongly urged to exercise greater care in monitoring this program and are cautioned against letting children under the age of 14 watch unattended. This program may contain one or more of the following: intensely suggestive dialogue (D), strong coarse language (L), intense sexual situations (S), or intense violence (V).

Mature Audiences Only
This program is specifically designed to be viewed by adults and therefore may be unsuitable for children under 17. This program may contain one or more of the following: crude indecent language (L), explicit sexual activity (S), or graphic violence (V).

Data from: TV Parental Guidelines Monitoring Board, www.tvguidelines.org, accessed February 20, 2019.

develop increasingly sophisticated market-research methods to determine consumer preferences and media use, such as direct-mail diaries, television meters, phone surveys, telemarketing, and eventually Internet tracking. In many instances, product companies paid consumers a small fee to take part in these studies. (To see how companies today track consumer habits and media use with sophisticated algorithms, see "The Digital Turn Case Study: Artificial Intelligence Gets Personal" on page 437.)

The Digital Turn

CASE STUDY

Artificial Intelligence Gets Personal

If you've used an online streaming service or shopping site—everything from Spotify to Amazon Prime to Netflix—you know that one of the first things you see when you open the app is a list of recommended songs, movies, or other products. When you encounter this type of recommendation engine, you are experiencing a form of *artificial intelligence* (AI)—a computer program that uses data and algorithms to try to predict what you will listen to, watch, or buy.

The evolution of Netflix's recommendation model helps explain the logic behind this kind of AI. At its founding, Netflix used a website to rent out DVDs through the mail. Back then it would ask customers to rate favorites, look at what they had ordered, and base recommendations on that information. Now, thanks to the rise of streaming, Netflix's algorithm can collect data on what users watched, how long they watched, when they watched, and what kind of device they used. This data populates an interface with categories of recommendations based on a variety of factors. According to Netflix's vice president of innovation, the company is always improving its algorithm with a particular goal in mind: "We should get to the point where you just turn on your Netflix app and automatically a video starts to play that you're very happy with."[1]

Netflix provides just one example of how data run through an algorithm dictates what you do (and don't) see on various sites. For example, the stories you see on your Facebook feed are determined by an algorithm, and the list of results you get from a Google search is based in part on past results and where you are physically located when you perform the search. Amazon's algorithm receives information based on what people watch on its streaming service, listen to on its music service, and purchase from its online retail sites. Amazon even has Echo Look, an algorithm-enabled camera interface that serves as a style and wardrobe assistant.[2]

Digital companies are investing in AI technology as a way to better understand customer behaviors—and boost corporate income. These AI programs are designed not just to provide entertainment recommendations but also to influence which ads are targeted to consumers. And as the marketing software gets better at tracking a person across multiple platforms and websites (see Chapter 11), that data becomes fodder for the AI program.

This move toward personalization through artificial intelligence creates concerns and questions for media critics, as well as areas of study for media scholars. After all, these algorithms are created by people who work for companies with specific financial interests, which are not necessarily in line with true user preferences. For example, does Netflix have an incentive to feature its own content more prominently than other content? Does Facebook have an obligation to filter out—or at least impede—the spread of fake news? Media researchers have set out to answer questions like these in order to better understand the relationship between media, data, privacy, and audience behavior.

> ### ▶ Web Clip
>
> **YouTube.com** features many videos that reference the algorithms of successful companies. For example, search for "Introducing Echo Look. Love your look. Every day" by amazonfashion. What do you see as the pros and cons of a device like Echo Look tracking your fashion choices? What types of questions do you think media scholars might have about this product and how it operates?
>
>

Research on Media Effects

Concerns about public opinion measurements, propaganda, and the impact of media on society intensified just as journalism and mass communication departments gained popularity in colleges and universities. As these forces dovetailed, media researchers looked increasingly to behavioral science as the basis for their work. Between 1930 and 1960, "who says what to whom with what effect" became the key question "defining the scope and problems of American communications research."[12] To address this question, media effects researchers asked more specific questions, such as, "If children watch a lot of TV cartoons (stimulus or cause), will this influence their behavior toward their peers (response or effect)?" New models arose to measure and explain such connections.

Early Models of Media Effects

Between the 1930s and the 1970s, media researchers developed several theories about how media affect individuals' behavior: the hypodermic-needle model, the minimal-effects model, and the uses and gratifications model. While more recent research has added nuance to these models and informed the creation of new ones, these early models helped shape an important branch of mass communication research.

Hypodermic Needle

The notion that powerful media adversely affect weak audiences has been labeled the **hypodermic-needle model**, or *magic bullet theory*. This model suggests that the media "shoot" their effects directly into unsuspecting victims.

One of the earliest challenges to this model came from a study of Orson Welles's legendary October 30, 1938, radio broadcast of *War of the Worlds*. The broadcast presented H. G. Wells's Martian-invasion novel in the form of a news report, which frightened millions of listeners who didn't realize it was fictional (see Chapter 6). In 1940, radio researcher Hadley Cantril wrote a book-length study of the broadcast and its aftermath, titled *The Invasion from Mars: A Study in the Psychology of Panic*. Cantril argued that

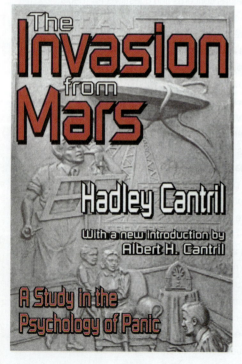

▼ In *The Invasion from Mars: A Study in the Psychology of Panic*, Hadley Cantril (1906–1969) argued against the hypodermic-needle model as an explanation for the panic that broke out after the *War of the Worlds* radio broadcast. A lifelong social researcher, Cantril also did a lot of work in public opinion research, even working with the government during World War II.

contrary to what the hypodermic-needle model suggested, not all listeners thought the radio program was a real news report. In fact, the relatively few listeners who thought there was an actual invasion from Mars were those who not only tuned in late and missed the disclaimer at the beginning of the broadcast but also were predisposed (because of religious beliefs) to think that the end of the world was actually near. Although social scientists have since disproved the hypodermic-needle model, many people still subscribe to it, particularly when considering the media's impact on children.

Minimal Effects

Cantril's research helped lay the groundwork for the **minimal-effects** (or limited-effects) **model**, proposed by some media researchers. With the rise of empirical research techniques, social scientists began discovering and demonstrating that media alone do not cause people to change their attitudes and behaviors. After conducting controlled experiments and surveys, researchers argued that people generally engage in **selective exposure** and **selective retention** with regard to media. That is, people expose themselves to media messages most familiar to them, and retain messages that confirm values and attitudes they already hold. Minimal-effects researchers have argued that in most cases, mass media *reinforce* existing behaviors and attitudes rather than change them.

Indeed, Joseph Klapper, in his 1960 research study *The Effects of Mass Communication*, found that mass media influenced only those individuals who did not already hold strong views on an issue. Media, Klapper added, had a greater impact on poor and uneducated audiences. Solidifying the minimal-effects argument, Klapper concluded that strong media effects occur largely at an individual level and do not appear to have large-scale, measurable, and direct effects on society as a whole.[13]

Uses and Gratifications

The **uses and gratifications model** arose to challenge the notion that people are passive recipients of media. This model holds that people actively engage in using media to satisfy various emotional or intellectual needs—for example, turning on the TV in the house not only to be entertained but also to create an "electronic hearth," making the space feel warmer and more alive. Researchers supporting this model use in-depth interviews to supplement survey questionnaires. Through these interviews, they study the ways in which people use media. Instead of asking, "What effects do media have on us?" these researchers ask, "Why do we use media?"

Although the uses and gratifications model addresses the *functions* of the mass media for individuals, it does not address important questions related to

launchpadworks.com

Media Effects Research
Experts discuss how media effects research informs media development.

Discussion: Why do you think the question of media's effects on children has continued to be such a big concern among researchers?

the impact of the media on society. Consequently, the uses and gratifications model has never become a dominant or enduring paradigm in media research. However, the rise of Internet-related media technologies has triggered a resurgence of uses and gratifications research in order to understand why people use new media.

Conducting Media Effects Research

As researchers investigated various theories about how media affect people, they also developed different approaches to conducting their research. These approaches vary depending on whether the research originates in the private or the public sector. *Private research*, sometimes called *proprietary research*, is generally conducted for a business, a corporation, or even a political campaign. It typically addresses some real-life problem or need. *Public research* usually takes place in academic and government settings. It tries to clarify, explain, or predict—in other words, to theorize about—the effects of mass media rather than to address a consumer problem.

▲ In 1952, audience members at the Paramount Theater in Hollywood donned 3-D glasses for the opening-night screening of *Bwana Devil*, the first full-length color 3-D film. The uses and gratifications model of research investigates the appeal of various mass media, such as going out to the movies. J. R. Eyerman/Getty Images

Most of this kind of research today focuses on the effects of media in such areas as learning, attitudes, aggression, and voting habits. This research employs the **scientific method**, which consists of seven steps:

1. Identify the problem to be researched.
2. Review existing research and theories related to the problem.
3. Develop working hypotheses or predictions about what the study might find.
4. Determine an appropriate method or research design.
5. Collect information or relevant data.
6. Analyze results to see whether they verify the hypotheses.
7. Interpret the implications of the study.

The scientific method relies on *objectivity* (eliminating or reducing researcher bias and prejudices), *reliability* (getting the same answers or outcomes from a study or measure during repeated testing), and *validity* (demonstrating that a study actually measures what it claims to measure).

A key step in using the scientific method is posing one or more **hypotheses**: tentative general statements that predict either the influence of an *independent variable* on a *dependent variable* or relationships between variables. For example, a researcher might hypothesize that frequent TV viewing among adolescents (independent variable) causes poor academic performance (dependent variable). Or a researcher might hypothesize that playing first-person-shooter video games (independent variable) is associated with aggression in children (dependent variable).

Researchers using the scientific method may employ experiments or survey research in their investigations. To supplement these approaches, researchers also use content analysis to count and document specific messages that circulate in mass media.

Experiments

Like all studies that use the scientific method, **experiments** in media research isolate some aspect of content; suggest a hypothesis; and manipulate variables to discover a particular medium's impact on people's attitudes, emotions, or behavior. To test whether a hypothesis is true, researchers expose an *experimental group*—the group under study—to selected media images or messages. To ensure valid results, researchers also use a *control group*, which is not exposed to the selected media content and thus serves as a basis for comparison. Subjects are picked for each group through **random assignment**, meaning that each subject has an equal chance of being placed in either group.

For instance, suppose researchers wanted to test the effects of violent films on preadolescent boys. The study might take a group of ten-year-olds and randomly assign them to two groups. The experimental group would then watch a violent action movie that the control group would not see. Later, both groups would be exposed to a staged fight between two other boys, and researchers would observe how each group responds. If the control subjects tried to break up the fight but the experimental subjects did not, researchers might conclude that the violent film caused the difference in the groups' responses (see the "Bobo doll" experiment photos on page 443).

When experiments carefully account for independent variables through random assignment, they generally work well to substantiate cause-effect hypotheses. Although experiments are sometimes conducted in field settings, where people can be observed using media in their everyday environments, researchers have less control over variables in these settings. Conversely, a weakness of more carefully controlled experiments is that they are often conducted in the unnatural conditions of a laboratory environment, which can affect the behavior of study participants.

Survey Research

Through **survey research**, investigators collect and measure data taken from a group of respondents regarding their attitudes, knowledge, or behavior. Using random sampling techniques that give each potential subject an equal chance to be included in the survey, this research method draws on much larger populations than those used in experimental studies. Researchers can conduct surveys through direct mail, personal interviews, telephone calls, e-mail, and websites, thus accumulating large quantities of information from diverse cross sections of people. These data enable researchers to examine demographic factors along with responses to questions related to the survey topic.

Surveys offer other benefits as well. Because the randomized sample size is large, researchers can usually generalize their findings to the larger society as well as investigate populations over a long period. In addition, they can use the extensive government and academic survey databases now widely available to conduct **longitudinal studies**, in which they compare new studies with those conducted years earlier.

But like experiments, surveys also have several drawbacks. First, they cannot show cause–effect relationships; rather, they can show only **correlations**—or associations—between two variables. For example, a random survey of ten-year-old boys that asks about their behavior might demonstrate that a correlation exists between acting aggressively and watching violent TV programs. But this correlation does not identify the cause and the effect. (Perhaps people who are already aggressive choose to watch violent TV programs.) Second, surveys are only as good as the wording of their questions and the answer choices they present. Thus, a poorly designed survey can produce misleading results.

Content Analysis

As researchers developed theories about the mass media, it became increasingly important to more precisely describe the media content being studied. As a corrective, they developed a method known as **content analysis** to systematically describe various types of media content.

Content analysis involves defining terms and developing a coding scheme so that whatever is being studied—acts of violence in movies, representations of women in television commercials, the treatment of political candidates in news reports—can be accurately judged and counted. One content analysis study is conducted by GLAAD each year to count the quantity, quality, and diversity of lesbian, gay, bisexual, transgender, and queer (LGBTQ) characters on television. In 2018, GLAAD's *Where We Are on TV* report used content analysis to examine overall diversity and LGBTQ representation on prime-time scripted network television, plus LGBTQ representation on cable networks and streaming services. According to the study, the overall number of "series regular" LGBTQ characters is slowly rising across all platforms, hitting an all-time high on network television at 8.8 percent. GLAAD points out that this is still proportional underrepresentation when compared to the general public and is calling on television producers to reach 10 percent by 2020. The GLAAD report also notes that the racial diversity of LGBTQ characters is up significantly.[14]

Content analysis has its own limitations. For one thing, this technique does not measure the effects of various media messages on audiences or explain how those messages are presented. Moreover, problems of definition arise. For instance, how do researchers distinguish slapstick cartoon aggression from the violent murders or rapes shown during an evening police drama?

Contemporary Theories of Media Effects

By the 1960s, several departments of mass communication began graduating Ph.D.-level researchers schooled in experiment and survey research techniques as well as content analysis. These researchers began developing new theories about how media affect people. Five particularly influential contemporary theories emerged. These are known as social learning theory, agenda-setting, the cultivation effect, the spiral of silence, and third-person effect.

Social Learning Theory

Some of the best-known studies suggesting a link between mass media and behavior are the "Bobo doll" experiments, conducted on children by psychologist Albert Bandura and his colleagues at Stanford University in the 1960s. Although many researchers criticized the use of Bobo dolls as an experimental device

▼These photos of the "Bobo doll" experiments show that the children who observed an adult punching and kicking the Bobo doll were more likely to imitate the adult's behavior when returned to a room full of toys. Courtesy of Albert Bandura

(since the point of playing with Bobo dolls is to hit them), Bandura argued that the experiments demonstrated a link between violent media programs, such as those on television, and aggressive behavior. Bandura developed **social learning theory** (later modified and renamed *social cognitive theory*), which he believed involved a four-step process:

1. *attention* (the subject must attend to the media and witness the aggressive behavior)
2. *retention* (the subject must retain the memory for later retrieval)
3. *motor reproduction* (the subject must be able to physically imitate the behavior)
4. *motivation* (there must be a social reward or reinforcement to encourage modeling of the behavior)

Supporters of social learning theory often cite real-life imitations of aggression depicted in media (such as the Columbine massacre) as evidence that the theory is correct. Critics argue that real-life violence actually stems from larger social problems (such as poverty or mental illness), and that the theory makes mass media the scapegoat for those larger problems.

Agenda-Setting

Researchers who hold to the **agenda-setting** theory believe that when mass media focus their attention on particular events or issues, they determine—that is, set the agenda for—what people discuss and what they pay attention to. Media thus do not so much tell us *what* to think as what to think *about*.

▶ A consequence of agenda-setting is that the stories that don't get attention from the mass media don't make it onto the public and political agendas. Despite causing catastrophic damage to the island of Puerto Rico back in 2017, the landfall of Hurricane Maria on the U.S. territory drew a negligible amount of U.S. media coverage, especially compared to the coverage devoted to the large hurricanes that made landfall in the continental United States just weeks before. Carolyn Cole/Los Angeles Times via Getty Images

In the 1970s, Maxwell McCombs and Donald Shaw compared issues cited by undecided voters on election day with issues covered heavily by the media. Since then, researchers exploring this theory have demonstrated that the more stories the news media do on a particular subject, the more importance audiences attach to that subject. For instance, when the media seriously began to cover ecology issues after the first Earth Day in 1970, a much higher percentage of the population began listing the environment as a primary social concern in surveys. When *Jaws* became a blockbuster in 1975, the news media started featuring more shark attack stories; even landlocked people in the Midwest began ranking sharks as a major problem, despite the rarity of such incidents worldwide.

The Cultivation Effect

The **cultivation effect** theory holds that heavy viewing of TV leads individuals to perceive the world in ways consistent with television portrayals. The major research into this hypothesis grew from the TV violence profiles of George Gerbner and his colleagues, who attempted to make broad generalizations about the impact of televised violence. Beginning in the late 1960s, these social scientists categorized and counted different types of violent acts shown on network television. Using a methodology that combines annual content analyses of TV violence with surveys, the cultivation effect suggests that the more time individuals spend viewing television and absorbing its viewpoints, the more likely their views of social reality will be "cultivated" by the images and portrayals they see on television.[15] For example, Gerbner's studies concluded that although fewer than 1 percent of Americans are victims of violent crime in any single year, people who watch a lot of television tend to overestimate that percentage.

Some critics have charged that cultivation research has provided limited evidence to support its findings. In addition, some have argued that the cultivation effects recorded by Gerbner's studies have been minimal. When compared side by side, these critics argue, perceptions of heavy television viewers and nonviewers regarding how dangerous the world is are virtually identical.

The Spiral of Silence

Developed by German communication theorist Elisabeth Noelle-Neumann in the 1970s and 1980s, the **spiral of silence** theory links mass media, social psychology, and public opinion formation. The theory proposes that those who believe that their views on controversial issues are in the minority will keep their views to themselves for fear of social isolation. The theory is based on social psychology studies, such as the classic conformity studies of Solomon Asch in 1951. In Asch's study on the effects of group pressure, he demonstrated that a test subject is more likely to give clearly wrong answers to questions about line lengths if everyone else in the room (all secret confederates of the experimenter) unanimously state an incorrect answer. Noelle-Neumann argued that this effect is exacerbated by mass media, particularly television, which can quickly and widely communicate a real or presumed majority public opinion.

Noelle-Neumann acknowledges, however, that not everyone keeps quiet if they think they hold a minority view. In many cases, "hard-core nonconformists" exist and remain vocal even in the face of possible social isolation. These individuals can even change public opinion by continuing to voice their views.

The Third-Person Effect

Identified in a 1983 study by W. Phillips Davison, the **third-person effect** theory suggests that people believe others are more affected by media messages than they are themselves. In other words, this theory posits the idea that "we" can escape the worst effects of media while still worrying about people who are younger, less educated, less informed, or otherwise less capable of guarding against media influence.

Under this theory, we might fear that other people will, for example, believe fake news, imitate violent movies, or get addicted to the Internet, while dismissing the idea that any of those things could happen to us. It has been argued that the third-person effect is instrumental in censorship, as it would allow censors to assume immunity to the negative effects of any supposedly dangerous media they must examine.

Evaluating Research on Media Effects

Media effects research has deepened our understanding of the mass media. This wealth of research exists partly because funding for studies on media's impact on young people remains popular among politicians and has drawn ready government support since the 1960s. But funding restricts the scope of some media effects research, particularly if the agendas of government agencies, businesses, or other entities do not align with researchers' interests. Moreover, because media effects research operates best in examining media's impact on individual behavior, few of these studies explore how media shape the larger community and social life. Some research has begun to address these deficits, as well as to explore the impact of media technology on international communication.

Cultural Approaches to Media Research

In the 1960s, cultural approaches to media research emerged to challenge social scientific media effects theories and to compensate for those theories' limitations. In contrast to media effects research, the *cultural studies* mode of media research involves interpreting written and visual "texts" or artifacts as symbols that contain cultural, historical, and political meanings. For example, researchers might argue that the wave of police and crime shows that flooded the TV landscape in the mid-1960s was a response to Americans' fears about urban unrest and income disparity. A cultural approach thus offers interpretations of the stories, messages, and meanings that circulate throughout society.

Like media effects research, cultural studies media research has evolved in the decades since it first appeared.

Early Developments in Cultural Studies Media Research

In Europe, media studies have always favored interpretive rather than scientific approaches. Researchers there have approached the media from the perspective of literary or cultural critics rather than experimental or survey researchers. These approaches were built on the writings of political philosophers such as Karl Marx and Antonio Gramsci, who investigated how mass media support existing hierarchies in society.

In the United States, early criticism of media effects research came from the Frankfurt School, a group of European researchers who emigrated from Germany to America to escape Nazi persecution in the 1930s. Under the leadership of Max Horkheimer, T. W. Adorno, and Leo Lowenthal, this group advocated augmenting experimental approaches with historical and cultural approaches to investigate mass media's long-range effects on audiences.

Since the time of the Frankfurt School, criticisms of the media effects tradition and its methods have continued, with calls for more interpretive studies of the rituals of mass communication. Academics who have embraced a cultural approach to media research try to understand how media and culture are tied to the actual patterns of communication in daily life. For example, in the 1970s, Stuart Hall and his colleagues studied the British print media and the police, who were dealing with an apparent rise in crime and mugging incidents. Arguing that the close relationship between the news and the police created a form of urban surveillance, the authors of *Policing the Crisis: Mugging, the State, and Law and Order* demonstrated that the mugging phenomenon was exacerbated, and in part created, by the key institutions assigned the social tasks of reporting on crime and controlling it.[16]

Contemporary Cultural Studies Approaches

Cultural research investigates daily experiences, especially through the lenses of race, gender, class, sexuality, and imbalances of power and status in society. Such research emphasizes how some groups have been marginalized and ignored throughout history, particularly African Americans, Native Americans, Asians and Asian Americans, Arabic peoples, Latinos, Appalachians, LGBTQ individuals, immigrants, and women. Cultural studies researchers also seek to recover these lost or silenced voices. The major approaches they use are textual analysis, audience studies, and political economy research.

◂ Media critic Jack Shaheen analyzes the cultural messages behind portrayals of Arabs and Arab Americans in film and TV, such as in the Bugs Bunny cartoon shown here. Media Education Foundation

Textual Analysis

Textual analysis entails a close reading and interpretation of cultural messages, including those found in books, movies, and TV programs—such as portrayals of Arab and Arab American characters in popular films.[17] Whereas media effects research approaches media messages with the principles of modern science in mind—replicability, objectivity, and data—textual analysis looks at rituals, narratives, and meaning.

Although textual analysis has a long and rich history in film and literary studies, it gained new significance for mass media in the early 1970s with the work of Stuart Hall in the United Kingdom, who theorized about how messages were sent and understood (encoded and decoded) via television, and with the publication of American Horace Newcomb's *TV: The Most Popular Art*—the first academic book to analyze television shows. Newcomb studied why certain TV programs and formats—such as *The Beverly Hillbillies*, *Bewitched*, and *Dragnet*—became popular. Trained as a literary scholar, Newcomb argued that content analysis and other social scientific approaches to popular media often ignored artistic traditions and social context.

Both Newcomb and Hall felt that textual analysis, which had largely focused on "important," highly regarded works of art—debates, film, poems, and books—should also be applied to popular culture. As Hall argued, things like television and popular music were important because they were what most people were using or experiencing most of the time. By the end of the 1970s, a new generation of media studies scholars, who had grown up on television and rock and roll, began studying less elite forms of culture. By shifting the focus to daily popular culture, such studies shone a spotlight on the more ordinary ways that "normal" people (not just military, political, or religious leaders) experience and interpret their daily lives through media messages (see also "Media Literacy Case Study: Does Art Imitate Life or Life Imitate Art? TV Depictions of Suicide and Copycat Fears" on pages 450–451). Researchers still examine the cultural meaning of messages in popular television, music, movies, and books consumed by those "normal" people; however, they have pushed that examination into post–digital turn mass media, from video games to social media to the use of smartphone technology.

Audience Studies

Audience studies differ from textual analysis in that the subject being researched is the audience for the text, not the text itself. For example, for her book *Reading the Romance: Women, Patriarchy, and Popular Literature*, Janice Radway studied a group of midwestern women who enjoyed reading romance novels. Using her training in literary criticism and employing interviews and questionnaires, Radway investigated the meaning of romance novels to these women. In the book, she argues that reading romance novels functions as personal time for many of the women. She also suggests that these particular romance-novel fans identified with the active, independent qualities of the romantic heroines they most admired.

As a cultural study, Radway's work did not claim to be scientific, and her findings cannot be generalized to all women. Rather, Radway investigated and interpreted the relationship between reading popular fiction and ordinary life for a specific group of women.[18] Such studies help define culture as comprising both the *products* a society fashions (such as romance novels) and the *processes* that forge those products.

Political Economy Research

A focus on the production of popular culture and the forces behind it is the topic of **political economy research**, which examines interconnections among economic interests, political power, and ways in which that power is used. Major concerns of such studies include the increasing consolidation of media ownership. With this consolidation, the production of media content is being controlled by fewer and fewer organizations, investing those for-profit companies with more and more power to dominate public discourse. The theory is that money—not democratic expression—is now the driving force behind public communication and popular culture. Political economy research also considers the profit motive behind certain company behaviors, such as how a company might gather data on customers (see "The Digital Turn Case Study: Artificial Intelligence Gets Personal" on page 437).

Political economy studies work best when combined with textual analysis and audience studies to provide fuller context for understanding a media product: the cultural content of the media product, the economics and politics of its production, and audiences' responses to it.

Media Literacy

CASE STUDY

Does Art Imitate Life or Life Imitate Art? TV Depictions of Suicide and Copycat Fears

Is it ever possible to depict suicide in a television show without also glamorizing it? That was the predicament for the creators of *13 Reasons Why*, a 2017 series on Netflix adapted by Brian Yorkey from the 2007 debut young-adult novel of the same name by Jay Asher.

The story, which spins out in thirteen episodes in its first Netflix season, follows teenager Clay Jensen (Dylan Minnette) as he returns home from school to find a mysterious box with his name on it lying on his porch. Inside he discovers cassette tapes recorded by Hannah Baker (Katherine Langford)—his classmate and crush—who tragically died from suicide two weeks earlier. On tape, Hannah explains that there are thirteen reasons why she decided to end her life. The reasons catalog betrayals, bullying, slut shaming, binge drinking, drunk driving, drug use, and rape. Hannah's suicide is depicted in the final episode. A reviewer for the *Guardian* concluded that the series was "too bleak to binge," but plenty of people did binge on it, leading to a second season in 2018 and a third in 2019.[1]

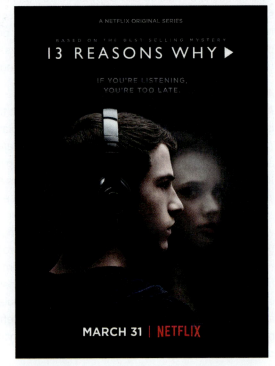

▲ Hit Netflix original series *13 Reasons Why* raises important questions about teenage suicide. But does it go too far? Netflix/Photofest

Like the book, the series prompted a debate about bullying, depression, sexual consent, drug and alcohol abuse, and self-harm. From a media effects perspective, there was concern that portrayals of suicide might glamorize suicide and induce copycats.

Mark Henick, a mental health advocate, argued that TV programs like *13 Reasons Why* can have several problematic features in their portrayal of suicide, including simplifying or romanticizing it, and presenting it as a viable option instead of seeking proper care for mental health issues. He argues that graphic representations of suicide can also harm viewers, especially young and impressionable ones.[2]

In 2017, the *Atlantic* reported on a study in which public health researchers found that "Google queries about suicide rose by almost 20 percent in 19 days

▶ **Visit LaunchPad** to watch a clip from *13 Reasons Why*. What messages about suicide do you think this clip sends to an audience?

launchpadworks.com

after the show came out, representing between 900,000 and 1.5 million more searches than usual regarding the subject."[3] The concern among many experts—referred to as the contagion effect—is that although the television series can increase awareness of the tragedy of suicide, it can also idealize it.

The show's creators defended the program and its story.[4] Nevertheless, about two months after the 2017 release of 13 Reasons Why (which was already rated TV-MA), Netflix added stronger advisory warnings at the beginning of certain episodes and supplementary content to its companion 13ReasonsWhy.info website. The site contains videos addressing a number of the show's disturbing topics, such as sexual assault; a discussion guide; and links to mental health resources for help, including the Crisis Text Line and the National Suicide Prevention Lifeline. In a statement, Netflix said, "While many of our members find the show to be a valuable driver for starting important conversation with their families, we have also heard concern from those who feel the series should carry additional advisories."[5] The Netflix page for the series states, "This series contains scenes that viewers may find disturbing, including graphic depictions of sexual assault, substance abuse, and suicide. If you or anyone you know needs help finding support or crisis resources, please go to 13ReasonsWhy.info for more information."[6]

Dan Reidenberg, psychologist and executive director of the national organization Suicide Awareness Voices of Education (SAVE), weighed in: "Although it's created a conversation about suicide, it's not the right conversation." When Reidenberg was contacted by Netflix for guidance before the release of 13 Reasons Why, he recommended that the company not release the show. That, of course, did not happen. In response, SAVE issued talking points for 13 Reasons Why for people to share in order to try to create the right conversation. The first point was this: "13 Reasons Why is a fictional story based on a widely known novel and is meant to be a cautionary tale."[7]

APPLYING THE CRITICAL PROCESS

DESCRIPTION Do an online search for news articles discussing 13 Reasons Why and concerns about copycat suicides. Pick three articles in a variety of publications that seem current, relevant, and detailed. Summarize each article, noting the following information: whether the article's author seemed to be troubled by the depiction of suicide in the show, the name of the publication in which the article was published, and the sources the article cites.

ANALYSIS Put your information into chart form, noting how the topic of suicide is discussed. Are certain arguments or concerns more common than others? Are there patterns? Are any opposing viewpoints given?

INTERPRETATION If you identified patterns during your analysis, what might these patterns mean? Were you surprised by any of the arguments given in the articles?

EVALUATION Which of the arguments presented in the articles seem most compelling? Why? Do you find yourself agreeing or disagreeing with the articles that express concerns over the portrayal of suicide in the series? Why or why not?

ENGAGEMENT Now that you have spent time reading about 13 Reasons Why, watch several episodes of the program. Compare your personal observations and impressions with the information you found in the articles you read, and write a blog post about your thoughts on how suicide is addressed in this program.

Evaluating Cultural Studies Research

A major strength of cultural studies research is that researchers can more easily examine the ties between media messages and the broader social, economic, and political world, since such research is not bound by precise control variables. For instance, media effects research on politics has generally concentrated on election polls and voting patterns. But cultural research has broadened the discussion to examine class, gender, and cultural differences among voters and the various uses of power by individuals and institutions in positions of authority.

Yet just as media effects research has its limits, so does cultural studies media research. Sometimes cultural studies have focused exclusively on the meanings of media programs or "texts," ignoring their effect on audiences. Some cultural studies have tried to address this deficiency by incorporating audience studies. Both media effects and cultural studies researchers have begun to look more closely at the limitations of their work and to borrow ideas from each other to better assess media's meaning and impact.

Media Research in a Democratic Society

One charge frequently leveled at academic studies is that they don't address the everyday problems of life and thus have little practical application. To be sure, media research has built a growing knowledge base and dramatically advanced what we know about mass media's effect on individuals and societies. But the larger public has had little access to the research process, even though cultural studies research tends to identify with marginalized groups. Any scholarship is self-defeating if its complexity removes it from the daily experience of the groups it examines. Researchers themselves have even found it difficult to speak to one another because of differences in the discipline-specific language they use to analyze and report their findings.

In addition, increasing specialization in the 1970s began isolating many researchers from life outside the university. Academics were criticized as being locked away in their ivory towers, concerned with seemingly obscure matters to which the general public could not relate. However, academics across many fields moved to mitigate this isolation, becoming increasingly active in political and cultural life in the 1980s and 1990s. For example, essayist and cultural critic Barbara Ehrenreich has written frequently about labor and economic issues for such magazines as *Time* and the *Nation* and has written several books on such issues.

In recent years, public intellectuals have also encouraged discussion of the new challenges posed by media production in a digital world. Harvard

University law professor Lawrence Lessig has been a leading advocate of efforts to rewrite the nation's copyright laws to enable noncommercial "amateur culture" to flourish on the Internet. He publishes his work in print and online. American University's Pat Aufderheide, longtime media critic for the alternative magazine *In These Times*, worked with independent filmmakers to develop the *Documentary Filmmakers' Statement of Best Practices in Fair Use*. The statement calls for documentary filmmakers to have reasonable access to copyrighted material for their work.

Like journalists, public intellectuals based on campuses help advance the conversations taking place in larger society. They actively circulate the most important new ideas of the day—including those related to mass media—and serve as models for how to participate in public life.

CHAPTER ESSENTIALS

Review

- Scientific approaches to mass media research did not emerge until the late 1920s and 1930s.

- Between 1930 and 1960, four trends contributed to the rise of modern media research: **propaganda analysis**, public opinion research, social psychology studies, and marketing research.

- Between the 1930s and the 1970s, **media effects** researchers (or *social scientific* media researchers) developed several models about how media affect individuals' behavior. These include the **hypodermic-needle model** (or *magic bullet theory*), the **minimal-effects** (or *limited effects*) **model**, and the **uses and gratifications model**.

- At the same time, researchers developed different approaches to conducting their research. Most media effects research today focuses on media's impact and employs the **scientific method**, which includes the key step of posing one or more **hypotheses**. Researchers using the scientific method may conduct **experiments**, employ **survey research**, or use **content analysis** in their investigations.

- When conducting survey research, researchers can use the extensive government and academic survey databases now widely available to conduct longitudinal studies, in which they compare new studies with those conducted years earlier. Surveys can show only correlations—or associations—between two variables, not demonstrable causes and effects.

- By the 1960s, media effects researchers began developing new theories about how media affect people, including **social learning theory**, **agenda-setting**, the **cultivation effect**, the **spiral of silence**, and the **third-person effect**.

- In the 1960s, cultural approaches to media research emerged to challenge mainstream media effects theories. Early **cultural studies** research was built on the writings of political philosophers such as Karl Marx and Antonio Gramsci and the criticisms of media effects research from the Frankfurt School.

- Contemporary cultural studies approaches focus on research, such as **textual analysis**, **audience studies**, and **political economy research**.

- Although media research has advanced what we know about mass media's effect on individuals and society, most people do not have access to the actual research process, which makes it hard to connect scholarship to the daily experience of the groups such research examines.

LaunchPad

Visit LaunchPad for *Media Essentials* at **launchpadworks.com** for additional learning tools:

- **REVIEW WITH LEARNINGCURVE**
  LearningCurve adaptive quizzing helps you master the concepts you need to learn from this chapter.
- **MEDIA LITERACY PRACTICE**
  This activity challenges you to develop a critical perspective and apply it to everyday encounters with communication media.

- We rely on public intellectuals to help advance the conversations taking place in larger society and culture. These individuals encourage discussion of the new challenges posed by media.

Key Terms

media effects research, p. 432
cultural studies, p. 432
propaganda analysis, p. 434
pseudo-polls, p. 435
hypodermic-needle model, p. 438
minimal-effects model, p. 439
selective exposure, p. 439
selective retention, p. 439
uses and gratifications model, p. 439
scientific method, p. 440
hypotheses, p. 441
experiments, p. 441
random assignment, p. 441
survey research, p. 441
longitudinal studies, p. 442
correlations, p. 442
content analysis, p. 442
social learning theory, p. 444
agenda-setting, p. 444
cultivation effect, p. 445
spiral of silence, p. 445
third-person effect, p. 446
textual analysis, p. 448
audience studies, p. 449
political economy research, p. 449

Study Questions

1. What are ways in which the mass media might be implicated in social problems like the growth of hate groups and the spread of their messages, and how might the media effects and cultural studies research traditions respond differently to these problems?

2. What are pseudo-polls, and what about them makes them less reliable than social scientific polls and surveys?

3. What are the main ideas behind social learning theory, agenda-setting, the cultivation effect, the spiral of silence, and the third-person effect?

4. Why did cultural studies develop in opposition to media effects research?

5. What role do media researchers play in public debates about the mass media?

Notes

1 Mass Communication: A Critical Approach

1. Alicia Garza, "Herstory: Creation of a Movement," accessed August 4, 2018, http://blacklivesmatter.com/herstory; Elizabeth Day, "#BlackLivesMatter: The Birth of a New Civil Rights Movement," *Guardian*, July 19, 2015, www.theguardian.com/world/2015/jul/19/blacklivesmatter-birth-civil-rights-movement; Dayna Evans, "Black Lives Matter's Opal Tometi Explains How Words Can Change Human Behavior," *New York Magazine*, March 22, 2016, http://nymag.com/thecut/2016/03/black-lives-matter-opal-tometi.html.
2. Monica Anderson et al., "An Analysis of #BlackLivesMatter and Other Twitter Hashtags Related to Political or Social Issues," *Activism in the Social Media Age*, July 11, 2018, www.pewinternet.org/2018/07/11/an-analysis-of-blacklivesmatter-and-other-twitter-hashtags-related-to-political-or-social-issues.
3. Monica Anderson et al., "Appendix A: Detailed Tables," *Activism in the Social Media Age*, July 11, 2018, www.pewinternet.org/2018/07/11/social-media-activism-appendix-a-detailed-tables.
4. Deron Dalton, "The Three Women behind the Black Lives Matter Movement," *Madame Noire*, May 4, 2015, http://madamenoire.com/528287/the-three-women-behind-the-black-lives-matter-movement.
5. For a historical discussion of culture, see Lawrence Levine, *Highbrow/Lowbrow: The Emergence of Cultural Hierarchy in America* (Cambridge, Mass.: Harvard University Press, 1988).
6. For overviews of this position, see Neil Postman, *Amusing Ourselves to Death: Public Discourse in the Age of Show Business* (New York: Penguin Books, 1985), 19; Stuart Ewen, *Captains of Consciousness: Advertising and the Social Roots of the Consumer Culture* (New York: McGraw-Hill, 1976).
7. James W. Carey, *Communication as Culture: Essays on Media and Society* (Boston: Unwin Hyman, 1989).

THE DIGITAL TURN CASE STUDY: FOMO in a Digital World, p. 13

1. Lev Grossman and Matt Vella, "iNeed?" *Time*, September 22, 2014, p. 44.
2. "Fear of Missing Out," J. Walter Thompson Intelligence, May 2011, www.jwtintelligence.com/production/FOMO_JWT_TrendReport_May2011.pdf.
3. Andrew K. Przybylski et al., "Motivational, Emotional, and Behavioral Correlates of Fear of Missing Out," *Computers in Human Behavior* 29 (2013): 1841–1848.
4. Ethan Kross et al., "Facebook Use Predicts Declines in Subjective Well-Being in Young Adults," *PLOS ONE* 8, no. 8 (2013), doi:10.1371/journal.pone.0069841.
5. Oscar Oviedo-Trespalacios et al., "Should I Text or Call Here? A Situation-Based Analysis of Drivers' Perceived Likelihood of Engaging in Mobile Phone Multitasking," *Risk Analysis* 38, no. 10 (October 2018), doi:10.1111/risa.13119.
6. Ed Diener and Robert Biswas-Diener, *Happiness: Unlocking the Mysteries of Psychological Wealth* (Malden, Mass.: Wiley-Blackwell, 2008), 51.

MEDIA LITERACY CASE STUDY: Masculinity and the Media, p. 24 [pp. 24–25]

1. Mark Follman, Gavin Aronsen, and Deanna Pan, "A Guide to Mass Shootings in America," *Mother Jones*, February 15, 2019, www.motherjones.com/politics/2012/07/mass-shootings-map. See also John Wihbey, "Mass Murder, Shooting Sprees and Rampage Violence: Research Roundup," October 1, 2015, http://journalistsresource.org/studies/government/criminal-justice/mass-murder-shooting-sprees-and-rampage-violence-research-roundup.
2. Jackson Katz, "Memo to Media: Manhood, Not Guns or Mental Illness, Should Be Central in Newtown Shooting," *Huffington Post*, updated February 17, 2013, www.huffingtonpost.com/jackson-katz/men-gender-gun-violence_b_2308522.html.
3. Ibid.
4. Rachel Kalish and Michael Kimmel, "Suicide by Mass Murder: Masculinity, Aggrieved Entitlement, and Rampage School Shootings," *Health Sociology Review* 19, no. 4 (2010): 451–464.
5. Ralph Ellis and Sara Sidner, "Deadly California Rampage: Chilling Video, but No Match for Reality," CNN, May 27, 2014, www.cnn.com/2014/05/24/justice/california-shooting-deaths.

2 Books and the Power of Print

1. "Comics and Graphic Novels One of Highest Growth Categories in Publishing, Reports NPD," NPD Group, October 6, 2017, www.npd.com/wps/portal/npd/us/news/press-releases/2017/comics-and-graphic-novels-one-of-highest-growth-categories-in-publishing-reports-npd.
2. Heidi Macdonald, "NY Times Ignores 400 Publishing Industry Pros' Pleas to Return Graphic Novel Bestseller Chart," *The Beat*, February 9, 2018, www.comicsbeat.com/ny-times-ignores-400-publishing-industry-pros-pleas-to-return-graphic-novel-bestseller-chart.
3. "Comics and Graphic Novels."

4. Ibid.

5. Michael Cavna, "Rep. John Lewis's National Book Award Win Is a Milestone Moment for Graphic Novels," *Washington Post*, November 17, 2016, www.washingtonpost.com/news/comic-riffs/wp/2016/11/17/rep-john-lewiss-national-book-award-win-is-a-milestone-moment-for-graphic-novels.

6. Calvin Reid, "Comics Industry Asks 'NYT' to Restore Graphic Bestseller Lists," *Publishers Weekly*, February 7, 2018, www.publishersweekly.com/pw/by-topic/industry-news/comics/article/75998-comics-industry-asks-nyt-to-restore-graphic-bestseller-lists.html.

7. Susana Polo, "The *New York Times* Gave Up on Graphic Novels," *Polygon*, January 26, 2017, www.polygon.com/2017/1/26/14401436/new-york-times-graphic-novel-list.

8. Olsen, quoted in Reid, "Comics Industry."

9. Elizabeth Eisenstein, *The Printing Press as an Agent of Change* (Cambridge: Cambridge University Press, 1980).

10. For a comprehensive historical overview of the publishing industry and the rise of publishing houses, see John A. Tebbel, *A History of Book Publishing in the United States*, 4 vols. (New York: R. R. Bowker, 1972–81).

11. "Highlights from Student Watch Attitudes and Behaviors toward Course Materials 2017–18 Report," National Association of College Stores, accessed August 17, 2018, www.nacs.org/research/studentwatchfindings.aspx.

12. "Book Publisher Revenue Estimated at More Than $26 Billion in 2017," Association of American Publishers, July 20, 2018, http://newsroom.publishers.org/book-publisher-revenue-estimated-at-more-than-26-billion-in-2017.

13. "Religious Books Sales Revenue in the United States from 2011 to 2017 (in Million U.S. Dollars)," Statista, accessed August 1, 2018, www.statista.com/statistics/251467/religious-books-sales-revenue-in-the-us.

14. "U.S. Publishing Industry's Annual Survey Reveals Nearly $28 Billion in Revenue in 2015," Association of American Publishers, July 11, 2016, http://newsroom.publishers.org/us-publishing-industrys-annual-survey-reveals-nearly-28-billion-in-revenue-in-2015.

15. Jim Milliot, "2017 Sales Had Small Decline," *Publishers Weekly*, April 25, 2018, www.publishersweekly.com/pw/by-topic/industry-news/financial-reporting/article/77552-2017-sales-had-small-decline.html.

16. Jim Milliot, "Bad News about E-books," *Publishers Weekly*, January 20, 2017, www.publishersweekly.com/pw/by-topic/digital/retailing/article/72563-the-bad-news-about-e-books.html.

17. Betty Kelly Sargent, "Surprising Self-Publishing Statistics," *Publishers Weekly*, July 28, 2014, www.publishersweekly.com/pw/by-topic/authors/pw-select/article/63455-surprising-self-publishing-statistics.html.

18. "Book Publisher Revenue Estimated at More Than $26 Billion in 2017."

19. Milliot, "2017 Sales Had Small Decline."

20. "Book Publishing Revenue Worldwide from 2012 to 2021 (in Billion U.S. Dollars)," Statista, accessed August 1, 2018, www.statista.com/statistics/307299/global-book-publishing-revenue.

21. David Leonhardt, "Save Barnes & Noble!" *New York Times*, May 6, 2018, www.nytimes.com/2018/05/06/opinion/save-barnes-noble.html.

22. Alexandra Alter and Tiffany Hsu, "Barnes & Noble Is Sold to Hedge Fund After a Tumultuous Year," *New York Times*, June 7, 2019, www.nytimes.com/2019/06/07/books/barnes-noble-sale.html.

23. Carmen Nobel, "How Independent Bookstores Have Thrived in Spite of Amazon.com," Harvard Business School, November 20, 2017, https://hbswk.hbs.edu/item/why-independent-bookstores-haved-thrived-in-spite-of-amazon-com.

24. "February 2017 Big, Bad, Wide and International Report: Covering Amazon, Apple, B&N, and Kobo Ebook Sales in the US, UK, Canada, Australia, and New Zealand," Author Earnings, February 2017, http://authorearnings.com/report/february-2017.

25. "January 2018 Report: US Online Book Sales, Q2–Q4 2017," Author Earnings, January 2018, http://authorearnings.com/report/january-2018-report-us-online-book-sales-q2-q4-2017.

26. Andrew Perrin, "Nearly One-in-Five Americans Now Listen to Audiobooks," Pew Research Center, March 8, 2018, www.pewresearch.org/fact-tank/2018/03/08/nearly-one-in-five-americans-now-listen-to-audiobooks.

THE DIGITAL TURN CASE STUDY: The Epic Rise of Instapoets, p. 47

1. "Instapoets Rekindling U.S. Poetry Book Sales, the NPD Group Says," NPD Group, April 5, 2018, www.npd.com/wps/portal/npd/us/news/press-releases/2018/instapoets-rekindling-u-s--poetry-book-sales--the-npd-group-says.

2. Ibid.

3. Carl Wilson, "Why Rupi Kaur and Her Peers Are the Most Popular Poets in the World," *New York Times*, December 15, 2017, www.nytimes.com/2017/12/15/books/review/rupi-kaur-instapoets.html.

4. Lavanya Ramanathan, "From Instapoets to the Bards of YouTube, Poetry Is Going Viral. And Some Poets Hate That," *Washington Post*, May 6, 2018, www.washingtonpost.com/lifestyle/style/from-instapoets-to-the-bards-of-youtube-poetry-is-going-viral-and-some-poets-hate-that/2018/05/06/ea4240fa-4329-11e8-8569-26fda6b404c7_story.html?utm_term=.c74916326456.

5. "U.S. Trends in Arts Attendance and Literary Reading: 2002–2017," National Endowment for the Arts, September 2018, www.arts.gov/sites/default/files/2017-sppapreviewREV-sept2018.pdf, p. 12.

MEDIA LITERACY CASE STUDY: Banned Books and "Family Values," p. 52 [pp. 52–53]

1. Brigid Alverson, "Roundtable: Why All the Drama about 'Drama'"? *School Library Journal*, April 20, 2015, http://blogs.slj.com/goodcomicsforkids/2015/04/20/roundtable-why-all-the-drama-about-drama.
2. "Interview with Raina Telgemeier," *TeenReads*, September 7, 2012, www.teenreads.com/authors/raina-telgemeier/news/interview-090712.

3 Newspapers to Digital Frontiers: Journalism's Journey

1. Brooke Kroeger, *Nellie Bly: Daredevil, Reporter, Feminist* (New York: Times Books/Random House, 1994).
2. David T. Z. Mindich, "Edwin M. Stanton, the Inverted Pyramid, and Information Control," *Journalism Monographs* 140 (August 1993).
3. Michael Schudson, *Discovering the News: A Social History of American Newspapers* (New York: Basic Books, 1978), 23.
4. Enn Raudsepp, "Reinventing Journalism Education," *Canadian Journal of Communication* 14, no. 2 (1989): 1–14.
5. Curtis D. MacDougall, *The Press and Its Problems* (Dubuque, Iowa: William C. Brown, 1964), 143, 189.
6. Walter Lippmann, *Liberty and the News* (New York: Harcourt, Brace and Howe, 1920), 92.
7. For another list and an alternative analysis of news criteria, see the Missouri Group, *News Reporting and Writing*, 13th ed. (New York: Bedford/St. Martin's, 2020), 8–10.
8. For a full discussion of the *New York Times* and mainstream journalism's treatment of the LGBTQ community and the early days of the AIDS epidemic, see Edward Alwood, *Straight News: Gays, Lesbians, and the News Media* (New York: Columbia University Press, 1996); Larry Gross, *Up from Invisibility: Lesbians, Gay Men, and the Media in America* (New York: Columbia University Press, 2001).
9. Emily Guskin, "5 Facts about Ethnic and Gender Diversity in U.S. Newsrooms," Pew Research Center, July 18, 2013, www.pewresearch.org/fact-tank/2013/07/18/5-facts-about-ethnic-and-gender-diversity-in-u-s-newsrooms.
10. "The 2017 ASNE Newsroom Diversity Survey," ASNE, October 10, 2017, https://www.asne.org/diversity-survey-2017.
11. Ibid.
12. "QuickFacts," U.S. Census Bureau, accessed August 1, 2018, www.census.gov/quickfacts/fact/table/US/PST045217.
13. Bob Papper, "RTDNA 2018 Research: Women and People of Color in Local TV and Radio News," June 27, 2018, https://rtdna.org/article/2018_research_women_and_people_of_color_in_local_tv_and_radio_news.
14. Don Hewitt, interview conducted by Richard Campbell on *60 Minutes*, CBS News, New York, February 21, 1989.
15. Bureau of Labor Statistics, U.S. Department of Labor, *Occupational Outlook Handbook*, July 2, 2018, www.bls.gov/ooh/media-and-communication/reporters-correspondents-and-broadcast-news-analysts.htm and www.bls.gov/ooh/media-and-communication/public-relations-specialists.htm.
16. Herbert Gans, *Deciding What's News* (New York: Pantheon, 1979), 42–48.
17. For reference and guidance on media ethics, see Clifford Christians, Mark Fackler, and Kim Rotzoll, *Media Ethics: Cases and Moral Reasoning*, 4th ed. (White Plains, N.Y.: Longman, 1995); Thomas H. Bivins, "A Worksheet for Ethics Instruction and Exercises in Reason," *Journalism Educator* (Summer 1993): 4–16.
18. *SPJ Code of Ethics*, Society of Professional Journalists, 1996, www.spj.org/ethicscode.asp.
19. Bob Papper, "Research: TV News Employment Surpasses Newspapers," RTDNA, April 16, 2018, https://rtdna.org/article/research_tv_news_employment_surpasses_newspapers.
20. "Newspapers Fact Sheet," *State of the News Media*, Pew Research Center, June 13, 2018, www.journalism.org/fact-sheet/newspapers.
21. Ibid.
22. Robert Kuttner and Hildy Zenger, "Saving the Free Press from Private Equity," *American Prospect*, December 27, 2017, http://prospect.org/article/saving-free-press-private-equity.
23. "Digital News Fact Sheet," *State of the News Media*, Pew Research Center, June 6, 2018, www.journalism.org/fact-sheet/digital-news; Kristen Bialik and Katerina Eva Matsa, "Key Trends in Social and Digital News Media," Pew Research Center, October 4, 2017, www.pewresearch.org/fact-tank/2017/10/04/key-trends-in-social-and-digital-news-media.
24. Alex Hern, "Facebook and Twitter Are Being Used to Manipulate Public Opinion—Report," *Guardian*, June 19, 2017, www.theguardian.com/technology/2017/jun/19/social-media-proganda-manipulating-public-opinion-bots-accounts-facebook-twitter.
25. Malcolm Gladwell, "The Satire Paradox," *Revisionist History* (podcast), August 17, 2016.
26. Heather L. LaMarre, Kristen D. Landreville, and Michael A. Beam, "The Irony of Satire: Political Ideology and the Motivation to See What You Want to See in *The Colbert Report*," *International Journal of Press/Politics* 14 (April 2009): 212–231.
27. Craig Silverman and Lawrence Alexander, "How Teens in the Balkans Are Duping Trump Supporters with Fake News," BuzzFeed, November 3, 2016, www.buzzfeed.com/craigsilverman/how-macedonia-became-a-global-hub-for-pro-trump-misinfo?utm_term=.eeM09nYqBw#.rkZJEqp7PD.

28. Laura Sydell, "We Tracked Down a Fake-News Creator in the Suburbs. Here's What We Learned," NPR, Nov 23, 2016, www.npr.org/sections/alltechconsidered/2016/11/23/503146770/npr-finds-the-head-of-a-covert-fake-news-operation-in-the-suburbs.
29. Madeline Conway, "Accused 'Pizzagate' Shooter Faces Federal Charges," *Politico*, December 13, 2016, www.politico.com/story/2016/12/edgar-maddison-welch-pizzagate-charges-232570.
30. David Uberti, "The Real History of Fake News," *Columbia Journalism Review*, December 15, 2016, www.cjr.org/special_report/fake_news_history.php.
31. Mike Wendling, "The (Almost) Complete History of 'Fake News,'" BBC, January 22, 2018, www.bbc.com/news/blogs-trending-42724320.
32. "Don Beyer Says 97 Percent of Scientists Believe Humans Contribute to Global Warming," *PolitiFact*, April 4, 2016, www.politifact.com/virginia/statements/2016/apr/04/don-beyer/don-beyer-says-97-percent-scientists-believe-human.
33. Chas Danner, "News Anchors Reciting Sinclair Propaganda Is Even More Terrifying in Unison," *New York Magazine*, April 1, 2018, http://nymag.com/daily/intelligencer/2018/04/anchors-reciting-sinclair-propaganda-is-terrifying-in-unison.html.
34. William P. Davis, "Enemy of the People: Trump Breaks Out This Phrase during Moments of Peak Criticism," *New York Times*, July 19, 2018, www.nytimes.com/2018/07/19/business/media/trump-media-enemy-of-the-people.html.
35. Scott Simon, "Calling the Press the Enemy of the People Is a Menacing Move," NPR, August 4, 2018, www.npr.org/2018/08/04/635461307/opinion-calling-the-press-the-enemy-of-the-people-is-a-menacing-move.
36. Brian Stelter, "Trump Calls Journalists 'Bad People' at a Rally a Week after Newsroom Shooting," CNN, July 6, 2018, https://money.cnn.com/2018/07/06/media/trump-montana-rally-media-attacks/index.html.
37. Nikki Battiste, "Man Charged with Making Death Threats Against Journalists over Trump Editorials," CBS News, August 30, 2018, www.cbsnews.com/news/robert-chain-charged-death-threats-boston-globe-journalists-editorials; Zachary Fagenson and Bernie Woodall, "Florida Man Charged after Bombs Sent to Trump Critics," Reuters, October 27, 2018, www.reuters.com/article/us-usa-packages/florida-man-charged-after-bombs-sent-to-trump-critics-idUSKCN1N10E7.
38. Freedom of the Press Foundation and Committee to Protect Journalists, "U.S. Press Freedom Tracker: Physical Attack," accessed January 9, 2019, https://pressfreedomtracker.us/physical-attack.
39. Phillip Rucker, "Trump Accuses 'Very Unpatriotic' Journalists of Putting the 'Lives of Many' in Peril," *Washington Post*, July 29, 2018, www.washingtonpost.com/politics/trump-says-he-called-media-enemy-of-the-people-in-meeting-with-ny-times-publisher/2018/07/29/fec5adee-9330-11e8-810c-5fa705927d54_story.html?utm_term=.e426fc5ca6e8.
40. Tess Townsend, "Washington Post's Marty Baron: 'We're Not at War with the Administration, We're at Work,'" Recode, February 14, 2017, www.recode.net/2017/2/14/14615824/marty-baron-not-at-war-trump.

MEDIA LITERACY CASE STUDY: Investigative Journalism: In the "Spotlight," p. 68 [pp. 68–69]

1. Scott Allen, "A Distinguished History of Digging Up the Truth," *Boston Globe*, June 22, 2012, www.bostonglobe.com/news/special-reports/2012/06/22/distinguished-history-digging-truth/koYXOjPVD3CfTuRBtp0ZnM/story.html.
2. Investigative Reporters and Editors, "About IRE," www.ire.org/about.
3. Kristen Hare, "Report for America Aims to Get 1,000 Journalists in Local Newsrooms in Next 5 Years," Poynter, September 18, 2017, https://www.poynter.org/tech-tools/2017/report-for-america-aims-to-get-1000-journalists-in-local-newsrooms-in-next-5-years.
4. Iowa Watch, "About Us," accessed August 4, 2018, www.iowawatch.org/about/about-us.

THE DIGITAL TURN CASE STUDY: Attacking Journalism: Trolls and State-Sponsored Troll Armies, p. 92

1. "MSNBC's Katy Tur Explains How Trump's Rhetoric on the Press Puts Journalists' Lives and Safety at Risk," *Media Matters*, August 3, 2018, www.mediamatters.org/video/2018/08/03/msnbcs-katy-tur-explains-how-trumps-rhetoric-press-puts-journalists-lives-and-safety-risk/220902.
2. Sherry Ricchiardi, "Female Journalists Fight Online Harassment," Global Investigative Journalism Network, September 28, 2017, https://gijn.org/2017/09/28/scourge-of-the-profession-online-harassment-of-female-journalists.
3. "Online Harassment of Journalists: Attack of the Trolls," Reporters Sans Frontières, July 25, 2018, https://rsf.org/sites/default/files/rsf_report_on_online_harassment.pdf.

4 Magazines in the Age of Specialization

1. "Cosmopolitan Demographic Profile 2018," Cosmomediakit.com, accessed September 2, 2018, www.cosmomediakit.com/r5/showkiosk.asp?listing_id=4785154&category_code=demo&category_id=77109.
2. Sammye Johnson, "Promoting Easy Sex without the Intimacy: *Maxim* and *Cosmopolitan* Cover Lines and Cover Images," in *Critical Thinking about Sex, Love, and Romance in the Mass Media*, ed. Mary-Lou Galician and Debra L. Merskin (Mahwah, N.J.: Erlbaum, 2007), 55–74.
3. Jennifer Benjamin, "How Cosmo Changed the World," May 3, 2007, www.cosmopolitan.com/lifestyle/a1746

/about-us-how-cosmo-changed-the-world. See also Theodore Peterson, *Magazines in the Twentieth Century* (Urbana: University of Illinois Press, 1964), 5.

4. "Wired Media Group 2017 Media Kit," *Wired.com*, accessed September 6, 2018, www.wired.com/wp-content/uploads/2015/03/WMG_Media_Kit_2017_v3.pdf.

5. Gloria Steinem, "Sex, Lies and Advertising," *Ms.*, July–August 1990, pp. 18–28.

6. *Magazine Media Factbook 2018/2019*, Association of Magazine Media, www.magazine.org/Magazine/Research_and_Resources/MPA_Factbook/Magazine/Research_and_Resources_Pages/MPA_Factbook.aspx?hkey=f422c440-7e9c-48aa-876a-daba93eaadfe.

7. Matt Drange, "Peter Thiel's War on Gawker: A Timeline," *Forbes*, June 21, 2016, www.forbes.com/sites/mattdrange/2016/06/21/peter-thiels-war-on-gawker-a-timeline/#6dacc54d7e80.

THE DIGITAL TURN CASE STUDY: Snapchats and Podcasts: Magazine Publishing Turns New Pages, p. 119

1. "Voyages: Travel Sounds from the World," *New York Times Magazine*, September 21, 2018, www.nytimes.com/interactive/2018/09/21/magazine/voyages-travel-sounds-from-the-world.html.

2. Zach Brooke, "How National Geographic Is Dominating Social Media as an Historic Magazine," *American Marketing Association*, March 12, 2018, www.ama.org/publications/MarketingNews/Pages/national-geographic-social-media-success.aspx.

3. Lauren Johnson, "What National Geographic Did to Earn 3 Million Snapchat Discover Subscribers in Just 3 Months: A New Streamlined Design Plays Up More Photos and Less Text," *Adweek*, October 5, 2017, www.adweek.com/digital/what-national-geographic-did-to-earn-3-million-snapchat-discover-subscribers-in-just-3-months.

4. "Magazine Media 360° Brand Audience Report Shows That Media Mix Has Shifted, Total Audience Remains Strong," Association of Magazine Media, March 7, 2018, www.magazine.org/magazine/News_Pages/Press_Releases/MPA_Press_Releases/MM360_BAR_Media_Mix_Shifted.aspx.

5 Sound Recording and Popular Music

1. Joe Coscarelli, "Chance the Rapper Says His Apple Music Deal Was Worth $500,000," *New York Times*, March 17, 2017, www.nytimes.com/2017/03/17/arts/music/chance-the-rapper-apple-deal.html.

2. Dan Rys and Ben Austen, "How Chance the Rapper Turned Down Leading Labels, Then Teamed with Apple Music," *Billboard*, August 11, 2016, www.billboard.com/articles/columns/hip-hop/7469373/chance-the-rapper-manager-interview.

3. Kaye Foley, "The Magnificent Rise of Chance the Rapper," interview by Katie Couric, Yahoo! News, February 27, 2017, www.yahoo.com/katiecouric/chance-the-rapper-talks-grammys-chicago-and-why-he-doesnt-need-a-label-211356146.html.

4. David Drake, "Chance the Rapper Puts on Magnificent Show for 'Coloring Day' Festival in Chicago," *Billboard*, September 26, 2016, www.billboard.com/articles/columns/hip-hop/7518992/chance-the-rapper-magnificent-coloring-day-festival.

5. Kim Bellware, "Local Media Needs Security. What Chance the Rapper's Purchase of Chicagoist Means," *New York Times*, July 31, 2018, www.nytimes.com/2018/07/31/opinion/culture/chance-the-rapper-chicagoist.html; Lisa Respers France, "Netflix Snags Cardi B, Chance and T.I. for Music Competition Show," CNN, November 14, 2018, www.cnn.com/2018/11/14/entertainment/cardi-b-ti-chance-netflix/index.html.

6. Foley, "Magnificent Rise of Chance the Rapper."

7. Mark Coleman, *Playback: From the Victrola to MP3* (Cambridge, Mass.: Da Capo Press, 2003).

8. "Spotify Technology S.A. Announces Financial Results for Third Quarter 2018," Spotify Press Release, November 1, 2018, https://investors.spotify.com/financials/press-release-details/2018/Spotify-Technology-SA-Announces-Financial-Results-for-Third-Quarter-2018/default.aspx.

9. Mick Jagger, quoted in Jann S. Wenner, "Jagger Remembers," *Rolling Stone*, December 14, 1995, 66.

10. Mac Rebennack (Dr. John) with Jack Rummel, *Under a Hoodoo Moon* (New York: St. Martin's Press, 1994), 58.

11. Ken Tucker, quoted in Ed Ward, Geoffrey Stokes, and Ken Tucker, *Rock of Ages: The Rolling Stone History of Rock and Roll* (New York: Rolling Stone Press, 1986), 521.

12. "2017 Year-End Music Report: U.S.," Nielsen Music, January 3, 2018, www.nielsen.com/us/en/insights/reports/2018/2017-music-us-year-end-report.html.

13. "The 'Nashville Sound' Begins," *Living in Stereo*, September 19, 2006.

14. Michael D'Arcy and Sherry Anderson, "What Is Countrypolitan Music?" January 2001, www.michaelfitz.net/blog/countrypolitan_101.

15. "Mid-Year 2018 RIAA Music Revenues Report," Recording Industry Association of America, www.riaa.com/wp-content/uploads/2018/09/RIAA-Mid-Year-2018-Revenue-Report-News-Notes.pdf.

16. "News and Notes on 2017 RIAA Revenue Statistics," Recording Industry Association of America, www.riaa.com/wp-content/uploads/2018/03/RIAA-Year-End-2017-News-and-Notes.pdf; Tim Ingham, "Independents Ruled Global Market Share in 2017—but Universal Was King of Streaming," *Music Business Worldwide*, April 25, 2018, www.musicbusinessworldwide.com/independents-ruled-global-market-share-in-2017-but-universal-was-king-of-streaming.

17. IFPI, *Music Consumer Insight Report 2018*, www.ifpi.org/downloads/Music-Consumer-Insight-Report-2018.pdf.

18. "*Billboard*'s Genre Album Charts Will Now Incorporate Streams and Track Sales," *Billboard*, January 26, 2017, www.billboard.com/articles/columns/chart-beat/7669133/billboard-genre-album-charts-consumption-streams-track-sales; Paul Resnikoff, "Billboard's New Math: 1,500 Streams = One Album Sale; Digital Music News," November 20, 2014, www.digitalmusicnews.com/2014/11/20/billboards-new-math-1500-streams-one-album-sale.
19. Cary Sherman, "2016: A Year of Progress for Music," *Medium*, March 30, 2017, https://medium.com/@RIAA/2016-a-year-of-progress-for-music-4e9b77022635.

MEDIA LITERACY CASE STUDY: The New Masters of Music Modernization: Daniel Ek, Spotify, and Streaming Services, p. 132 [pp. 132–133]

1. Daniel Ek, "A Playlist for Entrepreneurs" interview by Chi-Hua Chien, Venture Boldly with Stanford University, May 16, 2012, https://ecorner.stanford.edu/video/a-playlist-for-entrepreneurs-entire-talk.
2. Dorian Lynskey, "Is Daniel Ek, Spotify Founder, Going to Save the Music Industry . . . or Destroy It?" *Guardian*, November 10, 2013, www.theguardian.com/technology/2013/nov/10/daniel-ek-spotify-streaming-music.
3. "News and Notes on 2017 RIAA Revenue Statistics," Recording Industry Association of America, March 22, 2018, www.riaa.com/wp-content/uploads/2018/03/RIAA-Year-End-2017-News-and-Notes.pdf.
4. Bill Rosenblatt, "Here Are the Loopholes Closed by the Music Modernization Act," *Forbes*, October 11, 2018, www.forbes.com/sites/billrosenblatt/2018/10/11/music-modernization-act-now-law-leaves-one-copyright-loophole-unclosed/#3a6cc9437272.
5. William Frankel and Judy He, "A Tune of Modernity: The Music Modernization Act," *National Law Review*, October 17, 2018, www.natlawreview.com/article/tune-modernity-music-modernization-act.
6. Rosenblatt, "Here Are the Loopholes Closed by the Music Modernization Act."
7. Jason Murdock, "10 Years of Spotify: How the Platform Revolutionized the Music Industry—and Where Does It Go from Here?" *Newsweek*, October 9, 2018, www.newsweek.com/ten-years-spotify-how-platform-revolutionized-music-industry-1160004.

THE DIGITAL TURN CASE STUDY: 360 Degrees of Music, p. 151

1. Sara Karubian, "360-Degree Deals: An Industry Reaction to the Devaluation of Recorded Music," *Southern California Interdisciplinary Law Journal* 18, no. 395 (2009): 395–462, www-bcf.usc.edu/~idjlaw/PDF/18-2/18-2%20Karubian.pdf.
2. Clarisse Loughrey, "Katy Perry Tops *Forbes* List of Highest Paid Female Musicians, Beating Lady Gaga, Beyoncé, and Taylor Swift," *Independent*, November 21, 2018, www.independent.co.uk/arts-entertainment/music/news/katy-perry-richest-highest-paid-forbes-net-worth-lady-gaga-beyonce-taylor-swift-pink-a8644406.html.

6 Popular Radio and the Origins of Broadcasting

1. Brendan Regan, "Podcasts Took Off This Year; What Will the New Year Bring?" *Newsweek*, December 26, 2017, www.newsweek.com/podcasts-took-year-what-will-new-year-bring-758304.
2. "Best of the Blogs: What Kind of Shows Dominate Podcasting?" *Inside Radio*, December 6, 2017, www.insideradio.com/free/best-of-the-blogs-what-kind-of-shows-dominate-podcasting/article_57b18af4-da5e-11e7-9d35-9bf13c627d23.html; "2018's Top Programming Trend Isn't a Format: It's Podcasting," *Inside Radio*, January 3, 2018, www.insideradio.com/s-top-programming-trend-isn-t-a-format-it-s/article_eee906ae-f057-11e7-a4e2-bb5440d19573.html; Rebecca Mead, "How Podcasts Became a Seductive—and Sometimes Slippery—Mode of Storytelling," *New Yorker*, November 19, 2018, www.newyorker.com/magazine/2018/11/19/how-podcasts-became-a-seductive-and-sometimes-slippery-mode-of-storytelling.
3. "Best of the Blogs"; "2018's Top Programming Trend Isn't a Format."
4. Juliette De Maeyer, "Podcasting Is the New Talk-Radio," *Atlantic*, May 24, 2017, www.theatlantic.com/technology/archive/2017/05/how-podcasting-is-shaping-democracy/524028.
5. "Study: How to Use Podcasts to Bring Ears to Radio," *Inside Radio*, February 7, 2017, www.insideradio.com/free/study-how-to-use-podcasts-to-bring-ears-to-radio/article_42865dd4-ed07-11e6-b430-6fda005c6b66.html.
6. "2018's Top Programming Trend Isn't a Format."
7. Tom Lewis, *Empire of the Air: The Men Who Made Radio* (New York: HarperCollins, 1991), 181.
8. Margaret Cheney, *Tesla: Man Out of Time* (New York: Touchstone, 2001).
9. William J. Broad, "Tesla, a Bizarre Genius, Regains Aura of Greatness," *New York Times*, August 28, 1984, http://query.nytimes.com/gst/fullpage.html?res=9400E4DD1038F93BA1575BC0A962948260&sec=health&spon=&partner=permalink&exprod=permalink.
10. Michael Pupin, "Objections Entered to Court's Decision," *New York Times*, June 10, 1934, p. E5.
11. For a full discussion of early broadcast history and the formation of RCA, see Eric Barnouw, *Tube of Plenty* (New York: Oxford University Press, 1982); Susan Douglas, *Inventing American Broadcasting, 1899–1922* (Baltimore: Johns Hopkins University Press, 1987); Christopher Sterling and John Kitross, *Stay Tuned: A Concise History of American Broadcasting* (Belmont, Calif.: Wadsworth, 1990).

12. Michele Hilmes, *Radio Voices: American Broadcasting, 1922–1952* (Minneapolis: University of Minnesota Press, 1997).
13. *Amos 'n' Andy Show,* Museum of Broadcast Communications, accessed January 25, 2019, www.museum.tv/eotv/amosnandy.htm.
14. NPR, "NPR Factsheet," January 2019, www.npr.org/about/press/NPR_Fact_Sheet.pdf.
15. Regan, "Podcasts Took Off This Year."
16. Mike Murphy, "FCC Urges Apple to Activate FM Radio Chips in iPhones—but Newer Models Can't," MarketWatch, September 29, 2017, www.marketwatch.com/story/fcc-urges-apple-to-activate-fm-radio-chip-in-iphones-but-newer-models-cant-2017-09-28.
17. Ibid.
18. Sam Matheny, "Setting the Record Straight on FM Radio in iPhones," *Policy Blog*, National Association of Broadcasters, October 18, 2017, https://blog.nab.org/2017/10/18/setting-the-record-straight-on-fm-radio-in-iphones.
19. Arjun Panchadar and Vibhuti Sharma, "Sirius XM to Buy Pandora in $3.5 Billion Streaming Push," Reuters, September 24, 2018, www.reuters.com/article/us-pandora-m-a-sirius-xm-holdings/sirius-xm-to-buy-pandora-in-3-5-billion-streaming-push-idUSKCN1M418P.
20. "How America Listens: The American Audio Landscape," April 5, 2018, www.nielsen.com/us/en/insights/news/2018/how-america-listens-the-american-audio-landscape.html.
21. Emily M. Reigart, "U.S. Commercial Radio Revenue Down in 2017," *RadioWorld*, April 5, 2018, www.radioworld.com/news-and-business/radio-revenue-down-in-2017.
22. Federal Communications Commission, "Broadcast Station Totals as of September 30, 2018," October 3, 2018, www.fcc.gov/document/broadcast-station-totals-september-30-2018.
23. Larry Miller, "Terrestrial Radio Ducks Music Modernization Act, but Still Must Face the Music," *Billboard*, October 5, 2018, www.billboard.com/articles/news/politics/8478501/terrestrial-radio-music-modernization-act-essay.
24. Glenn Peoples, "How 'Playola' Is Infiltrating Streaming Services: Pay for Play Is 'Definitely Happening,'" *Billboard*, August 19, 2015, www.billboard.com/articles/business/6670475/playola-promotion-streaming-services. See also Robert Cookson, "Spotify Bans 'Payola' on Playlists," *Financial Times*, August 20, 2015, https://next.ft.com/content/af1728ca-4740-11e5-af2f-4d6e0e5eda22.
25. Peter DiCola, "False Premises, False Promises: A Quantitative History of Ownership Consolidation in the Radio Industry," Future of Music Coalition, December 2006, https://futureofmusic.org/article/research/false-premises-false-promises.
26. David Allison, "Radio Giant Cumulus Media Completes Bankruptcy Restructuring," *Atlanta Business Chronicle*, June 5, 2018, www.bizjournals.com/atlanta/news/2018/06/05/radio-giantcumulus-media-completes-bankruptcy.html; "iHeartMedia Unveils Post-Bankruptcy Board of Directors," *Variety*, November 14, 2018, https://variety.com/2018/biz/news/iheartmedia-unveils-post-bankruptcy-board-of-directors-1203028375.
27. "Statement of FCC Chairman William E. Kennard on Low Power FM Radio Initiative," March 27, 2000, www.fcc.gov/Speeches/Kennard/Statements/2000/stwek024.html.

MEDIA LITERACY CASE STUDY: How Did Talk Radio Become So One-Sided?, p. 174 [pp. 174–175]
1. *Audio Today 2018: How America Listens*, April 2018, www.nielsen.com/content/dam/corporate/us/en/reports-downloads/2018-reports/audio-today-report-apr-2018.pdf.
2. "Top Talk Audiences," *Talkers*, December 2018, www.talkers.com/top-talk-audiences.
3. Robert L. Hilliard and Michael C. Keith, *Waves of Rancor: Tuning in the Radical Right* (Armonk, N.Y.: M.E. Sharpe, 1999), 15.
4. Hilliard and Keith, *Waves of Rancor*, 17.
5. Kathleen Hall Jamieson and Joseph N. Cappella, *Echo Chamber: Rush Limbaugh and the Conservative Media Establishment* (New York: Oxford University Press, 2008), 46.
6. "Top Talk Audiences," *Morning Edition*, 2018, www.nationalpublicmedia.com/npr/programs/morning-edition.
7. *Audio Today 2018*.

THE DIGITAL TURN CASE STUDY: Streaming Services Set Their Sights on Broadcast Radio, p. 178
1. Cherie Hu, "Spotify vs. Pandora: Which Radio Competitor Is Winning at the Ad-Supported Game?" *Billboard*, June 1, 2018, www.billboard.com/articles/business/8458166/spotify-pandora-ad-supported-streaming-analysis.
2. Jem Aswad, "Traditional Radio Faces a Grim Future, New Study Says," *Variety*, August 30, 2017, https://variety.com/2017/music/news/traditional-radio-faces-a-grim-future-new-study-says-1202542681.
3. Hu, "Spotify vs. Pandora."
4. "National Association of Broadcasters, Nielsen Respond to Study Predicting Terrestrial Radio's Downfall," *Variety*, August 30, 2018, https://variety.com/2017/music/news/national-association-of-broadcasters-responds-to-silly-study-predicting-terrestrial-radios-downfall-guest-post-1202543318.
5. Hu, "Spotify vs. Pandora."

7 Movies and the Impact of Images

1. Douglas Gomery, *Shared Pleasures: A History of Movie Presentation in the United States* (Madison: University of Wisconsin Press, 1992), 18.
2. Douglas Gomery, *Movie History: A Survey* (Belmont, Calif.: Wadsworth, 1991), 167.

3. Mike McPhate, "Hollywood's Inclusion Problem Extends beyond the Oscars, Study Says," *New York Times*, February 22, 2016, www.nytimes.com/2016/02/23/movies/hollywoods-inclusion-problem-extends-beyond-the-oscars-study-says.html.
4. Time's Up, January 1, 2018, www.timesupnow.com.
5. "Record Number of Films Produced," UNESCO, March 31, 2016, http://uis.unesco.org/en/news/record-number-films-produced; "Indian Feature Films Certified during the Year 2017," Film Federation of India, 2017, www.filmfed.org/IFF2017.html; Zheping Huang, "China's Top 10 Box Office Hits of All Time Include Four Domestic Films Released in 2017," *Quartz*, January 2, 2018, https://qz.com/1169192/chinas-all-time-top-10-box-office-list-has-four-domestic-films-released-in-2017-including-wolf-warrior-2.
6. Daniel Kreps, "'Hunting Ground' Team Plan Hollywood Sexual Assault Documentary," *Rolling Stone*, October 23, 2017, www.rollingstone.com/movies/news/hunting-ground-team-plan-hollywood-sexual-assault-film-w509976.
7. Nancy Tartaglione, "Worldwide Box Office Poised for Record $41.7B in 2018: ComScore," *Deadline*, December 27, 2018, https://deadline.com/2018/12/worldwide-box-office-record-2018-domestic-international-china-1202526458/.
8. Matt Krantz et al., "Disney Buys Lucasfilm for $4 Billion," *USA Today*, October 30, 2012, www.usatoday.com/story/money/business/2012/10/30/disney-star-wars-lucasfilm/1669739/; Matthew S. Schwartz, "Disney Officially Owns 21st Century Fox," NPR, March 20, 2019, www.npr.org/2019/03/20/705009029/disney-officially-owns-21st-century-fox.
9. Julianne Pepitone, "Americans Now Watch More Online Movies Than DVDs," CNN/Money, March 22, 2012, http://money.cnn.com/2012/03/22/technology/streaming-movie-sales/index.htm.
10. See Eric Barnouw, *Tube of Plenty: The Evolution of American Television*, rev. ed. (New York: Oxford University Press, 1982), 108–109.

MEDIA LITERACY CASE STUDY: Breaking through Hollywood's Race Barrier, p. 200 [pp. 200–201]
1. Douglas Gomery, *Shared Pleasures: A History of Movie Presentation in the United States* (Madison: University of Wisconsin Press, 1992), 155–170.
2. Scott Mendelson, "Box Office: Marvel's 'Black Panther' Tops $1.1 Billion Worldwide," *Forbes*, March 14, 2018, www.forbes.com/sites/scottmendelson/2018/03/14/box-office-marvels-black-panther-tops-1-1-billion-worldwide/#6d47c4935ecb.
3. Jamil Smith, "The Revolutionary Power of *Black Panther*," *Time*, February 19, 2018, http://time.com/black-panther.

THE DIGITAL TURN CASE STUDY: Attracting an Audience in a Digital Age, p. 212 [pp. 212–213]
1. "Ryan Reynolds Might Have Leaked *Deadpool*'s Test Footage," YouTube video, February 10, 2016, www.youtube.com/watch?v=5Sq0_MGriXc.
2. Shannon Liao, "All the Ridiculous Deadpool 2 Marketing Stunts You May Have Missed," *The Verge*, May 18, 2018, www.theverge.com/tldr/2018/5/18/17365998/deadpool-2-marketing-stunts-deadpool-x-david-beckham-forever.
3. Seb Joseph, "Movie Marketing Moves into the Digital Age," *Marketing Week*, February 3, 2014, www.marketingweek.com/2014/02/03/movie-marketing-moves-into-the-digital-age.
4. "A Case Study in Gaining Exposure for Your Film," *Vimeo Blog*, October 17, 2012, https://vimeo.com/blog/post/a-case-study-in-gaining-exposure-for-your-film.

8 Television, Cable, and Specialization in Visual Culture

1. Quinn Keaney, "When You Find Out How Many People Watched *Stranger Things* Season 2, Your Jaw Will Drop," Pop Sugar, November 8, 2017, www.popsugar.com/entertainment/How-Many-People-Watch-Stranger-Things-44215482.
2. A. J. Katz, "Evening News Ratings: Week of October 15," *Adweek*, October 23, 2018, www.adweek.com/tvnewser/evening-news-ratings-week-of-oct-15-2/381563.
3. See Horace Newcomb, *TV: The Most Popular Art* (Garden City, N.Y.: Anchor Books, 1974), 31, 39.
4. Michael Schneider, "These Are the 100 Most-Watched TV Shows of the 2017–18 Season: Winners and Losers," IndieWire, May 25, 2018, www.indiewire.com/2018/05/most-watched-tv-shows-2017-2018-season-roseanne-this-is-us-walking-dead-1201968306.
5. "Estimated Total of Cable Channels Offered in 2014," NCTA, accessed January 23, 2019, www.ncta.com/chart/estimated-total-of-cable-channels-offered-in-2014.
6. Anthony Crupi, "Streaming Services Outpace Linear TV Production for the First Time," *Ad Age*, December 13, 2018, https://adage.com/article/media/a-good-thing/315962.
7. *United States v. Midwest Video Corp.*, 440 U.S. 689 (1979).
8. Bill Carter, "Cable TV, the Home of High Drama," *New York Times*, April 5, 2010, pp. B1, B3.
9. Maureen Ryan and Cynthia Littleton, "TV Series Budgets Hit the Breaking Point as Costs Skyrocket in Peak TV Era," *Variety*, September 26, 2017, http://variety.com/2017/tv/news/tv-series-budgets-costs-rising-peak-tv-1202570158.
10. Brian Beers, "How Netflix Pays for Movie and TV Show Licensing," Investopedia, October 18, 2018, www.investopedia.com/articles/investing/062515/how-netflix-pays-movie-and-tv-show-licensing.asp.

11. Benjamin Bullard, "Netflix Cuts First Original Series Syndication Deal to Cable TV—Could More Follow?" SyFy.com, July 26, 2018, www.syfy.com/syfywire/netflix-cuts-its-first-original-series-syndication-deal-to-cable-tv-could-more-follow.

MEDIA LITERACY CASE STUDY: Race, Gender, and Sexual Orientation in TV Programming, p. 234 [pp. 234–235]
1. Larry Gross, *Up from Invisibility: Lesbians, Gay Men, and the Media in America* (New York: Columbia University Press, 2001). See also Liesbet Van Zoonen, *Feminist Media Studies* (Thousand Oaks, Calif.: Sage, 1994); Angela McRobbie, *The Uses of Cultural Studies* (Thousand Oaks, Calif.: Sage, 2005).
2. Edward Alwood, *Straight News: Gays, Lesbians, and the News Media* (New York: Columbia University Press, 1996). See also Gaye Tuchman, *Making News: A Study in the Construction of Reality* (New York: Free Press, 1978).

THE DIGITAL TURN CASE STUDY: Bingeing Purges Traditional Viewing Habits, p. 243
1. "Distribution of Binge Viewers in the United States in 2017, by Age," Statista, accessed December 15, 2018, www.statista.com/statistics/289628/streaming-binge-viewing-tvs-shows-us.
2. "Netflix Declares Binge Watching Is the New Normal," PR Newswire, December 13, 2013, www.prnewswire.com/news-releases/netflix-declares-binge-watching-is-the-new-normal-235713431.html.

9 The Internet and New Technologies: The Media Converge

1. NBCDFW.COM, "Man Hacks Texas Family's Baby Monitors, Threatens to Kidnap Infant: Report," December 18, 2018, www.nbcdfw.com/news/local/Man-Hacks-Texas-Familys-Baby-Monitors-Threatens-to-Kidnap-Infant-503013171.html; see also Amy B. Wang, "'I'm in Your Baby's Room': A Hacker Took Over a Baby Monitor and Broadcast Threats, Parents Say," *Washington Post*, December 20, 2018, www.washingtonpost.com/technology/2018/12/20/nest-cam-baby-monitor-hacked-kidnap-threat-came-device-parents-say/?utm_term=.4dff2835967a.
2. M. L. Nestel, "South Carolina Parents Say Baby Monitor Was Hacked After Camera Lens Moved on Its Own," *ABCNews*, June 4, 2018, https://abcnews.go.com/US/south-carolina-parents-baby-monitor-hacked-camera-lens/story?id=55633540.
3. Simon Hill, "Is Your Smartphone Listening to Everything You Say? We Asked the Experts," *Digital Trends*, January 15, 2017, www.digitaltrends.com/mobile/is-your-smartphone-listening-to-your-conversations.
4. "Broadband vs. Dial-Up Adoption over Time," Pew Research Center, June 10, 2015, www.pewinternet.org/chart/broadband-vs-dial-up-adoption-over-time.
5. "Search Engine Market Share Worldwide, Dec 2017–Dec 2018," StatCounter Global Stats, accessed January 20, 2019, http://gs.statcounter.com/search-engine-market-share.
6. Chris Anderson and Michael Wolff, "The Web Is Dead. Long Live the Internet," *Wired*, August 17, 2010, www.wired.com/magazine/2010/08/ff_webrip. See also Charles Arthur, "Walled Gardens Look Rosy for Facebook, Apple—and Would-Be Censors," *Guardian*, April 17, 2012, www.guardian.co.uk/technology/2012/apr/17/walled-gardens-facebook-apple-censors.
7. Arthur, "Walled Gardens."
8. "Situation Syria Regional Refugee Response," Operational Data Portal, United Nations High Commissioner for Refugees, https://data2.unhcr.org/en/situations/syria; "Death Tolls," I Am Syria, www.iamsyria.org/death-tolls.html.
9. Renee Guarriello Heath, Courtney Vail Fletcher, and Ricardo Munoz, eds., *Understanding Occupy from Wall Street to Portland: Applied Studies in Communication Theory* (Lanham, Md.: Lexington Books, 2013).
10. Brendan I. Koerner, "Why ISIS Is Winning the Social Media War," *Wired*, March 2016, www.wired.com/2016/03/isis-winning-social-media-war-heres-beat.
11. Tim Berners-Lee, James Hendler, and Ora Lassila, "The Semantic Web," *Scientific American*, May 17, 2001, www.scientificamerican.com/article/the-semantic-web.
12. Jane C. Hu, "How One Lightbulb Could Allow Hackers to Burgle Your Home," *Quartz*, December 18, 2018, https://qz.com/1493748/how-one-lightbulb-could-allow-hackers-to-burgle-your-home.
13. Ibid.
14. Farhad Manjoo, "The Great Tech War of 2012: Apple, Facebook, Google, and Amazon Battle for the Future of the Innovation Economy," *Fast Company*, October 19, 2011, www.fastcompany.com/magazine/160/tech-wars-2012-amazon-apple-google-facebook.
15. Ad Age, *Marketing Fact Pack 2019*, http://adage.com/d/resources/resources/whitepaper/marketing-fact-pack-2019, p. 14.
16. Julie Bernard, "Five Bleeding-Edge Mobile Marketing Trends in 2017," *Ad Age*, January 5, 2017, http://adage.com/article/digitalnext/mobile-marketing-trends-2017/307343.
17. Mark Zuckerberg, "Our Commitment to the Facebook Community," Facebook, November 29, 2011, www.facebook.com/notes/facebook/our-commitment-to-the-facebook-community/10150378701937131.
18. "Online Tracking: Understanding Cookies," Federal Trade Commission, June 2016, www.consumer.ftc.gov/articles/0042-cookies-leaving-trail-web.

19. See Federal Trade Commission, *Privacy Online: Fair Information Practices in the Electronic Marketplace*, May 2000, www.ftc.gov/sites/default/files/documents/reports/privacy-online-fair-information-practices-electronic-marketplace-federal-trade-commission-report/privacy2000.pdf.
20. "Internet/Broadband Fact Sheet," Pew Research Center, February 5, 2018, www.pewinternet.org/fact-sheet/internet-broadband.
21. Ibid.
22. GSMA, "The Mobile Economy North America 2018," www.gsma.com/mobileeconomy/northamerica.
23. Ibid.

THE DIGITAL TURN CASE STUDY: Social Media Fraud and Elections, p. 264 [pp. 264–265]

1. Alan Finlayson, "Facebook: The Election's Town Square," *Guardian*, February 14, 2010, www.theguardian.com/commentisfree/2010/feb/14/social-networking-facebook-general-election.
2. Omar L. Gallaga, "We've Reached a Turning Point for Facebook—and Its Users," *Dayton Daily News*, December 3, 2016, D6.
3. Bill Priestap, "Statement Before the Senate Select Committee on Intelligence" (Washington, D.C., June 21, 2017), www.fbi.gov/news/testimony/assessing-russian-activities-and-intentions-in-recent-elections.
4. Elizabeth Weise, "Russian Fake Accounts Showed Posts to 126 Million Facebook Users," *USA Today*, October 30, 2017, www.usatoday.com/story/tech/2017/10/30/russian-fake-accounts-showed-posts-126-million-facebook-users/815342001.
5. Jessica Guynn, "Twitter: There Were More Russian Trolls Than We Thought," *USA Today*, January 19, 2018, www.usatoday.com/story/tech/news/2018/01/19/twitter-there-were-more-russian-trolls-than-we-thought/1050091001.
6. Wiese, "Russian Fake Accounts."
7. Scott Shane and Sheera Frenkel, "Russian 2016 Influence Operation Targeted African-Americans on Social Media," *New York Times*, December 17, 2018, www.nytimes.com/2018/12/17/us/politics/russia-2016-influence-campaign.html.
8. Dana Priest and Michael Birnbaum, "Europe Has Been Working to Expose Russian Meddling for Years," *Washington Post*, June 25, 2017, www.washingtonpost.com/world/europe/europe-has-been-working-to-expose-russian-meddling-for-years/2017/06/25/e42dcece-4a09-11e7-9669-250d0b15f83b_story.html.

MEDIA LITERACY CASE STUDY: Net Neutrality, p. 272 [pp. 272–273]

1. Rebecca R. Ruiz, "F.C.C. Sets Net Neutrality Rules," March 12, 2015, *New York Times*, www.nytimes.com/2015/03/13/technology/fcc-releases-net-neutrality-rules.html.
2. Federal Communications Commission, "Fact Sheet: Chairman Wheeler Proposes New Rules for Protecting the Open Internet," accessed May 9, 2015, https://apps.fcc.gov/edocs_public/attachmatch/DOC-331869A1.pdf.
3. Ted Johnson, "State Attorneys General File Suit over FCC's Net Neutrality Repeal," *Variety*, January 16, 2018, http://variety.com/2018/biz/news/net-neutrality-fcc-state-attorneys-general-sue-1202665803. See also "Montana Pushes Back on FCC Ruling to Enforce Net Neutrality," NPR, January 27, 2018, www.npr.org/2018/01/27/581343532/montana-pushes-back-on-fcc-ruling-to-enforce-net-neutrality.
4. Tim Wu, "Why the Courts Will Have to Save Net Neutrality," *New York Times*, November 22, 2017, www.nytimes.com/2017/11/22/opinion/courts-net-neutrality-fcc.html.

10 Digital Gaming and the Media Playground

1. Megan Farokhmanesh, "First Game Tournament, 'Intergalactic Spacewar Olympics,' Held 40 Years Ago," Polygon, October 20, 2012, www.polygon.com/2012/10/20/3529662/first-game-tournament-intergalactic-spacewar-olympics-held-40-years. See also Chris Baker, "Stewart Brand Recalls First 'Spacewar' Video Game Tournament," *Rolling Stone*, May 25, 2016, www.rollingstone.com/culture/news/stewart-brand-recalls-first-spacewar-video-game-tournament-20160525.
2. Andrew Paradise, "The History Behind a $5 Billion eSports Industry," TechCrunch, November 3, 2016, https://techcrunch.com/gallery/the-history-behind-a-5-billion-esports-industry.
3. "U Unveils Roster for First Varsity eSports Team," University of Utah, October 4, 2017, https://unews.utah.edu/university-of-utah-unveils-roster-for-first-varsity-esports-team. See also Aaron Reiss, "What It's Like to Be a Varsity Esports Player," *Sports Illustrated*, January 4, 2017, www.si.com/tech-media/2017/01/04/varsity-esports-team-columbia-college-league-legends.
4. Activate, *Activate Tech & Media Outlook 2018*, October 17, 2017, www.slideshare.net/ActivateInc/activate-tech-media-outlook-2018. See also Paradise, "History Behind."
5. Phuc Pham, "Facebook's Giant Step into eSports May Be a Look at Its Future," *Wired*, January 18, 2018, www.wired.com/story/facebook-esl-esports-streaming-partnership.
6. Irwin A. Kishner, "Esports Leagues Set to Level Up with Permanent Franchises," *Forbes*, October 3, 2017, www.forbes.com/sites/kurtbadenhausen/2017/10/03/esports-leagues-grow-up-with-permanent-franchises/#3f3f9be121d6.
7. Phuc Pham, "Esports Zerg-Rush the Olympics—but Can They Become Official Events?" *Wired*, February 9, 2018, www.wired.com/story/esports-pyeongchang-olympics.
8. Erkki Huhtamo, "Slots of Fun, Slots of Trouble: An Archaeology of Arcade Gaming," in Joost Raessens and Jeffrey Goldstein, eds., *Handbook of Computer Game Studies* (Cambridge, Mass.: MIT Press, 2005), 6–7.
9. Ibid., 9–10.

10. Seth Porges, "11 Things You Didn't Know about Pinball History," *Popular Mechanics*, September 1, 2009, www.popularmechanics.com/technology/g284/4328211-new.

11. "Magnavox Odyssey," PONG-Story, accessed April 6, 2015, www.pong-story.com/odyssey.htm.

12. Eddie Makuch, "Number of PS Plus Paying Members, PSN Users Rise to New Heights," GameSpot, May 22, 2018, www.gamespot.com/articles/number-of-ps-plus-paying-members-psn-users-rise-to/1100-6459137.

13. Asher Madan, "Xbox Live Grows to 59 Million Active Users," Windows Central, January 31, 2018, www.windowscentral.com/xbox-live-grew-59-million-active-users-last-quarter.

14. "Global Unit Sales of Current Generation Video Game Consoles from 2008 to 2018 (in Million Units)," Statista, accessed March 11, 2019, www.statista.com/statistics/276768/global-unit-sales-of-video-game-consoles.

15. "Dedicated Video Game Sales Units," Nintendo, December 31, 2018, www.nintendo.co.jp/ir/en/finance/hard_soft/index.html.

16. Associated Press, "Sony to Stop Selling PlayStation Portable by End of Year," *Time*, June 3, 2014, http://web.archive.org/web/20140603143428/http://time.com/2816781/sony-to-stop-selling-playstation-portable-by-end-of-year.

17. Sal Romano, "PS Vita Production to End in 2019 in Japan," September 20, 2018, Gematsu, https://gematsu.com/2018/09/ps-vita-production-to-end-in-2019-in-japan#emS8aeu018gW6CAo.99.

18. Brian Crecente, "'Overwatch' Tops 40 Million Players as Game Hits Two-Year Anniversary," *Variety*, May 24, 2018, https://variety.com/2018/gaming/news/overwatch-two-year-anniversary-1202820958.

19. Fantasy Sports Trade Association, "Industry Demographics," accessed January 9, 2019, http://fsta.org/research/industry-demographics.

20. Henry Jenkins, "Interactive Audiences? The 'Collective Intelligence' of Media Fans," in Dan Harries, ed., *The New Media Book* (London: British Film Institute, 2002).

21. Haroon Siddique, "*Sea Hero Quest*: The Mobile Phone Game Helping Fight Dementia," *Guardian*, November 16, 2016, www.theguardian.com/society/2016/nov/16/sea-hero-quest-the-mobile-phone-game-helping-fight-dementia; Alan Wen, "*Before I Forget*: The Video Game That Tackles Dementia," *Guardian*, June 6, 2018, www.theguardian.com/games/2018/jun/06/before-i-forget-early-onset-dementia-video-game.

22. Douglas A. Gentile et al., "Pathological Video Game Use among Youths: A Two-Year Longitudinal Study," *Pediatrics* 127, no. 2 (2011), doi:10.1542/peds.2010-1353.

23. Peter Gray, "Sense and Nonsense about Video Game Addiction: What Does Research Really Tell Us about the Brain Effects of Video Gaming?" *Psychology Today*, March 11, 2018, www.psychologytoday.com/us/blog/freedom-learn/201803/sense-and-nonsense-about-video-game-addiction.

24. Daniel Loton et al., "Video Game Addiction, Engagement and Symptoms of Stress, Depression and Anxiety: The Mediating Role of Coping," *International Journal of Mental Health and Addiction* 14 (2016): 565–578, https://core.ac.uk/download/pdf/42142317.pdf.

25. Laura Stockdale and Sarah M. Coyne, "Video Game Addiction in Emerging Adulthood: Cross-Sectional Evidence of Pathology in Video Game Addicts as Compared to Matched Healthy Controls," *Journal of Affective Disorders* 225 (2018): 265–272, www.ncbi.nlm.nih.gov/pubmed/28841491 (abstract).

26. Patrick Markey and Charlotte N. Markey, "Vulnerability to Violent Video Games: A Review and Integration of Personality Research," *Review of General Psychology* 14, no. 2 (2010): 82–91.

27. National Center for Women & Information Technology, "NCWIT Factsheet," accessed June 26, 2012, www.ncwit.org/sites/default/files/resources/ncwitfactsheet.pdf. See also Claire Cain Miller, "Technology's Man Problem," *New York Times*, April 5, 2014, www.nytimes.com/2014/04/06/technology/technologys-man-problem.html.

28. Entertainment Software Association, "2018 Sales, Demographic and Usage Data: Essential Facts about the Computer and Video Game Industry," www.theesa.com/wp-content/uploads/2018/05/EF2018_FINAL.pdf.

29. Entertainment Software Association, "U.S. Video Game Sales Reach Record-Breaking $43.4 Billion in 2018," January 22, 2019, www.theesa.com/article/u-s-video-game-sales-reach-record-breaking-43-4-billion-2018; Peter Warman, "Newzoo Cuts Global Games Forecast for 2018 to $134.9 Billion; Lower Mobile Growth Partially Offset by Very Strong Growth in Console Segment," Newzoo, November 2, 2018, https://newzoo.com/insights/articles/newzoo-cuts-global-games-forecast-for-2018-to-134-9-billion.

30. Ian Hamilton, "Blizzard's World of Warcraft Revenue Down," *Orange County Register*, November 8, 2010, www.ocregister.com/articles/blizzard-543767-world-warcraft.html.

31. "John Madden Net Worth," CelebrityNetworth.com, accessed April 5, 2012, www.celebritynetworth.com/richest-athletes/nfl/john-madden-net-worth.

32. "ESRB Ratings Guide," Entertainment Software Rating Board, accessed March 13, 2019, www.esrb.org/ratings/ratings_guide.jsp.

33. Evan Narcisse, "Supreme Court: 'Video Games Qualify for First Amendment Protection,'" *Time*, June 27, 2011, http://techland.time.com/2011/06/27/supreme-court-video-games-qualify-for-first-amendment-protection.

34. Ibid.
35. Todd VanDerWerff, "#Gamergate: Here's Why Everybody in the Video Game World Is Fighting," *Vox*, October 13, 2014, www.vox.com/2014/9/6/6111065/gamergate-explained-everybody-fighting.
36. Angela McRobbie, *The Uses of Cultural Studies* (Thousand Oaks: Sage, 2005).

THE DIGITAL TURN CASE STUDY: Games in the Great Wide Open: *Pokémon Go* and the Future of Mobile Gaming, p. 299

1. J. V. Chamary, "Why 'Pokémon GO' Is the World's Most Important Game," *Forbes*, February 10, 2018, www.forbes.com/sites/jvchamary/2018/02/10/pokemon-go-science-health-benefits/#2d728a153ab0.
2. See "'Pokémon Go': 10 Strangest Pokéstop Locations," *Rolling Stone*, July 13, 2016, www.rollingstone.com/culture/pictures/pokemon-go-10-worst-pokestop-locations-20160713; Paul Tassi, "Niantic and 'Pokémon GO' Have Turned an Important Corner This Past Week," *Forbes*, November 24, 2017, www.forbes.com/sites/insertcoin/2017/11/24/niantic-and-pokemon-go-have-turned-an-important-corner-this-past-week/#646df3d472d1.
3. Rene Ritchie, "Pokémon Go Events for March 2019," iMore, March 6, 2019, www.imore.com/pokemon-go-events.
4. "New Augmented Reality Mobile Game *Harry Potter: Wizards Unite* Announced," Pottermore, November 8, 2017, www.pottermore.com/news/new-augmented-reality-mobile-game-harry-potter-wizards-unite-announced.

MEDIA LITERACY CASE STUDY: Fighting the Dark Side of Gaming Culture: Anita Sarkeesian and Feminist Frequency, p. 302 [pp. 302–303]

1. Anita Sarkeesian, "It's Game Over for 'Gamers': Anita Sarkeesian on Video Games' Great Future," *New York Times*, October 28, 2014, www.nytimes.com/2014/10/29/opinion/anita-sarkeesian-on-video-games-great-future.html?_r=0.
2. VanDerWerff, "#Gamergate."
3. Jen Yamato, "Anita Sarkeesian on Life after Gamergate: 'I Want to Be a Human Again,'" *Daily Beast*, September 23, 2016, www.thedailybeast.com/articles/2016/09/23/anita-sarkeesian-on-life-after-gamergate-i-want-to-be-a-human-again.html.

Advertising and Commercial Culture

1. Rani Molla, "Billboards—Yes Billboards—Are Having a Heyday in the Digital World," September 25, 2018, Recode.net, www.recode.net/2018/9/25/17897656/billboards-outdoor-advertising-ads.
2. Patrick Sisson, "Why Billboards and Outdoor Ads Are Booming in a Smartphone Age," Curbed.com, December 19, 2018, www.curbed.com/2018/12/19/18148818/outdoor-digital-advertising-billboard.
3. S. A. Whitehead, "McDonald's Invests Billions for Digital Signage, Kiosk Makeover," Digital Signage Today, August 14, 2018, www.digitalsignagetoday.com/articles/mcdonalds-invests-billions-for-digital-signage-kiosk-makeover.
4. Ad Age, *Marketing Fact Pack 2019*, http://adage.com/d/resources/resources/whitepaper/marketing-fact-pack-2019, p. 14.
5. Sisson, "Why Billboards."
6. Larissa Faw and Steve McClellan, "With Some Concerns about the Economy, Forecasters See Modest Ad Growth in 2019," MediaPost, December 3, 2018, www.mediapost.com/publications/article/328770/with-some-concerns-about-the-economy-forecasters.html.
7. Ad Age, *Marketing Fact Pack 2019*, 18–19.
8. Ibid., 14, 16.
9. Jordan Robertson, "E-Mail Spam Goes Artisanal: Scammers Are Turning to Small-Batch Attacks to Beat Today's More Sophisticated E-mail Filters," January 19, 2016, www.bloomberg.com/news/articles/2016-01-19/e-mail-spam-goes-artisanal.
10. See Bettina Fabos, "The Commercialized Web: Challenges for Libraries and Democracy," *Library Trends* 53, no. 4 (Spring 2005): 519–523.
11. "Google's Ad Revenue from 2001 to 2017 (in Billion U.S. Dollars)," Statista, accessed January 4, 2019, www.statista.com/statistics/266249/advertising-revenue-of-google.
12. Ad Age, *Marketing Fact Pack 2019*, 20, 24.
13. "Facebook's Advertising Revenue Worldwide from 2009 to 2017 (in Million U.S. Dollars)," Statista, accessed January 4, 2019, www.statista.com/statistics/271258/facebooks-advertising-revenue-worldwide.
14. Ad Age, *Marketing Fact Pack 2019*, 16.
15. "Worldwide Net Mobile Advertising Revenues of Google from 2014 to 2018 (in Billion U.S. Dollars)," Statista, accessed January 5, 2019, www.statista.com/statistics/539477/google-mobile-ad-revenues-worldwide; Felix Richter, "Facebook's Growth Is Fueled by Mobile Ads," Statista, July 26, 2018, www.statista.com/chart/2496/facebook-revenue-by-segment; "Facebook's U.S. and Non-U.S. Advertising Revenue from 2014 to 2018 (in Billion U.S. Dollars)," Statista, accessed January 23, 2018, www.statista.com/statistics/544001/facebooks-advertising-revenue-worldwide-usa.
16. Ad Age, *Marketing Fact Pack 2019*, 5, 11, 17.
17. Chris Kane, "When Deterministic Identity Isn't Good Enough: The Case for Probabilistic Data," *Medium*, July 24, 2015, https://medium.com/jounce-media-blog/when-deterministic-identity-isn-t-good-enough-d974105f70cd.
18. Ad Age, *Marketing Fact Pack 2019*, 5, 11, 17.
19. See Alexandra Ilyashov, "That Dress You Saw All Over Instagram Last Year Might Be a *Really* Expensive Mistake," March 15, 2016, www.refinery29.com/2016/03/106064/lord-and-taylor-ootd-ads-campaign-ftc-settlement.

20. "Global Top 100 Brands 2018," BrandZ, accessed March 11, 2019, http://brandz.com/charting/54.

21. Michael Schudson, *Advertising: The Uneasy Persuasion* (New York: Basic Books, 1984), 36–43; Andrew Robertson, *The Lessons of Failure* (London: MacDonald, 1974).

22. Centers for Disease Control, "Tobacco Industry Marketing," updated May 4, 2018, www.cdc.gov/tobacco/data_statistics/fact_sheets/tobacco_industry/marketing/index.htm.

23. Ad Age, *Marketing Fact Pack 2019*, 12.

24. Alix Spiegel, "Selling Sickness: How Drug Ads Changed Healthcare," National Public Radio, October 13, 2009, www.npr.org/templates/story/story.php?storyid=113675737.

25. Jason Millman, "It's True: Drug Companies Are Bombarding Your TV with More Ads Than Ever," *Washington Post*, March 23, 2015, www.washingtonpost.com/news/wonk/wp/2015/03/23/yes-drug-companies-are-bombarding-your-tv-with-more-ads-than-ever/?utmterm=.1ffecb80be78.

26. Liz Szabo, "Health Care Industry Spends $30 Billion a Year on Marketing," NBC News, January 8, 2019, www.nbcnews.com/health/health-news/health-care-industry-spends-30-billion-year-marketing-n956251.

27. See Truth Initiative, "Let's Be the Generation to Finish It," www.thetruth.com/about-truth; "Truth® Campaign," https://truthinitiative.org/truth%C2%AE-campaign; "Saving Lives through Truth," https://truthinitiative.org/saving-lives-through-truth (all accessed June 15, 2018).

28. Center for Responsive Politics, "Cost of Election," OpenSecrets.org, accessed January 29, 2019, www.opensecrets.org/overview/cost.php.

29. Ashley Balcerzak, "Update: Federal Elections to Cost Just under $7 Billion, CRP Forecasts," Center for Responsive Politics, November 2, 2016, www.opensecrets.org/news/2016/11/update-federal-elections-to-cost-just-under-7-billion-crp-forecasts.

30. Nicholas Confessore and Karen Yourish, "$2 Billion Worth of Free Media for Donald Trump," *New York Times*, March 15, 2016, www.nytimes.com/2016/03/16/upshot/measuring-donald-trumps-mammoth-advantage-in-free-media.html?register=google&smprod=nytcore-iphone&smid=nytcore-iphone-share&_r=1&mtrref=undefined.

31. Michael Hiltzik, "Les Moonves, CBS, and Trump: Is TV's Business Model Killing Democracy?" *LA Times*, March 15, 2016, www.latimes.com/business/hiltzik/la-fi-hiltzik-trump-moonves-snap-htmlstory.html.

THE DIGITAL TURN CASE STUDY: Does the Digital Turn Spell Doom for Network TV?, p. 328

1. Ad Age, *Marketing Fact Pack 2019*, 14.

2. See Emily Steel and Sydney Ember, "Networks Fret as Ad Dollars Flow to Digital Media," *New York Times*, May 10, 2015, www.nytimes.com/2015/05/11/business/media/networks-fret-as-ad-dollars-flow-to-digital-media.html.

3. Ad Age, *Marketing Fact Pack 2019*, 18.

MEDIA LITERACY CASE STUDY: Idiots and Objects: Stereotyping in Advertising, p. 332 [pp. 332–333]

1. Gene Demby, "That Cute Cheerios Ad with the Interracial Family Is Back," National Public Radio, January 30, 2014, www.npr.org/blogs/codeswitch/2014/01/30/268930004/that-cute-cheerios-ad-with-the-interracial-family-is-back.

2. Joanne Kaufman, "A Sign of 'Modern Society': More Multiracial Families in Commercials," *New York Times*, June 3, 2018, www.nytimes.com/2018/06/03/business/media/advertising-multiracial-families.html.

3. Ibid.

4. Tara John, "Crackdown on Sexist Ads Outlaws Bad Female Driver and Inept Dad Commercials," CNN, December 14, 2018, www.cnn.com/2018/12/14/health/gender-stereotype-ad-ban-gbr-scli-intl/index.html.

5. Ibid.

12 Public Relations and Framing the Message

1. Mark Fainaru-Wada and Steve Fainaru, "NFL-NIH Research Partnership Set to End with $16M Unspent," ESPN, July 28, 2017, www.espn.com/espn/otl/story/_/id/20175509/nfl-donation-brain-research-falls-apart-nih-appears-set-move-bulk-30-million-donation.

2. Michael McCann, "Will New CTE Findings Doom the NFL Concussion Settlement?" *Sports Illustrated*, August 15, 2017, www.si.com/nfl/2017/08/15/new-cte-study-effect-nfl-concussion-settlement.

3. "NFL Issues Response to CTE Research Report," NFL, July 26, 2017, www.nfl.com/news/story/0ap3000000822159/article/nfl-issues-response-to-cte-research-report.

4. Louis Bien, "The NFL Is Going to Insulting Lengths to Prove That CTE Isn't a Problem," SB Nation, August 31, 2017, www.sbnation.com/2017/8/31/16233630/nfl-concussion-study-funding-cte-horse-jockeys.

5. "NFL Announces Play Smart. Play Safe., a New Commitment to Improve Player Health and Safety," NFL Communications, September 14, 2016, https://nflcommunications.com/Pages/NFL-Announces-Play-Smart.-Play-Safe.,-a-New-Commitment-to-Improve-Player-Health-and-Safety.aspx.

6. Bien, "NFL Is Going to Insulting Lengths."

7. Jacob Feldman, "Five Former Players Accused of Sexual Harassment in Lawsuit," *Sports Illustrated*, December 13, 2017, www.si.com/nfl/2017/12/13/nfl-network-sexual-harassment-marshall-faulk-themmqb-newsletter.

8. Kevin Draper, "NFL Network Executive Resigns after Reports of Sexually Explicit Tweets," *New York Times*, December 20, 2017, www.nytimes.com/2017/12/20/sports/football/david-eaton-nfl-network-resigns.html.

9. Associated Press, "Saints Ex-Cheerleader Says NFL Team's Policies Discriminate," March 26, 2018, www.apnews.com/152ddd9294044a2d9f5885774371cae0.

10. Matthew J. Culligan and Dolph Greene, *Getting Back to the Basics of Public Relations and Publicity* (New York: Crown, 1982), 100.
11. Marvin N. Olasky, "The Development of Corporate Public Relations, 1850–1930," *Journalism Monographs* 102 (April 1987): 15.
12. Michael Schudson, *Discovering the News: A Social History of American Newspapers* (New York: Basic Books, 1978), 136.
13. "Lobbying: Overview," OpenSecrets.org, accessed March 4, 2019, www.opensecrets.org/lobby.
14. Philip Shenon, "3 Partners Quit Firm Handling Saudis' P.R.," *New York Times*, December 6, 2002, www.nytimes.com/2002/12/06/world/threats-and-responses-publicists-3-partners-quit-firm-handling-saudis-pr.html?mtrref=www.google.com&gwh=30F94D721B9BCA74A8B8049DBE5EB732&gwt=pay.
15. PRSA, "PRSA Statement on 'Alternative Facts,'" January 24, 2017, http://media.prsa.org/news-releases/prsa-opinions-and-commentary/prsa-makes-statement-on-alternative-facts.htm.
16. Jane Dvorak, Twitter.com, March 22, 2017, https://twitter.com/jkdjane?lang=en.
17. Video of "Eisenhower Answers America" commercials available online at www.c-span.org/video/?188176-1/eisenhower-answers-america.

MEDIA LITERACY CASE STUDY: The Invisible Hand of PR, p. 354 [pp. 354–355]

1. Jennifer Lee, "Big Tobacco's Spin on Women's Liberation," *New York Times*, October 10, 2008, https://cityroom.blogs.nytimes.com/2008/10/10/big-tobaccos-spin-on-womens-liberation.
2. John Stauber, "Corporate PR: A Threat to Journalism?" *Background Briefing: Radio National*, March 30, 1997, www.abc.net.au/radionational/programs/backgroundbriefing/corporate-pr-a-threat-to-journalism/3563876.

THE DIGITAL TURN CASE STUDY: Military PR in the Digital Age, p. 358

1. Marc Chacksfield, "U.S. Army Spends $32.8 Million on Propaganda Video Game," TechRadar, December 10, 2009, www.techradar.com/news/gaming/us-army-spends-32-8-million-on-propaganda-videogame-657121; Cecilia D'Anastasio, "The U.S. Army Has a New Plan to Recruit Gamers," Kotaku, December 4, 2018, https://kotaku.com/the-u-s-army-has-a-new-plan-to-recruit-gamers-1830850297.
2. Erik Ortiz, "String of Social Media Scandals Plagues Military," NBC News, February 17, 2014, www.nbcnews.com/news/military/string-social-media-scandals-plagues-military-n40501.
3. Cori E. Dauber, *YouTube War: Fighting in a World of Cameras in Every Cell Phone and Photoshop on Every Computer*, Strategic Studies Institute, U.S. Army War College, November 2009, https://ssi.armywarcollege.edu/pubs/download.cfm?q=951.

13 Legal Controls and Freedom of Expression

1. Allan J. Lichtman, "Who Rules America?" *Hill*, August 12, 2014, http://thehill.com/blogs/pundits-blog/civil-rights/214857-who-rules-america.
2. Bradley Jones, "Most Americans Want to Limit Campaign Spending, Say Big Donors Have Greater Political Influence," Pew Research Center, May 8, 2018, www.pewresearch.org/fact-tank/2018/05/08/most-americans-want-to-limit-campaign-spending-say-big-donors-have-greater-political-influence.
3. Center for Responsive Politics, "Cost of Election," OpenSecrets.org, 2018, www.opensecrets.org/overview/cost.php.
4. Gene Policinski, "Amendment to Undo Citizens United Won't Do," First Amendment Center, September 21, 2011.
5. Lawrence Lessig, "An Open Letter to the Citizens against *Citizens United*," *Atlantic*, March 23, 2012, www.theatlantic.com/politics/archive/2013/03/an-open-letter-to-the-citizens-against-citizens-united/254902.
6. See Douglas M. Fraleigh and Joseph S. Tuman, *Freedom of Speech in the Marketplace of Ideas* (New York: St. Martin's Press, 1998), 77.
7. Fred Siebert, Theodore Peterson, and Wilbur Schramm, *Four Theories of the Press* (Urbana: University of Illinois Press, 1956).
8. Hugo Black, quoted in *New York Times Co. v. United States*, 403 U.S. 713 (1971), www.law.cornell.edu/supct/html/historics/USSC_CR_0403_0713_ZC.html.
9. Sameepa Shetty, "Julian Assange and Daniel Ellsberg Mount Snowden Defense," *Fortune*, June 20, 2013, http://fortune.com/2013/06/20/julian-assange-and-daniel-ellsberg-mount-snowden-defense.
10. Robert Warren, quoted in *United States v. Progressive, Inc.*, 467 F. Supp. 990 (W.D. Wis. 1979), https://law.justia.com/cases/federal/district-courts/FSupp/467/990/1376343.
11. See Edward W. Knappman, ed., *Great American Trials: From Salem Witchcraft to Rodney King* (Detroit, Mich.: Visible Ink Press, 1994), 517–519.
12. "Live-Blogging and Tweeting from Court," Digital Media Law Project, March 31, 2019, www.dmlp.org/legal-guide/live-blogging-and-tweeting-from-court.
13. L. David Russell, Christopher C. Chiou, and Sean D. Nelson, "Litigation in Twitter Nation: When You Can and Can't Tweet in #Court," Law.com, February 6, 2017, www.law.com/legaltechnews/almID/1202778824883/Litigation-in-Twitter-Nation-When-You-Can-and-Cant-Tweet-in-Court/?mcode=1202617687205&curindex=21.
14. *Mutual Film Corp. v. Industrial Communication of Ohio*, 236 U.S. 230 (1915).
15. Brooks Boliek, "Sorry, Ms. Jackson: FCC Hits New Record," *Politico*, September 10, 2014, http://www.politico.com/story/2014/09/fcc-net-neutrality-record-110818.html.

THE DIGITAL TURN CASE STUDY: Is "Sexting" Pornography?, p. 385

1. Richard Wortley and Stephen Smallbone, "Child Pornography on the Internet," U.S. Department of Justice, May 2006, https://ccoso.org/sites/default/files/import/child-porn-on-the-internet..pdf.
2. Sheri Madigan et al., "Prevalence of Multiple Forms of Sexting Behavior among Youth: A Systematic Review and Meta-analysis," *JAMA Pediatrics* 172, no. 4 (2018): 327–335, doi:10.1001/jamapediatrics.2017.5314.
3. Pavielle Bookman and Alesha D. Williams, "A Closer Look at Teen Sexting in a Digital Age," American Bar Association, March 19, 2018, www.americanbar.org/groups/young_lawyers/publications/tyl/topics/criminal-law/a-closer-look-teen-sexting-the-digital-age.
4. Sameer Hinduja and Justin W. Patchin, "State Sexting Laws," Cyberbullying Research Center, November 26, 2018, https://cyberbullying.org/state-sexting-laws.

MEDIA LITERACY CASE STUDY: Fake News, the First Amendment, and Fighting Propaganda, p. 398 [pp. 398–399]

1. Craig Silverman, "This Analysis Shows How Viral Fake Election News Stories Outperformed Real News on Facebook," BuzzFeed, November 16, 2016, www.buzzfeednews.com/article/craigsilverman/viral-fake-election-news-outperformed-real-news-on-facebook.
2. Louis W. Tompros et al., "The Constitutionality of Criminalizing False Speech Made on Social Networking Sites in a Post-*Alvarez*, Social Media–Obsessed World," *Harvard Journal of Law and Technology* 31 no. 1 (Fall 2017): 108–109, https://jolt.law.harvard.edu/assets/articlePDFs/v31/31HarvJLTech65.pdf.
3. See "Fake News: Home," Indiana University East Library Guide, accessed March 11, 2017, http://iue.libguides.com/fakenews/index; Joyce Valenza, "Truth, Truthiness, Triangulation: A News Literacy Toolkit for a 'Post-Truth' World," *Neverending Search*, *School Library Journal*, November 26, 2016, http://blogs.slj.com/neverendingsearch/2016/11/26/truth-truthiness-triangulation-and-the-librarian-way-a-news-literacy-toolkit-for-a-post-truth-world.
4. Melissa Zimdars, "False, Misleading, Clickbait-y, and/or Satirical 'News' Sources," 2016, https://docs.google.com/document/d/10eA5-mCZLSS4MQY5QGb5ewC3VAL6pLkT53V_81ZyitM/preview.

14 Media Economics and the Global Marketplace

1. Larry Page, "Google's Larry Page Explains the New Alphabet," CNET, August 10, 2015, www.cnet.com/news/googles-larry-page-explains-the-new-alphabet.
2. Conor Dougherty, "Google to Reorganize as Alphabet to Keep Its Lead as an Innovator," *New York Times*, August 10, 2015, www.nytimes.com/2015/08/11/technology/google-alphabet-restructuring.html?smid=pl-share&_r=0.
3. Dyllan Furness, "Google's Balloon Internet Is Coming to Kenya in 2019," Digital Trends, November 15, 2018, www.digitaltrends.com/cool-tech/loon-balloon-internet; Google, "Project Loon," accessed February 18, 2019, https://loon.com.
4. Dougherty, "Google to Reorganize as Alphabet."
5. Douglas Gomery, "The Centrality of Media Economics," in Mark R. Levy and Michael Gurevitch, eds., *Defining Media Studies* (New York: Oxford University Press, 1994), 202.
6. David Harvey, *The Condition of Postmodernity: An Enquiry into the Origins of Cultural Change* (Oxford: Basil Blackwell, 1989), 171.
7. Katerina Eva Matsa, "The Acquisition Binge in Local TV," Pew Research Center, May 12, 2014, www.pewresearch.org/fact-tank/2014/05/12/the-acquisition-binge-in-local-tv; "TV Stations," Sinclair Broadcast Group, accessed February 16, 2019, http://sbgi.net/tv-stations.
8. Kristal Brent Zook, "Blacks Own Just Ten U.S. Television Stations. Here's Why," *Washington Post*, August 17, 2015, www.washingtonpost.com/posteverything/wp/2015/08/17/blacks-own-just-10-u-s-television-stations-heres-why.
9. Nathan Reiff, "AT&T and Time Warner Merger Case: What You Need to Know," Investopedia, December 7, 2018, www.investopedia.com/investing/att-and-time-warner-merger-case-what-you-need-know; Diane Bartz and Dave Shepardson, "U.S. Justice Department Will Not Appeal AT&T, Time Warner Merger after Court Loss," Reuters, February 26, 2019, www.reuters.com/article/us-timewarner-m-a-at-t/us-justice-department-will-not-appeal-att-time-warner-merger-after-court-loss-idUSKCN1QF1XB.
10. Wesley Morris and James Poniewozik, Why 'Diverse TV' Matters: It's Better TV. Discuss," *New York Times*, February 10, 2016, www.nytimes.com/2016/02/14/arts/television/smaller-screens-truer-colors.html.
11. Shira Ovide, "Amazon Is Defined by Billions, but Its Workers' Median Pay Is $28,446," *Los Angeles Times*, April 19, 2018, www.latimes.com/business/la-fi-amazon-median-pay-20180419-story.html; Daniel Wagner and Mike Baker, "Warren Buffett's Mobile Home Empire Preys on the Poor," *Center for Public Integrity*, April 6, 2015, https://publicintegrity.org/business/warren-buffetts-mobile-home-empire-preys-on-the-poor.
12. Lawrence Mishel and Jessica Schieder, "CEO Compensation Surged in 2017," Economic Policy Institute, August 16, 2018, www.epi.org/publication/ceo-compensation-surged-in-2017.
13. Thomas Geoghegan, "How Pink Slips Hurt More Than Workers," *New York Times*, March 29, 2006, p. B8.
14. Edward Herman, "Democratic Media," *Z*, January–March 1992, 23.

THE DIGITAL TURN CASE STUDY: Are the Big Digital Companies Too Big?, p. 411

1. Dylan Byers, "Artificial Future: The Forever Companies," *Pacific*, May 24, 2018, https://mailchi.mp/cnn/pacific-may-24-2018?e=e6767fbebc.
2. Amanda Lotz, "'Big Tech' Isn't One Big Monopoly—It's 5 Companies All in Different Businesses," *Conversation*, March 23, 2018, https://theconversation.com/big-tech-isnt-one-big-monopoly-its-5-companies-all-in-different-businesses-92791.
3. Christopher Mims, "Tech's Titans Tiptoe toward Monopoly: Amazon, Facebook and Google May Be Repeating the History of Steel, Utility, Rail and Telegraph Empires Past—While Apple Appears Vulnerable," *Wall Street Journal*, May 31, 2018, www.wsj.com/articles/techs-titans-tiptoe-toward-monopoly-1527783845.
4. Charles Duhigg, "The Case against Google," *New York Times Magazine*, February 20, 2018, www.nytimes.com/2018/02/20/magazine/the-case-against-google.html.

MEDIA LITERACY CASE STUDY: Netflix and Change: The Streaming Revolution and the Business of Content Creation, p. 422 [pp. 422–423]

1. "Netflix's View: Internet Entertainment Is Replacing Linear TV," updated January 22, 2018, https://ir.netflix.com/netflixs-view-internet-tv-replacing-linear-tv.
2. Netflix Form 10-K (2018 Annual Report), January 29, 2019, https://ir.netflix.com/node/29631/html; Netflix, "Overview," https://ir.netflix.com.
3. John Koblin, "Netflix Studied Your Binge-Watching Habit. That Didn't Take Long," *New York Times*, June 8, 2016, www.nytimes.com/2016/06/09/business/media/netflix-studied-your-binge-watching-habit-it-didnt-take-long.html.
4. "Apple's Revenue Worldwide from 2004 to 2018 (in Billion U.S. Dollars)," Statista, accessed March 2, 2019, www.statista.com/statistics/265125/total-net-sales-of-apple-since-2004.

15 Social Scientific and Cultural Approaches to Media Research

1. Campbell Robertson, Christopher Mele, and Sabrina Tavernise, "11 Killed in Synagogue Massacre; Suspect Charged with 29 Counts," *New York Times*, October 27, 2018, www.nytimes.com/2018/10/27/us/active-shooter-pittsburgh-synagogue-shooting.html.
2. "Alek Minassian Toronto Van Attack Suspect Praised 'Incel' Killer," BBC News, April 25, 2018, www.bbc.com/news/world-us-canada-43883052.
3. Elizabeth Chuck, Alex Johnson, Corky Siemaszko, "17 Killed in Mass Shooting at High School in Parkland, Florida," NBC News, February 14, 2018, www.nbcnews.com/news/us-news/police-respond-shooting-parkland-florida-high-school-n848101.
4. Julie Turkewitz and Kevin Roose, "Who Is Robert Bowers, the Suspect in the Pittsburgh Synagogue Shooting?" *New York Times*, October 27, 2018, www.nytimes.com/2018/10/27/us/robert-bowers-pittsburgh-synagogue-shooter.html.
5. Bill Morlin, "The Alt-Right Is Still Killing People," *Intelligence Report: Rage against Change*, Spring 2019, www.splcenter.org/fighting-hate/intelligence-report/issues/rage-against-change.
6. Steve Fore, "Lost in Translation: The Social Uses of Mass Communications Research," *Afterimage* 20 (April 1993): 10.
7. James Carey, *Communication as Culture: Essays on Media and Society* (Boston: Unwin Hyman, 1989), 75.
8. Daniel Czitrom, *Media and the American Mind: From Morse to McLuhan* (Chapel Hill: University of North Carolina Press, 1982), 122–125.
9. Ibid., 123.
10. Harold Lasswell, *Propaganda Technique in the World War* (New York: Alfred A. Knopf, 1927), 9.
11. W. W. Charters, *Motion Pictures and Youth: A Summary* (New York: Macmillan, 1934); Garth Jowett, *Film: The Democratic Art* (Boston: Little, Brown, 1976), 220–229.
12. Czitrom, *Media and the American Mind*, 132; see also Harold Lasswell, "The Structure and Function of Communication in Society," in Lyman Bryson, ed., *The Communication of Ideas* (New York: Harper and Brothers, 1948), 37–51.
13. Joseph Klapper, *The Effects of Mass Communication* (New York: Free Press, 1960).
14. *Where We Are on TV, 2018–2019* (New York: GLAAD Media Institute, 2018), www.glaad.org/whereweareontv18.
15. See Nancy Signorielli and Michael Morgan, *Cultivation Analysis: New Directions in Media Effects Research* (Newbury Park, Calif.: Sage, 1990).
16. See Stuart Hall et al., *Policing the Crisis: Mugging, the State, and Law and Order* (London: Macmillan, 1978).
17. See Jack G. Shaheen, *Reel Bad Arabs: How Hollywood Vilifies a People* (Northampton, Mass.: Interlink Publishing Group, 2001).
18. See Janice Radway, *Reading the Romance: Women, Patriarchy, and Popular Literature* (Chapel Hill: University of North Carolina Press, 1984).

THE DIGITAL TURN CASE STUDY: Artificial Intelligence Gets Personal, p. 437

1. Gus Lubin, "How Netflix Will Someday Know Exactly What You Want to Watch as Soon as You Turn Your TV On," *Business Insider*, September 21, 2016, www.businessinsider.com/how-netflix-recommendations-work-2016-9.

2. Jon Markman, "Amazon Using AI, Big Data to Accelerate Profits," *Forbes*, June 5, 2017, www.forbes.com/sites/jonmarkman/2017/06/05/amazon-using-ai-big-data-to-accelerate-profits/#361f90fe6d55.

MEDIA LITERACY CASE STUDY: Does Art Imitate Life or Life Imitate Art?: TV Depictions of Suicide and Copycat Fears, p. 450 [pp. 450–451]

1. Rebecca Nicholson, "*13 Reasons Why* Review—Sex, Drugs and Mixtapes in Netflix's High-School Horror Show," *Guardian*, March 31, 2017, www.theguardian.com/tv-and-radio/2017/mar/31/13-reasons-why-review-sex-drugs-and-mixtapes-in-netflix-high-school-horror-show.

2. Mark Henick, "Why *13 Reasons Why* Is Dangerous," CNN, May 4, 2017, https://edition.cnn.com/2017/05/03/opinions/13-reasons-why-gets-it-wrong-henick-opinion/index.html.

3. Sophie Gilbert, "Did *13 Reasons Why* Spark a Suicide Contagion Effect?" *Atlantic*, August 1, 2017, www.theatlantic.com/entertainment/archive/2017/08/13-reasons-why-demonstrates-cultures-power/535518.

4. Joyce Chen, "Selena Gomez Defends *13 Reasons Why* as Honest Depiction of Teen Suicide," *Rolling Stone*, June 7, 2017, www.rollingstone.com/culture/news/selena-gomez-defends-13-reasons-why-as-honest-w486466.

5. Jon Blistein, "Netflix Adds More Advisory Warnings to *13 Reasons Why*," *Rolling Stone*, May 2, 2017, www.rollingstone.com/tv/news/netflix-adds-more-advisory-warnings-to-13-reasons-why-w480108.

6. Netflix, *13 Reasons Why*, 2018, www.netflix.com/title/80117470.

7. "*Thirteen Reasons Why* Talking Points," Suicide Awareness Voices of Education, 2017, https://save.org/13-reasons-why.

Glossary

A&R (artist & repertoire) agents talent scouts of the music business who discover, develop, and sometimes manage performers.

access channels in cable television, a tier of nonbroadcast channels dedicated to local education, government, and the public.

account executives in advertising, client liaisons responsible for bringing in new business and managing the accounts of established clients.

account reviews in advertising, the process of evaluating or reinvigorating an ad campaign, which results in either renewing the contract with the original ad agency or hiring a new agency.

acquisitions editors in the book industry, editors who seek out and sign authors to contracts.

actual malice in libel law, a reckless disregard for the truth, such as when a reporter or an editor knows that a statement is false and prints or airs it anyway.

ad impressions in advertising, how often ads are seen.

adult contemporary (AC) one of the oldest and most popular radio music formats, typically featuring a mix of news, talk, oldies, and soft rock.

affiliate stations radio or TV stations that, though independently owned, sign a contract to be part of a network and receive money to carry the network's programs; in exchange, the network reserves time slots, which it sells to national advertisers.

agenda-setting a media-research argument that says that when the mass media pay attention to particular events or issues, they determine—that is, set the agenda for—the major topics of discussion for individuals and society.

album-oriented rock (AOR) the radio music format that features album cuts from mainstream rock bands.

AM (amplitude modulation) a type of radio and sound transmission that stresses the volume or height of radio waves; this type of modulation was sufficient for radio content such as talk, but not ideal for music.

analog in television, standard broadcast signals made of radio waves (replaced by digital standards in 2009).

analog recording a recording that is made by capturing the fluctuations of the original sound waves and storing those signals on record grooves or magnetic tape—analogous to the actual sound.

analysis the second step in the critical process, it involves discovering significant patterns that emerge from the description stage.

anthology drama a popular form of early TV programming that brought live dramatic theater to television; influenced by stage plays, anthologies offered new teleplays, casts, directors, writers, and sets from week to week.

arcade an establishment gathering multiple coin-operated games together in a single location.

ARPAnet the original Internet, designed by the U.S. Defense Department's Advanced Research Projects Agency (ARPA).

association principle in advertising, a persuasive technique that associates a product with some cultural value or image that has a positive connotation but may have little connection to the actual product.

astroturf lobbying phony grassroots public affairs campaigns engineered by public relations firms; coined by U.S. Senator Lloyd Bentsen of Texas (named after AstroTurf, the artificial grass athletic field surface).

Atari a video game development company that released Pong, the first big-hit arcade game, and established the home video game market through a deal with Sears.

audience studies cultural studies research that focuses on how people use and interpret cultural content. Also known as *reader-response research*.

audiotape lightweight magnetized strands of ribbon that make possible sound editing and multiple-track mixing; instrumentals or vocals can be recorded at one studio and later mixed onto a master recording in another studio.

authoritarian model a model for journalism and speech that tolerates little criticism of government or public dissent; it holds that the general public needs guidance from an elite and educated ruling class.

avatar an identity created by an Internet user in order to participate in a form of online entertainment, such as *World of Warcraft* or *Second Life*.

bandwagon effect an advertising strategy that incorporates exaggerated claims that everyone is using a particular product, so you should, too.

barter in TV, giving a program to a local station in exchange for a split in the advertising revenue.

basic cable in cable programming, a tier of channels composed of local broadcast signals, nonbroadcast access channels (for local government, education, and general public use), a few regional PBS stations, and a variety of popular channels downlinked from communication satellites.

Big Five the five major Hollywood studios that currently rule the commercial film business: Warner Brothers, Paramount, Universal, Columbia Pictures, and Disney.

blacklisted when the film industry began to self-regulate in the 1920s, and actors and movie extras with minor police records or involvement in scandals were put on a list of people who would subsequently not be hired by any movie studio.

block booking an early tactic of movie studios to control exhibition involving pressuring theater operators to accept marginal films with no stars in order to get access to films with the most popular stars.

blocking broadband providers prohibiting access to legal content and services.

block printing a printing technique developed by early Chinese printers, who hand-carved characters and illustrations into a block of wood, applied ink to the block, and then printed copies on multiple sheets of paper.

blues originally a kind of black folk music, this music emerged as a distinct category in the early 1900s; it was influenced by African American spirituals, ballads, and work songs in the rural South, and by urban guitar and vocal solos from the 1930s and 1940s.

book challenge a formal complaint to have a book removed from a public or school library's collection.

boutique agencies in advertising, small regional ad agencies that offer personalized services.

branded content specialized print, online, or video content produced and funded by individual advertisers.

broadband data transmission over a fiber-optic cable—a signaling method that handles a wide range of frequencies.

broadcasting the transmission of radio waves or TV signals to a broad public audience.

catfishing the practice of pretending to be another person, even a person of a different gender, to trick someone into having an online relationship.

cathode ray tube (CRT) a key component of early television and computer screens that allowed the display of images.

CATV (community antenna television) early cable systems that originated where mountains or tall buildings blocked TV signals; because of early technical and regulatory limits, CATV contained only twelve channels.

celluloid a transparent and pliable film that can hold a coating of chemicals sensitive to light.

chapter shows in television production, situation comedies or dramatic programs whose narrative structure includes self-contained stories that feature a problem, a series of conflicts, and a resolution from week to week (for contrast, see **serial programs**).

cinema verité French term for *truth film*, a documentary style that records fragments of everyday life unobtrusively; it often features a rough, grainy look and shaky, handheld camera work.

citizen journalism a grassroots movement wherein activist amateurs and concerned citizens, not professional journalists, use Internet tools like blogs to disseminate news and information.

click-throughs in online advertising, how often users land briefly on a site before clicking through to the next site.

codex an early type of book in which paperlike sheets were cut and sewed together along the edge, then bound with thin pieces of wood and covered with leather.

collective intelligence video game tips and cheats shared by players of the games, usually online.

commercial speech any print or broadcast expression for which a fee is charged to the organization or individual buying time or space in the mass media.

common carrier a communication or transportation business, such as a phone company or a taxi service, that is required by law to offer service on a first-come, first-served basis to whoever can pay the rate; such companies do not get involved in content.

compact discs (CDs) playback-only storage discs for music that incorporate pure and very precise digital techniques, thus eliminating noise during recording and playback.

conflict of interest considered unethical, a compromising situation in which a journalist stands to benefit personally from the news report he or she produces.

consensus narrative cultural products that become popular and command wide attention, providing shared cultural experiences.

console a device used specifically to play video games.

contemporary hit radio (CHR) originally called Top 40 radio, this radio format encompasses everything from hip-hop to children's songs; it appeals to many teens and young adults.

content analysis in social science research, a method for systematically studying and coding media texts and programs.

cookies information profiles about a user that are usually automatically accepted by the web browser and stored on the user's own computer hard drive.

copy editor the person in magazine, newspaper, and book publishing who attends to specific problems in writing, such as style, content, and length.

copyright the legal right of authors and producers to own and control the use of their published or unpublished writing, music, and lyrics; TV programs and movies; or graphic art designs.

Corporation for Public Broadcasting (CPB) a private, nonprofit corporation created by Congress in 1967 to funnel federal funds to nonprofit radio and public television.

correlation an observed association between two variables.

country claiming the largest number of radio stations in the United States, this radio format includes such subdivisions as old-time, progressive, country-rock, western swing, and country-gospel; also a musical form in which all styles share one element: the country voice, inflected by a twang or drawl.

cover music songs recorded or performed by musicians who did not originally write or perform the music; in the 1950s, cover music was an attempt by white producers and artists to capitalize on popular songs by blacks.

critical process the process whereby a media-literate person or student studying mass communication employs the techniques of description, analysis, interpretation, evaluation, and engagement.

cultivation effect in media research, the idea that heavy television viewing leads individuals to perceive reality in ways that are consistent with the portrayals they see on television.

cultural imperialism the phenomenon of American culture (e.g., media, fashion, and food) dominating the global market and shaping the cultures and identities of other nations.

cultural studies in media research, the approaches that try to understand how the media and culture are tied to the actual patterns of communication used in daily life; these studies focus on how people make meaning, understand reality, articulate values, and interpret their experiences through the use of stories and symbols.

culture the symbols of expression that individuals, groups, and societies use to make sense of daily life and to articulate their values.

data mining the unethical gathering of data by online purveyors of content and merchandise.

deadheading the practice in the early twentieth century of giving reporters free rail passes as bribes for favorable stories.

deficit financing in television, the process whereby a TV production company leases its programs to a network for a license fee that is actually less than the cost of production; the company hopes to recoup this loss later in rerun syndication.

demographic editions national magazines whose advertising is tailored to subscribers and readers according to occupation, class, and zip-code address.

demographics in market research, the gathering and analysis of audience members' age, gender, income, ethnicity, and education in order to better target messages to particular audiences.

description the first step in the critical process, it involves paying close attention, taking notes, and researching the cultural product to be studied.

design manager publishing industry employee who works on the look of a book, making decisions about type style, paper, cover design, and layout.

developmental editor in book publishing, the editor who provides authors with feedback, makes suggestions for improvements, and obtains advice from knowledgeable members of the academic community.

development budget the money spent designing, coding, scoring, and testing a video game.

digital communication images, texts, and sounds that use pulses of electric current or flashes of laser lights and are converted (or encoded) into electronic signals represented as varied combinations of binary numbers, usually ones and zeros; these signals are then reassembled (decoded) as a precise reproduction of a TV picture, a magazine article, or a telephone voice.

digital divide the socioeconomic disparity between those who do and those who do not have access to digital technology and media, such as the Internet.

digital recording music recorded and played back by laser beam rather than by needle or magnetic tape.

digital turn the shift in media use and consumption resulting from the emergence of the Internet as a mass medium, which enables an array of media to converge and be easily shared.

digital video the production format that is replacing celluloid film and revolutionizing filmmaking because the cameras are more portable and production costs are greatly reduced.

digital video recorder (DVR) a device that enables users to find and record specific television shows (and movies) and store them in computer memory to be played back at a later time or recorded onto a DVD.

digitization a process through which information in analog form (such as text or pictures) is translated into binary code—a series of ones and zeros that can be encoded in software and transmitted between computers.

dime novels sometimes identified as pulp fiction, these cheaply produced and low-priced novels were popular in the United States beginning in the 1860s.

direct broadcast satellites (DBS) satellite-based services that for a monthly fee downlink hundreds of satellite channels and services; they began distributing video programming directly to households in 1994.

documentary movie or TV news genre that documents reality by recording actual characters and settings.

e-book a digital book read on a computer or on an electronic reading device.

e-commerce electronic commerce, or commercial activity, on the web.

electromagnetic waves invisible electronic impulses similar to visible light; electricity, magnetism, light, broadcast signals, and heat are part of such waves, which radiate in space at the speed of light, about 186,000 miles per second.

electronic publisher a communication business, such as a broadcaster or a cable TV company, that is entitled to choose what channels or content to carry.

e-mail electronic mail messages sent by the Internet; developed by computer engineer Ray Tomlinson in 1971.

engagement the fifth step in the critical process, it involves actively working to create a media world that best serves democracy.

Entertainment Software Rating Board (ESRB) the video game industry's self-regulating system, designed to inform parents of sexual and violent content that might not be suitable for younger players.

episodic series a narrative form well suited to television because main characters appear every week, sets and locales remain the same, and technical crews stay with the program; episodic series feature new adventures each week but establish a handful of ongoing characters with whom viewers can regularly identify (see also **chapter shows** and **serial programs**).

ethnocentrism an underlying value held by many U.S. journalists and citizens, it involves judging other countries and cultures according to how they live up to or imitate American practices and ideals.

evaluation the fourth step in the critical process, it involves arriving at a judgment about whether a cultural product is good, bad, or mediocre; this requires subordinating one's personal taste to the critical assessment resulting from the first three stages (description, analysis, and interpretation).

evergreens in TV syndication, popular, lucrative, and enduring network reruns, such as *The Andy Griffith Show* or *I Love Lucy*.

evergreen subscriptions magazine subscriptions that automatically renew on subscribers' credit cards.

experiments in regard to the mass media, research that isolates some aspect of content, suggests a hypothesis, and manipulates variables to discover a particular text's or medium's impact on attitudes, emotions, or behavior.

Fairness Doctrine repealed in 1987, this FCC rule required broadcast stations to both air and engage in controversial-issue programs that affected their communities and, when offering such programming, to provide competing points of view.

famous-person testimonial an advertising strategy that associates a product with the endorsement of a well-known person.

feature syndicates commercial outlets or brokers, such as Andrews McMeel Syndication and Tribune Content Agency, that contract with newspapers to provide work from well-known political writers, editorial cartoonists, comic-strip artists, and self-help columnists.

Federal Communications Act of 1934 the far-reaching act that established the FCC and the federal regulatory structure for U.S. broadcasting.

Federal Communications Commission (FCC) an independent U.S. government agency charged with regulating interstate and international communications by radio, television, wire, satellite, and cable.

Federal Radio Commission (FRC) an organization established in 1927 to oversee radio licenses and negotiate channel problems.

fiber-optic cable thin glass bundles capable of transmitting thousands of messages converted to shooting pulses of light along cable wires; these bundles can carry broadcast channels, telephone signals, and all sorts of digital codes.

fin-syn (Financial Interest and Syndication Rules) FCC rules that prohibited the major networks from running their own syndication companies or from charging production companies additional fees after shows had completed their prime-time runs; most fin-syn rules were rescinded in the mid-1990s.

flipper bumper an addition to the pinball machine that transformed the game from one of chance into a challenging game of skill, touch, and timing.

FM (frequency modulation) a type of radio and sound transmission that offers static-free reception and greater fidelity and clarity than AM radio by accentuating the pitch or distance between radio waves.

focus group a common research method in psychographic analysis in which a moderator leads a small-group discussion about a product or an issue, usually with six to twelve people.

folk music music performed by untrained musicians and passed down through oral traditions; it encompasses a wide range of music, from Appalachian fiddle tunes to the accordion-led zydeco of Louisiana.

format radio the concept of radio stations developing and playing specific styles (or formats) geared to listeners' age, race, or gender; in format radio, management, rather than deejays, controls programming choices.

Fourth Estate the notion that the press operates as an unofficial branch of government, monitoring the legislative, judicial, and executive branches for abuses of power.

fringe time in broadcast television, the time slot either immediately before the evening's prime-time schedule (called *early fringe*) or immediately following the local evening news or the network's late-night talk shows (called *late fringe*).

gag orders legal restrictions prohibiting the press from releasing preliminary information that might prejudice jury selection.

gangster rap a style of rap music that depicts the hardships of urban life and sometimes glorifies the violent style of street gangs.

general-interest magazine a type of magazine that addresses a wide variety of topics and is aimed at a broad national audience.

genres narrative categories in which conventions regarding similar characters, scenes, structures, and themes recur in combination.

grunge rock music that takes the spirit of punk and infuses it with more attention to melody.

HD radio a digital technology that enables AM and FM radio broadcasters to multicast two to three additional compressed digital signals within their traditional analog frequency.

hegemony the acceptance of the dominant values in a culture by those who are subordinate to those who hold economic and political power.

hidden-fear appeal an advertising strategy that plays on a sense of insecurity, trying to persuade consumers that only a specific product can offer relief.

high culture a symbolic expression that has come to mean "good taste"; often supported by wealthy patrons and corporate donors, it is associated with fine art (such as ballet, the symphony, painting, and classical literature), which is available primarily in theaters or museums.

hip-hop music that combines spoken street dialect with cuts (or samples) from older records and bears the influences of social politics, male boasting, and comic lyrics carried forward from blues, R&B, soul, and rock and roll.

Hollywood Ten the nine screenwriters and one film director subpoenaed by the House Un-American Activities Committee (HUAC) and sent to prison in the late 1940s for refusing to discuss their memberships or to identify communist sympathizers.

HTML (HyperText Markup Language) the written code that creates web pages and links; a language all computers can read.

human-interest stories news accounts that focus on the trials and tribulations of the human condition, often featuring ordinary individuals facing extraordinary challenges.

hypodermic-needle model an early model in mass communication research that attempted to explain media effects by arguing that the media shoot their powerful effects directly into unsuspecting or weak audiences; sometimes called the *magic bullet theory*.

hypotheses in social science research, tentative general statements that predict a relationship between a dependent variable and an independent variable.

illuminated manuscripts books from the Middle Ages that featured decorative, colorful designs and illustrations on each page.

indecency the government may punish broadcasters for indecency or profanity after the fact; over the years, a handful of radio stations have had their licenses suspended or denied due to indecent programming.

indie rock independent-minded rock music, usually distributed by smaller labels.

indies independent music and film production houses that work outside industry oligopolies; they often produce less mainstream music and film.

individualism an underlying value held by most U.S. journalists and citizens, it favors individual rights and responsibilities over group needs or institutional mandates.

infotainment a type of television program that packages human-interest and celebrity stories in the style of TV news.

intellectual properties the material in video games—stories, characters, personalities, music, and so on—that requires licensing agreements.

Internet radio online radio stations that either "stream" simulcast versions of on-air radio broadcasts over the web or are created exclusively for the Internet.

Internet service provider (ISP) a company that provides Internet access to homes and businesses for a fee.

interpretation the third step in the critical process, it asks and answers the "What does that mean?" and "So what?" questions about one's findings.

interpretive journalism a type of journalism that involves analyzing and explaining key issues or events and placing them in a broader historical or social context.

inverted pyramid a style of journalism in which news reports begin with the most dramatic or newsworthy information—answering *who*, *what*, *where*, and *when* (and less frequently *why* or *how*) questions at the top of the story—and then tail off with less significant details.

irritation advertising an advertising strategy that tries to create product-name recognition by being annoying or obnoxious.

jazz an improvisational and mostly instrumental musical form that absorbs and integrates a diverse body of musical styles, including African rhythms, blues, big band, and gospel.

kinescope before the days of videotape, a 1950s technique for preserving television broadcasts by using a film camera to record a live TV show off a studio monitor.

kinetograph an early movie camera developed by Thomas Edison's assistant in the 1890s.

kinetoscope an early film projection system that served as a kind of peep show in which viewers looked through a hole and saw images moving on a tiny plate.

libel in media law, the defamation of character in written or broadcast expression.

libertarian model a model for journalism and speech that encourages vigorous government criticism and supports the highest degree of freedom for individual speech and news operations.

limited competition in media economics, a market with many producers and sellers but only a few differentiable products within a particular category; sometimes called *monopolistic competition*.

linotype a technology introduced in the nineteenth century that enabled printers to set type mechanically using a typewriter-style keyboard.

lobbying in government public relations, the process of attempting to influence the voting of lawmakers to support a client's or an organization's best interests.

lobbyists professionals who seek to influence the voting of lawmakers to support a client's or an organization's best interests.

longitudinal studies a term used for research studies that are conducted over long periods of time, or the practice of comparing new studies with those conducted years earlier; these studies often rely on large government and academic survey databases.

low (popular) culture a symbolic expression allegedly aligned with the questionable tastes of the masses, who enjoy the commercial "junk" circulated by the mass media, such as soap operas, rock music, talk radio, comic books, and monster truck pulls.

low-power FM (LPFM) a class of noncommercial radio stations approved by the FCC in 2000 to give voice to local groups lacking access to the public airwaves; the 10-watt and 100-watt stations broadcast to a small, community-based area.

magalogs a combination of a glossy magazine and retail catalogue that is often used to market goods or services to customers or employees.

magazine a nondaily periodical that comprises a collection of articles, stories, and ads.

malware malicious software that hackers sneak onto computers, tablets, smartphones, and high-tech household appliances.

manuscript culture a period during the Middle Ages when priests and monks advanced the art of bookmaking.

market research in advertising and public relations agencies, the department that uses social science techniques to assess the behaviors and attitudes of consumers toward particular products before any ads are created.

mass communication the process of designing and delivering cultural messages and stories to diverse audiences through media channels as old as the book and as new as the Internet.

mass customization the process whereby product companies and content providers customize a web page, a print ad, or some other media form for an individual consumer.

massively multiplayer online role-playing game (MMORPG) an online fantasy game set in a virtual world in which users develop avatars of their own design and interact with other players.

mass market paperbacks low-priced paperback books sold mostly on racks in drugstores, supermarkets, and airports, as well as in bookstores.

mass media the cultural industries—the channels of communication—that produce songs, novels, news, movies, online services, and other cultural products and distribute them to a large number of people.

media buyers in advertising, the individuals who choose and purchase the types of media that are best suited to carry a client's ads and reach the targeted audience.

media convergence the first definition involves the technological merging of content across different media channels; the second definition describes a business model that consolidates various media holdings under one corporate umbrella.

media effects research a form of research that attempts to understand, explain, and predict the effects of mass media on individuals and society.

media literacy an understanding of the mass communication process through the development of critical-thinking tools—description, analysis, interpretation, evaluation, and engagement—that enable a person to become more engaged as a citizen and more discerning as a consumer of mass media products.

mega-agencies in advertising, large firms or holding companies that are formed by merging several individual agencies and that maintain worldwide regional offices; they provide both advertising and public relations services and operate in-house radio and TV production studios.

megaplex a movie theater facility with fourteen or more screens.

microprocessors miniature circuits that process and store electronic signals, integrating thousands of electronic components into thin strands of silicon along which binary codes travel.

minimal-effects model a mass communication research model based on tightly controlled experiments and survey findings; it argues that the mass media have limited effects on audiences, reinforcing existing behaviors and attitudes rather than changing them. Also called the *limited effects* model.

modding the most advanced form of collective intelligence in gaming, this term is slang for modifying game software or hardware.

modern era period from the Industrial Revolution to the twentieth century that was characterized by working efficiently, celebrating the individual, believing in a rational order, and rejecting tradition and embracing progress.

monopoly in media economics, an organizational structure that occurs when a single firm dominates production and distribution in a particular industry, either nationally or locally.

Morse code a system of sending electrical impulses from a transmitter through a cable to a reception point; it was developed in the 1840s by the American inventor Samuel Morse.

movie palaces ornate, lavish single-screen movie theaters that emerged in the 1910s in the United States.

MP3 short for MPEG-1 Layer 3, an advanced type of audio compression that reduces file size, enabling audio to be easily distributed over the Internet.

muckrakers reporters who used a style of early-twentieth-century investigative journalism that emphasized a willingness to crawl around in society's muck to uncover a story.

multichannel video programming distributors (MVPDs) a term the television industry used to use for its largest revenue generators, including cable companies and DBS providers.

multiple-system operators (MSOs) large corporations that own numerous cable television systems.

multiplex a contemporary type of movie theater that exhibits many movies at the same time on multiple screens.

must-carry rules rules established by the FCC requiring all cable operators to assign channels to and carry all local TV broadcasts on their systems, thereby ensuring that local network affiliates, independent stations (those not carrying network programs), and public television channels would benefit from cable's clearer reception.

narrative films movies that tell a story, with dramatic action and conflict emerging mainly from individual characters.

narrowcasting any specialized electronic programming or media channel aimed at niche viewer groups.

National Public Radio (NPR) noncommercial radio established in 1967 by the U.S. Congress to provide an alternative to commercial radio.

net neutrality the principle that every website and every user—whether a multinational corporation or you—has the right to the same Internet network speed and access.

network a broadcast process that links, through special phone lines or satellite transmissions, groups of radio or TV stations that share programming produced at a central location.

network era the period in television history, roughly from the mid-1950s to the late 1970s, that refers to the dominance of the Big Three networks—ABC, CBS, and NBC—over programming and prime-time viewing habits; the era began eroding with a decline in viewing and with the development of VCRs, cable, and new TV networks.

news the process of gathering information and making narrative reports—edited by individuals in a news organization—that create selected frames of reference and help the public make sense of prominent people, important events, and unusual happenings in everyday life.

news/talk the second most popular radio format in the nation, this format is dominated by news programs and talk shows.

newshole the space left over in a newspaper for news content after all the ads are placed.

newspaper chains large companies that own several papers throughout the country.

newsreels weekly ten-minute magazine-style compilations of filmed news events from around the world, organized in a sequence of short reports; prominent in movie theaters between the 1920s and the 1950s.

newsworthy the often-unstated criteria that journalists use to determine which events and issues should become news reports, including timeliness, proximity, conflict, prominence, human interest, consequence, usefulness, novelty, and deviance.

nickelodeon the first type of movie theater; these small, makeshift theaters were often converted cigar stores, pawnshops, or restaurants redecorated to mimic vaudeville theaters.

objective journalism a modern style of journalism that distinguishes factual reports from opinion columns; reporters strive to remain neutral toward the issue or event they cover, searching out competing points of view among the sources for a story.

obscenity expression that is not protected as speech if these three legal tests are met: (1) the average person, applying contemporary community standards, would find that the material as a whole appeals to prurient interest; (2) the material depicts or describes sexual conduct in a patently offensive way; (3) the material, as a whole, lacks serious literary, artistic, political, or scientific value.

offset lithography a technology that enabled books to be printed from photographic plates rather than from metal casts, reducing the cost of color and illustrations and eventually permitting computers to perform typesetting.

oligopoly in media economics, an organizational structure in which a few firms control most of an industry's production and distribution resources.

online fantasy sports games in which players assemble teams of real-life athletes and use actual sports results to determine scores.

online piracy the illegal uploading, downloading, or streaming of copyrighted material, such as music or movies.

open-source software noncommercial software shared freely and developed collectively on the Internet.

opinion and fair comment a defense against libel that states that libel applies only to intentional misstatements of factual information rather than expressions of opinion and therefore protects said opinion.

opt-in policies policies favored by consumer and privacy advocates that require websites to gain explicit permission from online consumers before they can collect users' personal data.

opt-out policies policies favored by data-mining corporations that allow websites to automatically collect personal data unless the consumer fills out a specific form to restrict the practice.

Pacifica Foundation a radio broadcasting foundation established in Berkeley, California, by journalist and World War II pacifist Lewis Hill; he established KPFA, the first nonprofit community radio station, in 1949.

paid prioritization the practice of favoring some Internet traffic over other lawful traffic in exchange for payment, thereby creating a "fast lane" for those who pay and a "slow lane" for all others.

paperback books books made with less expensive paper covers, introduced in the United States in the mid-1800s.

papyrus one of the first substances to hold written language and symbols; obtained from plant reeds found along the Nile River.

Paramount decision the 1948 Supreme Court decision that ended vertical integration in the film industry by forcing the studios to divest themselves of their theaters.

parchment treated animal skin that replaced papyrus as an early pre-paper substance on which to document written language.

partisan press an early dominant style of American journalism distinguished by opinion newspapers, which generally argued one political point of view or pushed the plan of the particular party that subsidized the paper.

pass-along readership the total number of people who come into contact with a single copy of a magazine.

payola the unethical (and often illegal) practice of record promoters paying deejays or radio programmers to favor particular songs over others.

pay-per-view (PPV) a cable-television service that allows customers to select a particular movie for a fee, or to pay $25 to $40 for a special one-time event.

paywall an arrangement restricting website access to paid subscribers.

penny arcade an early version of the modern video arcade, with multiple coin-operated mechanical games gathered together in a single location.

penny papers (also *penny press*) newspapers that, because of technological innovations in printing, were able to drop their price to one cent beginning in the 1830s, thereby making papers affordable to the working and emerging middle classes and enabling newspapers to become a genuine mass medium.

phishing an Internet scam that begins with phony e-mail messages that pretend to be from an official site and request that customers send their credit card numbers, passwords, and other personal information to update the account.

photojournalism the use of photos to document events and people's lives.

pinball machine a mechanical game in which players score points by manipulating the path of a metal ball on a play field in a glass-covered case, and an early ancestor of today's electronic games.

plain-folks pitch an advertising strategy that associates a product with simplicity and the common person.

podcasting the practice of making audio files available on the Internet so that listeners can download and listen to them on their electronic devices.

political advertising the use of ad techniques to promote a candidate's image and persuade the public to adopt a particular viewpoint.

political economy research an area of academic study that specifically examines interconnections among economic interests, political power, and how that power is used.

pop music popular music that appeals either to a wide cross section of the public or to sizable subdivisions within the larger public based on age, region, or ethnic background; the word *pop* has also been used as a label to distinguish popular music from classical music.

populism a political idea that attempts to appeal to ordinary people by setting up a conflict between "the people" and "the elite."

portable listening an effect of the digital turn that resulted in people listening to music using contemporary portable audio devices, such as iPods and smartphones.

postmodern period a contemporary historical era spanning the 1960s to the present; its social values include celebrating populism, questioning authority, and embracing technology.

premium channels in cable programming, a tier of channels that subscribers can order at an additional monthly fee over their basic cable service; these may include movie channels and interactive services.

press agents the earliest type of public relations practitioner, who sought to advance a client's image through media exposure.

press releases in public relations, announcements—written in the style of a news report—that give new information about an individual, a company, or an organization and simultaneously pitch a story idea to the news media.

prime time in television programming, the hours between 7 and 11 P.M. (or 7 and 10 P.M. in the Midwest), when networks have traditionally drawn their largest audiences and charged their highest advertising rates.

printing press a fifteenth-century invention whose movable metallic type technology spawned modern mass communication by creating the first method for mass production; it reduced the size and cost of books, made them the first mass medium affordable to less-affluent people, and provided the impetus for the Industrial Revolution, assembly-line production, modern capitalism, and the rise of consumer culture.

prior restraint the legal definition of censorship in the United States, which prohibits courts and governments from blocking any publication or speech before it actually occurs.

product placement the advertising practice of strategically placing products in movies, TV shows, comic books, and video games so that the products appear as part of a story's set environment.

professional books technical books that target various occupational groups and are not intended for the general consumer market.

Progressive Era the period of political and social reform lasting roughly from the 1890s to the 1920s that inspired many Americans—and mass media—to break with tradition and embrace change.

propaganda in advertising and public relations, a communication strategy that tries to manipulate public opinion to gain support for a special issue, program, or policy, such as a nation's war effort.

propaganda analysis the study of propaganda's effectiveness in influencing and mobilizing public opinion.

pseudo-events in public relations, any circumstance or event created solely for the purpose of obtaining coverage in the media.

pseudo-polls typically call-in, online, or person-on-the-street polls that do not use random samples and whose results thus do not represent the population as a whole.

psychographics in market research, the study of audience or consumer attitudes, beliefs, interests, and motivations.

Public Broadcasting Act of 1967 the act by the U.S. Congress that established the Corporation for Public Broadcasting, which oversees the Public Broadcasting Service (PBS) and National Public Radio (NPR).

Public Broadcasting Service (PBS) the noncommercial television network established in 1967 as an alternative to commercial television.

public domain the end of the copyright period for a cultural or scientific work, at which point the public may begin to access it for free.

publicity in public relations, the positive and negative messages that spread controlled and uncontrolled information about a person, a corporation, an issue, or a policy in various media.

public relations the total communication strategy conducted by a person, a government, or an organization attempting to reach and persuade its audiences to adopt a point of view.

public service announcements (PSAs) reports or announcements, carried free by radio and TV stations, that promote government programs, educational projects, volunteer agencies, or social reform.

pulp fiction a term used to describe many late-nineteenth-century popular paperbacks and dime novels, which were constructed of cheap machine-made pulp material.

punk rock rock music that challenges the orthodoxy and commercialism of the recording business; it is characterized by simple chord structures, catchy melodies, and politically or socially defiant lyrics.

radio wireless transmission of voice and music.

Radio Act of 1912 the first radio legislation passed by Congress, it addressed the problem of amateur radio operators increasingly cramming the airwaves. This act required all radio stations on land or at sea to be licensed and assigned special call letters.

Radio Act of 1927 the second radio legislation passed by Congress; in an attempt to restore order to the airwaves, it stated that licensees did not own their channels but could license them as long as they operated in order to serve the "public interest, convenience, or necessity."

Radio Corporation of America (RCA) a company developed during World War I that was designed, with government approval, to pool radio patents; the formation of RCA gave the United States almost total control over the emerging mass medium of broadcasting.

radio waves a portion of the electromagnetic wave spectrum that was harnessed so that signals could be sent from a transmission point and obtained at a reception point.

random assignment a social science research method for assigning research subjects; it ensures that every subject has an equal chance of being placed in either the experimental group or the control group.

rating in TV audience measurement, a statistical estimate expressed as a percentage of households tuned to a program in the local or national market being sampled.

reference books dictionaries, encyclopedias, atlases, and other reference manuals related to particular professions or trades.

regional editions national magazines whose content is tailored to the interests of different geographic areas.

responsible capitalism an underlying value held by many U.S. journalists and citizens, it assumes that businesspeople compete with one another not primarily to maximize profits but to increase prosperity for all.

retransmission fee a fee that cable service providers and satellite services have to pay to broadcast networks to carry network channels and programming.

rhythm and blues (R&B) music that merged urban blues with big-band sounds.

right to privacy a person's right to be left alone, without his or her name, image, or daily activities becoming public property.

rockabilly music that mixed bluegrass and country influences with those of black folk music and early amplified blues.

rock and roll music that mixed the vocal and instrumental traditions of popular music; it merged the black influences of urban blues, gospel, and R&B with the white influences of country, folk, and pop vocals.

rotation in format radio programming, the practice of playing the most popular or best-selling songs many times throughout the day.

satellite radio pay radio services that deliver various radio formats nationally via satellite.

saturation advertising the strategy of inundating a variety of print and visual media with ads aimed at target audiences.

scientific method a widely used research method that studies phenomena in systematic stages; it includes identifying the research problem, reviewing existing research, developing working hypotheses, determining appropriate research design, collecting information, analyzing results to see if the hypotheses have been verified, and interpreting the implications of the study.

search engines computer programs that allow users to enter key words or queries to find related sites on the Internet.

Section 315 part of the 1934 Communications Act; it mandates that during elections, broadcast stations must provide equal opportunities and response time for qualified political candidates.

selective exposure the phenomenon whereby audiences seek messages and meanings that correspond to their preexisting beliefs and values.

selective retention the phenomenon whereby audiences remember or retain messages and meanings that correspond to their preexisting beliefs and values.

serial programs radio or TV programs, such as soap operas, that feature continuing story lines from day to day or week to week (see **chapter shows**).

share in TV audience measurement, a statistical estimate of the percentage of homes tuned to a certain program, compared with those simply using their sets at the time of a sample.

shield laws laws protecting the confidentiality of key interview subjects and reporters' rights not to reveal the sources of controversial information used in news stories.

situation comedy (sitcom) a type of comedy series that features a recurring cast and set as well as several narrative scenes; each episode establishes a situation, complicates it, develops increasing confusion among its characters, and then resolves the complications.

sketch comedy short television comedy skits that are usually segments of TV variety shows; sometimes known as *vaudeo*, the marriage of vaudeville and video.

slander in law, spoken language that defames a person's character.

small-town pastoralism an underlying value held by many U.S. journalists and citizens, it favors the small over the large and the rural over the urban.

snob appeal an advertising strategy that attempts to convince consumers that using a product will enable them to maintain or elevate their social status.

social learning theory a theory within media effects research that suggests a link between the mass media and behavior; later modified and renamed *social cognitive theory*.

social media varied Internet websites that share certain characteristics that make them "social"—most commonly some combination of the ability to share information, pictures, videos, jokes, memes, news articles, and other content with a network of friends or with the public.

social responsibility model a model for journalism and speech, influenced by the libertarian model, that encourages the free flow of information to citizens so that they can make wise decisions regarding political and social issues.

social scientific research the mainstream tradition in mass communication research, it attempts to understand, explain, and predict the impact—or effects—of the mass media on individuals and society.

soul music that mixes gospel, blues, and urban and southern black styles with slower, more emotional, and melancholic lyrics.

space brokers in the days before modern advertising, individuals who purchased space in newspapers and sold it to various merchants.

spam a computer term referring to unsolicited e-mail.

Spanish-language radio one of radio's fastest-growing formats, concentrated mostly in large Hispanic markets, such as Miami, New York, Chicago, Las Vegas, California, Arizona, New Mexico, and Texas.

spiral of silence a theory that links the mass media, social psychology, and the formation of public opinion; it proposes that people who find their views on controversial issues in the minority tend to keep those views silent.

split-run editions editions of national magazines that tailor ads to different geographic areas.

spyware software with hidden codes that enable commercial firms to spy on users and gain access to their computers.

state model a model for journalism and speech that places control in the hands of an enlightened government, which speaks for ordinary citizens and workers in order to serve the common goals of the state.

stereo the recording of two separate channels or tracks of sound.

storyboard in advertising, a blueprint or roughly drawn comic-strip version of a proposed advertisement.

studio system an early film production system that constituted a sort of assembly-line process for moviemaking; major film studios controlled not only actors but also directors, editors, writers, and other employees, all of whom worked under exclusive contracts.

subliminal advertising a 1950s term that refers to hidden or disguised print and visual messages that allegedly register on the subconscious, creating false needs and seducing people into buying products.

subsidiary rights in the book industry, selling the rights to a book for use in other media forms, such as a mass market paperback, a CD-ROM, or the basis for a movie screenplay.

supermarket tabloids newspapers that feature bizarre human-interest stories, gruesome murder tales, violent accident accounts, unexplained phenomena stories, and malicious celebrity gossip.

superstations local independent TV stations, such as WTBS in Atlanta or WGN in Chicago, that have uplinked their signals onto a communication satellite to make themselves available nationwide.

survey research in social science research, a method of collecting and measuring data taken from a group of respondents.

syndication leasing TV stations the exclusive right to air older TV series.

synergy in media economics, the promotion and sale of a product (and all its versions) throughout the various subsidiaries of a media conglomerate.

talkies movies with sound, beginning in 1927.

targeted advertising ads targeted to a consumer based on information that various websites have gathered about that individual.

Telecommunications Act of 1996 the sweeping update of telecommunications law that brought cable fully under federal oversight and led to a wave of media consolidation.

telegraph invented in the 1840s, this device sent electrical impulses through a cable from a transmitter to a reception point, transmitting Morse code.

textbooks books made for the el-hi (elementary and high school) and college markets.

textual analysis in media research, a method for closely and critically examining and interpreting the meanings of culture, including architecture, fashion, books, movies, and TV programs.

third-person effect theory suggesting that people believe others are more affected by media messages than they are themselves.

throttling intentionally impairing or degrading Internet performance based on content or source.

time shifting the process whereby television viewers record shows and watch them later, when it is convenient for them.

Top 40 format the first radio format, in which stations played the forty most popular hits in a given week, as measured by record sales.

trade books the most visible book industry segment, featuring hardbound and paperback books aimed at general readers and sold at bookstores and other retail outlets.

trade publications specialty magazines that supply information relevant to specific manufacturing trades, professional fields, and business sectors.

transistor invented by Bell Laboratories in 1947, this tiny technology, which receives and amplifies radio signals, made portable radios possible.

TV newsmagazine a TV news program format, pioneered by CBS's *60 Minutes* in the late 1960s, that features multiple segments in an hour-long episode, usually ranging from a celebrity-focused or political feature story to a hard-hitting investigative report.

university press the segment of the book industry that publishes scholarly books in specialized areas.

urban contemporary one of radio's more popular formats, primarily targeting African American listeners in urban areas with dance, R&B, and hip-hop music.

uses and gratifications model a mass communication research model, usually employing in-depth interviews and survey questionnaires, that argues that people use the media to satisfy various emotional desires or intellectual needs.

Values and Lifestyles (VALS) a market-research strategy that divides consumers into types and measures psychological factors, including how consumers think and feel about products and how they achieve (or do not achieve) the lifestyle to which they aspire.

vellum a handmade paper made from treated animal skin, used in producing the first Gutenberg Bibles.

vertical integration in media economics, the phenomenon of controlling a mass media industry at its three essential levels: production, distribution, and exhibition; the term is most frequently used in reference to the film industry.

videocassette recorders (VCRs) recorders that used a half-inch video format known as VHS (video home system), which enabled viewers to record and play back programs from television or watch movies rented from video stores.

video news release (VNR) in public relations, the visual counterpart to a press release; it pitches a story idea to the TV news media by mimicking the style of a broadcast news report.

video-on-demand (VOD) cable television technology that enables viewers to instantly order programming, such as movies, to be digitally delivered to their sets.

video subscription services a term referring to cable and video-on-demand providers, introduced to include streaming-only companies like Hulu and Netflix.

viral marketing short videos or other content that marketers hope will quickly gain widespread attention as users share it with friends online or by word of mouth.

vitascope a large-screen movie projection system developed by Thomas Edison.

web browsers information-search services, such as Firefox and Microsoft's Internet Explorer, that offer detailed organizational maps to the Internet.

Wi-Fi a standard for short-distance wireless networking, enabling users of laptops, smartphones, and other devices to connect to the Internet in cafés, hotels, airports, and parks.

Wireless Ship Act the 1910 mandate that all major U.S. seagoing ships carrying more than fifty passengers and traveling more than two hundred miles off the coast be equipped with wireless equipment with a one-hundred-mile range.

wireless telegraphy the forerunner of radio, a form of voiceless point-to-point communication; it preceded the voice and sound transmissions of one-to-many mass communication that became known as *broadcasting*.

wireless telephony early experiments in wireless voice and music transmissions, which later developed into modern radio.

wire services commercial organizations, such as the Associated Press, that share news stories and information by relaying them around the country and the world, originally via telegraph and now via satellite transmission.

World Wide Web (WWW) a data-linking system for organizing and standardizing information on the Internet; the WWW enables computer-accessed information to associate with—or link to—other information, no matter where it is on the internet.

yellow journalism a newspaper style or era that peaked in the 1890s; it emphasized high-interest stories, sensational crime news, large headlines, and serious reports that exposed corruption, particularly in business and government.

zines self-published magazines produced on personal computer programs or on the Internet.

Index

A&R (artist and repertoire) agents, 148
AARP Bulletin, 112
AARP The Magazine, 112
ABC. *See* American Broadcasting Company (ABC)
above-the-line costs, 243
academics, 452–53
Academy Awards, 202–3
access channels, 238
account executives, 325
account planning, 322–23
account reviews, 325
acquisitions editors, 46
Action for Children's Television (ACT), 335
Activision Blizzard, 284
activism
　hashtag, 3–4
　political, 264
actual malice, 382
Ad Age, 339
Adams, Eddie, 107
Adams, John, 101, 377
Adamson, Allen, 333
Ad Council, 319
addiction, to gaming, 300
Adele, 125, 148
ad impressions, 326
Adobe Premiere Pro, 211
Adorno, T. W., 447
adult contemporary (AC), 173
Advanced Research Projects Agency (ARPA), 256
advance money, 46
Adventures of Huckleberry Finn, The (Twain), 52
advertisers, top, 324
advertising, 313–345
　alcohol, 337–38
　American society and, 318
　association principle, 330–31
　branding and, 316–17, 323
　cost of, 325
　deception in, 340, 398–99
　in a democratic society, 340–43
　digital out-of-home, 313–14
　digital turn in, 328
　early history of, 315–19
　evolution of, 319–329

food, 336–37
forms of, 314–15
industry monitoring, 338–350
influence of, 27, 335
in-game, 306
irritation advertising, 330
magazines, 115, 121
mobile, 320, 325, 326, 336
newspaper, 62
online, 270–71, 325–29, 411, 414
patent medicines, 317
persuasive techniques in, 329–331, 334
pharmaceutical, 338
planning and placing, 324–25
political, 340–42, 369
product placement, 334
vs. public relations, 348–49
radio, 164–65, 179–180
regulation of, 318–19, 335–340
saturation, 324
smoking, 337
social media, 326–27
stereotypes in, 331, 332–33
storytelling, 334
streaming services and, 178
subliminal, 319
targeting children and teens, 335–36
television, 224, 245, 246, 328, 335–36, 341, 342
of tobacco, 337
visual design in, 319–320
web, 325–27
word of mouth, 327
Advertising Age, 113–14
advertising agencies, 316, 320–25
　boutique, 320, 321–22
　global, 319–320
　mega-agencies, 320–21
　revenue, 320–21
　structure of, 320, 322–25
advertising and sales department, 116–17
advertising revenue
　Internet, 270–71, 326
　for media companies, 412
　newspaper, 83–84
advice columns, 103
Advocate, 113
Aeropagitica (Milton), 376, 377

Aerosmith, 145
affiliate stations, 227, 243
African Americans
　Civil Rights movement and, 70–71, 106, 137, 168
　directors, 200
　Hollywood race barrier and, 200, 202–3
　magazines targeted to, 113
　media ownership and, 409
　migration to north, 139
　police shootings of, 3
　stereotypes of, 332–33
　on television, 232–33
Agee, James, 93
Agence France-Presse, 85
agenda-setting theory, 444–45
age-specific magazines, 112
aggrieved entitlement, 24–25
AIDS epidemic, 76
Air America, 175
album-oriented rock (AOR), 173
albums, 129, 130, 149–150
alcohol advertising, 337–38
Aldean, Jason, 148
Alden Capital, 86
Alexa, 254
Alfred A. Knopf, 38
Alibaba Group, 331
Alice through the Looking Glass, 213
Alliance for Audited Media, 319
All Things Considered, 176
almanacs, 40
Alpert, Philip, 385
Alphabet, 411
alphabet, 6–7, 35
"alternative facts," 366
alternative magazines, 114
alternative rock, 144
alt-right, 431–32
Alwood, Edward, 232–33
Amanpour, Christiane, 72
amateur culture, 453
Amazon, 41, 42–43, 49–50, 210, 237, 239, 240, 269, 284, 331, 404, 410, 411
Amazon Echo, 254, 265
Amazon Fire TV Stick, 240
Amazon Music, 131, 149
Amazon Prime, 328

I-1

AMC Entertainment, 209
Amélie, 200
American Booksellers Association (ABA), 39
American Broadcasting Company (ABC), 168, 236, 246
American culture, 168, 417, 426
American Dream, 417
American Gods, 235
American Idol, 16, 230
American Library Association (ALA), 51, 52
American Magazine, 102
American Marconi, 161, 163
American Society of Composers, Authors and Publishers (ASCAP), 134
American Tobacco Company, 353, 354
American values, 14
Amos 'n' Andy, 167, 168, 232, 233
AM radio, 170
analog recording, 130
analog standard, 223
analysis, 22, 23
Anderson, Lynn, 146
Andreessen, Marc, 260
Andrews McMeel Syndication, 85
Andrews Sisters, 136
animated films, 418–421
anime, 306
anorexia, 336
anthology dramas, 229
anti-paparazzi laws, 384
antitrust laws, 410, 424–25
anti-vaccination campaigns, 21
AOL, 260–61, 410
Apple, 41, 118, 131, 177, 269, 331, 386–87, 404, 407, 410, 411, 422–23
Apple Music, 125–26, 131, 147, 149, 150, 179, 181, 423
Apple News, 88, 118
Apple Watch, 269
apps, 263
App Store, 263, 305
AR-15-style rifles, 24
Arab Americans, 448
Arab Spring, 264
Arbuckle, Fatty, 389
Arcade Fire, 144
arcades, 286–89
archives, digital, 274
Aristotle, 81
Armstrong, Edwin, 170
Armstrong, Louis, 135
Arnaz, Desi, 232

Aro, Jessikka, 92
ARPA. *See* Advanced Research Projects Agency (ARPA)
ARPAnet, 256–57, 259
Arrow, 44
artificial intelligence, 437
ASCAP, 152
Asch, Solomon, 445
Asian Week, 113
Assassin's Creed, 305
Associated Press (AP), 63, 85
Association of American Publishers (AAP), 39, 51
association principle, 330–31
Asteroids, 288
astroturf lobbying, 362
AT&T, 163, 164–65, 223, 248, 261, 331, 351, 406–7, 409–10, 424
Atari, 287–88, 289–290
Atlanta, 228
atlases, 40
Atwood, Margaret, 41, 44
Audible, 43, 50
audiences, global, 421
audience share, 244–45
audience studies, 449
audio books, 43
Audion vacuum tube, 162
audiotapes, 129–130
Audit Bureau of Circulation (ABC), 319
Aufderheide, Pat, 453
augmented reality, 115, 300
authoritarian model, 378
authority
  questioning of, 20–21
  resistance to, 8
authors
  advance money, 46
  royalties for, 46
  self-published, 18, 42–43
Authors Guild, 51
Autobiography of Malcolm X, The, 51
Avalon, Frankie, 138
Avatar, 188
avatars, 289
Avenger series, 43
Avengers: Infinity War, 198, 209
Axelrod, David, 368
Azalea, Iggy, 145

Bachelor, The, 231
Back to the Future II, 208

Baer, Ralph, 287
Baez, Joan, 142
Baidu, 262
BAM Tech, 284
Bandura, Albert, 443–44
bandwagon effect, 330
banned books, 52–53
Banned Books Week, 51
banner ads, 325–26
Baran, Paul, 257
Barnes & Noble, 41, 48–49
Barney, 231
Barnum, P. T., 350
Baron, Marty, 95
barter deals, 244
Bashi, Kishi, 148
basic cable, 234–35
Beatles, 140, 141, 143
Beauty and the Beast, 419
beauty standards, 336
Bechdel, Alison, 31
Beck, Glenn, 174
Bee, Samantha, 89, 90
Bee Gees, 144
Before I Forget, 299
Bell, Chichester, 128
Bell Labs, 197
below-the-line costs, 242–43
Bennett, Chancellor Johnathan, 125–26
Bennett, James Gordon, 61–62
Benny, Jack, 166
Bentham, Jeremy, 81
Berkshire Hathaway, 413
Berlin, Irving, 136
Berliner, Emile, 128–29
Bernays, Edward, 351, 352–53, 354, 358, 367–68, 415–16
Berners-Lee, Tim, 260, 265
Bernstein, Carl, 68
Berry, Chuck, 137, 138, 140
Bertelsmann, 44, 45
Best Buy, 150
bestsellers, 43
BET, 418
Better Business Bureau, 318
Better Homes and Gardens, 111
Bezos, Jeff, 49, 413
bias, 75–76, 94
Bible, 7, 35, 36, 40
Big Bang Theory, 219, 227, 328
Big Brother and the Holding Company, 143
big data, 326

Bigelow, Kathryn, 199
Big Five film companies, 208
Big Five movie studios, 208
Big Five publishing houses, 44
Biggest Loser, The, 334
Big Machine Records, 148
Big Mac Theory, 19
Big Tech, 411
billboards, digital, 313–14
Bill of Rights, 50, 376, 377, 388
binary code, 255
Bing, 262, 326
binge watching, 241
bin Laden, Osama, 107
Birther movement, 342
Birth of a Nation, The, 197
Biswas-Diener, Robert, 13
Black, Hugo, 378–79
black cinema, 202–3
Black-ish, 232, 233
BlacKkKlansman, 203, 215
blacklisting, 390
Black Lives Matter movement, 3–4, 264, 348
Black Mirror, 229
black music, 139
Black Panther, 203
black theaters, 202
Blair, Jayson, 78
Blair Witch Project, The, 213
Bland, Sandra, 89
Blizzard Entertainment, 293, 294
block booking, 195–96
Blockbuster, 239
blockbusters, 203
blocking, 273
block printing, 34, 36
bloggers, 329
blogging, 88–89
blogs, 263, 364
Blondie, 143
blues music, 136
Blumlein, Alan, 129
Blu-ray, 206, 210
Bly, Nellie, 57–58
Bobo doll experiments, 443–44
Bohannon, Jim, 174
BoJack Horseman, 244
Bollea, Terry G., 121, 384
Bollywood, 200–201
Bolt, Beranek and Newman (BBN), 257
book agents, 46

book challenge, 51
Book Industry Study Group (BISG), 39
book publishing, 36–50
  early history of, 36–37
  evolution of, 38–41
  influence of television and film on, 43–44
  largest publishers, 44–45
  organization and economics of, 44–50
  self-publishing, 42–43
  structure of, 46, 48–50
  trends in, 41–44
books
  audio, 43
  bestsellers, 43
  censorship of, 51
  comic, 43
  demand for, 37, 38
  in a democratic society, 50–51
  digitization of, 50–51
  early history of, 34–37
  e-books, 41–43, 49–50
  graphic novels, 31–32, 43
  influence of television and film on, 40–41
  marketing, 46
  mass market paperbacks, 40
  as mass media, 32
  number published annually, 33
  online sales, 49–50
  paperback, 37, 40
  physical deterioration of, 50–51
  preservation of, 50–51
  print, 39–41
  printing press and, 7, 36–37
  professional, 40
  publishing industry, 36–50
  reference, 40
  religious, 40
  revenue from, 48
  role of, 32
  selling, 48–50
  textbooks, 39
  trade, 31–32, 39
  types of, 39–41
  university press, 40–41
bookstores, 48–49, 50
Boone, Daniel, 61
Boone, Pat, 137
Borders, 48
Born a Crime (Noah), 43
Boston Globe, 68, 95
Boswell Sisters, 136
bots, 88, 92, 267

Bourke-White, Margaret, 108
boutique agencies, 320, 321–22
Bowers, Robert, 431
boxed game/retail model, 304
box office sales, 207
Boys' Life, 112
BP oil rig explosion, 359–360
Bradford, Andrew, 102
branded content, 116
branding, 316–17
brand names, 323, 331
BrandZ, 331
Bravo, 418
Brennan, William Jr., 375
brick-and-mortar stores, 48–49, 50
Brin, Sergey, 404
Britain, 267, 333
British Marconi, 161, 163
British rock, 140–41
broadband connections, 261, 272–73, 277–78
broadcasting, 160–62
  deregulation of, 408–9
  First Amendment and, 391–95
  regulation of, 392–93
  toll, 164–65
Broadcast Music, Inc. (BMI), 152
broadcast networks, 76, 226–233, 236–37, 243, 246–47
Broadway, 135
Broken Bow Records, 148
Brooklyn Nine-Nine, 228
Brooks, Garth, 146
Brown, Helen Gurley, 100
Brown, James, 141
Brown, Michael, 3
Brown v. Board of Education, 137
Brussels, 267
Bryan, Luke, 146
Buckley v. Valeo, 373–74
Budweiser, 323, 337
Buffalo Bill, 350
Buffett, Warren, 413
Bugs Bunny, 448
bulletin boards, 258
bureau reporters, 85
Burger King, 355
Burke, John, 350
Burke, Tarana, 113
Burns, Alan, 158
Burson-Marsteller, 360–61
Burstyn v. Wilson, 390

Burton, Tim, 199
Bushnell, Nolan, 287–88
business model
  of journalism, 82–84
  of newspapers, 82–84
business trends, 414–15
Buzzcocks, 143
BuzzFeed, 398

cable companies, 409
cable news, 71–72, 75
cable television, 207, 221, 225–26, 248
  advertising, 246
  basic cable, 234–35
  digital cable, 235
  distribution, 243
  economics of, 242–48
  evolution of, 10, 231, 234–36
  global audiences, 421
  local monopolies and, 425
  ownership and consolidation in, 247–48
  premium cable, 235–36
  production of, 243
  regulatory challenges for, 236–39
  subscription fees, 246
Cambridge Analytica, 271, 276
cameras in courtrooms, 387–88
Cameron, James, 188
campaign contributions, 373–74
Campbell, Clive, 145
Campbell, Glen, 146
Campbell Soup Co., 316
Campion, Jane, 199
Candy Crush Saga, 295
Cantril Henry, 438–39
capitalism, 8, 413, 425
  music and, 153
  responsible, 79
Capitalism: A Love Story, 215
Carlin, George, 393
Carson, Rachel, 50
Carter, Jimmy, 408
Carter, Troy, 178
Casablanca, 198
Cash, Johnny, 146
Cash Money Records, 148
cassettes, 129, 130
Castile, Philando, 89
categorical imperative, 81
catfishing, 276–77
cathode ray tubes (CRTs), 287
Catholic Church, investigation of, 68

CATV, 225–26
CBS. *See* Columbia Broadcasting System (CBS)
CBS Access, 220
CBS Morning News, 71
CBS News, 67, 70
CBS Records, 129
CBS-TV News, 227
CDs, 127
celebrity endorsements, 327, 329
cell phone, 9
celluloid, 190
censorship, 51, 137–38, 277, 377–79
Center for Digital Democracy, 396
Center for Media and Democracy (CMD), 354
Chance the Rapper, 125–26, 145, 151
Channel One, 336
Chaplin, Charlie, 194
chapter shows, 229–230
Charles, Ray, 137
Charter Communications, 248, 261
Cheerios, 332–33
Chen, Steve, 404
Chicago Edison, 351
child pornography, 385
children
  ads targeting, 335–36
  gaming and, 295
Children's Internet Protection Act, 277
Children's Television Act of 1990, 335–36
China
  block printing, 36
  books in ancient, 35
  cyber-attacks from, 92
  invention of moveable type in, 36
Chrome, 270
Chromecast, 270
chronic traumatic encephalopathy (CTE), 347–48
Cincinnati Enquirer, 66
Cinderella, 192
Cinemark USA, 209
cinematograph, 191
cinema verité, 201
Cineplex Entertainment, 209
circulation and distribution department, 117–18
Citadel, 86
citizen journalism, 89
Citizen Kane, 188

Citizens United v. Federal Elections Commission, 341, 373, 374
Civil Rights movement, 26, 70–71, 106, 137, 168, 382
clans, 295–96
Clark, Dick, 137
Clash, 143
Clash of Clans, 295
classified ads, 83, 325
"clear and present danger" criterion, 380
Clear Channel Communications, 181
click-throughs, 326
climate change, 93–94
climate change denial, 21, 93–94
Cline, Patsy, 146
Clinton, Bill, 408
Clinton, Hillary, 91, 106
Cloud Player, 269
CNN, 71–72, 87, 95, 226, 227
coaxial cable, 225
Coca-Cola, 323, 331
Cochrane, Elizabeth "Pink," 57
codex, 34, 35
Cody, William F., 350
Colbert, Stephen, 89, 90
Colbert Report, The, 90
Cold War, 67, 256, 377, 425
Coler, Jestin, 91
Colgate-Palmolive, 168
collective intelligence, 296
college texts, 39
Collier's, 105
colonial magazines, 102
colonial newspapers, 59–60
Colony, George, 364
color television, 223–24
Columbia Broadcasting System (CBS), 165–66, 236, 237, 246
Columbia Journalism Review, 91
Columbia Pictures, 193, 208
Columbia University, 67
Comcast, 11, 210, 220, 237, 241, 243, 247, 248, 261, 272, 324, 395, 404, 410, 418, 422, 424
comedians, 89–90
Comedy Central, 244
comedy shows, 227–28
comic books, 43
comics, 31–32
comic strips, 64
Commercial Alert, 334, 338–39
commercial culture, 5, 26

commercial speech, 335, 340, 369
Committee of Advertising Practice (CAP), 333
Committee on Public Information (CPI), 353
common carriers, 238
common sense, 416–17
Common Sense (Paine), 9
communication
 need for, 4–5
 process of, 12–16
 wireless, 160–62
Communications Act of 1934, 238, 392, 394, 395
communications industry, regulation of, 408–9
communities, gaming, 295–97
community newspapers, 86
community relations, 361–62
compact discs (CDs), 130, 147, 149, 150, 152
company websites, 363–64
computer gaming, 293
computer-generated imagery (CGI), 198, 211
computer networks, 256–57
Condé Nast, 116
conflict of interest, 81
conglomerates. *See* media conglomerates
Conrad, Frank, 163–64
consensus narratives, 214–15
consoles, 289–290
conspiracy theories, 91
consumer choice, 425–26
consumer control, 425–26
consumer culture, 8, 138, 316, 317–18
consumer products, 14
consumer relations, 361–62
contemporary hit radio (CHR), 173
content analysis, 442–43
content creation, 422–23
control groups, 441
controlled circulations, 117
controversial content, 277
conventions, gaming, 297
Coogler, Ryan, 200, 203
Cook, Fred, 392
Cooke, Janet, 78
cookies, 271, 276
Coolidge, Calvin, 165, 368
Cooper, Anderson, 72
Coppola, Francis Ford, 199
Coppola, Sofia, 199, 204

copycat suicides, 450–51
copy editors, 46
copyright, 380–81
Copyright Act of 1970, 380
copyright infringement, 381
"cord-cutting," 221
corporate mergers. *See* mergers and acquisitions (M&As)
corporate radio, 181–82
Corporation for Public Broadcasting (CPB), 176, 231
correlations, 442
Correll, Charles, 168
Cosby Show, The, 232
Cosmopolitan, 99–100, 105, 111, 120
counterculture, 143
Counterintuitive CEO, The, 364
country music, 139, 146, 172
Couric, Katie, 126
courtrooms, cameras in, 387–88
cover music, 137
Cox Communications, 261
craigslist, 325
Crazy Rich Asians (Kwan), 44
creative development, 323
Crimean War, 106
Crisis, 113
critical perspective, benefits of, 26–27
critical process, 22, 23, 26
critical thinking, 399
Crockett, Davy, 61
Cronkite, Walter, 227
crooners, 136
Crosby, Bing, 136
cross-ownership rules, 407
Crown, The, 243
Cruz, Nikolas, 431
Cuaron, Alfonso, 199
Cucumbers Biting, 295
Cullors, Patrisse, 3
cultivation effect theory, 445
cultural imperialism, 426
cultural model, 18–19
cultural studies, 432–33, 446–452
culture
 amateur, 453
 American, 168, 417, 426
 commercial, 5, 26
 consumer, 8, 316, 317–18
 defined, 16
 high, 18–19, 138
 low, 19, 138

 manuscript, 7, 35
 popular, 19
 urban, 144
"culture as map" metaphor, 19
"culture as skyscraper" metaphor, 18–19
Cumulus, 181
Curb Your Enthusiasm, 235
Cure, the 144
customer data, 326–27
CW Television, 44
cyberspace, 260
Czitrom, Daniel, 433–34

Daily Show, The, 240
Daily Show with Jon Stewart, The, 90
Daily Show with Trevor Noah, The, 90
Dancing with the Stars, 231
Daniels, Lee, 202
Daredevil, 44
Dash, Julie, 202, 203
Das Kapital (Marx), 51
data mining, 271, 326–27
data security, 275–76
Daughters of the American Revolution, 14
Daughters of the Dust, 203
Dave & Buster's, 288
da Vinci, Leonardo, 189
Davison, W. Phillips, 446
Day, Benjamin, 61
Daye, Stephen, 37
DBS. *See* direct broadcast satellite (DBS)
deadheading, 351
Deadpool, 212–13
Deadpool 2, 213
Dean, James, 206
Death Race, 307
deejays, 145, 171, 180
Deepwater Horizon, 359–360
Deezer, 131, 181
deficit financing, 243
De Forest, Lee, 162
DeGeneres, Ellen, 26
De Maeyer, Juliette, 158
de Martinville, Édouard-Léon Scott, 128
democracy
 advertising and, 340–43
 books and, 50–51
 digital gaming and, 307–9
 First Amendment and, 396–97
 free markets and, 425
 Internet and, 277–79
 journalism and, 58, 68–69, 93–95

democracy *(continued)*
  magazines and, 120–21
  media and, 26
  media as watchdog for, 5
  media marketplace and, 426–27
  media research and, 452–53
  movies and, 214–15
  music and, 152–53
  printing press and, 37
  public relations and, 367–69
  radio and, 182–83
  social media and, 263–64
  television and, 248–49
Democracy Now! 427
demographic editions, 117
demographics, 322
demos, 148
De Palma, Brian, 199
department stores, 317–18
dependent variables, 441
Depp, Johnny, 213, 383
Depression Quest, 309
deregulation, 237, 246, 406, 408–9
description, 22, 23
desegregation, 137
design managers, 46
desktop publishing, 115
Destiny, 306
detective journalism, 58
deterministic identity, 327
developmental editors, 46
development budget, 306
development stage, of new medium, 12
Diamond Sutra, 36
Diary of a Young Girl (Frank), 52
Dick, Kirby, 201
Dickson, William Kennedy, 191
dictionaries, 40
Diddley, Bo, 138
Diener, Ed, 13
digital archiving, 274
digital cable, 235
digital communication, 6, 10–12, 261
digital companies, 411
digital divide, 277–78, 279
digital era, 10–12
Digital First Media, 86
digital gaming, 283–311
  See also video games
  advertising, 306
  alternate voices in, 308–9
  children's market, 295

  classic games, 288–290
  communities, 295–97
  computer gaming, 293
  conventions and expos, 297
  convergence and, 292
  culture of, 302–3, 308–9
  in a democratic society, 307–9
  early history of, 285–88
  economics of, 304–7
  evolution of, 288–295
  in-game chat, 296
  immersion and addiction, 297–300
  misogyny and, 300–301, 302–3
  mobile, 292, 300, 308–9
  popularity of, 285
  royalties in, 306–7
  self-regulation of, 307
  on smartphones and tablets, 292
  social gaming, 293–95
  on social networking sites, 295
  tie-ins and licensing, 305–6
  trends and issues in, 295–303
  violence, 300–301
  virtual reality and, 297–98
digital magazines, 114–15, 117–18
Digital Millennium Copyright Act, 381
digital movie distribution, 210–13
digital music, 127, 130–31, 132–33, 147–152
digital newspaper subscriptions, 84
digital out-of-home (DOOH) marketing, 313–14
digital photography, 106–7
digital publishing, 41–43
digital recording, 129–130
digital revenue, 84
digital television, 239–242
digital turn
  advertising and, 326–27
  books and, 41, 42, 48, 49
  defined, 6, 10–11
  digital gaming and, 304
  journalism and, 72–73, 88
  magazines and, 100, 115
  media companies and, 404, 410
  movies and, 210–13
  music industry and, 127, 130–31, 147, 153
  newspapers and, 83
  radio and, 176–77, 180
  television and, 237
Digital Turn case studies

artificial intelligence, 437
digital companies, 411
Fear of Missing Out (FOMO), 13
film industry, 212–13
Instapoets, 47
magazines, 119
military PR, 358
mobile gaming, 299
music industry, 151
network television, 328
sexting, 385
social media fraud and elections, 266–67
streaming services and radio, 178
television bingeing, 241
trolls, 92
digital video, 211, 212–13
digital video recorders (DVRs), 239
digitization, 255
Digster, 181
dime novels, 37
direct broadcast satellite (DBS), 221, 242, 248
directors, 199, 202–3
DirecTV, 242, 247, 248
dirty words, 393–94
disc jockeys, 170
disco, 144
Dish, 242, 247, 248
Disney, 16, 208, 209, 210, 213, 215, 220, 237, 243, 246, 247, 404, 410, 418–421, 422, 423, 424
Disney, Walt, 418–19
Disney+, 220, 420, 421, 423
Disney Channel, 418
distributed denial-of-service (DDoS) attacks, 276
distributed networks, 257
diversification, 424–25
diversity, in the newsroom, 77–78
DJ Kool Herc, 145
documentaries, 201
Domino, Fats, 137
Donkey Kong, 288
Do-Not-Track legislation, 276
Doors, 143
Dope, 202
Dorsey, Tommy, 135
Dota 2, 284
Do the Right Thing, 203
Doubleday & McClure Company, 38
downsizing, 415

doxxing, 92
Doyle Dane Bernbach, 323
Drake, 145, 148
Drama (Telgemeier), 52
dramas, 228–230
dramatic programs, 168
dramedy, 228
Drew, Robert, 201
drinking, promotion of, 337–38
Drive, 120
drop capitals, 35
Drunk History, 228
Du Bois, W. E. B., 113
DuVernay, Ava, 200
DVDs, 206
DVD/video sales and rentals, 207, 210
Dvorak, Jane, 366
DVRs, 246, 314
Dylan, Bob, 142

earned media, 327
Eastman, George, 190
Eastman Kodak, 190
easyJet, 355
Ebony, 113
e-books, 41–43, 49–50
Echo, 269
EchoStar Communications, 248
e-commerce, 271
Economist, 45
Edelman, 356
Edge, 260
Edison, Thomas, 12, 128, 161, 190–91, 193, 195
editorial department, 116
editors
  acquisitions, 46
  copy, 46
  developmental, 46
  magazine, 116
  news, 84–85
Ed Sullivan Show, The, 168, 230
efficiency, 20
Egypt, 34–35
Ehrenreich, Barbara, 452–53
Eisenhower, Dwight, 256, 368
Eisner, Michael, 419
Ek, Daniel, 132–33
elections
  See also politics; presidential elections
  influence over, 373–74
  social media fraud and, 266–67

electromagnetic waves, 160
Electronic Communications Privacy Act of 1986, 386
Electronic Entertainment Expo (E3), 297
electronic era, 9–10
electronic publishing, 41–43, 238
11.22.63, 44
el-hi texts, 39
elite class, 8
elite magazines, 112–13
Ellen, 232
Ellen DeGeneres Show, The, 244
Ellsberg, Daniel, 377–78
e-mail, 257, 261
e-mail interviews, 72–73
EMI, 407
Eminem, 145
Empire, 229, 232, 328
Encore, 248
encyclopedias, 40
endorsements, 327, 329
engagement, 22, 23, 26
ENIAC, 255
entertainment magazines, 111–12
entertainment shows, 227–230
Entertainment Software Association (ESA), 300–301
Entertainment Software Rating Board (ESRB), 307
entrepreneurial stage, of new medium, 12
E. P. Dutton, 38
Epic of Gilgamesh, The, 47
episodic series, 229–230
equal opportunity laws, 394
e-readers, 41, 269
ESL, 284
Espionage Acts, 380
ESPN, 246, 305
eSports, 283–84
Essence, 113
ethics
  applying, 81
  cameras in the courtroom and, 387–88
  data gathering and, 275–76
  endorsements and, 329
  lobbying and, 362
  news media, 79–81, 93–94
  photojournalism and, 106
  professional codes of, 80
  public relations and, 366–67
ethnocentrism, 79
Etsy, 263

E.T.: The Extra-Terrestrial, 208
Euripides, 14
Europe
  data protection regulations in, 276
  early magazines in, 102
  Russian propaganda and, 267
evaluation, 22, 23
Evans, Walker, 93
evergreens, 244
evergreen subscriptions, 117
everyday life, media's role in, 14–16
executive compensation, 85, 415, 416
experimental groups, 441
experiments, 441
Explorer, 256
expos, gaming, 297

Fabian, 138
Facebook, 87–88, 262, 263, 270, 331, 404, 405, 411
  advertising, 271, 326, 327
  customization and, 279
  "fake" news and, 91, 398
  FOMO and, 13
  fraud and elections and, 266–67
  as news source, 27
  privacy issues and, 271, 276
  rise of, 410
Facebook Watch, 284
Factcheck.org, 398
Fairbanks, Douglas, 194
Fairness Doctrine, 174–75, 394–95
fair use doctrine, 381
fair wages, 413
"fake" news, 90–91, 396, 398–99
Fallon, Jimmy, 212
false advertising, 398–99
false equivalency, 93–94
Falwell, Jerry, 383
family values, banned books and, 52–53
famous-person testimonials, 330
Famous Players Film Company, 194
fantasy sports, 294
Fargo, 230
Farm Heroes Saga, 295
Farnsworth, Philo, 222–23
Fat Boys, 145
fax machine, 9
FCC. *See* Federal Communications Commission (FCC)
FCC v. Pacifica Foundation, 393–94
Fear of Missing Out (FOMO), 13

feature-length films, 197
feature syndicates, 85
Federal Communications Act of 1934, 167
Federal Communications Commission (FCC)
  cable television and, 237–38
  communications industry and, 409
  cross-ownership rules and, 407
  Internet and, 395
  net neutrality and, 272–73
  product placement and, 334
  radio and, 167–68, 174, 182
  regulation of broadcasting by, 236–37, 391–94
  television standards, 223–24
Federal Food and Drugs Act, 317
Federalist Party, 377
Federal Radio Commission (FRC), 167
Federal Trade Commission (FTC), 271, 276, 318, 329, 334, 338, 340, 364
feedback, 17
female gamers, 302–3, 308
female models, 336
Feminine Mystique, The (Friedan), 332
femininity, 138–39
Feminist Frequency, 302–3
Fenton, Roger, 106
Fessenden, Reginald, 161
Fibber McGee and Molly, 167
fiber-optic cable, 256, 259
fiction, pulp, 37
film exchange system, 195
film festivals, 204
film industry
  See also movies
  box office sales, 207
  conglomerations and synergy in, 208–9
  economics of, 207–11
  First Amendment and, 388–391
  gender problem in, 199–200
  global cinema, 200–201, 421
  Hollywood, 193–200
  independent film companies, 195, 201, 204
  Indian, 200–201
  minorities and, 202–3
  narrative style in, 198–200
  power of, 215
  role of, 188–89
  studio system, 193–96
  television and, 205–6
  theaters and, 209–10
  transformation of, 204–6
film noir, 198
films. *See* movies
film technology, 189–191, 205–6, 211, 212–13
Filo, David, 261
Filtr, 181
Financial and Syndication Rules, 236–37
Financial Times, 45
Finding Nemo, 420
fin-syn, 236–37
Firefox, 260
"fireside chats," 70, 167
First Amendment, 50, 60, 153, 238, 285, 308
  advertising and, 335
  broadcasting and, 391–95
  debates over, 375
  in a democratic society, 396–97
  elections and, 373, 374
  "fake" news and, 398–99
  film and, 388–391
  Internet and, 392, 395
  limits on, 379–387
  movies and, 214
  origins of, 376–77
  vs. Sixth Amendment, 387–88
first-run syndication, 244
first-run theaters, 196
Fitzgerald, F. Scott, 38
Flash, The, 44
Fleischman, Doris, 353, 354
flexible markets, 414–15
flipper bumper, 286–87
Florida Georgia Line, 146, 148
Flynt, Larry, 383
FM radio, 170, 177
focus groups, 322
folk music, 135, 142
food industry, 336–37
foreign distribution, of films, 207
foreign films, 200–201
format radio, 170–73
Fortnite, 293, 295
45-rpm records, 129
Fourth Estate, 378
Four Tops, the, 142
Fox, 237
Fox, William, 194
Fox News, 72, 77, 342
France, 267
Francis, Connie, 138
Frank, Anne, 52
Frankenstein, 17
Frankfurt School, 447
Franklin, Aretha, 141
Franklin, Benjamin, 37, 60, 102
FRC. *See* Federal Radio Commission (FRC)
Freed, Alan, 137
freedom of expression, 373–401
  See also First Amendment
  censorship and, 377–79
  debates over, 375
  indecency and, 393–94
  Internet and, 395
  interpretations of, 377
  origins of, 377–388
  unprotected expression and, 379–387
freelance writers, 116
free markets, 425–26
freemium games, 305
Free Press, 396, 427
free press, 60
  origins of, 377–388
free speech, 51, 214, 285, 307–8, 335, 373, 375
  See also freedom of expression
free-to-play games, 304–5
Fresh Air, 176
Friedan, Betty, 332
Friedkin, William, 199
fringe time, 244
Frozen, 199, 419
FTC. *See* Federal Trade Commission (FTC)
Full Frontal, 89, 90
Furious Five, 145
Future, 145

gag orders, 387
Gallagher, Mike, 174
Game Boy, 292
game development, 306–7
Game of Thrones, 44, 235, 243
#GamerGate, 302–3
games. *See* video games
gamespeak, 296
GameSpot, 296
GameStop, 305
gaming. *See* digital gaming
gaming conventions and expos, 297
gaming sites, 296–97
Gandhi, 108
gangster rap, 145
Gannett, 85, 86

Gans, Herbert, 79
Ganz, 295
Garner, Eric, 89
Garsd, Jasmine, 157
Garza, Alicia, 3, 4
GateHouse, 86
gatekeepers, 17
Gawker, 121, 384, 386
Gaye, Marvin, 135, 142
gay rights, 76
gender
 film industry and, 199–200
 gaming and, 302–3, 308
 stereotypes, 332–33
 suicide behaviors and, 24–25
 television and, 232–33
general assignment reporters, 85
General Data Protection Regulation (GDPR), 276
General Electric (GE), 161, 163, 165, 246, 410
general-interest magazines, 105, 109–10
General Magazine, and Historical Chronicle, 102
genres
 film, 198–99
 video game, 291
Gentleman's Magazine, 102
geo-based games, 300
Gerbner, George, 445
Germany, 267
Gerwig, Greta, 199
Get Out, 334
Girl with the Dragon Tattoo, The, 200
Gjoni, Eron, 302
GLAAD, 442–43
Gladwell, Malcolm, 90
global audiences, 421
global brands, 331
global cinema, 200–201, 421
globalization, 418
global village, 426
Globe, 114
Gmail, 261
Godey's Lady Book, 103
Golden Age, of Hollywood, 196–200
golden mean, 81
Goldsmith, Thomas T., 287
Goldwyn, Sam, 199
Gomery, Douglas, 192
Gone Home, 309

Gone with the Wind, 198
Good Housekeeping, 111
Goodman, Amy, 427
Good Morning America, 71
Good Place, The, 228
Goodwin, Hannibal, 190
Google, 210, 262, 263, 270, 320, 325, 326, 331, 403–4, 410, 411
Google Analytics, 357
Google Apps, 270
Google Assistant, 254
Google Books Library Project, 50–51
Google Cardboard, 298
Google Chrome, 260
Google Chromecast, 240
Google Home, 265
Google News, 88
Google Play, 149, 270, 305
Google Play Music, 131
Gordy, Berry, 142
Gore, Lesley, 138
Gosden, Freeman, 168
government, control of press by, 8
government relations, 362–63
government surveillance, 275
G. P. Putnam, 38
GQ, 120
Grammy Awards, 125
gramophones, 128–29
Gramsci, Antonio, 447
Grandmaster Flash, 145
Grand Ole Opry, 172
Grand Theft Auto, 301
graphical user interface (GUI), 260
graphic novels, 31–32, 43
graphophones, 128
Grateful Dead, 143
Great Britain. *See* Britain
Great Depression, 38, 70, 93, 106, 109, 134, 200, 413
Great Gatsby, The (Fitzgerald), 38
Great Recession, 85
Great Train Robbery, The, 192
Green Day, 144
Green Hornet, The, 167
Griffith, D. W., 194, 197
grunge, 144
Grupo Planeta, 45
Guardian, 266
Guess Who's Coming to Dinner? 202
guilds, 295–96
gun industry, 25

Gutenberg, Johannes, 7, 36
Gutenberg Bible, 36
Guthrie, Arlo, 142
Guthrie, Woody, 135, 142

Habermas, Jurgen, 398
Hachette Livre, 45
hackers, 265
hacking, 253–54
Hall, Stuart, 309, 447, 448
Hamilton, Andrew, 60
handheld consoles, 292
Handmaid's Tale, The (Atwood), 41, 44
Hannity, Sean, 72, 174
happiness, 13
"happy talk," 71
Hare, Jimmy, 106
Harper & Bros., 38
Harper & Row, 38
HarperCollins, 38
Harris, Benjamin, 60
Harry, Debbie, 144
Harry Potter book series, 43, 300
Harry Potter film series, 43
Hartmann, Thom, 174
hashtag activism, 3–4
hate groups, 431–32
hate speech, 277
Hate You Give, The (Thomas), 44
Hauptmann, Bruno, 387
Hawks, Howard, 199
Hawthorne, Nathaniel, 45, 52
Hays, Will, 390
HBO, 44, 226, 231, 235, 243
HD radio, 179
Heard, Amber, 213, 383
Hear It Now, 70
Hearst, William Randolph, 64, 100, 114
Hearst Corporation, 100, 120
Hefner, Hugh, 111
hegemony, 415–17
Hello, 110
Hell's Kitchen, 231
Hendrix, Jimi, 143
Henick, Mark, 450
Hertz, Heinrich, 160
Hewitt, Don, 78
Hewitt, Hugh, 174
hidden-fear appeal, 330
hieroglyphics, 35
high culture, 18–19, 138
Highlights for Children, 112

Hill, Lewis Kimball, 176
Hilliard, Robert, 174–75
Hine, Lewis, 106
hip-hop, 135, 144–46
History Channel, 418
Hitchcock, Alfred, 199
Hole, 144
Holly, Buddy, 139
Hollywood
　See also film industry; movies
　anti-communism and, 214
　cultural imperialism and, 426
　directors, 199
　gender problem in, 199–200
　genres, 198–99
　Golden Age of, 196–200
　narrative style in, 198–200
　race barrier in, 200, 202–3
　self-regulation in, 389–391
　studio system, 193–96
　transformation of, 204–6
Hollywood Ten, 214
Holmes, Oliver Wendell, 380
HoloLens, 268
Holt, Lester, 77
home entertainment, 206
HomePod, 269
home video and recording, 239–240
home-viewing market, 207
Honeymooners, The, 228
Horkheimer, Max, 447
Houghton Mifflin, 38
household products, 318
House Un-American Activities Committee (HUAC), 214
Howlin' Wolf, 136
HTML (hypertext markup language), 260
Hulk Hogan, 121, 384, 386
Hulu, 41, 44, 206, 210, 220, 239, 240, 244, 247, 292, 328, 420, 421, 423, 424
human-interest stories, 61, 74
Hunt, Jonathan, 119
Hunting Ground, The, 201
Hurley, Chad, 404
Hurricane Maria, 444
Hüsker Dü, 144
Hustler, 383
Hynde, Chrissie, 144
hypertext, 260
hypodermic-needle model, 438–39
hypotheses, 441

IBM 360, 256
iBookstore, 41
Ice-T, 145
iCloud, 269
iconoscope, 223
identity theft, 275
Iger, Robert, 421
IGN, 296
iHeartMedia, 18, 158
iHeartRadio, 177
illuminated manuscripts, 35
illustration, 103
I Love Lucy, 227–28
immersion, in gaming, 297–98
Ince, Thomas, 194–95
Incredibles 2, 198
indecent speech, 393–94
independent bookstores, 49, 411
independent film companies, 195, 201
independent film distribution, 207–8
independent film festivals, 204
independent films, 204, 213
independent publishers, 45
independent variables, 441
India, film industry in, 200–201
indie rock, 144
indies, 147–48, 201, 204
individualism, 8–9, 20, 79
Industrial Revolution, 8, 60, 285, 315, 349
information, digitization of, 255
information economy, transition to, 406–10
information security, 274–77
infotainment, 236
in-game advertising, 306
in-game chat, 296
Ingraham, Laura, 174
innovation, 403–4
Instagram, 47, 87–88, 263, 266, 270, 326
Instapoets, 47
Instructions Not Included, 200
InStyle, 110
intellectual properties, 307
intellectuals, 452–53
interest films, 201
Internet, 6, 12, 253–281
　access, 277–78, 279
　advertising, 270–71, 325–29, 411, 414
　archiving, 274
　beginnings of, 254–55
　broadband, 261, 272–73, 277–78
　censorship, 277
　commercialization of, 259–262, 278–79
　communication policy and, 395
　control of, 268–270
　controversial content on, 277
　customization and, 278–79
　in a democratic society, 277–79
　early history of, 256–59
　economics of, 268–274
　evolution of, 259–265
　expansion of, 258–59
　First Amendment and, 392
　hate groups on, 431–32
　impact on media industries, 413–14
　as information superhighway, 254–55
　journalism and, 72–73, 75
　meaning-making process and, 17–18
　media convergence and, 255, 262–64
　movies and, 206, 210–13
　net neutrality, 272–73, 395
　noncommercial, 274
　online magazines, 114–15
　online news, 83–84
　ownership, 278–79
　public relations and, 363–64
　search engines, 261–62, 270
　security, 274–77
　Semantic Web, 265
　social gaming, 293–95
　social media and, 262–64
　television and, 240
　video streaming, 219–220, 221
Internet Archive, 274
Internet Explorer, 260
Internet gaming disorder (IGD), 300
Internet of things, 253–54, 265
Internet radio, 131, 134, 176, 177
Internet service providers (ISPs), 260–61, 272
interpretation, 22, 23
interpretive journalism, 65, 67
interviews, e-mail, 72–73
inverted pyramid, 63, 76
investigative journalism, 64, 68–69
Investigative Reporters and Editors (IRE), 69
invisible stereotyping, 332
Invisible War, The, 201
io9.com, 213
IowaWatch, 69
iPads, 42
iPhone, 269, 386–87
iPods, 131, 177, 269, 422

Iraq, 264
IRE. *See* Investigative Reporters and Editors (IRE)
irritation advertising, 330
Ishibashi, Kaoru, 148
ISIS, 264
iTunes, 131, 150, 152, 240, 269, 410, 422–23

Jagger, Mick, 139
jazz, 135
Jazz Singer, The, 188, 197–98
J. B. Lippincott, 38
Jefferson, Thomas, 101, 377
Jefferson Airplane, 143
Jeffries, Jim, 389
Jenkins, Barry, 200, 203
Jennings, Waylon, 146
Jessica Jones, 21, 44
Jet, 113
Jett, Joan, 144
Jobs, Steve, 269
Joe Camel, 337
Johnson, Jack, 389
Johnson, John H., 113
Johnson, Lyndon, 227, 231
Johnson, Robert, 136, 140
Johnson & Johnson, 360–61
Jolson, Al, 197
Joplin, Janis, 143
journalism, 57–97
    See also news
    across media, 67, 70–73
    attacks on, 92, 94–95
    blogging and, 88–89
    cable news and, 71–72
    changes, challenges, and threat to, 87–91
    citizen, 89
    in a democratic society, 58, 68–69, 93–95
    detective, 58
    early history of, 59–64
    economics of, 82–86
    ethics and, 79–81, 93–94
    evolution of newspaper, 65–67
    future of, 94–95
    "golden age" of, 75
    human-interest stories, 61
    Internet and, 72–73
    interpretive, 65, 67
    inverted pyramid reports, 63, 76
    investigative, 64, 68–69

muckraking, 104–5
neutrality in, 75–76
news culture, 73–81
objective, 66
objectivity and, 65
photojournalism, 103, 105–7
professionalization of, 65–67
professional standards in, 78–79
public relations and, 364–67
radio and, 70
satiric, 89–90
social media and, 87–88
spin strategies and, 369
television and, 70–72
values in American, 75–79
watchdog, 94
wire services, 63
yellow, 63–64
journalistic principles, 73–74
journalists
    conflicts of interest for, 81
    credibility of, 58, 75–76
    demographics of, 77–78
    employment outlook for, 82
    harassment of, 92, 94–95
    layoffs of, 86
    social responsibility of, 93–94
    training of, 66–67
    TV, 70–71
Jovovich, Milla, 305
Joyce, James, 52, 383
jukeboxes, 171
juvenile delinquency, rock music and, 138

Kaepernick, Colin, 348
Kalish, Rachel, 24–25
Kanopy, 249
Kant, Immanuel, 81
Karim, Jawed, 404
Katz, Jackson, 24, 25
Kaur, Rupi, 47
KDKA, 163–64
Keith, Michael, 174–75
Kennard, William E., 182
Kennedy, John F., 106, 368
Keyhole, 357
Khashoggi, Jamal, 95
Kickstarter, 308
Kimmel, Jimmy, 89
Kimmel, Michael, 24–25
Kindle, 41, 269
Kindle Fire, 42, 269

kinescopes, 227
kinetograph, 191
kinetoscope, 191
King, Stephen, 44
Kinks, the, 141
Klapper, Joseph, 439
Klear, 357
knowledge, access to, 37
Korean War, 67
Kotaku, 296
Kraft, Robert, 348
Kristofferson, Kris, 146
Kwan, Kevin, 44

labor, cheap, 414–15
labor unions, 414–15
Ladies' Home Journal, 105, 111
Ladies' Magazine, 103
Lamar, Kendrick, 145
Lasswell, Harold, 434
Last Week Tonight, 90, 240
Late Show with Stephen Colbert, The, 90
Latina, 113
Lauer, Matt, 77
League of Legends, 293
Learning Tree, The, 202
Leave It to Beaver, 232
Leaves of Grass (Whitman), 52
Lee, Ang, 200
Lee, Harper, 52
Lee, Ivy Ledbetter, 351–52
Lee, Spike, 200, 202, 203, 215
Lego Movie, The, 208
leisure magazines, 111–12
leisure time, 286
L'Engle, Madeleine, 44, 200
Le Prince, Louis Aimé Augustin, 190
Lessig, Lawrence, 453
Let Us Now Praise Famous Men (Agee), 93
leveraged purchases, 86
Levin, Mark, 174
Lewis, Jerry Lee, 139
Lewis, John, 31
LGBTQ community, 232–33, 309, 442–43
libel, 60, 381–83
libertarian model, 378
Liberty and the News (Lippmann), 433
Liberty Media, 248
libraries, research, 50
licenses
    music, 132–33
    music industry, 150

licensing fees, 150, 208, 305–7
Lieberman, Joe, 307
Life, 105, 106, 108, 109
Life of an American Fireman, The, 192
Lifetime, 418
Limbaugh, Rush, 172, 174, 175, 394
limited competition, 407–8
limited-effects model, 439
Lindbergh, Charles, 165–66, 198
linear model, 17–18
LinkedIn, 262, 356
linotype, 37
Linux, 274
Lippmann, Walter, 67, 433
literacy, spread of, 8
literacy rates, 8
lithography, offset, 37
Lithuania, 267
Little, Brown, 38
Little Mermaid, 419
Little Richard, 139, 140
Living Desert, The, 419
living wage, 413
Lizzo, 145
LL Cool J, 145
lobbying, 362–63, 368–69
lobbyists, 351
local monopolies, 425
local radio stations, 171, 176, 180, 182
Lolita (Nabokov), 52
Lone Ranger, The, 167
longitudinal studies, 442
long lines, 165
long-playing records (LPs), 129
Look, 109
Lord & Taylor, 329
Lotz, Amanda, 411
low culture, 19, 138
Lowenthal, Leo, 447
low-power FM (LPFM), 182
LPs. *See* long-playing records (LPs)
LSD, 143
Lucas, George, 187, 199
Lucasfilm, 209, 421
Lucky Strike campaign, 354, 355
Lumière, Auguste, 191
Lumière, Louis, 191
Lumino City, 309
Lynch, Roger, 178

M*A*S*H, 228
Macklemore, 125, 145

Macmillan, 38
Madden, John, 307
Madden NFL, 294
Maddow, Rachel, 72
magalogs, 120
magazine chains, 118, 120
magazines, 99–123
　advertisements in, 116–17, 121
　age-specific, 112
　alternative, 114
　circulation and distribution, 103–4, 117–18
　defined, 101
　in a democratic society, 120–21
　demographic editions, 117
　departments, 115–18
　digital distribution of, 117–18
　distribution and production costs, 104
　early history of, 101–3
　in eighteenth-century America, 102
　elite, 112–13
　entertainment, leisure, and sports, 111–12
　evolution of modern, 103–10
　general-interest, 105, 109–10
　international editions of, 120
　limited-distribution, 120
　media convergence and, 119
　men's and women's, 111
　minority, 113
　muckrakers and, 104–5, 108, 120
　in nineteenth-century America, 102–3
　online, 114–15, 117–18
　organization and economics of, 115–120
　origins of, 102
　photojournalism and, 105–7, 108
　regional editions, 116–17
　religious, 102–3
　role of, 100
　self-published, 114
　specialty, 111–12
　split-run editions, 117
　supermarket tabloids, 114
　top 10 by circulation, 110
　trade, 113–14
　in twentieth century, 103
　types of, 110–15
　women's, 103
magic lantern, 189–190
Magnavox, 287
Magnolia Story, The (Gaines and Gaines), 40
Maine, USS, 106
Malcolm X, 51, 203

male stereotypes, 332
malware, 276
Manchester by the Sea, 269
M&M commercials, 334
manga, 31, 306
Man in the High Castle, The, 269
Mann, Estle Ray, 287
Manning, Chelsea, 379
manufacturing-based economy, 406
manuscript (written) culture, 6–7, 35
manuscripts, illuminated, 35
March for Our Lives, 18
Marconi, Guglielmo, 160–61
Marconi Wireless Telegraph Company, 161, 163
Marcus Theatres, 209
marketing
　See also advertising
　books, 46
　digital out-of-home, 313–14
　Internet, 325–29
　movies, 211, 212–13
　research, 435–36
　viral, 323, 327
market research, 322
Marlboro, 331
Martin, George R. R., 44
Martin, Trayvon, 3, 264
Marvel, 43, 209
Marvel Entertainment, 421
Marvelettes, 142
Marvel films, 209
Marvelous Mrs. Maisel, The, 269
Marx, Karl, 51, 447
masculinity, 24–25, 138–39
mass communication
　defined, 6
　digital era of, 10–12
　electronic era of, 9–10
　evolution of, 6–12
　oral era of, 6–7
　print era of, 7–9
　written era of, 6–7
mass customization, 279
massively multiplayer online role-playing games (MMORPGs), 293
mass market paperbacks, 40
mass media
　commercialism of, 15
　criticism of, 5
　defined, 6
　diversity of, 21

evolution of, 12, 14
information economy and, 406–10
journalism across, 67, 70–73
process of communication and, 12–16
social impact of, 14–15
mass medium stage, 14
mass production
of books, 8
of consumer products, 8
mass shootings, 24
Masterpiece Theatre, 229
Maxim, 111
Maxwell, James, 160
McCarthy, Joseph, 70
McCombs, Maxwell, 445
McDonald's, 331
McGraw-Hill Book Company, 38
McGraw-Hill Education, 45
McLure's, 105
McQueen, Steve, 202
Meat Inspection Act, 105
mechanical gaming, 286–87
mechanical royalties, 152
media
See also mass media; news media; social media
criticism of, 5
critiquing, 21–23, 26–27
democracy and, 26
evolution of, 12, 14
masculinity and the, 24–25
role of, 4–5, 14–16
study of the, 16–21
as watchdog for democracy, 5
Media Access Project, 396
media buyers, 324
media conglomerates
in book publishing, 38, 44–45
control of commercial speech by, 340
democracy and, 426–27
in film industry, 208–9
global audiences and, 421
global marketplace and, 404–5
international, 215
in magazine industry, 115, 118, 120
in newspaper industry, 86
in radio industry, 181–82
rise of, 409–10
synergy and, 418
in television, 237
media consolidation, 11–12, 147, 246–48, 406, 409

media consumption, by platform, 15
media convergence, 6, 11–12, 14, 21, 72–73
e-books and, 41–42
gaming and, 292
Internet and, 255, 262–64
magazines and, 119
movies and, 210–13
radio and, 176–79
television and, 239–240, 246, 248–49
media corporations, 86, 404–5
deregulation and, 408–9
downsizing by, 415
hegemony of, 415–17
operation of, 412–13
profits of, 411
revenue sources for, 412–13
size of, 411
media economics, 403–29
analyzing, 412–17
social issues in, 424–26
media effects, 438–446
media effects research, 432
media industries, 5
business trends in, 414–15
evolution of, 12
financial power of, 15–16
Internet and, 413–14
structure of, 406–8
media literacy, 5
case studies
banned books and "family values," 52–53
dark side of gaming culture, 302–3
evolution of photojournalism, 106–7
fake news and propaganda, 398–99
investigative journalism, 68–69
Hollywood's race barrier, 202–3
masculinity and the media, 24–25
music modernization, 132–33
Netflix and streaming revolution, 422–23
net neutrality, 272–73
public relations, 354–55
race, gender, and sexual orientation in TV programming, 232–33
stereotyping in advertising, 332–33
talk radio, 174–75
TV depictions of suicide and copycats, 450–51
critical process behind, 22, 23, 26
cultural model of, 18–19

linear model of, 17–18
media marketplace, in a democratic society, 426–27
media partnerships, 424–25
media portrayals
negative impact of, 26
positive impact of, 26
media relations, 359–361
media research, 431–456
conducting, 440–43
contemporary media effects theories, 443–46
content analysis, 442–43
cultural approaches to, 446–452
in a democratic society, 452–53
early methods, 433–36
experiments, 441
marketing research, 435–36
media effects, 438–446
propaganda analysis, 434
public opinion research, 434–35
social psychology studies, 435
social scientific research, 438–446
survey research, 441–42
medium, 6
Meet the Press, 227
mega-agencies, 320–21
megaplexes, 210
Méliès, Georges, 187–88, 192
Men's Health, 111, 120
Men's Journal, 25
men's magazines, 111
Meredith Corporation, 118, 120
mergers and acquisitions (M&As), 44–45, 237, 238–39, 404–5, 406, 407, 409, 424–25
"Message, The" (Grandmaster Flash and the Furious Five), 145
#MeToo movement, 4, 77–78, 113, 200, 348
Meyers, Seth, 89
MGM, 193
Miami Herald Publishing Co. v. Tornillo, 392–93
Mickey Mouse, 380–81, 418–19
microprocessors, 256, 258
Microsoft, 268, 290, 323, 331, 410, 411
Middle Ages, 35
middle class, 8, 60–61
Midwest Video case, 238
military PR, 358
Milk and Honey (Kaur), 47

Mill, John Stuart, 81
Miller, Stephanie, 174
Miller v. California, 383–84
Milton, John, 376, 377
Minaj, Nicki, 148
Minassian, Alek, 431
Minhaj, Hasan, 90
minimal-effects model, 439
miniseries, 230
minority groups
  gaming and, 308–9
  media ownership and, 409
  stereotypes of, 332–33
  on television, 232–33
minority journalists, 77
minority magazines, 113
Minutemen, the, 144
Miracle, The, 390
misinformation, 91
misogyny, in gamer culture, 300–303
Mister Rogers' Neighborhood, 231
Miyamoto, Shigeru, 290
Miyazaki, Hayao, 199
mobile devices
  See also smartphones
  advertising on, 320, 325, 326, 336
  podcasts on, 158
mobile gaming, 292, 300, 308–9
mobile magazine editions, 118–19
mobile video, 240
modding, 296
modern era, 20
Modern Maturity, 112
mom bloggers, 364
monopolies, 163, 406–7, 408, 409–10, 425
Moonlight, 203
moonshots, 403
Moonves, Les, 342
Moore, Michael, 215
moral codes, 81
Morning Edition, 175, 176
morning news programs, 71
Morrison, Jim, 143
Morse, Samuel, 160
Morse code, 160, 161
Mortal Kombat, 308
Mosaic, 260
Motion Picture Association of America (MPAA), 205, 390–91
Motion Picture Patents Company, 193–94
Motion Picture Producers and Distributors of America (MPPDA), 390

Motion Picture Production Code, 205, 390, 435
motivation, 444
motor reproduction, 444
Motown, 141–42
moveable type, 7, 34, 36
movie directors, 199, 202–3
movie palaces, 196
movies, 9–10, 187–217
  See also film industry
  animated, 418–421
  in a democratic society, 214–15
  Disney, 215, 419–421
  distribution of, 195, 207–8, 210–13
  documentaries, 201
  early history of, 189–193
  exhibition of, 195–96, 209–10
  feature-length, 197
  First Amendment and, 388–391
  game-inspired, 305–6
  genres, 198–99
  home entertainment, 206
  independent, 204, 213
  marketing, 211, 212–13
  media convergence and, 210–13
  narrative, 191–92
  nickelodeons, 192–93
  production of, 194–95, 207
  product placement in, 334
  ratings system, 205, 390–91
  silent, 14, 192, 196–97
  special effects, 198, 211
  talkies, 197–98
movie streaming services, 206
movie studios, 193, 208
movie theaters, 195–96
  black, 202
  nickelodeons, 192–93
Movietone, 198
MP3 format, 127, 130–31
MSNBC, 72
muckrakers, 104–5, 108, 120
Muddy Waters, 136
multichannel video programming distributors (MVPDs), 247
multimedia ads, 325
multiplayer online battle arenas (MOBAs), 293–94
multiple-system operators (MSOs), 247
multiplexes, 210
Murdoch, Rupert, 405
Murrow, Edward R., 67, 70

music
  blues, 136
  country, 139, 146, 172
  cover, 137
  democracy and, 152–53
  digital, 127, 130–31, 132–33, 147–152
  disco, 144
  distribution of, 147, 149–150
  folk, 135, 142
  gangster rap, 145
  grunge, 144
  hip-hop, 135, 144–46
  jazz, 135
  licensing, 132–33, 150
  pop, 134–146
  popular, 125–26
  power structure in, 147–48
  punk rock, 143–44
  R&B, 136, 137
  recorded, 129–130
  rock, 134–140, 143–44, 153
  rockabilly, 139
  sales, 149–150, 151
  sheet, 135
  soul, 141–42
  streaming, 131, 132–33, 134, 149, 150, 152, 178, 180–81
music industry, 18
  censorship and, 138
  digital music streaming and, 131, 132–33
  economics of, 146–152
  evolution of, 126–134
  indies, 147–48
  international, 150
  market share of major labels, 148
  new forms of distribution in, 125–26
  profits in, 150, 151, 152
  radio and, 134, 135, 180
  royalties, 150, 152, 180
  360-degree agreements, 151
  Tin Pan Alley, 135
music labels, 144, 147–48, 180
Music Modernization Act (MMA), 132–33, 150
must-carry rules, 238
Mutual v. Ohio, 389
Muybridge, Eadweard, 190
MySpace, 405

NAB. *See* National Association of Broadcasters (NAB)
Nabokov, Vladimir, 52

Nader, Ralph, 338
NAFTA. *See* North American Free Trade Agreement (NAFTA)
Napster, 130
narrative films, 191–92
narrative techniques
 Hollywood, 198–200
 in silent film, 196–97
narrowcasting, 160, 234
Nashville sound, 146
National Association for the Advancement of Colored People (NAACP), 113, 168, 197
National Association of Broadcasters (NAB), 174, 178, 237–38
National Association of Television Program Executives (NATPE), 244
National Book Award, 31
National Broadcasting Company (NBC), 77, 165, 236, 246
National Dairy Council, 336
National Enquirer, 114
National Football League (NFL), 347–48
National Geographic, 111–12, 119
nationalism, 8
National Press Photographers Association (NPPA), 80
National Public Radio (NPR), 95, 158, 173, 175, 176
National Science Foundation (NSF), 258
national security, 162–63, 379
National Security Agency (NSA), 275
National Television Systems Committee (NTSC), 223
nation-states, 8
Native Peoples, 113
NBC. *See* National Broadcasting Company (NBC)
NBC Nightly News, 27, 77
NC-17 rating, 391
negative publicity, 359–360
negative stereotypes, 332–33
Negro Digest, 113
Nelson, Ricky, 138
Nelson, Willie, 146
Netflix, 44, 204, 210, 219–220, 237, 239, 241, 243, 244, 246, 328, 421, 422–23, 437
net neutrality, 272–73, 395
Netscape, 260
network era, 236
network news, 227, 232–33

network system, of radio, 164–66, 180
network television, 75, 248, 328
neutrality, in news reporting, 75–76
Newcomb, Horace, 448
news, 59
 See also journalism
 culture of, 73–81
 defined, 74–75
 evaluation of, 398–99
 network, 227, 232–33
 reporting, 73–81
 scoops, 78
 sources of, 27
 "spun," 369
 wire services, 63
news aggregation, 88–89
news and talk radio, 172, 174–75, 394
newscasters, 71
News Corp., 405, 409
news delivery, 6
news editors, 84–85
newshole, 83
news media
 attacks on, 94–95
 business model of, 82–84
 cable news, 71–72, 75
 consolidation in, 85–86
 diversity in, 232–33
 downsizing in, 415
 ethics and, 79–81, 93–94
 "fake" news and, 90–91, 396, 398–99
 false equivalency and, 93–94
 Internet, 72–73, 75, 83–84
 public relations and, 364–67
 radio, 70
 social media and, 87–88
 television, 70–72
newspaper chains, 86, 94
newspapers, 6
 advertisements, 62, 83–84
 business model of, 82–84
 business outlook for, 82–83
 colonial, 59–60
 community, 86
 consolidation of, 85–86
 evolution of journalism, 65–67
 expansion of, 62–63, 65
 expenses for, 84–85
 future of, 94–95
 online, 72–73
 op-ed pages, 67
 operations, 84–85

paywalls, 84
penny papers, 60–63, 65
newsreels, 198, 201
news reporters, 84–85
 See also journalists
newsroom
 cutbacks in, 86, 94
 demographics of, 77–78
 employment in, 82
 male-dominated, 77–78
news stories, 78–79
newsworthy, 74
New Yorker, 113
New York Journal, 64
New York Morning Herald, 61–62
New York Sun, 61
New York Times, 14, 27, 32, 65–66, 76, 84, 85, 88
New York Times Magazine, 119
New York Times v. Sullivan, 381–82
New-York Weekly Journal, 60
New York World, 57–58, 64
NFL concussion crisis, 347–48
Niantic Labs, 300
niche markets, 14, 110, 414, 418
niche programming, 234, 249
Nickelodeon, 418
nickelodeons, 192–93
Nielsen Corporation, 244–45, 246
1984 (Orwell), 50
ninjas, 296
Nintendo, 290, 292, 299, 300, 304
 DS, 292
 Entertainment System, 289–290
 eShop, 305
 Game Boy, 292
 Switch, 290, 292
 3DS, 292
 Wii, 297
Nipkow, Paul, 222
Nirvana, 144
Nixon, Richard, 68, 378
Noah, Trevor, 43, 90
Noelle-Neumann, Elisabeth, 445–46
Nolan, Christopher, 199
noncommercial web, 274
nonprofit radio, 173
noobs, 296
Nook, 41
Noory, George, 174
North, music in, 139

North American Free Trade Agreement (NAFTA), 418
novels, dime, 37
novelty stage, of new medium, 12
NPPA. *See* National Press Photographers Association (NPPA)
NSFNET, 258, 260
N. W. Ayer, 316

Oakley, Annie, 350
Obama, Barack, 107, 368
obesity, 336–37
objective journalism, 66
objectivity, 65
obscene material, 277
obscenity, 383–84
Ocasio-Cortez, Alexandria, 368
Occupy Wall Street movement, 264
Ochs, Adolph, 65–66
Ochs, Phil, 142
Oculus VR, 270, 298
Odyssey, 287
Office for iPad, 268
Office Mobile, 268
off-network syndication, 244
offset lithography, 37
offshoring, 418
Ohio Theatre, 196
oligopoly, 147, 193, 205, 246, 407–8, 425
Oliver, John, 27, 89, 90, 240
Olsen, Charlie, 32
Olympics, 284
Once Upon a Deadpool, 213
OneDrive, 268
online advertising, 325–29, 411, 414
online book sales, 49–50
online engagement, 4
online fantasy sports, 294
online fraud, 275
online games, 293–95
online harassment, 92
online magazines, 114–15, 117–18
online music streaming, 131, 134, 149–150, 180–81
online news, 72–73, 75, 83–84
online piracy, 130–31, 150
online predators, 276–77
online radio, 131, 134, 177
online sales, of books, 49–50
op-ed pages, 67
open-source software, 274
opinion and fair comment, 382–83

opposing viewpoints, 93–94
Oprah's Book Club, 43
Oprah Winfrey Show, The, 43
opt-in policies, 276
opt-out policies, 276
oral communication, 6–7
Orange Is the New Black, 23, 228, 422
O'Reilly, Bill, 77
Orwell, George, 50
Oscars, 202–3
#OscarSoWhite, 203
Osmond, Marie, 146
Outcault, R. F., 64
outdoor advertising, 313–14
Outlander, 235
outsourcing, 418
overeating, 336–37
overleveraged, 86
Overwatch, 293, 294
Oxford University Press, 41

Pacifica Foundation, 176
Pac-Man, 288, 289
Page, Larry, 403, 404
Pai, Ajit, 177, 273, 395
paid prioritization, 273
paid search, 326
Paine, Thomas, 9, 101
Palacio, R. J., 44
Paley, William S., 70, 166
Pandora, 131, 177, 178, 179
paper, 35, 37
paperback books, 37, 39, 40
papyrus, 34, 35
Paramount, 193, 208
Paramount decision, 204–5
parchment, 34, 35
Parker, George, 352
Parks, Gordon, 202
Parks, Gordon, Jr., 202
partisan press, 59–60
Parton, Dolly, 146
pass-along readership, 108
patent medicines, 317
Patreon, 308
Patriot Act with Hasan Minhaj, 90
Patton, Charley, 136
PAX, 297
pay models, in gaming industry, 300, 304–6
Payne Fund Studies, 435
payola, 180–81

pay-per-view (PPV), 235–36
pay-to-play system, 373–74
paywalls, 84
Pearl Jam, 144
Pearson, 44–45
Penguin Random House, 45
Penn, William, 317
Pennsylvania Gazette, 60
Penny Arcade, 297
penny arcade, 286–87
penny papers, 60–63, 65
penny press, 60–63
Pentagon Papers, 75, 377–79
People, 109–10, 114, 116, 120
People en Español, 113
performance royalties, 152
Perkins, Carl, 139
Perry, Tyler, 202
personal computers (PCs), 258, 293
personalization, 437
personal safety online, 276–77
persuasive techniques, in advertising, 329–331, 334
Peter, Paul, and Mary, 142
Peter Pan, 224
Pew Research, 4, 84
pharmaceutical advertising, 338
Philip Morris, 331
phishing, 275
phonographs, 128, 135
photojournalism, 103, 105–7, 108
photo researchers, 46
Photoshop, 107
Pickett, Wilson, 141
Pickford, Mary, 194, 195
pinball machines, 286–87
Pinterest, 263
piracy, music, 130–31, 150
pirate radio stations, 182
Pittsburgh Dispatch, 57
Pixar, 209, 420
Pixies, the, 144
Pizzagate, 91
plagiarism, 78
plain-folks pitch, 330
Plato, 14
Playboy, 111
playlists, 180–81
Play Smart, Play Safe initiative, 348
PlayStation, 290
PlayStation 4, 290
PlayStation Portable (PSP), 292

PlayStation Store, 305
PlayStation Vita, 292
podcasts, 119, 157–58, 176, 177
Pod Save America, 157
poetry, 47
point-to-point communication, 160, 163
Pokémon Go, 298, 299
police shooting, of black people, 3
political action committees (PACs), 374
political activism, 264
political advertising, 340–42, 369
political broadcasts, 394
political campaigns, 341, 367–69, 373–74
political economy studies, 449
political elections, social media fraud and, 266–67
political talk radio, 394
politics
  media conglomerates and, 426–27
  pay-to-play system, 373–74
  public relations and, 367–69
  social media and, 10, 368
PolitiFact.com, 398
Polo, Susana, 32
POM Wonderful Presents: The Greatest Movie Ever Sold, 334
Pong, 284, 287, 289
pop (popular) music, 125–26
  alternative rock, 144
  blurring of boundaries and, 138–140
  British invasion, 140–41
  censorship and, 137–38
  country, 146
  evolution of, 140–152
  folk music, 142
  gangster rap, 145
  genres, 134–35
  grunge, 144
  hip-hop, 144–46
  Motown, 141–42
  punk, 143–44
  race and, 137, 139
  rise of, 135–36
  rock and, 134–140
  rock and roll, 136–38
Popov, Alexander, 161
popular culture, 19
populism, 20
pop-under ads, 325
pop-up ads, 325
pornography, 277, 385
portable cassette players, 130

portable consoles, 292
Porter, Edwin S., 192
Portlandia, 228
postmodern period, 20–21
Precious, 202
premium cable, 235–36
Prentice Hall, 38
presidential elections
  "fake" news and, 90–91, 398–99
  public relations and, 367–69
  social media fraud and, 266–67
  of 2016, 88, 91, 92, 266–67, 341, 398–99
Presley, Elvis, 137, 138, 139, 146, 230
press
  See also journalists; news media
  control of, by government, 8
  government control of the, 378
  partisan, 59–60
  penny, 60–63
  responsibilities of, 67
  tensions between PR and, 364–67
  vilification of, 94–95
press agents, 350–51
press freedom. *See* free press
press releases, 357
Prevention, 120
Price Is Right, The, 168
Pride, Charlie, 146
prime time, 225, 243, 244–45
Prime Time Access Rule (PTAR), 236
print books, 39–41
print era, 7–9
printing, block, 36
printing press, 7, 8, 34, 36–37
print shops, 37
prior restraint, 377, 379
Privacy Act of 1974, 386
privacy issues
  Facebook and, 271, 276
  on Internet, 254, 274–77
privacy rights, 384, 386–87
private equity firms, 86
private research, 440
private-sector monopoly, 163
probabilistic identity, 327
Procter & Gamble, 324
product differentiation, 199, 317
production and technology department, 116
product placement, 334
product placement fees, 208
product reviews, 329

product standardization, 199
professional books, 40
professional codes of ethics, 80
professionalization, of journalism, 65–67
profit maximization, 412–13
Progressive Era, 20
Progressive magazine, 379
Project Loon, 403
Project Runway, 168
propaganda, 263, 264, 356–57, 358, 368
propaganda analysis, 434
proprietary research, 440
Protestant Reformation, 8
PR Watch, 354, 366
PRWeek, 366
PSAs. *See* public service announcements (PSAs)
pseudo-events, 361
pseudo-polls, 435
psychedelic rock, 143
Psycho, 199
psychographics, 322
PTAR. *See* Prime Time Access Rule (PTAR)
Public Broadcasting Act of 1967, 176, 231
Public Broadcasting Service (PBS), 176, 231
Public Citizen, 338
public domain, 370
Public Enemy, 145
public good, 413
publicity, 213, 350
Publick Occurrences, Both Forreign and Domestick, 60
Public Opinion (Lippmann), 433
public opinion research, 434–35
public relations (PR), 79, 347–371
  vs. advertising, 348–49
  agencies, 353, 356, 369
  communications, 357
  community and consumer relations, 361–62
  defined, 349, 353
  in a democratic society, 367–69
  early history of, 350–53
  emergence of professional, 351–53
  ethics and, 366–67
  evolution of, 353–364
  functions, 356–57, 359–363
  in-house services, 353, 356
  image of, 366
  in Internet age, 363–64

public relations (PR) *(continued)*
  invisible hand of, 354–55
  lobbying, 362–63
  media relations, 359–361
  military, 358
  NFL, 347–48
  research by, 357
  role of, 348–49, 368–69
  social media and, 364
  special and pseudo-events, 361
  tensions between press and, 364–67
Public Relations Society of America (PRSA), 353, 366, 367
public research, 440
public service announcements (PSAs), 319, 339, 359
public sphere, 398
public television, 231
publishing houses
  early, 38
  independent, 45
publishing industry
  Amazon and, 49–50
  conglomerates, 38, 44–45
  consolidation in, 44–45
  early, 37
  electronic and digital publishing, 41–43
  evolution of modern, 38–41
  influence of television and film on, 43–44
  organization and economics of, 44–50
  self-publishing and, 42–43
  structure of, 46, 48–50
  trade organizations, 39
  trends in, 41–44
puffery, 340
PUGs (pick-up groups), 295–96
Pulitzer, Joseph, 57, 64, 67
Pulitzer Prize, 64, 66, 67, 78, 113
pulp fiction, 37
punctuation, 35
punk rock, 143–44
Pure Food and Drug Act, 105, 317

Quake, 284
Quaker Oats, 317
Queen Latifah, 145
Queer Eye for the Straight Guy, 19
Quinn, Zoe, 302
quiz shows, 168, 224–25

race
  barriers in Hollywood and, 202–3
  media ownership and, 409
  television and, 232–33
"race" charts, 136
race relations, 137, 139, 168
radicalization, online, 431–32
radio, 6, 9–10, 67, 70, 156–185
  advertising, 164–65, 179–180
  AM, 170
  authority of, 168–69
  characteristics of contemporary, 171–79
  convergence and, 176–79
  as cultural mirror, 168
  in a democratic society, 182–83
  digital turn in, 176–79
  early history of, 159–169
  early programming, 167–68
  economics of, 179–182
  evolution of, 169–171
  FM, 170, 177
  format, 170–73
  golden age of, 157, 167–69
  impact of television on, 169
  Internet, 131, 134, 176
  invention of, 159–160, 162
  music industry and, 134, 135, 180
  networks, 164–66, 180
  news and talk, 172, 174–75, 394
  noncommercial, 175
  nonprofit, 173, 176
  ownership, 181–82
  payola, 180
  playlists, 180–81
  podcasts and, 157–58, 177
  programming, 180–81
  regulation of, 162–64, 166–67, 392
  role of, 158–59
  satellite, 179, 180
  streaming, 178, 179
  talk, 10
  topless, 393
  transistor, 169–170
Radio Act of 1912, 162
Radio Act of 1927, 166–67
Radio Corporation of America (RCA), 41, 129, 163, 164, 165, 168, 223
Radiohead, 125, 151
radio stations, 163–66, 170–73, 176, 180, 181–82, 407–8
  HD, 179

Radio Television Digital News Association (RTDNA), 80
radio waves, 160
Radway, Janice, 449
railroads, 315, 351, 368–69
Rainey, Ma, 136
Ramones, 143
Ramsey, Dave, 174
Rand Corporation, 257
Rand McNally, 38
random assignment, 441
Random House, 38, 45
Ranger Rick, 112
rap music, 144–46
"Rapper's Delight" (Sugarhill Gang), 145
Rascal Flatts, 148
ratings system, 244–46, 307, 390–91
rational order, 20
Ray Donovan, 235
RCA. *See* Radio Corporation of America (RCA), 41
Readers' Digest, 105, 109, 120
reading, resiliency of, 51
Reagan, Ronald, 174, 408
reality shows, 168, 230–31
Real World, The, 230
Rebel without a Cause, 206
record companies, 138
recorded music, 129–130
recording industry. *See* music industry
recording labels, 150, 151, 153
recording sessions, 148
record players, 128–29
records, 128–29, 130, 147
recreational drugs, 143
RedBox, 240
Redding, Otis, 141
Red Lion Broadcasting Co. v. FCC, 392
Reese, Rhett, 212
Reeves, Jim, 146
reference books, 40
Regal Entertainment Group, 209
regional editions, 116–17
regulation
  of advertising, 318–19, 335–340
  of broadcasting, 392–93, 393–94
  of communications industry, 408–9
  of films, 388–391
  of monopolies, 408
  of radio, 162–64, 166–67, 392
  of television, 236–39
  of video games, 307

Reidenberg, Dan, 451
relationships, close, 13
religion, rock music and, 139–140
religious books, 40
religious magazines, 102–3
RELX Group, 44, 45
R.E.M., 144
Report for America (RFA), 69
research, media. *see* media research
research libraries, 50
Resident Evil, 305, 306
resistance, to authority, 8
responsible capitalism, 79
retail music sales, 150
retail stores, 316–17
retention, 444
retransmission fees, 243
Reuters, 85
Review, 102
review boards, 389
Reynolds, Ryan, 212
rhythm and blues (R&B), 136, 137
right to privacy, 384, 386–87
Rihanna, 125
Riis, Jacob, 106
Riot Games, 284
RKO, 193
rockabilly, 139
rock and roll, 136–38
Rockefeller, John D., Jr., 352
Rockefeller, John D., Sr., 105, 407
"Rocket 88," 139
rock music, 134–140, 153
  alternative, 144
  arrival of, 136–38
  boundary blurring, 138–140
  British invasion, 140–41
  grunge, 144
  indie, 144
  psychedelic, 143
  punk, 143–44
Rodale Press, 120
Rodriguez, Gina, 232
Rodriguez, Robert, 204
Rogers, Kenny, 146
Rogue One: A Star Wars Story, 209
Roku, 240
Rolling Stone, 111
Rolling Stones, 139, 140, 141, 143
"Roll Over Beethoven" (Berry), 138
Roosevelt, Franklin Delano, 70, 167, 413
Roosevelt, Theodore, 105

Roots, 230, 232
Rose, Charlie, 78
Roseanne, 232
Ross, Bob, 213
Ross, Diana, 142
Ross, Harold, 112
rotary presses, 37
rotation, of songs on radio, 171
Roundhay Garden Scene, 190
Rowling, J. K., 300
royalties
  book industry, 42, 46
  gaming industry, 306–7
  music industry, 150, 152, 180
RTDNA. *See* Radio Television Digital News Association (RTDNA)
Run-DMC, 145
Rushdie, Salman, 51
Russia, 92, 266–67

Salon, 115
Salt-N-Pepa, 145
Sanford and Son, 232
Sarkeesian, Anita, 301, 302–3
Sarnoff, David, 170
Satanic Verses, The (Rushdie), 51
satellite radio, 179, 180
satellite television, 221, 226, 234, 242, 248, 421
satiric journalism, 89–90
saturation advertising, 324
Saturday Evening Post, 103, 105, 108, 109
Saturday Night Live, 90, 228
Saudi Arabia, 363
Savage, Michael, 174
Scalia, Antonin, 308
scanning disk, 222
Scarlet Letter, The (Hawthorne), 52
Schenck, Charles T., 380
Schenck v. United States, 380
Scholastic, 45
School Library Journal, 398
School of Journalism, University of Missouri, 67
school shootings, 18
scientific method, 440–41
scoops, 78
Scorsese, Martin, 199
Scott, Walter, 89
Scribner's, 38
scripted programming, 237
scrolls, 35

Sea Hero Quest, 299
Seal Island, 419
search engines, 261–62, 263, 270, 326
Seau, Junior, 347
Section 315, 394
security
  Internet, 253–54, 274–77
  smart devices and, 265
sedition, 380
Sedition Act, 377, 380
seditious libel, 60
Seeger, Pete, 142
See It Now, 70
Sega Dreamcast, 290
Sega Genesis, 289
Seinfeld, 237
selective exposure, 439
selective retention, 439
self-published magazines, 114
self-publishing, 42–43
Selma, 200
Semantic Web, 259, 265
senders, 17, 18
sensationalism, 15, 63–64
"separate but equal" laws, 137
September 11, 2001, 363
Serial, 157
serial programs, 230
Sernoff, David, 165
Sesame Street, 231
Seventeen, 112
78s, 129
Sex and the Single Girl (Brown), 100
Sex Pistols, 143
sexting, 385
sexual harassment, 77–78, 200, 348
sexual identity, 138–39
sexual orientation, 138–39, 232–33
sexual predators, 276–77
Shadow, The, 167
Shaheen, Jack, 447, 448
shareholder dividends, 85
shares, 245
Shaw, Donald, 445
sheet music, 135
shield laws, 387
shootings, 431
Showtime, 235
Shyamalan, M. Night, 200
silent film, 14, 192, 196–97
Silent Spring (Carson), 50
Simon, Scott, 95

Simon & Schuster, 38
Simpson, O. J., 388
Sinatra, Frank, 136, 166
Sinclair Broadcast Group, 94, 409
Singing Fool, The, 197
Singleton, John, 200, 202
Siouxsie and the Banshees, 143
Siri, 254, 265
Sirius, 179
SiriusXM, 179
Sitting Bull, 350
situation comedy (sitcom), 228
Sixth Amendment, 376, 387–88
60 Minutes, 78, 230
sketch comedy, 228
slacktivism, 4
slander, 381
Slate, 115
Sleater-Kinney, 144
Slovakia, 267
small-town pastoralism, 79
smart devices, 265
smartphones, 6, 278
   See also mobile devices
   advertising on, 326
   citizen journalism and, 89
   e-books on, 42
   gaming on, 292
   iPhone, 269
   radio and, 176, 177
   television and, 240
smart TVs, 240
"Smells Like Teen Spirit" (Nirvana), 144
Smillie, Ella, 333
Smith, Bessie, 136
Smith, Jamil, 203
Smith, Kevin, 204
Smith, Patti, 144
smoking advertising, 337
smoking prevention campaigns, 339
Snapchat, 119, 261, 263, 326
snob appeal, 330
Snopes.com, 398
Snowden, Edward, 275, 379
Snow White and the Seven Dwarfs, 419
soap operas, 168, 230
social anxiety, 13
social cognitive theory, 444
social fragmentation, 11
social gaming, 293–95
social impact, of mass media, 14–15
social issues, 424–26

social learning theory, 443–44
social media
   activism using, 3–4
   advertising, 326–27
   democracy and, 263–64
   FOMO and, 13
   fraud and elections and, 266–67
   impact of, 4
   journalism and, 87–88
   meaning-making process and, 17–18
   military PR and, 358
   movie marketing and, 213
   politics and, 10, 368
   power of, 4
   public relations and, 364
   trolls, 92
   types of, 262–63
social movements, 142
social networking sites, 87–88, 262–63, 295
social protest, 143, 264
social psychology studies, 435
social reform, 104–5, 120
social responsibility, 93–94
social responsibility model, 378
social scientific research, 438–446
   See also media effects; media research
   conducting, 440–43
   contemporary media effects theories, 443–46
   early models of media effects, 438–440
   evaluating, 446
Society of European Stage Authors and Composers (SESAC), 152
Society of Professional Journalists (SPJ), 80
socioeconomic classes, 8
Socrates, 14
software, open-source, 274
Solo: A Star Wars Story, 209
songwriters, 152, 180
Sonic Youth, 144
Sony, 41, 181, 290, 418
Sony Music Entertainment, 147
Sopranos, The, 235
Sorry to Bother You, 199
soul music, 141–42
sound bites, 71
SoundCloud, 131
Soundgarden, 144
sound recording, 124–155
   in a democratic society, 152–53
   early history of, 127–134

   economics of, 146–152
   invention of, 126–27
   pop music and, 134–146
   radio and, 134
   sales, 149–150
South, music in, 139
Southern Poverty Law Center, 277, 432
Soviet Union, 256
space brokers, 316
Space Invaders, 289
space race, 256
Spacewar! 284
spam, 325–26
Spanish-American War, 106
Spanish language magazines, 113
Spanish-language radio, 173
special effects, 198, 211
special events, 361
specialization, 418, 419
specialty magazines, 111–12
specialty reporters, 85
Specific Media, Inc., 405
Spectator, 102
Spectrum, 261
Spider-Man: Homecoming, 306
Spielberg, Steven, 199
spiral of silence theory, 445–46
SPJ. *See* Society of Professional Journalists (SPJ)
split-run editions, 117
spokespersons, 330
sponsored links, 279
Sports Illustrated, 111, 116–17, 120
sports magazines, 111–12
Spotify, 131, 132–33, 147, 149, 150, 178, 179, 181, 423
Spotlight team, 68–69
Springer Nature, 45
"spun" news, 369
Sputnik, 256
spyware, 276
Standard Oil Company, 105, 352, 407
Staples, Vince, 145
Star, 114
Starbucks, 360
Star Wars, 16, 187–88, 213, 298, 306, 421
Star Wars: Episode VII: The Force Awakens, 187, 209
Star Wars: Episode VIII: The Last Jedi, 187, 209
Star Wars: The Old Republic, 304–5

Star Wars: Episode IX: The Rise of Skywalker, 187
Starz, 235, 248
state model, 378
state-sponsored trolls, 92
station owners, 170–71
Stauber, John, 354–55
Steam, 297, 305
stereo, 129
stereophonic sound, 129
stereotypes, 26, 232–33, 331, 332–33
Stern, Howard, 172
Stewart, Jon, 90
Stockham, Thomas, 130
storyboards, 323
storytelling, 334
Storz, Todd, 170–71
Stowe, Harriet Beecher, 43, 50
S-Town, 157
Strand Theatre, 196
Stranger Things, 219, 243
Strategic Business Insights, 322–23
streaming music, 131, 134, 150, 152, 179, 180–81
streaming services, 131, 132–33, 147, 149, 150, 178
streaming video services, 210, 219–220, 237, 239–240, 241, 243–44, 246, 328, 421, 422–23
studio system, 193–96, 204, 205–7
stunt journalism, 58
subliminal advertising, 319
subscription fees, 246
   newspaper, 83, 84
   streaming music, 131
   television, 243, 246
   video games, 304–5
subsidiary rights, 46
suburbanization, 202, 205, 206
Sugarhill Gang, 145
suicide, TV depictions of, 450–51
suicide behaviors, 24–25
Sullivan, Ed, 141
Sullivan, L. B., 382
Sulzberger, A. G., 95
Sumeria, 35
Summer, Donna, 144
Sun and Her Flowers, The (Kaur), 47
Sunday Night Football, 325
Sunday Times, 106
Super Bowl ads, 325, 337, 343
Supergirl, 44, 232

Super Mario Odyssey, 292
Super Mario World, 290
supermarket tabloids, 114
super PACs, 341, 374
superstations, 234
Supremes, 142
Surface tablet, 268
survey research, 441–42
Survivor, 168
sweatshops, 414
Sweden, 267
swing bands, 135
Switch, 290
symbols, 6
syndicated television, 207, 236–37, 244
syndication, 244
synergy, 38, 209, 418, 419–420
Syria, 264

tablets, 240, 292
tabloids, 114
Tainter, Charles Summer, 128
talkies, 197–98
"talking head" pundits, 72
Talking Heads, 143
talk radio, 10, 172, 174–75, 394
talk shows, 230
Tarantino, Quentin, 199
Tarbell, Ida, 105
targeted advertising, 270–71
Tatler, 102
Technicolor, 205
technology, 5
   embrace of, 21
   privacy issues and, 254, 271, 276, 386–87
   radio, 159–162
   sound recording, 126–27
   television, 222
   video game, 287–88
teenagers
   ads targeting, 335–36
   sexting by, 385
teen magazines, 112
teen smoking, 339
Telecommunications Act of 1996, 181, 238–39, 408–9
telegraph, 6, 9, 159–160, 315
telegraphy, wireless, 160–61
telephone, 164, 165
teleplays, 229
television, 6, 9–10, 67, 219–251

advertising, 224, 245, 246, 319, 328, 335–36, 341, 342
binge watching, 241
cable, 71–72, 221, 225–26, 231, 234–36, 246, 421
channels, 221, 223
Civil Rights movement and, 26
color, 223–24
comedies, 227–28
consolidation in, 246–48
control of content on, 224
decline in viewership, 328
in a democratic society, 248–49
development of, 222–23
digital, 239–242
distribution, 243–44
diversity of programming, 413, 442–43
dramas, 228–230
early history of, 222–26
economics of, 242–48
global audiences for, 420–21
home video and recording and, 239–240
impact on film industry, 205–6
impact on radio, 169
Internet and, 240
media convergence and, 239–240, 246, 248–49
minorities on, 232–33
network, 75, 248, 328
network era, 236
network programming, 226–233
news, 70–72, 227, 232–33
niche programming, 249
prime time, 225, 244–45
production, 242–43
product placement in, 334
programming, 232–33
programs, 224, 227–231
public, 231
quiz show scandal, 224–25
ratings, 244–46
reality, 230–31
regulatory challenges for, 236–39
revenue sources, 243–44
role of, 220–21
satellite, 221, 226, 234, 242, 248, 421
spectaculars, 224
streaming, 219–220
suicide depictions on, 450–51
syndicated, 207, 236–37, 244
talk shows, 230

television *(continued)*
  technical standards, 223
  violence, 15, 445
Television Critics Association (TCA), 89
Telgemeier, Raina, 52
Tencent, 331
terrorist groups, 358
terrorist organizations, 264
Tesla, Nikola, 161
testimonials, 330
Tetris, 289
textbooks, 39
textual analysis, 448–49
Texture app, 118
thaumatrope, 190
theaters, 209–10
Thiel, Peter, 121
third-person effect theory, 446
13 Reasons Why, 450–51
Thomas, Angie, 44
Thomson Reuters, 44, 45
360-degree agreements, 151
throttling, 273
Tidal, 131
tie-in sales, 305–6
Tikkun, 113
TikTok, 263
Timberlake, Justin, 405
Time, 105, 108, 117, 120
Time Inc., 120
time shifting, 239
Time's Up, 200
Time Warner, 410, 424
Tin Pan Alley, 135
Tip Top Weekly, 37
Titanic, 162
TMZ, 110
tobacco advertising, 337
Tocqueville, Alexis de, 433
Today, 71, 224
Today Show, 418
To Kill a Mockingbird (Lee), 52
toll broadcasting, 164–65
Tomason, Audrey, 106–7
Tomb Raider, 305
Tometi, Opal, 3
Tomlinson, Ray, 257
Tonight Show, 224, 230
Top 40 charts, 141
Top 40 programming, 134, 171, 173
Top Chef, 168
topless radio, 393

Topsify, 181
Torvalds, Linus, 274
touring bands, 151
Townsquare Media, 181
Toyota, 323
Toy Story, 420
trade agreements, 418
trade books, 31–32, 39
trade magazines, 113–14
tradition, rejection of, 20
transatlantic cable, 160
transistor radios, 169–170
Transparent, 269
Travel Notes of a Geechee Girl, 203
travelogues, 201
Treasure Island, 419
Tribune Content Agency, 85
Trip to the Moon, A, 187–88, 192
Trojan horses, 276
trolls, 92, 266, 296
True Detective, 230, 235
Truman, Harry, 137
Trump, Donald, 272, 273, 341, 342, 395
  "alternative facts" and, 366
  attacks on journalists by, 92, 94–95
  "fake" news and, 91
  tweeting by, 88, 368
Trust, the, 193–94, 195
Truth Initiative, 339
Tucker, Ken, 143
Tur, Katy, 92
Turner, Ike, 141–42
Turner, Tina, 141–42
turntables, 128–29
TV Guide, 109
TV newsmagazines, 230
TV parental guidelines, 436
TV stations, 223
Twain, Mark, 45, 52
Twain, Shania, 146
12 Years a Slave, 202
Twentieth Century Fox, 193, 194
21st Century Fox, 208, 209, 210, 220, 247, 410, 421, 423
24/7 news cycle, 72, 78, 227
Twenty-One, 225
Twitch, 262, 284
Twitter, 87–88, 262, 266, 326, 327, 342
  advertising, 329
  hashtag activism and, 3–4
  politics and, 368

  public relations and, 357
Twitter Analytics, 357
2 Dope Queens, 157
Tylenol tragedy, 360–61

Uchitelle, Louis, 415
Ulysses (Joyce), 52, 383
Uncle Tom's Cabin (Stowe), 43, 50
Underwood, Carrie, 146
United Artists, 193, 194
United Mine Workers, 352
United Press International (UPI), 85
Universal, 193, 208, 407, 410
Universal Music Group, 147, 181
Universal Pictures, 418
University of Missouri, 67
university presses, 40–41
urban contemporary, 173
urban culture, 144
urbanization, 9
USA Patriot Act, 275, 386
USA Today, 86
U.S. book revenue, 48
U.S. Constitution, 50, 58, 60, 153, 335, 376–77
  See also First Amendment
U.S. Defense Department, 256
U.S. economy, 406–10
uses and gratifications model, 439–440
U.S. Navy, 163
U.S. Press Freedom Tracker, 95
US Weekly, 114

Vallée, Rudy, 136
values
  in American journalism, 75–81
  changes in, 19–21
  mass media and, 15
Values and Lifestyles (VALS) strategy, 322–23
Vampire Weekend, 144, 148
Vandidades, 113
Van Doren, Charles, 225
Vanishing Lady, The, 192
Vanity Fair, 120
Variety, 114
variety shows, 168, 228
vaudeville shows, 14, 135, 195
vellum, 36
Velvet Underground, 381
Verizon FiOS, 261

Index

vertical integration, 193
Vevo, 131
VHS, 206
Viacom, 246, 424
Victrolas, 129
videocassette recorders (VCRs), 239
videocassettes, 206
video games
   See also digital gaming
  arcade games, 288–89
  classic games, 288–290
  consoles, 289–290
  digital distribution of, 305
  early, 287–88
  free speech and, 307–8
  genres, 291
  misogyny and, 300–301, 302–3
  production of, 306–7
  sales, 304–6
  tournaments, 283–84
  violent, 300–301, 307
video game stores, 305
video news releases (VNRs), 357, 359
video-on-demand (VOD), 236
videos
  mobile, 240
  smartphone, 89
video sales and rentals, 207, 239–240
video streaming, 207, 210–13, 219–220, 237, 239–240, 241, 243–44, 246, 328, 421, 422–23
video subscription services, 247
Vietnam War, 106, 107, 143, 377–78
Village People, 144
Vimeo, 213, 262
vinyl albums, 129, 130, 149–150
violence
  against journalists, 94–95
  media, 15, 445
  school shootings, 18
  shootings, 431
  video games and, 300–301
viral marketing, 323, 327
virtual communities, 295–96
virtual reality (VR), 270, 297–98
Visa, 331
visual design, 319–320
visual language, power of, 70–71
vitascope, 191
VNRs. *See* video news releases (VNRs)
vocational texts, 39
Vogue, 120

voice-controlled assistants, 254, 265
VOID, 298
Volkswagen, 323

wage gap, 415, 416
wages, 413, 414–15
Wales, Jimmy, 364
Walker, John Brisben, 99
Walking Dead, The, 244
Walmart, 150, 210, 411
Walt Disney Company, 418–421
Wang, Wayne, 200
Wang Chieh, 36
War Advertising Council, 319
Warhol, Andy, 381
Warner, Jack L., 214
Warner Brothers, 188, 193, 197–98, 208, 214
WarnerMedia, 424
Warner Music Group, 147, 181
War of the Worlds, 168–69, 438–39
Warren, Robert, 379
war reporting, 106, 107, 108
War Robots, 293
Washington Post, 68, 73, 78, 88, 95, 398
watchdog journalism, 94
watchdog organizations, 318, 334
Watergate scandal, 68, 75
Waters, Muddy, 140
Watson, Emma, 47
Waymo, 403
WBAI, 393
WEAF, 164
Weaver, Sylvester "Pat," 224
Weavers, the, 142
web advertising, 270–71, 325–27
web browsers, 260
Webkinz, 295
websites, 11, 19, 49, 60, 64, 81, 88, 115, 151, 177, 240, 259–264, 271, 276–77, 363–64
  See also Internet
webzines, 110, 114–15
Weebly, 263
Weinstein, Harvey, 4, 112–13, 200, 201
Welch, Edgar Maddison, 91
Welles, Orson, 188
Wells, H. G., 168, 438
Wells, Orson, 168–69
Wernick, Paul, 212
Wertmüller, Lina, 199
West, Mae, 393

Westinghouse, 163–64, 165
Westworld, 235
WhatsApp, 270
"What's Going On" (Gaye), 135
Wheel of Fortune, 244
"White Christmas" (Berlin), 136
white flight, 202, 205, 206
white music, 139
Whitman, Walt, 52
Who, The, 141
Who Framed Roger Rabbit? 419
Who Wants to Be a Millionaire, 168
Wi-Fi, 240, 265
Wii, 290, 297
Wii Fit, 290
Wii Sports, 290
Wikipedia, 364
Wiley, 45
Will and Grace, 232
Williams, Brian, 80
Williams, Serena, 330
Wilson, Woodrow, 353
Windows Phone 8, 268
Winfrey, Oprah, 27, 43, 200
Wired, 114–15
wireless communication
  invention of, 160–62
  regulation of, 162–64
Wireless Ship Act, 162
wireless telegraphy, 9, 160–61
wireless telephony, 161
wire services, 63, 85
Witherspoon, Reese, 200
Wix, 263
WNBC, 164
Wolters Kluwer, 44, 45
Woman's Day, 111
women
  film industry and, 203
  gaming and, 301–3, 308
  journalists, 77
  smoking by, 354
  stereotypes, 332–33
  on television, 232–33
women's magazines, 103, 111
Wonder (Palacio), 44
Wonderwall, 110
Wonder Woman films, 23, 43
Wood, Natalie, 206
Woodstock, 143
Woodward, Bob, 68
word-of-mouth advertising, 327

WordPress, 263, 279
World of Warcraft, 293, 304–5
World Trade Organization (WTO), 418
World War I, 163, 353, 358, 380
World War II, 70, 108, 129, 202, 205, 319, 357
World Wide Web, 259–264
worms, 276
Wozniak, Steve, 269
Wrinkle in Time, A (L'Engle), 44, 200
writers
   See also journalists
   freelance, 116
   magazine, 116
written communication, 6–7
WTO. *See* World Trade Organization (WTO)

Wu, Constance, 200
Wu, Tim, 273

Xbox, 268, 290
Xbox Games Store, 305
Xbox LIVE, 290
Xbox One, 290
XL Recordings, 148
XM, 179

Yahoo! 261, 326
Yandex, 262
Yang, Gene Luen, 31
Yang, Jerry, 261
Yardbirds, the, 141
yellow journalism, 63–64
Yellow Kid, 64

Young Frankenstein, 17
youth population, 138
YouTube, 18, 131, 150, 213, 240, 243, 262, 266, 327, 404, 414
YouTube Gaming, 284

Zenger, John Peter, 60
Ziering, Amy, 201
Zimdars, Melissa, 398
Zimmerman, George, 3, 264
zines, 114
zoetrope, 190
Zook, Kristal Brent, 409
Zuckerberg, Mark, 263, 270, 276, 405
Zukor, Adolph, 194, 195–96
Zworykin, Vladimir, 222–23

Video Program for *Media Essentials*, Fifth Edition

Media Essentials doesn't just teach convergence—it also practices convergence, converging print and video with LaunchPad and a variety of recommended web clips.

LaunchPad Videos with Quizzing

LaunchPad for *Media Essentials* includes a full e-book as well as a library of video clips that complement text material. Here's a list of all the LaunchPad videos featured in the book by chapter, each of which is accompanied by assignable critical-thinking questions that report to the gradebook.

Chapter 1: Mass Communication: A Critical Approach
Agenda Setting and Gatekeeping, p. 14
Masculinity on Screen: *Tough Guise 2*, p. 24
The Media and Democracy, p. 28

Chapter 2: Books and the Power of Print
Based On: Making Books into Movies, p. 43
Amazon's Brick-and-Mortar Bookstores, p. 50
Banned Books on Screen: *Huck Finn*, p. 52

Chapter 3: Newspapers to Digital Frontiers: Journalism's Journey
Investigative Journalism on Screen: *Spotlight*, p. 68
Newspapers and the Internet: Convergence, p. 86
The Objectivity Myth, p. 96
Community Voices: Weekly Newspapers (see LaunchPad)
Newspapers Now (see LaunchPad)

Chapter 4: Magazines in the Age of Specialization
Magazine Specialization Today, p. 110
Narrowcasting in Magazines, p. 115
Magazines on Screen: *13 Going on 30*, p. 119
Essence Magazine, p. 122

Chapter 5: Sound Recording and Popular Music
Sound Recordings from a Century Ago, p. 129
Recording Music Today, p. 130
Touring on Screen: Katy Perry, p. 151
Streaming Services, p. 154
Alternative Strategies for Music Marketing (see LaunchPad)

Chapter 6: Popular Radio and the Origins of Broadcasting
Going Visual: Video, Radio, and the Web, p. 177
Radio: Yesterday, Today, and Tomorrow, p. 180

Chapter 7: Movies and the Impact of Images
Storytelling in *Star Wars*, p. 188
Breaking Barriers with *12 Years a Slave*, p. 200
A Hollywood Blockbuster: *Black Panther*, p. 202
More Than a Movie: Social Issues and Film, p. 215
The Theatrical Experience and *The Hobbit*, p. 216

Chapter 8: Television, Cable, and Specialization in Visual Culture
Television Networks Evolve, p. 225
Television Drama: Then and Now, p. 229
Race in TV Programming: *Black-ish*, p. 232
Bingeable Series: *Stranger Things*, p. 241
Changes in Prime Time, p. 250

Chapter 9: The Internet and New Technologies: The Media Converge
The Rise of Social Media, p. 262
The Internet in 1995: *The Net*, p. 265
Reddit CEO on Net Neutrality, p. 272
User-Generated Content, p. 280

Chapter 10: Digital Gaming and the Media Playground
Anita Sarkeesian and #GamerGate, p. 302
Video Games at the Movies: *Resident Evil*, p. 306
Tablets, Technology, and the Classroom, p. 310

Chapter 11: Advertising and Commercial Culture
Advertising in the Digital Age, p. 325
Internet vs. TV Ad Spending, p. 328
Advertising and Effects on Children, p. 335
Blurring the Lines: Marketing Programs across Platforms, p. 344
Product Placement in the Movies: *E.T.* (see LaunchPad)

Chapter 12: Public Relations and Framing the Message
Give and Take: Public Relations and Journalism, p. 366
Going Viral: Political Campaigns and Video, p. 370
Filling the News Hole: Video News Releases (see LaunchPad)

Chapter 13: Legal Controls and Freedom of Expression
MTV Explores Sexting and the Law, p. 385
Bloggers and Legal Rights, p. 387
The First Amendment and Student Speech, p. 400
Freedom of Information (see LaunchPad)

Chapter 14: Media Economics and the Global Marketplace
The Impact of Media Ownership, p. 411
Disney's Global Brand: *Frozen*, p. 421
The Money behind the Media, p. 428

Chapter 15: Media Effects and Cultural Approaches to Media Research
Media Effects Research, p. 439
Suicide on TV: *13 Reasons Why*, p. 450

Recommended Web Clips

There are many interesting and informative videos available on the web. Listed below are recommended third-party videos included in a number of case study boxes throughout the text. Each clip is paired with an accompanying discussion question, which makes these prompts especially useful for in-class or small-group discussion.

Social Media and FOMO, p. 13
Rupi Kaur: Instapoet, p. 47
Global Attacks on Journalism, p. 92
The Power of Photojournalism, p. 106
Spotify and Streaming, p. 132
News/Talk Radio on YouTube, p. 174
Streaming Music Videos, p. 178
Digital Marketing for Popular Movies, p. 212
Understanding Social Media Fraud, p. 266
Pokémon Go and Mobile Gaming, p. 299
Parodying Ad Stereotypes, p. 332
The Influence of Edward Bernays, p. 354
Military PR and Lady Gaga, p. 358
Stopping the Spread of Fake News, p. 398
Netflix on YouTube, p. 422
Amazon's Powerful Algorithm, p. 437